AP* Achiever Advanced Placement American History Exam Preparation Guide

to accompany

American History: A Survey

Thirteenth Edition

Alan Brinkley

Prepared by
Jason George
Jerald Brown

Revised by
George W. Henry, Jr.

* Pre-AP, AP, and Advanced Placement program are registered trademarks of the College Entrance Examination Board, which was not involved in the production of and does not endorse these products.

Boston   Burr Ridge, IL   Dubuque, IA   New York   San Francisco   St. Louis
Bangkok   Bogotá   Caracas   Kuala Lumpur   Lisbon   London   Madrid   Mexico City
Milan   Montreal   New Delhi   Santiago   Seoul   Singapore   Sydney   Taipei   Toronto

The **McGraw·Hill** Companies

AP* Achiever Advanced Placement American History Exam Preparation Guide to accompany
AMERICAN HISTORY: A SURVEY, THIRTEENTH EDITION
ALAN BRINKLEY

Published by McGraw-Hill Higher Education, an imprint of The McGraw-Hill Companies, Inc., 1221 Avenue of the Americas, New York, NY 10020. Copyright © 2010 by The McGraw-Hill Companies, Inc. All rights reserved.

1 2 3 4 5 6 7 8 9 0 QPD/QPD 0 9

ISBN: 978-0-07-892750-8

MHID: 0-07-892750-1

www.mhhe.com

* Pre-AP, AP, and Advanced Placement program are registered trademarks of the College Entrance Examination Board, which was not involved in the production of and does not endorse these products.

About the Authors

Jason George

Jason George has been teaching History at the Bryn Mawr School in Baltimore, Maryland, since 1999 and has been teaching an AP United States History Seminar since 2003. He was an instructor and teaching assistant at Ohio University in Athens, Ohio, between 1993 and 1999. Jason received his Ph.D. from Ohio University in 2003 with a dissertation titled, "The View from Afar: Russian Perceptions of the United States, 1776–2002." He has served as United States History Content Advisor for the College Board's AP Central Program since 2003 and has been a reviewer for AP Central since 2002. He has participated in the AP U.S. History Reading since 2004. He also contributed teaching exercises on the 1960s Cultural Revolution to Columbia University's American History Online program and had his course syllabus published in the 2005–2006 College Board Teachers' Guide.

Jerald Brown

Jerald Brown received his Ph.D. in American History from the University of New Hampshire, and presently teaches United States History and Economics at the Bryn Mawr School in Baltimore, Maryland. He is the author of *The Years of the Life of Samuel Lane* (New Hampshire Historical Society). He first taught AP United States History in 1985 and has taught the college survey course at several colleges and universities. He has been a reader for the College Board in United States History since 1999.

George W. Henry, Jr.

George Henry is in his thirty-third year of teaching in the public and private schools of Salt Lake City, Utah. He has served as teacher, department chair, curriculum specialist, and student council advisor at South High School, Highland High School, and Rowland Hall-St. Marks School. George has also served as a member of the Educational Testing Services Achievement Test Development committee in United States History, and for the past 17 years as Faculty Consultant at the AP U.S. History reading. In addition, George was part of the development team on the College Board Social Studies Vertical Teams Project, and co-authored *Pre AP topics for Vertical Teams: Improving Student Writing*.

George has served the Western Region of the College Board in the capacity of Regional Council member, Academic Assembly Chair, and Regional Council Chair. He is a consultant for AP U.S. History, Building Success, and AP Vertical Teams workshops. George has a strong commitment to equity and access for all students to AP programs, and focuses his attention specifically on how to increase paths of access for minority and underrepresented students in AP courses. He has also served on the National Academic Advisory Committee of the College Board. Currently he teaches Advanced Placement United States History at Rowland Hall-St. Mark's School in Salt Lake City, and is an Adjunct Instructor specializing in teaching methods in the History Department at the University of Utah.

Contents

INTRODUCTION

We cannot promise you any "magic formula" to score well on your Advanced Placement United States History Exam, but this book can help. There is no substitute for working hard in your history course throughout the year so that you know your American History. You probably will not be successful on the exam if you attempt to cram in a great deal of information at the last minute. That said, you can use this book to help you build upon what you learn throughout the course of the year. The history of the United States is exciting and will help you better understand the society in which you live, making you a more informed citizen. Knowing our nation's history is important in and of itself, and doing well on the AP Exam should simply be a by-product of having this important knowledge.

The purpose of this introduction is two-fold. The first section provides an overview of the goals of the AP Course and AP Exam, helping you to understand the basic format of the exam and the rationale behind its structure and format. The second section offers a series of strategies and tips meant to help you with each of the major sections of the exam. This comes from feedback from our students and from our experience as AP Readers and teachers.

Once you have become familiar with the format of the exam through the introduction, you will then have the opportunity to practice the skills that you will need when you take the exam. In addition to a summary of the contents of the chapters from Alan Brinkley's *American History: A Survey,* we have included multiple-choice questions, two sample essay questions, and a document-based exercise for each chapter. All of these exercises are meant to reflect the types of questions that you will find on the AP Exam.

PURPOSE AND SCOPE OF THE EXAMINATION

The Advanced Placement Course is meant to replicate a college-level introductory United States History Survey Course and thus give you the skills and knowledge for more specialized courses in American History. While there are an infinite variety of ways to present an AP Course, there are certain things that everyone should get out of such a course. These include an understanding of the chronological framework of American History, especially an understanding of how events and trends are related, rather than simply memorizing a collection of facts and dates. In addition, you should come out of an AP Course with certain skills, including the ability to critically analyze both primary and secondary sources; to develop a thesis or argument and support it with concrete historical evidence; and to understand the major interpretive frameworks that historians have used to explain the American past.

The College Board and the Educational Testing Service, which administer the AP Exam, survey over 100 college and university instructors across the country to get a sense of what is being taught in introductory college survey courses. A Test Development Committee, which consists of three college or university professors and three high school teachers, uses this information to create an examination that reflects the experience that most undergraduate students receive. It is administered in early May. The AP United States History Exam is then scored by a group of nearly 1,000 AP high school teachers, college and university professors who serve as AP Exam Readers. These teachers gather for a week in early June and receive training in how to score the exams and then spend the rest of the week reading and scoring your essays. We have both served as AP Exam Readers for a combined total of over ten years.

Colleges and universities often grant credits equivalent to that which is offered for their introductory United States History survey course to those students who successfully complete the AP Exam. The criteria for receiving credit vary widely from institution to institution and you should find out from each college and university what their standards are; you choose to have your scores sent to colleges and universities to which you are applying. The AP Exam is scored on the following 5-point scale: 5 is "extremely well-qualified"; 4 is "well qualified"; 3 is "qualified"; 2 is "possibly qualified"; 1 is "no recommendation."

EXAMINATION FORMAT

There are two sections to the Advanced Placement United States History Examination: a multiple-choice section and a free-response section. The free-response section consists of one document-based question (DBQ) and two free-response essay questions usually referred to as FRQs. The examination lasts for three hours and five minutes, with fifty-five minutes for multiple choice and one hundred and thirty minutes for the essay sections. The multiple-choice and free-response questions each count for 50 percent of your score. Within the free-response section, the DBQ counts for 45 percent and the free-response essays count for 55 percent, of your score, respectively.

1. *Multiple Choice*—You have fifty-five minutes to answer the eighty multiple-choice questions. The overall level of difficulty of these questions is such that most students who receive scores of three (3) or above on the examination answer between 60 and 80 percent of the questions correctly. Therefore, you should not expect that you will answer every question correctly or become unnerved if you encounter material that is not familiar to you. Do not assume that you are not well prepared for the examination if there is something on the exam that you did not study in class. It is impossible to cover everything about United States history from its origins to the present in the course of a year, especially when most courses end their coverage of new material in mid to late April in order to leave time for review. Perhaps it will make you feel better to know that even veteran AP teachers sometimes see questions that stump them!

   The time period for the multiple-choice questions is as follows: approximately 20 percent of the questions cover the pre-Columbian period to 1789; 45 percent cover the period from 1790 to 1914; 35 percent cover the period from 1915 to the present mainly up to 1980, although recent exams have included a few questions covering the period since then. The multiple-choice questions are also broken down by topic as follows: Political History—35 percent; Social History, including cultural and intellectual developments—45 percent; Diplomatic History—15 percent; Economic Developments—10 percent.

2. Free Response
   DBQ—You have one hour to devote to the DBQ: a mandatory 15-minute reading and planning period and 45 minutes for writing. The DBQ is labeled "Part A" on the second section of the AP Exam. The DBQ score counts for 22.5 percent of your score for the AP Exam. The DBQ consists of approximately eight to ten documents, ranging widely in type: speeches, letters, visual sources such as political cartoons and photographs, as well as charts, maps and graphs.

   Essays are scored on a 9-point scale, which is based primarily on the clarity and overall strength of your thesis in responding to the question, appropriate use of a substantial number of documents; writing and organization; use of relevant outside information; and thorough and accurate analysis of the question and the historical time period. The scoring for the APUSH Exam is done holistically, and there is no specific factual information that you must include to receive a certain score. You must simply have a preponderance of the elements listed under each category in the rubric in order to receive that score. Following is a sample rubric similar to the one used by AP Readers to score DBQs. The rubric for free-response questions is similar, without the inclusion of the criteria about the documents.

Scoring

The 8–9 Essay:
• Contains a well-developed thesis
• Contains effective analysis dealing with all parts of the question
• Effectively uses a substantial number of documents
• Supports the thesis with relevant and substantial outside information
• Is clearly organized and well-written
• May contain minor errors

The 5–7 Essay:
• Contains a thesis that addresses the question
• Provides some relevant supporting information
• Provides limited analysis of the question
• Makes effective use of some documents
• Has acceptable organization and writing
• May have errors that do not seriously detract from the quality of the essay

The 2–4 Essay:
• Contains a limited or undeveloped thesis—deals with the question in a general, simplistic, superficial manner
• Provides little relevant outside or information is inaccurate or irrelevant
• Quotes or cites briefly some of the documents
• Contains little outside information
• Contains little or no analysis
• Is poorly organized
• May have major errors

The 0–1 Essay:
• Contains no thesis or has one that is irrelevant to the question posed
• Contains no analysis and does not reflect understanding of the question
• Makes little or no use of the documents
• Is organized in a way that makes it difficult to understand
• Has numerous and substantial factual errors

FRQs—These will not cover the same time period as that covered in the DBQ. For example, if the DBQ deals with the impact of the French and Indian War over a twenty-five or thirty-year period, the free-response questions might deal with the social impact of the American Revolution or the political events leading up to the Civil War.

In this book, we have included a full sample DBQ in several chapters, because we believe this mimics the scope and format of the questions that you will encounter on the AP Exam. DBQs on the AP Exam often cover broader themes and time periods than those you will encounter in one chapter of this or any other textbook, and thus are drawn from multiple chapters. They will require that you synthesize a broad range of factual information. A DBQ on the period leading up to the Civil War might ask you to incorporate social, political, and economic factors that would be found in three separate chapters. We have included shorter document-based exercises that are meant to help you with both content and skills in the chapters without a full DBQ.

FREE-RESPONSE QUESTIONS

You have seventy minutes to answer both free-response essay questions. A general rule of thumb is to spend five minutes organizing and thirty minutes writing for each question. These questions cover the period from the earliest European exploration to 1980. The FRQs count for 27.5 per cent of the total AP Exam score.

The free-response essays are divided into two parts. These are labeled "Part B" and "Part C" in the second section of the AP Exam. Generally speaking, questions from Part B cover the period from the Columbian arrival in the Western Hemisphere until the Civil War and Reconstruction; questions from Part C cover the period from the Civil War and Reconstruction until the late twentieth century. Questions in these sections might have comparative questions that involve discussion of earlier or later periods, asking you, for example, to compare American social reform in the 1840s with that of the 1960s.

In addition, these questions are usually balanced thematically, so that a question dealing with a topic that asks you to exhibit an understanding of social or cultural themes might be paired with a question that involves more traditional political, economic, or diplomatic topics.

THINKING ABOUT THE EXAM

Besides your teacher, your textbook, and this book (of course!), one other indispensable resource to help you in preparing for the AP Exam is the College Board's AP Central Site (*apcentral.collegeboard.com*). The AP Central United States History section includes sample multiple-choice questions, as well as DBQs and free-response essays from the past five years, along with sample student responses and scoring explanations. In addition, it includes the College Board's Course Outline, which identifies twenty-eight major periods in United States history from the pre-Columbian period to the present, subdivided by topic.

The College Board introduced twelve themes to help prepare you for the AP Exam. These include the following: American Diversity; American Identity; Culture; Demographic Changes; Economic Transformations; Environment; Globalization; Politics and Citizenship; Reform; Religion; Slavery and Its Legacies in North America; War and Diplomacy. These themes can be used in a variety of different manners. More information about themes in AP United States History and their use in Advanced Placement courses can be found on AP Central).

In this book, each chapter begins with a brief discussion of how its contents relate to major AP themes. Please note that this is not meant to be exhaustive—you may well find ways to relate other themes to the chapter's contents; we have just tried to point out some of the most prominent connections. Some chapters clearly lend themselves more than others to certain themes—War and Diplomacy, for example, will be much more relevant to a chapter on World War II than other themes. Given the ever-present time pressures and the increasing chronological scope and amount of information that you must cover in United States history, you will likely be at an advantage if you can find ways to study material in a thematic way and make connections across time and topic rather than sticking to a straight chronological approach in an attempt to cover everything. A recent survey of college and university professors noted that most survey courses in higher education are spending at least 15 percent of their courses on the period since 1975.

Trying to look into a crystal ball to anticipate exactly what will be on the AP Exam is a distracting and fruitless exercise. Many people often look to past years in order to see if they can guess what the upcoming DBQ or free-response questions might be. To reiterate what we said earlier, the best way to prepare for the exam is to learn overall chronology, events, and themes of United States History. You will not know every period equally well, but the degree of choice on the two free response essays should allow you to find questions that you feel comfortable answering. Similarly, your knowledge and historian's skills should enable you to navigate a DBQ on almost any topic.

COOKING ON THE AP EXAM—STRATEGIES AND TIPS

Once again doing good work in your American History course at school means doing well on the Advanced Placement United States History Exam—this is not rocket science. Over and above that you can increase your chances of doing well by using the strategies here and using the AP Central website. Each section of the AP Exam gives you the opportunity to demonstrate your skills and knowledge; make the most of that by knowing what to expect before you open the exam booklet in May. The following are tips and strategies for each of the AP Exam's two sections: multiple choice, the document-based question and the two free-response questions.

MULTIPLE-CHOICE SECTION

It is important to work hard in your history course to have command of the people, events, ideas and their interplay that are important to understanding our nation's history. This detail will be particularly important for success on the multiple-choice section, Section I, of the AP Exam.

The multiple-choice section:
- is fifty-five minutes long, consists of eighty questions, and counts as 50 percent of your overall exam grade
- assumes that a score of approximately 60 percent (48/80), with reasonable essays, meaning essay scores of 5 and above on the nine point scale shouldearn you an exam score of 3
- assesses a 1/4-point penalty for each incorrect answer
- puts questions in order of difficulty with the easier questions first
- may place questions in chronologically ordered groups of eight to twelve questions; after one group ends another chronological sequence begins.

Knowing this about the format of the multiple-choice section will allow you to prepare a personal strategy to follow when taking the exam. You may find the following tips helpful:
- Read the question and *all five choices* before recording your answer. You must choose the BEST right answer. There may be more that one correct answer. Read carefully to determine the subtle differences between a correct answer, and the best correct answer. Choices that indicate a rigid position with no flexibility are rarely correct. If the answer contains "always," "never," or similar terms, beware!
- Stay alert for questions that use "except," "not," or "least": for example, "All of the following characterize . . . EXCEPT." The factually "right" answers in this type of question are often wrong. Look for the answer that indicates a reverse trend from the other answers. If four of the choices point left and one points right, go right.
- Be sure to look at what is measured on both axes when considering questions with graphs, tables, or charts.
- When considering questions referring to specific quotations, be aware that you are rarely required to identify the quotation itself, but you must be familiar with the ideas or policies it expresses, or the historical context in which the statement was made.
- Use clues in cartoons, photographs, or art to help answer the question. The source attribution often gives important information such as the date and the publication. These can be very helpful.

- Remember that there are no questions on specific military history in the multiple-choice section.
- Understand the historical context and ideas of a period. None of the questions asks for memorized facts alone. They ask you to demonstrate understanding and analysis of the question.
- Be ready to skip questions the first time through; you don't want to spend lots of time pondering any one question. Go through and answer all the questions you are sure about. Then read through the test again and work on those about which you know something. If you don't have a clue about any question, leave it blank.
- Use the general theme of the question to point you toward what the answer might be.
- Remember there is a 1/4-point penalty for each wrong answer; a blank answer is *not* penalized. Use the process of elimination to eliminate wrong answers. You may not be comfortable answering a question unless you are sure of the answer. However, if you can eliminate at least one choice it is statistically to your advantage to guess the answer among the four remaining choices. Devise a formula that works for you and your comfort level. That may mean guessing among the four, three, or two remaining choices. Again, remember that *some degree of guessing is a good strategy.*

The many multiple-choice questions in this book are designed to help you learn our history and to mimic exam questions. The questions are linked to specific chapters in *American History: A Survey,* and there are two sample exams. The more you practice with this type of question, the better you will know the content, and the better your multiple-choice score on the AP Exam will be.

THE FREE-RESPONSE QUESTIONS

The free-response, or essay, questions are found in Section II of the AP Exam. Getting a good score on free-response essays requires two elements: a strong thesis which fully addresses every aspect of the prompt, takes a position with regard to the prompt, and provides categories for analysis. You essay must also include substantial supporting evidence. This requires you to bring background material to your essay. Make sure that you answer the question asked. Study the verb or verbs used to ask the question. If the question is to "compare and contrast" or to "analyze," make sure you do that in your answer. Also strive for balance when the question asks you to explore several aspects of an event such as political, economic, and ideological significance. Address all three in this instance. An imbalance among your treatment of the topics will diminish your score significantly.

READY-MADE THESES

When you are searching for a thesis around which to frame your answer to a free-response question, the following categories might help. Almost every free-response question can be answered using one of the following themes as a basis for a thesis. Remember that these themes are not the gospel—be flexible and adapt them to the particular question you choose to answer. If the question involves:

- *Foreign policy*–consider continuation of, or departure from *isolation and neutrality.*
- *Political Issues*–consider political parties; impact of presidential decisions; political parties; concepts such as democracy, freedom, liberty, as well as major events in United States history; states rights vs. federal authority; the Supreme Court and Congress; the relationship between the states and the national government; and the relationship between the branches of government and the growth of American democracy.

- *Social issues*–consider race, class, gender, religion, education, organized labor, social movements such as Civil Rights, Women's rights, Immigration *minority vs. majority rights*
- *Economics*–consider *laissez-faire vs. government intervention; economic depressions; the influence of business and industry;* and *government programs such as the New Deal, Great Society*
- *Culture*–consider *conformity vs. change literature, art, music,* and *architecture.*

Use the following tips for essay writing in general:
- Organize your response according to the verbs in the question.
- Decide what the question is asking, and what the question is asking you to do.
- Create a clear precise thesis that fully addresses the question, takes a position, and provides organizational categories for analysis.
- Analyze rather than describe; that is, give reasons for reasons.
- Do not assume that the readers know what you are trying to say—you must explain in detail.
- Provide clear commentary that demonstrates your analysis
- Offer accurate historical evidence. Do not make up factual evidence
- Relate the evidence you use to your thesis and to the other evidence.
- Defend your thesis, that is provide accurate, relevant factual information that supports what you argue
- Address major arguments that run counter to yours.
- *Introductory paragraph*—include a thesis that directly addresses all aspects of the question. Be precise—limit this to what you will discuss in the essay.
- *Body Paragraphs*—include a topic sentence from the organizational statement in your thesis. Provide factual evidence to support the sentence, analysis of the factual information, and commentary that answers the question, "so what?". Provide a clincher sentence that ties together all that you have said in the paragraph, and then provide a transition sentence to the next paragraph so that your essay has continuity.
- *Concluding paragraph*—This is the impression that the reader leaves with—reserve time to make it good. Reiterate and summarize main points; don't introduce new ideas. Reinforce your strong thesis. Offers a sentence or two on the historical significance of your argument. Do not contradict your thesis.

THE DOCUMENT-BASED QUESTION

The document-based question is the first essay you are asked to write. It has a fifteen-minute reading and planning period and allows forty-five minutes for writing. The DBQ can cover any period of American history up to 1980. The DBQ generally asks about a major topic in United States history. You must use both the documents provided as well as your own knowledge of both the time period and topic in your answer. An essay that simply lists the documents and what they say, or mean, will not suffice. Readers refer to that as the "laundry list"; that strategy will not earn you a high score. Your job is to use a *substantial* number of documents, usually more than half, supported by your own knowledge and analysis to answer the question. The DBQ usually contains eight to ten documents, which might be a combination of written documents, pictures, photographs and paintings, maps, charts, and tables.

First of all you must determine what the question is asking (content) and what the question asks you to do, (process); read it several times and dissect its various components. Focus on the verbs; important words are: *how, why, account for, list, compare, contrast, define, discuss, illustrate, explain, defend, describe, differentiate, outline, summarize, assess, evaluate, analyze, how successful,* and *to what extent.* They indicate what you are being asked to do and the readers of your essay take them very seriously. Also note if the question asks you to explore various aspects of a bigger topic. These categories are sometime social, political, military, diplomatic, ideological, economic, and cultural, among others. If the question asks you to look at more than one area, you must do so, and try to provide balanced analysis between the several areas. It is rare for an essay to score well if it focuses mainly on one topic when the question requires analysis of several.

Use the reading period to read the documents and plan your essay. One strategy is to write down everything you can think of that relates to the question before you read through the documents, and to continue that as you go through them. You must use outside information if you wish to score well.

Your job is to select what documents to use, and then arrange them to support your argument in providing an answer to the question. DO NOT QUOTE from any document extensively. Choose a short phrase or idea from the document and use that to refer to the entire document. This test is not evaluating how well you can copy, but your knowledge, analytical skills, and ability to write clear prose. Also, use the information given about the source to help you in identifying both it and its significance. The date, author, and any other information may be crucial in helping you evaluate its significance, perspective, and the context in which it falls.

Once you have analyzed the documents and created a document key, you should decide on a thesis, that fully addresses every aspect of the question, takes a position with regard to the question, and provides categories for analysis. The document key is merely a synthesis of your analysis of the documents. It will help you decide what information from each document is most important to use in your essay. If you are at a loss in this area, or simply want some guidance, try to fit the question into one of the five categories offered earlier. Develop your thesis before you start to write. It should appear clearly and prominently in the first paragraph of your essay. Your thesis should be supported with evidence from the documents and from your own (outside) knowledge. Make sure that the body of your essay is linked to your thesis. Refer to your thesis as you develop the body paragraphs. Link your interpretation of the factual evidence from the documents and your outside information to your thesis. Interweave your own background knowledge into your analysis. A well-developed thesis is essential to a high score in this section.

Considering counterarguments is a good way to add substance to your essay, so look at the ways your arguments could be criticized and address them. For example, if your thesis about the New Deal argues that it was not revolutionary, but worked to preserve the capitalistic system, take some of your arguments and show why they are stronger than those which contend it was revolutionary. This will demonstrate critical analysis and knowledge, and will make your essay stronger.

If you have time, revise your essay. You can cross out and add to your essay, but try to do it neatly. The readers really will try to do their best to follow what you intend, but it is best to present a well-crafted, clearly articulated essay. The readers understand that your essay is a draft, and do not expect a polished essay, even to receive the highest scores. Make sure that your thesis is prominent; it is best to state it in the first paragraph, and to reiterate in the last.

Spend some time making your last paragraph strong; that is the last impression you make before the reader puts a score on your essay.

FREE-RESPONSE QUESTIONS—THE STANDARD ESSAYS

You are required to answer two out of four possible questions in this section of the exam. You must answer one question from the two in Part B, and one of the two questions in Part C. The questions in Part B are from the time period from Colonial America through the Civil War and Reconstruction. Questions in Part C are from the Gilded Age to about 1980. There is some chronological overlap, and the time divide is not rigid. Each section allows you five minutes to plan out your answer, and thirty minutes to write. You must provide all the relevant evidence to support your argument in these essays.

The same format and skills that you will use in the DBQ are applicable here. The only difference is that there are no documents accompanying these questions. You should clearly state your thesis in your introductory paragraph and reiterate it in your conclusion, referring to your thesis throughout the body paragraphs. Create clear organizational statements in your thesis and use them as the topic sentences of each of your body paragraphs. Carefully organized and well-written body paragraphs that analyze and synthesize rather than describe the factual information will earn high scores on this section of the exam. You can do the essays in any order, but clearly mark what question you are answering.

These questions often ask you to compare some topic over time, or aspects of a subject by demographic groups, regions, or themes. You should seek balance by offering substantial analysis of each category raised in the question.

To summarize the main points covered here:

MULTIPLE-CHOICE SECTION
- Read the questions and the all choices very carefully. Most errors are caused by hasty reading of the question. Realize you have less than one minute per question.
- Earlier questions tend to be less difficult—don't spend too much time agonizing over later questions if earlier ones are blank.
- If you can eliminate at least one or two of the answers it pays to make an educated guess. There is a 1/4-point penalty for wrong answers.
- If you are unsure whether to change an answer once you have answered the question, you probably should leave it alone in this scenario—too many people change the right answer to a wrong one.
- Make sure the question number on your answer sheet matches the test question—check frequently.

FREE-RESPONSE QUESTIONS
- • Read the directions carefully. Especially be sure to answer *one* essay from Part B and *one* from Part C.
- Read the questions carefully and *answer what is asked*—note the time period and perspective. Remember that if the question asks "to what extent," you should evaluate the degree to which something happened, not whether it happened or not.
- Develop a thesis and put it in the reader's face, or at least in the first paragraph. Develop your thesis and refer to it throughout your essay.
- Use the reading period to plan your essays—know what the question is asking you to do.
- Use the ready-made theses noted earlier to shape your answers when applicable.
- Support your contentions with specific evidence.

- Revise your essay—as necessary, but try to present a clearly organized essay. You can cross out words and move phrases, but take care not to confuse the readers.
- Use the best penmanship possible—making the reader happy is good strategy.

DBQ RULES
- Read the question several times to determine what specific tasks it asks you to perform.
- Note outside information that pertains to the question.
- Read the documents for both context and content—the source lines give much useful information.
- When logical, group the documents to accomplish the tasks asked by the question. Don't simply list them, or quote extensively from them.
- Develop a thesis.
- Write good prose and refer back to the question to maintain your focus.

BASIC APUSH BROMIDES

- **Prepare** for the exam—that means study consistently all year in your AP U.S. History class. Good luck and providence play no role in achieving a good score on the AP Exam.
- Get to the exam site early with all the equipment you need (tissues, pencils and pens, and a watch).
- Get plenty of sleep the night before—napping during the exam is not recommended.
- Confidently display what you know. You have worked hard to learn about our nation's past—this is an opportunity to excel. Be creative—you have nothing to lose and everything to gain.

CHAPTER 1
The Meeting of Cultures

AP THEMES

- **American Diversity:** Pre-English colonization in the Americas points particularly to the influence of the Spanish, French, Native Americans, and Africans in North America. Early settlement explains the presence of these cultures in the United States.
- **Culture:** The cultural diversity represented in early America created both synthesis and tension. All groups adopted ways of the others, whether wittingly or not, but conflict was perhaps more prevalent between the groups. Non-European cultures were either subsumed, but more commonly almost destroyed by their contact with the English; the French and Spanish made greater attempts to accommodate non-Europeans.
- **Religion:** The introduction of Catholicism to the Americas is the most significant religious development, followed by the Treaty of Tordesillas dividing the Americas between the Spanish and the Portuguese. Catholicism on the continents lured Catholics to the Americas as well as creating religious conflict in both politics and society.
- **Slavery:** The introduction of slaves to the Americas by the Dutch and the Portuguese established a model that was followed by the North American colonists. Acceptance of a racial hierarchy provided the Americas with an ample labor supply, but its legacy of white supremacy did, and continues to, contradict principles upon which the nation was founded.

EXAM TIPS

Don't spend a great deal of time with this chapter. The AP Exam will not have a significant number of questions about America before the seventeenth century. Know the *general characteristics* of the major civilizations, especially the Native Americans of North America and the French and Spanish societies in America. Your time can be put to better use than learning specific details from this chapter.

CHAPTER SUMMARY

Substantial diversity and sophistication existed in pre-Columbian American societies. In Mexico, South America, and Central America, **Incan, Mayan,** and **Aztec** civilizations thrived with cities that rivaled or exceeded the population of Europe's largest cities; these civilizations hosted complex social and political structures that required elaborate public ceremonial architecture. Their economies depended primarily on agriculture and trade.

North American civilizations were not as complex as those in the south but were large and varied. They were organized around hunting, gathering, and fishing. The Northwest Indians and **Eskimos** primarily hunted and fished. Western tribes in arid regions relied on hunting and fishing, while southwestern tribes built pueblos and irrigated their crops. Eastern **woodland** societies engaged in farming, hunting, gathering, and fishing. Substantial cities were linked by trade, and tribes were loosely associated by common language roots. As in other areas of the world American Indian societies experienced an agricultural revolution and consequent population growth, a result being more sedentary societies. Tasks were divided by gender, and women tended to have more power in the family than their European counterparts. Religions were based on the natural world.

Although early Norse explorers had knowledge of the Americas since the eleventh century there was little incentive for westward expansion until the fifteenth century. Population growth, commercial prosperity, and the development of powerful nation-states prompted European monarchs to look abroad for wealth. Portugal's Prince Henry the Navigator looked to Africa and India while in 1492 Spain's Isabella and Ferdinand sponsored the first of Christopher Columbus's three voyages west to find China. Columbus explored the Bahamas, Cuba, Hispaniola, the Caribbean, and the north coast of South America, but the continents he discovered for Europe were named after merchant and chronicler Amerigo Vespucci, at least in part because Columbus did not acknowledge that he was in a new world. In 1494 the Treaty of Tordesillas divided the Americas between Spain and Portugal.

Spain began to consider the Americas as a source of wealth and established a considerable empire there in the sixteenth century. Hernando Cortés, aided by smallpox epidemics, captured the Aztec capital Tenochtitlán and established his reputation as a conquistador. Others followed in search of gold and silver bullion stretching the Spanish Empire from Peru north to present-day New Mexico and east to Florida. The conquistadors exhibited both extraordinary bravery and brutality in their quest for wealth and nearly exterminated the native populations they encountered.

New World riches made Spain wealthy and powerful, and toward the end of the sixteenth century the Spanish attempted colonization rather than conquest and subjugation. Later settlers established an agricultural society with the Catholic Church at its core. The most common settlement was the mission, which had conversion of the natives as its primary goal, and presidios which were fortified garrisons. Missionaries aggressively spread the Gospel. A major settlement arose at St. Augustine in Spanish Florida in 1565.

A larger venture moved into present-day New Mexico near Santa Fe. Settlers were issued *encomiendas,* or licenses, to subjugate native labor and wealth. Over time relations with natives improved and the Spanish settlement grew, with livestock at the center of its economy. Most Pueblos outwardly converted to Christianity; however, in 1680 Spanish authorities tried to suppress all practice of native religious practices. The Pueblos revolted, killing hundreds of Europeans and driving them from the region. Popes Rebellion forced the Spanish out of New Mexico for twelve years. Realizing that constant conflict did not foster prosperity, the Spanish turned to assimilation and intermarriage, and developed a less oppressive labor system. This won peace but without significant immigration the Spanish population remained small and disease ravaged the native population.

Bullion made Spain fabulously wealthy but its mercantile restrictions stifled commercial development in its American empire. Unlike other European colonies, a small European population ruled over a large native population and the dream of a Spanish agricultural empire never materialized. However, lines separating the races were less distinct in Spanish America than throughout North America and significant exchanges took place. European disease was catastrophic and caused the death of millions. That coupled with brutal colonial policies of extermination, of both peoples and of cultures, was designed to eliminate any opposition to Spanish rule. Europeans did import items of benefit to American natives including sugar cane, bananas, cattle, pigs, sheep, and horses. Important to Europeans were the American crops they adopted such as corn, squash, pumpkins, beans, sweet potatoes, tomatoes, peppers, and potatoes. The overwhelming preponderance of men in Spanish America induced intermarriage, resulting in people of mixed race called *mestizos.* The social hierarchy was quite fluid and race did not prohibit one from holding positions of power. Many of the natives also adopted Catholicism.

Natives were coerced into providing the main source for labor in the colonies. With the native population declining this did not provide sufficient labor, and by the beginning of the sixteenth century the Dutch and Portuguese began to import **slaves** from Africa to the Caribbean and South America.

English exploration in North America initially focused on finding a **Northwest Passage** to China. With a strong commercial incentive to sell manufactured goods and merchant capital to finance new ventures, **chartered companies** pooled merchant capital and made enormous profits. The economic system known as **mercantilism** prompted England to establish colonies in the Americas for raw materials and markets. Religion also played a role as **Puritans** dissented from the **Church of England** and the **Stuart Kings** persecuted opposition. England's first attempt at colonization was **Ireland.** The English considered the Irish people savage and created **plantations** to eliminate the native population and customs. This model was used in America. Among England's early attempts at North American settlement in 1585 was the unsuccessful **Roanoke** or **"the Lost Colony."** It was not until 1606 that James I issued a charter for **Jamestown,** the first permanent English colony in the New World.

The French and Dutch also were settling in America. The French founded **Quebec** in 1608 and formed close relationships with natives. **Jesuit missionaries** lived among the Indians and *Coureurs des Bois,* or fur traders and trappers, developed extensive trading networks. The Dutch settled **New Amsterdam** in 1624 and established fur trading posts along rivers into the interior.

The motives for European expansion into the Americas were wealth, religious persecution, missionary work, and the search for **"Utopia."** This movement had profound and catastrophic consequences for all involved. The great American civilizations prior to European contact were diverse, substantial, sophisticated, and in many ways equivalent to European and Asian civilizations, and native populations were destroyed.

$\frac{7}{10} = \frac{6}{10}$ for AP Test

Multiple-Choice Questions

1. Civilizations in the Americas before the arrival of Columbus
   a. were only small bands of hunters and gatherers.
   b. were substantial cultures with superior technology compared to Europe.
   c. included elaborate and sophisticated cultures that rivaled those of Europe.
   d. were nomadic tribes that used horses for hunting.
   e. had no written language, public buildings, or agriculture.

2. The Treaty of Tordesillas contained a provision to
   a. give Spain all rights to settle in the Americas.
   b. end Aztec domination in Mexico.
   c. end the rebellion of the Pueblos in New Mexico.
   d. divide the Americas between Spain and Portugal to colonize.
   e. allow England to colonize North America and Spain to colonize Central and South America.

3. Which of the following originated in the Americas and were taken to Europe?
   a. horses
   b. potatoes
   c. bananas
   d. cattle
   e. sugar cane

4. Groups in English society sought colonies in the Americas for all of the following reasons *except*
   a. to convert natives to Catholicism.
   b. to expand trade routes.
   c. to acquire raw materials for manufacturing enterprises.
   d. to search for refuge from repressive religious persecution.
   e. to further mercantile goals by gaining wealth.

5. Europeans in Central and South America relied on all of the following systems for meeting their labor needs except
   a. Indians used as slaves by the Spanish and Portuguese.
   b. a restrictive wage system where Indians were unable to leave their jobs without consent of their employers.
   c. slaves from Africa.
   d. large numbers of Spanish and Portuguese immigrants.
   e. a system by which Indian labor was licensed by the king to work on large estates.

6. The Coureurs des Bois relationship with Indians differed from the English because
   a. they formed successful partnerships with Indians by becoming a part of native society and intermarrying.
   b. they did not wish to trade with Indians for furs but stole pelts during a series of wars.
   c. there were so many French immigrants that the Indian population was overwhelmed.
   d. like the conquistadors, the Coureurs used brutal methods to convert Indians to Christianity.
   e. they did not respect Indian culture and subjugated them ruthlessly.

7. A principle of the economic theory of mercantilism was that
   a. centralized control of the economy was essential to increasing a nation's wealth.
   b. free trade and the market system would increase a country's productivity.
   c. the world's wealth increased as the population grew.
   d. importing goods from other countries would conserve a nation's resources and make it wealthier.
   e. government should not be involved in a nation's economy.

8. Puritans in England were discontented with the Church of England because
   a. Anglicans stressed spiritual matters more than worldly concerns.
   b. Puritans wanted to worship as they pleased in their own congregations, contrary to English law.
   c. they wanted more elaborate rituals in the Church of England services.
   d. they wanted a more powerful role for bishops of the Church.
   e. Puritans wanted English Catholics to have the right to worship freely.

9. An assumption that the English learned in Ireland and brought to their American settlements was
   a. native populations were civilized and sophisticated and should be treated with respect.
   b. Irish loyalty to the Catholic Church was not an obstacle to their becoming members of the British Empire.
   c. Irish culture and language could be adopted by English settlers.
   d. that the Irish fought bravely and in a civilized manner.
   e. English colonial settlements must remain separated from native populations.

10. The first permanent English settlement in North America was
    a. Roanoke Island.
    b. Quebec.
    c. New Amsterdam.
    d. Jamestown.
    e. Newfoundland.

Free-Response Question—Exam Tip

Free-response questions dating from this era can focus on relations between Indians and the Europeans. Note the major characteristics of the various Native American and European cultures and how they interacted with one another.

Free-Response Question

1. Evaluate the success of the Spanish in assimilating native populations into their colonial society in the Americas.

Document-Based Question—Exam Tip

Use all the information in the documents to help answer the document-based question. The source attribution can give very helpful hints; in this case it is a drawing by a European, and most likely an Englishman. The place and date point to the first settlement at Roanoke Island. Recognizing the point of view and using it to develop evidence will give your analysis more substance.

Document-Based Question

Knowing that the artist has a European point of view allows you to make some observations about the aspects of Indian society that are illustrated, including housing, diversified agriculture, hunting, and religion. White appears to have superimposed his European values on the scene. The geometrically shaped fields neatly tended, a straight and broad main road running through the center of the village, and the neat arrangement of the buildings quite probably is an indication of what White thinks the village should look like rather than what Secoton actually looked like. Using outside knowledge that settlers had to be lured to emigrate to America, one might surmise that White was creating a scene to invite rather than intimidate, emphasizing the promise of this new land to the viewer, and promoting immigration to America. Motive played an important role in descriptions of the Americas. In order to promote immigration the Americas were portrayed as inviting, with native cultures that imitated the world Europeans would be leaving. Portrayed as both an opportunity and a familiar environment, this illustration might induce European migration to America.

Source: British Museum

*The Indian Village of
Secoton in North Carolina*
(ca. 1585)
by John White

Multiple-Choice Answers

1. c. The Mesoamerican cultures had large populations with cities that rivaled those in
   Europe. However, Europe had a more sophisticated and advanced technological base.

2. d. The Treaty of Tordesillas was drafted by the Pope in 1494 to prevent conflict and give
   these two Catholic nations rights to settlement in Africa and America.

3. b. In this group of alternatives, potatoes are the only crop or animal that migrated from
   America to Europe. The others were either from Europe or its colonies and were brought
   to the American mainland.

4. a. The English did not seek to convert Indians as a primary reason for migrating to the
   Americas. They did have economic motives, and wanted to escape religious persecution.

5. d. The Spanish and Portuguese colonies did not attract large numbers of European
   immigrants, and as a result they relied on Indians or Africans to meet their labor needs.

6. a. The French forged the most peaceful relationships with the Indians of North America by respecting Native American culture, joining their society, and adopting their customs.

7. a. Mercantilism held that wealth was fixed and that a nation must export more than it imported to funnel wealth into the country. Central control was necessary to make sure this happened.

8. b. Puritans believed that the Church of England was too Catholic and "Popish," with elaborate services and an emphasis on this world rather than the next. They wanted to follow the dictates of their conscience and worship accordingly, but were prevented from doing so.

9. e. The English considered the Irish savage and uncivilized, and in the sixteenth century established plantations in Ireland that kept them separate. They carried this assumption to America, where "heathen" Indians were looked at in the same light. English settlements were erected apart from natives.

10. d. Jamestown barely survived, whereas Roanoke, about 20 years earlier, did not. The other colonies listed were not English but French and Dutch. Newfoundland was claimed by the English but not settled early.

Free-Response Question Commentary

1. This question asks you to assess the success of Spanish policies and practices in assimilating natives into their colonial society; the most sophisticated answers will tackle both sides of the issue and make a determination as to both success and failure. Consider Spanish attempts to incorporate the Indian population into its mainstream colonial society, such as conversion to Catholicism, intermarriage, and the blurring of racial lines so that an Indian could become "Spanish" and rise in the social and political hierarchy. The Spanish made few attempts to completely isolate the Native Americans from their communities, and the relatively small stream of Spanish immigration from Europe promoted the process of assimilation. Mitigating this was the critical need for labor colonists faced in mines, ranches, and farms. This led to brutal subjugation of native populations, and attempts to obliterate Indian culture (perhaps an argument for forced assimilation). Indians were actually or virtually enslaved by the encomienda system, and also remained a racial underclass in the Spanish colonies. The Pueblo Revolt is an example of Indian resistance to these aspects of Spanish colonization.

CHAPTER 2
Transportations and Borderlands

AP THEMES

- **Religion:** Religion or its absence played an important role in the settlement of all the North American colonies. Religious freedom was not a dominant feature of the early colonies. Rhode Island was founded with religious freedom as a principle. The many denominations founded in the post-Reformation era assured that diversity would characterize religion in the North American colonies.

- **Demographic Changes:** The contrast between New England and Virginia is most evident in demographic data. New Englanders emigrated in family groups, settled in a relatively healthy climate with compact settlement, and enjoyed a long life expectancy. In contrast, Virginians were mostly male, settled in a disease-ridden region, had a dispersed settlement, and suffered high mortality. Immigration continued throughout the seventeenth century and westward migration continued as the century progressed.

- **American Identity:** The Puritan idea of creating a "city on a hill" as an example to a corrupt England embedded a sense of mission into the American identity. The Puritans wished to transmit their idea of utopia to the rest of the world. Other distinct characteristics established during this early period were slavery, democratic foundations, and ethnic and religious diversity.

- **American Diversity:** Although England sponsored settlement in the North American colonies, settlers came from throughout Europe, the Caribbean, and Africa to live with Native Americans. Africans quickly became an underclass upon which a system of white superiority was based throughout the colonies. The Scots-Irish, resistant to authority in their European homes, settled in western frontier areas away from imperial and colonial control. In the middle and southern colonies a variety of people from mainland Europe settled and created a heterogeneous population.

- **Environment:** The abundance of land differentiated America from Europe. This led Americans to use and then abandon resources rather than to conserve and reuse them. Coastal lands were abandoned and farmers moved to the west. Population growth and the clearing of lands eliminated forests and created pollution in the increasingly densely populated seaports.

CHAPTER SUMMARY
The Early Chesapeake

The early attempts to transplant and replicate English society in North America were carried out by **joint-stock companies** chartered by the Crown. The **Virginia Company** settled the first permanent colony in Virginia in 1607. **Jamestown** was hampered by a high **mortality rate.** The site was low, swampy, and in the territory of the powerful **Powhatan** Indians. Settlers were prone to diseases such as malaria. The settlers were almost entirely men with few useful skills; no sense of community developed.

Captain John Smith was the leader of the Jamestown settlers. In 1608, he imposed order and discipline, with the result that few deaths occurred during the second winter. However, soon after he left for England problems arose again even though the colony received more immigrants and supplies. Initially the Powhatan Indians showed the English how to cultivate corn, or **maize,** but by the winter of 1609–1610, known as the starving time, relations turned sour. The survivors were reinforced by continued immigration, and governors achieved some stability by implementing harsh regimes. The institution of private property, **John Rolfe's** introduction of **tobacco,** an influx of skilled workers and **indentured servants** due to the Headright system, political participation in the House of Burgesses, and the introduction of **African labor** helped Virginia achieve stability and modest success.

Virginia's expansion came at the expense of the local Powhatan Indians. In 1622 the Powhatan attacked Jamestown, killing one-quarter of the population. In the aftermath the colonists pursued a strategy of suppression that ended the Powhatan threat by 1644. However, the 1622 attacks drove the Virginia Company into bankruptcy, and the king revoked its charter in 1624, bringing the colony under the control of the crown as a **royal colony.**

The Catholic Calvert family was awarded **Maryland** as a **proprietary colony** in 1632. **Lord Baltimore, Cecilius Calvert,** saw this as both a commercial venture and a refuge for English Catholics. To fulfill the commercial goal, he invited Protestants to live in Maryland. As a result, they almost immediately outnumbered Catholics. To protect the Catholic minority, Maryland adopted the Act of Toleration in 1649; however, frequent conflict between the two denominations ensued. Large land grants from the proprietors established a powerful landed aristocracy, and instability in Maryland resulted from warfare among the settlers rather than with the Indians. Maryland also used the Headright system, indentured servants, and ultimately slaves to cultivate the labor-intensive tobacco crop.

By the middle of the seventeenth century Virginia was prospering largely as a result of tobacco. As the colonists expanded west, conflicts with Indians increased. The governor, **Sir William Berkeley,** attempted to resolve these conflicts by setting aside land areas for the natives and restricting English settlement in those areas. This furthered the existing schism between the land-hungry western "backcountry gentry" and the eastern aristocracy. In 1676 this erupted into revolt when **Nathaniel Bacon,** a backcountry landowner, attacked Indians in defiance of the Governor. Twice, Bacon attacked Jamestown, but Berkeley regained control. Bacon died of dysentery and troops arrived from England. Bacon's Rebellion left the Indians in a weaker position with less territory. The episode revealed the unwillingness of the English to honor agreements with Indians, the bitterness between eastern and western interests, and the dangers of an unstable landless population.

The Growth of New England

Puritan dissenters from the Church of England known as Pilgrim Separatists founded the first lasting settlement in New England after first moving to Holland to escape **Anglican** repression. They obtained permission to settle in America, and in 1620 a small group aboard the *Mayflower* settled at **Plymouth,** north of Cape Cod. The Separatists established a civil government based on majority rule in the Mayflower Compact. The Massachusetts Indians were less able to resist the European settlement than the Powhatans because the Massachusetts Indians had been weakened by disease. Even with assistance from **Squanto** and Samoset, half the Pilgrims perished during the first winter. Their belief that they were fulfilling God's will sustained the community.

Another group, the **Puritans,** many of whom were merchants, obtained a charter for the Massachusetts Bay Company and 1,000 colonists arrived in the area around Boston in 1630.

The Massachusetts charter served as a foundation for the government and **John Winthrop** was chosen governor. Puritan villages each regulated their own affairs. Seeing themselves as an example of a godly community to purify England, they created **"a city upon a hill"** to be an example to the world. The clergy and government worked closely together and, for all intent and purpose, created a theocracy. Only male church members, the **"saints"** as they were known, could vote or hold office. The strong sense of community, a continuing influx of immigrants, aid from the Indians and Pilgrims, and a strong sense of religious purpose promoted rapid growth and prosperity, Puritans left England to practice their religion, but they did not support religious freedom. Those who did not accept Puritan orthodoxy were forced to leave Massachusetts. **Thomas Hooker,** a Puritan minister, settled with his congregation in the fertile Connecticut River Valley at **Hartford** in 1639 and adopted a written constitution, the Fundamental Orders of Connecticut, with a more inclusive male franchise than in Massachusetts Bay. The New Haven Colony merged with Hartford in 1662.

Puritan minister **Roger Williams,** who argued for the complete **separation of church and state,** was banished from Massachusetts in 1635. He bought land from the Narragansett Indians and founded Providence in Rhode Island. Granted a royal charter in 1644, Rhode Island had no **established church** and supported religious freedom. A charismatic and pious Boston woman, **Anne Hutchinson,** preached in her home what was criticized as the Antinomian heresy: that only those who had a conversion experience could be one of the **elect,** and that **good works** alone were not sufficient proof of sainthood. She criticized the established clergy, crossed the boundary of a woman's proper role, and claimed to have direct communication with God. She too was banished to Newport, Rhode Island, in 1637. Three years later, dissident **John Wheelwright,** an adherent of Hutchinson, founded New Hampshire.

Because European diseases had decimated their populations, the northern Indians were in a less advantageous position than those to the south. They provided assistance to the settlers, sold their lands, and traded furs to the European settlers. They taught the Europeans about local crops—corn, beans, pumpkins, and potatoes—and agricultural techniques. However, conflicts arose as the settlers moved inland. Also, Puritans were increasingly critical of the "heathen" Indians and their threat to godly Puritan communities. Although some tried to convert the natives, most Puritans came to accept removal or extermination as the way to solve the Indian "problem." At the same time the Indians' way of life was threatened as colonists cleared forests, drove off game, allowed roaming livestock to destroy native crops, introduced alcohol, and infected natives with disease. The native populations declined precipitously.

More than anything else competition over land and power prompted conflict. In the 1637 **Pequot War** Puritans were particularly brutal, killing Indian women and children. English incursion on native lands led **Metacomet,** or **King Philip,** a **Wampanoag** chief, to strike back in 1675. Settlers allied with the **Mohawk** tribe against the Wampanoags, and **King Philip's War** took a heavy toll on all sides. The Indian threat to the English diminished but was not eliminated. Casualties were high in part because Indians adopted English technology and strategy, such as the **flintlock** rifle and forts where bloody battles occurred.

The Restoration Colonies

Events in England always had an effect on the American colonies, and the **English Civil War** and the **Restoration** of Charles II to the throne in 1660 was no exception. Charles rewarded his followers with land grants in the colonies. Eight proprietors received a grant of land from Virginia to Georgia with nearly absolute power to rule and named the area **Carolina;** they hoped to profit as landlords and land speculators. Aided by philosopher **John Locke,** the proprietors drafted a constitution, but actual settlement followed a different pattern. Family subsistence farming developed in the north. In the more cosmopolitan and aristocratic south, cultivation of **rice** and trade were the major commercial ventures. **Barbadian** emigrants brought **African slaves** to the colony, and a **plantation**-based society arose. Tensions between the north and south ended when the king separated them into two royal colonies in 1729.

The Atlantic commercial rivalry between the Dutch and English intensified when Charles II granted the Duke of York, his brother James, land between the Connecticut and Delaware Rivers that had been occupied by the Dutch since 1624. York established his claim to the former **New Netherland** in 1664 when an English fleet captured **New Amsterdam.** Renamed **New York,** the colony boasted an extraordinarily diverse population from a variety of European countries, as well as Africans and Native Americans. Religious toleration was guaranteed, and political authority rested in a governor and council, and local governments. The large Dutch estates, called **patroons,** remained, and similar land grants were made by the proprietor. Agriculture, the fur trade, and commerce supported the economy. James granted his lands south of New York to **John Berkeley** and **George Carteret.** **The colony of New Jersey** contained enormous ethnic and religious diversity. After a decade New Jersey became a royal colony.

William Penn, a **Quaker** from the **Society of Friends,** was owed a large debt from the king, who repaid it by a grant of land between New York and Maryland. Rejecting the Puritan concepts of predestination and original sin, Quakers believed all people contained an **inner light** that could lead them to salvation. Women assumed a position equal to that of men in the church. Generally democratic, pacifist, and unpopular in England, Quakers looked to America as a refuge, and Penn provided it. He successfully attracted settlers from throughout Europe, and Pennsylvania became the most cosmopolitan American colony. Penn purchased land for the Indians, and his holy experiment practiced some degree of democracy with its representative assembly. The 1701 **Charter of Liberties** limited the proprietor's power.

Borderlands and Middle Grounds

Although Spain claimed all the **Caribbean islands,** it settled only a few and England settled others without contest. Sugarcane, with its potential to be distilled into rum, became the cash crop, and enslaved Africans became the labor force. The small, white ruling class governed a larger number of Africans and natives, creating much instability. Slave mortality was high because of the climate and harsh treatment. Slave revolts took place despite legal codes to ensure white supremacy, and other forms of resistance also developed. The Caribbean was an important part of the Atlantic **triangular trade** with sugar, rum, and slaves being sent to the mainland and England. These islands provided models for the North American plantation system.

To the south and west lay the Spanish Empire. The Spanish established **presidios** along the Californian coast and **missions** throughout the southwest to convert natives, who were forced to work on estates and died in great numbers. These Spanish borderlands were neither vibrant nor growing, nor did they attempt to displace native populations. Unlike the

English, the Spanish intermarried with natives. The two societies were blended, even if the Spanish did not treat natives well as a group.

The Spanish in Florida were a more direct threat to the English than in the Southwest. Settlement was centered around **St. Augustine** in the east and Pensacola on the Gulf Coast. Tension between the English and Spanish arose frequently. Florida ceased to be a threat only after the French and Indian War in 1763.

In part to counter this Spanish threat, King George granted a charter for land between the Carolinas and Florida to a group led by **James Oglethorpe** in 1732. These trustees hoped to provide a buffer from the Spanish and be a refuge for debtors and the poor. To meet these goals, compact settlement was encouraged, Africans were excluded, rum was prohibited, and trade with Indians was regulated. Few English debtors settled in Georgia, but other European colonists came from throughout Europe. The restrictive laws stifled early development, and the trustees ultimately removed them, but growth took place slowly.

Along the western borders English colonists were too few to dominate and learned to live in an uneasy truce with Native Americans. Indians resented this European intrusion but looked to the French and British for gifts, weapons, and mediation of internal disputes and conflicts between tribes. The French quickly learned this role, but French influence waned by the mid-1700s and was replaced by the English, who never completely accepted the efficacy of gifts, ceremony, and mediation, and ultimately turned to conquest and subjugation.

The Evolution of the British Empire

By 1650 the continued success of the colonial system demanded a more organized imperial structure. England embraced **mercantilism,** an economic theory aimed at increasing a nation's wealth by prohibiting colonies from trading with foreign nations, using colonies for raw materials, and selling manufactured goods in colonial markets. To counter Dutch shipping competition and colonial trade with Americans, Britain passed a series of laws to regulate trade called **Navigation Acts.** These laws required colonial trade to be carried in British ships, certain products to be sent directly to England, and goods from Europe to first pass through England before going to the colonies. The laws encouraged the colonial shipbuilding industry and created demand for colonial goods in England. Despite the presence of customs officials and colonial protests, the Navigation Acts served both Britain and its colonies well.

Britain had been increasing imperial control over the American colonies by gradually converting them to **royal colonies;** Massachusetts joined this group in 1684. In a further attempt at control, the crown united the New England colonies into the Dominion of New England in 1686, and later added New York and New Jersey. James II abolished the existing representative assemblies and appointed a single governor, **Edmund Andros,** whose rigid enforcement of the Navigation Acts quickly made him unpopular.

The Catholic King James II was losing support in England as well as in America. In 1688 Parliament invited his Protestant daughter **Mary,** and her husband, **William of Orange,** to assume the throne. James fled, and northern colonists dissolved the Dominion of New England. News of this **Glorious Revolution** inspired **Jacob Leisler,** a German immigrant merchant, to challenge the ruling New York elite. He ruled for two years but was ultimately tried for treason and hanged. In Maryland, **John Coode** revolted against the proprietor's government, drove out the ruling officials, and established a committee to govern the colony. Although these actions in the wake of the Glorious Revolution validated certain rights of Englishmen, the colonies were more closely bound to royal authority by the end of the century than before.

Multiple-Choice Questions

1. One of the problems in Jamestown that led to a high mortality rate in the early years was
    a. Captain John Smith's lack of leadership and inability to impose order and discipline on the settlers.
    b. the settlement lay outside the territory of the helpful Powhatan tribe.
    c. the family groups were more susceptible to disease than single male settlers.
    d. the initiation of the Headright system, which promoted private property and migration of skilled workers.
    e. the cultivation of the staple crop tobacco for trade instead of grain.

2. The immediate event that sent the Virginia Company into bankruptcy and prompted James I to revoke its charter in 1624 was
    a. the creation of the House of Burgesses.
    b. the "starving time" when a vast majority of the settlers died.
    c. the introduction of African labor to the colony.
    d. John Rolfe's marriage to Pocahontas.
    e. savage Powhatan attacks on the settlement.

3. All of the following individuals were involved in colonization of the Chesapeake *except*
    a. John Winthrop.
    b. Sir William Berkeley.
    c. John Rolfe.
    d. Opechancanough.
    e. Cecilius Calvert.

4. The Calvert family adopted the Toleration Act in 1649 because
    a. Catholics found Protestants friendly and helpful.
    b. warfare between Indians and settlers was destabilizing the colony.
    c. indentured servants refused to join the Catholic Church.
    d. the Calverts decided to abandon the original goal of providing a refuge for Catholics.
    e. Protestants quickly outnumbered Catholics in the colony.

5. The main reason for conflict between Native Americans and European settlers in the early English colonies was
    a. little exchange of agricultural methods and crops.
    b. the Native American alliances with the French.
    c. expansion by the Indians on established English settlements.
    d. diseases contracted by the English from Native Americans.
    e. population pressures on the English settlers to expand westward.

6. All of the following contributed to a foundation of democratic government in America *except* the
   a. Mayflower Compact.
   b. House of Burgesses.
   c. Dominion of New England.
   d. Fundamental Orders of Connecticut.
   e. Maryland Act of Toleration.

7. Resentment of a powerful coastal ruling class by western farmers and of Indian attacks instigated
   a. Leisler's Rebellion.
   b. John Coode's Rebellion.
   c. Bacon's Rebellion.
   d. the Pequot War.
   e. the founding of Rhode Island.

8. Puritan theology included a belief that
   a. every individual contained an "inner light" that could lead to salvation.
   b. the Bishop would chose ministers for each church.
   c. man was innately good, and free from sin.
   d. God chose who was saved before they were born.
   e. good works and faith would lead to salvation.

9. Slavery emerged in the Chesapeake region
   a. upon the first arrival of Africans at Jamestown in 1619.
   b. over time as labor demand increased and the flow of indentured servants decreased.
   c. when colonists learned that Indians made poor servants.
   d. when cotton became the primary crop in the region.
   e. when colonists emulated the Barbadian plantation system.

10. A leader in establishing the principle of religious freedom and diversity in America was
    a. Roger Williams of Rhode Island.
    b. John Winthrop of Massachusetts.
    c. Jacob Leisler of New York.
    d. William Berkeley of Virginia.
    e. King Philip of Massachusetts.

11. Spanish and French colonization patterns differed from those of the English by
    a. settling around areas already occupied by Indians so there was little contact.
    b. including Indians in their society and intermarrying with them.
    c. respecting native religion and making no attempt at conversion to Christianity.
    d. sending large armies to America to subdue the hostile Indians.
    e. sponsoring large numbers of emigrants to settle in North America.

12. The contention that colonial events were directly influenced by actions and events in England is illustrated by which of the following correctly paired events?
    a. restoration of Charles II—Founding of Georgia
    b. persecution of Roman Catholics in Ireland—Maryland Act of Toleration
    c. John Locke's political philosophy—Fundamental Orders of Connecticut
    d. Dutch and English commercial rivalry—Penn's Charter of Liberties
    e. the Glorious Revolution—Leisler's Rebellion

13. The Dominion of New England was an attempt
    a. to rationalize colonial policy and consolidate it in the Crown.
    b. to strengthen defenses against hostile Indians.
    c. by Massachusetts to gain power in the region.
    d. by the Puritan church to spread its religion throughout the Northeast colonies.
    e. to counter the economic restrictions of the Navigation Acts.

14. John Winthrop's characterization of Massachusetts Bay as "a city on a hill" implied that
    a. Boston would be settled on high, defensible ground.
    b. Massachusetts Bay would be an example for England to emulate.
    c. Puritans were superior in their theology to the Pilgrims.
    d. Massachusetts Puritans offered religious freedom to all settlers.
    e. Puritans should leave England and immigrate to the colonies.

Free-Response Questions—Exam Tips

The early colonial free-response questions often explore problems of settlement, relations with Native Americans, imperial relations with England, religion, and comparisons between the colonies of France, England, and Spain.

Free-Response Questions

1. To what extent did English attempts to increase imperial control over the colonies during the seventeenth century succeed in making the colonies dependent on England in political and economic terms?
2. Evaluate the significance of religion in colonial development in sixteenth-century British North America.

Document-Based Question—Exam Tips

Consider the following when using documents in the document-based question:
- Most documents are written—use the information contained in the document, the clues from the source identification, and information from the question itself to help you learn about how to use the document to help support your argument.
- Documents should always be analyzed in the context of the prompt.
- Consider the author, date, audience, point of view, and purpose to draw conclusions from the document to use in your answer.
- Use the information to connect to other documents, your own background knowledge, and the question.
- Do not quote extensively (such as more than one sentence) from the document. Instead, use as short a quotation as possible to demonstrate your analysis of the document within the context of the question. You should paraphrase, that is, condense the main idea, into a short statement to convey its meaning, which supports your thesis.

Document-Based Question

Use the documents that follow as well as your own background knowledge to write a paragraph answering the following:
- In Virginia's early years of settlement, how do you reconcile its high mortality rates with the ability of the Virginia Company to entice people to migrate there?

Document A	**Document B**
Source: Captain John Smith, *Works*: 1608–1631	*Source*: Richard Frethorne, *Letter to his mother and father*, March 20, April 2 and 3, 1623, in the Records of the Virginia Company of London.
The mildness of the aire, the fertilitie of the soile, and the situation of the rivers are so propitious to the nature and use of man as no place is more convenient for pleasure profit, and man's sustenance. Under that latitude or climat, here will live any beasts, as horses, goats, sheep, asses, hens, &c. as appeared by them that were carried thither… …So then here is a place a nurse for souldiers, a practice for mariners, a trade for marchants, a reward for the good, and that which is most of all a businese (most acceptable to God) to bring such poore infidels to the true knowledge of God and his holy Gospell.	Loveing and kind father and mother… this is to let you vnderstand that I yo' Child am in a most heavie Case by reason of the nature of the Country…is such that it Causeth much sickness, as the scurvie and the bloody flix, and divers other diseases, wch maketh the bodie very poore, and Weake…since I came out of the ship, I never at [ate] anie thing but pease, and loblollie (that is water gruell) as for deare or venison I never saw anie since I came into this land… …if you love me you will redeeme me suddenlie, good ffather doe not forget me, but have m^{o}cie [mercy] and pittye my miserable Case.

Multiple-Choice Answers

1. e. Although settlers were starving, the lure of wealth from tobacco cultivation pushed them to grow it rather than foodstuffs.

2. e. 1622 Powhatan attacks killed nearly 25 percent of the Jamestown population and led to the bankruptcy.

3. a. John Winthrop was governor of the Massachusetts Bay Colony.

4. e. With a Protestant majority, the Toleration Act would ensure Maryland Catholics the freedom to worship.

5. e. Although other issues caused conflict between Indians and settlers, the English encroachment on Indian land created continual tension.

6. c. The Dominion of New England in 1686 suspended the local assemblies of New England colonies and put them under royal control.

7. c. Virginian Nathanial Bacon confronted the tidewater elite and attacked Indian tribes against the Governor's orders, starting a rebellion.

8. d. Predestination was a central tenant of Puritan theology.

9. b. The first African workers were most likely indentured servants. Slavery for life developed over time as fewer indentured servants migrated to the colonies.

10. a. Roger Williams was banished from Massachusetts for advocating the separation of church and state because he thought the state would corrupt the church.

11. b. The English tried to transplant English society in America, a vision that did not include Indians. The mostly male Spanish and French colonists created a society that included Indians.

12. e. Leisler assumed power in New York only after the royal governor lost his authority because of the fall of James II in England.

13. a. In his attempts to consolidate power within the empire James II created the Dominion of New England.

14. b. As religious reformers, John Winthrop and the Puritans hoped to establish a religious utopia for England to follow and mimic.

Free-Response Questions Commentary

1. In geographic terms the colonies lay largely outside of the effective control of England, although events in the mother country often had important effects in the colonies. Both charter colonies and proprietary colonies were converted to royal colonies over time, which increased royal control. Also, the Navigation Acts attempted to centralize control of the imperial economy and keep the colonies as suppliers of raw materials and markets for manufactured goods. The colonies did depend on England for manufactured goods and as a market for colonial goods, but tended toward self-government in political terms and often thwarted the will of the royal governors. Lax enforcement and inattention by the king and Parliament meant that the colonies depended on England for their economy but were in the process of creating their own governing systems.

2. Both the presence and absence of religion played a vital role in the early colonies. It was central to colonies in New England, providing both motivation for settlement and patterns for settlement to take place. Puritanism was central to compact settlement, town meetings, and the idea of majority rule as embodied in the Mayflower Compact. Education, culture, politics, and society all revolved around varieties of Puritan theology.

   The mid-Atlantic colonies were more diverse. The New York population practiced a number of different religions, which set it on a path of both secularism and religious toleration. Quakerism in New Jersey, and particularly Pennsylvania, provided ideologies leading to religious toleration and freedom, acceptance of different European cultures, rejection of slavery, and relatively fair dealings with Native Americans.

   Maryland's Catholic purpose and Protestant majority allowed for the Toleration Act, but the two denominations fought one another for the better part of the century. Virginia differed markedly from its Chesapeake neighbor. Although the established church was Anglican, religion was conspicuous by its absence, and dispersed settlement resulted from no religious centers to hold the population. Instability and disorder were endemic in Virginia, in part because of religion's minimal role.

Document-Based Question Commentary

This question asks about the seeming contradiction between the high mortality rates in the Virginia Colony at Jamestown and the steady flow of immigrants over the course of the seventeenth century.

Background Information: To set the historical context of this question you might include information about the poor English economy, poverty, the hopelessness of ever acquiring any land, persecution, and political unrest. The situation in Virginia was dire, with disease, Indian attacks, and starvation killing a high percentage of settlers. The Virginia Company tried to lure settlers by use of both the Headright and by publishing exaggerated accounts of Virginian benefits.

The Documents: The documents present contradictory portraits of life in the Chesapeake. In Document A, John Smith's description of Virginia is predictable. A member of the Virginia Company who hoped to profit from the venture, he writes in glowing terms about the colony and its prospects. He is a promoter hoping to increase both immigration and the chances of success. Since this cannot have been written after 1631, the colony was on the edge of failure, and one must not take it at face value.

Document B is written by a servant suffering in Virginia. He writes of disease, starvation, and deprivation and begs his father to bring him back to England. However, Freethorne may have exaggerated his plight in the hopes that his family would act more quickly to redeem him.

Use both documents to explain the tension. Many prospective emigrants to Virginia would have only accounts like those of Smith upon which to decide to go to Virginia. He paints a rosy picture to someone who has no hopes in England and who can gain a Headright in the Chesapeake. However, the Virginia reality was harsh, and only a continual influx of people from Europe maintained the population.

Comparative Exercise: Review the following chart comparing the Chesapeake and New England colonies from 1607 to 1670.

Trait	Chesapeake	New England
Motives for Settlement	This was a commercial and profit-seeking venture.	Commercial but, most important, religious—Puritans sought to establish a religious utopia, "a city on a hill."
Settler Demographics	Young, single men who spear out in dispersed settlements. Few women or families went to Virginia. Indentured servants, and later, African slaves.	Families with a variety of skills settled in compact settlements. Unlike Virginia, natural increase added to the population by 1650.
Economic System	Commercial farming and tobacco was the staple crop, and the economy centered on its cultivation and the plantation system.	Small family "self-sufficient" farms would sell any surplus in the market; soil was good for livestock. Small commercial ventures, lumber, and fish.
Social Patterns	Many lower-class workers. Small families that were complex because of early death. A plantation aristocracy held disproportionate social and political power to its numbers.	Settled by the "middling sort," there was not a great gap between rich and poor. A religious hierarchy exercised social and political power.
Political Structures	The planter aristocracy held power, and a representative assembly, the House of Burgesses, was established in 1619.	A religious hierarchy held power, and the General Court, the charter's governing board, became the assembly. Town Meetings exercised power on the local level.
Religion	Anglican, but not significant. Its absence led to instability and disorder.	Puritan, it permeated every aspect of life and all institutions were informed by its theology.
Labor System	A combination of free labor, indentured servitude, and later slavery.	Free labor and indentured servitude abounded. Slavery existed, but played a very minor role.
Indian Relations	There were good relations at the very beginning, but they soon soured. The English goal ultimately was to remove or exterminate the Indians.	The Indians helped the settlers survive the first winters, but land competition led to conflict. Once conversion was abandoned, Puritans wanted to remove or exterminate the Indians.

CHAPTER 3
Society and Culture in Provincial America

AP THEMES

- **American Identity:** Contradictory trends were taking place in the American colonies to the mid-eighteenth century. Colonists had come to America for a variety of reasons, but many had been forced out of their countries because of economic hardship and political and religious persecution. These migrants harbored antiauthoritarian characteristics and often settled in regions with others of like-minds. The grasp of both English culture and authority over the colonies was strengthening; the Crown attempted to increase its control as English goods and fashions came into the colonies. Both autonomy and integration were taking place simultaneously.

- **Culture:** Continued immigration injected various cultural streams into the American colonies; this is particularly the case with religion, where European sects joined colonial dissenters to form new denominations. Puritan New England placed a stronger emphasis on education than the southern colonies. The hubs of learning and scientific inquiry were the cities such as Cambridge, which hosted the first college in America. The Massachusetts School Act, passed in 1647, provided for public education for white Americans only.

- **Demographic Changes:** An increasing stream of immigrants flowed to the American colonies by the end of the seventeenth century. Deteriorating conditions in mainland Europe pushed German and French Protestants to the colonies, and Scot-Irish began to replace the English as economic conditions in England improved. Most significant was the increasing stream of black laborers from Africa and the Caribbean who replaced the declining number of indentured servants. Mortality rates decreased more so in the northern colonies than in the south, and by the mid-seventeenth century New England's population was increasing naturally. The southern colonies depended on immigration to grow until the eighteenth century. The European population doubled nearly every twenty-five years.

- **Economic Transformations:** After the early years when survival was the first order, a thriving colonial economy developed accompanied by a growing consumer culture. Throughout English America agriculture was the dominant economic activity. In the Carolinas, rice and later indigo became important crops. The Navigation Acts were a boon to shipbuilding in New England, as well as to other manufacturing ventures that used the region's abundant water power. Commercial farming in the middle colonies provided foodstuffs for New England, the Caribbean, and Europe. The slave trade between Africa, the Caribbean, and America flourished. This all occurred in the context of a complex trading network labeled the "triangular trade." As Americans searched for markets throughout the Atlantic a more apt label would be the "Atlantic polygon."

- **Religion:** Religion and religious intensity affected the various regions differently. The Anglican Church was most common in Virginia, but was not a commanding presence. Maryland's conflict between Catholics and Protestants diminished in the late seventeenth century. In New England religious declension worried many. Reaction ran from witchcraft hysteria to religious revivals during the Great Awakening. Both point to the fact that religion played an important role in people's lives.

- **Slavery and Its Legacies in North America:** As American society matured, the black population developed a distinct slave culture that blended both European and African tradition. The slave family grew beyond the nuclear family into an extended kinship network that provided for those left behind when families were separated. The church and religion provided solace and hope for freedom—if not in this life, then in the next. Slaves also developed the ability to cope with slavery's harsh realities. Unique dialects forged from a mix of African and English were used by slaves. In some areas of the United States, these dialects still exist today.

CHAPTER SUMMARY
The Colonial Population

Immigrants, coming from various areas of the Atlantic world, contributed to heterogeneous and divergent societies in distinct American regions. Most depended on England for goods, literature, and culture. Their common English heritage played an important role even as the regional differences caused tension and even conflict in the colonial period.

By the late seventeenth century natural increase and immigration made the European and African populations a majority in the colonies. A salient feature of the population was **indentured servitude.** A majority of immigrants came from the lower or working classes. Convicts, orphans, vagrants, and paupers were sent to the colonies. The population contained an unstable mix of single men and landless families. Indentured servitude declined by the late seventeenth century and African slavery grew in its place.

High mortality rates diminished by 1700, and New England saw a natural increase in population as early as the 1650s primarily because of exceptional longevity. In the Chesapeake, mortality rates remained high for another 100 years, and population there increased primarily by immigration. Throughout the colonies, the ratio of men to women gradually improved.

In the Chesapeake, patterns of male authority were undermined as women often outlived their husbands. Childbearing was the most frequent cause of female mortality. Infant mortality was also high. Women enjoyed more power and freedom than in other regions. Regardless of gender, early death created blended families where the children often were not the biological offspring of either adult. There were also a high number of orphans. As mortality rates declined women began to lose their authority to men. Lower mortality rates in New England promoted more stable and traditional families. Child bearing and rearing dominated women's lives. With sons dependent on parents for land and daughters dependent on parents for **dowries,** parents had more control over their children. By both religion and tradition, authority was held by men. The family was the central economic and religious unit of society in New England. The scarcity of labor in the southern colonies created increased demand for slaves, which were scarce until England chartered the Royal African Company and the Dutch and French also joined in the **slave trade.** Most slaves came to North America from the Caribbean islands. The direct African trade grew after 1690 when the English monopoly lapsed. The **middle passage** was deadly for slaves. Initially, a preponderance of males limited the slave population, but this changed by the eighteenth century. The assumption of black inferiority and the development of specific slave codes gradually pushed Africans from the status of servant to slave for life. The **slave codes** were enacted one law at a time, gradually ensuring white supremacy.

With English prosperity increasing and conditions in other parts of Europe deteriorating, the mix of immigrants to America changed. Religious persecution drove French **Huguenots** and German Protestants to the colonies. Many Germans settled in Pennsylvania and were known as the **Pennsylvania Dutch** (Deutsch). Other immigrants went to North Carolina. Disdaining authority, **Scotch-Irish** Presbyterians migrated to the frontier and helped establish Presbyterianism as an important denomination. The European population in the colonies doubled nearly every twenty-five years.

The Colonial Economies

Commerce was the primary economic activity of most of the colonies. After some early problems, the British colonists quickly established trade with the Indians, as well as with the French and Spanish. The result was an expanding and increasingly complex Atlantic economy. However, agriculture dominated in all sections. Overproduction of **tobacco** in the Chesapeake caused serious price fluctuations and economic instability. Rice production in South Carolina and Georgia used slaves who came from African cultures with knowledge about its cultivation and were better adapted to this work. During the 1740s **indigo,** the source of blue dye, was introduced and complemented rice cultivation. Focus on these **staple crops** limited the growth of commerce and industry in the southern economy.

Areas in southern New England and the middle colonies were better suited for commercial farming. Home industries and craft enterprises grew, and larger enterprises that used **water power** ground **grain,** cut **timber,** and processed cloth. **Shipbuilding** prospered. An early **Ironworks at Saugus,** Massachusetts, was a technological success. **Navigation Acts** including the **Iron Act** restricted this and other manufacturing industries. Nonagricultural commerce dependent on extracting natural resources such as minerals, timber, and fish thrived.

Throughout the colonies many households were too isolated or poor to afford many basic goods and tools, but a few households were self-sufficient. They had to buy what they could not make. The colonial economy was unable to provide sufficient manufactured goods and commerce expanded to fill this demand. Despite disorder and the lack of currency in the Atlantic economy, a vibrant coastal trade, including extensive trade with the West Indies and England, developed. The complex **triangular trade** involved the American colonies, England, Africa, and Europe. Seaport cities developed a growing merchant class whose commerce was protected from foreign competition by the **Navigation Acts.** American merchants developed markets in the French, Spanish, and Dutch West Indies in violation of English law. Growing prosperity and the increasing supply of consumer goods resulted in **consumerism.** Material goods were considered virtuous and refined and raised a family's social status.

Patterns of Society

Circumstances in America—abundant land and a small population—reflected a reality opposite that of England's. As a result, the American aristocracy rested on consumerism, manufacturing, and the ability to control labor. There was substantial social mobility in the American colonies.

There were a few large southern plantations but most were modest farms with few or no slaves. These yeoman farmers and their families worked alongside the servants. Profits varied widely from year to year, and **dispersed settlement patterns** led plantations to strive for self-sufficiency. Slavery had profound social consequences in all households. White women on large plantations relied on black servants for domestic chores and were able to devote more time to family. Sexual relations between white men and black women caused resentment and anxiety among all women. Disproportionately small in numbers, the plantation gentry wielded economic and political power in the community. Consequently, small farmers were dependent on the gentry to sustain their livelihood.

By mid-eighteenth century, slaves developed an independent culture based on African tradition, family, language, and religion. Extended kinship networks emerged to support families that might have been broken up at any time. **Mixed race** children were seldom recognized by their fathers and remained slaves. Interaction with white society was constant, and treatment of slaves varied but was frequently brutal. Slave reactions ranged from rare but bloody uprisings such as the South Carolina **Stono Rebellion** to more passive forms of resistance and running away. On larger plantations slaves might learn trades and could be hired out. A few bought their freedom, adding to the small free black population.

In New England the basic social unit was the town based upon a religious and social **covenant.** A **town meeting** of adult males ran the affairs of the community. Full membership in the church depended upon evidence of **grace. Compact settlement** provided each family a home lot in the village with outlying farm lots. A family's land distribution depended upon its size, wealth, and social standing. Fathers divided family land among all sons rather than following the English practice of **primogeniture.** As land within towns became scarce due to population growth, sons moved to areas of more plentiful land. This tended to erode the authority of both the town and fathers.

With community cohesion eroding in the late seventeenth century and as new communities were developed, tensions occasionally arose between older and newer settlements. An extreme case was the 1692 **witchcraft** hysteria in Salem, Massachusetts. Adolescent girls began acting strangely and initially blamed a West Indian servant named Tituba. Witchcraft accusations spread, and nineteen Salem residents were executed for the crime of witchcraft. Generally, the accused were women of low social status who did not attend church, were accused of other crimes, or who owned substantial property and violated gender norms and inheritance patterns. Although some of the girls later recanted their stories, the witchcraft hysteria in Salem and other areas illustrates the highly contentious nature of this society.

Colonial cities, small by modern standards, served as markets for farm goods and for international commerce. The inequality of wealth was particularly evident in cites. Social problems surfaced in these densely populated areas. Eventually cities became cosmopolitan intellectual centers.

Awakenings and Enlightenments

Traditional emphasis on God vied with the Enlightenment's emphasis on science and reason as a force in individuals' lives. This created tension throughout the eighteenth century. Religious toleration existed in America only because conditions made it impossible to impose a single religion. Decline in the importance of religion was a growing concern among Puritans during the seventeenth century. The religious leaders hoped **Jeremiads** would lead people from sin to renewed piety.

The Great Awakening, a religious revival, sought to stem religious decline in the 1730s and 1740s. **Itinerant** evangelists preached that grace was available to all who renewed their relationship with God. Englishmen **John and Charles Wesley** and **George Whitefield** visited the colonies and spread the revival. Puritan preacher **Jonathan Edwards** preached the absolute sovereignty of God and rejected the idea of easy salvation. The Great Awakening challenged traditional authority and divided many congregations between revivalist **new lights** and traditional **old lights.** Ultimately, this led to the formation of new denominations. **The Enlightenment** argued that reason and scientific inquiry led to progress. This undermined traditional authority and encouraged education and independent thinking. Puritans valued education from the beginning, and Massachusetts required every town to support a **public school.** In 1647, some religious sects such as Quakers operated schools. Few people received more than a primary education. Slaves and Indians were left largely outside this system. Literacy was high among both men and women in New England. Early colleges included **Harvard,** founded in 1636, and **The College of William and Mary,** which was founded in 1693. These schools primarily trained preachers. Secular schools and curricula appeared by the mid-eighteenth century. **Benjamin Franklin** published a widely read **Almanac** and was America's most famous scientist for his experiments with lightening and electricity. Puritan minister **Cotton Mather** encouraged smallpox inoculation in Boston. Other eighteenth-century American Enlightenment thinkers include **Thomas Jefferson, Thomas Paine,** and **James Madison.**

The Enlightenment influenced the English political and legal systems that had been transplanted to the colonies. **John Peter Zenger's** trial for libel redefined that concept in America. America's isolation from centers of authority instilled the concept of self-government. Colonial assemblies began to assume the powers of Parliament, and limited the power of the colonial governors. Largely because of salutary neglect, England did not actively govern the American colonies, and provincial governments began to act independently.

Multiple-Choice Questions

1. The labor force in colonial America included which of the following over the course of the early eighteenth century?
    - I.   African slaves
    - II. Indentured servants
    - III. Free labor from continental Europe
    - IV. Women began to assume male working roles
    - V.   Indians were forced to work for colonists
    - a. I, II, III
    - b. II, III
    - c. I, III
    - d. I, IV, V
    - e. I, III, IV

2. The colonial population changed during the first half of the eighteenth century for all of the following reasons except
    - a. the flow of slaves from both Africa and the Caribbean increased.
    - b. Huguenots emigrated from France to escape persecution.
    - c. German Protestants left Germany for Pennsylvania.
    - d. Scots-Irish arrived and settled close to the frontier.
    - e. the number of indentured servants from England increased as the English economy declined.

3. The Navigation Acts
   a. helped the colonial economy by supporting shipbuilding and protecting trade from foreign competition.
   b. had more significance for trade on the frontier than on the coast.
   c. had a greater impact on coastwise trade in British North America than on its Atlantic trade.
   d. were irksome because of the great number of customs officials stationed in the colonies.
   e. hurt colonial trade by limiting trade excessively.

4. Which of the following regions is correctly matched with the products that region was known to produce?
   a. New England—shipbuilding, commercial farming of grain, livestock
   b. Carolinas—rice and indigo
   c. Middle colonies—timber, commercial farming of grain, commerce
   d. Chesapeake—tobacco, shipbuilding
   e. Georgia—trade, shipbuilding, indigo

5. Slavery in the plantation system
   a. was harsh without exception and allowed few freedoms.
   b. did not specify that offspring of relationships between white masters and slave women would be slaves.
   c. provided labor for a majority of plantations and farms in the South.
   d. provided for some flexibility and some slaves were able to buy their freedom.
   e. trained slaves only for domestic work or field work in gangs.

6. Enlightenment thought influenced the colonies by
   a. the development of the calculus at Harvard College.
   b. the colonial assemblies assuming the powers of Parliament within the colonies.
   c. the rejection of using inoculation to prevent smallpox epidemics.
   d. John Peter Zenger's trial narrowing the definition of liable in the colonies.
   e. lessening tension between religious and secular interests.

7. "New lights" during the Great Awakening
   a. pushed for a renewal of traditional Puritan religion.
   b. embraced and combined scientific discoveries with religion.
   c. challenged traditional authority and divided congregations.
   d. appealed mostly to older men and few women.
   e. opposed the message of itinerant preachers such as George Whitefield.

8. Puritan theologian Jonathan Edwards strayed from Puritan orthodoxy in his belief that
   a. few would be saved and individuals could do nothing to affect their salvation.
   b. salvation was available to all and easy to gain.
   c. God and ministers shared power to save sinners.
   d. God's power was absolute, but one could work toward salvation although it was difficult to gain.
   e. bishops could determine who in the congregation would be saved.

9. Religious toleration developed in America because
   a. Puritans who fled persecution in England and migrated to America for religious freedom offered it to others.
   b. so many immigrants with different religious backgrounds settled in America, it was impossible to impose a single religion.
   c. the king included it as one of the liberties contained in the colonies' charters.
   d. Native American religious were pervasive and had to be accepted by all the colonies.
   e. most of the English settlers were Quakers who were both pacifists and very tolerant of others.

10. The 1692 witchcraft crisis in Salem illustrates
    a. the pervasive presence of witches and Satan in colonial Massachusetts.
    b. that religion played a small role in people's lives if they could believe in witchcraft.
    c. that the Enlightenment and scientific revolution must have had little effect in New England.
    d. demonstrable proof that witches existed.
    e. that the weak in society were open to persecution by the majority.

11. After the first few decades of settlement in British North America
    a. mortality remained high and immigration provided what population growth there was.
    b. the trend was for colonies to convert from royal colonies to charter colonies.
    c. conflicts with Indians continued as settlers pushed westward and settled on lands claimed by Indians.
    d. conflicts decreased because settlers came to accept the practice of buying land from the Indians.
    e. the ratio of men to women remained extremely unbalanced as women continued to avoid settling in the wild American colonies.

12. Seaports became important centers in Colonial America for all of the following reasons except
    a. that markets centered there for products coming from inland and going to international markets.
    b. they were centers of culture drawing cosmopolitan influences from England and Europe.
    c. wealth concentrated there because of commerce and trade.
    d. institutions of learning tended to be established there.
    e. they avoided all the problems of inland cities such as disease, crime, and poverty.

Free-Response Questions—Exam Tips

Questions on this period will focus on the relationship between society, culture, religion, economics, and political changes taking place.

The establishment of new colonies with more heterogeneous populations, the Great Awakening and its tumultuous consequences for all the colonies, the development of slavery, and the integration of the American colonies into the Atlantic economy all combined to shape politics within the colonies and the relationships between the colonies and England. Be prepared for questions that raise these issues.

Free-Response Questions

1. Evaluate the consequences of slavery for the economy and society of Colonial America from 1650 to 1750.

2. Assess the changing relationships between Indians and European settlers in the Chesapeake and New England areas before 1750.

Document-Based Question—Exam Tips

Questions from this period most typically venture into the pre-Revolutionary era and consider the issues of American identity, unity, politics, and the economy. Try to make connections between specific evidence and your thesis about the nature of America at the time.

Document-Based Question

Cite key pieces of evidence from the documents and draw on outside knowledge of the period in your essay.

- By 1763 the British Colonies in North America had created a separate identity as Americans. Assess the validity of this contention.

Document A

Source: Hugh Jones, *The Present State of Virginia* (1724, rpt. Chapel Hill, 1947) [in David Hackett Fischer, *Albion's Seed Four British Folkways in America* (New York, Oxford: Oxford University Press, 1989), p. 219.]

The habits, life, customs, computations, etc., of the Virginians are much the same as about London, which they esteem their home…for the most part [they] have contemptible notions of…country places in [other parts of] England and Scotland, whose language and manners are strange to them…they live in the same manner, dress after the same fashion, and behave themselves exactly as the gentry in London.

Document B

Source: Gabriel Thomas, *An Historical and Geographical Account of the Province and Country of Pennsylvania*, London 1698. [Daniel J. Boorstin, ed. *American Primer*. New York and Scarborough, New American Library, 1966]

…[farmers] can have…Land for a very small matter, or next to nothing in comparison of the Purchase of Lands in England… [and American farmers] commonly will get twice the encrease of Corn for every Bushel they sow, that the Farmers in England can from the richest Land they have.

Document C

Source: *Historical Statistics of the United States Colonial Times to 1970*. Part 2, U.S. Bureau of the Census, Washington, DC 1975. pp. 1176–77.

Value of Exports To and Imports From England by American Colonies
(In pounds sterling)

Year	Exports	Imports
1700	395,021	344,341
1710	249,814	293,659
1720	468,188	319,702
1730	572,585	536,860
1740	718,416	813,382
1750	814,768	1,313,083

Document D

Source: Jonathan Edwards, *Sinners in the Hands of an Angry God*. 1742. Sermon.

… The bow of God's wrath is bent, and the arrow made ready on the string, and justice bends the arrow at your heart, and strains the bow, and it is nothing but the mere pleasure of God, and that of an angry God, without any promise or obligation at all, that keeps the arrow one moment from being made drunk with your blood. Thus all you that never passed under a great change of heart, by the mighty power of the spirit of God upon your souls, all you that were never born again, and made new creatures, and raised from being dead in sin, to a state of new, and before altogether unexperienced light and life are in the hands of an angry God.

Document E

Source: *Laws of New Jersey*, c. IX, 1704. An Act for regulating Negro, Indian, and mulatto slaves within this province of New Jersey.

…And whereas the baptizing of slaves is thought by some to be a sufficient reason to set them at liberty, which being a groundless opinion and prejudicial to the inhabitants of this province, be it further enacted by the authority aforesaid, that the baptizing of an Negro, Indian, or mulatto slave shall not be any reason or cause for setting them, or any of them, at liberty…

Document F

Source: Rev. Thomas Barnard, Massachusetts, 1763. Sermon.

Aspicious Day! When Britain, the special Care of Heaven, blessed with a patriot-Sovereign, served by wise and faithful Councellors, brave Commanders, successful Fleets and Armies, seconded in her Efforts by all her Children, and by none more zealously than by those of New England…

America, mayest well rejoice, the Children of New England may be glad and triumph, in Reflection, on Events past, and Prospect for the future…

Now commences the Era of our quiet Enjoyment of those Liberties which our Fathers purchased with the Toil of their whole Lives, their Treasure, their Blood, Safe from the Enemy of the Wilderness, safe from the gripping Hand of arbitrary Sway and cruel Superstition, here shall be the late founded Seat of Peace and Freedom. Here shall our indulgent Mother, who has most generously rescued and protected us, be served and honored by growing Numbers, with all Duty, Love and Gratitude, till Time shall be no more.

Multiple-Choice Answers

1. a. Slaves, indentured servants (in relatively smaller numbers), and free labor all came to America in the early eighteenth century.

2. e. The economy in England was prospering, so economic hardship forced fewer people to seek passage to America as indentured servants.

3. a. The Navigation Acts affected primarily the colonial Atlantic trade, and were beneficial for the most part, especially by promoting shipping and shipbuilding and protecting trade from competition.

4. b. South Carolina produced both rice and indigo; New England produced ships, livestock, timber, and commerce; the middle colonies produced grain and commerce; and the Chesapeake produced tobacco.

5. d. Although most farms had no slaves, those that did trained slaves for various occupations, provided for some flexibility, and allowed some slaves to earn money on their own account.

6. b. Enlightenment thinking introduced more secular thought in the colonies, and provided an intellectual foundation for self-rule in the rise of the colonial assemblies.

7. c. "New lights" or the Awakeners challenged not only Puritan orthodoxy, but also local ministers and their congregations. Many new churches were formed.

8. d. Edwards reacted to many Awakeners by adopting a stricter Calvinist theology than other Awakeners that emphasized the sovereignty of God but also the ability of one to work toward his or her salvation.

9. b. Many colonists did not embrace religious toleration, but the variety of religions represented by immigrants made worship in a single church impossible.

10. e. The witchcraft crisis in Salem was an extreme example of many reports of witches in America, but illustrates the religiosity of the age. The accused were often weak, vulnerable, and the least able to defend themselves.

11. c. Conflicts with Indians continued throughout the seventeenth century as European settlers moved inland onto Indian lands, often breaking previous treaties.

12. d. Although acting as cultural, economic, and social centers, seaports created an unequal distribution of wealth and resulted in disease, crime, and poverty.

Free-Response Questions Commentary

1. This question will focus mostly on the southern colonies as the number of slaves in the north was insignificant and slavery as an institution was inconsequential to the economic development of the region. All the colonies, with the exception of Pennsylvania and Georgia originally, recognized and allowed slavery. Some New England merchants participated in the slave trade, but in general, slaves had little effect on New England's social structure.

   However, in the southern colonies, slavery played a role in both the economy and the social structure. Slaves provided labor for the plantations and smaller farms. They came to represent a substantial amount of southern capital along with the land they worked. Most slaves worked in agriculture, but some slaves were household workers. Other slaves learned trades and could be hired out. The system was not rigid, and some slaves were able to make money on their own account, and a few bought their freedom.

   Socially, racial slavery provided the foundation upon which the caste system rested. Although almost three-quarters of southern whites owned no slaves, large plantation owners dominated southern politics and society. In plantation households the offspring of masters and slaves (the practice of miscegenation) caused considerable tension within Southern society. Slave codes were created to define the social position of slaves. Slaves created a society of their own with extended kin networks, churches, and language. Thus, slaves had an influence on white culture. At the same time, they adopted European customs to enable their survival and make their own cultural world.

2. The pattern of relationships between Indians and settlers differed little in general between New England and the Chesapeake. At first settlement relations were cordial as each group found out about the other, and looked for ways to use the other to their advantage. The Indians helped the colonists establish their settlements, provided food, and taught the Europeans agricultural and hunting techniques. However, relations deteriorated soon thereafter.

   In the Chesapeake the initial truce ended quickly. Initially, the Powhatan hoped to ally with the English against their enemies. That never developed. The desperate settlers stole food from the Indians and warfare was the result. As the Europeans moved onto Indian lands there were a series of confrontations—the 1622 attacks that drove the colony to bankruptcy, the 1640s war, and the conflicts during Bacon's Rebellion—which ended any effective Indian resistance. The two cultures exchanged technology, with the English learning how to cultivate native crops such as corn and the Indians acquiring European firearms.

   New England did not differ greatly. The Indians were already weakened by disease and so posed a less serious threat during the early Puritan settlement. The first Thanksgiving is an indication of early cooperation. The settlers hoped to convert the Indians to Christianity. That goal faded as the natives did not easily abandon many of their religious rituals and traditions, although Puritans such as John Eliot tried to settle Indians in villages committed to their conversion. Competition over land led to bloody conflicts—the Pequot War and King Philip's War—which effectively ended Native American resistance. In the colonial wars between Britain and France, Native Americans sided with the opposing European nations. This did not end until 1763.

Document-Based Question Commentary

This is an abbreviated DBQ containing only six documents and looking at the period before and including the French and Indian War. It asks you to assess whether the American colonies had developed an identity and society separate from that of England. The heart of the question is about *both* identity and society, and how alike and different they are from one another.

The documents here divide neatly into opposing categories. Documents A, C, and F make connections between England and America's similarities, while documents B, D, and E illustrate differences. Arranging them into these groups raises some issues to consider, all of which relate to identity and society: land, the economy, patriotism, religion, and slavery. The abundance of American land and lack of a hereditary landed aristocracy, religious pluralism, the evangelical nature of American religion, and the existence of slavery all point to a new American identity. On the other hand, after victory in the French and Indian War, Americans took pride in being English. The mercantile links and consumer culture that rested on status arising from ownership of English goods and the colonial elite's desire to mimic English fashions and culture demonstrate colonial satisfaction with their relationship with the English.

A wide variety of outside information can be brought to bear in this question. The relatively widespread nature of political participation in the colonies; a heterogeneous population coming from Europe, the Caribbean, and Africa; the sense of separation colonial militias experienced when fighting alongside the British; and the American sense of individualism arising from both democratic institutions and relative isolation from authority all can be used to argue a unique American identity and society. Contrary evidence could include a common British heritage and language, respect for English political institutions, dependence on the Empire for economic prosperity, and pride in a king and country that was engaged in warfare with, and ultimately defeated, rivals France and the Indians.

A sophisticated answer will balance these two competing trends and develop a thesis that argues one side of the debate or the other, but tempers the sameness or difference with elements from the opposing side. For example, one could argue that land was the basis for developing a unique American identity and bring in immigration, politics, and religion. On the other hand, one can temper this by referencing American pride in English tradition and culture and the strong economic ties between England and the colonies.

CHAPTER 4
The Empire in Transition

AP THEMES
- **American Identity:** During the French and Indian War and its aftermath, events led many American colonials to reassess what it meant to be British. For many colonists the war was the first close contact they had with British individuals and they found it unsettling. With the end of salutary neglect and changes in empirical policy, Americans began to question just how British they really were.
- **Economic Transformations:** After 1763, as political tensions heightened, Americans came to see their economy as somewhat independent of Britain and powerful in its own right. Americans also realized that boycotts of British goods could become an effective means of protest.
- **Politics and Citizenship:** A wholesale reassessment of the colonial political system within the context of empire occurred in the dozen years after the French and Indian War. Issues of sovereignty, representation, and taxation came to the fore as both the British and Americans questioned their status as subjects of both the individual colonies and the Crown. An American political ideology emerged.
- **War and Diplomacy:** This period was sandwiched between two wars, both of which transformed America's place within the British Empire and its place in the world. The French and Indian War marked a shift in British policy toward its American colonies and ended the French presence on the North American continent. The beginning of the Revolutionary War marked a giant stride toward independence from England.

EXAM TIP

This is an important chapter because the events after the French and Indian War leading to independence often find their way into exam questions. Pay particular attention to political ideology and its evolution as America moved toward independence.

CHAPTER SUMMARY
Loosening Ties

Americans at mid-eighteenth century were proud to be British and enjoyed many advantages of membership in the British Empire, including trade, protection, political stability, and the fact that the government left the colonies alone. However, during the 1760s and 1770s, changes in both international and domestic political circumstances led to a new imperial relationship that sharpened differences between England and its American colonies.

Although the Crown converted many colonies to royal status during the first half of the eighteenth century and more strict **Navigation Laws** were passed, there were no serious enforcement efforts and the colonies exercised substantial autonomy. After the **Glorious Revolution** Parliament exercised increasing authority over the king and tighter imperial organization was not a priority.

Royal officials in America were often corrupt and dependent upon the colonial assemblies for expenses. Colonial **assemblies** had significant authority—claiming the right to tax, spend, appoint officials, and legislate—and came to see themselves as sovereign in their respective colonies. Colonists considered themselves loyal British subjects and felt closer ties to England than to the other colonies. Despite the inter-colonial trade and communication that bound the colonies together, they still refused to approve the **Albany Plan of Union** in 1754 when confronted with a common foe.

The Struggle for Continent

The century-old struggle between England and France for Atlantic supremacy in trade and naval power sparked four colonial wars: **King William's War, Queen Anne's War, King George's War,** and ended with England's 1763 victory in the **Seven Years' War.** Known in the American colonies as the **French and Indian War,** this struggle affected three powers, the English, French, and Iroquois. English dominance in North America brought into focus tensions in the imperial relationship.

Over the eighteenth century the French attempted to establish their dominance in the **Ohio Valley.** The French were better at forming relations with Indians than were the English. One exception was the **Iroquois Confederacy,** which traded with the English and Dutch as well as the French and was adept at playing the Europeans against each other. After King George's War the Iroquois granted trading concessions to the English, which prompted the French to construct a series of forts in the Ohio Valley. The English countered, and the Virginia militia led by George Washington attacked **Fort Duquesne.** Washington was defeated, and the **French and Indian War** commenced.

From 1754 to 1756 the colonists fought without much assistance from Britain. Receiving little help from Iroquois allies, British General **Edward Braddock** was defeated. When the war expanded to Europe, Prime Minister **William Pitt,** realizing the consequences of a French victory in North America, took control of the war and supported the colonial effort with British troops. Pitt used forced enlistments, **impressments,** and confiscation of goods without payment to secure a British victory. These actions engendered colonial resistance. In 1758, Pitt sent many more soldiers to America. A series of major British victories followed, most significantly the fall of **Quebec** and **Montreal.** The war ended in 1763 with the Peace of Paris. All French territory in North America was ceded to England. However, as a result of the war, Britain's national debt grew dramatically, and the British were embittered by the Americans' resistance to its policies, military ineptitude, meager financial support of the war effort, and wartime profiteering. This led to a move for colonial reorganization with increased imperial authority. The French and Indian War had a profound effect on the colonies. They had united against a common foe and resisted British interference in local affairs. The American militia, fighting alongside British regulars, noted stark contrasts with their English countrymen. Indians earned British enmity, and the Iroquois Confederacy began to unravel.

The New Imperialism

With peace in 1763 Britain faced an enormous debt and new responsibilities with its expanded empire. A new British government adopted the strategy of more governmental involvement in colonial affairs. This response is characterized by historians as the end of **salutary neglect,** that the British inattention to colonial matters before 1763 had benefited both England and her colonies. This new policy reflected a shift in philosophy from **commercial** to **territorial imperialism.** Officials began to value the land itself, apart from the commerce it produced, and the new lands made governing more complex. The staggering debt combined with already high British taxes pointed to a policy of taxing the colonies. The new king **George III** wanted to be an involved monarch but had intellectual and psychological limitations. He replaced stable Whig governments, beginning with a ministry headed by **George Grenville.** Grenville believed the colonies should obey the law and pay their share of the cost of governing and maintaining the empire.

An Indian attempt to stem the tide of colonial migration westward, **Pontiac's Rebellion,** pointed to the urgency of western issues. Grenville issued **The Proclamation of 1763** to limit conflicts with Indians and control trade, migration, and land speculation. The Proclamation failed to meet these goals and the line was continually moved west at the Indian's expense. Grenville soon followed with other acts to assert imperial authority by stationing troops and ships in the colonies, the **Quartering Act;** collecting duties, reorganizing the duties on sugar and molasses, the **Sugar Act;** establishing vice-admiralty courts in America, stopping the use of paper currency, the **Currency Act;** and taxing documents, the **Stamp Act.** This program collected much more revenue but created common grievances, antagonized nearly all interest groups in the colonies, and promoted increasing economic anxiety already fueled by a postwar depression, particularly in the cities. Grenville's program violated the colonial belief in self-government and the authority of the provincial assemblies to control public finance. Tension between coastal and western settlers, the **Paxton Boys,** and the North Carolina **Regulator Movement** diverted colonial attention away from the new British policies until the Stamp Act Crisis.

Stirrings of Revolt

The Stamp Act of 1765 focused colonial antagonism to, and unification against, new British policies. Americans had accepted English taxes for the purpose of regulating trade, not to raise revenue. The Virginia House of Burgesses adopted the **Virginia Resolves** introduced by **Patrick Henry,** proclaiming Americans had the same rights as Englishmen and only their representative assemblies could tax them. That fall, the delegates from nine colonies met at New York as the **Stamp Act Congress** and petitioned the king and Parliament. They argued that they were loyal British citizens, but they could not be taxed by Parliament. In Massachusetts, organized resistance to the Stamp Act came from the **Sons of Liberty,** which encouraged mob action and sacked Lt. Governor Thomas Hutchinson's house. Parliament repealed the Stamp Act in 1766, more because of pressure from London merchants losing profits from the colonial boycotts rather than from colonial pressure or violence. However, Parliament simultaneously passed the **Declaratory Act,** upholding Parliament's authority to pass laws affecting the colonies **"in all cases whatsoever."**

Charles Townshend assumed leadership of the English government and dealt with colonial noncompliance of the **Quartering Act** by suspending the New York Assembly. To raise revenue he accepted the colonial distinction between **internal** and **external** taxes. Parliament then levied a new set of taxes, the **Townshend Duties,** which taxed lead, paint, paper, glass, and tea. These actions stirred the colonies to action. The **Massachusetts Circular Letter** was sent by its assembly to the other colonies urging them to resist all taxes. When Townshend established a **Board of Customs Commissioners** in America, the colonies established a **non-importation agreement** and promoted American production. **Homespun** became fashionable. All the duties except the tax on tea were repealed in 1770.

To protect the Board of Customs Commissioners from harassment, troops were sent to Boston. This action created significant tension, in part because the British troops were vying with Bostonians for menial jobs. In March 1770, a mob harassed troops with snowballs and rocks and the troops fired on the crowd, an event known as the **Boston Massacre.** Five colonists were killed including a black sailor, **Crispus Attucks.** Bostonian **Samuel Adams** led a **Committee of Correspondence** to propagandize Bostonian grievances. This sparked a resistance network throughout the colonies.

While Puritan theology was a source of revolutionary ideology, **Whig ideology** from England, which argued that men were inherently evil and government existed to protect individuals, was also a source of Americans' revolutionary thinking. Americans believed that government too was prone to abuses of power. A balanced government with power distributed as it was in England was the ideal and would avoid corruption and tyranny. Whigs feared the king and his ministry was becoming a single center of power and corruption. Americans also believed that people could be taxed only by their consent as expressed through their direct representatives. They did not accept the idea of **virtual representation**—that Parliament legislated for the nation as a whole—but believed in **actual representation,** legislation by a body of their peers directly accountable to them. In theory, Americans accepted Parliament's **sovereignty** in some areas, but they also believed that their colonial assemblies had authority.

After the Boston Massacre an uneasy calm settled on the colonies. Corrupt customs officials continued to antagonize merchants and in 1772 Rhode Islanders burned the British revenue cutter *Gaspee.* In 1773, with the **British East India Company** verging on bankruptcy, Parliament passed the **Tea Act,** which allowed the company to sell tea directly to the colonies without paying the tea duty; this would bypass American merchants and establish a tea **monopoly.** The colonial response was another boycott that united the colonies. Women played a major role by avoiding English goods and producing domestic substitutes. They participated in riots and formed the **Daughters of Liberty,** which often chided its male counterpart, the Sons of Liberty, as not being radical enough. Many ports prohibited the unloading of tea, but in Boston in 1773, townsmen dressed as Indians dumped the tea in the harbor. This radical event known as the Boston Tea Party set off a series of retaliatory events both in England and in America. Boston refused to pay, and Parliament passed a series of laws known as the **Coercive Acts** in England and as the **Intolerable Acts** in the colonies. These acts closed the port of Boston, limited Massachusetts' power of self-government, required the quartering of troops in private houses, and permitted royal officials to be tried in England. Soon after, the **Quebec Act** gave the province of Quebec a self-governing structure and freedom to practice Catholicism. Combined, these acts spelled tyranny to the Americans. The colonies unified in their resistance to these actions by passing resolves and extended the colonial boycott.

Cooperation and War

Traditions of local autonomy were strong, and new **extralegal** bodies emerged as royal authority in the colonies crumbled in the face of these new laws. The **Sons of Liberty** directed vigilante action. The **Committee of Correspondence** formed inter-colonial groups, and most importantly, the **First Continental Congress** met in Philadelphia in 1774. The congress endorsed grievances, approved the **Suffolk Resolves** that recommended military preparation to defend against the British, approved a **Continental Association** to enforce a total boycott of British goods, and agreed to meet the following spring. These actions ratified the autonomous status of the colonies within the empire. England's response, the **Conciliatory Propositions,** was too late. Having imposed martial law in Massachusetts, **General Thomas Gage,** Britain's commander in Boston, sent troops to **Lexington and Concord** in April of 1775. They were to arrest **Samuel Adams** and **John Hancock** and seize a cache of gunpowder. Alerted by **Paul Revere** and **William Dawes, minutemen** resisted and eight were killed. The British troops burned what little powder they found. They were attacked by minutemen as they returned to Boston. Nearly two dozen British soldiers were killed in the ambush. The colonial version of the events at Lexington and Concord rallied Americans to the patriot cause and brought into clearer focus the view that had been emerging since the end of the French and Indian War, that there were significant ideological and political differences between Americans and their English countrymen.

Multiple-Choice Questions

1. No concerted efforts were made to increase English control over its empire in America during the first half of the eighteenth century because
   a. Parliament was focused on increasing its authority over the king.
   b. the colonial assemblies were weakened and posed no threat to imperial authority.
   c. rigorous enforcement of the Navigation Acts maintained a British presence in America.
   d. there were no threats to the colonies so tight control was not necessary.
   e. the Albany Plan of Union exercised a good deal of authority over the colonies by the British government.

2. A major reason for the French construction of fortresses in the Ohio Valley in the mid-eighteenth century was
   a. its desire to protect French farmers settled in the area from the English.
   b. ongoing wars with the Iroquois and other Indian nations because of French encroachment on Indian lands.
   c. tension between the French merchant aristocracy on the coast and French settlers inland.
   d. to counter rising English influence when the Iroquois granted them trading concessions.
   e. to protect overzealous Jesuit priests undertaking a new campaign to convert the natives to Catholicism.

3. The change in William Pitt's strategy that finally led to victory in the French and Indian War was
   a. confiscation of goods from colonists without compensation.
   b. devoting more financial resources and soldiers to the war in America.
   c. reorganization of the colonial militia so that it better integrated with British regulars.
   d. the forced enlistment of colonial soldiers in areas where fighting with the French was taking place.
   e. encouraging the colonies to unite in the formation of a single fighting force supported by uniform taxes throughout the colonies.

4. As a result of the French and Indian War
   a. the colonies were more dependent on Britain because they relied on English soldiers for protection.
   b. the French agreed to stay within the boundaries of Louisiana and Canada and not incite Indians to attack western British settlements.
   c. the French and the Indians agreed to a peace that lasted until the Revolutionary War.
   d. the British regarded Americans as loyal subjects, good soldiers in the cause, and strong financial supporters of the war.
   e. the colonists resented British interference in local affairs, and American militia noted marked differences between themselves and their English brethren.

5. Which of the following was the first to signal a change in British policy to the American colonists?
   a. the Townshend Duties
   b. the Tea Act
   c. the Proclamation of 1763
   d. the Coercive Acts
   e. the appointment of Thomas Hutchinson as Massachusetts Governor

6. The declaration from the Stamp Act Congress "That the people of these colonies are not, and from their local circumstances cannot be, represented in the House of Commons . . ." was based on a repudiation of
   a. the theory that the king could not legislate for his subjects in overseas colonies.
   b. John Locke's ideology of the rights of Englishmen.
   c. the idea of virtual representation in the British Empire as a whole.
   d. the idea that only the colonial assemblies could impose taxes on their respective colonies.
   e. the colonial governors' authority to veto laws passed in the colonial assemblies.

7. At the conclusion of the Stamp Act Crisis, Parliament reasserted its authority to legislate for the colonies "in all cases whatsoever" in the
   a. Coercive Acts.
   b. Declaratory Act.
   c. Mutiny Act.
   d. Regulator Movement.
   e. Proclamation of 1763.

8. British North American colonists accepted the Navigation Act duties before the Sugar Act because
   a. mercantilism was the accepted economic policy of the time.
   b. the Sugar Act raised the rates on sugar and molasses to unprecedented levels.
   c. the Navigation Acts were external, not internal taxes.
   d. the purpose of the Sugar Act was to regulate trade, not to raise revenue.
   e. the Navigation Acts did not impact the colonies.

9. The actions of corrupt and overbearing customs officials were highlighted most clearly in the
   a. Boston Massacre because the British troops were stationed in Boston to protect customs officials.
   b. burning of the Gaspee because customs officials had antagonized Rhode Island merchants by their abuse of authority.
   c. enforcement of the Stamp Act with its ridiculously high duty on imported sugar and molasses.
   d. Continental Association, which was formed to publicize the unjust actions of customs collectors.
   e. Boston Port Act, in which the customs officials ordered the port closed because of the smuggling of goods on which duties were not paid.

10. The political philosophy of Whig ideology
   a. viewed concentration of power as the biggest threat to liberty, leading to corruption and tyranny.
   b. believed men were inherently good and needed little governance.

c. supported the king's policy of organizing government with more authority so that it was effective and efficient.

d. accepted that balanced government with evenly distributed power among its branches would lead to disorder and anarchy.

e. viewed government by consent of the governed as political heresy.

11. The Quebec Act both infuriated and threatened American colonists by
    a. allowing France to resume political control of Quebec Province.
    b. forcing Canada to accept the Church of England and the religious authority of an Anglican Bishop.
    c. granting Quebec Province a self-governing structure and the freedom to practice Catholicism.
    d. granting trading rights to the American interior through the St. Lawrence River rather than through Atlantic port cities.
    e. prohibiting any intercourse between Indians of that province and the French settlers remaining after the French and Indian War.

12. British troops were sent to Lexington and Concord in 1775 to
    a. arrest John Hancock and Samuel Adams and to seize patriot ammunition stored there.
    b. retaliate for the dumping of tea in Boston Harbor during the Boston Tea Party.
    c. arrest the members participating in the First Continental Congress meeting there.
    d. show British resolve to quell the rebellion by attacking Massachusetts hotbeds of resistance.
    e. use a British show of force so that Americans would end their boycott of English goods.

Free-Response Questions—Exam Tips

- It is important to keep in mind that even though protest was violent in this period, most Americans were loyal subjects of the king until just before Independence was declared in 1776.
- A question about relations between Indians and the three main European colonial cultures may be asked in the period before the Revolution.
- A good knowledge of the economic and political structure of the British Empire is important in answering questions in this period.

Free-Response Questions

1. Defend England's changes in policy toward the colonies after the conclusion of the French and Indian War.

2. Analyze the relationship between Native Americans and European colonists over the course of the eighteenth century to the end of the French and Indian War.

Document-Based Question

In what ways and to what extent did colonial response to changes in English policies contribute to a coherent ideology of protest against concentrated power before the American Revolution?

Use the documents and your knowledge of the period 1754–1775 in constructing your response.

Document A

Source: George Washington, letter to Robert Orme, aide-de-camp to General Edward Braddock, March 15, 1755

"It is true Sir, that I have...expressed an inclination to serve the ensuing Campaigne as a volunteer; and this inclination is not a little increased since it is likely to be conducted by a Gentleman of the General's Experience. But, besides this and the laudable desire I may have to serve (with my best abilities) my King & Country, I must be ingenuous enough to confess, that I am not a little biased by selfish considerations. To be plain, Sir, I wish earnestly to attain some knowledge of the Military Profession: and believing a more favourable opportunity cannot offer, than to serve under a Gentleman of General Braddock's abilities and experience."

Document B

Source: Massachusetts Soldiers, Diary, 1758

"No regard is paid...to sacred time. This day I heard a band of music at the commanding officer's tent while [officers] were dining which was very delightful, though in my opinion not so seasonable on such days of sacred appointment."

Source: Anderson, *A People's Army*, p. 117. Samuel Jenks and Caleb Rea

After the British defeat at Ticonderoga, "...horrid cursing and swearing there is in the camp, more especially among the regulars; and, as a moral cause I can't help but charge our defeat on this sin, which so much prevails, even among the chief commanders."

Document C

Source: Farmer Samuel Lane's *Almanack*, 1760, Stratham, NH

"...Lost a good King, George yᵉ [2ⁿᵈ on the] 25ᵗʰ of October. In the [77ᵗʰ year of his] age & 34ᵗʰ of his R[eign]" [New Hampshire Historical Society]

Document D

Source: James Otis' Speech Against the Writs of Assistance, 1761

"...Every one with this writ may be a tyrant; if this commission be legal, a tyrant in a legal manner also may control, imprison, or murder any one within the realm...A man is accountable to no man for his doings...Now one of the most essential branches of English liberty is the freedom of one's house. A man's house is his castle; and whilst he is quiet, he is as well guarded as a prince in his castle. This writ, if it should be declared legal, would totally annihilate this privilege."

Document E

Source: Benjamin Franklin, testimony before Parliament, February 1766.

Question: "What was the temper of America towards Great Britain before the year 1763?"

Answer: "The best in the world. They submitted willingly to the government of the Crown, and paid, in all their courts, obedience to Acts of Parliament...They had not only a respect, but an affection, for Great Britain, for its laws, for its customs and manners, and even a fondness for its fashions, that greatly increased the commerce. Natives of Britain were always treated with particular regard..." [Colbert, *Eyewitness to America*, 54]

Document F

Source: Resolutions of the Stamp Act Congress, Oct 19, 1765

"...That the only representatives of the people of these colonies are persons chosen therein by themselves, and that no taxes ever have been, or can be constitutionally imposed on them, but by their respective legislatures."

Document G

Source: Petition of London Merchants Against the Stamp Act, Jan 17, 1766

"...an act... for granting and applying certain stamp duties...are represented to have been extended in such a manner to disturb legal commerce and harass the fair trader, have so far interrupted the usual former most fruitful branches of their commerce, restrained the sale of their produce, thrown the state of several provinces into confusion, and brought on so great a number of actual bankruptcies..."

Document H

Source: Burstein Collection / Corbis

The Boston Massacre (1770), by Paul Revere

Document I

Document I

Source: Declaration of the Causes and Necessity of Taking Up Arms, July 6, 1775

"In our own native land, in defense of the freedom that is our birth-right, and which we ever enjoyed till the late violation of it-for the protection of our property, acquired soley by the honest industry of our forefathers and ourselves, against violence actually offered, we have taken up arms. We shall lay them down when hostilities shall cease on the part of the aggressors…"

Multiple-Choice Answers

1. a. Parliament was focused on the French threat and on the king's increasing power within the British government rather than on the colonies. Historians call this the period of salutary neglect because the Empire prospered.

2. d. There was not a significant population of Europeans in New France and their relations with Indians were generally good. The France forts were to establish a French presence in an area where English settlers were moving.

3. b. Earlier British strategy was to force the colonies to supply men and equipment with little help from British forces. When England took a bigger role and stopped pressing the colonies for support, its fortunes turned. The last alternative was the failed Albany Plan of Union.

4. e. As this war was the first time that many colonists had any personal contact with the English, a significant result was that the Americans saw themselves as quite different from the English.

5. c. The Proclamation was issued not long after the Treaty of Paris was signed. This direct interference in colonial settlement patterns indicated a larger English involvement in colonial affairs.

6. c. Associating their representatives with the colonial assemblies, colonists believed in the principle of actual representation. They did not believe that Parliament, sitting in Great Britain, could represent their interests.

7. b. During the Stamp Act Crisis the colonies had begun serious questioning of their relationship to the Empire. Parliament's response to colonial protest was repeal of the Stamp Act and passage of the Declaratory Act, which confirmed authority over the colonies.

8. a. Even though the Sugar Act lowered rates on sugar and molasses, the fact that its purpose was to raise revenue rather than regulate trade (its formal name was the Revenue Act) led colonists to protest. Revenue had always been incidental before this, and regulation was the goal of duties.

9. b. The burning of the Gaspee was a direct response to corrupt customs officials' seizing of ships and cargoes in Rhode Island. The other events caused colonial protests but they were not primarily responding to corruption.

10. a. Adherents of Whig ideology were most concerned with concentration of power leading to tyranny and corruption. Their solution to this was a vigilant and virtuous public and balanced government.

11. c. On top of the threats to colonial liberty since 1763 by the English government and the king, the Quebec Act gave Quebec and its French inhabitants liberties that were denied English colonists and added the threat of a neighboring Catholic state to the largely Protestant English colonies.

12. a. General Gage wanted to quell the rising unrest and rebellion. He hoped to capture Massachusetts leaders and capture munitions to forestall any armed rebellion in the colony he commanded.

Free-Response Questions Commentary

1. This question asks you to support the change in colonial policy George Grenville sponsored after 1763. That year is considered a watershed because not only were the French eliminated as a presence in North America, but England turned its sights to those colonies. Grenville studied the North American colonies and discovered that it cost the British treasury more to run them than they produced in revenue. Also, the British debt had grown enormously as a result of the war. Grenville's solution was to have the colonies pay a greater share of the cost. By separating colonists and Indians by the Proclamation of 1763 he hoped to lower the cost of defending the frontier. On the other side his plan was to increase revenue with a succession of duties and taxes, the Sugar Act, Stamp Act, and Townshend duties. Given that the colonists paid fewer taxes than the English and that England had helped defend the colonies from the French in four wars over the course of the century, this appeared eminently reasonable from an English point of view.

2. Perhaps the easiest way to organize this question is to look at the relations between Native Americans and the three main groups of European settlers—the Spanish, French and English. After the brutal Spanish conquests of the sixteenth and seventeenth centuries, the Spanish tended to assimilate Indians into their culture, intermarry, and convert many to Catholicism. Indians and mestizos had some limited mobility in Spanish society and could become "Spanish" to some extent. The small French population posed no competition for land, intermarried, and more easily accepted the Indian notions of ceremony and kinship. Jesuits allowed Indians to commingle native religion with Catholicism, and the French developed a working relationship fulfilling roles that Indians desired: mediating internal and external conflicts and gift giving. The English were not as successful as the French at maintaining positive relationships with Native Americans, but slowly adapted to Indian ways, and became more demanding as French influence declined by the mid-eighteenth century. The exception was the Iroquois Confederacy, which was interested in preserving its independence and sided with neither European nation and played each against the other.

Document-Based Question Commentary

This question asks you to consider colonial protest to alleged abuses of power and determine how such abuses contributed to a coherent set of principles of protest. You would do well to put this in the context of eighteenth-century Whig ideology and point to the development of grievances based on concentration of power, which denied rights and ultimately led to independence.

The documents can be categorized into different types of protest. Economic responses are one category, as illustrated in Documents F and G; the frequent use of the boycott by patriots was an effective protest of the centralized mercantile economy. Source D represents the desire of colonials to have the rights of Englishmen. The Lockean idea of natural rights to life and property is demonstrated by the wildly inaccurate Revere engraving of the Boston Massacre. Finally the use of violence in Documents H and I implies a growing reliance on Locke's idea of the right to rebel.

Opposing this trend are Documents A, C, and E, which demonstrate an affection for Britain and its king. Pointing out that the population was divided and some only slowly moved toward the Patriot cause, will add substance to your analysis here.

You can use Whig ideology or John Locke's political philosophy to tie the various elements together to create an argument. Using his natural rights of life, liberty, and property along with the American tendency to use English ideology to resist shows the American desire to remain within the Empire. Out of the continual flaunting of natural rights by the imperial government and in American responses you can argue that a coherent ideology of protest emerged.

CHAPTER 5
The American Revolution

AP THEMES

- **American Diversity:** Divisions between those who supported independence produced a major division in the population during the Revolution. Also, ethnic groups often divided along these lines. By the end of the war many Loyalists left for other parts of the British Empire.
- **Globalization:** This period marks the first in which America engaged with the outside world as an independent political entity. From its appeal to the world in the Declaration of Independence to its alliances with European nations for financial and military aid, this era was a sharp break with its colonial past.
- **Politics and Citizenship:** Politics in America was revolutionized on both the state and national level by the end of British government in America. State governments with written constitutions emerged, and America's first national government as an independent nation, the Articles of Confederation, helped pave the way for a more permanent political system.
- **Reform:** The American Revolution produced dramatic social as well as political changes. The departure of many of the former elite, the Loyalists, opened up the political and social structures to new people. The relative positions of religious denominations shifted, and slave emancipation gained strength in northern states. Women joined in Revolutionary activity and assumed the role of "republican mothers." Native American loyalty was divided between the British and the patriots, and in general, Native Americans found themselves in a weaker position.
- **War and Diplomacy:** The Revolutionary War mobilized the entire population as no previous war had. George Washington played the prominent role in keeping an army in the field to resist British forces. Fighting a defensive war, the American forces finally outlasted the English political will to fight. America's alliance with France proved critical to the success of the Revolution.

EXAM TIP

Focus on the political, social, and cultural changes resulting from the war in this chapter. There are rarely multiple-choice questions on the military aspects of the war. The essay questions tend to ask you to analyze the changes brought about by the Revolution.

CHAPTER SUMMARY
The States United

In 1775 the colonies were neither prepared for nor united to fight a war with England. In fact, the Revolution encompassed two struggles: a military conflict with Great Britain and a domestic political struggle. Once fighting began, Americans' opinions ranged from wanting complete independence to wanting no change in the imperial relationship. Within a month of Lexington and Concord, the **Second Continental Congress** attempted reconciliation with Great Britain with the **Olive Branch Petition.** The king's response was to try to stop the rebellion by force. The English tried to recruit slaves, Indians, and **mercenaries** as soldiers and eventually blockaded American ports. Both the congress and the public became more radical over the course of the first year. Sentiment for independence strengthened, especially in January 1776 with the publication of Thomas Paine's widely read pamphlet *Common Sense.*

As imperial governments crumbled, the colonies established governments apart from British authority. On July 4, 1776, the congress adopted a **Declaration of Independence.** Written mainly by **Thomas Jefferson,** it borrowed heavily from the political theories of **John Locke** and the protest rhetoric of the past decade. The Declaration made America a **sovereign** nation but resistance to independence continued. **Loyalists,** called **Tories** by **Patriots,** remained loyal to the king. The former colonies, now states, began to write constitutions and were sovereign in the new national government. The **Articles of Confederation** were ratified in 1781 near the end of the war. This new government was purposely designed to create a weak central government with stronger state governments.

America's greatest challenge was keeping a well-equipped army in the field, and paying for it. Foreign nations, particularly France, provided much of the financing for the war. The government could not force states to provide money or troops and had difficulty selling bonds. They thus resorted to printing **paper money.** The result was **inflation.** The continental army depended heavily on what weapons they were able to capture from the British. As the war continued, patriotism faded, and the nation had difficulty raising troops. **George Washington,** the commander in chief of the **Continental Army,** was mainly responsible for keeping the army and the new nation together.

The War for Independence

Although Britain appeared to have the advantage of a large army and navy, abundant resources, and centralized command, Americans were fighting at home and were committed to their cause. They were able to get substantial foreign aid. English commanders also made major errors. From 1775 to 1776, British opinion held that the conflict was a local rebellion around Boston. **General Thomas Gage's** army in Boston was besieged by the American forces that lost the **Battle of Bunker Hill** but not before they inflicted heavy casualties on the English. This helped change British perceptions about the conflict. In early 1776, when it became apparent that the war was a larger conflict than the British initially realized, the British evacuated Boston. Elsewhere, the Americans invaded Canada without success, and the British met resistance in the South.

During the second phase of the war from 1776 to early 1778, the British were in the best position to win. **General William Howe** moved British forces to New York City. The Patriots were successful in defeating **Hessian** troops at **Trenton** on Christmas Eve in 1776, but otherwise Washington's forces suffered a series of defeats. In 1777 Howe adopted a **pincer's strategy** to divide the United States along the Hudson River, separating New England from the rest of the colonies. The plan fell apart when Howe decided to occupy Philadelphia rather than moving up the Hudson Valley to meet **General John Burgoyne,** whose army was moving south into New York from Canada. In October 1777, British forces suffered defeats at **Oriskany** and **Bennington,** and Burgoyne surrendered at **Saratoga.** This proved to be a turning point because it led to an alliance between France and America. British mistakes were monumental during this period; Burgoyne was left to fight alone and Washington was allowed to regroup his forces after defeats. Some have questioned Howe's loyalty to the British cause.

When fighting first began America sent diplomats abroad to enlist support, and France provided covert aid. **Benjamin Franklin** went to France and, aided by the news of the British defeat at Saratoga in 1778, France recognized the United States and provided loans, munitions, and army and naval forces. Spain and the Netherlands also provided aid and all three nations went to war with England. After maintaining neutrality in past conflicts, the tribes of the **Iroquois Confederacy** were divided over support for the British or Americans. Some of the Iroquois leaders hoped that an alliance with the British would slow the advance of Americans onto Indian lands. However, Patriots retaliated by destroying Iroquois villages and forcing many to flee to Canada.

After the defeat at Saratoga, British public opinion, which was never fully behind the war, forced a limited commitment. In this final phase of the war, the strategy shifted to the South where the British erroneously believed that there was significant Loyalist support. Although the British enjoyed some military successes, they found themselves fighting a guerrilla war. This misguided tactic aroused segments of the American population that previously had been detached from the conflict. The politicization of the populous made the war "revolutionary" and deepened support for the Patriot cause. Accepting failure of this strategy, **Lord Cornwallis,** commander of the southern forces, retreated to **Yorktown,** Virginia, to rendezvous with a fleet to evacuate his troops. Trapped there by a combined Franco-American army and the French navy, he surrendered in October 1781. This marked the end of major fighting, and public opinion in England shifted in favor of a negotiated peace. The **Treaty of Paris** in 1783 recognized an independent United States stretching from Canada to Florida and west to the Mississippi River.

War and Society

The Revolution was both a social and political revolution. Many Americans remained loyal to Britain and many were forced to flee the country, some leaving behind large estates and positions of authority in the former colonies. Although this **Loyalist** property was confiscated, the overall distribution of wealth did not change dramatically. The **Anglican Church** was **disestablished,** and many Anglican clergy left the United States. Quaker pacifism also weakened that sect's influence in the United States. The position of the Catholic Church improved as Catholic Patriots such as **Charles Carroll** and the alliance with Catholic France gave Catholicism new validity in America. Maryland's **John Carroll** became the first American bishop in 1789.

Tension existed between the ideal of liberty and the reality of slavery. Many southern blacks were exposed to the Revolutionary ideals of liberty. British policy and presence in the South freed some slaves, but many more remained in bondage. Some white Southerners were ambivalent toward the Revolution because of slavery. Whites opposed British efforts at **emancipation** but also feared that Patriot ideology might prompt slave revolts. In the North, revolutionary ideals combined with **evangelical Christianity** to spread antislavery sentiments. In the South, churches developed a rationale that painted slavery as essential to the liberty of whites. Indian groups mostly tried to remain neutral in the conflict although some tribes sided with the British. They saw the Americans as more hostile and the British as protectors from American westward settlement. Some simply took advantage of the situation to attack American settlements on the frontier. Mostly, the war weakened the Native American tribes. The American victory spurred western settlement and many resented Indian alliances with the British. Deep divisions developed among tribes, and many found it difficult to unify to resist further American encroachment on their lands.

The Revolution had a significant effect on women, who often ran farms and businesses in their husbands' absence. The war created an unstable population of poor women. As the war progressed, increasing numbers of women known as **camp followers** joined the camps of the Patriot army. Although discouraged by many officers, the women provided household services to the army and increased morale. The Revolution raised issues about women's rights and role in society. British author **Mary Wollstonecraft's *Vindication of the Rights of Women* in 1792** articulated these ideas. There was little change in the legal restrictions of married women. The participation of women in the Revolution led to a new role for them as Republican mothers who were responsible for teaching the virtues of republicanism to their children.

Freedom from the British Navigation System strengthened the American economy. New trading venues opened up in the Caribbean, South America, and later in China. During the war, **privateering** was profitable for ship-owners and trade between American states also increased. Entrepreneurial energy was funneled into commerce but not industry.

The Creation of State Governments

State governments were the first political creations of the Revolution. They revolved around the idea of a republican government with power emanating from virtuous landowning citizens. Despite this, men without property, blacks, Native Americans, and women were denied rights of citizens. The Revolutionary struggle inspired written constitutions with limited executive power and bicameral legislatures. The upper chamber was to represent the elite, which demonstrates that democracy was not completely accepted.

In the midst of the war, the state governments were having trouble governing, which many attributed to too much democracy. Massachusetts revised its constitution and significantly strengthened the power of the executive. This provided a model for the other states. Many states moved in the direction of complete religious freedom. Virginia adopted Thomas Jefferson's **Statute of Religious Liberty** in 1786, which completely separated church and state. Slavery, already weak in New England and Pennsylvania, was abolished in some northern states, but it continued in the southern states. Racist assumptions about blacks and the significant financial investment in slaves left many Americans without a viable option to end slavery, even if they had moral reprehension for the institution.

The Search for a National Government

As the war raged with England many sought a weak national government with sovereignty resting in the states. The result was the **Articles of Confederation** adopted in 1777 and ratified in 1781. This government had little authority over the states and no executive or courts. It could not regulate trade or tax or raise armies. Each state had a single vote, and a majority of nine was necessary for approval of bills. Its record was mixed during its existence from 1781 to 1789. The Confederation commanded little respect in the world. After the war Britain continued to violate aspects of the Treaty of Paris, and full access to English markets was never achieved. An important accomplishment was resolution of western land issues. The **Land Ordinance of 1785** created a system of surveying and selling lands in rectangular sections. In 1787 the **Northwest Ordinance** provided for settlement and government of the **Northwest Territory,** guaranteeing freedom of religion and prohibiting slavery there. A postwar depression from 1784 to 1787 exposed the economic weakness of the new nation. Without the ability to tax, the Confederation could not pay its debts and states increased taxes to pay their debts. Massachusetts' farmers pressed by higher taxes joined **Daniel**

Shays, a western Massachusetts farmer and veteran who closed courts to prevent farmers from losing their property. With the national government unable to act the revolt was extinguished by a local militia financed by wealthy merchants. Shays' Rebellion exposed fundamental weaknesses in the government and strengthened the movement to revise the Articles.

Multiple-Choice Questions

1. After the battles at Lexington and Concord, the Continental Congress sent the Olive Branch Petition to the king to
   a. acknowledge the colonies' independence and lay the groundwork for the Declaration of Independence to follow.
   b. seek a reconciliation with the Crown by stating colonial grievances.
   c. declare complete submission to the king and the intent to rebel no longer.
   d. declare the colonial intent to resist English rule by force until the king withdrew his forces from America.
   e. inform him of the colonial association's boycott of British goods until the British troops left Boston.

2. The sentiment expressed in this phrase from the Declaration of Independence, "[T]hat whenever any form of government becomes destructive of these ends [securing life, liberty and property], it is the right of the people to alter or abolish it," best expresses the political philosophy of
   a. Baron de Montesquieu.
   b. Thomas Hobbs.
   c. John Locke.
   d. Voltaire.
   e. William Pitt.

3. The Battle of Bunker Hill was significant because
   a. this early American defeat lowered Patriot morale and made recruiting troops much harder.
   b. the British suffered significant casualties that made efforts to suppress the rebellion much more difficult.
   c. this British victory made Boston safe for the British army to keep its headquarters there.
   d. it showed the British that the American resistance was organized and determined, and more than a local conflict.
   e. losing this battle made the British troops evacuate Boston.

4. The major consequence of the American Revolution for the Iroquois Confederacy was
   a. division among the various tribes of the Confederacy as some abandoned its traditional policy of neutrality and supported the British against the Americans.
   b. unity among the tribes in support of the British, which ultimately left the Confederacy weaker at the end of the war with American victory.
   c. strong support for the Americans in hopes that it would help Indians resist white settlement of their lands after the war.
   d. total disaster as both American and British troops attacked villages that would not give them military support.
   e. insignificant, as the Iroquois remained neutral and were largely unaffected by the warfare between the British and American colonists.

5. The following map illustrates the British strategy of
   a. moving its large armies in river valleys to ease transportation burdens.
   b. centering the battles in New York, where there were more Loyalists than in other colonies.
   c. anticipating the collapse of the rebellion after dividing New England from the rest of the colonies.
   d. moving away from major urban areas and trying to attract rural Americans to the Loyalist side.
   e. using Indian allies as a major source of troops in their tribal areas to defeat the continental armies.

(a)

(b)

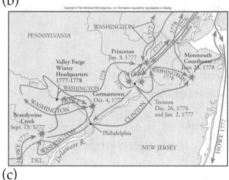

(c)

6. The Battle of Yorktown most clearly demonstrated which of the following?
   a. the overwhelming superiority of American troops toward the end of the Revolutionary War
   b. the inability of Britain to support its armies across the Atlantic Ocean
   c. the waning support of the British public to continue support of a war to retain its colonies in British North America
   d. the misplaced emphasis British generals put on support from Loyalists in its southern strategy
   e. the significance of French aid to the Patriot cause

7. The Treaty of Paris at the end of the Revolutionary War contained provisions for
   a. an end to the fighting and provisions for America and France to divide Britain's North American possessions.
   b. recognition of the United States' independence and Britain's withdrawal from the North American continent.
   c. treaties of trade and alliance between France and the United States.

    (d.) the United States western boundary to be the Mississippi River and British recognition of its independence.

    e. an end to fighting and a return to the status quo antebellum.

8. A consequence for religion in America as a result of the Revolutionary War was
    a. the Anglican Church became more established in areas where Loyalist sympathies remained strong.
    b. Quaker sects increased membership because their pacifism attracted Americans tired of fighting a long and drawn-out war.
    c. Catholicism was afforded a new respect because of the American alliance with France.
    (d.) a new wave of evangelical Christianity swept through the states in the unsettled times of war and social upheaval.
    e. more states adopted established churches to support.

9. The Revolution had a significant effect on women's status due to
    a. lifting of restrictions on property ownership for married women.
    b. their gaining the right to vote in local, but not national, elections.
    c. acceptance of women in jobs previously reserved for men only.
    (d.) their new role as teachers of republican virtue to their children.
    e. their elevated role in politics because of their organization of boycotts.

10. The republican ideology of equal rights and liberty that was fundamental to the Revolution
    a. caused a great antislavery outcry throughout the nation when the war ended.
    b. pushed some states to distribute confiscated Loyalist property to the poor to promote equality.
    c. influenced the British to promise freedom to slaves in areas that they controlled.
    d. led to massive slave revolts in the South after the war was over.
    (e.) helped push New England states to abolish slavery in their new constitutions.

11. The first state constitutions after the Revolution began were replaced because
    (a.) their executive branches were weak and they had difficulty governing.
    b. they were not democratic enough for people fighting and sacrificing for their rights.
    c. they contained no provisions for a separation of powers.
    d. Loyalists were gaining political power under the less restrictive governing structures.
    e. as pressures lessened at the end of the war, state governments with less central authority were possible.

12. The national government under the Articles of Confederation was particularly successful in
    a. repaying the nation's domestic and foreign war debt.
    b. quelling opposition movements such as Shays' Rebellion in Massachusetts.
    (c.) the resolution of western land issues in the Northwest Territory.
    d. forcing Britain to adhere to all the provisions of the Treaty of Paris.
    e. -opening trade to areas closed to American merchants because of the war.

Free-Response Questions

1. Assess the advantages and disadvantages of either the British or the Americans that affected the outcome in the Revolutionary War.

2. Evaluate the economic and social changes that were a result of the Revolutionary War.

Document-Based Question—Exam Tip

Thinking About the American Revolution as a Civil War

Historian Carl Becker saw the American Revolution as more than a fight for independence Becker saw a two-sided political problem that raised two questions: "The first was the question of home rule; the second was the question of who should rule at home." Sophisticated analyses often must deal with the Revolution as a civil war since the population was divided between Patriots, Loyalists, and a variety of positions in between. The following documents help with this issue.

Documents A and B refer to treatment of Loyalists by state governments and by local Patriots. New Hampshire named seventy-eight people "enemies" and proceeded to confiscate their property that lay within the state in 1778. Revenues from the sales of these estates helped the war effort, but the estates were sometimes sold below market value to privileged Patriots. This broke up large landed properties and equalized the distribution of wealth to some extent. The woodcut of a Loyalist editor being hung in effigy points to another persecution of Loyalists by local committees that appropriated political power. Loyalists viewed this behavior as anarchy and the natural outcome of the lawless overthrow of the Crown's government of the colonies. Many fled to England, and asked for compensation from the Crown for their losses for remaining loyal. Most were disappointed.

Patriots however, regarded Loyalists as traitors, and that alone justified their actions. They attempted to convert them to the Patriot cause, but if that was not possible, any action up to execution was used to silence opposition. The passion for the cause in Document C is evident, and fighting for the cause even crossed gender lines, with women ready to fight to defend their country.

Many questions ask to what extent an event had specified results. These documents point to the idea of looking at both sides of issues. Many Loyalists were wealthy and politically powerful under imperial rule. The Revolution gave those out of political and economic power the opportunity to appropriate that in the former colonies. You can use these types of documents to illustrate and analyze that issue in an essay on the Revolution.

Document A

Source: Laws of New Hampshire, November 28, 1778. [*Original Acts*, Vii, 99.]

"Whereas John Wentworth, Esq. . . . [inserted here is a list of loyalists] . . . & James Rogers Esq have since the commencement of Hostilities between Great brittain and the united states of America left this and the other united states and gone over to and joined the enemys thereof and have to the utmost of their power aided abetted and assisted the said enemys in their cruel designs of wresting from the good people of said states their said Liberties civil and religious. . . . Be it Therefore Enacted . . . that the whole estate real and personal . . . of each of them lying and being within this state be & hereby is declared to be forfeited to this state and that the same be for the use thereof."

Document B

Mr. Rivington, Loyalist editor, hanged in effigy, 1775

Document C

"Awake, Americans, to a sense of your danger. No time is to be lost. Instantly banish every Tory from among you. Let America be sacred alone to freemen.

Drive far from you every baneful wretch who wishes to see you fettered with the chains of tyranny. Send them where they may enjoy their beloved slavery to perfection-send them to the island of Britain; there let them drink the cup of slavery and eat the bread of bitterness all the days of their existence-there let them drag out a painful life; despised and accursed by those very men whose cause they have had the wickedness to espouse. Never let them return to this happy land-never let them taste the sweets of that independence which they strive to prevent."

Document D

Source: Collection of the New York Historical Society in HM, "The History Companion" CD.

Woodcut from *New Touch on the Times by a Daughter of Liberty Living in Marblehead.* 1779

Multiple-Choice Answers

1. b. It took the colonies more than a year after Lexington and Concord to declare Independence. Most colonists still acknowledged the king but wanted him to accept colonial republican ideals concerning representation and taxation.

2. c. In his treatise concerning England's Glorious Revolution, John Locke stated that a people have the right to overthrow a government that does not protect natural rights of life, liberty, and property.

3. d. Although the British loss of troops was considerable, the Patriot show of force showed the British that their estimation of poor American fighting capabilities was wrong.

4. a. The Iroquois Confederacy abandoned its policy of neutrality when confronted with conflict among Europeans in America. Some of the tribes supported the British in hopes of slowing American westward expansion, and the Confederacy lost unity and strength.

5. c. This British pincers strategy had a goal of dividing New England, the supposed center of rebellion, from the other colonies. Cut off from Patriot leadership centered in Boston, the British felt that the rebellion would then die.

6. e. The temporary superiority of the French fleet in the Chesapeake cut off any means of retreat for Cornwallis.

CHAPTER 6
The Constitution and the New Republic

AP THEMES
- **Globalization:** America now had to deal with politics and economics in the Atlantic world as an independent nation. As both France and England vied for hegemony, the United States wished to engage in commerce and trade while remaining neutral in political affairs.
- **Politics and Citizenship:** This chapter focuses on the creation of the republic based on the Constitution. The intent of the founders was often challenged by others in the early years, but those patterns set lasting precedents. A major development was the formation of political parties whose basic ideologies animate our political system today.
- **War and Diplomacy:** Neither Europe nor America had unabashed confidence that the United States would last, and a major task of the new government was to show the world that the American republic was viable. Despite efforts to steer clear of European politics it proved impossible. Conflicts with both Britain and France arose during Federalist rule, and treaties with foreign nations sometimes led to conflict at home between regions.

CHAPTER SUMMARY
Framing a New Government

Despite the opposition to central authority evidenced during the Revolution, as the 1780s progressed there was much dissatisfaction with the Articles of Confederation. The Confederation Congress had proven ineffective in key areas: funding veterans' pensions, promoting trade, the Indian threat, creating a stable currency, social unrest, and retiring debt. At the **Annapolis Convention** in 1786 **Alexander Hamilton** proposed that a special convention meet to strengthen the Articles, and after Shays' Rebellion Washington supported this.

Hosting delegates from all states except Rhode Island, the Constitutional Convention met at Philadelphia in 1787; Washington was chosen to preside. Delegates agreed on a government with three branches—legislative, executive, and judicial—but competing plans were presented concerning representation and slavery. Large states favored the **Virginia Plan,** which called for representation based on population; the **New Jersey Plan** gave each state equal representation and was favored by the small states. The **Great Compromise** resolved this divide with the lower house representation based on population, and the upper house based on equal representation by state. Slavery was given protections by prohibiting taxes on exports, limiting the tax on imported slaves, and prohibiting Congress from interfering with the slave trade for twenty years. With respect to taxation and representation slaves would be counted as **three-fifths** of a free person. The Constitution omitted a definition of citizenship, as well as a list of individual rights.

James Madison was crucial to the creation of the Constitution and to the resolution of two critical issues: sovereignty and limiting power. Sovereign authority would come from the people, not the national or state governments between which power was divided. The problem of concentrated power was resolved by adopting the ideas of **Baron de Montesquieu. A federal system** with power divided between states and the nation, and

separation of powers and **checks and balances** within the federal government would prevent tyranny. Madison also successfully argued that a large republic was less susceptible to tyranny, countering contemporary political thought. **Tyranny of the people** was checked by frequent and indirect elections, as well as other devices.

The supporters of the Constitution, such as Washington and **Benjamin Franklin,** were called **Federalists.** Their cause was publicized by **Alexander Hamilton, James Madison, and John Jay** in *The Federalist Papers.* Critics were known as **Anti-federalists.** They saw in the new Constitution a potentially tyrannical state that would subjugate the states and end liberty. Their biggest complaint was the omission of a **bill of rights.** They feared the power of the state more than the anarchy of the people. Federalists feared that the unchecked power of the masses would result in chaos. A heated debate ended in June 1788 when the required nine states ratified the document.

The first elections in early 1789 chose Washington as president. He was inaugurated in New York, the national capital at the time. Congress's first task was to draft the Bill of Rights. The **Judiciary Act of 1789** set up the system of federal courts, and Congress established three executive departments: the Treasury Department with Alexander Hamilton at its head, the State Department with **Thomas Jefferson,** and the War Department with **Henry Knox** as head.

Federalists and Republicans

Political controversy arose during the 1790s over the nature of the new government. **Alexander Hamilton** led the **Federalists** (not the same group supporting ratification), who believed that the United States needed a strong central government supporting a commercial economy, which together would earn international stature for the United States. The **Republicans,** led by **James Madison** and **Thomas Jefferson,** saw America as predominantly a rural and agrarian nation, with the preponderance of power resting not in the central government, but in the states and the people.

George Washington favored Federalist ideas and he supported Hamilton's programs. To gain support of the country's elite and provide a strong financial basis for the country, Hamilton's program included **funding** the national debt at its face value or **at par;** the assumption of state debts accumulated during the Revolution; the creation of a **national bank;** and in his **Report on Manufacturing,** an **excise tax** on distilled liquor and a **protective tariff** on imported goods. His reports offered a grand vision for the new nation but ran into varying degrees of opposition. The **Assumption Bill** passed only after reaching a compromise in which the new national capital would be located in the south. The Bank Bill was the most controversial, with many arguing that the Constitution gave no explicit power to create it, but it passed, and the **Bank of the United States** received a twenty-year charter in 1791. The **Funding Bill** and whiskey excise tax also passed, as did a tariff that was much more modest than Hamilton wanted. Hamilton's program restored public credit and satisfied many with the exception of small farmers.

Most philosophers of the age believed that political parties or **factions** were dangerous. Madison detailed their danger and the republican solution to them in **"Federalist Number 10."** However, both political groups formed organizations to support their visions for the United States. The **first party system** consisted of the **Federalists,** who supported an urban and commercial economy with a strong central government to provide order, stability, and the protection of property, and the Republicans, who were adherents of a rural and **agrarian** economy and wanted a strong state governments and a relatively weak federal government to prevent tyranny and the loss of liberty. The Federalists felt rule should rest with the wealthy and the commercial elite, whereas Republicans felt authority should rest with the independent, landowning farmer.

Establishing National Sovereignty

During their twelve-year tenure, Federalists helped secure western lands and strengthened America's international position. In 1794 western-Pennsylvania farmers refused to pay the whiskey tax. Washington raised and led an army to put down the **Whiskey Rebellion.** During this time several western territories were admitted as states. This served to tie westerners more closely to the federal government. The struggle with Native Americans for control of lands continued. Under the Constitution, Indian tribes were legal entities but not considered foreign nations; individual Indians were not citizens of the United States. With settlers encroaching on Indian lands violence heightened in the 1790s. Despite several Indian victories in Ohio, they eventually capitulated at the **Battle of Fallen Timbers** in 1794. A year later the **Miami** Indians ceded their lands in the **Treaty of Grenville.**

Establishing legitimacy with Great Britain was a major goal but difficult to achieve. The relationship was tested in 1793 when France and England went to war. Washington issued a **Proclamation of Neutrality,** which was ignored by a French diplomat, **Citizen Edmond Genêt.** Anti-British feeling arose when the Royal Navy began seizing American ships trading with the French in the Caribbean. Washington sent Federalist **John Jay** to settle affairs with England. Unable to secure the goals in his instructions, Jay did establish American sovereignty in the Northwest and a satisfactory commercial relationship with Great Britain. After much debate, the Senate ratified **Jay's Treaty** in 1794. That treaty led the way to settling conflicts with Spain in **Pickney's Treaty** signed in 1795. Its provisions gave American's the right to deposit their goods at the mouth of the Mississippi River and to settle the northern border of Florida and secured a promise that Spain would prevent Indian raids over the border.

The Downfall of the Federalists

The Federalist belief in stable government over personal liberty ended them as an effective political force by 1800. Declining a third term Washington highlighted the dangers of foreign influence and political parties in his **Farewell Address.** In 1796 John Adams and Thomas Jefferson ran for president. Adams's political opponent, Jefferson, was second in electoral balloting and became vice president. Adams was a superb statesman but a poor politician. Leading a divided party, Adams faced a crisis when France seized American ships. In the face of his party's calls for war, Adams preferred diplomacy and sent a mission to France in 1797. The group was met by three French agents who demanded a bribe before negotiating. The **XYZ Affair** infuriated America and led to an undeclared naval war with France. Ultimately France chose to negotiate, averting war.

Politically strengthened by this conflict, Federalists passed the **Alien and Sedition Acts** in 1798 to stifle Republican opposition. The Republican response was the **Virginia and Kentucky Resolutions,** which used John Locke's **compact theory** to introduce the concept of state **nullification** of federal laws.

Party strife engulfed the 1800 presidential election. Adams and Jefferson were candidates again. However, in the electoral college both Jefferson and his vice presidential running mate, **Aaron Burr,** received 73 electoral votes; Adams received 65. The House of Representatives chose Jefferson as President. The judiciary was now the only branch dominated by Federalists, and the **lame duck** Federalist Congress strengthened its hold on the courts by passing the **Judiciary Act of 1801,** which provided for the last-minute installation of several Federalist judges, known as the **midnight appointees.**

Multiple-Choice Questions—Exam Tips

- Questions from this era often ask you to discuss political, economic, and social changes that resulted from the American Revolution.
- Interpretations of the Articles of Confederation vary from it being a dark "critical period" in which little was accomplished to its successes in winning the war, negotiating the peace, and settling the West. There is evidence to support both viewpoints.
- Pay particular attention to the issue of compromise in the Constitution, especially over the issues of representation and slavery.
- Political parties emerged during Washington's first administration. Take care to understand the Federalist and Republican ideologies.

Multiple-Choice Questions

1. Those pushing for reform of the Articles of Confederation government at the Annapolis Convention did so because
   a. the government did not give the states enough sovereign power.
   b. it did not provide for the settlement of the new territories granted to the United States in the Treaty of Paris.
   c. its central authority violated principles that Patriots fought for during the Revolution.
   d. the commercial economy was in a depression, but western Massachusetts farmers were thriving.
   e. the government's authority proved insufficient to provide solutions in several key areas.

2. Divisions in the 1787 Constitutional Convention resulted in the omission of which of the following in the Constitution?
   a. a bill of rights and the definition of citizenship
   b. provisions protecting slavery and the slave trade
   c. plans for counting slaves in the census
   d. plans to provide representation for both the states and the people
   e. provisions for a strong executive branch

3. The principle of sovereignty in the Federal Constitution was derived from the political philosophy of
   a. the Baron de Montesquieu, whose concept of the separation of powers would keep the people in control.
   b. David Hume, who favored a large republic with many different interests that could be heard by the government.
   c. James Madison, who believed in government by the consent of the governed.
   d. Alexander Hamilton, whose belief in a strong central government could protect democratic rule by the people.
   e. Thomas Hobbes, whose Leviathan was controlled and run by popular rule.

4. During the ratification debate over the new Constitution, essays in The Federalist Papers argued that
   a. the Constitution betrayed Revolutionary principles by establishing a strong and potentially tyrannical government.
   b. a small republic could better serve the people than a large government because all voices would be heard.
   c. the proposed government would increase taxes, destroy state power, and destroy individual liberty.
   d. the large republic as proposed would have so many different interests that none would dominate and liberty would be preserved.
   e. slavery and individual liberty were not contradictory because slaves were not citizens and therefore did not deserve freedom.

5. All of the following provisions of Hamilton's financial plan for the new nation were adopted *except*
   a. assumption of state debts because they were contracted during a war that benefited the nation as a whole.
   b. the creation of a national bank to do the government's banking business and provide stability to the nation's finances.
   c. funding the existing debt at face value even though many of the bonds issued during the Revolutionary War were purchased by speculators at a discounted price.
   d. adopting an excise tax on whiskey to provide funding of the national debt and revenue for government expenses.
   e. enacting a tariff high enough to both provide revenue and protect American industry from foreign competition.

6. Republican opposition to Washington's support for the Federalist program rested in a national vision for the United States that included
   a. strong support for commercial interests by a strong federal government to provide economic prosperity.
   b. a country of small independent landowners whose interests were protected and promoted by the states more than the federal government.
   c. the ability of the states to nullify any federal action with which they did not agree.
   d. a country that should include only people who were Americans at ratification and therefore pursue an anti-immigration policy.
   e. a passion for the order and stability that England appeared to enjoy in contrast to the anarchy of the French Revolution.

7. Under the Constitution the status of Indians and Indians tribes was
   a. unclear because tribes were considered legal entities but not foreign nations, and individual Indians were not United States citizens.
   b. clarified as Indian lands were ceded to the United States government and Indians were required to live on reservations.
   c. to be determined by the state in which the tribe resided, and that state could determine the Indians' status as it saw fit.
   d. determined by the three-fifths compromise, in which Indians were counted as three-fifths of a person for taxation and representation purposes.
   e. to be renegotiated because all treaties approved under the Articles of Confederation were declared null and void.

8. The first major challenge to Washington's Proclamation of Neutrality in 1793 was
    a. from Great Britain, which failed to send a diplomat to the United States after the Treaty of Paris.
    b. begun by John Jay, whose treaty with England in 1794 failed to achieve any goals set out by Washington.
    c. from Spain's refusal to abide by the provisions outlined in Pinckney's Treaty concerning goods at New Orleans.
    d. made by Citizen Genêt, who solicited American support for France in its war against England and other European nations.
    e. made from western expansionists who gathered together an army to invade and annex Canada.

9. The Republican response to the Alien and Sedition Acts passed during the administration of John Adams was
    a. Washington's Farewell Address, which cautioned against the party politics reflected in the acts.
    b. the XYZ Affair, in which Republicans worked with French agents to undermine Federalist foreign policy.
    c. the Virginia and Kentucky Resolutions, which drew on John Locke's compact theory of government.
    d. the Revolution of 1800, in which Republicans and Federalists physically fought in Congress.
    e. the Proclamation of Neutrality, which prohibited foreign aliens from immigrating to the United States.

10. The federal system embodied in the Constitution
    a. balanced competing needs for protection from tyranny with the need for an effective central government.
    b. gave states sovereign authority in nearly all areas of government but defense and foreign policy.
    c. ultimately gave preference to large states by having representation in the House of Representatives based on population.
    d. made the Constitution the "supreme law of the land" and opened the door for the unchecked exercise of power by the federal government.
    e. relied exclusively on pure democratic principles for decisions to be made, with "We, the people" making all major decisions.

11. Both elections of 1796 and 1800 resulted in ambiguous initial outcomes because
    a. there was no clear popular majority for any of the candidates running for president.
    b. neither Republican nor Federalist parties could agree on a candidate once Washington decided not to seek reelection.
    c. the voting mechanism of the electoral college led to unintended consequences in the choices for president and vice president.
    d. the popular vote and the vote in the electoral college did not agree with each other.
    e. the losing candidate would not concede the election once the votes were counted and certified.

12. After Washington was inaugurated president in 1789, Congress's first major task was to fulfill anti-federalist expectations by
    a. adopting Hamilton's Report on Manufacturing to get the economy moving forward.
    b. drafting a bill of rights protecting individual liberties from a powerful government.
    c. establishing a federal court system in the Judiciary Act of 1789.
    d. putting down the protest to the whiskey excise tax in western Pennsylvania.
    e. declaring war on England for inciting Indians in the Northwest to attack American settlements there.

Free-Response Questions

1. Analyze the issues that led to the formation of the Federalist and Republican Parties during the Federalist era.

2. How did the United States attempt to achieve independence and stature in foreign affairs during the Washington and Adams administrations?

Document-Based Question—Exam Tip

Evaluate whether the Articles of Confederation or the Federal Constitution best fulfilled the principles for which the Revolutionary War was fought.

Use the documents and your knowledge of the period 1765–1790 in constructing your response.

Document A

Source: "Declaration and Resolves of the First Continental Congress, 10/14/1774.

"…the foundation of English liberty, and of all free governments, is a right in the people to participate in their legislative council: and as the English colonists are not represented, and from their local and other circumstances cannot properly be represented in the British parliament, they are entitled to a free and exclusive power of legislation in their several provincial legislatures, where their right of legislation can alone be preserved, in all cases of taxation and internal polity…" [W.C. Ford, ed. *Journals of the Continental Congress*, 1904, I, 63.

Document B

Source: Thomas Paine, *Common Sense*, 1776.

"…the powers of governing still remaining in the hands of the king, he will have a negative over the whole legislation of this continent. And he has shown himself such an inveterate enemy to liberty, and discovered such a thirst for arbitrary power, is he, or is he not, a proper person to say no to these colonies, 'You shall make no laws but what I please!'"
[Paine, *Common Sense*, 1856]

Document C

Source: Articles of Confederation, Art. 2.

"Each state retains its sovereignty, freedom and independence, and every power, jurisdiction and right, which is not by this confederation expressly delegated to the United States, in Congress assembled."

Document D

Source: Land Survey: Ordinance of 1785.

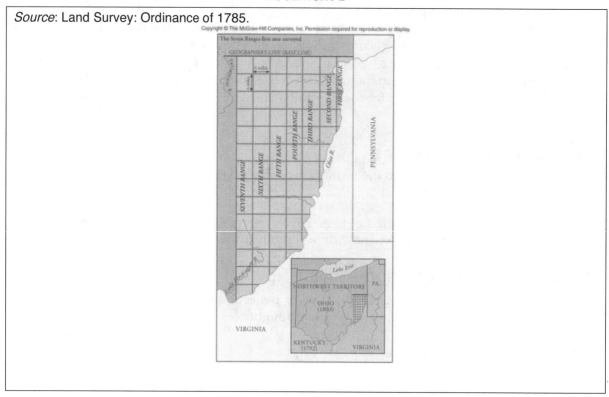

Document E

Source: Letter from George Washington to James Madison, 11/5/1786.

"Without an alteration in our political creed, the superstructure we have been seven years in raising at the expense of so much treasure and blood, must fall. We are fast verging to anarchy and confusion…What stronger evidence can be given of the want of energy in our government than these disorders?…Thirteen sovereignties pulling against each other, and all tugging at the federal head, will soon bring ruin on the whole…" [Washington, *Writings*, XXIX, 52.]

Document F

Source: Letter from Thomas Jefferson to William S. Smith, 11/13/1787.

"God forbid we should ever be 20 years without such a rebellion…What country can preserve its liberties, if their rulers are not warned from time to time that this people preserve the spirit of resistance? Let them take arms!…What signify a few lives lost in a century or two? The tree of liberty must be refreshed from time to time with the blood of patriots and tyrants." [Jefferson, *Papers*, XII, 356.]

Document G

Source: Speech of Patrick Henry during the debate in the Virginia Ratifying Convention, June 1788.

"...This proposal of altering our federal government is of the most alarming nature! Make the best of this new government—say it is composed of anything but inspiration—you ought to be extremely cautious, watchful, jealous of your liberty: for, instead of securing your rights, you may lose them forever. If a wrong step be now made, the republic be lost forever. If this new government will not come up to the expectation of the people and they shall be disappointed, their liberty will be lost, and tyranny must and will arise." [Eliot, III in *Annals of America*, III, 280-81]

Document H

Source: Alexander Hamilton, *The Federalist No. 1*, 1787.

"...the vigor of government is essential to the security of liberty; that, in the contemplation of a sound and well-informed judgment, their interest can never be separated; and that a dangerous ambition more often lurks behind the specious mask of zeal for the rights of the people than under the forbidding appearance of zeal for the firmness and efficiency of government." [From *Annals of America*, III, 215]

Document I

Source: The United States Constitution, Article Six, Clause 2, 1787.

"This Constitution, and the laws of the United States which shall be made in pursuance thereof, and all treaties made, or which shall be made, under the authority of the United States, shall be the supreme law of the land, and the judges in every state shall be bound thereby, anything in the constitution or laws of any state to the contrary notwithstanding."

Multiple-Choice Answers

1. e. Government under the Articles had several successes but proved too weak to effectively govern. States were sovereign, and the Confederation Congress had no right to tax or raise an army. The economy was depressed at the same time.

2. a. When the Constitution was ratified it did not contain a bill of rights; the Bill of Rights were amendments that were added later. The States defined who its citizens were until after the Civil War when constitutional amendments defined citizenship.

3. c. James Madison, borrowing from John Locke, was the architect of this principle.

4. d. "Federalist Number 10" countered contemporary political theory by pointing to the virtue of a large republic. This theory had never been tested.

5. e. Congress passed a tariff to fund government operations but it was not the high protective tariff Hamilton proposed to protect American infant industries from European competition.

6. b. Republican principles were opposite to those of Hamilton. Their greatest fear was tyranny, whether from concentrated political or economic power. Virtue for Republicans rested in the yeoman farmer.

7. a. Native American legal status under the Constitution was ambiguous, which put them in a vulnerable position when dealing with whites in the American legal and political system. Policies have shifted over time as attitudes toward Indians changed.

8. d. Despite Washington's warnings, Genêt tried to rally Americans around France's cause. Washington had him recalled.

9. c. The Nullification Theory was first articulated by Jefferson and Madison in these Resolutions. Propounding that the federal government was a creation of the states, they theorized that a state could declare a federal law null and void within that state.

10. a. The federal system embodies the idea of divided sovereignty, with powers being divided between the states, the federal government, and the people. This prevents concentration of power.

11. c. The original method for electing the president in the electoral college specified that the top vote getter would be president, and the next place would go to the vice president. In 1796 this led to opposition politicians, Adams and Jefferson, being in the same government. In 1800 Jefferson and his running mate, Aaron Burr, tied in the electoral college, but Burr would not concede. Jefferson narrowly won the House vote, which breaks a presidential electoral deadlock.

12. b. A bill of rights was the congressional priority as the promise of these protections was the only reason many ultimately voted for ratification.

Free-Response Questions Commentary

1. The formation of a two-party system happened during the early years of the republic. The major issue that defined the two groups was the national bank. Republicans came down on the side of strict construction and that the Bank was not "necessary" and not enumerated in the Constitution. They also objected to a government institution that would favor commercial interests and enhance governmental power. On the other hand, Federalists believed that it was "proper" to charter a bank, an "implied" constitutional power. It would encourage commerce and stabilize the financial system. Nearly every aspect of Hamilton's Financial Plan divided Federalists along these lines. Republicans favored states' rights to preserve liberty while Federalists believed that liberty rested in the protection of property and order. Federalists also differed on foreign policy, with Federalists favoring Britain and Republicans favoring France.

   One can argue that financial policy determined the lines between the two political groups, which tended to divide between commercial and agricultural interests.

2. As war broke out in the Atlantic between England and France in the 1790s, the United States was drawn into foreign affairs. Washington's response was the 1793 Proclamation of Neutrality in an attempt to maintain independence. Washington reinforced this in his farewell address. All during this period Washington was trying to open up the British West Indies to American trade. Citizen Genêt contested this policy without success. Washington's emissaries negotiated treaties with both England and Spain, and the payment of America's foreign debt raised its international stature. This strategy broke down in the late 1790s as the French began to seize American ships. Federalists called for war, but Adams resisted and the crisis passed. Washington's policy of neutrality served the country well and allowed the country a period of peace to establish stability in both domestic and foreign affairs.

Document-Based Question Commentary

There is ample evidence to support an answer that falls on either side of this question. Revolutionary principles were founded upon Whig ideology, which resisted concentrations of power that it believed would lead to corruption and tyranny. Thus the strong executive, power to tax, and lack of a bill of rights that characterized the Federal Constitution appeared to parallel the British government that America had only years before overthrown. Document B addresses issue of power, which would argue for the Articles. The Confederation excerpt, Document C, places sovereignty in the people and the States, decentralized power that is close to the people themselves—a Revolutionary virtue. Document D illustrates one of the Confederation's major successes, the orderly settlement of the Old Northwest. An Anti-federalist could also point to the winning of the war against Britain and the successful peace, and the enjoyment of liberties that were extinguished under the heavy hand of England's powerful government.

On the other hand, Federalists pointed to weaknesses in the Articles of Confederation that they claimed destroyed the notion of liberty. You can use Document A to argue either side of the debate depending upon what aspect you choose to stress—the state delegation of the Confederation, or the bicameral Congress of the Constitution. Trusting in order and stability as foundations of freedom, the weak powers of the Confederation government promoted the disorder of Shays' Rebellion referred to in Washington's letter, Document E, and Hamilton warns of the dangers of unchecked ambition in Document H. You can use other weaknesses of the Confederation to bolster your argument: the government commanded little respect in the world and Britain continued to violate the Treaty of Paris, it could not pay its debts without the power to tax, and a lingering postwar depression showed its inability to act in that area.

When answering this question it is important to articulate Revolutionary principles first; then your choice of either the Confederation or the Constitution should address the counterarguments on the other side.

CHAPTER 7
The Jeffersonian Era

AP THEMES

- **Culture:** America began to exert its cultural independence during this time. Private education flourished as republican ideology sought to produce virtuous citizens. American authors began producing a genre of national schoolbooks, dictionaries, literature, and histories.
- **Economic Transformations:** The Republican era beginning with Jefferson marked the beginning of the first Industrial Revolution in the United States. Powered by the Northeast's fast-flowing rivers, manufacturing enterprise sprouted, particularly in textiles. In turn this spurred growth in southern agriculture and shipping. The Lowell System provided work outside of the home for farm girls.
- **Environment:** The acquisition of Louisiana by Jefferson in 1803 had a profound impact on how Americans viewed their environment and its resources. Doubling the size of the national domain, Louisiana projected notions of abundance, expansion, and unlimited wealth. Jefferson predicted that the area would not be settled for 100 years, and together these ideas promoted waste of natural resources.
- **Politics and Citizenship:** The Revolution of 1800 and the Republicans in office promoted a more democratic and open political system than under Federalist rule. Land remained the basis for the franchise, and Jefferson cemented one aspect of political ideology in the American mind, that large government is a threat to individual liberty.
- **Religion:** The rationalism of the American Enlightenment was overtaken by evangelicalism during the early nineteenth century, and this became, and still remains, America's dominant religious characteristic.
- **War and Diplomacy:** Jefferson ushered in the Republican tendency to seek solutions to international disputes through diplomacy rather than war. Nevertheless, during the Republican tenure the United States did not hesitate to use force against Indians opposing white expansion westward, and it reluctantly went to war against Great Britain and the Barbary States to uphold American honor, provide security to western settlers, and establish its credibility in the international sphere.

CHAPTER SUMMARY
The Rise of Cultural Nationalism

The cultural life in Jeffersonian America both embraced and strayed from Republican ideals. Ironically, once in power, Jeffersonian Republicans reluctantly adopted the Federalist procedures they once resisted. Cities, industry, and commerce grew; religious revivals expanded, and American culture exhibited a vigorous nationalism.

True to their ideals, Republicans wanted to create a national public school system to produce an enlightened and virtuous citizenry. Although Massachusetts had supported the idea of public education, by 1815 no state had a comprehensive system. Southern private schools were sponsored by religious groups while northern private academies were secular. **Republican motherhood** made education for females more accessible, but there was little desire to educate Indians or blacks. Higher education was limited to training in the classics and religion. Professional training had little support.

Nationalism inspired cultural independence. **Noah Webster** published *The American Spelling Book* and a **dictionary,** which created a national linguistic standard. American authors tended to follow trends in British literature. However, American author **Washington Irving** became widely read, and patriotic historians, such as **Mercy Otis Warren** and **Parson Weems,** were also popular.

The Revolution weakened Americans' commitment to institutional religion but most still held strong religious convictions. Rationalism promoted theologies such as **deism,** which accepted God as the creator of the universe saw him as uninvolved with the daily interactions of human beings. To combat these theologies, various denominations promoted evangelical movements. Itinerant Presbyterian, Methodist, and Baptist ministers sought converts. **Cane Ridge, Kentucky,** hosted the first **camp meeting** of outdoor preaching and fervent responses. The theology was straightforward if not entirely consistent: accept God as an active force, and grace could be attained through faith and good works. Women played a vital role in revivals, and in some areas, blacks were admitted and enthusiastically embraced the appeal of salvation. In Virginia, **Gabriel Prosser's** aborted slave rebellion was inspired by this kind of revival preaching. Revivals for Native Americans combined Christian and Indian imagery and created a movement to defend native lands and traditions and to reject the white man's ways. By 1801, evangelicalism eclipsed the influence of rational theology and became the dominant force in American religion.

Stirrings of Industrialism

Although overwhelmingly rural and agrarian, America was moving slowly in the direction of an urban industrial society. British attempts to prohibit the export of manufacturing expertise failed in 1790 when English immigrant **Samuel Slater** established a spinning mill in Pawtucket, Rhode Island. The most important inventions were **Eli Whitney's cotton gin** and **interchangeable parts.** The cotton gin gave new life to southern agriculture and slavery and prompted New England's textile industry. A coherent transportation system began to develop. **Robert Fulton** perfected the **steamboat** in 1807 and private companies built turnpikes. Longer roads were later built and maintained by federal and state governments. As a result, cities grew and became centers of commerce, education, and affluence.

Jefferson the President

In office, Jefferson tried to reconcile Republicans and Federalists. He stressed Republican simplicity and did not entirely repudiate Federalist policies. As a shrewd politician he used his party and presidential powers to strengthen republican ideals. He was overwhelmingly reelected in 1804.

Jefferson was successful in reversing the Federalist trend of a large central government by repealing the whiskey tax, reducing government spending, retiring half the national debt, and reducing the size of the army and navy. Jefferson stood firm and stopped appeasing the **Barbary States** by refusing to continue the payment of **tribute.** He reached an agreement in the Mediterranean by expanding the American fleet in the region.

The Federalists' last stronghold was the judicial branch of government where judges were appointed for life. In 1803 the Supreme Court expanded its power in the case of *Marbury* v. *Madison* by ruling that it was the role of the court to decide on the constitutionality of laws. This concept is known as **judicial review.** Chief Justice **John Marshall** served as chief justice of the United States until 1835. Marshall often furthered the Federalist ideal of a strong national government.

Doubling the National Domain

Napoleon had dreams of establishing a New World Empire and quietly regained control of Louisiana from Spain. At the same time, Spain closed the port of New Orleans to American shipping. Westerners dependent on the Mississippi to ship their produce to market were outraged. Jefferson instructed America's minister in Paris, **Robert Livingston,** to purchase New Orleans. Napoleon, whose army in Santo Domingo was decimated by disease while quelling a revolt by **Toussaint L'Overture,** offered to sell the entire Louisiana Territory. Jefferson questioned whether he should buy the land, given that there was no explicit authority in the Constitution to acquire territory. His advisers convinced him that his treaty powers allowed him to do so, and America purchased all of Louisiana for $15 million.

The Louisiana Purchase doubled the United States territory. Even before the purchase Jefferson commissioned **Meriwether Lewis** and **William Clark** to explore the continent. They received aid from **Sacajawea,** a Shoshone woman, in 1804–1805. **Zebulon Pike** explored the Upper Mississippi Valley and left the impression that much of the land was uncultivable desert.

Expansion and War

The **Napoleonic Wars** in Europe and conflicts with Native Americans in the west together created pressures to declare **War in 1812.** Napoleon instituted the **Continental System** to keep Britain and its allies from trading with Europe, and England replied with its **Orders in Council** effectively blockading Europe from trade with America. America's large merchant marine became a pawn in the conflict, and America's rights as a neutral nation were violated. Exacerbating these humiliations was England's **impressment** policy. The British warship *Leopard* stopped the American naval frigate *Chesapeake* and removed four sailors in 1807. When the news reached America, popular outrage called for war, which Jefferson was determined to avoid.

To avoid maritime incidents Jefferson instituted an **embargo,** stopping trade with all nations, but it precipitated a serious depression in the United States. James Madison won the election of 1808 and modified the embargo several times, but Napoleon's manipulation led America to stop trading with Great Britain alone, and consequently the stage was set for war.

Competition for western lands increased tensions between whites and Native Americans. The Indians looked to the British, and the British to the Indians, to protect their native lands and to defend Canada. Two Indian brothers, **the Prophet,** a charismatic religious leader who preached the evils of white culture, and **Tecumseh,** a Shoshone chief who tried to unite all the Indians of the Mississippi Valley, attempted to stop the white onslaught. William Henry Harrison, governor of the Indiana Territory, attacked the Indians in 1811 and scored a strategic victory at the **Battle of Tippecanoe.**

Like northern expansionists with respect to Canada, southerners wanted to annex Spanish Florida, where slaves escaped to and Indians crossed the border to attack American settlements. In 1810 Madison annexed Baton Rouge, and the acquisition of Florida became another motivation for war with Britain, a Spanish ally. The elections of 1810 sent a number of western nationalists, expansionists, and war proponents, or **war hawks,** to Congress. Two important new leaders were **Henry Clay** and **John C. Calhoun.** Pressure for war mounted, and in 1812, President Madison capitulated.

The War of 1812

Already at war in Europe, the British relegated the conflict in America to the backburner until late 1813. The war did not go well for America. An **invasion of Canada** was repulsed and Indians captured Chicago. America's early naval victories were a result of England's preoccupation with the war in Europe. On the Great Lakes, American forces burned York (Toronto) and gained control of both Lake Ontario and Lake Erie. On Lake Erie, **Oliver Hazard Perry** defeated a British fleet, which paved the way for another Canadian invasion. In Florida, **Andrew Jackson,** a Tennessee planter, defeated the Creek Indians at the **Battle of Horseshoe Bend,** and the tribe later ceded its territory to the United States. Jackson went on to Spanish Florida and seized Pensacola.

England imposed a blockade on the United States and invaded America after Napoleon's surrender in 1814. British troops burned public buildings in Washington, including the White House, but withdrew from Baltimore after bombarding **Fort McHenry.** It was at this battle that **Francis Scott Key** wrote **"The Star-Spangled Banner."** American forces commanded by Andrew Jackson overwhelmingly defeated the British at the **Battle of New Orleans,** which took place after the peace treaty was signed, but news of the war's end had not reached America.

Opposition to the war, especially from Federalists in New England, increased with military failures. A political minority in national politics, Federalists convened the **Hartford Convention** in late 1814, proposed constitutional amendments designed to protect New England's political influence, and hinted at secession. News of victory at New Orleans and the peace treaty discredited the Federalists in the eyes of the country and ended their influence in national politics.

The **Treaty of Ghent** ended the fighting and solved little else. Later Britain granted America commercial privileges in the Empire and the Great Lakes were disarmed in the 1817 **Rush-Bagot Agreement.** The war was another disastrous blow to the ability of Native Americans to resist white expansion.

Multiple-Choice Questions

1. Which of the following was a primary role of education for children in the New Republic?
   a. training in religion to serve as ministers in various denominations during the Second Great Awakening
   b. technical education for operatives to work in the growing manufacturing sector, especially textiles
   c. education for women to become midwives and assistants to doctors
   d. education to create a nation of virtuous citizens to make political decisions
   e. teaching reading so that children would be able to read the Bible

2. The Second Great Awakening produced which of the following?
   a. strong support for the secular theologies of the American Enlightenment
   b. rebellion by some slaves who acted on the egalitarian message of the revivals
   c. an end to open-air camp meetings and a return to traditional, but enthusiastic services
   d. acceptance of Christianity by Indian tribes and their acquiescence to white demands for assimilation
   e. a return to the strict theology of the Puritan religion with its rejection of good works as a means to salvation

3. The basis for the Industrial Revolution during the Republican era lay in the
   a. manufacture of textiles in New England factories.
   b. use of steam power to run factories cheaply.
   c. transportation of finished goods via Robert Fulton's newly perfected steamboat.
   d. opening of the Mississippi Valley to manufacturing with the purchase of Louisiana.
   e. growth of major cities along the eastern seaboard.

4. As president, Jefferson's most difficult decision and challenge to his Republican ideology was his decision to
   a. avoid war and negotiate with the Barbary States.
   b. retire a large proportion of the national debt because it required raising taxes from the people.
   c. repeal the Whiskey Tax when the government needed that revenue.
   d. reduce the size of the army and navy when America faced several threats from European nations.
   e. purchase the Louisiana Territory because he was uncertain whether the Constitution gave him that authority.

5. The Supreme Court decision in Marbury v. Madison was significant for which of the following reasons?
   a. It expanded the power of the federal judiciary by establishing its right to review whether a law was constitutional.
   b. It gave Marbury the right to claim his commission as a justice of the peace.
   c. It settled the issue of life tenure for judges.
   d. It established John Marshall as chief justice for the next three decades.
   e. It validated Madison's claim as president in the disputed election of 1808.

6. The immediate effect of the Embargo Act in 1807 was
   a. that Britain stopped all trade with the United States.
   b. that the United States stopped trade with both Britain and France because they seized American ships.
   c. an economic depression in the United States when all foreign trade stopped.
   d. the end of all trade between the United States and its western territories until Indian hostilities ceased.
   e. economic prosperity as American industry grew to replace trading losses.

7. America went to war in 1812 for all of the following reasons except
   a. the British navy policy of impressment of American sailors.
   b. America's refusal to pay tribute to the Barbary States for safe passage in the Mediterranean for American ships.

c. British actions to incite Indians to attack American settlements in the Indiana Territory.

d. British trade policy blockading European trade with America.

e. the war hawks' demands for war to address western issues.

8. Andrew Jackson gained national stature during the War of 1812

   a. as commander of troops at the Battle of New Orleans.

   b. for leading the successful invasion of Canada at the beginning of the war.

   c. for successfully defending Baltimore from attack at Fort McHenry.

   d. for slowing the British attack on Washington and keeping several public buildings from being burned.

   e. as commander of troops that defeated the British at the Battle of Lake Erie.

9. Which of the following contained proposals for the constitutional amendments to admit new states and declare war only by a two-thirds vote of Congress and to restrict Congress's power to lay an embargo?

   a. the Virginia and Kentucky Resolutions

   b. the Rush-Bagot Agreement

   c. the Connecticut Compromise

   d. The Hartford Convention

   e. the declaration of war in 1812

10. A consequence for America as a result of the Treaty of Ghent was

    a. further westward expansion by white settlers as Indian defenses weakened.

    b. creation of an Indian buffer state in the Northwest.

    c. British renunciation of its impressment policy.

    d. cession of large parts of Canada to the United States.

    e. a military alliance with France.

11. Historians might contend that Jefferson's characterization of his election as the Revolution of 1800 was incorrect for which of the following reasons?

    a. Growth in this period expanded the ideal of a simple rural and agrarian republic.

    b. The size and the power of the federal government dramatically decreased under the Republican presidents.

    c. The national debt grew rather than decreased in size.

    d. The nation's cities and commercial economy were growing and becoming more important.

    e. The army and navy grew in size and the government was more prone to look to military rather than diplomatic solutions.

12. In domestic political terms the War of 1812 ushered in a period of

    a. bitter party rivalry between the Federalists and Republicans over the issue of federal power.

    b. growing popular support for Federalist candidates who opposed the war with England.

    c. a growing number of slave states relative to free states as new slave states were formed in the Louisiana Territory.

    d. the emergence of a new nativist party that opposed any attempts at trade or alliance with England.

    e. the end of Federalist support and influence, resulting in little partisan strife.

Free-Response Questions—Exam Tips

The Timeless Political Debate

Alexander Hamilton and Thomas Jefferson outlined the two major views of American democracy in the late eighteenth century. Their respective ideas on government are often characterized as "big" or "small" government. Hamilton believed a strong central government was essential to curbing human appetites and passions, a Hobbesian viewpoint; only through a powerful government's protection of property and maintenance of order could liberty flourish. On the other hand, Jefferson believed human nature was essentially good and people virtuous, John Locke's position, so no strong central government was necessary to maintain order and, in fact, that strong central government would destroy individual liberty. For Jeffersonians concentration of power inevitably led to corruption and tyranny. Much of the political debate throughout our history has stemmed from this fundamental philosophical difference.

Free-Response Questions

1. How did the Constitution regard Native Americans, and how did their position change with respect to the United States government in the period between ratification and the end of the War of 1812?

2. In what ways did both eastern and western interests lead to the declaration of war in 1812?

Document-Based Question—Exam Tips

The documents that follow are from the writings of Thomas Jefferson and Alexander Hamilton. They articulate two very different and competing visions for America. Use these documents and your background knowledge to describe what those visions were and to what extent America was moving toward them in the period from 1789 to 1815.

Document-Based Question

Document A

Source: Alexander Hamilton, *Federal Constitution Debates*, June 18, 1787.

"All communities divide themselves into the few and the many. The first are the rich and the wellborn, the other the mass of the people…The people are turbulent and changing; they seldom judge or determine right. Give therefore to the first class a distinct, permanent share in the government. They will check the unsteadiness of the second, and they cannot receive any advantage by a change, they therefore will ever maintain good government."

Document B

Source: Alexander Hamilton, *Opinion on the Constitutionality of the Bank*, February 23, 1791.

"If the end be clearly comprehended within any of the specified powers, and if the measure have an obvious relation to that end, and it is not forbidden by any particular provision of the Constitution, it may be safely deemed to come within the compass of the national authority."

Document C

Source: Alexander Hamilton, *Report on Manufactures*, December, 1791.

". . . the establishment of manufactures is calculated not only to increase the general stock of useful and productive labor, but even to improve the state of agriculture in particular—certainly to advance the interest of those who are engaged in it...Not only the wealth but the independence and security of a country appear to be materially connected with the prosperity of manufactures. Every nation, with a view to those great objects, ought to endeavor to possess within itself, all the essentials of national supply."

Document D

Source: Thomas Jefferson, *Notes on the State of Virginia, Query 19*. 1781–1785.

"Those who labor in the earth are the chosen people of God, if ever he had a chosen people, whose breasts He has made his particular deposit for substantial and genuine virtue."

Document E

Source: Thomas Jefferson, Letter to Colonel Edward Carrington, January 16, 1787.

"The basis of our government being the opinion of the people, the very first object should be to keep that right; and were it left to me to decide, whether we should have a government without newspapers, or newspapers without a government, I should not hesitate a moment to prefer the latter."

Document F

Source: Thomas Jefferson, *Writings*, February 15, 1791.

"I consider the foundation of the Constitution as laid upon this ground—that all powers *not delegated to the United States by the Constitution, nor prohibited by it to the states, are reserved to the states, or to the people*...To take a single step beyond the boundaries thus specifically drawn around the powers of Congress is to take possession of a boundless field of power, no longer susceptible of any definition."

Document G

Source: Thomas Jefferson, Letter to John Dickinson, August 9, 1803.

"...there is a difficulty in this acquisition [Louisiana Purchase] which presents a handle to the malcontents among us...Our confederation is certainly confined to the limits established by the Constitution. The general government has no powers but such as the Constitution has given it, and it has not given it a power of holding foreign territory, and still less of incorporating it into the Union. An amendment to the Constitution seems necessary for this. In the meantime we must ratify and pay our money...for a thing beyond the Constitution, and rely on the nation to sanction an act done for its great good, without its previous authority."

Multiple-Choice Answers

1. d. The success of the republic depended on a virtuous and vigilant citizenry to make good political decisions and detect corruption. This role largely fell on mothers.

2. b. The egalitarian message of the Great Awakening that all could be saved and acquire "grace" inspired revolts in oppressed groups, especially African Americans and Native Americans.

3. a. New England's water power, ports, and commercial spirit became the basis for the Industrial Revolution.

4. e. Jefferson believed in strict construction of the Constitution and so agonized over the purchase of Louisiana. The land furthered his agrarian vision for America, but he did not recognize any constitutional authority to purchase land from foreign nations.

5. a. Before Marbury the judiciary was not on an equal footing with the two other branches. The power to review actions and laws put it on an equal footing.

6. c. Jefferson's embargo stopped trade with all nations, which was disastrous to the American economy.

7. b. The conflict with the Barbary States occurred several years before the War of 1812. The causes for the war had roots in eastern maritime commerce and western expansionist and security issues.

8. a. Jackson was already known for his prowess as an Indian fighter, but the great victory at New Orleans made him a patriotic hero.

9. d. The Hartford Convention, in opposition to its Federalist political principles, tried to restrict the power of the federal government to protect its waning influence. As the nation grew and expanded westward the New England Federalists' power declined.

10. a. The Treaty of Ghent provided for the status quo antebellum, or the same status as before the war. There was no exchange of territory with England, but Indian tribes, weakened by the war and their support of Britain, were forced to give up more lands east of the Mississippi.

11. d. The irony of the Republicans in power was that even though the national domain expanded, industrialism, commercialism, and the growth of cities were becoming increasingly important to the American economy and society.

12. e. This is known as "the Era of Good Feelings" because the Federalists lost significant political stature and authority at the Hartford Convention. For practical purposes there was only one political party for several years, and thus little partisan strife.

Free-Response Questions Commentary

1. The Constitution left Native Americans with an ambiguous status with respect to the new United States. Tribes were given legal status but were not foreign nations, and individual Indians were not considered citizens. Congress was given the power to regulate commerce with the tribes. The Constitution bound the government to respect treaties signed under the Confederation government. Although the Constitution implied some measure of sovereignty, that ultimately depended on control of the land Indians occupied. This vagueness left the relationship up to treaties, judicial decisions, and wars.

   The Revolution divided Indians among supporters of the British and the Americans, and left them in a weaker position. As settlers continued their move westward after the war, a series of agreements ceded Indian lands to the Confederation, although Indians offered armed resistance. After a series of defeats at the hands of Little Turtle in Ohio, the Miami tribe was defeated in 1794 at the Battle of Fallen Timbers; the Treaty of Greenville ceded substantial land to the American government. The conflict over land continued and William Henry Harrison defeated a unified force under Tecumseh at the Battle of Tippecanoe in 1811. Some tribes sided with the British during the War of 1812, and United States forces under the command of Andrew Jackson inflicted a harsh defeat on the Southwest Indians at Horseshoe Bend in 1814. More land was ceded. The War of 1812 weakened Native American resistance as white momentum for expansion increased.

2. The declaration of war in 1812 resulted from a confluence of diverse interests. Since the renewal of war in Europe in the early nineteenth century, both Britain and France were violating American rights as a neutral nation. The Berlin and Milan Decrees and the Orders in Council both prohibited trade between America and European nations. Britain seized American ships and impressed American seamen. Jefferson's response was the Embargo Act, which sent America into economic depression. Ultimately, machinations by the French over trade policy led to the declaration.

   In addition to neutral rights a group of nationalistic western congressmen called the war hawks supported territorial expansion and disliked the British support of Indians in the Northwest. Henry Clay and John Calhoun were members of this group. They pushed for war with England to eliminate barriers to expansion. Madison, losing influence in Congress, succumbed to the combined pressures and approved the declaration of war against England.

Document-Based Question Commentary

The series of quotations from Alexander Hamilton and Thomas Jefferson highlight two different conceptions of the American republic. Hamilton and Washington's Federalist program interpreted the Constitution broadly, as Document B demonstrates. Believing property a natural right, and the government's role to protect property, essentially they believed those who owned the country should govern it. This excepted most of the population from politics, as Document A suggests. Hamilton's economic vision was that of commerce and manufacturing, Document C, and links to Britain through trade, and a reverence of the British led Federalists to favor England in foreign affairs.

The Jeffersonian Republicans were on the opposite end of the political spectrum in most of these matters. Document D points to the vision of an agricultural America with virtue and liberty resting in the independent farmer. Both Documents E and F point to the benefit to liberty of a small central government that emphasizes states' rights. Therefore, he favored a strict construction of the Constitution, and Document G indicates the anguish he harbored with his decision to purchase the Louisiana Territory.

By 1812 you can point to the country moving in both directions. The Louisiana Purchase, development of the Nullification Doctrine, war with England, decline of the Federalist Party, and efforts at reducing the size and authority of the federal government all point to Jefferson's vision. The Hamiltonian vision is evident in the beginnings of the Industrial Revolution, strong federal authority, support of commerce with the declaration of war, and a federal judiciary that supported property rights and federal power. At this point you can make either argument.

CHAPTER 8
Varieties of American Nationalism

AP THEMES

- **American Identity:** This period ushered in explosive westward growth and shaped the expansionist character that Americans espoused throughout the nineteenth century. Distinct sectional development threatened but did not overpower strong nationalist forces.
- **Demographic Changes:** The irony of American development in this period and over the course of its history is that as the United States acquired more land and its population migrated to the vast agricultural regions of the West and the South, the nation was becoming more urban and industrialized.
- **Economic Transformations:** The factory system took shape during this era using the Lowell System as a model. The national government lent support with internal improvements and a protective tariff. The country was shifting its support to Hamilton's vision for America.
- **Environment:** Particularly in the cotton culture of the South abundance and waste went together. As cotton and tobacco depleted soils in the Old South, westward migration of the plantation system followed. Population growth fostered the opening up of new land throughout the country.
- **Slavery and Its Legacies in North America:** Not since the debates in the Constitutional Convention had slavery been so contentious an issue. The Missouri Compromise exposed issues of federal versus state power, regional lifestyles, and economic prosperity. However, the controversy was short-lived, and the Compromise appeased both sides for the three following decades.

CHAPTER SUMMARY

After the War of 1812, a rising tide of vigorous American nationalism overshadowed regional differences, but the 1820 Missouri Compromise brought the divisive issue of slavery to the center of national attention.

A Growing Economy

A postwar boom and subsequent panic in 1819 exposed weaknesses in the United States' financial and economic systems. Disruptions in commerce and banking during the War of 1812 led to a charter for the **Second Bank of the United States** in 1816. Industrial growth was led by textiles and the innovations of **Francis Cabot Lowell,** who developed a power loom and combined the spinning and weaving processes in one factory at Waltham, Massachusetts, employing young women workers from New England farms. British dumping of goods in America prompted Congress to pass a **protective tariff** in 1816 to protect **infant industries** from foreign competition. Farmers protested higher prices for manufactured goods, but the Hamiltonian dream of an industrial economy prevailed.

The British blockade of American ports during the war highlighted weaknesses in the transportation system, and an increasing proportion of the population living west of the Appalachians fueled the demand for **internal improvements.** However, controversy arose over whether the Constitution authorized funding for internal improvements. The **National**

Road was built with federal support in 1811. This along with other privately financed roads and travel by steamboat lowered transportation costs. Congress passed a bill for funding roads and canals, which Madison vetoed in 1817 on the grounds that it was the responsibility of private enterprise and the states, not the federal government, to build this infrastructure.

Expanding Westward

Although the population in eastern cities was growing most Americans were farmers, and improved transportation such as the **Erie Canal** in 1825 made the plentiful lands in the **Old Northwest** increasingly attractive. Additionally, the institution of the **factor system** made Indian tribes more dependent on white America, and Indian resistance declined.

Settlers often traveled in groups and formed communities together. However, rising land prices and poor conservation practices prompted many to move on and settle new lands after a few years' time; thus mobility was great. As lands in the Old South wore out but demand for cotton continued to grow, planters migrated to lands in Alabama and Mississippi; there they formed a **planter aristocracy.** Within five years of the end of the War of 1812, four new states entered the Union.

Upon its independence from Spain in 1821, Mexico opened its commerce to America and lively trade ensued. In Oregon, **John Jacob Astor** established a fur-trading outpost but moved his interests to the Great Lakes at the war's end. Substantial numbers of French-Canadian and Anglo-American **mountain men** followed, trapping on their own as well as trading with the Indians for furs. Many mountain men took Native American and Hispanic women as wives. Several explorers, such as **Stephen H. Long,** described the Great Plains as uninhabitable. Most Anglo Americans accepted this image of the West.

The "Era of Good Feelings"

The **Virginia dynasty** referred to a succession of presidents from Virginia. They inspired some dissatisfaction among Northerners, but Virginian **James Monroe,** who was elected in 1816, chose government officials from all areas of the nation and from both parties. Consequently, a vibrant nationalism superseded partisan politics for a time. In 1818 Monroe took a **goodwill tour** of the country and was acclaimed by all sections.

Secretary of state **John Quincy Adams** was a former Federalist, a nationalist, and expansionist. Adams acted on the strong sentiment for annexing Florida and opened negotiations with Spain. At the same time, Andrew Jackson invaded Florida without authorization to stop raids by the Seminole Indians, a conflict known as the **Seminole War.** The United States then claimed responsibility for the attack and pressed Spain to cede Florida to the United States. This was accomplished in the **Adams-Onis Treaty** of 1819.

Speculation in land, weak banks, and the tightening of credit by the Bank of the United States led to the **Panic of 1819,** an economic depression lasting six years. The depression reopened debate about the Bank of the United States and its role in the country's expansion.

Sectionalism and Nationalism

Strong sectional feelings emerged briefly in 1819 and 1820, but nationalism prevailed. In 1819 Missouri applied for statehood as a slave state, and Maine then applied for statehood as a free state. In the **Missouri Compromise** both states were admitted, maintaining the balance in the Senate between slave and free states, and slavery was prohibited in the remaining Louisiana Territory above the **36°30′ line.** This compromise stalled the movement toward disunion for a time, as it set a geographic boundary on where slavery was allowed.

A strong nationalist, **John Marshall** served as chief justice of the Supreme Court from 1801 to 1835. Marshall left an indelible imprint on the nation. Under his leadership the Court increased the power of the judiciary and the federal government. Tackling the constitutionally murky relationship between Indian tribes and the United States, the **Marshall Court** declared tribes sovereign entities with property rights, but stipulated that the federal government had ultimate authority in tribal affairs.

The weakening Spanish Empire and growing democratic ideology in the Atlantic world led to revolutions in South and Central America. President James Monroe recognized five new nations in 1822 despite nominal neutrality in the conflicts. In 1823 the **Monroe Doctrine** asserted American authority in the western hemisphere. It warned European nations that the Americas were closed to future colonization and assured them that the United States would not interfere with existing colonies.

The Revival of Opposition

During the 1820s, political parties and partisan conflict was renewed over the issues of federal authority and national expansion. The system for picking presidential candidates, the **Congressional caucus,** was replaced by **nominating conventions** of state legislatures. The new, more open process produced four candidates in 1824, with the result that no one received a majority of either electoral or popular votes. The decision went to the House of Representatives, where John Quincy Adams trailed **Andrew Jackson** until nationalist candidate **Henry Clay** endorsed Adams. Once in office Adams appointed Clay secretary of state, and Jackson's supporters, outraged by his loss, labeled this a **"corrupt bargain."**

President Adams proposed an ambitious program paralleling Clay's **American System** that created a national market with western farms supporting eastern industry protected by high tariffs. Most of his program was blocked by Jackson supporters. Adams's greatest setback came with the politically distorted tariff of 1828, which southerners labeled the **"tariff of abominations."**

Two new party organizations emerged by the election of 1828. Adams supporters, who called themselves **National Republicans,** promoted economic nationalism. Opposing this were Jackson adherents, who now called themselves **Democrats.** The Democrats opposed privilege and supported a widening of opportunity. In reality, the election had little to do with issues but revolved around the personalities of the candidates. Jackson won handily, but his support was largely from the South and the West. Adams carried New England, and he had strong support in the mid-Atlantic.

Although nationalism characterized the period, after the War of 1812 deep divisions were growing over issues of federal authority, national growth, the emerging industrial economy, and slavery.

Multiple-Choice Questions

1. The War of 1812 promoted all of the following except
   a. cotton planters who moved into the fertile southwestern lands.
   b. expansionists who immediately called for the annexation of Canada.
   c. manufacturers who moved to fill the void created by the embargo of trade with England.
   d. farmers who could expand westward with diminished resistance from Indians.
   e. merchants who no longer were threatened with the seizure of their ships and sailors by both the British and the French.

2. Which of the following statements does the accompanying chart refute?
   a. In most cases imports and exports follow each other closely.
   b. Except in times of conflict, Americans appeared to be dependent on manufactured goods from England and Europe.
   c. American commercial warfare in the period before the War of 1812 was effective in slowing trade.
   d. The protective tariff of 1816 was effective in limiting foreign imports as intended.
   e. The War of 1812 boosted America's foreign trade and commerce.

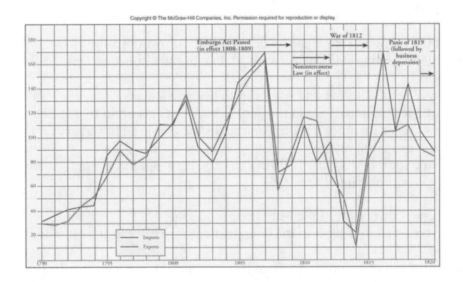

Copyright © The McGraw-Hill Companies, Inc. Permission required for reproduction or display.

3. Americans during the early nineteenth century viewed the American West as uninhabitable because
   a. John Jacob Astor failed in his trading ventures in the Pacific Northwest.
   b. William Henry Harrison lost to Indian warriors at Tippecanoe.
   c. James Monroe's "goodwill tour" failed to gain any support for western settlement.
   d. Stephen Long and others described the west as arid and barren.
   e. Lewis and Clark found little of commercial interest on their expedition west.

4. The period after the War of 1812 is known as the "Era of Good Feelings" because
    a. the United States handily won the war with Great Britain and was finally free of British influence.
    b. the Federalist Party lost so much influence that there was little partisan conflict.
    c. Americans could concentrate on the unifying effects of westward expansion and development rather than foreign affairs.
    d. the United States gained Florida without fighting Spain over that territory.
    e. the Erie Canal opened, so trade and communication with the West tied the country together.

5. In 1817 Madison vetoed a bill for federal support of roads and canals on the grounds that
    a. his strict interpretation of the Constitution did not authorize funding for internal improvements.
    b. he had vetoed the bill for a National Road in 1811 and this bill was no different.
    c. it was not practical to build canals because railroads were a much more efficient means of transportation.
    d. the Constitution only allowed federal funding for projects that were wholly within a single state and did not cross state lines.
    e. there was no need for internal improvements since so few Americans lived in the West at the time.

6. Which of the following statements about the Missouri Compromise is true?
    a. It prohibited slavery north of the 36°30' line in the Louisiana Territory except for Missouri.
    b. It allowed for California and Missouri to become states.
    c. It introduced an imbalance in the Senate between slave and free states.
    d. It allowed each territory in Louisiana to decide the issue of slavery on the basis of popular sovereignty.
    e. It allowed for the Missouri Territory to have between three and five states and slavery was prohibited there.

7. The Supreme Court under John Marshall ruled that
    a. Indian tribes were subject to the laws and authority of the state in which the tribe resided.
    b. the federal government could force Indian tribes to move west to Indian Territory set aside in Oklahoma.
    c. Indian tribes had no rights to property when states claimed it.
    d. Indian tribes were sovereign foreign nations and the government had to respect that status.
    e. Indian tribes were sovereign and independent of state governments but the federal government had ultimate authority over tribes.

8. The Monroe Doctrine asserted which of the following with respect to American affairs?
    a. The United States had the authority to invade any Latin American country to ensure its security.
    b. European nations were to grant independence to their colonies in the Americas.
    c. The United States would not interfere with any already-existing European colonies in the Americas.

d. Latin American colonies were not free to declare their independence and overthrow existing colonial rule.

e. Mexico had to turn over Texas to the United States or risk invasion.

9. Those who claimed a "corrupt bargain" occurred in the election of 1824 believed

a. that Andrew Jackson should have been president because he received more popular and electoral votes than any other candidate.

b. if the congressional caucus system had not been replaced that Andrew Jackson would have taken office.

c. Adams's unethical support of Jackson in the House voting turned the election in Jackson's favor.

d. Clay's support for Adams in the House balloting was in return for his appointment as secretary of state.

e. that Clay supported Jackson in return for Jackson's support of his American System.

10. The political debate that arose during the contests between Andrew Jackson and John Quincy Adams centered mainly on issues of

a. foreign policy and trade issues with England.

b. the expansion of slavery in the territories.

c. economic nationalism and government support of privilege.

d. the admittance of Missouri as a slave state.

e. renewal of the charter of the Bank of the United States.

11. Henry Clay's American System contained provisions for

a. high tariffs to promote industry, which would provide funds for internal improvements linking western farmers to growing cities.

b. regional economic development so that different regions could prosper independently of other sections.

c. growing connections between cotton growers in the South and western farmers.

d. the elimination of political parties and partisan conflict so that orderly economic growth could continue.

e. bringing the newly independent American republics into the United States economic system.

12. All of the following were projects supported by the federal government during the early nineteenth century except

a. the Second Bank of the United States.

b. the National Road.

c. the Monroe Doctrine.

d. the establishment of Indian Reservations east of the Mississippi River.

e. the protective tariff.

Free-Response Questions—Exam Tips

Many of the essay questions on the AP Exam ask you to determine the degree to which an idea, trend, or movement has manifested itself over our history. Very often tensions arise from competing movements, and this chapter highlights this pattern in the conflict between nationalism and sectionalism. This is a popular topic in the nineteenth century before the Civil War. These types of questions might have the following formats: *to what extent or degree, in what ways, how successful,* or *how effective.* Most of the better essays will be able to determine the extent to which changes were occurring rather than providing an all-or-nothing answer. Identify opposing movements in your essay, and be able to use evidence that allows you to argue, "sectional interests were growing, yet on the other hand an increasingly national and integrated economy and culture drew the sections closer together."

Free-Response Questions

1. How and why was a compromise reached over the admission of Missouri as a state in 1820?

2. Analyze the significance of the War of 1812 for American economic development.

Document-Based Question

Explain how the competing forces of nationalism and sectionalism affected national unity in the early nineteenth century.

Use the documents and your knowledge of the period 1800–1840 to construct your essay.

Document A

Source: U.S. Bureau of the Census in *Historical Statistics of the United States Colonial Times to 1970*, Part 1, p. 8.

Area and Population of the United States

Year	Land area (square miles)	Population	Percentage population increase from preceding census	Population per square mile of land area
1800	864,746	5,308,483	35.1	6.1
1810	1,681,828	7,239, 881	36.4	4.3
1820	1,749,462	9,638,453	33.1	5.5
1830	1,749,462	12,866,020	33.5	7.4
1840	1,749,462	17,069,453	32.7	9.8

Document B

Source: U.S. Bureau of the Census in *Historical Statistics of the United States Colonial Times to 1970*, Part 1, p. 139.

United States Labor Force and Employment (in thousands)

Year	Free laborers	Slave laborers	Agriculture	Manufacturing
1800	1,370	530	1,400	2
1810	1,590	740	1,950	75
1820	2,185	950	2,470	NA
1830	3,020	1,180	2,965	NA
1840	4,180	1,480	3,570	500

Document C

Cotton Production (in thousands of bales)

Year	Cotton production
1800	73
1810	178
1820	335
1830	732
1840	1,348

Document D

Investment in Canals by Region (in millions of dollars)

Year	Total investment	Northeast	South	West
1820	1.1	.8	.3	---
1830	7.5	6.1	.5	1.0
1840	14.3	8.4	1.2	4.7

Multiple-Choice Answers

1. b. All of the groups except expansionists felt immediate benefits from the conclusion of the War of 1812. Expansionists later called for the annexation of Canada, but it was not prevalent in 1815.

2. e. As the chart indicates, trade before and during the war was small relative to before the Embargo Act.

3. d. On surveys in the 1820s, Long labeled the Midwest plains as "the Great American Desert." Most Americans believed the area was unfit for agriculture.

4. b. The bitter conflict that characterized politics since the founding of the republic ended with the demise of the Federalists after the Hartford Convention, thus the name "the Era of Good Feelings."

5. a. Unlike his Republican predecessor Jefferson, who approved the National Road, Madison did not interpret the Constitution as authorizing internal improvements.

6. a. This Compromise dealt with the issue of slavery only within the Louisiana Territory, and Congress prohibited slavery in the northern portion above 36°30'.

7. e. In *Worcester* v. *Georgia* the Marshall Court protected Indian tribes from state power in the states where they resided. However, this order was largely disregarded and the many eastern tribes were forced to relocate to the west.

8. c. The Monroe Doctrine established the western hemisphere as the United States' sphere of influence. While warning European nations that the Americas were no longer open to any new colonization, the Monroe Doctrine reassured colonial powers that their existing colonies were safe from American interference.

9. d. Since no candidate had a clear majority in the electoral college, the election of the president fell to the House of Representatives. Ultimately, Clay threw his electoral support behind Adams, who took office and then named Clay secretary of state. Since Jackson had received more popular and electoral votes than any of the other candidates, his supporters saw this as a perversion of democracy and claimed an underhanded or "corrupt bargain" had taken place between Adams and Clay.

10. c. These were the main issues in both the elections of 1824 and 1828. Adams supported strong federal support of the economy, while Jackson saw a more limited federal role. Jackson opposed elitism and privilege, especially as a product of government largesse.

11. a. Clay's economic program linked the industrial northeast to western agriculture. Prosperous industries protected by tariffs would spawn a growing labor force that would be fed by western farmers. Government-supported internal improvement would link the regions.

12. d. The United States government gave its support to all except Indians occupying lands east of the Mississippi River. Although the Supreme Court gave tribes the rights to traditional lands, the legislative and executive branches supported removal to the west, and carried that out in the 1830s and 1840s.

Free-Response Questions Commentary

1. Prior to 1820 the issue of slavery had remained relatively dormant after ratification of the Constitution. However, with acquisition of Louisiana in 1803, and rapid westward expansion after the War of 1812, the question of slavery arose with Missouri's application for statehood in 1819 as a slave state. There was a growing opposition to slavery in the Northeast, although most Americans tolerated it in the South at the least. The spread of slavery had political implications for both the North and the South. With its more rapid population growth the North prevailed in the House, and there was a balance in the Senate between slave and free states, which gave southerners some security. Missouri's admission would have tipped the Senate balance to the slave states. Political power lay at the heart of the controversy and prompted Jefferson to call the crisis "a firebell in the night."

   The Compromise was engineered by Henry Clay and matched the admission of a slave Missouri with a free Maine, maintaining the Senate balance. An amendment provided a formula for the rest of the Louisiana Territory and prohibited slavery north of latitude 36°30' with the exception of Missouri. Although that area was much larger than the area open to slavery, the South was satisfied because most of it was considered unfit for cultivation. Thus both interests perceived both gains and security by the Compromise, and it lasted until the acquisition of new territories again upset the balance in the 1840s.

2. The War of 1812 had important consequences for United States economic development. The embargo and ensuing warfare disrupted trade and spurred self-sufficiency in the

guise of domestic manufactures. This coincided with technological advances and the institution of the factory system, especially in New England, whose fast-flowing rivers provided power. In addition, stress from the war exposed weakness in both the financial and transportation systems. It led the way to the recharter of the Second Bank of the United States and a more stable currency; even Republicans, opponents of the First Bank, lent support the second time around. Hamilton proposed a protective tariff in his Report on Manufactures in 1791, but it was defeated then. Congress, now recognizing the importance of a strong manufacturing sector, passed a tariff in 1816 to protect infant American industries.

The British blockade of American ports highlighted the difficulty of moving goods and people around the expanding nation. The government supported the National Road in 1811, but Madison vetoed a bill for federally funded roads and canals in 1817. At this time most internal improvements were funded privately or received local and state, but not federal, support, such as the Erie Canal.

Document-Based Question Commentary

The document-based question often includes tables with statistical data for you to use as evidence when answering the question. Be careful not to over-analyze the data when using statistical tables. These questions ask you to use the documents to support your argument. You must use outside information in constructing your answer and demonstrate analysis and integration of both the documents and outside information. Both are crucial if you are to construct a good answer. When considering data take care to determine just what the information is telling you. This requires a good sense of the historical context from which the data was derived. The tables in this exercise provide evidence for both national and sectional feelings in the first four decades of the nineteenth century. The fairly straightforward statistics about financial investment in canal construction in Document D provide several insights about America's nationalism. This was the "canal age" and the dramatic increases in investment are clear. The opening of the Erie Canal in 1824 fits into this scenario. The regional differences in investment also shed light on the subject. The canals linked regions but also point to regional differences. Without much industry, the South did not build many canals when compared to the Northeast and the West. With growing westward migration, investment in western canals increased at more than twice the rate of the northeast. In addition, you might also note that the increases here just preceded the growth of railroads, which soon replaced canals as a major form of freight transportation. The other tables provide important insights about this issue. In the end, you must determine what the data means by placing it in solid historical context.

CHAPTER 9
Jacksonian America

AP THEMES

- **American Diversity:** Jackson reflected the nation's attitude toward Native Americans as uncivilized and unable to be civilized. The use of paternalism to justify the seizure of Indian lands persisted for the next century, and Jackson both clarified and articulated this policy in his message supporting the Indian Removal Act in 1830.
- **American Identity:** A strong states' rights movement arose during this period, with slavery in the background and the tariff in the foreground. South Carolina, supported by other southern slave states, emerged as the champion of the nullification theory. Political ideology began to regionalize during 1832 and 1833. This set the foundation for the divisive decade of the 1850s.
- **Politics and Citizenship:** Modern politics were born in this era. The franchise was extended to all white males, divorcing property from citizenship rights. In addition, Jackson was the first president to use the power of the office to lead the country. His use of the veto and patronage and party and his vision of the executive as the embodiment of the popular will set out the course of the modern presidency.

CHAPTER SUMMARY
The Rise of Mass Politics

The expansion of democracy, the hallmark of the **Age of Jackson,** was more rhetoric than reality for poorer Americans and those without power. However, **Tocqueville's** observation that a "general equality of condition" prevailed did characterize the fluid social and economic system. Jackson's primary goal was to keep entrenched eastern elites from closing avenues of opportunity to the rising western commercial classes.

While politics were transformed, the distribution of wealth changed little. During this period; restrictions on the **franchise** either disappeared or were reduced in all states. However, politics continued to be reserved for white males. Women, blacks, and Indians were excluded. Between 1824 and 1840, voter participation in presidential elections increased from 27 to 80 percent. Citizenship replaced property as the source of political authority.

The eighteenth-century view that political parties were evil gave way to the idea that a two-party system was essential to democracy's success. **Patronage** and loyalty became the foundation of party, with ideology becoming less important. Two parties emerged: the Jacksonian Democrats and the Whigs, who opposed them. Jackson's Democratic Party embraced no coherent ideology but simply looked to establish equality of opportunity and rights to all citizens. He first tried to open up federal offices that had become dominated by an entrenched **bureaucracy.** Jackson reasoned that offices were the people's property, and that any intelligent man could do the job. Although he removed no more than one-fifth of federal officials, he established the idea of the spoils system, where elected officials had the right to distribute **patronage** in the form of government positions. Jackson also pushed for a more open nominating process for presidential candidates, resulting in the **political convention** to replace the **congressional caucus.**

"Our Federal Union"

Jackson believed in the supremacy of the federal government of which he was the head, even though he wished to reduce its power. Early in his tenure a dangerous theory surfaced to challenge federal supremacy and view of the president as the embodiment of the popular will. South Carolina proposed the **theory of nullification,** which held that a state had the authority to decide whether federal law was unconstitutional. First articulated in the 1798 **Virginia and Kentucky Resolutions,** its underlying foundation was that the Union was a **compact** created by the states. South Carolina threatened to declare the 1828 Tariff of Abominations "null and void" within its borders. While it did not do so, this set the stage for a later confrontation.

Robert Y. Hayne, a South Carolina senator, and **Daniel Webster,** a Massachusetts Whig, engaged in a debate over the nature of the Union and states' rights in 1830. Hayne defended nullification, but Jackson later renounced nullification in a toast: "Our Federal Union: It must be preserved." His vice president, John C. Calhoun, replied, "The Union, next to our liberty most dear."

The 1832 a new tariff bill initiated a crisis concerning these opposing views. The new tariff kept rates high, and South Carolina nullified both it and the tariff of 1828. Jackson believed nullification was treason, and in 1833, Congress passed the **Force Bill,** which authorized the president to use the military to enforce federal law. **Henry Clay** once again proposed a compromise tariff bill that would lower rates gradually. South Carolina rescinded its ordinance of nullification, but unwilling to cede the point, nullified the Force Bill, which had no real effect, and which Jackson ignored.

The Removal of the Indians

President Jackson's attitude toward Indians mirrored that of most Americans—he wanted them moved west of the Mississippi, separate from white America. Americans had come to see Indians not as **noble savages,** but simply as savages who could not be civilized. In response, American Indians created new and larger organizations of tribes that were relatively weak and divided in their negotiations with the federal government. Refusing to recognize the legality of treaties signed by rival factions in 1831, the **Sauk** and **Fox** tribes in Illinois mounted the last resistance in the Old Northwest. During the **Black Hawk War,** named for chief Black Hawk, ruthless treatment and slaughter of the Indians by federal troops and Illinois militia drove them from that state.

Many of the remaining southeastern tribes had formed agricultural societies that mimicked white civilization. The Cherokee Nation adopted a formal constitution in 1827. Despite Supreme Court rulings that Indian tribes were sovereign nations within the states, southern states passed laws regulating tribes. In addition, Congress passed the **Removal Act** in 1830, which aimed to move Indian tribes west. Despite Supreme Court rulings, such as *Worcester v. Georgia* in 1832, affirming Indian rights to tribal lands, Jackson did not enforce the rulings. In 1835 a minority of Cherokees approved the exchange of their Georgia lands for $5 million and a reservation in the West. Many others refused to leave and in 1838 were forced to go to the Indian territory set aside in present-day Oklahoma. As many as one-eighth of the Native Americans died during this march, which is known as the **Trail of Tears.** Virtually all Native Americans were removed from the South, with the exception of the Seminole tribe of Florida. Helped by escaped slaves and led by **Chief Occeola,** the Seminoles defended their lands in the Seminole War, which began in 1835. Frustrated by guerilla tactics in the Everglades, the federal government withdrew in 1842. Many Seminoles had moved or were killed, but some remained.

Overall, Indians exchanged 100 million acres of eastern land for $68 million and 32 million acres on reservations west of the Mississippi. The British attitude toward Indians from the colonial period persisted after independence, with removal being the only acceptable solution to most Americans, even though successful assimilation had taken place among the Indians, Spanish, and French.

Jackson and the Bank War

Jackson's belief in federal supremacy did not extend to using federal power to concentrate economic power either in the government or in its allied institutions. He vetoed the **Maysville Road Bill** in 1830 because the road lay entirely within Kentucky and thus was not interstate commerce. The charter of the **Second Bank of the United States** was to expire in 1836. It was the most powerful economic institution in the United States, held the government's funds, did considerable general private banking, and provided stability for the nation's banking system. Jackson's opposition to the bank was based on a personal experience with paper credit and his dislike of **privilege** and of the bank's president, **Nicholas Biddle.** Others opposed the bank over support for or against the issue of paper money. Biddle applied for a new charter in 1832, four years early, hoping to make the re-charter of the bank a campaign issue in the presidential election. Congress complied, and passed the re-charter bill, but Jackson vetoed it and then went on to be overwhelmingly reelected.

To diminish the influence of the bank as quickly as possible, Jackson withdrew federal funds and deposited them in state banks, which came to be known as **pet banks.** In an effort to demonstrate the bank's necessity and gain support for another re-charter bill, Biddle began to tighten credit, which sent the country into a recession. This played to Jackson's political hand as he decried a privileged bank with the power to ruin the economy. Biddle's policies doomed any chances for another charter, and the country was left with an unstable and weak banking system for more than a century.

Jackson replaced chief justice John Marshall with **Roger B. Taney** in 1835. Taney, who earlier had served as Jackson's Secretary of the Treasury and complied with his request to withdraw federal funds from the federal bank, did not shift the direction of the Supreme Court dramatically but tempered the **Marshall Court's** strong economic nationalism. Where the previous Supreme Court upheld rights of property and contract rigorously, Taney ruled in *Charles River Bridge* v. *Warren Bridge* that the general welfare preceded private property rights, and the monopoly in this case exercised unwarranted privilege. Taney's ruling in this case demonstrated the fundamental principle of Jacksonian politics.

The Changing Face of American Politics

Jackson's extraordinary use of presidential power led his opponents to label him **King Andrew I** and gave birth to both a new party, the **Whigs,** and the **second party system.** Political parties began to focus on the single goal of getting their candidates elected, and their ideologies, constituencies, and leadership reflected this. **Jacksonian Democrats** emphasized states' rights, limited federal government, the abolition of privilege, and opportunity for the common man, which attracted support from labor, small merchants, and western farmers, people who favored agriculture and small-scale commercial enterprises. **Whigs,** whose name came from the English opposed to the king, were from all sections of the country and were commercially oriented, whether it be farming, manufacturing, or trade. Large planters and farmers, and substantial merchants and manufacturers tended to gravitate to the Whig Party. Whigs adopted **Anti-Freemasonry** as a cause, which gave them a less aristocratic label. The newer Irish and German Catholic immigrants tended to support the Democratic Party, while evangelical Christians favored Whigs. But in 1836 the Whigs did not have a leader behind which to unite, and so the Democrat and Jackson's heir apparent, **Martin Van Buren,** easily won the presidency.

Jackson was a hard act to follow and economic hardship contributed to Van Buren's burdens. Van Buren was elected in the midst of an economic boom, with rising prices and easy credit. Speculation in public lands left the country debt-free and with a surplus, a situation that has never been repeated. The boom ended suddenly in early 1837: The government withdrew its reserves from the pet banks, distributed its surplus to the states, and Jackson, shortly before leaving office in 1837, issued the **Specie Circular,** which stipulated that only specie be used to purchase public lands. Credit tightened, causing the worst recession in our history to that point. Van Buren's response may have been counterproductive. He created an **independent treasury** system to replace the Bank of the United States in 1840 and instituted a **ten-hour work day** on federal projects.

In 1840 the Whigs settled on one candidate, **William Henry Harrison,** a famous Indian fighter. Although Harrison was from an aristocratic Virginian family, the Whigs appealed to the common man by associating Harrison, **"Old Tippecanoe,"** with log cabins and hard cider, and he easily won the election.. Harrison died after one month in office and **vice president John Tyler** succeeded him. Tyler, a former Democrat, had few firm ties to the Whig Party, and as president, he drifted back to his roots, abolishing the new treasury system, raising tariff rates, and vetoing internal improvements.

Relations with England were tense because of issues with Canada. A series of skirmishes over the boundary separating Maine and Canada was labeled the **Aroostook War.** In 1842 the **Webster-Ashburton Treaty** settled this dispute and put relations on an improved footing. Under Tyler the United States initiated diplomatic relations with China. An 1844 treaty gained **most-favored nation** status for the United States in China. This gave the United States the same trading rights as England, as well as **extraterritoriality,** which is the right of Americans accused of crimes in China to be tried in America. Trade with China increased. With few other successes, the Whigs lost the White House in 1844.

In sum, Jacksonian America heralded a new age of politics in which more men participated, philosophy became subordinate to gaining office, and parties became an accepted feature of the political landscape.

10/12

Multiple-Choice Questions

1. Popular ideas about political parties during the Jacksonian era
   a. changed from the idea that parties were evil and divisive to the idea that parties were essential to the success of democracy.
   b. slowly changed from considering permanent parties as essential to represent interests in the political process to the idea that they would only divide the country.
   c. became hostile to parties as bitter and personal campaigning hid issues from the people.
   d. believed that party should restrict the suffrage to only property holders and keep politics an elitist activity.
   e. returned to Washington's advice in his farewell address to avoid permanent political parties.

2. The Whig Party that arose during Jackson's administrations
   a. supported Jackson's strong stand on states' rights as long as it did not conflict with federal authority.
   b. believed in equality of opportunity and equal protection for all citizens.
   c. held that patronage had no place in politics and that government positions should be above party.
   d. had a nationalist outlook and opposed Jackson's exercise of power as being tyrannical.
   e. believed in the Republican program of Jefferson with its vision of an America of independent farmers.

3. South Carolina nullified which of the following in 1832?
   a. internal improvements
   b. charter of the Bank of the United States
   c. tariff
   d. fugitive slave law
   e. spoils system

4. Jackson believed the executive branch superseded all other authority in the federal government because
   a. states could declare any laws passed by Congress null and void within their state.
   b. the president's veto power could stop any bill from becoming law.
   c. the judiciary had no power of enforcement so its rulings were not important.
   d. the president was the only federal official that all citizens could vote for.
   e. federal law was the supreme law of the land.

5. Jackson supported removal of the Indians from their traditional lands east of the Mississippi to
   a. allow Indians to assimilate with whites in more settled eastern areas.
   b. civilize the Indians so that they could come to learn to live with white Americans.
   c. separate the two groups because the Indian and white civilizations would compete with one another.
   d. reservations in the Mississippi Valley where they could pursue their nomadic lifestyle.
   e. the West because Indians could not be civilized and interaction with white society would destroy white society.

6. Jackson's policy with respect to the Bank of the United States was grounded in
   a. his belief that the Bank harbored eastern privilege and limited opportunity.
   b. his respect for Nicholas Biddle and the stability the Bank brought to the financial system.
   c. his acknowledgement of the need for sound paper money in the American economy.
   d. the access to funds it gave westerners for the purchase of western lands.
   e. his support for centralized control of the American economy.

7. Roger Taney modified the direction of his predecessor, John Marshall, by
   a. refusing to accept that the courts had to exercise judicial review.
   b. accepting that private property rights must account for the general welfare.
   c. rejecting the idea that contracts are a form of property.
   d. hearing cases involving suits over Indian lands east of the Mississippi.
   e. recognizing that slaves were United States citizens.

8. The election of 1840 is considered by many to be a modern election campaign for the reason that
   a. there were only two candidates running for president.
   b. both parties worked at getting their candidate elected.
   c. the parties designed their campaigns and candidates to appeal to the common man.
   d. William Henry Harrison was a famous Indian fighter and military hero.
   e. William Henry Harrison was the first candidate from the West.

9. President John Tyler's diplomatic measures included
   a. the annexation of Texas from Spain.
   b. settling the boundary with Canada from the Great Lakes to the Pacific Ocean.
   c. opening diplomatic relations with China and gaining trading rights there.
   d. ending the underground slave trade with African nations.
   e. the peaceful evacuation of the Seminole tribe from Florida.

10. The result of the Specie Circular for the American economy was
    a. to loosen credit and create a boom in the public land market.
    b. reduce the amount of specie in circulation and make people rely on paper money.
    c. end the use of paper money to settle debts in the financial markets.
    d. to tighten credit and create a financial panic.
    e. to retire the public debt by using revenue from public land sales.

11. All of the following are characteristics of the party system that included the Whigs and the Democrats except
    a. Whigs adopted Anti-Freemasonry to soften criticism of them as aristocratic. ✓
    b. Democrats emphasized states' rights and limited federal government. ✓
    c. large planters and farmers, and substantial merchants and manufacturers, tended to be Whigs. ✓
    d. recent Irish and German Catholics favored the Democratic Party. ✓
    e. supporters of agriculture and small-scale commercial enterprises favored Whigs.

12. In the "Age of Jackson" coherent ideology in party politics took a secondary position to
    a. party loyalty, patronage, and election results.
    b. support for sectional issues, rather than national issues.
    c. the personality cult of presidential politics.
    d. raising money to support national campaigns.
    e. building congressional alliances to gain support in elections such as that in 1824.

Free-Response Questions—Exam Tips

Although social and cultural phenomena were significant during the early republic, political topics are generally more prevalent. It is important to demonstrate your understanding of the following:

- Constitutional interpretations and their consequences; strict and loose construction
- Political parties and changes in the system *Republican-Demo → Whig*
- Wars and foreign policy—Republican foreign policy ideology

Be able to distinguish between the first and second party systems.

First Party System—1790–1820: Federalist and Jeffersonian Republican
- Federalist: Leader—Alexander Hamilton, loose constitutional construction, strong central government, support of the Bank of the United States, and commercial and manufacturing interests, regional strength in New England and southern ports.
- Jeffersonian Republicans: Leaders—Thomas Jefferson and James Madison, strict constitutional construction, limited government, states' rights, opposed Bank of the United States, support on frontier and rural south and west.

Transitional Period—1816–1828
- 1816–1828—As the Federalists disintegrated, the Era of Good Feelings displayed little party strife.
- 1824–1828—Supporters of John Q. Adams were known as the National Republicans and endorsed active federal government, nationalism, and support for the tariff and internal improvements. Regional support in New England and the mid-Atlantic.
- 1824–1828—Democrat-Republicans: Leader—Andrew Jackson, support for government reform, improved opportunity and end of eastern privilege, political patronage, the spoils system, states' rights but not at the expense of federal supremacy.

Second Party System—1828–1854
- Democrat: see earlier Democratic Republican.
- Whig: Leader—Henry Clay, J.Q. Adams, strong nationalism and strong, active federal government, support for Bank of the United States, internal improvements, and the tariff. The name "Whig" derives from opposition to Jackson's policies. Support comes from New England, the mid-Atlantic, and larger commercial interests in the South.

Free-Response Questions

1. Analyze the reasons for the growing support of the Nullification Doctrine during the Andrew Jackson administration.

2. How successful was the Missouri Compromise at resolving the issues that precipitated that crisis in 1820?

Document-Based Question

"Washington's precedents established the patterns upon which our government and political system rests." Assess the validity of this statement with specific reference to the years 1797–1825.

Use the following documents and your knowledge of the period 1797–1825 to construct your response.

Document A

Source: George Washington, April 1789.

". . . this government must be less obnoxious to well-founded objections than most which have existed in the World. And in that opinion I am confirmed on three accounts: first, because every government ought to be possessed of power adequate to the purpose for which it was instituted; secondly, because no other or greater powers appear to me to be delegated to this government than are essential . . .; and thirdly because it is clear to my conception that no government before introduced among mankind ever contained so many checks and such efficatious [effective] restraints to prevent it from degenerating into any specious of oppression. . . ." [Washington, *Writings*, XXX, 299-300]

Document B

Source: Washington's Farewell Address, September 17, 1796.

". . . Let me now take a more comprehensive view, and warn you in the most solemn manner against the baneful effects of the spirit of party generally. . . ."

"The great rule of conduct for us in regard to foreign nations is, in extending our commercial relations to have with them as little political connection as possible. So far as we have already formed engagements let them be fulfilled with perfect good faith. Here let us stop. It is our policy to steer clear of permanent alliances with any portion of the foreign world. . . ." [Richardson, ed. *Messages and Papers*, I, 213.

Document C

Source: The Kentucky Resolutions written by Thomas Jefferson, November 16, 1798.

"Resolved, That . . . whensover the general government Assumes undelegated powers its acts are unauthoritative, void, and of no force. . . . That the government created by this compact was not made the exclusive or final judge of the extent of the powers delegated to itself. . . ." [Elliot, ed., *debates in the Several State Conventions*, IV, 540-1]

Document D

Source: Cartoon of the celebrated fight in Congress between Republican Matthew Lyon and Federalist Roger Griswold, 1798.

Congressional Brawlers

Document E

Source: The Embargo Act, December 22, 1807.

"Be it enacted, That an embargo be, and hereby is laid on all ships and vessels in the ports and places within the Limits or jurisdiction of the United States. . . ." [*US Statutes at Large*, II, 451]

Document F

Source: President James Madison's war message to Congress, June 1, 1812.

"British cruisers have been in the continued practice of violating the American flag on the great highway of nations, and of seizing and carrying off persons sailing under it...British cruisers have been in the practice also of violating the rights and the peace of our coasts. They hover over and harass our entering and departing commerce...In reviewing the conduct of Great Britain toward the United States, our attention is necessarily drawn to the warfare just renewed by the savages on one of our extensive frontiers..." [Richardson, ed. *Messages and Papers*, II, 485.]

Document G

Source: Speech regarding the conscription bill by Federalist Daniel Webster to the House of Representatives, December 9, 1814.

The administration asserts the right to fill the ranks of the regular army by compulsion. . . . Where is it written in the Constitution, in what article or section is contained, that you may take children from their parents, and parents from their children, and compel them to fight the battles of any war in which the folly or wickedness of the government may engage it? . . . If the secretary of war has proved the right of Congress to enact a law enforcing a draft of men out of the militia into the regular army, he will at any time be able to prove quite as clearly that Congress has power to create a dictator."

Document H

Source: Henry Clay speech to the House of Representatives, April 26, 1820.

"Now, as when we arranged the existing tariff, is the auspicious moment for government to step in and cheer and countenance them [domestic manufactures]. We did too little then and I endeavor to warn this House of the effects of inadequate protection." [*The life and Speeches of Henry Clay*, 139-41 from *Annals*, IV, 612.

Document I

Source: The Monroe Doctrine delivered to Congress, December 2, 1823.

". . . Our policy in regard to Europe…is, not to interfere in the internal concerns of any of any of its powers; . . . But in regard to these continents circumstances are . . . different. It is impossible that the allied powers should extend their political system to any portion of either continent without endangering our peace and happiness. . . ." [Richard, ed. *Messages and Papers of the Presidents*, II, 776.

Multiple-Choice Answers

1. a. Washington's warning about the evils of "factions" gave way to a belief in the two-party system as a mechanism to check concentrated power and protect liberty.

2. d. The Whigs derived their name from the English political party that opposed the king's policies. Jackson's use of the power of the presidential office caused his opponents to see him in that light.

3. c. The Tariff of 1828 and its slightly lower predecessor, the Tariff of 1832, were unacceptable to South Carolina, the foremost proponent of states' rights. It nullified the latter.

4. d. Since all Americans voted for the president, Jackson believed that office embodied the popular will and therefore was the prominent branch of government.

5. e. Jackson held Native Americans in low esteem, and believed that in a direct competition with white Americans, the Indians would not survive.

6. a. A financial failure early in his career that he attributed to paper money as well as his belief that the bank favored eastern interests led him to oppose the Bank's re-charter.

7. b. In *Charles River Bridge* v. *Warren Bridge,* Taney ruled that private property, in this case contract, could not counter the public interest. Marshall had always supported the rights of private property.

8. c. This election was a watershed in that both the record and reality of the candidates was set aside for images created to appeal to the majority of voters.

9. c. One of Tyler's major accomplishments was sending a mission to China and gaining a privileged trade status with that nation.

10. d. Because speculation in public lands was rampant and relied on paper money payments, the Specie Circular caused a restriction of the money supply and a financial depression.

11. e. With their nationalistic outlook, Whigs tended to be owners of larger enterprises, whether commercial or agricultural.

12. a. The devotion to principle that characterized the first party system diminished during the 1830s and 1840s. Building strong support for elections became the major goal and an uncompromising ideology took a backseat.

Free-Response Questions Commentary

1. Nullification became an increasingly significant political doctrine in the decades preceding the Civil War. First articulated in the Virginia and Kentucky Resolutions, it surfaced again at the Hartford Convention, although ironically there it was used by the Federalists. A brainchild of the Jeffersonian Republicans in response to the Alien and Sedition Acts, it was later adopted by Democrats such as John C. Calhoun.

   The tariff controversies of the late 1820s and 1830s brought the Doctrine back into political discourse. Southerners, but South Carolinians especially, opposed the 1828 Tariff of Abominations, which placed a burden on non-manufacturing regions like the agricultural South. Although nullification was considered then, and the Compact Theory was more clearly defined, South Carolina took no action. The Tariff of 1832 with slightly lower rates satisfied no one and the state nullified it. Although Jackson believed in states' rights, he was committed to the Constitution and its supremacy clause. He threatened to use the military, via the Force Bill in 1833, to enforce collection of the tariff. A compromise tariff ended the crisis.

   One could argue that the results of 1832–1833 turned back the nullification tide as Jackson's nationalism prevailed. On the other side, as southern interests became more distinct from the other sections, nullification became both a justification and defense of the southern lifestyle and slavery. For Americans leery of federal power, it was an ideology used to protect regional characteristics.

2. The immediate issue in 1819 was the admission of Missouri to the Union as a slave state, and its significance was both social and political, although mainly the latter. As the slave culture and economy gained strength in the South, sectional differences became more visible. Slavery was well established in Missouri and its admission would upset the balance between slave and free states in the Senate, which stood at eleven each in 1819. Proposals to admit Missouri on the condition that slavery would eventually be abolished led to bitter controversy. Coincidently, Maine, formerly part of Massachusetts, applied for statehood as a free state.

Maine's application provided the basis for compromise. Admitting the two states together maintained the numerical balance in the Senate, and anxiety over political power threatening a regional way of life subsided. An amendment also provided a resolution for the rest of Louisiana by prohibiting slavery above Missouri's southern border, 36° 30'. Since most of this area was considered unfit for agriculture, the South did not object. Since this was the extent of United States territory at the time, this agreement resolved the crisis.

The compromise settled the immediate issues in 1820, a crisis Jefferson called a "firebell in the night," but the underlying issue of slavery and its expansion was highlighted and set in place to become a central issue in national politics as the United States territory expanded. Then the Compromise no longer held, even within the Louisiana Territory. You might argue that in the short run it resolved issues, but not in the long run as the country added territory in the 1840s.

Document-Based Question Commentary

Washington's precedents established a governing model for the nation in certain respects, but not all of his advice was heeded or followed as the nation developed. You can argue either side of this issue. One way to approach this would be to describe Washington's precedents and the vision for the United States he held. Then you can use the documents and background knowledge to show where the country deviated from that model.

Arranging the documents according to those that support Washington's ideas and those that contradict it provides one way to approach an answer. Documents A and B give clues about Washington's vision that government needs sufficient power to carry out its duties, but that authority should be checked. Other aspects of his vision would appear to follow Hamilton's Federalist view. Use the elements of the financial plan to outline strong central government and Washington's distrust of political factions and support for neutrality in foreign affairs. His farewell address warns against the establishment of domestic political parties and permanent alliances in foreign affairs.

The other documents appear to separate support for and opposition to Washington's ideas in broad domestic and foreign affairs categories. One can consider documents supporting Washington to be Document G, Webster's opposition to conscription, but the act itself suggests use of governmental authority, and might be paired with Washington's suppression of the Whisky Rebellion in 1794. Also, Document H supports a protective tariff and was part of Hamilton's financial plan. The Monroe Doctrine also supports Washingtonian neutrality. Other documents contradict Washington: Document C opposes a strong federal government and supports states' rights; Document D points to the rise of permanent political parties; and Documents E and F show America's involvement in European affairs. Document G can be used for either side. Outside information might point out that the federal government increasingly exercised its power despite the growing movement of states' rights.

Therefore, one way to "assess the validity" would be to use the domestic and foreign policy categories and argue that in foreign affairs America stood more firmly with Washington than in domestic political affairs.

CHAPTER 10
America's Economic Revolution

AP THEMES

- **American Diversity**: This chapter raises the issue of European immigration as an unwanted component of American society. After nearly two centuries of trying to attract immigrants to America, the influx of Irish Catholics in the 1840s stirred popular resentment and political movements with goals of keeping Irish Catholics and other immigrants as a distinct underclass in American society.
- **Demographic Changes**: Lower mortality rates and immigration made the period before the Civil War one of rapid population growth. The geographical center of the population was shifting westward also. One great irony of American population shifts is that as more western lands were settled, the country as a whole became more urban. Cities grew relatively faster than the country in general.
- **Economic Transformations**: During this first Industrial Revolution the legal, economic, and social foundations for Hamilton's vision of America were established. Manufacturing began to eclipse trade as the central focus of the commercial economy, and the factory system created new wealth. As America industrialized the gap between rich and poor grew.
- **Globalization**: As western agricultural production grew and transport of goods from the interior to the coast improved, America developed as an exporter of agricultural products, further linking her to the Atlantic economy. Cotton played a major role as England's textile mills took a large share of America's expanding output.
- **Reform**: Industrialism changed the face and the role of labor in the United States. People left farms for manufacturing jobs in the city. For a brief period women labored in factories under the Lowell System until cheaper immigrant labor replaced them. With wages diminishing and working conditions deteriorating, a fledgling labor movement began to take shape. Workers began to realize that in a world of large corporations, organization was the only way for labor to achieve its goals. That realization alone may have been the major success of the period; no substantial labor reforms occurred.

EXAM TIPS

Certain events instigate significant social, political, and cultural change; war and economic transformation are two of the most important. The first American Industrial Revolution demonstrates this clearly. The following items relate to economic change:
- Society and gender—Women's roles were affected by underlying economic change. In this period opportunity expanded with the Lowell System, but also diminished with the cult of domesticity.
- Relations between labor and capital—Industrialism sharpened differences between owners and workers, and stirred the beginnings of organized labor. Violent strikes, fears of anarchy, and the threat to property threatened stability in the public mind.
- Urbanization—Industrialism provided economic opportunity for workers and they flocked to cities where industry located.

- Culture and communication—Industrialism lowered the price of books and newspapers, making them more accessible, and higher incomes supported cultural endeavors such as the theatre.
- Standard of living—Although the distribution of income usually becomes less equal, the absolute standard of living for all generally increases with the advent of lower-priced consumer goods.
- Politics—Government has tended to promote the interests of business more than those of labor. Protection of property favors the owners of factories, as do tariffs.
- Family—Economics often underlies changes in the family structure, including family size and child labor.

AP exam questions often will ask you to assess the impact of economic change on society, culture, and politics.

CHAPTER SUMMARY

By the eve of the Civil War, westward expansion and growing cities spurred growth in commercial farming and manufacturing. The southern cotton economy boomed, although commercial development in the South was less strong than in other sections of the country. There was also a radical difference in the labor system of the South. As cotton and textile manufacturing unified the nation, other economic developments sharpened the division between the North and the South.

The Changing American Population

A large and growing population, unified transportation and communication systems, technological advances, and business organization combined to promote an American industrial revolution. The population grew from 10 to 17 million between 1820 and 1840. Improvements in public health decreased mortality, and high birth rates were augmented by increasing immigration, especially from **Ireland** and **Germany.** City populations bolstered by immigrants and Americans leaving farms grew relative to the general population.

Increasing immigration spurred **nativism,** a movement hostile to foreigners and their cultures. The most prominent organization was the **American Party** called the **Know Nothings.** Particularly strong in the Northeast, this party peaked in the 1854 election and declined thereafter. Its short life contributed to the demise of the second party system.

Transportation, Communications, and Technology

The Appalachian Mountains forced most commerce from the West south to New Orleans. Turnpikes provided no solution to this barrier, but for a short period in the early nineteenth century, canals filled this void. The most successful was the 350-mile **Erie Canal** from Buffalo on Lake Erie to the Hudson River. Opened in 1825, the Erie Canal funneled western produce away from New Orleans and other coastal cities to New York and distanced the northern and southern economies.

Soon after, **railroads** began to challenge canals, as railroads were a more efficient means of transportation. In the 1820s and 1830s, railroads were in the experimental stage and played no significant role in the country's transportation system. However, a series of technological innovations such as heavier iron rails, passenger and freight cars, and more powerful locomotives soon demonstrated the efficiency of this system relative to canals. Railroad mileage increased dramatically in the two decades preceding the Civil War, with most of it in America's Northern regions. Tracks spanned the Mississippi at several points. Consolidation of shorter lines into **trunk lines** diverted traffic from rivers and provided a direct route between the Northeast and the Northwest, which further weakened ties with the South. Both domestic and foreign investment helped finance railroads, but there was substantial assistance from state and local governments, and by 1860 the federal government had granted over 30 million acres of land to railroad companies.

Samuel F. B. Morse's telegraph revolutionized communication in 1844 but further isolated the South from the rest of the country. The telegraph complemented railroads by assisting with train schedules and made news immediately available. By 1860 most of the 50,000 miles of telegraph wire were controlled by the **Western Union Telegraph Company,** including a link between New York and San Francisco. Technology also revolutionized journalism with the invention of the **rotary press** in 1846. Newspapers could now be printed cheaply, and most cities hosted newspapers such as **Horace Greeley's *Tribune*** in New York. Northern publishers contributed to growing awareness of the differences between sections in the decades preceding the Civil War.

Commerce and Industry

The emerging capitalist economy produced enormous wealth, which affected groups and regions differently. Innovative **entrepreneurs** organized businesses more productively. Retail stores began to **specialize,** and businesses organized as **corporations,** pooling the resources of many and offering them **limited liability.** Banks printed **paper notes,** alleviating the shortage of money and credit, but the lack of government regulation led to bank failures and financial instability.

The efficiency of the factory system spread to industries other than textiles. In 1860 the value of manufactured goods exceeded the value of agricultural products for the first time in United States history. Industry was centered in the Northeast, which produced two-thirds of the manufactured goods and employed the vast majority of industrial workers. American manufactured goods were often inferior to those made in Europe, but rapid technological advances improved their quality. The **machine tool industry** was vital and flourished with government support, particularly with orders for military goods. Eli Whitney's principle of **interchangeable parts** was the foundation for most of this new industrial growth. **Coal** began to replace water power, and industrial **patents** for new technology exploded prior to 1860.

Merchant capitalists were central to financing, organizing, and transporting the products of the Industrial Revolution, but they were in decline by the mid-century as manufacturing profits grew relative to profits in trade. Drawing financial backing from many individuals, **industrial capitalists** began to overtake merchants as the new upper class.

Men and Women at Work

Finding a labor supply to work in factories in predominantly rural and agrarian America was no easy task. However, more productive midwestern farms and improved transportation pushed people out of farming in the less productive areas, especially in New England. Two employment patterns emerged: families might work in factories, which introduced child labor but at least with parental supervision, unlike Europe. The other pattern was the **Lowell System,** which employed young farm women who worked in the factories and lived in boarding houses. Typically, girls would work for several years, save their wages, and return home to marry. Factory owners took care to provide a clean moral environment but the transition to long hours of regulated factory work was often not easy. As wages declined over the period, hours increased, and conditions deteriorated, the women founded several organizations, such as the **Factory Girls Association,** and organized **strikes** to improve their wages and working conditions, but by then women's role in the factory labor force was declining.

Increased immigration after 1840 provided a large pool of cheap labor for the expanding factory economy as well as for internal improvement projects. **Irish immigrants** flooded New England and built canals, turnpikes, and railroads. With few skills and plagued by anti-Irish prejudice, they commanded low wages and worked under poor conditions. The Irish began to displace women in textile factories, which furthered already-deteriorating working conditions under pressure from foreign competition.

The economic and social position of skilled artisans declined as less expensive manufactures replaced hand-crafted goods. Craftsmen likened themselves to the Jeffersonian **yeoman farmer** also challenged by industry. Like factory women, artisans in major cities began to organize **labor unions** and **workingmen's political organizations** to defend their status. In an increasingly unified economy, workers soon realized the advantages of organization and, in 1834, joined forces in the **National Trades' Union.** Printers and shoemakers also formed unions. These organizations had little standing in a legal system that considered them illegal conspiracies. The Panic of 1837 further weakened the fledgling labor movement.

Workers had little overall success in improving their position. Several state legislatures passed laws prohibiting child labor and restricting work to ten-hour days, but the laws were weak and easily avoided. The Massachusetts Supreme Court in 1842 ruled that labor unions and strikes were legal in *Commonwealth* v. *Hunt.* In general, labor organizations had little power or influence because many forces beyond their control marginalized the labor movement.

Patterns of Industrial Society

The Industrial Revolution transformed social relationships and made society more imbalanced. Average American income increased dramatically but its distribution became progressively more unequal. By 1860, 5 percent of families owned 50 percent of the nation's wealth. In cities merchants and industrialists displayed their wealth in mansions, carriages, household goods, and social clubs. At the same time a significant number of poor people lived marginal lives, with some immigrant groups, the Irish in particular, and free blacks suffering most due to racial prejudice.

Despite the growing gulf between rich and poor, America avoided much of the unrest Europe experienced. The absolute **standard of living** for most workers was improving, even if their relative position was not. Social, geographic, and economic **mobility** provided hope for the worker that his lot and that of his children would improve.

Historian **Frederick Jackson Turner** later theorized that open western land provided a **"safety valve"** for social discontent. However, few workers had the resources or inclination to move to a western farm. Geographic mobility offered workers opportunities and, at the same time, discouraged them from organizing to protest their plight. A more open political system became the safety valve offering opportunity for the worker.

Commercial and industrial development opened doors for many to own or work in businesses, and a middle-class culture developed around the household, which was beginning to separate from the workplace. Women tended to stay in the home, and inventions such as the stove made housework easier. American diets improved as the result of a greater variety of foods. Houses were also more elaborately furnished in the early Victorian style.

As families left the farm, children often left home earlier in search of work. Commercial farming relied less heavily on the family and more on hired help. Farm women performed domestic tasks rather than working at farm production. This resulted in a decline in the **birth rate,** from seven to five children per woman from 1800 to 1860. Changes in sexual behavior and efforts to limit family size in an increasingly secular and commercial world were the most important factors in the declining birth rate.

Growing distinctions between public world and the private sphere of the home drew sharper distinctions in the roles of men and women. Opportunities for women continued to be restricted, and marriage often further restricted their legal rights. Women were expected to remain at home and create a moral and virtuous household to balance their husbands' secular and business interests. Historians have labeled this idea of a **separate sphere** for women in the home as **the cult of domesticity.** It isolated women from the public world and made work outside the home less acceptable, especially for middle class women, although teaching and nursing were acceptable professions for women.. Domestic service also was an alternative for working women. Although elementary education was considered sufficient for women, formerly all-male **Oberlin College** began accepting women in 1837, and in the same year, **Mount Holyoke College** opened as an all-women's college.

The Agricultural North

Responding to national and international markets, agriculture in the Northeast declined while it flourished in the Northwest. Climate and soil conditions made the Northeast relatively unproductive. Northeastern farmers turned to opportunities presented by the Industrial Revolution, providing fruits, vegetables, and dairy products to the growing cities, producing hay for livestock, and growing potatoes. Even so the agricultural population in the Northeast declined, as did the value of its product relative to industrial production.

Urban growth and industrialization in the Old Northwest centered on agriculture, either by producing farm machinery or refining agricultural produce. Rising world prices for farm goods provided incentives for **commercial farming** and specialization in one **staple** crop. New agricultural technology and farming methods spurred production. New strains of grains, better breeds of animals, and, most important, new equipment reduced the need for labor. **John Deere's steel plow** made cultivation easier, and **Cyrus McCormick's automatic reaper** reduced the amount of labor needed for harvesting by almost half. Industrialization tied the Northeast and the Northwest more closely together with the important exchange of manufactured and agricultural goods, but this further isolated the South from the other parts of the country.

Community was less evident as one moved westward. Religion might be in a formal church setting, or in a household in the further western reaches. Families united to accomplish tasks that required more labor than a single family could muster, such as with a **barn raising.** Women gathered for both social and productive reasons in **bees.** However, farm families were isolated from the popular culture of towns and cities.

Multiple-Choice Questions

1. Population growth in the United States in the three decades before the Civil War grew primarily for which of the following reasons?
   a. families beginning earlier and women having many more children
   b. decreasing mortality rates and increasing immigration from Europe
   c. increased immigration from Africa and Asia
   d. very low birth rates by world standards but decreased mortality
   e. population expanded to settle western lands on the frontier.

2. The first, but brief revolution in the transportation of goods from the West to the East came about as a result of
   a. turnpikes.
   b. railroads.
   c. steamboats.
   d. wagon trains.
   e. canals.

3. By decreasing the use of the Mississippi River, new transportation developments
   a. weakened economic ties between the Northern and Southern states.
   b. tied the western and Southern states more closely together.
   c. diminished the reality of Henry Clay's American System.
   d. linked the economies of the Atlantic and Pacific coasts more closely.
   e. made the agricultural economies of the Midwest less important to American growth.

4. The Lowell System was initially designed to use which of the following groups as its factory labor force?
   a. fugitive slaves and free blacks
   b. Irish immigrants
   c. children from poor houses and orphanages
   d. rural farm women
   e. unemployed men from large cities

5. All of the following contributed to the growing isolation of the Southern slave states from the rest of the nation *except*
   a. new transportation patterns that bypassed Southern cities and ports.
   b. cheap newspapers and magazines, which pointed out the sectional differences.
   c. the growth of a Northern textile industry.
   d. a growing commercial agricultural sector in the Northwest.
   e. the installation of telegraph lines along established rail routes.

6. One of the consequences for the family of the commercialization of agriculture was
   a. large farms relied less on family, and more on hired help.
   b. large families were more important than ever to provide labor.
   c. farm women took over a larger share of farm production.
   d. the birth rate increased by over one-quarter.
   e. the trend for young workers to move from cities to work on farms.

7. Frederick Jackson Turner's theory emphasized the significance of
   a. a permanent working class sowing social disorder.
   b. the growing isolation of the South up to the outbreak of Civil War.
   c. women as a revolutionary force for social change.
   d. labor unions in promoting the best interests of workers.
   e. western lands as a "safety valve" preventing social discontent.

8. One of the main consequences of the "cult of domesticity" for women was
   a. a blurring of the social roles of men and women.
   b. stronger legal rights for both unmarried and married women.
   c. work outside the home was proper and fashionable.
   d. increased detachment of women from the world outside the home.
   e. the promotion of higher education for women.

9. The political philosophy of the American or Know Nothing Party promoted
   a. economic nationalism above all other issues.
   b. a strong central government to quell any appearance of nullification.
   c. the gradual abolition of slavery in all American territory.
   d. the end of public support for education above the elementary level.
   e. anti-immigrant legislation and hostility toward foreigners.

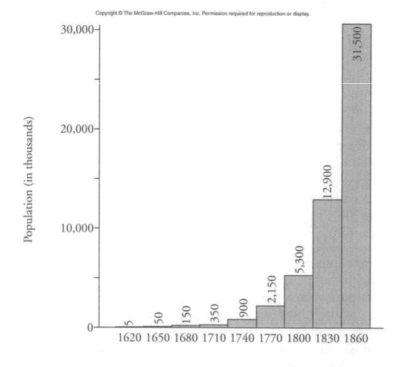

10. The accompanying graph on the previous page supports which of the following statements?
   a. Population growth was faster in the last three decades shown than in the first three.
   b. Most of the growth of the population during the nineteenth century came from immigration.
   c. Population growth was faster in the first three decades shown than in the last three.
   d. The availability of western lands promoted population growth in the nineteenth century.
   e. A bigger population spurred economic growth.

11. All of the following were necessary for America's Industrial Revolution to take place before the Civil War except
   a. the use of electricity as a source of power.
   b. a large population to produce and consume goods.
   c. a transportation system to move goods and people.
   d. the corporation as a way to organize business.
   e. interchangeable parts technology for mass production.

12. In *Commonwealth* v. *Hunt* the Massachusetts Supreme Court decided
   a. labor unions were combinations in restraint of trade.
   b. male free black laborers had the right to vote.
   c. women could only participate in the professions of teaching and nursing.
   d. both strikes and labor unions were legal.
   e. all workers had the right to a ten-hour work day.

Free-Response Questions
1. Analyze the factors that led to America's economic revolution before the Civil War.

2. Compare and contrast the changing roles of women in American society in two of the following periods:
   - 1700–1725
   - 1775–1800
   - 1825–1850

Document-Based Question
Account for the differing views of labor developed by Americans during the first Industrial Revolution.

Use the documents and your knowledge of the period 1820–1850 in constructing your response.

Document A

Source: American Textile History Museum, Lowell, Massachusetts

Middlesex Co. Woolen Mill, Lowell, Massachusetts

Document B

Source: Editor of the *Boston Reformer* Theophilus Fisk's address, "Capital Against Labor," to the mechanics of Boston in 1835. [*New York Evening Post*, 6/6/1835 in *Annals* VI, 118.]

"Eight hours for work, eight hours for sleep, and eight hours for amusement and instruction is the equitable allotment for the twenty-four. But to a great majority of the buyers of labor even the granting of your present just demand that ten hours shall constitute a day's work seems preposterous in the extreme."

Document C

Source: A communication in the *Pennsylvanian*, a pro-labor newspaper attributed to J.C., February 1836. [*Annals* VI: 245.]

"As proof of the power of employers' power over single societies, it would be well to know that, previous to the formation of the union, there were not more than six or eight trades in Philadelphia that had control over their own labor, whereas at this time there are more than fifty. . . .If it was right in individuals of one trade to unite, it was equally just and proper for them to call in their brethren of other trades to assist them in establishing just rules and regulations for their trade, consequently upon their capital, the labor of their hands. . . ."

Document D

Source: Resolutions of the "Employers, Curriers and Leather Dealers, of the City of New York and Brooklyn," March 1836. [*Annals* VI: 228.]

". . . Resolved, that while we acknowledge the right of every man, in his individual capacity, to demand whatever price he chooses for his labor; and while we are willing to give our journeymen such wages for their services as shall amply compensate them and enable them to prosper, and ourselves to compete successfully in open market with our neighbors; yet, we deny the rights and deprecate the policy of combining and conspiring to dictate terms on which journeymen shall be employed, or by which their labor shall be regulated."

Document E

Source: The opinion of Lemuel Shaw, Chief Justice of the Massachusetts Supreme Court, in *Commonwealth of Massachusetts* v. *Hunt*, 1842. [*Annals* Vii: 65.]

"We think, therefore, that associations may be entered into, the object of which is to adopt measures that may have a tendency to impoverish another, that is, to diminish his gains and profits, and yet so far from being criminal or unlawful, the object may be highly meritorious and public spirited. The legality of such an association will therefore depend upon the means to be used for its accomplishment. If it is to be carried into effect by fair or honorable and lawful means, it is to say innocent; if by falsehood or force, it may be stamped with the character of conspiracy."

Multiple-Choice Answers

1. b. Improvements in public health and the decrease in mortality from epidemics combined with increased immigration after 1830, especially from Ireland, Germany, England, and other northern European nations.

2. e. The "canal age" was short-lived but provided more efficient transportation than turnpikes before the advent of railroads in the 1830s.

3. a. Before canals and railroads directly connected the markets of the West to the Northeast, most western production flowed down the Mississippi to New Orleans before transshipment to East Coast markets. The Erie Canal and later railroads cut out some of this commerce and began to alienate the South.

4. d. At the beginning of the Industrial Revolution most laborers lived on farms. The Lowell System tapped this source of labor by employing women who would work for several years and then return home.

5. c. Economic developments slowly worked to separate the slave states from the free states of the North. The strong link that remained was cotton, which the South provided to Northern textile mills.

6. a. In many respects farms mirrored factories by mechanizing also. The labor formally provided by the farm family was replaced by machines and hired help.

7. e. Turner's frontier thesis emphasizes the significance of an expanse of open land on American development until 1890 when the frontier was declared closed. One aspect of this was the frontier's function as a "safety valve" that drew population away from the cities, therefore diminishing pressure for social and economic revolution, unlike in Europe.

8. d. Women's roles narrowed as the nineteenth century progressed. The ideal woman in the Victorian Age oversaw the raising of children and the running of the household. There was little public life for women.

9. e. Nativist attitudes were the foundation of the American Party, which arose largely in response to the growing number of Irish and German Catholics immigrating to the United States. Begun as a secret society, the movement evolved into an open political party with an anti-immigrant platform.

10. c. The chart provides data only on total population growth. In the first three decades from 1620 to 1650 the population grew from 5 to 50 thousand, a ten-fold increase. From 1830 to 1860 the population grew from 12.9 to 31.5 million, a less than three-fold increase.

11. a. Practical use of electricity did not occur until the end of the nineteenth century. Water power provided the energy for the first Industrial Revolution.

12. d. Massachusetts was the exception in this area of the law. Unions were considered obstacles to free trade by most Americans, were held in low esteem, and found it difficult to become established at this time.

Free-Response Questions Commentary

1. This is a straightforward question asking about the factors that led to America's first Industrial Revolution. The thrust of the question is to identify the elements, and to explain their impact on the great increase in American production and productivity before the Civil War. One can easily categorize the developments into three categories: labor and entrepreneurship, capital, and technology. These usually work for any period of economic transformation.

   Changing demographics, immigration, and migrating farm workers provided an industrial labor force that accumulated in America's growing cities. The embargo and the War of 1812 provided a stimulus for domestic manufactures, and fortunes made through trade and during the war provided a ready pool of capital for investment in new ventures. Finally, technological improvements combined entire manufacturing processes in a single factory. Eli Whitney's innovation of interchangeable parts in machinery made this possible. Textiles, particularly cotton fabrics, were the major product. In addition, first canals and later railroads and the telegraph helped create a national market. These factors combined the demand for and supply of goods that inspired the Industrial Revolution before the Civil War.

2. Many free-response questions ask you to compare and contrast something over time, and give you the option to choose the time periods you wish to analyze. This question follows that format.

In early colonial America you can draw a distinction between the Chesapeake and New England. In the Chesapeake the small numbers of women gave them more power and independence in the seventeenth century. As their numbers increased, this diminished in the early eighteenth century. As life stabilized in the eighteenth century the gender balance equalized and women lost some of their authority; households became more patriarchal, although women's roles included working in the home as well as assisting in farm production. In New England, where families dominated and mortality was low, women could claim less independence. Also, parental control was greater in the Northeast. Most women's lives were dominated with child rearing, and both custom and religion supported a patriarchal structure. Women were expected to be submissive, work on the farm, and serve the household. There was little thought given to more than a rudimentary education for women.

The Revolution placed new demands on women and revolutionized their role, at least for a time. Women heeded the call of Revolutionary ideology and pushed for equal roles as they too resisted English rule by boycotts and political organizations such as the Daughters of Liberty. Some fought in the Continental Army. However, the Revolution did little to change women's legal or social status; patriarchy persevered. After the war women adopted a new role as "Revolutionary mothers," the teachers of republican virtue to children. Republican motherhood gave women a political role but it did not extend outside of the family structure.

In antebellum America women fell into one of several roles. Farm women or lower-class urban women might work outside the home in factories; the Lowell System was designed to employ girls from the farm. Farms became less dependent on family labor, and women performed increasingly domestic tasks, remaining in the home to provide for husband and family. Historians have labeled this the "cult of domesticity." Work outside the home was discouraged, but was accepted in domestic service, teaching, and nursing.

You should choose two of the eras given to compare and contrast. You can divide the woman's role into social, economic, and political categories, which might make it easier to point out similarities and differences.

Document-Based Question Commentary

Although there had been clashes between employers and employees previous to the Industrial Revolution during colonial times and the early republic, these were local and on a small scale. The Industrial Revolution more clearly defined the two groups and their interests, and increased the numbers of laborers while decreasing their individual power within the workplace.

The documents point out several perspectives on labor in America during this first wave of industrialism. America's traditional values of individualism, free trade, and private property generally favored business, but attitudes often reflected personal interests. Documents A and D favor employer interests, with the painting from the Lowell Mills showing a clean environment with women laborers. Document D appeals to the right of the individual to bargain and be justly compensated, but denies the right of labor to conspire and disrupt free trade. By the 1840s most Americans accepted labor unions, but acceptance did not extend to the right to strike.

The remaining documents favor the labor perspective. Document B seeks support for an eight-hour day, in an age when ten- and twelve-hour days were standard. Some states and the federal government in 1840 limited the length of the workday. Document C shows the necessity of unions to promote labor interests, and Document E is the Massachusetts landmark ruling making both unions and strikes legal in that state.

The growing rift between capital and labor would be important to highlight, as well as the American public attitudes toward both groups. You can also include in your argument slavery, immigration, and gender.

CHAPTER 11
Cotton, Slavery, and the Old South

AP THEMES

- **American Diversity:** Race is the central fact of American slavery. Social and legal constructs were necessary to separate and define racial groups and maintain slavery in America.
- **Culture:** To cope with the harsh burdens of slavery, blacks supported a culture that assimilated their African, Caribbean, and American heritages. These traditions continue today in song, religion, family, and language, but have remained largely out of the cultural mainstream until recently.
- **Economic Transformations:** The growing differentiation between the Northern industrial and Southern agricultural economies is more sharply delineated in this period. As the Southern economy grew with cotton at its core, it also became more dependent on outside economic forces. Southerners recognized this, and came to fear its consequences.
- **Environment:** The migration into the Southwest cotton kingdom gives a clear view of a movement that occurs throughout United States history: westward movement. Wasteful agricultural techniques exhausted the soil, and Americans abandoned that land and sought new lands to the west.
- **Slavery and Its Legacies in North America:** This theme is central. An important element is recognizing the two viewpoints represented in slave accounts. While whites observed laziness and incompetence in slave work, slaves often did this deliberately as a form of resistance.

CHAPTER SUMMARY

As the South grew and prospered in the decades preceding the Civil War, its reliance on agriculture and slave labor differentiated it from the North's capitalist economy and society. The **plantation system** dominated Southern society and politics. But as the cotton economy became more closely tied to national and international markets, it also came to feel threatened by those very same forces.

The Cotton Economy

Cotton came to be the most important crop in the South as tobacco prices declined and economic factors limited the growth of rice and sugar. The durability of **short-staple cotton** together with the invention of the **cotton gin** and increasing demand for cotton in the industrial North increased production from 500,000 bales in 1820 to nearly 5 million bales in 1860. Concurrent with the boom was a rush to settle and cultivate the fertile lands of the lower South, and Southern economic power shifted to that region, which was known as the **"cotton kingdom."** The slave population and profits grew also, in part from the sale and migration of slaves from the upper to the lower South.

In contrast to the explosive growth in the Southern agricultural economy, industry and commerce in the South grew slowly. Most business enterprise was associated with agriculture and served the needs of the plantation economy. Southerners relied heavily on the North for financial backing and began to recognize the dangers of a **colonial economic relationship** between the sections. Louisiana's *De Bow's Review* warned of the dangers of colonialism and pleaded with the South to develop a manufacturing sector. However, profits in cotton provided ample incentive to continue investment in plantation agriculture. Also, Southern values of **chivalry,** leisure, and elegance tended to discourage commerce. Southerners found Yankee acquisitiveness antithetical to their ideal image of the **cavalier.**

White Society in the South

No more than one quarter of white Southerners owned slaves, and only a small proportion owned slaves in large numbers, so images of a large **planter aristocracy** were mythical. The few owners of large plantations with many slaves were at the top of a hierarchical social order to which most everyone else deferred. Unlike the upper South, in the newly settled lower South this group was new to wealth and power, had struggled to get there, and ardently defended the system.

An intricate system of **chivalry** prevailed and public dignity, morality, and bravery were badges of honor. **Dueling** continued as a practice long after it was outlawed in the North. **Preston Brooks,** vilified by Northerners for caning Senator **William Sumter,** was considered a hero in the South. In many respects the household-centered lives of Southern white women paralleled those of Northern middle-class women. However, male conceptions of Southern women placed females in an even more subordinate role. Women were largely defenseless and dependent on their husbands. In reality, most women lived on isolated farms and participated actively in household production. There was little opportunity for schooling and nearly one-quarter of white women over age twenty were illiterate. In slave-owning households, marriage relations were constantly threatened by sexual relationships between masters and female slaves. Despite this, upper-class white women were often the most outspoken defenders of the Southern way of life.

Despite the plantation ideal, most white Southerners lived on modest farms, owned no slaves, and were subsistence farmers. There was little opportunity to better their position, but many still supported the system. Kinship ties between the classes, an unusually high participation in politics, and a general acceptance of hierarchy mustered support for this social arrangement. An exception were the inhabitants of the Appalachian hill country who rejected the plantation system, did not support secession or the Confederacy, and valued independence and freedom above all. Despite the gulf between the planter aristocracy and the plain folk, race became a unifying factor for whites. No matter how poor or desperate Southern whites were, they considered themselves superior to slaves.

Slavery: The "Peculiar Institution"

In the western hemisphere, only the United States, Brazil, Puerto Rico, and Cuba practiced slavery, and this further isolated the South. Paradoxically, slavery both created a bond between blacks and whites and also created two distinct cultures based on racial separation. No single generalization can describe the practice of slavery in the antebellum South. In theory **slave codes** regulated both slave and free behavior and served to maintain a superior position for whites. However, enforcement of these strict codes varied widely and in certain circumstances slaves could achieve a degree of autonomy and a measure of freedom within prescribed limits. The size of the plantation was often a main factor in determining the relationship between master and slave. On smaller farms, slaves and white owners often worked alongside each other and might live in the same house. Larger plantations with many slaves often employed **overseers** and slave **drivers** to supervise slaves, and the master was remote. In rice cultivation, the **task system** was used, where slaves were given a task to accomplish in a given period of time. More common was the **gang system** in which slaves worked in groups overseen by a driver who determined when work began and ended.

Slave masters had incentive to keep slaves healthy but still only provided a minimal amount of food, shelter, and clothing. Plantation owners often hired other workers, usually poor, landless whites, to do the most arduous and dangerous jobs. Although slaves were less healthy than Southern whites, they fared better than slaves in other parts of the Americas where the climate and work were far more severe. Ironically, some scholars argue that slaves enjoyed a better standard of living than Northern industrial workers or European peasants and workers.

The slave population grew through natural increase but at a considerably slower pace than white America. Women had particular burdens as they were expected to work on the plantation in addition to their household chores as wives and mothers. Work in the fields was harder than domestic work in the master's household, but slaves often preferred the former because of privacy issues and their desire to be with other slaves. Female slaves were always vulnerable to sexual abuse.

Most whites found slavery incompatible with city living because of the lack of close supervision and consequent liberties city slaves enjoyed relative to those on plantations. City slaves had considerable freedom of movement during the day and contact with whites and free blacks. Slaves were often hired out both as skilled and unskilled labor for work on the docks or in construction. In the city, lines between slave and free were blurred, and over time the urban slave population declined. Fearing insurrection, whites sold male slaves to the plantations and introduced more rigid slave codes. On the eve of the Civil War, there were about 250,000 free blacks living in the slave states, the majority in Maryland and Virginia. Urban slaves might buy their freedom or be freed by their masters, but this became more difficult to do as the slave system became more rigidly enforced. In some cities free black communities existed relatively unmolested by whites.

With new cotton lands opening in the Southwest the trade in slaves between the upper and lower South flourished. At auction slaves were examined like livestock, and a prime male field hand could cost from $500 to $1,700 in the 1840s and 1850s; a female might cost even more. The **foreign slave trade** was banned in 1808, but the smuggling of slaves continued.

The common slave stereotypes were that of **"Sambo,"** the slow, obsequious, deferential slave, or the rebel. Formal rebellion was rare, but the white South was obsessed by the possibility. Two rebellions, **Gabriel Prosser's** in 1800 in Richmond, Virginia, and **Denmark Vesey's** in 1822 in Charleston, South Carolina, were uncovered and foiled before any violence against whites occurred. In each case many of the conspirators were executed. In 1831 **Nat Turner,** a slave preacher, led a successful slave revolt that killed 60 whites before it was suppressed. Over 100 of his followers were executed. More typical resistance involved either running away, which became more successful after the initiation of the **Underground Railroad,** or small but recurring instances of passive resistance, such as, slow work, breaking tools, or performing tasks incorrectly. Subtlety characterized the vast majority of slave resistance and fed into the negative perception whites had of slaves.

The Culture of Slavery

One survival mechanism for slaves was to create a culture of their own. Although some slaves maintained native languages, **pidgin** incorporated both English and African languages. Music relying heavily on rhythm played an important role. It could accompany dance, but the voice and song were primary. **Spirituals,** imbued with faith, combined hope for freedom and a lament of servitude.

Although most slaves worshipped in their master's churches, **blacks** held illegal, secret church services at night on plantations. Slaves developed their own brands of religion, often blending Christianity with African religions and **voodoo.** More emotional and ecstatic than whites, participants in these worship services above all prayed for freedom from slavery, although it was often couched in Christian theology. Separate black churches in cities had both slave and free black congregations.

Along with the church, **family** was central to black culture, adapting to obstacles that banned legal marriage between blacks. The economics of slavery prevented a condemnation of premarital pregnancy; slave couples often met at night, and families might be broken apart by the sale of a family member. Extended **kinship networks** evolved to compensate for the breakup of nuclear families. **Miscegenation** was a heinous practice that, at bare minimum, stressed both slave and master's families. The relationship between master and slave was complex but embodied a paternalism that bound slaves to their masters and that masters used as a form of control.

Southern circumstances—natural resources, environment, culture and society, and most of all a slave labor system—increasingly differentiated and isolated the Southern states from other regions and the Atlantic world. As cotton bound sections together economically, differences became more evident and, therefore, more profound.

Multiple-Choice Questions

1. Cotton came to dominate the Southern economy for all of the following reasons except
   a. tobacco prices were unstable and declining.
   b. sugar growers had to compete with established Caribbean sugar plantations.
   c. the growing textile industry increased the demand for cotton.
   d. Southern textile factories switched from woolen to cotton.
   e. short-staple cotton was hardy and technology made it easier to process.

2. As settlement rapidly pushed into the Southwest during the 1840s and 1850s, plantations
   a. in the lower South relied less on slave labor and reinstituted indentured servitude.
   b. in the lower South smuggled a large number of slaves to the United States from the Caribbean to work the new lands.
   c. from the upper South sold slaves to the lower South to maintain their profits.
   d. in South Carolina gave up rice cultivation entirely because slaves did not have adequate skills.
   e. in the lower South were small and used fewer slaves than the large plantations of the upper South.

3. In the antebellum era, the South never developed a significant industrial economy because
   a. there was no way to raise sufficient capital in the South for industry.
   b. the rural Southern home production satisfied all the needs for manufactured goods.
   c. cotton prices were high and provided adequate incentives for Southerners to continue investment in that sector.
   d. there were not enough natural resources to support industry in the Southern states.
   e. the capitalistic and inquisitive nature of Southern society was better suited to a plantation economy.

4. Which of the following aspects of plantation life is illustrated by the accompanying map?

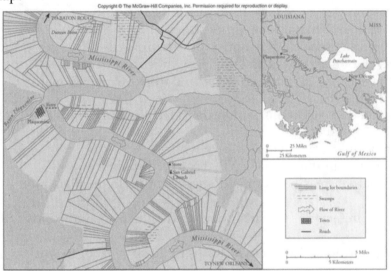

Copyright © The McGraw-Hill Companies, Inc. Permission required for reproduction or display.

   a. There was little need to cross rivers so it was necessary to build few bridges.
   b. The most important stretch of the Mississippi River lay between Baton Rouge and New Orleans.
   c. The river had little effect on the profitability of cotton cultivation because most plantations did not border a river.
   d. Slave labor was more important on the long, narrow lots where growing cotton was more labor-intensive.
   e. Any river frontage was important for the ease of shipping goods and for transportation.

5. The ideal of the "Southern lady" embodied which of the following characteristics?
   a. lives centered in the home as wives and mothers rather than as public figures
   b. home production such as spinning and weaving to increase family income
   c. little reliance on servants to do work, which demonstrated a lady's usefulness to the plantation economy
   d. employment outside of the home to show their capabilities and equality with men
   e. extensive education to illustrate refinement and culture

6. Even though divided by a large gap in income and wealth, Southern plain folk were linked to the planter aristocracy
   a. because life on small family farms was not very different from large plantations.
   b. because there was considerable social mobility and many small farmers rose into the ranks of the planter class.
   c. since race and kinship ties linked the two groups.
   d. for the reason that few participated in politics so despite economic differences, they could agree on issues.
   e. because many hill country farmers supported the social hierarchy that characterized their region.

7. In practice, before the Civil War slave codes
   a. instituted a rigid caste system with little flexibility for slaves.
   b. were designed to regulate only the behavior of slaves.
   c. allowed marriage between slaves but not mixed-race marriages.
   d. regulated the behavior of both blacks and whites with respect to each other.
   e. kept any slaves from learning to read and write, and from owning property.

8. Some historians maintain that conditions for Northern factory workers were worse than those of slaves for the reason that
   a. slaves had a lower mortality rate than Southern whites.
   b. planters had an economic incentive to keep their slaves healthy.
   c. some slaves had a relatively easy life doing domestic chores in the plantation household.
   d. children did not work in factories but they were used regularly for all kinds of slave labor.
   e. slaves were plentiful and some Northern factories hired slave labor to work in the mills.

9. Growing resistance to slavery in the cities was a result of
   a. white fears of insurrections by the relatively unsupervised slaves.
   b. the shortage of housing for slave labor in rapidly growing cities.
   c. increased manufacturing employing slaves instead of free labor.
   d. declining demand for unskilled labor in cities.
   e. Irish immigration to the South, which took jobs formerly held by slaves.

10. Looking at the overall economy of the United States before 1860
   a. the Southern economy was becoming less connected to the national economy because of its use of slave labor in agriculture.
   b. the Southern transportation system kept Southern produce largely out of Northern markets.
   c. Southern cotton had a relatively minor impact on exports as a whole.
   d. Northerners were apprehensive about their growing dependence on Southern cotton for economic prosperity.
   e. Southerners feared economic colonialism, with the Northern economy becoming their master.

11. How might an historian today interpret the following 1849 statement?

"[N]either mule nor Negro can be made to do more than a certain amount of work; and that amount so small in comparison to the amount done by the white laborers at the North it is a universal observation at the South."

    a. White labor was vastly more productive than slave labor.
    b. Slaves were little better than animals in accomplishing the tasks at hand.
    c. The gang system was better than the task system to complete work.
    d. Deliberate resistance may have decreased slave productivity.
    e. Northern labor was among the most productive in the world at the time.

12. All of the following were survival mechanisms for slaves except
    a. music in which spirituals mixed faith with hope and lamentation.
    b. miscegenation, which made the master and slave relationship more complex.
    c. pidgin, which made it harder for masters to understand slaves.
    d. religion, which included Christianity, African religions, and voodoo.
    e. kinship networks that replaced the nuclear slave family.

Free-Response Questions—Exam Tip
Using the Slave Narrative in Free-Response Answers

The slave narrative is one of the most important primary sources available to help historians understand slavery and the South, and Frederick Douglass's *Narrative* is a classic in this genre. Be sure to look for the point of view from both a slave and slaveholder perspective. Important ideas in slave narratives are identity, literacy, slavery's injury to blacks and whites, and irresponsible power.

Be sure to evaluate and use all Document-Based Question documents in the same manner when constructing your arguments. Read them critically, and look for subtle meaning to strengthen your essay.

Free-Response Questions
1. Compare the development of the Northern economy with that of the South in the three decades before the Civil War.

2. Account for the variety in the administration of slavery that led to flexibility and coping systems for slaves.

Document-Based Question
The selections shed some light on the following two questions: What was Douglass's goal in writing the *Narrative,* and how does the slave point of view compare and contrast with that of the slaveholder?

Document A

Source: All of the following come from Frederick Douglass, *Narrative of the Life of Frederick Douglass*, published in Boston by the Anti-Slavery Office in 1845.

"…One of my [Frederick Douglass] greatest faults was that of letting his horse run away, and go down to his father-in-law's farm, which was about five miles from St. Michael's. I would then have to go after it. My reason for this kind of carelessness, or carefulness, was, that I could always get something to eat when I went there…I never left there hungry…"

Document B

"My new mistress proved to be all she appeared when I first met her at the door – a woman of the kindest heart and finest feelings. She had never had a slave under her control previously to myself…But, alas! This kind heart had but a short time to remain such. The fatal poison of irresponsible power was already in her hands, and soon commenced its infernal work. That cheerful eye, under the influence of slavery, soon became red with rage; that voice, made all of sweet accord, changed to one of harsh and horrid discord; and that angelic face gave place to that of a demon."

Document C

[Douglass's master about Douglass] "Learning would spoil the best nigger in the world. Now," said he, "if you teach that nigger (speaking of myself) how to read there would be no keeping him. It would forever unfit him to be a slave…These words sank deep into my heart…I now understood what had been to me a most perplexing difficulty – to wit, the white man's power to enslave the black man…From that moment, I understood the pathway from slavery to freedom."

Multiple-Choice Answers

1. d. The opening up of southwestern lands where short staple cotton would grow together with the growing textile industry made cotton "king," and other crops faced limitations. The South did not have a large factory sector.

2. c. As tobacco profits declined, a trade in slaves between the upper and lower South grew, which helped the older areas remain profitable. The Southwest cotton plantations relied heavily on slave labor.

3. c. A strong and growing market for cotton made its production very profitable. Also, the growing disagreements between sections made Southerners wary of capitalistic manners.

4. e. As waterways were the most important means of transport in the South, having land bordering a river was important. The long lots illustrate this; any frontage, no matter how small, was access to transportation and markets.

5. a. The "ideal" was a lady in a household with servants so that she needed to do no manual labor. She was to care for her husband and children in a refined atmosphere.

6. c. Race and kinship were the main links between plain folk and gentry. There was little social mobility, but most poor farmers aspired to become planters.

7. d. Slave codes, if strictly enforced, would have instituted a rigid caste system with little flexibility for slaves. They were enforced neither consistently nor strictly so slaves had some small freedom from those rules. Black codes regulated white behavior also so that racial lines remained clear.

8. b. Since slaves were considered property and represented a significant investment planters wanted to keep them relatively healthy. Northern workers were not protected by any sense of paternalism from factory owners.

9. a. Slaves in the city regularly mingled with whites and free blacks and this relative freedom became increasingly unsettling to whites, who feared that unsupervised associations would lead to conspiracies.

10. e. Since Southern planters were dependent on the North for their cotton markets, transportation, capital needs, and manufactured goods, they began to see themselves in a dependent colonial economic relationship and feared that they were becoming slaves to Northern industry.

11. d. Slave resistance took many forms, the least of which was outright rebellion and disobeying orders. Much was subtle: work slowdowns, breaking of tools, and poorly done work. Historians today interpret white observations of low slave productivity in this light.

12. b. Slaves maintained much of their African and Caribbean heritage as an anchor against the harshness of slavery. Miscegenation was a burden that stressed slave families, and a particular hardship for slave women.

Free-Response Questions Commentary

1. The question asks you to compare and contrast the regional economies of the North and the South in the antebellum period. The contrasts are more prevalent but there are similarities to be made also. You could begin by pointing out that the economy was becoming more national and integrated in many ways, and that the South was industrializing, but on a much smaller scale. Agriculture was important to both regions, but was an overwhelming sector in the Southern economy.

   The contrasts are more striking. An overall theme could be the dichotomy of the Hamiltonian vision in the North and the Jeffersonian in the South. Northern commercial culture, the energy from water power, and poor agricultural conditions all contrasted with the South. The cotton gin made cotton production economically feasible, and its growth was tremendous. In addition, the labor systems were opposite. You can also support the differences in culture and society that supported the economy in both sections.

2. This chapter shows the complexity and complicated nature of Southern slave society. You might argue that the rules were too rigid for both blacks and whites to follow, and therefore the system allowed for considerably more flexibility in practice than the theory suggests. The cost of following all the prescribed rules was simply too high.

Therefore, even though the system tried to eliminate a sense of humanity for slaves, they devised ways to deal with their servitude: extended family, language, religion, music, and private property. The rules and slave codes prohibited much of this, but slaves found ways around the rules, or kept knowledge of these subversive activities from their masters.

Document-Based Question Commentary

Each of the three documents shows a former slave's analysis of the system. It is important to note how Douglass interpreted slavery and its consequences. In Document A the use of "carelessness" and "carefulness" helps explain the pervasive nature of slave resistance. The evil effect of slavery on both blacks and whites is illustrated by Document B; Douglass hoped this would help gain support for abolition among whites. Finally, Document C emphasizes the significance of literacy and knowledge in maintaining power over the slave.

Be sure to be rigorous in your analysis of this specific type of document, and all others, in your essay. Being able to show how actions might be interpreted differently by two different interest groups will make your essay stronger and show a higher degree of interpretation and analysis.

CHAPTER 12
Antebellum Culture and Reform

AP THEMES

- **Culture:** A cultural outpouring characterizes antebellum America. Building upon patriotism and nationalism of the early republic, romanticism awakened visions of unlimited human potential on the grand American landscape. In both literature and visual arts optimism was the theme.
- **Environment:** Americans began to view the environment differently at this time. Rather than viewing it as an obstacle to be overcome, tamed, or destroyed, intellectuals found power, wonder, and grandeur in nature. Transcendentalists believed nature to be the medium through which one could find one's inner self and truth.
- **Reform:** Social changes brought about by industrialization were unsettling to many Americans and optimistic movements to improve society and perfect individuals arose. Fueled by simultaneous but contradictory impulses seeking to liberate people from social tyranny and to impose order on an increasingly chaotic social system, grassroots movements arose. Major movements addressed temperance, health, education, rehabilitation, Native Americans, feminism, and abolition.
- **Religion:** The Second Great Awakening was another protestant revival with strong evangelical underpinnings. It absorbed optimistic impulses and preached that every individual was capable of achieving salvation, and that individual efforts at redemption could pave the way. This evangelical strain entered the American mainstream, and was a powerful incentive for American reform.

CHAPTER SUMMARY

Before the Civil War Americans saw promise but felt uneasy amidst the social, economic, and political changes taking place. A number of reform movements arose to correct society and seek perfection of the individual. Drawing on European **romanticism** and American optimism, some reformers sought to free the human spirit. Coincidentally, the disorder arising from growth and industrialism inspired others to search for order and stability. Both impulses sought answers in reform, which became another dividing line between the North and the South.

The Romantic Impulse

Borrowing from European romanticism, American intellectuals sought to liberate the human spirit. The American environment led artists to depict the grandeur and power of nature. The large **Hudson River School** paintings of **Frederick Church** and **Albert Bierstadt** portrayed nature and the American landscape as the fount of power, spirit, and wisdom.

Slowly, American writers began to replace European authors for popular reading in America. **Washington Irving** was superseded by America's first great novelist, **James Fenimore Cooper,** who in *The Last of the Mohicans,* recounted tales of the American frontier with an independent individual searching for some order in the untamed wilderness. Later, **Walt Whitman's** poems in the 1855 *Leaves of Grass* celebrated the democratic individual. **Herman Melville** and **Edgar Allan Poe** looked at the darker side of the human spirit.

Southern literature of the period followed two general patterns: historical romances embodying and defending the cavalier spirit of the plantation system or more realistic novels about ordinary people that set the stage for the regional humor of later writers, such as **Mark Twain.**

A group of New Englanders called the **transcendentalists** viewed society's conventions as limiting human knowledge and potential. Their leader Ralph Waldo Emerson was the leading intellectual of the time. In his most famous essay, **"Self-Reliance,"** Emerson sought to unite the individual with the universe. **Henry David Thoreau** spent two years in isolation on Walden Pond to free himself from social restrictions. *Walden* (1854) was a chronicle of his insights during his two-year commune with nature. Thoreau promoted the idea of **"civil disobedience,"** or a citizen's responsibility to disobey unjust laws. By focusing on the unity between man and nature, transcendentalists hoped to overcome the human limitations caused by social constraints and achieve perfection.

Others sought utopia and individual freedom in communal living. **Brook Farm** outside of Boston was formed in 1841 by transcendentalist **George Ripley** to support self-exploration. Based on equal work and leisure among its members, the experiment folded six years later. One resident was **Nathaniel Hawthorne,** who later wrote about the dangers of separation from society in *The Scarlet Letter* (1851). Other utopian experiments were based on ideas from Europeans **Charles Fourier** and **Robert Owen. Owen** founded an Indiana community based on total equality at **New Harmony** in 1825; it was an economic failure.

The relationship between women and men was a particular concern of many reformers. **Margaret Fuller's** example and writings promoted an early feminist agenda. New York's **Oneida Community** founded in 1848 rejected traditional family and marriage; its founder, **John Noyes,** declared all members married to each other with the goal of liberating women. The **Shakers,** a religious sect founded by **Ann Lee,** went further in its promotion of equality by espousing complete celibacy. Women exercised more power than men, and the group sought to separate itself from the chaos of American society. The movement spawned more than twenty communities.

The most successful and lasting utopian effort is **The Church of Jesus Christ of the Latter Day Saints,** or the **Mormons.** Founded by **Joseph Smith,** who published the **Book of Mormon** (1830), his followers sought a place to settle free from outside interference. Most established communities rejected the Mormons because of their radical theology, their practice of polygamy, and their secrecy. Smith was killed by a mob in 1844, and his successor, **Brigham Young,** led 12,000 Mormons to Salt Lake City in Utah, where they finally found isolation and security to practice their faith.

Remaking Society

Goals of the reform movements in the nineteenth century were diverse and reflected the coincidental impulses to both free individuals from social restrictions and also to impose order on a rapidly changing society. Two philosophical strains pushed America down the road of reform: romantic optimism and evangelical Protestantism. The **Second Great Awakening** ushered in a powerful force for social reform with its belief that individuals could gain salvation through their own efforts. This revival movement was particularly strong along the Erie Canal in what came to be known as the **Burned-Over District.** The revival leader was Presbyterian preacher **Charles Grandison Finney.** Many of his followers had benefited from the economic revolution, but felt threatened by its accompanying social changes. For this group religion became not only a means of salvation, but also a call for reform and order in the larger community.

The average male in 1830 drank nearly three times the amount of alcohol as today, and alcohol was considered a major cause for social ills such as crime, disorder, and poverty. Evangelical Protestantism's focus on individual redemption provided the foundation for reform. The **American Society for the Promotion of Temperance** founded in 1826 used revival techniques to urge abstinence and later movements used former alcoholics as models of redemption. In Maine the movement pressured the legislature to ban the sale and consumption of alcohol in 1851. It caused tensions between Protestants and newly arrived Irish Catholics, whose social customs included alcohol consumption.

Public health issues contributed to Americans' sense of insecurity at this time. Periodic epidemics were deadly. In 1833, nearly one-quarter of the New Orleans population perished in a cholera epidemic. Americans sought many options to improve health: spas were popular among the rich, the study of the skull's shape and texture (phrenology) was practiced by others, and some promoted new diets. The field of medicine tended to attract many unqualified men to its ranks. There were no general theories about disease and ignorance of bacteria as the cause of infections resulted in few practical cures. Smallpox vaccination in the eighteenth century and anesthesia were discovered by chance. In 1843 **Oliver Wendell Holmes** surmised that disease could be transmitted between people and this led to the practice of disinfecting surgical instruments, with positive results.

The first secretary of the Massachusetts Board of Education in 1837 was **Horace Mann.** He believed education was essential to democracy, and that labor needed protection from dominant capital. Mann lengthened the academic year, increased teachers' salaries, enhanced the curriculum, and introduced professional training for teachers. Other states followed suit, providing public funds for education and creating teachers colleges. These reforms had less influence in the West and the South, but by the time of the Civil War, America enjoyed one of the highest literacy rates in the world. The promise of human potential also inspired institutions to help the handicapped, the network of which became known as the **Benevolent Empire.**

The redemption impulse underlay the **asylum movement,** which sought to rehabilitate criminals and the mentally ill. At this time jails imprisoned criminals and the mentally ill together under poor conditions. Newly designed **penitentiaries** disciplined prisoners and provided opportunities for them to consider their wrongs to society. Also, laws imprisoning debtors were eliminated. The asylum movement included the mentally ill, orphans, and the poor and built institutions designed to lead inmates in the direction of more productive lives. **Dorothea Dix** led the movement for the improved treatment of the mentally ill.

Resting on the idea of protection of Native Americans, the **reservation system** was instituted in the 1840s and 1850s. In part it was a benevolent solution to the Indian problem; reservations provided a protected area for Indians to develop so eventual **assimilation** into white society was possible. It also moved Indians off the valuable lands whites wanted.

Women played a pivotal role in the various reform movements and questioned their role in a male-dominated society. The **cult of domesticity** served to tie women more closely to the household and limit their actions. As proponents of reform, especially as abolitionists, women noted parallels between their bondage and slavery. Denied access to antislavery conventions, a group of women including **Lucretia Mott, Elizabeth Cady Stanton,** and **Susan B. Anthony** organized a women's rights convention at **Seneca Falls** in 1848, at which they adopted a **"Declaration of Sentiments and Resolutions"** modeled on the Declaration of Independence. They called for **women's suffrage,** which was not achieved until 1920. Many of the movement's leaders were Quakers, a sect that embraced sexual equality. Little concrete progress was made for women in antebellum America and women's issues were mostly subordinated to other reform issues.

The Crusade Against Slavery

There were efforts in the seventeenth century to end slavery in America, and powerful antislavery movements existed in Europe, but it was not until after 1830 that abolition gained prominence in the United States.

The earliest nineteenth-century efforts to abolish slavery in the United States embraced **colonization,** or settling of slaves in foreign lands. The **American Colonization Society** founded **Liberia** on the west coast of Africa in 1830 but few freed slaves ever settled there. It was costly and many American slaves did not want to go. The antislavery movement was revitalized by the appearance of **William Lloyd Garrison.** Garrison, an assistant to the publisher of the *Genius of Universal Emancipation,* **Benjamin Lundy,** grew disillusioned with its moderate stance and struck out on his own in 1831. That year he published the *Liberator* in which he outlined a revolutionary program. He urged his readers to adopt the black man's perspective and acknowledge the damage slavery did to the individual slave. The solution should then be evident: immediate emancipation and citizenship for freed slaves. Garrison attracted an immediate following and he founded the **New England Antislavery Society** in 1832 followed by the **American Antislavery Society** in 1833. Membership grew rapidly to 250,000 by 1838. His success was partly due to the coincidence of abolition and general reform ideals.

The 250,000 free blacks in the North in 1850 confronted substantial prejudice and economic deprivation, but they were aware that their lowly social status was partly due to the existence of slavery. **Sojourner Truth,** a freed slave, was an eloquent antislavery advocate, and **Frederick Douglass,** also a freed slave, were powerful examples of the individual liberation reformers sought. Douglass lectured in America and Europe and published an antislavery newspaper, the *North Star.* He became widely known for his autobiography, published in 1845.

Abolitionists were always a minority in all regions, and they provoked a powerful reaction by those who feared the political consequences of growing sectionalism and those who feared the social consequences of a great number of free blacks; both threatened the existing social system. Some abolitionists were attacked; Garrison was mobbed on Boston's streets in 1835 and an Illinois mob attacked and killed abolitionist **Elijah Lovejoy** and burned his print shop. Although few anti-abolitionists resorted to violence, they shared sentiments with those who did.

This violence and Garrison's radicalism persuaded some abolitionists to adopt a more moderate stance. Abolitionists secured passage of **personal liberty laws** in several Northern states forbidding officials to assist in the capture and return of runaway slaves, but never organized into a political party. The **Liberty Party,** formed in 1840, promoted **free soil** or the abolition of slavery in the territories. The party had a racist element and many hoped to exclude African Americans as well. Some New England abolitionists took more drastic measures, supplying money and arms to violent abolitionists. Others used propaganda to arouse sympathy for the cause. The publication of *Uncle Tom's Cabin* in 1852 by **Harriet Beecher Stowe** was the most significant of these works. Combining the emotion of romantic fiction with an abolitionist political agenda, this novel changed the nature of the antislavery debate in America. It sold more than 300,000 copies in its first year and expanded the abolition audience greatly. Although few accepted the abolitionist argument completely, in the decades before the Civil War it more sharply defined the divisions produced by slavery in America.

Multiple-Choice Questions

1. Nineteenth-century romanticism differed from America's traditional Protestant values by assuming
   a. an individual's inner spirit needed only to be released for its goodness to be evident.
   b. an individual's innate evil was an obstacle to be overcome through discipline and virtue.
   c. God was all powerful and individuals could do nothing to affect their fate.
   d. the universe reflected a divine mechanism put in motion by a supreme being.
   e. the American frontier marked the divide between good and evil.

2. All of the following represent aspects of romanticism in nineteenth-century American culture except
   a. Walt Whitman's Leaves of Grass.
   b. James Fenimore Cooper's The Last of the Mohicans.
   c. Frederick Church and the Hudson River School.
   d. Noah Webster's American Spelling Book.
   e. Edgar Allan Poe's "The Raven."

3. New England's transcendentalists embraced nature because
   a. it provided the natural resources necessary to sustain the Industrial Revolution.
   b. there the individual could leave society's artificiality and find truth.
   c. settlement required transcending and clearing nature's forests to settle new lands.
   d. increasing settlement was destroying America's natural beauty and ruining the environment.
   e. nature was a place where race-based slavery did not exist.

4. Which of the following utopian communities is correctly matched with one of its major characteristics?
   a. Mormons allowed each resident to achieve their individual potential by equally sharing work and leisure.
   b. Brook Farm rejected traditional notions of marriage and family, thereby liberating women.
   c. New Harmony set up a rigid social order that they believed reflected nature's laws.
   d. Shakers embraced sexual equality by limiting contact between men and women and practicing celibacy.
   e. Oneida adopted traditional social values with men working in factories and women staying in the home doing domestic chores.

5. The reform impulse in antebellum America was philosophically divided between supporters of
   a. Andrew Jackson and John Quincy Adams.
   b. government intervention and anarchy.
   c. religion and atheism.
   d. evangelism and deism.
   e. individualism and social order.

6. The Second Great Awakening differed from the First Great Awakening in that
   a. the Second stressed the omnipotent power of God to save or damn.
   b. the First held that reason alone allowed one to communicate with God.
   c. the Second believed that each individual contained the capacity for salvation.
   d. the Second rejected both reason and emotion as ways to understand God's message.
   e. women played a more important role in the evangelical First Great Awakening.

7. Temperance was one of the most influential reform movements of the antebellum period because
   a. government reformers found alcohol difficult to control and tax.
   b. social reformers believed it was responsible for almost all social ills.
   c. it used scarce agricultural sources of grain for alcohol instead of food.
   d. it caused revolution in western areas as typified by the Whisky Rebellion.
   e. public water supplies were often unhealthy.

8. Reform movements before the Civil War were distinctive because
   a. women played a major role as both members and leaders of the various movements.
   b. this was the federal government's first attempts to reform the individual.
   c. men played the major role in all the reform associations.
   d. there was no place in the reforms for government on any level to play a role.
   e. reformers all came from the ranks of white America.

9. In the 1840s and 1850s the new idea for reform of Native Americans centered around
   a. relocation of Indians away from white settlement because competition with whites would destroy Indians.
   b. warfare to eliminate any obstacles to continued westward white expansion.
   c. immediate assimilation of Indians into American society to improve the lives of Native Americans.
   d. the protection and promotion of Indian culture in traditional tribal lands so native ways would not be lost.
   e. promotion of reservations to protect Indians until they developed to the point where they could assimilate into white society.

10. The main thrust of the "Declaration of Sentiments" adopted at the Seneca Falls Convention in 1848 was
    a. a separate sphere for women and men should have no access to it.
    b. all men were created equal so that slavery should be abolished immediately.
    c. women deserved special protection in the law such as a shorter work day.
    b. women and men were created equal and had the same inalienable rights.
    e. political rights, including the vote, should be extended to all male citizens.

11. Harriet Beecher Stowe's Uncle Tom's Cabin gave abolition an important boost because
    a. it portrayed slavery accurately by giving the account of a former slave.
    b. it provided an exaggerated and distorted view of slavery but claimed the stories were true.
    c. its romantic appeal and sentimental characters personalized slavery and gained a new audience for abolitionists.
    d. it was a best-selling book and the proceeds went to support the abolition movement.
    e. it gave a balanced account of slavery and left the readers to judge for themselves the issue of slavery.

12. William Lloyd Garrison's approach to abolition began to fragment the movement in the 1830s because
    a. he accepted slavery where it existed but opposed its expansion in the western territories.
    b. his approach to abolition was too moderate for those who saw slavery as a moral wrong.
    c. his Quaker upbringing prevented him from entering into violent conflict with others.
    d. his push for immediate emancipation prompted anti-abolitionists to use violence against the antislavery movement.
    e. he joined with radicals advocating violence against slaveholders and the slave system.

Free-Response Questions—Exam Tips

- Free-response questions dealing with social issues often focus on reform in the antebellum period because it touches on so many issues and groups that do not fit into the political or social mainstream.
- Pay particular attention to the role of women during this period. Not only were women a major force in the reform movement, but women's rights was a reform movement in its own right.
- Associate each major movement with a prominent leader, such as Dorothea Dix in the asylum movement and Horace Mann in education reform.
- Be able to identify the motivating forces underlying reform; the impulses stretch across the broad range of reform. Demonstrate an understanding of transcendentalism as an important force in the reform movements.

Free-Response Questions

1. Analyze the contributions of TWO of the following in helping establish a distinct national identity in the period from ratification of the Constitution to the Civil War:
   • Literature and Fine Arts
   • Politics Religion

2. "Reformers were far more numerous in the North and Northwest than in the South. . . ." Assess the validity of this statement in antebellum America.

Document-Based Question

How successful were women in providing ideas, support, and leadership to achieve the goals of reform movements in antebellum America?

Use the documents and your knowledge of the period 1835–1860 in constructing your response.

Document A

Source: A Report on Female Labor given at the National Trades' Union Convention held in Philadelphia in 1836. [*Annals* VI: 256.]

"The system of female labor, as practiced in our cities and manufacturing towns, is surely the most disgraceful escutcheon on the character of American freemen, and one, if not checked by some superior cause, will entail ignorance, misery, and degradation on our children, to the end of time. "The physical organization, and natural responsibilities, and moral sensibility of women prove conclusively that her labors should be only of a domestic nature.'"

Document B

Source: Dorothea Dix's Memorial to the Legislature of Massachusetts reporting on her visits to jails and Almshouses, 1843. [Commanger, *Documents of American History*, 302–303.]

"Springfield. In a jail, one lunatic woman, furiously mad, a State pauper, improperly situated, both in regard to the prisoners, the keepers, and herself . . . Lincoln. A woman in a cage. . . . Men of Massachusetts, I beg, I implore, I demand pity and protection for these of my suffering, outraged sex. . . . Become the benefactors of your race, the just guardians of the solemn rights you hold in trust."

Document C

Source: Library of Congress

The Drunkard's Progress

Document D

Source: The "Declaration of Sentiments" adopted by the Seneca Falls Convention in New York, 1848. [*Annals* VII:438–439.]

"The history of mankind is a history of repeated injuries and usurpations on the part of man toward woman, having in direct object the establishment of an absolute tyranny over her. To prove this, let facts be submitted to a candid world.

He has never permitted her to exercise her inalienable right to the elective franchise....

...He has made her, if married, in the eye of the law, civilly dead.

...He has denied her the facilities for obtaining a thorough education, all colleges being closed against her..."

Document E

Source: Madison County Historical Society, Oneida, NY.

FUGITIVE SLAVE LAW CONVENTION
Abolitionists gathered in Cazenovia, New York, in August 1850 to consider how to respond to the law recently passed by Congress requiring northern states to return fugitive slaves to their owners. Frederick Douglass is seated just to the left of the table in this photograph of some of the participants. The gathering was unusual among abolitionist gatherings as it included substantial numbers of African Americans.

Document F

Source: Harriet Beecher Stowe's *Uncle Tom's Cabin*, first published as a novel in 1853. [*Annals* VIII: 202.]

"Legree [the overseer]...at last burst forth...

'What! Ye blasted black beast! Tell me ye don't think it right to do what I tell ye! What have any of you cussed cattle to do with thinking what's right? I'll put a stop to it! Why, what do ye think ye are? May be ye think ye're a gentleman, master Tom, to be telling your master what's right and what ain't! So you pretend it's wrong to flog the gal!'

'I think so Mas'r,' said Tom, 'the poor crittur's sick and feeble; 't would be downright cruel, and it's what I never will do, not begin to. Mas'r, if you mean to kill me, kill me; bbut as to my raising my hand agin anyone here, I never shall – I'll die first.'"

Document G

Source: Feminist and editor Margaret Fuller, *Woman in the Nineteenth Century*, 1855.

"We would have every path laid open to Woman as freely as to Man...then will mankind be ripe for this, when inward and outward freedom for Woman as much as for Man shall be acknowledged as a right, not yielded as a concession. As a friend of the Negro assumes that one man cannot by right hold another in bondage, so should the friend of Woman assume that Man cannot by right lay even well meant restrictions on Woman."
[*Annals* VII: 299]

Document H

Source: From an official report to the New York State Legislature on women's rights, 1856. [in Kennedy, *The American Spirit* I:328, from Stanton et al. *History of Woman Suffrage* (1881) I: 629–630.]

"In such case [where husband and wife have both signed the same petition], they [the committee] would recommend the parties to apply for a law authorizing them to change dresses, so that the husband may wear petticoats, and the wife breeches, and thus indicate to their neighbors and the public the true relation in which they stand to each other."

Multiple-Choice Answers

1. a. Romanticism emphasized the goodness of every individual and rejected traditional religious values of original sin.

2. d. Noah Webster's American spelling book was first published in the 1780s before romanticism permeated American culture. His reasoned approach sought a national standard for speech and writing.

3. b. Transcendentalism embraced every individual's ability to find beauty and truth once liberated from obstacles erected by society.

4. d. The Shaker sect was founded and led by a woman, and practiced sexual equality. New members came from outside the community, often orphans or children from poor families.

5. e. Reform movements worked toward two opposite goals: liberation of individuals oppressed by society including slaves and women, and social order in the midst of the chaos created by political, social, and economic developments.

6. c. The Second Great Awakening accepted that all people could be redeemed through good works and acceptance of God as the Savior. The First Great Awakening moved away from Puritan predestination, but placed a much greater emphasis on an all powerful God granting salvation.

7. b. In antebellum America, alcohol was considered the root of all evil by many. Reformers believed it led to abuse of women, the breakdown of families, accidents in the workplace, and all manner of social problems.

8. a. Women were at the forefront of reform in America at this time. They took up the mantle of Republican mothers and extended it to social as well as political America.

9. e. Reformers, and even Andrew Jackson, felt that Indians needed protection from white society. With ever advancing white settlement on Indian lands, the reservation system was to give Indians a protected area in which to develop and then join white society.

10. d. The "Declaration of Sentiments" was modeled on the "Declaration of Independence" but demanded equal rights for men and women.

11. c. Stowe's novel combined the popular sentimental literary style with a political agenda personalizing slaves and slaveholders, and awakened many Americans to slavery's evils.

12. d. Garrison's uncompromising stance on immediate emancipation led him to not only attack slaveholders, but also the United States government and Constitution. His stand prompted violent responses, and the antislavery movement began to divide over what tactics to use.

Free-Response Commentary

1. This question asks you to choose two of the three areas to discuss an emerging American identity. A national culture grew slowly in the early republic, and expanded rapidly in antebellum America. Heroic portraits of the Revolution and Revolutionary leaders gave way to the romantic landscapes of the Hudson River School. In literature, nationalistic histories such as Webster's books on language and Irving's stories were replaced by Emerson, Thoreau, Cooper, Poe, and Whitman, all of whom investigated the democratic individual in an American context.

   Politics became more democratic and the two-party system became established. Increased male suffrage, a more open presidential nominating process, the spoils system, and a fluid social structure helped justify this period as "The Age of the Common Man."

   Religion continued to be deeply embedded in American life. Christian evangelism became a dominant theme, and revivals focused energies on making the world better. Churches prospered and spawned movements for reform. The potential for redemption injected optimism into American life.

   Other aspects to consider might be the divisive role of slavery in politics, and the use of religion to justify both antislavery and proslavery arguments on the national scene.

2. This question provides you the opportunity to consider reform in the sectional context. It appears that the impetus for reform came largely from the Northern tier, especially since abolition was such a prominent movement.

   You can draw out the differences between the Northern and Southern cultures with Northern commerce, industrialism, and urbanization contrasting with rural Southern chivalry and agriculture. Many of the ills reformers wanted to eliminate were in part consequences of industrialism and urbanization, and therefore not as pressing in the Southern states. Also, Southerners avoided the reform ideal of individual liberty, which contradicted the slave labor system. There were exceptions such as the Grimke sisters, but the South was committed to the status quo, so the Southern urge for reform was weak.

Document-Based Question Commentary

The question asks you to consider how successful women were in providing ideas, support, and leadership to achieve the goals of the reform movements. You should take care to address every aspect of the prompt, take a clear position in your thesis, and fully analyze all three categories.

Read the documents carefully and note the subtleties. Document D from asylum movement leader Dix begs *men* to fix the plight of incarcerated women, from which you can infer that she does not hold much power. Fuller, in Document G, acknowledges this. You can also gauge the male attitude toward women in Documents A and H. On the other hand, the photograph of the Frederick Douglass at the Abolitionist Convention displays a number of women on the platform, Dix propelled the asylum movement, and Stowe's novel breathed fresh life into the antislavery movement.

You can develop your argument in a number of ways. You might associate the various movements with women's contributions to assess the success of the movements in achieving their goals. Another strategy would be to categorize the various movements by success and failure and then assess the role of women. Organize your answer to this question in broad terms in order to provide sufficient analysis and evidence to support your thesis.

CHAPTER 13
The Impending Crisis

AP THEMES
- American Diversity: Manifest Destiny and the acquisition of the western reaches of North America infused a Hispanic population and culture into American society.
- Demographic Changes: The addition of new lands furthered the movement of the American population westward. As settlement pushed westward, the geographic center of the American population also moved westward.
- Politics and Citizenship: Manifest Destiny rekindled the issue of the expansion of slavery in the new territories. During the 1850s in particular, the political system broke down as regional political interests overcame national politics.
- War and Diplomacy: The Mexican War had dramatic consequences for the United States by increasing its territory. It also established a pattern of brittle relations with Mexico that continues to the present.

EXAM TIPS
This is a very important period in United States history, and AP exam questions often include information from this chapter. In studying this chapter, you should do the following:
- Understand Manifest Destiny and continental expansion, especially as it relates to the sectional balance achieved in 1820.
- Pay particular attention to the reasons for the breakdown of the party system in the 1860s.
- Focus on the issue of compromise in the Constitution and during the early republic. Reasons for the inability to reach compromise in antebellum America are often found in AP exam questions.
- Think about the events in Kansas and Nebraska during this decade as a rehearsal for the Civil War. The issues, opposing sides, and violence all set the stage for what was to come.

CHAPTER SUMMARY
An uneasy peace in the sectional conflict between the South and the North held until the 1840s, when western expansion and slavery intersected. The nationalism that helped unify the country also inspired territorial growth, and that ultimately tore the nation apart.

Looking Westward
Westward expansion characterized settlement since America's very beginnings. In the 1840s, that movement gained momentum and adopted an ideological justification, known as **Manifest Destiny.** This vision of a territorial empire embodied pride in the American democratic experiment and ideals of social perfection, while it overlooked the displacement and genocide of Native Americans. In 1845, editor **John L. O'Sullivan** called the movement to gain new territory **Manifest Destiny,** and imbued it with a religious sanction; others pointed to the burden of the "American race" to fulfill the democratic promise. The movement grew in the 1840s, partly fueled by the new **"penny press."** Others, such as Henry Clay, feared its consequences because the slavery question would be reopened.

Americans moved into Texas in the 1820s, encouraged by the Mexican government and lured by fertile lands suitable for cotton cultivation. In 1830 there were twice as many Americans as Mexicans in Texas. Missourian **Stephen F. Austin** established the first legal settlement in 1822, and by 1835 there were over 30,000 Americans in Texas. Many of the American settlers were dissatisfied with Mexican rule, and the discontent grew after **General Santa Anna** seized power and attempted to exert more autocratic control over the Mexican provinces. Increasing conflict led American settlers living in Texas to declare independence from Mexico in 1836. The Mexican forces were ruthless in subduing the rebellion and had several military successes including the **Alamo.** However, a force led by **General Sam Houston** captured Santa Anna, defeated his army at the **Battle of San Jacinto** in 1836, and forced Santa Anna to accept an independent Texas. Houston sought annexation by the United States, but Northern politicians, as well as President Andrew Jackson, fearing sectional calamity with the addition of more slave territory, opposed the plan. Texas would remain the independent **Lone Star Republic** until alliances between Texas and European nations spurred Americans to reopen the question in 1844.

The **Oregon Territory,** a vast territory including parts of present-day British Colombia, Oregon, Washington, Idaho, and Montana, had been jointly administered by both the United States and Great Britain since the 1818 **Transcontinental Treaty.** Until the 1820s there was little interest in the area except among fur traders such as **John Jacob Astor.** However, efforts to convert the Indians and counteract Canada's Catholic influence attracted American evangelicals. Two of the most famous missionaries were **Narcissa** and **Marcus Whitman,** whose efforts were largely unsuccessful; they were killed by hostile Indians in 1847. However, by the 1840s numerous settlements had been established and many urged America to take possession of Oregon.

Migration happened in waves and generally in times of economic prosperity. Settlers moved west for a variety of reasons, but many hoped for economic advancement. Southerners went to Texas, but most western migrants came from the **Old Northwest,** and some had moved several times before settling permanently in the West. The main westward route was the 2,000-mile **Oregon Trail** from Independence, Missouri, to either California or the Oregon coast. Over 300,000 traveled the trails between 1840 and 1860. Contrary to myth and belief, Indians were more helpful than harmful to those on the trail, and despite its hardships, the death rate was not much higher than in the United States as a whole. Most migrated in family groups and attempted to re-create patterns of life that they left on the trail. Women not only walked much of the day, they also were responsible for domestic tasks when the travel day ended. Overland travel was a collective experience, with families and often communities moving together.

Expansion and War

Pressure from the increasing number of white settlers west of the Mississippi eventually pushed America to war with Mexico. The main issue of the election of 1844 was expansion, and the Democrat **James K. Polk** ran on that platform against Whig **Henry Clay.** By combining the annexation of Texas and Oregon under one umbrella, Polk hoped to attract both Northerners and Southerners, and he won the election. By the time Polk took office Congress had already approved the annexation of Texas. Polk proposed that Oregon be divided along the 49th parallel. When Britain rejected his offer America considered a military solution as expressed in the slogan **"Fifty-four forty or fight!"** Neither country wanted war, so Britain accepted Polk's terms in 1846.

Tensions were developing over the boundary with Mexico in the wake of the Texas annexation. Mexico had broken diplomatic ties with Washington after annexation and claimed the Nueces River as the boundary of Texas. America claimed more territory with Rio Grande as the boundary. Polk sent a small army commanded by **General Zachary Taylor** to defend Texas. Polk was also interested in the Mexican provinces of New Mexico and California; both areas had substantial populations of white settlers. Polk sent secret instructions to seize those territories if war should break out.

Having made preparations for war, Polk sent envoy **John Slidell** to arrange for a purchase of the territories. When Mexico rejected the offer, Polk ordered troops across the Nueces River to the Rio Grande. Although it is not clear what actually happened, the United States claimed that Mexico attacked the American troops, and in 1846, Congress declared war. There was considerable opposition to the war, which mounted alongside costs and casualties. An American force under **General Winfield Scott** captured Mexico City, the government fell, and a new government expressed a willingness to negotiate. In New Mexico **Stephen W. Kearny** captured Santa Fe and California. In 1848 Congress ratified the **Treaty of Guadalupe Hidalgo** in which Mexico ceded California and New Mexico to the United States and accepted the Rio Grande as the border of Texas. The United States agreed to pay Mexico $15 million and accept any financial claims settlers held against the Mexican government. The vast new territory held great promise but also created some troubling issues for the United States.

The Sectional Debate

Polk accomplished his goals of expanding United States territory; however, each section of the country came to believe he did so to its detriment. In 1846, with the Mexican War raging, Pennsylvanian **David Wilmot** proposed the prohibition of slavery from any territory that was acquired from Mexico. The **Wilmot Proviso** was countered by other proposals regarding slavery, such as extending the **Missouri Compromise Line t**o the West Coast or **squatter** or **popular sovereignty,** a plan to allow the residents of each territory to decide for themselves the issue of slavery. The election of 1848 produced the **Free Soil Party,** which supported the Wilmot Proviso. Military hero and Whig **Zachary Taylor** won a narrow victory, but the existence of this new party signaled the inability of the existing party system to deal with the issue of slavery.

The discovery of gold in California at **Sutter's Mill** in 1848 started a migration that increased California's population from 14,000 to over 220,000 in slightly less than four years. Overwhelmingly male and ambitious, the **forty-niners** created a volatile society. The lure of gold drew people from China, Europe, South America, and Mexico to California. Although relatively few found fortunes in the gold fields, many remained in California on farms and in cities, and this sharpened the national crisis over slavery. President Taylor saw statehood as the answer to the question of slavery in the territories and pushed for California to be admitted to the Union as a free state in 1849; he also suggested that New Mexico also should decide its status and become a state. At the same time other sectional issues clouded the horizon. Antislavery efforts to abolish slavery in Washington as well as Northern **personal liberty laws** prompted opposition from slavery forces, which called for stricter legal guarantees for the return of fugitive slaves. Southern fears about the growing number of free states creating an imbalance in the Senate were foremost, and some Southern leaders began to consider **secession** as a solution.

National leaders worked to craft a compromise to address several issues arising from the bid for California's statehood in 1849 and 1850. Henry Clay proposed an **omnibus bill** that included the admission of **California** as a free state, the creation of territorial governments in the other lands acquired from Mexico with no restrictions on slavery, the abolition of the slave trade—but not slavery—in Washington, and a more stringent fugitive slave law. A prolonged debate followed, ending with the defeat of the omnibus bill. New leaders stepped in, and employing both pragmatism and self-interest were able to achieve a compromise. Upon the death of **President Taylor,** who opposed the measures, **Senator Stephen A. Douglas** from Illinois proposed each of Clay's measures separately and crafted a series of deals that secured passage of each. Unlike the **Missouri Compromise** twenty years earlier, the **Compromise of 1850** was not based on common national ideals, but in sectional self-interest, and was therefore not long-lived.

The Crises of the 1850s

An uneasy sectional truce amid economic prosperity descended upon the nation after 1850, but conflict emerged again in the 1852 election. Democrat **Franklin Pierce** won mainly because antislavery Whigs defected to the **Free Soil Party.** In office Pierce stood aside and avoided the slavery issue while Northerners attempted to prevent the enforcement of the fugitive slave law and alarmed Southerners saw their positions in the Compromise of 1850 erode. Hoping to divert attention from domestic controversy, Pierce looked to expand American ideals and influence abroad. A proposal to annex Cuba by force outlined in the **Ostend Manifesto** and an attempt to annex Hawaii both fell to defeat at the hands of antislavery and proslavery forces in 1854.

The issue of slavery in the territories became connected to the route for a transcontinental railroad. Northerners and Southerners both pushed for the eastern terminus in their respective sections, and diplomat **James Gadsden** acquired land from Mexico suitable for a southern route. Senator Stephen A. Douglas of Illinois was vying for the railroad hub to be in Chicago. He proposed a bill to organize the Nebraska territory to the west and allow the slavery question to be decided by the territorial legislature, or **"popular sovereignty."** To gain Southern support he amended the bill to include a repeal of the Missouri Compromise and the division of Nebraska into two territories, Nebraska and Kansas. Called the **Kansas-Nebraska Act,** it became law in 1854 with the support of all Southerners and Northern Democrats. However, this act had disastrous consequences for the party system. The Democrats were badly divided along sectional lines, and the Whig Party had all but disappeared by 1856. In addition the Kansas-Nebraska Act prompted the creation of the **Republican Party,** which rested entirely on Northern support. The Republican Party gained significant support in the 1854 election.

Upon passage of the Kansas-Nebraska Act both pro- and antislavery settlers poured into Kansas. Proslavery forces formed a majority in the legislature and legalized slavery. Antislavery settlers met at Topeka, adopted a constitution prohibiting slavery, and applied for statehood. These settlers moved to Lawrence, and several months later, proslavery forces attacked and sacked the town. In retaliation, an ardent abolitionist **John Brown** murdered five proslavery settlers at **Pottawatomie Creek,** and civil war erupted in **"Bleeding Kansas."** Violence was not limited to Kansas. Abolitionist Senator **Charles Sumner** was attacked on the floor of the United States Senate by South Carolinian **Preston Brooks** after Sumner made a vicious speech, **"The Crime Against Kansas."** Both Sumner and Brooks became heroes in their respective sections of the country.

The root of the sectional hostility lay in deep economic and territorial differences of the American vision. The North embraced a "free soil" and "free labor" ideology in which all citizens would have the opportunity to control their labor and property. It claimed that slavery hurt all involved by denying both democracy and opportunity and that the Southern aristocratic society was stagnant and rejected progress. In the Northern mind, a Southern conspiracy existed to expand slavery and close avenues to opportunity. Republicans adhered to these principles and to a strong and powerful union.

Southern response tended to focus on slavery as a "peculiar institution," by which they meant to emphasize the paternalistic aspects of the institution. Beginning in 1832, **Thomas Dew** proclaimed slavery as a **"positive good"** rather than the earlier apology of it as a **"necessary evil."** It put slaves in a better position than Northern **"wage slaves"** and was a system in which the two races could live together in peace. Even more central was slavery's role as the basis for the orderly and civilized Southern way of life. In this view biologically inferior slaves fit in a hierarchical social order that provided security for all.

The presidential election of 1856 took place in the turmoil of this sectional discontent. Multiple candidates again divided the electorate. Democrat **James Buchanan** of Pennsylvania won a close contest, defeating Republican **John C. Fremont,** who opposed the Kansas-Nebraska Act and the expansion of slavery in the territories but supported internal improvements, and **Know Nothing** candidate **Millard Fillmore.** Buchanan proved to be a weak and indecisive president. He was plagued by an economic depression throughout his term of office. The Supreme Court enflamed sectional conflict when in 1857 the Court issued its decision in *Dred Scott v. Sanford.* Scott, a slave taken to free territories, sued for his freedom, arguing that residence in a free state liberated him from slavery. Scott who was once owned by an army surgeon had been taken from Missouri to Illinois and then into Wisconsin, which prohibited slavery. The Court, headed by **Roger Taney** of Maryland, decided that blacks were not citizens and had no right to sue in the courts. Further, the Court declared that Congress had no authority to deprive citizens of slave property and therefore the Missouri Compromise was unconstitutional. The case proved a spectacular victory for proslavery advocates. Tensions in Kansas continued to simmer, and Buchanan endorsed Kansas's admission as a slave state. Slavery was legal under the **Lecompton Constitution,** but Kansas voters had twice rejected this constitution. Kansas entered the Union in 1861 as a free state, after the Civil War had begun.

In 1858 the senate campaign between Democrat **Stephen A. Douglas** and Republican **Abraham Lincoln** placed both candidates in the national spotlight. Douglas was already a national figure, and even though Lincoln lost the contest, Lincoln's fame spread as a result. The two engaged in a series of **debates** that centered on the issue of slavery. Douglas took no moral stand on slavery and maintained the position of popular sovereignty for slavery in the territories. Lincoln argued that he was not an abolitionist but that he opposed slavery's expansion into the territories. According to Lincoln, American democratic principles rested on the principle of free labor.

John Brown's raid on **Harper's Ferry,** Virginia, hardened lines between the sections to the breaking point. The fanatic abolitionist overpowered the arsenal there, planning to arm slaves and lead a rebellion. His plan was thwarted by troops under the command of **Robert E. Lee.** Brown, along with six of his followers, was executed for treason. His actions provided positive proof to Southerners that there was a Northern conspiracy afoot to end slavery.

The presidential election of 1860 again demonstrated the continuing breakdown of the political party system in America. After several attempts and two conventions, the Democrats nominated two candidates: Northerners chose Stephen Douglas of Illinois and Southerners chose **John C. Breckenridge** of Kentucky. Conservative former Whigs nominated Tennessee's **John Bell,** putting Union above all else, and Republicans nominated Lincoln with a platform supporting measures to gain as wide a base as possible but opposing the expansion of slavery in the territories. In 1860 Lincoln won a majority in the electoral college but only 40 percent of the popular vote, all from Northern states. The message to many Southerners was unmistakable, and very soon after the election, the process of disunion began.

The strong forces promoting nationalism throughout the nineteenth century were eventually eclipsed by the central issue of slavery. Although slavery was essentially an economic issue, it became a social, moral, and political issue. When parties no longer had national constituencies or consensus, the political system broke down. Each section came to consider the other the enemy, and national unity collapsed.

Multiple-Choice Questions

1. Texas fought for its independence from Mexico because
   a. Mexico no longer wanted a territory largely peopled by United States exiles.
   b. settlers there claimed Texas was part of the Louisiana Purchase.
   c. Mexico's government tried to impose stricter control over its provinces in the 1830s.
   d. a state of civil war existed between American settlers and native Mexicans in Texas.
   e. Mexico wanted to legalize slavery in Texas.

2. John Jacob Astor's main business on the Northwest Pacific coast involved
   a. lumbering the vast forests.
   b. fur trapping and trading.
   c. fishing in the Northwest Pacific waters.
   d. trading cattle hides with the resident Spanish settlers.
   e. trading with the Russians who migrated from Alaska.

3. Some Americans were opposed to the Mexican War because
   a. pacifism was growing in the United States throughout the nineteenth century.
   b. they claimed Polk deliberately had staged circumstances to start conflict.
   c. they believed it would not further the cause of Manifest Destiny.
   d. America was already at war with England over Oregon.
   e. they did not think the massacre at the Alamo was a good reason to fight.

4. The Wilmot Proviso was continually defeated because
   a. Southern senators opposed its slavery prohibition as against their section's interests.
   b. many opposed its provision to extend the Missouri Compromise line to the West Coast.
   c. its provision for popular sovereignty in new territories angered Northerners.
   d. it did not deal with the issue of slavery in the territories.
   e. Northerners objected to its provisions for lower tariff rates.

5. All of the following characterized California during the gold rush except
   a. its population expanded dramatically from 1848 to 1852. ✓

b. the first Chinese immigrants were attracted to the United States. ✓
c. most immigrants gained wealth from finding gold.
d. immigrants included black and white Americans, Europeans, South Americans, and Mexicans.
e. the Native American population declined dramatically in the two decades following the discovery of gold.

6. The Compromise of 1850 and the Missouri Compromise were alike in that both
   a. maintained an equal balance of slave and free states in the Senate.
   b. designated territories open to slavery.
   c. strengthened the federal laws to return fugitive slaves.
   d. adopted popular sovereignty to determine slavery in the territories.
   e. settled sectional strife over slavery for a period of time.

7. The Young America movement
   a. supported the ideology underlying the Revolutions of 1848 in Europe.
   b. opposed the American acquisition of Cuba.
   c. supported expansion of slavery in the territories.
   d. opposed expansion of slavery in the territories.
   e. opposed the acquisition of Canada.

8. John Brown's actions in Kansas and Harper's Ferry
   a. convinced the North that abolition was a cause worthy of its wholehearted support.
   b. pushed the North to declare war on the seceding states.
   c. provided a reason for Harriet Beecher Stowe to write Uncle Tom's Cabin.
   d. offered proof to the South that an antislavery conspiracy existed.
   e. brought the country together in search of a compromise.

9. Democrat Franklin Pierce won the election of 1852 following a strategy of
   a. endorsing no expansion of slavery in the territories.
   b. repudiating the Compromise of 1850.
   c. avoiding the issue of slavery as much as possible.
   d. attacking Whigs as being slavery supporters.
   e. promoting defiance of the fugitive slave law in New Hampshire.

10. In the election of 1856, the Republican Party's platform included
    a. support for the Kansas proslavery petition for statehood.
    b. popular sovereignty in the territories.
    c. internal improvements and repudiation of the Kansas-Nebraska Act.
    d. an end to immigration and foreign influence in America.
    e. an expansion of the Missouri Compromise line to the Pacific.

11. The South believed that a Northern conspiracy to overwhelm the South politically and economically existed for all of the following reasons except
    a. John Brown's raid on Harper's Ferry. ✓
    b. the violent conflict in Kansas between the competing constitutions. ✓
    c. efforts to impose protective tariffs.
    d. personal liberty laws to inhibit the return of fugitive slaves.
    e. the decision in the Dred Scott case.

12. Using the information from the accompanying map, one could conclude which of the following about the election of 1860?

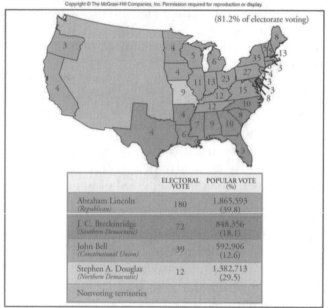

	ELECTORAL VOTE	POPULAR VOTE (%)
Abraham Lincoln (Republican)	180	1,865,593 (39.8)
J. C. Breckinridge (Southern Democratic)	72	848,356 (18.1)
John Bell (Constitutional Union)	39	592,906 (12.6)
Stephen A. Douglas (Northern Democratic)	12	1,382,713 (29.5)
Nonvoting territories		

a. Abraham Lincoln received a clear majority of both the popular and electoral vote.
b. The four candidates split the vote so the election was decided in the House of Representatives.
c. Abraham Lincoln received the greatest number of popular votes and thus won the election.
d. The vote for president divided along clear sectional lines.
e. Douglas carried Missouri because it was his home state.

Free-Response Questions

1. Describe the events relating to conflict over states' rights in TWO of the following periods listed. Analyze both issues and ideology in the periods you choose.
   • 1795–1815
   • 1820–1840 oregon - Texas
   • 1841–1861 kansas- nebraska , Lincoln's election

2. Compare and contrast Northern and Southern culture and economy in the three decades before the Civil War.

Document-Based Question

The following documents come from newspapers in the immediate aftermath of the caning of Massachusetts senator Charles Sumner on the Senate floor by South Carolina congressman Preston Brooks.

Use the editorials to analyze the breakdown of the political parties over the 1850s.

Document A

> *Source:* Charleston, South Carolina, *Mercury* [Democratic], (28 May 1856).
>
> As soon as the last lady had left the hall, Col. BROOKS went up to Mr. SUMNER, and facing him, said: "Mr. SUMNER, I have read your speech with great care, and all the impartiality in my power, and I have come to tell you that you have libelled my State, and slandered my relative, who is old and absent, and I deem it my duty to punish you, which I shall now proceed to do." Col. BROOKS thereupon struck Mr. SUMNER, who was rising, across the face with a gutta percha cane. He continued repeating the blows until Mr. SUMNER fell upon the floor, crying out for help. Col. BROOKS then desisted voluntarily, saying, "I did not wish to hurt him much, but only punish him." . . . SUMNER was well and elegantly whipped, and he richly deserved it. Senator TOOMBS, of Georgia, who was in the midst of it, said, "BROOKS, you have done the right thing, and in the right place." Gallant old Governor FITZPATRICK, of Alabama, who was in the midst of it, warmly sustained BROOKS also. . . . The whole South sustains BROOKS, and a large part of the North also. All feel that it is time for freedom of speech and freedom of the cudgel to go together.

Document B

> *Source:* Concord, New Hampshire, *New Hampshire Patriot* [Democratic], (28 May 1856).
>
> This assault will find no apologists among our people, as it has no justification. It meets, as it merits, the most unqualified reprehension, and deserves the severest punishment. We regard it as utterly disgraceful, a gross outrage, and we regret and condemn it as sincerely as any of the political friends of Mr. S. can do; even the malignant slander of an aged and absent relative, and the most insulting libel upon his State, do not justify the assailant. . . . But while we say and feel this, we must also say that Sumner's speech was of such a character as to provoke the result which has followed, and it seems to have been designed for that purpose. It was a most biting, and insulting tirade of personality, filled with the most wanton and malignant vituperation of men of the purest character, abounding in absolute vulgarity of invective and indecency of epithet and accusation against the conduct and motives and character of his opponents, imputing to them again and again the total want of veracity and honor; as well as utter ignorance and imbecility; all carefully prepared, and written out beforehand, thus showing a deliberate malignancy and settled purpose to insult, degrade and irritate his antagonists as much as possible.

Document C

> *Source:* Nashville, Tennessee, *Republican Banner and Nashville Whig* [American], (27 May 1856).
>
> His assault upon Mr. S., a member of the Senate, upon the floor of the Senate, was a great outrage upon that body, and cannot be justified or excused. As to Mr. Sumner, no Southern reader of his speech will be likely to feel any sympathy for him personally. But that circumstances should not prevent Southern men of all parties from raising their voices in strong and earnest rebuke and condemnation of the desecration, by such brutality, of the Halls of the National Legislature. The effect abroad of this occurrence can not fail to be deeply injurious to our national character. At home—in the non-slave-holding States—the effect will be to cause Mr. Sumner to be looked upon with increased consideration, and to strengthen the party to which he belongs. . . .

Document D

Source: Boston, Massachusetts, *Courier* [Whig], (23 May 1856).

. . . The speech of Mr. Sumner was exceedingly insulting towards some gentlemen who sit with him upon the Senate floor. It was not in consonance with the sort of arguments which people expect to hear from U.S. Senators upon a grave question. They do not want flowery adjectives or far-fetched allusions to, or illustrations from Greece and Rome, to give them an opinion as to how they shall act with regard to a practical question which is now before them. . . . We offer no palliation for the brutal assault which was made upon Mr. Sumner by a Representative from South Carolina. It is a well understood axiom and rule of the United States Congress, that no member shall be allowed to be held responsible for words spoken in debate. The member from South Carolina transgressed every rule of honor which should animate or restrain one gentleman in his connections with another, in his ruffian assault upon Mr. Sumner. There is no chivalry in a brute. There is no manliness in a scoundrel. If Mr. Brooks is a nephew to Senator Butler, as it is said that he is, the Senator has only cause to regret that his blood runs through such ignoble veins.

Document E

Source: Albany, New York, *Evening Journal* [Republican], (24 May 1856).

"Mr. Sumner, I have read your speech twice. It is a libel on South Carolina, and Mr. Butler, who is a relative of mine." . . . Charles Sumner did not libel South Carolina. Representing Massachusetts which furnished to the Revolutionary War 83,092 Continental troops and Militia, against 5,508(!) from South Carolina, it was suitable that in repelling the stale assumptions in behalf of the latter State and her sister Slave-labor communities, that Republican liberty was won by the arms and treasure, by the patriotism and good faith of the South, he should tell the truth as it is in the keeping of History. The record of the Revolutionary Struggle shows that South Carolina's Slavery, weakened South Carolina, so that she was a drag upon the fight not only, but a perpetual point of danger to the common cause, – a constantly open gate-way for invasion and general disaster. Then as now she held a foe in her bosom, which crippled her capacity for offensive war, and weakened her powers of defensive action – a foe dangerous to the Union, in its exceeding dangerousness to an assailable member of the Union.

Multiple-Choice Answers

1. c. Texas was a Mexican province settled by many United States migrants. Mexico's stricter policy inspired rebellion.

2. b. Astor's fur interests were centered at the mouth of the Columbia River.

3. b. Whig opponents of Polk claimed he staged the circumstances that led to war.

4. a. The Proviso contained provisions prohibiting slavery from any territories acquired from Mexico.

5. c. Most wealth resulted from commerce related to the gold rush, not from the gold itself.

6. b. Both Compromises permitted slavery in certain territories if the territories allowed it.

7. a. The Young America movement supported republican ideals and ideology beyond American borders. It took no position on slavery but supported expansion.

8. d. Brown's actions confirmed Southern fears that the North was actively working to overturn its slave economy and culture.

9. c. Pierce tried to maintain national unity by avoiding discussion of politically contentious issues in 1852.

10. c. The Republican platform combined antislavery sentiments with economic nationalism.

11. e. The Dred Scott decision was a victory for proslavery forces.

12. d. Only non-slave states voted Republican in 1860, and all were in the Northern United States or on the West Coast.

Free-Response Questions Commentary

1. This question asks you to describe events related to states' rights in the context of the issues and ideology in two of the three time periods listed. Your answer should include specific events, and a balanced discussion including the issues and political ideology on both sides of the conflict.

   The first period, 1795 to 1815, contains several events, the two most prominent being the Alien and Sedition Acts and the Hartford Convention. Analyzing the first appearance of the Nullification Doctrine in the Virginia and Kentucky Resolutions is a critical piece. You might comment on the Missouri Compromise and the tariff crisis in South Carolina in the second time period, and argue a sectional divide growing over the use of the Nullification Doctrine. The last period includes Manifest Destiny, the 1850s, and the election of Lincoln. The 1850s exhibited a growing attachment to the states' rights doctrine in Southern states and their use of it after the election of Lincoln in 1860 to support their claims to a right of secession

   Provide balance between the two time periods you choose in your answer, and be sure to analyze the events in terms of political thought and how the specific issues fit into the states' rights debate. One line of argument to take might be to comment on increasing divisions as the Nullification Doctrine and slavery became the overriding national issues.

2. This is a straightforward compare-and-contrast question looking at sectional culture and economics between 1830 and 1860. One way to look at this could be to use the Northern and Southern defenses for their respective way of life in contrast to the other. For example, use the Southern defense of slavery, which ultimately argued for the slave system as a "positive good," and combine the plantation economy with Southern culture; Southerners labeled the Northern labor system as "wage slavery." For Northerners, a commercial economy with free labor and independent "yeoman" farmers created an ideal of liberty and productivity. Balance between the economy and culture and between the North and the South will be important in your answer.

Document-Based Question Commentary

These five editorials were written in the immediate aftermath of representative Preston Brooks' assault with a cane on Senator Charles Sumner in May 1856. It fits into a chronology of events that increasingly hardened sectional lines and tensions. These editorials express both a political and regional point of view, and display some signs that parties and sections were unable to find common ground. Pay particular attention to the language used, and the ways in which different editors evaluate the speech of Sumner and the consequent action of Brooks. Consider how you might use these documents to analyze the role of politics leading to disunion four years later.

CHAPTER 14
The Civil War

AP THEMES

* **Globalization:** It is useful to view this war to preserve the Union as part of a larger global trend to consolidate and centralize nation-states. This also occurred in Europe, Russia, and Japan.
* **Politics and Citizenship:** Lincoln was a masterful political leader, perhaps America's greatest president. His use and some abuse of federal power and his conception of democracy as expressed in his "Gettysburg Address" have helped define modern America.
* **Slavery and Its Legacies:** The Civil War ended slavery in America. It is also important to note the active role that slaves themselves took to ensure that outcome, both in the Union and the Confederacy.
* **War and Diplomacy:** The Civil War had an extraordinary impact on all aspects of American life. The Union victory put an end to the question of federal supremacy and an end to slavery, although a caste system based on race remained.

CHAPTER SUMMARY

The election of 1860 signaled the breakdown of the American political system. It also indicated to many that two very different visions of America separated the South from the North. In an effort to resolve the issue of slavery in the territories, the federal government was no longer a benign and unobtrusive force, and the two-party system, once a force for compromise, led to deeper division. Regionalism overwhelmed nationalism, and Civil War followed.

The Secession Crisis

Before Lincoln took office seven slave states had seceded, led by South Carolina in December 1860. In February they met at Montgomery, Alabama, and formed the Confederate States of America. President Buchanan continued to be indecisive. He claimed that no state had the right to withdraw but assumed no authority to force states to remain in the Union. Congress sought a compromise to avert a crisis. Kentucky senator **John Crittenden** proposed several constitutional amendments guaranteeing slavery's right to exist, the return of fugitive slaves, and slavery in Washington, D.C., and also proposed extending the Missouri Compromise line in the territories. Southerners appeared willing to consider the **Crittenden Compromise,** but Republicans would not abandon their opposition to slavery's expansion. Lincoln's inaugural address laid out his position that the Constitution did not sanction secession and that any state attempting to do so was in rebellion.

The seceding states seized federal properties within their boundaries with the exception of offshore forts. **Fort Sumter** in Charleston Harbor, South Carolina, was running low on supplies. Lincoln declared his intention of re-supplying the Fort, and the Confederacy decided to take it by force. After two days of bombardment from the shore, the Union forces surrendered.

With the Civil War now underway, four more states seceded; however, four **border states,** Maryland, Delaware, Kentucky, and Missouri, remained in the Union under intense pressure from Washington. With the fighting intensifying and Americans believing that two distinct cultures had developed within the United States, Lincoln had little choice but to fight on to preserve the Union.

From the beginning of the war, it appeared that the North had important advantages in the contest. The Union had twice the population of the South, a developing industrial economy, and an integrated transportation system joined by railroads. However lacking in material advantages, the Confederacy was fighting for a cause in which it believed and was fighting a defensive war on its own soil amidst a friendly population. It also had hopes that both England and France would come to its aid to protect their textile industries' supply of American cotton.

The Mobilization of the North

With little political opposition in Congress after secession, both industry and agriculture enjoyed wartime prosperity under a Republican administration. With Lincoln's blessing the Republican Congress enacted its nationalistic economic program. In the West, the **Homestead Act** (1862) promoted western settlement on free soil, and the **Morrill Land Grant Act** (1862) created land grants to subsidize public education. **Protective tariffs** supported Northern industry, a **transcontinental railroad** was chartered with substantial **federal subsidies** of land grants and loans, and **National Bank Acts** (1863–1864) established a national banking system with a stable currency. Congress paid for the war through taxes, printing money, and borrowing. New taxes on goods and services and an income tax paid for only a small part of wartime expenses. Paper currency, or **greenbacks,** was not backed by specie, and the government used this infrequently, issuing only $450 million, but enough to cause high inflation. The war was primarily funded by loans, which finally totaled $2.6 billion.

The United States regular army numbered 16,000 troops in 1861 and eventually more than 2 million men served in the armed forces. Volunteers satisfied military needs for only a short time and the Union resorted to a draft in 1863. A man could provide a substitute or pay $300 to avoid service. Americans were unaccustomed to such an intrusive government and opposition to the draft was strong. Four days of rioting erupted in New York City, with Irish workers attacking blacks, believing them to be a cause of the war and the draft. Over 100 people died.

Only recently catapulted on to the national scene, Lincoln acted quickly to establish his authority. His cabinet reflected a broad range of Republican and Northern views, and Lincoln did not hesitate to use the powers of his office to preserve the Union. That goal was so important that at times he ignored the Constitution. He committed troops without a declaration of war and blockaded the Confederacy without congressional approval. To stem political opposition to the war, he suspended habeas corpus and arrested civilians. Two prominent opposition leaders who were arrested were Ohio congressman **Clement L. Vallandigham** and Maryland citizen **John Merryman.** Lincoln ignored the Supreme Court order to release Merryman.

Republicans lost some ground in the 1862 congressional elections, so there was significant uncertainty among Republicans as the election of 1864 approached. In an attempt to gain more popular support, Republicans created a new party, the **Union Party,** and nominated Lincoln as president and unionist Tennessee Democrat **Andrew Johnson** as vice president. General **George McClellan,** who had been relieved of his command by Lincoln, was the opposing Democratic candidate, although McClellan did not support negotiating a peace, which was a plank in the Democratic Party platform. Timely Northern victories, particularly the capture of Atlanta, turned the tide for Lincoln.

Although slavery had appeared to be a major cause of the war, it was secondary to preserving the Union. As war progressed it became apparent that, in order to save the Union, slavery must be abolished. Radicals such as **Thaddeus Stevens** of Pennsylvania, **Charles Sumner** of Massachusetts, and **Benjamin Wade** of Ohio wanted abolition to be a war goal. Lincoln was cautious and slowly embraced emancipation as the war continued. **Confiscation Acts** had freed slaves, and in 1862 Congress authorized Lincoln to use African Americans as soldiers. After the Union victory at Antietam in 1862, Lincoln issued the preliminary **Emancipation Proclamation,** declaring all slaves in rebellious states free as of January 1, 1863. This expansion of war aims breathed new life into the battle, even if few slaves were immediately freed as a result.

After the **Emancipation Proclamation** was issued, the number of blacks in the Union army increased quickly. About 186,000 African Americans served in a variety of roles, with most doing menial tasks supporting the white troops. Ironically, black mortality exceeded that of whites because of their work in unsanitary conditions behind the lines. The **Fifty-fourth Massachusetts Regiment** was an exception, but it suffered severe casualties in 1863. Paid less than whites and at greater risk if captured, discrimination haunted even those African Americans serving their country.

Wartime demand for industrial goods spurred economic growth in the North. Coal production rose, railroads improved and adopted the **standard gauge,** and farmers mechanized to compensate for labor shortages. Northern prices rose 70 percent while wages increased only 40 percent, so workers' standard of living declined. Immigrant labor and increased mechanization conspired to keep wages low.

War has a revolutionary effect on certain groups, and the Civil War provided new roles for women in teaching, retail sales, offices, factories, and particularly in nursing. **Dorothea Dix** headed the **U.S. Sanitary Commission a**nd organized women to work in hospitals, formerly occupations occupied by males. **Clara Barton** helped provide supplies to hospitals and went on to help found the **Red Cross.** Women came to be accepted in the nursing profession, and increased sanitation in medical procedures helped lower mortality due to disease, although unsanitary conditions still caused more deaths than combat. Other women worked to link emancipation and the women's suffrage movement, with little success.

The Mobilization of the South

Ironically, as the war progressed similarities between the United States and the Confederacy emerged that made the very real differences less evident. The Confederate Constitution was patterned on the Federal Constitution, but it guaranteed state sovereignty and slavery's right to exist. Mississippi's **Jefferson Davis** was president, and Georgia's **Alexander Stephens** was vice president; they held six-year terms. Like the Union, this government was dominated by western leaders. Despite the raucous support for secession, there was much dissention and disagreement within confederate politics. Jefferson Davis was never able to provide the necessary leadership to rally the country wholeheartedly behind the cause.

Securing financing for the Southern war effort proved impossible. With little specie and few liquid assets, the Confederate government relied heavily on printing paper money, which resulted in runaway **inflation** of 9,000 percent. Operating in an antiauthoritarian environment, the government instituted an income tax in 1863 that produced little revenue, and after the initial enthusiasm of Confederate nationalism and early military victories, few lent money to support the war. Finding men to fight also was a chore. Volunteers dropped off in late 1861, and the government enacted a **Conscription Act** the following year. The Conscription Act drafted white men between the age of 18 and 35 for three years of service. Exemptions and the ability to provide substitutes created class conflict. Desertions increased in 1864 and 1865, and the Conscription Act was broadened to include both young boys and old men. At the very end, the Confederate Congress renounced its founding principles by authorizing the conscription of black troops, but the war ended before this was enacted.

Perhaps the South's greatest weakness was the contradiction caused by its states' rights ideology. While the South attempted to create a centralized government, the doctrine of states' rights resisted centralization at every point. The kind of centralization necessary to win the war—taxation, conscription, seizing food, impressing slaves, government control of transportation, regulating industry, and limiting profits—made the Confederacy look suspiciously like the nation it had broken away from.

The Southern economy was devastated by the war. Cut off from northern and European markets, and deprived of its labor force, production declined by one-third. With nearly all the fighting taking place on Confederate soil, agriculture, industry, and infrastructure were destroyed. With its economic concentration in cotton, the South was never able to feed itself, and shortages appeared in all sectors. **Food riots** in major cities, and overt resistance to Confederate military and economic policy led to social instability. However, in the midst of the suffering, the war transformed society. Many women—now working and controlling households and plantations, teaching, nursing, and working in the government bureaucracy—began to question the assumption of a woman's restricted domestic sphere. In addition, a gender imbalance created by wartime casualties expanded the economic and social roles for women. Instability also provided opportunities for slaves. Many sought freedom behind Union lines; those who remained could resist authority more easily with male masters away.

Strategy and Diplomacy

The war posed different circumstances for the two sides. The Union had to take the military initiative to defeat the Confederacy while the diplomatic initiative lay with the South. Lincoln succeeded as a military commander because he realized and used the North's material advantage and was eventually able to combine this advantage with good military strategy. He targeted the Confederate armies and resources rather than territory, although it took him three years to find a commander who agreed with him. That commander was **Ulysses S. Grant.** Confederate president **Jefferson Davis** was a trained soldier who relied on General **Robert E. Lee** to command the forces in the field. This system of command never worked well for the Confederacy.

Sea power played an important role in the war, and the Union had the overwhelming advantage. Its **blockade** of the Southern ports grew in effectiveness as the war progressed, and its support of military operations was particularly important in the western river systems. Southern attempts to break the blockade ended in failure. The **ironclad** *Merrimac* (renamed *Virginia*) was neutralized by the Union ironclad *Monitor.* Other innovations such as torpedo boats and submarines did not play a major role in the Civil War.

Other than not losing on the battlefield, the Confederacy's most important task was to gain the diplomatic recognition of European nations, particularly England and France. Although there was some sympathy for the Southern cause in those nations, as well as an aversion to the growing economic power of the United States, strong antislavery sentiment in England squashed any moves to recognize the Confederacy as an independent nation. Two events threatened to drive a wedge between the Union and England. In 1861 a United States naval vessel stopped the British ship *Trent* and arrested two Confederate officials. Britain protested, and Lincoln eventually apologized and released the Confederates. More significant was the sale of six British ships designed to destroy commerce to the Confederacy. The most famous was the *Alabama.* Claims against Britain continued after the war ended.

The Course of Battle

New battlefield tactics, military strategies, and technology conspired to make the Civil War the deadliest in American history. **Repeating rifles** and improved artillery forced commanders to abandon fighting in static formations, and the armies resorted to elaborate fortifications to protect soldiers from more effective enemy fire. Armies also adapted civilian technologies to warfare. Hot air balloons were used for surveillance, railroads transported the large armies and supplies, and the telegraph improved communication between commanders.

After **Fort Sumter** fell in April, there was a lull as each side prepared and waited to see what the other would do. The first pitched battle took place at **Manassas (Bull Run)** in Northern Virginia. The Union retreat deflated Northern morale and dispelled the notion that the war would end quickly. Union forces boasted no significant victories in the East during the first year of fighting, but they had more success in the West. In early 1862 a fleet under the command of **David Farragut** captured **New Orleans,** closing the Mississippi to Confederate trade. Forces under the command of **Ulysses S. Grant** forced the Confederate troops out of Kentucky and western Tennessee. Grant then moved along the Tennessee River to **Shiloh,** where his army forced the enemy to withdraw. Union armies then controlled important rail centers and had control of the Mississippi south to Memphis.

In the East Union forces were less successful. **George McClellan** was reluctant to commit his forces to battle, and in the spring of 1862 he devised a strategy to attack Richmond by a roundabout route known as the **Peninsular Campaign.** He encountered forces led by **Robert E. Lee** and **Thomas "Stonewall" Jackson.** Lee's forces routed a Union army at the **Second Battle of Bull Run,** and then moved north in to Maryland. McClellan's army met him at **Antietam** in September. Lee's northern advance was stopped in the deadliest single day of the war. McClellan's caution may have cost him the decisive advantage and Lincoln removed him from command.

The year of 1863 proved to be the year that the tide turned in favor of the Union. In May, at the **Battle of Chancellorsville,** Lee's forces won, but his most trusted lieutenant, **Stonewall Jackson,** was killed. In the west Grant broke away from his supply lines and laid siege to **Vicksburg.** After six weeks it surrendered; the Union controlled the entire Mississippi River and achieved a major war aim of dividing the Confederacy. At the same time Lee's forces were making what was to be their last offensive into Northern territory. The opposing armies met at **Gettysburg, Pennsylvania,** and after three days of battle the Confederate forces retreated. In the fall **Chattanooga** fell to Union forces, which now controlled Tennessee and the Tennessee River. The war's momentum had turned.

Lincoln appointed Grant to take charge of all Union forces in early 1864. Grant's strategy mirrored Lincoln's, and Grant used all his resources to inflict greater cost on the enemy than he suffered. Grant moved toward **Richmond,** trying to maneuver Lee into a decisive battle. Both sides suffered huge losses but Richmond remained in Confederate hands. Grant changed his objective, hoping to capture the rail center at **Petersburg,** cutting off Richmond. The attack there settled into a nine-month siege.

In the West, Sherman advanced on **Atlanta,** which fell in early September, giving Lincoln some momentum in the presidential campaign. From there Sherman embarked on his famous **"March to the Sea,"** destroying everything in his path between Atlanta and Savannah. The sixty-mile wide corridor provided Sherman's army with supplies it needed, but everything else was destroyed to deprive the Confederacy of supplies and to break the Southern will to fight. From **Savannah** he continued his path of destruction into South Carolina. Meanwhile, in Virginia, Grant cut off rail lines from **Petersburg** and **Richmond,** and Lee fled, hoping to join what was left of his army with Confederate forces in North Carolina. With his escape blocked, he surrendered to Grant at **Appomattox Courthouse** on April 9, 1865. During the next few weeks remaining Confederate resistance crumbled.

The war claimed the lives of over 600,000 men and decided the troubling questions that had dogged America in the decades leading up to the war. America's future lay in commerce and industry. American slavery was ended. The American political system would prevail, and the nature of federalism was decided—the federal government was supreme.

Multiple-Choice Questions—Exam Tips

- Although there are no specific questions on military history in the multiple-choice section, battles and strategies can be important reference points for changes in politics, economics, and society. For example, the Union "victory" at Antietam gave Lincoln an opportunity to issue the Emancipation Proclamation.
- Wars are almost always instigators of social reform; the Civil War was no exception. Note its effect on African Americans, women, and immigrants.
- The Civil War is a good time to pay particular attention to presidential leadership. Lincoln expanded the powers of his office and of the federal government to confront the threat to the United States. Note both the military and political consequences of his actions during the Civil War.
- Technology and war go hand in hand. Because strategy lags behind, technology makes weapons more efficient, and therefore more deadly. The positive side is that what is learned from war often improves civilian standards of living.

Multiple-Choice Questions

1. The immediate cause of the first wave of secession in late 1860 and early 1861 was
   a. fears of slave uprisings in the wake of John Brown's raid on Harper's Ferry.
   b. Northern personal liberty laws that voided the fugitive slave law.
   c. the inability to reach a compromise over the proposals drafted by John Crittenden.
   d. the election of Republican Abraham Lincoln as president.
   e. Southern anger over the decision in the Dred Scott case.

2. Confederate advantages at the start of the Civil War included all of the following *except*
   a. it was fighting a defensive war on its own territory.
   b. its citizens had a strong commitment to the Confederate cause.
   c. its population exceeded the North's when slaves were included.
   d. it would be fighting among a friendly and supportive population.
   e. Northern armies needed long supply lines and Southern transportation was poor.

3. The largest source of financing for Union expenses during the Civil War came from
   a. confiscating Confederate property and selling it.
   b. printing greenbacks that were not backed by specie.
   c. loans from both American citizens and businesses.
   d. levying an income tax with rates as high as 10 percent.
   e. loans from foreign nations.

4. In the New York draft riots in 1863, some of the opposition to the draft was fueled by
   a. rich people who did not want to be forced to fight.
   b. black laborers who were not allowed to serve in the army.
   c. Southerners who had migrated to the city before the war began.
   d. Irish laborers who believed African Americans would compete for their jobs.
   e. former Whigs who believed a compromise could still be reached to stop the fighting.

5. Presidents Jackson and Lincoln acted similarly when they both
   a. chose to ignore treaties that had been made protecting Native American lands.
   b. used military force against South Carolina's refusal to obey federal law.
   c. worked to stop a national bank system from becoming established.
   d. agreed that slavery should not expand in the territories.
   e. ignored Supreme Court rulings with which they disagreed.

6. The strongest opposition to Lincoln's policies came from
   a. free northern blacks who pressed for immediate emancipation.
   b. army professionals who disliked Lincoln's war management.
   c. Copperheads in the Democratic Party.
   d. slavery supporters in the border states.
   e. immigrants who did not think the war was worth the Union.

7. Northern views on the emancipation of slaves
   a. changed little over the course of the war until victory was assured.
   b. always favored immediate freedom for all citizens.
   c. accepted emancipation as a war goal as the war progressed.
   d. accepted Lincoln's opinion that the nation could survive half-slave and half-free.
   e. overwhelmingly agreed that compensation should be paid to slave owners to end the fighting.

8. The Emancipation Proclamation was important to the Union military cause because
   a. a majority of Southern slaves left their plantations and joined the Union army.
   b. slaves in the border states were now free to fight for the Union.
   c. the Southern economy was weakened as most slaves refused to work for their former masters.
   d. Northern free African Americans had a reason to fight for the Union.
   e. it harnessed antislavery forces, giving the United States new momentum.

9. The experience of the Civil War for Northern labor
   a. improved their position because wages rose significantly.
   b. opened up skilled jobs as skilled labor went to fight.
   c. diminished union membership because jobs were plentiful.
   d. diminished labor's standard of living as prices rose more than wages.
   e. improved as immigration restrictions stopped the flow of foreign labor.

10. As the Civil War progressed, the Confederacy found itself
   a. becoming increasingly tied to its founding ideals of states, rights.
   b. more unified throughout the South in its war aims and goals.
   c. developing a more centralized government like the Union.
   d. increasingly accepted by European powers who lent support to the cause.
   e. able to develop industry to supply its army to an increasing degree.

11. The American Civil War was a part of the worldwide tendency of
   a. empires falling apart as groups broke away.
   b. forced labor being questioned by both people and governments.
   c. territorial expansion and the associated problems as a result.
   d. nations resorting to war to settle internal issues.
   e. countries to consolidate power and territory to create large nation-states.

12. The Civil War in the West was different from what happened in the East due to the fact that
   a. major fighting took place throughout the American West.
   b. the western states nearly all sided with the Confederacy.
   c. a vast majority of Indian tribes sided with the Union.
   d. pro- and antislavery forces lived together there, localized fighting was vicious.
   e. the western states and territories remained uninvolved because slavery issues did not involve them.

Free-Response Questions
1. Assess the importance of the battles of Antietam, Vicksburg, and Atlanta to the political and military situation of the Confederacy and the Union during the Civil War.

2. Compare and contrast the ways in which the Union and Confederacy mobilized for war between 1861 and 1865.

Document-Based Question
President Abraham Lincoln was a leader in peace as well as in war. Use the following speeches of the president to assess the validity of this assertion. Consider Lincoln as politician, moralist, and military leader.

Document A

Source: Speech given at the Republican State Convention, 1858.

If we could first know where we are, and whither we are tending, we could better judge what to do, and how to do it. We are now far into the fifth year since a policy was initiated with the avowed object and confident promise of putting an end to slavery agitation. Under the operation of that policy, that agitation has not only not ceased, but has constantly augmented. In my opinion, it will not cease until a crisis shall have been reached and passed. "A house divided against itself cannot stand." I believe this government cannot endure permanently half slave and half free. I do not expect the Union to be dissolved; I do not expect the house to fall; but I do expect it will cease to be divided. It will become all one thing, or all the other.

Document B

Source: First Inaugural Address, 1861.

Apprehension seems to exist among the people of the Southern States that by the accession of a Republican Administration their property and their peace and personal security are to be endangered. There has never been any reasonable cause for such apprehension. Indeed, the most ample evidence to the contrary has all the while existed and been open to their inspection. It is found in nearly all the published speeches of him who now addresses you. I do but quote from one of those speeches when I declare that—I have no purpose, directly or indirectly, to interfere with the institution of slavery in the States where it exists. I believe I have no lawful right to do so, and I have no inclination to do so.

Document C

Source: Speech given at Gettysburg, Pennsylvania, 1863.

It is for us the living, rather, to be dedicated here to the unfinished work which they who fought here have thus far so nobly advanced. It is rather for us to be here dedicated to the great task remaining before us—that from these honored dead we take increased devotion to that cause for which they gave the last full measure of devotion—that we here highly resolve that these dead shall not have died in vain—that this nation, under God, shall have a new birth of freedom—and that government of the people, by the people, for the people, shall not perish from the earth.

Document D

Source: Second Inaugural Address, 1865.

On the occasion corresponding to this four years ago all thoughts were anxiously directed to an impending civil war. All dreaded it, all sought to avert it. While the inaugural address was being delivered from this place, devoted altogether to *saving* the Union without war, urgent agents were in the city seeking to *destroy* it without war—seeking to dissolve the Union and divide effects by negotiation. Both parties deprecated war, but one of them would *make* war rather than let the nation survive, and the other would *accept* war rather than let it perish, and the war came…

With malice toward none, with charity for all, with firmness in the right as God gives us to see the right, let us strive on to finish the work we are in, to bind up the nation's wounds, to care for him who shall have borne the battle and for his widow and his orphan, to do all which may achieve and cherish a just and lasting peace among ourselves and with all nations.

Multiple-Choice Answers

1. d. There were two waves of secession. The first states seceded after Lincoln was elected; the second wave came after fighting began at Fort Sumter.

2. c. The Northern population was twice the size of the Confederate population including slaves.

3. c. Loans provided most of the financing; taxes and printing money were used, but not extensively.

4. d. The New York riots were mainly caused by the poor who resented the exemptions made for the rich and Irish labor who blamed their ills on black labor.

5. e. Jackson ignored Court rulings concerning Indians in Georgia, and Lincoln continued to imprison citizens without charging them with a crime.

6. c. Most of the opposition to Lincoln was political, from the Democrats.

7. c. The North entered the war to preserve the Union. After the Emancipation Proclamation, freeing the slaves became a war goal also.

8. e. Lincoln considered it a military measure to destabilize the Confederacy and to give the North more reason to continue fighting.

9. d. Northern labor had less buying power as prices rose faster than wages.

10. c. The Confederacy found it increasingly difficult to function with its ideology of decentralized power.

11. e. This was an era of consolidation as nations competed for world stature and power.

12. d. Fighting in the West was particularly violent as residents on both sides of the issue occupied those territories and states.

Free-Response Questions Commentary

1. This question asks you to assess the military importance of three battles and relate that to politics in both the Confederacy and the Union. A good answer will assess the significance of each of the battles and comment on issues such as public opinion, military position, and politics. Your assessment should include the ways each battle was significant to both the Union and Confederacy.

   Each of the battles had a different effect on the fortunes of both sides. For example, Antietam was a marginal Union victory that gave Lincoln the opportunity to issue the Emancipation Proclamation. However, McClellan allowed Lee's army to escape, and perhaps squandered a chance to end the war. Vicksburg was a clear Union victory and divided the Confederacy along the Mississippi River, furthering Union war goals and weakening the Confederacy. Atlanta, just before the election of 1864, helped Lincoln win reelection.

   You can argue that the first had positives and negatives for both sides while Vicksburg and Atlanta were clear Union victories. In addition, Atlanta buoyed Northern morale, and bolstered the wartime president's political fortunes. Stronger essays will take a position pointing out the different dimensions.

2. This is a straightforward question about the similarities and contrasts between how the Union and Confederacy prepared for and carried out the war effort. A strong answer will consider specific policies and actions, and how they responded to changes resulting from the war itself.

One way to approach this could be to look at the respective ideologies and how each side responded to both principle and necessity. In actuality both the Confederacy and the Union responded in similar ways, especially as the war progressed. The Confederacy centralized authority and increasingly violated the states' rights doctrine. Impressment, conscription, and taxes were actions both sides used. At the end of the war the Confederacy even passed a law to enlist slaves in the army, a violation of a cherished principle. On the other hand, the Confederate government had no authority over the individual states themselves to requisition men and materials, and that hindered the Confederate war effort. The Union labored under no restraints in exercising federal power over both states and individuals.

A powerful essay will consider both similarities and differences. Using the competing ideologies can help highlight these and adds a measure of analytical sophistication to your answer.

Document-Based Question Commentary

The four excerpts from Lincoln's speeches cover the period from the 1858 senatorial campaign to just before his assassination. Lincoln's use of language to make a point is powerful, and he was able to mobilize and direct public opinion through his speeches. In Document A, his "House Divided Speech," Lincoln delineated his vision for America and his strong support for Union above all else, even the issue of slavery. His devotion to the nation is clear and unmistakable. His efforts to maintain unity are clear, but were ultimately unheeded, as implied in Document B. His most well-known speech, "The Gettysburg Address," uses few words to redirect the reasons for fighting the Civil War, "a new birth of freedom." In Document D he shows his compassion, his unwavering devotion to the indivisibility of Union, and his lack of vindictiveness.

You can use these passages to show Lincoln as a leader who strove to instill both political and moral goals in a people at war. Despite the enormous sacrifices made, he also urged the nation to forgive, and to forge a new national unity without slavery, the cause of disunion in the first instance.

CHAPTER 15
Reconstruction and the New South

AP THEMES
- **American Diversity:** Reconstruction laid the foundations for a revolutionary change in the relationships of blacks and whites in America. It opened the door for black culture to be preserved and increasingly accepted in American life during the twentieth century.
- **Economic Transformations:** Two major economic transformations are explored in this chapter. The first is the abolition of slavery and its replacement, albeit imperfect, by a system of "free" labor in the South. The second is the rise of the "New South," which promoted the growth of industrial production.
- **Politics and Citizenship:** In the aftermath of civil war, the nation assumed the authority to define citizenship and, for a very brief period, created the most equal society America had ever experienced until very recently.
- **Slavery and Its Legacies in North America:** The social effects of slavery were evident in the Reconstruction South. Assumptions of black inferiority and white superiority permeated the culture. Because of this unchallenged tenet, freedmen were denied justice in spite of amendments to the Constitution.

EXAM TIPS
- This will be one of the most important chapters in your study of United States History. Americans were forced to deal with the problems of race without the economic buffer of slavery and black codes. The Reconstruction Amendments ended slavery, made African Americans citizens, and gave to black men the right to vote. As you study this chapter, it is essential that you understand the transformation in American society that these political changes set into motion. The problem of racism that would challenge twentieth-century America was born in this period. Learn the various viewpoints about race and their origins. These views will inform the struggle for civil rights and largely define the fight for equality of the past 140 years.
- Separate truth from fiction. Understand that, in reality, there was no such thing as "negro rule." Although freed slaves were protected by federal troops during Reconstruction, freed slaves never exercised a great deal of political or economic power, and any power that they held was short-lived.
- Andrew Johnson's impeachment set a pattern for congressional and executive relationships during the twentieth century. Modern American politics would see an executive and Congress from different parties; situations where the president was perceived to have gained, or did gain, power at the expense of the other branch; and executives who were unpopular, vulnerable, or both because of some sort of scandal.
- There are many visuals from this period. Among the most famous are Republican Thomas Nast's political cartoons. Be familiar with his point of view and analyze the meticulous detail in his drawings in order to understand this critical period of United States history.

CHAPTER SUMMARY
The era of Reconstruction was one of the most controversial in our nation's history. Southerners interpreted it as a vindictive North exacting revenge while Northerners viewed

the South as unrepentant and unwilling to abandon its slave culture. For African Americans throughout the nation, Reconstruction began a slow and tortured process to gain civil rights and freedoms in America.

The Problems of Peacemaking

As the Civil War ended, the physical destruction in the states of the former Confederacy was unparalleled in American History. Approximately 258,000 Confederate soldiers died, and a substantial proportion of private and public property was destroyed. In its defeat, the South embraced a myth of the **"Lost Cause,"** which looked back nostalgically to the South before the war. Almost 200,000 African Americans had served in the Union armies and others labored in Confederate service. At the end of the war, many left their former plantations to look for economic opportunities and to unite broken families, but they had no property and nowhere to go. In 1865, the South was in disarray.

What freedom would mean in the postwar United States was unclear. Most African Americans wanted the rights and freedom enjoyed by whites, but there was disagreement about what this meant. The Thirteenth Amendment abolished slavery, but no one was quite sure how society was to be structured and the labor force reestablished. Americans were not familiar with a large and intrusive national government. Both the government and the American people were unsure of how to proceed to turn the civil war victory into lasting changes in American society. For their part, African-American former slaves wanted land and opportunity for education. Some fought for a redistribution of property as a means to achieve that end. White southerners wanted freedom to restore some semblance of antebellum Southern society, free from Northern interference. Congress established the **Freedman's Bureau** in 1865 to distribute food, establish schools, provide economic assistance, and reunite families of both black and white Southerners.

The Republican Party had established an ambitious economic program favoring a national industrial economy. It was not clear how this would be developed in the agricultural lands of the South. The political system, which Republicans had dominated during the war, was certain to be altered as Southern Democrats rejoined the union. Republicans worried about losing their political majority if a united Democratic Party emerged after the war. Republicans were divided among themselves about how to reconstruct the nation. Conservatives wanted the abolition of slavery and a minimum of change in the South. **Radical Republicans** looked to punish the Confederacy, guarantee full political and civil rights for African Americans, and strengthen the Republican Party in the south in order to maintain their political power in the nation.

Lincoln was a moderate and proposed a lenient reconstruction policy known as the **10 percent plan.** He proposed a **general amnesty** for most Southerners and would allow states to reenter the Union when 10 percent of the number of 1860 voters took an oath of loyalty and accepted the abolition of slavery. In 1864, three states—Louisiana, Arkansas and Tennessee—fulfilled these conditions. Radical Republicans refused to seat the representatives from the "reconstructed" states or to count their electoral votes that year. They countered by passing the **Wade-Davis Bill,** which authorized the president to appoint a provisional governor for each conquered state. When a majority of those who had voted in the 1860 election took an oath of loyalty to the United States, a state constitutional convention consisting of delegates who swore *past* loyalty to the country, the **ironclad oath,** could write a constitution that abolished slavery, repudiated Confederate debts, and disenfranchised Confederate leaders. Like Lincoln's plan, political rights for African Americans were to be determined by the states. Lincoln pocket-vetoed this measure in 1864.

Lincoln's reconstruction plans ended with his **assassination** by **John Wilkes Booth** in April 1865 at Ford's Theatre in Washington, D.C. There was suspicion of a conspiracy by former Confederates, which was exploited by extreme Republicans to promote their political agenda. The intemperate, impolitic, and white supremacist **Andrew Johnson,** who was a former Democrat, Tennessee governor, and United States senator, assumed the presidency on Lincoln's death. Like Lincoln's plan for reconstruction, Johnson's plan, known as Presidential Reconstruction, extended amnesty to Confederates, excluding high-ranking Confederate officials and any Southerner with property worth more than $20,000, who needed individual presidential pardons. Otherwise, his plan was like the **Wade-Davis** plan. By the end of 1865, all former Confederate states had formed new governments and were ready to reenter the Union once Congress recognized them. However, Congress refused to seat these governments.

Radical Reconstruction

When Congress convened in late 1865, it created the **Joint Committee on Reconstruction** to institute its own policy. This inaugurated the period known as **Radical or Congressional Reconstruction.** Southern states had enacted **black codes** to ensure white control over former slaves and restrict freedmen's movement and labor. Congress responded by extending the life of the Freedman's Bureau and passing the **Civil Rights Act of 1866,** which protected freedmen's rights. Congress also proposed the **Fourteenth Amendment,** which defined American citizenship and provided **"due process"** and **"equal protection"** of the laws by both state and national governments. **Race riots** in Southern cities increased Northern support of the Radical Republicans, which sustained substantial majorities in the **1866 elections.**

That majority passed and overrode vetoes of three major reconstruction bills in 1867. Ultimately, the former Confederacy was divided into five military districts. The commander of each district was to register voters, including adult freedmen and excluding white males who had supported rebel governments. The district commanders were also to call conventions to draft new state constitutions that accepted the Fourteenth Amendment. By 1868 eight of the former Confederate states had been readmitted. A later requirement for readmission was ratification of the **Fifteenth Amendment,** forbidding the federal or state governments to deny the vote on the basis of race. Congress also passed the **Tenure of Office Act** designed to reduce the power of the president to subvert its plans. The act required the president to obtain the Senate's **advice and consent** to remove officials, thereby protecting Radical secretary of war **Edwin Stanton** from removal by Johnson. In 1867, the House of Representatives used Johnson's refusal to obey this act as grounds to **impeach President Johnson** after he dismissed Stanton without their advice or consent. The Senate failed to convict Johnson by only one vote, but by then Johnson's power to resist congressional will had dissipated.

The South in Reconstruction

African Americans played a significant role in the politics of Reconstruction governments but not in the ways nor to the extent that critics have claimed. Twenty blacks served in the House of Representatives, two in the Senate, and many in state legislatures and other state offices. But the myth of **"negro rule"** was just that, a myth. Restrictions on white suffrage were dropped quite quickly and only South Carolina had a **black majority** in its lower House for a short time. White Southern **scalawags** joined the Republican Party because it best matched their economic interests. White Northerners, earning the epithet of **carpetbaggers,** served as Republican leaders and also hoped to find fortune in the South. These governments were criticized for their inefficiency and corruption, but they were probably no more corrupt than governments in the North during this time period. The growing state debts resulted largely from rebuilding as a result of the war and increased government services, especially in education. Reconstruction governments began building a public education system for both blacks and whites, and a number of black colleges were started.

Concurrent with freedman's gains was the establishment of a system of segregation based on race. Initial attempts to integrate schools were abandoned when Democratic governments assumed control. Blacks and whites continued to be separated in economic terms. The few attempts at the redistribution of land to fulfill the freedman's dream of **"forty acres and a mule"** were abandoned in Mississippi, Georgia, and South Carolina. However, black land ownership increased while white land ownership decreased during Reconstruction. For both races the **crop-lien system** was the major way to gain access to land for farming. Merchants or landowners would loan farmers money and land with which to plant crops, charge high rates of interest, and use the crop as collateral. Individual debt grew, and many small landowners of both races lost their land and resorted increasingly to cash crops, especially cotton. This could result from either tenant farming or sharecropping.

Without slavery's restraints, black families began to adopt the structure of white families. Women increasingly inhabited the domestic sphere and men worked in the fields. However, poverty required many black women to work outside the home for wages.

The Grant Administration

Ulysses S. Grant ran on the Republican ticket in 1868 against Democrat **Horatio Seymour.** An inexperienced and somewhat naïve politician, Grant used patronage extensively, which ultimately inspired a good deal of corruption in his administration and split the Republican Party. **Crédit Mobilier,** a construction company chartered to help build the Union Pacific Railroad, defrauded the railroad and the federal government. This scandal came to light in 1872. Another scandal known as the **"whiskey ring"** involved Treasury officials and distillers who falsified reports of tax revenues. Several other smaller scandals tainted Grant's administration. **The Panic of 1873** was a severe depression lasting four years, and Grant's monetary policy, which was firmly based on the **gold standard,** made the depression worse.

During this time, Alaska was acquired by secretary of state **William Seward** for $7.2 million, but this move was derided at the time as **"Seward's Folly."** An active and forward thinking secretary of state, Seward also annexed the **Midway Islands.**

The Abandonment of Reconstruction

With mounting economic and political problems, the country turned away from Reconstruction's idealistic goals, and the overriding goal of the Republican Party became continued political dominance. Even so, by the end of Grant's tenure, seven of the former eleven Confederate states had been **"redeemed"** by the Democrats. In those states, secret societies such as the **Ku Klux Klan,** the **Knights of the White Camellia,** and **White Leagues** used violence and intimidation to solidify white supremacy and to exclude freedmen from exercising their political rights. Congress attempted to thwart this with the **Ku Klux Klan Acts** in 1870 and 1871, which authorized the federal government to enforce civil and political rights in the states. These acts were ineffectual. The federal government's commitment to enforce these rights waned soon after.

Northern support for Reconstruction diminished after ratification of the **Fifteenth Amendment.** Some Radicals moderated to the point of allying with Democrats, and white Southern Republicans defected to the Democratic Party. The Panic of 1873 also diverted support for the Reconstruction. The new philosophy of **Social Darwinism** also argued that blacks were inferior and destined to occupy a low station in society. Democrats won a majority in the House of Representatives in 1874, and growing Democratic political strength led to the disputed **election of 1877.** The contest between Republican **Rutherford B. Hayes** and Democrat **Samuel Tilden** would turn on disputed electoral votes from three states. Congress established a commission to settle the dispute, and its Republican majority awarded every questionable ballot to Hayes, who became president. Democrats and the South accepted **the Compromise of 1877** because Hayes agreed to withdraw all federal troops from the South, appoint a Southerner to the cabinet, and provide substantial economic aid to rebuild southern states. Republicans vainly hoped their accommodations would shore up Republican support in the South.

The Compromise ended the federal effort to establish political and civil rights for African Americans. There were no immediate or lasting gains. A deep-seated social conservatism and commitment to white supremacy along with a strong belief in private ownership of property and free enterprise thwarted substantial reform. The surprising result is that Reconstruction accomplished as much as it did. Most significantly, the ratification of the three Reconstruction amendments provided the constitutional basis for the civil rights revolution of the twentieth century.

The New South

The Republican goal of establishing a Republican Party in the South failed, and by the end of 1877 every Southern state was in Democratic control. These **redeemers** were mostly not the former planter class but a commercial class that promoted economic development of the South. These governments mirrored the rest of the country in their corruption, and they lowered taxes and reduced the services that Reconstruction governments had provided. Leaders hoped to build an industrial economy and were led by spokesmen such as **Henry Grady,** the editor of the *Atlanta Constitution.* In promoting the Northern values of thrift, industry, and progress that were so roundly denounced before the Civil War, Grady hoped to transform Southern culture. Industry expanded, particularly in textiles, tobacco processing, iron and steel, and railroads. Southern production and income increased but still lagged significantly behind that of the North. Agriculture, the most significant sector of the economy, was impoverished in the post-Reconstruction South. Farmers increasingly relied on a few cash crops, and by 1900, 70 percent of Southern farmers were tenants.

Many African Americans were attracted to the **"New South Creed"** of progress and some established a **black middle class.** Acquiring property, establishing business enterprises, and entering professions, these blacks offered services to their own race. This group embraced **education** as the basis of self-improvement, and with the support of Northern missionary societies created a network of colleges and institutes. **Booker T. Washington** founded and was president of Alabama's **Tuskegee Institute,** a trade school. He urged blacks to learn trades and adopt white middle-class values. Once they gained the respect of whites in the economic area, he believed, larger social gains would follow. He outlined this program in his 1895 **Atlanta Compromise** speech.

Washington's **Compromise** implied that the growing **segregation** in the South would not be challenged. In the 1883 **Civil Rights Cases,** the Supreme Court ruled that the Fourteenth Amendment prohibited states, but not private individuals or organizations, from discriminating against African Americans. In the 1896 *Plessy* v. *Ferguson* case, the Supreme Court ruling declared that **separate but equal** accommodations were constitutional. This legalized what came to be called **Jim Crow laws** authorizing segregation by race in America. In addition, Southern states passed laws restricting blacks from voting; **poll taxes, literacy tests,** and **grandfather laws** all tried to accomplish this. Both black and white voting dropped significantly, although the former was more dramatic. Restricting the vote of poor whites often served the interests of people in power. Another effort to maintain white control was **lynching,** and the rise of the anti-lynching movement did little to slow it.

Reconstruction solidified economic nationalism throughout the country, and although the exercise of political and civil rights by African Americans was relatively short-lived, a constitutional foundation for those rights was put in place. A network of black institutions was also established to help counter the effects of a society that believed in black inferiority. Although primarily agricultural, the New South accepted industry and commerce and many of the related values it had previously despised. The Reconstruction era was one of largely unfulfilled promises, but it laid the foundation for significant changes in America's future.

Multiple-Choice Questions

1. Lincoln's plan for the readmission of former Confederate states to the Union
   a. included provisions for providing freed slaves political and civil rights.
   b. prohibited any supporter of the Confederacy from voting.
   c. was included in the Wade-Davis Bill that Congress rejected.
   d. gained momentum and Radical support after his assassination.
   e. was relatively lenient to gain support for the Republican Party in the South.

2. Radical Republicans proposed the Fourteenth Amendment to the Constitution because
   a. they wanted the Constitution, not the Emancipation Proclamation, to acknowledge the end of slavery.
   b. Northern as well as Southern states were denying African Americans the right to vote.
   c. it would end all claims of white superiority in the former Confederacy.
   d. it defined citizenship and required the states to protect a citizen's rights.
   e. it allowed the government to commit federal forces in the states.

3. Corruption in Southern Reconstruction governments was
   a. a result of inexperienced politicians being taken advantage of by scalawags.
   b. at the hands of former Confederates seeking revenge on the federal government.
   c. part of the post–Civil War political culture throughout the nation.
   d. much more extensive than that found in Northern politics.
   e. extremely rare because military commanders supervised state spending.

4. The most convincing evidence that "negro rule" during Reconstruction was not a valid concept is
   a. carpetbaggers and scalawags ran local government at the time.
   b. freedmen controlled no state legislatures and no governorships.
   c. a majority of white Southerners were denied the vote.
   d. the "ironclad oath" never allowed Confederate soldiers to take office.
   e. the proportion of black officeholders exceeded the black population.

5. During Grant's first term as president, the Republican Party divided over
   a. the blatant use of patronage to solidify his support within the party.
   b. Southern blacks gaining the right to vote in federal elections.
   c. scandal and corruption at the highest levels of government.
   d. the use of force to subdue opposition to Reconstruction policy by force.
   e. the use of excessive greenbacks to repay the Civil War debt.

6. Republican support for the Compromise of 1877 came from
   a. wanting a Republican Party member in the cabinet.
   b. a desire to maintain office, and declining interest in civil rights for blacks.
   c. the political necessity to maintain troops in the Southern states.
   d. the overwhelming popular vote for Rutherford B. Hayes.
   e. Southern Republicans who wanted to avoid another armed conflict.

7. One of the most important legacies of Reconstruction for America was the
   a. declaration that segregation was unconstitutional in *Plessy* v. *Ferguson*.
   b. gaining momentum of the movement ending the culture of white supremacy.
   c. ratification of the Fourteenth and Fifteenth Amendments.
   d. granting of equal political rights to both African Americans and poor whites.
   e. acceptance of the principles of Social Darwinism and progress.

8. In the *Atlanta Constitution*, Henry Grady championed the idea that
   a. Southerners must not abandon the ideals embodied in the "Lost Cause."
   b. Southern agriculture and cotton could resurrect the Southern economy.
   c. African-American labor should migrate North, which would raise Southern wages.
   d. Southern culture and economy should adopt Northern commercial values.
   e. high tariffs would help both the Southern and Northern economies grow.

9. The crop-lien system in the South after the Civil War had all of the following effects *except*
   a. the growing reliance on a limited number of cash crops.
   b. the increase in tenant farming and sharecropping.
   c. the increased debt accrued by those making a living in agriculture.
   d. the decrease in land ownership among white farmers.
   e. the increased opportunity to establish farms that were mainly self-sufficient.

10. "Cast down your bucket where you are. Cast it down among the eight millions of Negroes whose habits you know" best expresses the ideas of
    a. Herbert Spencer's views on Social Darwinism.
    b. Rutherford B. Hayes in the presidential campaign of 1877.
    c. Charles Sumner on his plans for equal civil rights for freedmen.
    d. Henry Grady on the New South.
    e. Booker T. Washington in the "Atlanta Compromise."

11. The white power structure in the "redeemed" South designed voting laws to
    a. provide education for former slaves so that they would be more productive agricultural workers.
    b. give more political power to all whites at the expense of blacks.
    c. to stop the increasing number of lynchings of both blacks and whites.
    d. to stop both blacks and poor whites from politically uniting against them.
    e. share a limited amount of social and political power with African Americans to end race riots such as the one in New Orleans.

Free-Response Questions

1. Explain the economic and political motivations behind the Radical Reconstruction policy and program from 1867 to 1877.

2. How successful were "New South" proponents at instituting their vision from 1877 to 1900?

Document-Based Question

Assess how former slaves used political, social, and economic means to secure civil rights and economic power. Use the documents and your knowledge of the period 1865–1890 in constructing your response.

Document A

Source: Library of Congress

The Louisiana Constitutional Convention, 1868

Document B

Source: Northern Journalist Edward King questions a Natchez, Mississippi Planter, 1875.

"Do the Negroes on this plantation vote?"

"I reckon not (laughing). I don't want my niggers to have anything to do with politics. They can't vote as long as they stay with us, and these Alabama boys don't take no interest in the elections here."

"What do they receive as monthly wages?"

"From $10 to $16. It costs us about $15 per head to bring 'em from Alabama. These niggers likes wages better than shares. We keep a store here, and Saturday nights, most of the money they have earned comes back to us in trade. They're fond o' whiskey and good things to eat." [*Annals* X: 335]

Document C

Source: African-American Senator Blanche K. Bruce speech to the Senate, 1876.

The unanimity with which the colored voters act with a party is not referable to any race prejudice on their part. On the contrary, they invite the political cooperation of their white brethren, and vote as a unit because proscribed as such. They deprecate the establishment of the color line by the opposition, not only because it isolates them from the white men of the south, and forces them, in sheer self-protection and against their inclination, to act seemingly upon the basis of a race prejudice that they neither respect nor entertain." [*Annals* X: 350-51]

Document D

Source: The Newberry Library, Chicago, Illinois

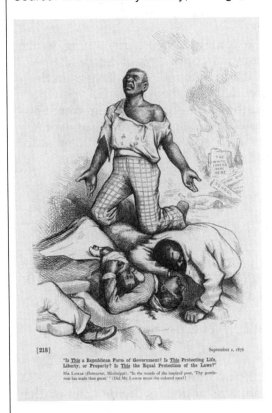

The caption of this 1876 Thomas Nast cartoon asks "Is this a Republican form of government? Is this protecting life, liberty, or property? Is this equal protection of the laws?"

Document E

Source: Library of Congress

Photograph of Tuskegee Institute, 1902, founded by Booker T. Washington for technical and industrial training.

Document F

Source: African-American Journalist John E. Bruce manuscript, 1889.

Under the present condition of affairs the only hope, the only salvation for the Negro is to be found in a resort to force under wise and discreet leaders. He must sooner or later come to this in order to set at rest, for all time to come, the charge that he is a moral coward ... I hate namby-pambyism, or anything that looks like temporizing, when duty calls. [*Annals* XI: 215]

Document G

Source: News article reporting a Negro lynching in the *Richmond Dispatch*, 1889.

RALEIGH, N.C., September 14—News was received here tonight of another lynching, which is the *thirteenth* this year. It occurred at Whiteville, Columbus County, night before last. A body of masked men, a hundred or more, entered the jail and demanded the keys from the jailer. With a score of revolvers pointed at him, he surrendered the keys, and the lynchers went to the cell where Sherman Farrier (colored) was confined for an outrage committed on an aged white woman, and took him and departed. Yesterday, suspended to the limb of a large oak about one mile from the jail, the body of Sherman Farrier was found with a placard pinned on his breast bearing the words: "We protect the virtue of our women. Beware." [*Annals* XI: 213.]

Document H

Source: *Atlanta Constitution* editor Henry Grady in a speech to Boston Merchants association, 1889.

It is claimed that this ignorant labor is defrauded of its just hire. I present the tax books of Georgia which show that the Negro, twenty-five years ago a slave, has in Georgia alone $10 million of assessed property, worth twice that much." [*Annals* XI: 244]

Source: Reverend Joshua A. Brackett, African Methodist Episcopal Church, reply to Henry Grady, 1890.

In Georgia, Mr. Grady's own state, the Negro's real wealth accumulated since the war, is $20 million. Its population of Negroes is 725,132. Twenty millions of dollars divided among that number will give to each person $27.58. [*Annals* XI: 251]

Multiple-Choice Answers

1. e. Lincoln hoped to reunite the nation as quickly as possible and to establish support for the Republican Party in the South.

2. d. This amendment made all freedmen citizens, and guaranteed "due process" and "equal protection."

3. c. Graft and corruption existed throughout the country; it was not confined to the South.

4. b. Although freedmen held state and federal offices, they never held controlling power in any state.

5. a. Liberals divided from Conservatives over the extensive use of patronage by Grant. During his second term scandals came to light.

6. b. Republicans wanted to hold on to the presidency, and the economic depression shifted attention away from the Radical program of civil rights.

7. c. Both amendments had little immediate effect but served as a foundation for civil rights in the twentieth century.

8. d. Grady championed the idea of the "New South," which accepted Northern commercial virtues and principles.

9. e. Many of the backcountry farms that had been largely self-sufficient resorted to cash crops to pay off debts.

10. e. Booker T. Washington wanted blacks to learn trades and become economically crucial to whites, and only then expect some degree of political and social equality.

11. d. Voting laws were designed to prevent freedmen from voting Republican, but also to prevent blacks and poor whites from politically uniting against upper-class whites.

Free-Response Questions Commentary

1. This is a relatively straightforward question about the Radical or congressional phase of Reconstruction from after the war until 1877. You must address economic and political motivations. Looking at who the Republican supporters were will help you explain the nationalistic economic program Republicans enacted. The political motivations are clear, and the mobilization of the freedman vote and disenfranchisement of the Southern Democrats will be an important part of your response.

   You can conclude with the Compromise of 1877, and explore the ultimate failure of the strategy in political but not economic terms. A Republican Party never became established in the South once it was "redeemed," and the political hegemony the Republicans desired did not last.

2. This question asks you to evaluate "how successful" New South proponents were in establishing their vision, so you will need to look at both successes and failures in your response. You can outline what the New South meant and follow up with specific ways it was or was not accomplished. It is important to acknowledge not only physical phenomenon but also the acceptance of ideas and attitudes.

You should address the important role of African Americans who accepted the creed of the New South, even as segregation laws hardened. Their role, the role of whites and the Democratic Party, and the relationship between the two is important in answering this question. Your task is to analyze how much and in what ways the South changed after 1877.

Document-Based Question Commentary

This question asks you to "assess" how former slaves acted to gain and maintain civil rights *and* economic power. To assess means that you must evaluate the ways in which former slaves acted. You should address both rights and economics. It also requires you to consider how freedmen used political, social, and economic methods to achieve those ends. Make sure that you cover all those bases in a balanced manner.

The documents do not all divide easily into those that support freedmen achieving civil rights and economic power and those that do not. Take a sophisticated stance. For example, you might look a Document E, the Tuskegee Institute in 1881, as evidence of black action for improvement. Yet, you can also see its other side, as a segregated school. Also bring in outside knowledge of Booker T. Washington's strategy of accommodation and restriction of blacks to manual labor. Several of the documents here can be used as evidence to support both African-American activism and their restraint or passivity.

The stronger answers will note the dual messages contained in some of the documents listed here, and use them to show both sides of the issue. There is no explicit evidence supporting Jim Crow, but it is implied here, so use your own background information to analyze the documents. To make a strong argument you may argue that former slaves used political and social means to establish their rights, but not economic means because of their lack of land ownership and the crop-lien system. There are a number of ways to craft a powerful essay. Create a strong thesis that fully addresses every aspect of the prompt, takes a clear position, and creates categories for analysis.

CHAPTER 16
The Conquest of the Far West

AP THEMES
- **American Identity:** This chapter is important for raising three issues: the experience of Native Americans during the white settlement of the West; the opening of the American political system to women; and the struggle of Asian immigrants and Hispanics in western development.
- **Demographic Changes:** The heart of this story is one of migration. White settlers moved west, and then reversed that trend as farming declined. Opportunity lured Chinese and other Asians to America. Native Americans under pressure from white settlement and federal policy were forced to move repeatedly.
- **Economic Transformations:** The West underwent several economic transformations. One way to think of this is as a succession of opportunities in mining, ranching, and farming. Overall, the West, like the East, was becoming industrialized in the overall national economic context.
- **Environment:** In his Frontier Thesis Frederick Jackson Turner wrote that the frontier, with its vast resources, promoted waste. Consumption, not conservation, was central to western development. Once a land area satisfied immediate economic goals and was exhausted, it was abandoned.

EXAM TIPS
- In the past there have been few free-response questions about the West itself as a topic. In many ways, the Civil War had been a contest between the North and the South for the economic control of the West. With the war over, the West would now develop its vast resources based on free labor. Keep this in mind as you study this chapter. Think of the West in the context of broader issues such as women, the economy, and Native Americans.
- Keep in mind that what happened in the West was not isolated from what was going on in the rest of the country. The economy, social developments, intellectual currents, and politics developed with regional distinctions, but reflected national characteristics.
- Be familiar with Turner's Frontier Thesis, which is one of the most influential historical essays ever written about America. It resonates with our self-image, but also be aware of its inaccuracies.
- This chapter's coverage of Native Americans, their resistance to white settlement, and shifting federal policy toward the tribes is important.

CHAPTER SUMMARY
During the nineteenth century the conquest of the West was not only physical but ideological. Emigrants found that it was not the "great American desert," too arid for cultivation, but a diverse environment, full of promise and opportunity. The vast western reaches were occupied by a diverse population of Indians, Hispanics, French, British Canadians, and Asians, and its development reflected these cultures. The West became a part of the expansive eastern capitalist economy, aided in its development by substantial support from the federal government.

The Societies of the Far West

Before the great white-American migration following the Civil War, the West was home to many Indian tribes. The **Cherokee** and **Creek** were forcibly moved west to present-day **Oklahoma.** The **Pueblos** of the Southwest were largely agricultural, lived in permanent villages of **adobe houses,** and irrigated their fields. Their relationship with the Spanish from Mexico produced a **hierarchical system** with the Spanish at the top and Indians from other tribes at the bottom. Increasing numbers of white Americans upset this society. Ultimately, the old Hispanic elite was forced out of political and economic power, and Mexicans became subordinate members of society.

The Plains Indians were a diverse society. Some farmed and others were nomadic hunters. The powerful **Sioux** subsisted by hunting **buffalo.** The Sioux dominated the Missouri River Valley and mounted the strongest opposition to white settlers' incursions into Sioux territory. However, the Sioux were unable to unite against their greatest enemies: disease and the technological advances of white society.

Chinese migration to California began even before the 1849 gold rush. Initially considered industrious, the Chinese had successes that turned white public opinion against them. A tax on foreign miners restricted their activity in mining, but new jobs opened up in railroad construction. The Chinese constituted 90 percent of the **Central Pacific Railroad** labor force. Like the rest of the country, economic opportunity was increasingly in cities, and the Chinese settled there also. **"Chinatowns"** developed, the largest in San Francisco; however, discrimination forced the Chinese into the less desirable occupations, one of which was **laundering clothes.** The conspicuous presence of the Chinese and their meager economic success fostered **anti-Chinese reactions,** the most extreme of which was the **Chinese Exclusion Act,** passed by Congress in 1882. It was made permanent in 1902 despite vigorous protest on the part of Chinese living in the United States.

After the Civil War, American migration from the East overshadowed all other demographic changes in the West, including the immigration of a substantial numbers of foreigners. Federal policy encouraged settlement of the West. The 1862 **Homestead Act** provided 160 acres for those who stayed for five years and improved the land. Modeled after farming in the East, the parcels proved too small to be economically viable. A series of subsequent legislation provided more land to homesteaders so that ultimately an individual could acquire 1,280 acres at little cost. With these incentives settlement was rapid. By 1900 only the Arizona and New Mexico territories had not gained statehood.

The Changing Western Economy

Commercial enterprise—**mining, timbering, ranching,** and **commercial farming,** among others—in the rapid settlement of the West forged strong ties to the industrial economy of the East. Recruiting labor was a major challenge, and the nature of the work, particularly in the mining industry, was often **boom and bust,** and conditions were dangerous. Workers were mostly single men who faced increasing competition from immigrants, particularly Chinese, Filipinos, Mexicans, and Indians. Supported by racial theories and **Social Darwinism,** a **dual labor system** developed, with white workers occupying the more attractive jobs. Although geographical mobility was significant among all western labor, upward social mobility was almost exclusively the preserve of white workers.

Mining of precious metals, especially **gold** and **silver,** was at the core of the first economic boom. Gold was discovered in California and Colorado's **Pike's Peak** while Nevada's **Comstock Lode** yielded silver. Although romance lay with mining gold and silver, in the long run resources such as **aluminum, lead, tin, quartz,** and **zinc** were more significant to the western and national economy. Few miners ever found fortunes in mines; corporations replaced individuals and reaped far larger profits over a long period of time. However, a spirit of optimism and opportunity gripped western towns. With a predominantly male population living without the sobering influence of family, lawlessness and disorder characterized western communities. **Vigilante committees** often formed when a lawless situation became intolerable, but those committees themselves often became part of the problem.

The second economic wave was **cattle ranching.** This industry followed patterns established by Mexicans and Texans in the Southwest. The **open range,** part of the vast **public domain,** provided lands for unrestricted grazing. **Longhorn cattle, horses** for **cowboys,** and cattle ranching methods such as **branding, roundups,** and the **long drives** all had Texan roots. Ranchers drove the herds over long trails such as the **Chisholm Trail** to Abilene to get to railroad centers. With increasing settlement, competition for the open range grew from sheep ranchers and farmers who fenced in the range. A series of **range wars** erupted between these groups. The great profits from cattle lured more investors, who put more livestock on the land. The cattle boom crashed in 1887 after two harsh winters and a dry summer decimated the western herds. The industry abandoned the open range and grazed cattle on fixed ranches. Ironically, the railroads both inspired and ultimately destroyed the open-range cattle industry; it provided the necessary access to eastern markets but also brought the farmers who ended the open range to the West.

There was a great gender imbalance in the West. The few women there often came with their husbands and generally performed traditional domestic roles. Single women and women with unemployed husbands worked as cooks, waitresses, tavern keepers, and in laundries. Some women broke the mold and seized opportunities previously unavailable. By 1890, more than 250,000 women owned farms or ranches. The biggest difference with their eastern counterparts was that western women increasingly participated in politics. Wyoming was the first state to grant women the vote, and throughout the West, women were a political presence. Considered a moral presence in politics, they also were needed to swell the voter population when applying for statehood.

The Romance of the West

The West, free from the unnatural influence of civilization, has been highly romanticized in American culture. Writers and artists embellished this ideal. The **Rocky Mountain School** of paintings followed in the steps of the earlier **Hudson River School,** portraying the majesty and awesome nature of the landscape. This inspired growing tourism once the Native American population had been contained on reservations, and railroads made travel to these vast areas possible. The **cowboy**—an example of individualism, morality, and ingenuity— struck a positive vein in American culture. That ideal differed greatly from the low-paid and rough life cowboys actually lived, but popular **Wild West shows** and novels made cowboys American heroes. The substantial number of African-American cowboys was omitted from the romanticized version of the American West. Literature also heralded the **frontier** as the last place one could seek refuge from organized society. The **1893 census** declared the frontier closed, and historian **Frederick Jackson Turner** argued that the frontier was the most important aspect of American development. His **"frontier thesis"** claimed an era of American History was over with the disappearance of the frontier. Although generally accepted as a valid perception of our history, Turner's contentions were generally inaccurate, but did capture the light in which Americans saw themselves. As the century closed and with it the "frontier," many Americans sensed foreboding with this loss of promise and opportunity.

The Dispersal of the Tribes

Both the Frontier Thesis and the popular image of the West portrayed it as unsettled and ignored the substantial Indian population and culture there. However, the federal government had searched since its beginning for a policy to minimize conflict between Indians and white settlers, while at the same time allowing white settlers access to Indian land. Two contradictory assumptions underlay that policy: that the tribes were both sovereign nations and wards of the American president. Earlier attempts at erecting a permanent frontier ended with settlers increasingly encroaching on tribal lands. The **concentration policy** of 1851 attempted to define lands for individual tribes in separate treaties. This divided the Indians and made them easier to control, but encouraged even more conflict. After the Civil War in 1867, a new **reservation policy** was adopted, creating two large reservations in Oklahoma and the Dakotas. Management of the reservations was left to incompetent and dishonest agents from the **Bureau of Indian Affairs.** Many tribes were tricked into accepting the new policy.

Equally as devastating to Indian life and culture was the slaughter of the **buffalo** herds. There was tremendous eastern demand for hides as souvenirs and symbols of the West. Migrants used the buffalo for food, and factories used the hides for machine belts. Railroads, slowed by herds on their tracks, encouraged and subsidized killing the buffalo for sport, and even some Indian tribes were drawn into this thriving market. In addition, the Bureau of Indian Affairs saw this as a way to weaken and control Indian tribes by eliminating their main source of food and supplies. The result was catastrophic; from 1865 to 1875 the herd declined from over 15 million to less than 1,000.

The elimination of the buffalo increasingly led to conflict, especially when the United States government committed more troops to the West after the Civil War. In 1864 a militia under the command of **Colonel J. M. Chivington** massacred Arapaho and Cheyenne Indians at **Sand Creek** in Colorado. Fighting continued throughout the 1870s both by the military and by white vigilantes who believed that Indians and white Americans could not coexist. Most encounters eventually resulted in white victories, but during the country's bicentennial in 1876, **George A. Custer** and his troops were annihilated by 2,500 Indians at the Battle of the **Little Big Horn.** The Indians did not remain united for long, which was one of their major weaknesses in the face of centralized United States forces.

Despite the stories and myths about atrocities committed by uncivilized Indians, white settlers and troops were more vicious, often slaughtering women and children when attacking Indian camps. Predicting the coming of a messiah, in 1890 a Native American prophet led a spiritual revival centered on a **Ghost Dance.** When fighting broke out between Indians and troops at **Wounded Knee** in South Dakota, troops turned machine guns on the Indians and ended Native American resistance. Just before this event, a final blow came to Indian culture with the passage of the **Dawes Act.** In a dramatic policy reversal, this legislation provided for the elimination of tribal lands and the transfer of 160-acre lots to individual Indians, with smaller allotments for each family member. This attempt at assimilation also included a provision for Native Americans to become citizens of the United States after twenty-five years. A system of boarding schools was developed to eradicate all evidence of Native American culture and speed the acceptance of American culture by Native American children.

The Rise and Decline of the Western Farmer

After the mining and ranching industries, farming became the dominant economic activity in the West. However, just as with the other occupations, farming also declined after a time. Railroads made western farming possible by bringing settlers to the West, and taking their produce back to eastern markets. Completion of the **transcontinental railroad** in 1869 and the construction of branch lines improved access to markets and the value of land. The railroads themselves received generous **government subsidies and loans.** In the 1870s, above-average rainfall also encouraged farming. The invention of **barbed wire** and methods of irrigation spurred agricultural development.

In the late 1880s, the weather pattern shifted to long periods of drought, which destroyed crops, and farm prices began a long period of decline. Many debt-ridden farmers unable to grow crops or pay their bills abandoned their farms and moved east in a reversal of the previous twenty-year migration. In place of the independent farmer, commercial farming began its rise. These farms specialized in cash crops that sold in national and international markets. The boom in American agricultural production was matched in other areas around the world. Farmers lost a degree of independence, having to rely on bank loans, railroad companies for transportation of their crops, and prices set elsewhere. In the 1880s, worldwide overproduction led to lower prices and increased indebtedness. Some commercial farms prospered, but the agricultural economy on the whole declined.

Farmers responded to this decline by targeting the immediate and obvious sources of their trouble: railroads and crop storage facilities, banks and the volume of money, and prices of their goods and what they needed to buy. Other forces were harder to identify but a sense that eastern manufacturers exploited farmers gained credence. In addition, farmers saw their social and economic position declining relative to that of city dwellers. Rural isolation and loneliness, inadequate education for children, lack of cultural activities, and the migration of farm children to the city all combined to create a sense of **agrarian malaise.**

The forces transforming the American West after the Civil War were significantly different than the romantic image of the West most Americans embraced. The growth of the West was influenced by the same capitalistic forces that were driving industrialization.

Multiple-Choice Questions

1. Railroad building in the West was not an example of a federal policy of laissez faire because
   a. the majority of laborers on the Central Pacific were Chinese.
   b. when the railroad was completed thousands of workers lost their jobs.
   c. strikes were ruthlessly put down by the railroad companies.
   d. the two railroad companies met at Promontory Point, Utah.
   e. millions of acres of land and low-cost loans subsidized its construction.

2. Railroads in the West had all of the following effects except
   a. bringing settlers to the West and returning to the East with natural resources.
   b. promoting settlement to increase the value of the lands they held.
   c. eliminating the buffalo herds that slowed trains on the open range.
   d. helping Indians by stimulating the market economy on reservations.
   e. providing jobs for workers who performed manual labor.

3. The 160-acre homesteads provided by the 1862 Homestead Act were
   a. purchased by both American-born citizens and foreigners at a high price.
   b. not taken advantage of because no market crop could be grown in the arid conditions.
   c. not large enough to sustain a farm family on the Great Plains.
   d. an economic disaster for the government, which lost significant revenue.
   e. ignored by most, who chose instead to prospect gold in California.

4. In the late nineteenth century ranching eventually gave way to farming because
   a. beef cattle could not survive on the open range.
   b. farmers began to fence the plains and end the practice of open-range grazing.
   c. profits in ranching declined after the end of the Civil War.
   d. hostile Indians were a constant threat to the rancher.
   e. a glut of cattle caused prices to drop.

5. The advance of white settlement affected the Plains Indians' economy most directly by
   a. annihilating the herds of buffalo on which the Indians depended for food and supplies.
   b. introducing an agricultural economy to Native Americans.
   c. drawing the Indians into the commercial market economy and away from traditional barter.
   d. creating large reservations for tribes from land originally owned by individual tribal chiefs.
   e. drawing Indian labor from tribes to work in mines.

6. The western frontier was romanticized by all of the following *except*
   a. Henry David Thoreau in Walden.
   b. Albert Bierstadt in his "Rocky Mountain School" paintings.
   c. Mark Twain in Roughing It.
   d. Frederic Remington in sculptures and paintings.
   c. Frederick Jackson Turner in his "frontier thesis."

7. With the 1887 Dawes Act, the federal government adopted an Indian policy of
   a. moving tribes to two large areas in Oklahoma and the Dakotas.
   b. assimilation by encouraging Indians to abandon tribal culture and settle on individual lots.
   c. concentration of each tribe on its own defined reservation confirmed by a treaty.
   d. elimination of remaining Native Americans by armed warfare.
   e. removal of all Indians from the West to eastern boarding schools to learn to assimilate to white culture.

8. The incidents at Sand Creek and Wounded Knee were examples of
   a. Indian barbarity with the senseless killing of white women and children.
   b. George Custer's heroic efforts to protect white settlers from Indian attacks.
   c. atrocities committed by white soldiers on Indian communities.
   d. large-scale battles in the Indian wars in which both sides suffered great casualties.
   e. Chief Joseph's unsuccessful attempts at negotiating a treaty to retain some Idaho lands.

9. The distinct difference in the status of women between the East and West was
   a. western women were nearly all single, and did not form families.
   b. women in the West could own and work the land, a right denied women in eastern states.
   c. the western labor scarcity that gave opportunities to women identical to those of men.
   d. in the West, the need for voters and a moral voice opened suffrage to women.
   e. Victorian domestic values were dominant in the East, but had no influence in the West.

10. A problem that contributed to the farmers' plight, but was not commonly recognized, was
    a. the need for more currency to inflate prices.
    b. the railroad monopoly that charged high rates to farmers.
    c. the power of bankers to charge high interest rates on loans.
    d. high prices for manufactured goods that farmers bought.
    e. expanding worldwide agricultural production, driving down prices.

11. The poor use of resources in the late-nineteenth-century West is best exemplified by
    a. irrigation of farmland by diverting water from rivers.
    b. fencing in the range with barbed wire.
    c. creating large Indian reservations on productive western farmland.
    d. commercial mining of lead, copper, and zinc in western territories.
    e. ranchers grazing longhorn cattle on the open range.

12. Western "ghost towns" were a result of
    a. Native American spiritual revivals such as the Ghost Dance.
    b. Indian raids on white settlements in Indian territory.
    c. farmers losing their land for failing to pay their mortgages.
    d. the boom-and-bust economy of the mining frontier.
    e. the loneliness of life on western farms that drove families to the East.

Free-Response Questions

1. Analyze the response of Native Americans to changes in government Indian policy between 1850 and 1900.

2. Compare and contrast the experience of two of the following groups with respect to the economy and society in the post–Civil War West:
   Miners
   Ranchers
   Farmers

Document-Based Question

Use the following excerpts from the document as evidence to show how Americans viewed themselves at the close of the nineteenth century.

"The Significance of the Frontier in American History," 1893
Frederick Jackson Turner

In a recent bulletin of the Superintendent of the Census for 1890 appear these significant words: "Up to and including 1880 the country had a frontier of settlement, but at present the unsettled area has been so broken into by isolated bodies of settlement that there can hardly be said to be a frontier line. In the discussion of its extent, its westward movement, etc., it can not, therefore, any longer have a place in the census reports." This brief official statement marks the closing of a great historic movement. Up to our own day American history has been in a large degree the history of the colonization of the Great West. The existence of an area of free land, its continuous recession, and the advance of American settlement westward, explain American development. . . .

In the settlement of America we have to observe how European life entered the continent, and how America modified and developed that life and reacted on Europe. Our early history is the study of European germs developing in an American environment. Too exclusive attention has been paid by institutional students to the Germanic origins, too little to the American factors. The frontier is the line of most rapid and effective Americanization. . . . Little by little he transforms the wilderness, but the outcome is not the old Europe, not simply the development of Germanic germs, any more than the first phenomenon was a case of reversion to the Germanic mark. The fact is, that here is a new product that is American. At first, the frontier was the Atlantic coast. It was the frontier of Europe in a very real sense. Moving westward, the frontier became more and more American. As successive terminal moraines result from successive glaciations, so each frontier leaves its traces behind it, and when it becomes a settled area the region still partakes of the frontier characteristics. Thus the advance of the frontier has meant a steady movement away from the influence of Europe, a steady growth of independence on American lines. And to study this advance, the men who grew up under these conditions, and the political, economic, and social results of it, is to study the really American part of our history. . . .

But the most important effect of the frontier has been in the promotion of democracy here and in Europe. As has been indicated, the frontier is productive of individualism. Complex society is precipitated by the wilderness into a kind of primitive organization based on the family. The tendency is anti-social. It produces antipathy to control, and particularly to any direct control. The tax-gatherer is viewed as a representative of oppression. Prof. Osgood, in an able article, has pointed out that the frontier conditions prevalent in the colonies are important factors in the explanation of the American Revolution, where individual liberty was sometimes confused with absence of all effective government. The same conditions aid in explaining the difficulty of instituting a strong government in the period of the confederacy. The frontier individualism has from the beginning promoted democracy. The frontier States that came into the Union in the first quarter of a century of its existence came in with democratic suffrage provisions, and had reactive effects of the highest importance upon the older States whose peoples were being attracted there. An extension of the franchise became essential. . . .

So long as free land exists, the opportunity for a competency exists, and economic power secures political power. But the democracy born of free land, strong in selfishness and individualism, intolerant of administrative experience and education, and pressing individual liberty beyond its proper bounds, has its dangers as well as its benefits. Individualism in America has allowed a laxity in regard to governmental affairs which has rendered possible the spoils system and all the manifest evils that follow from the lack of a highly developed civic spirit. In this connection may be noted also the influence of frontier conditions in permitting lax business honor, inflated paper currency and wild-cat banking. . . .

The result is that to the frontier the American intellect owes its striking characteristics. That coarseness and strength combined with acuteness and inquisitiveness; that practical, inventive turn of mind, quick to find expedients; that masterful grasp of material things, lacking in the artistic but powerful to effect great ends; that restless, nervous energy; that dominant individualism, working for good and for evil, and withal that buoyancy and exuberance which comes with freedom- these are traits of the frontier, or traits called out elsewhere because of the existence of the frontier. . . . Movement has been its dominant fact, and, unless this training has no effect upon a people, the American energy will continually demand a wider field for its exercise. But never again will such gifts of free land offer themselves. For a moment, at the frontier, the bonds of custom are broken and unrestraint is triumphant. There is not *tabula rasa*. The stubborn American environment is there with its imperious summons to accept its conditions; the inherited ways of doing things are also there; and yet, in spite of environment, and in spite of custom, each frontier did indeed furnish a new field of opportunity, a gate of escape from the bondage of the past; and freshness, and confidence, and scorn of older society, impatience of its restraints and its ideas, and indifference to its lessons, have accompanied the frontier. . . .

Multiple-Choice Answers

1. e. Railroad companies received subsidies of land grants and loans from all levels of government; government intervention was substantial.

2. d. Railroads, by dividing the plains, helped destroy the buffalo herds and the Indian lifestyle. Native Americans never joined the market economy to a significant degree.

3. c. The 160-acre homesteads were designed according to eastern farming patterns. The arid environment of the plains would not support a family on 160 acres.

4. b. By fencing in the open range, over time farmers hurt the ranchers' dependence on the open range. The winters of 1885–1887 ended open-range ranching.

5. a. The Indians subsisted mainly on buffalo for food and shelter.

6. a. Henry David Thoreau wrote about nature on Walden Pond in Massachusetts before the Civil War.

7. b. The Dawes Act attempted to end tribal culture and Americanize the Indian by eliminating reservations and encouraging Native American private property ownership.

8. c. Despite the myth of "savage" Indians, white soldiers committed atrocities more frequently than Indians.

9. d. Western women gained political rights denied eastern women. In part this resulted from the need for voters to apply for statehood.

10. e. Farmers blamed their economic woes on circumstances they could easily identify. Low prices due to a worldwide surplus of agricultural goods were not conspicuous to the western farmer.

11. e. Overgrazing on the open range led to disaster during the harsh weather in 1885–1887.

12. d. Towns depended on the economic activity from the mines. Once they played out, there was no basis for any economic activity and settlers left, creating ghost towns.

Free-Response Questions Commentary

1. This question asks you to evaluate Native American responses to white settlement on lands supposedly protected by prior treaties. There were three separate government policies during the period in question. Native Americans consistently resisted the policy changes by using force.

   You should outline the three policies of concentration, reservations, and assimilation and point out the effects of continued white settlement on Indian lands. Indian resistance continued, but diminished as their livelihood declined with the loss of the buffalo. The Dawes Act was the final blow and resistance ended with Wounded Knee.

   You can answer this question by arguing that Native American responses changed little, but were less effective as forces beyond their control weakened the economic and social position of the various tribes. The Dawes Act completed the process by depriving Indians of tribal land in the western territories and states.

2. This question asks you to choose two of the three major groups that settled the West—miners, farmers, and ranchers—and show how their experiences were alike and different in the late nineteenth century. A common element was the commercialism of the enterprise after the initial development. What began as individual enterprise often evolved into a commercial venture bigger than a single individual's ability to finance.

   Choose two of the three occupations and analyze the economic and social aspects of that group's existence and transformation. The economy should address the competition for resources between industries, and social aspects could include who settled, the role of women and families, and the part played by immigrants. A strong answer should show how development changed the nature of the economy and society, evaluate the similarities and differences of the change, and explain the transformation that occurred as that particular sector of the economy matured.

Document-Based Question Commentary

Frederick Jackson Turner's essay on the frontier in American History is perhaps the seminal example of United States historiography. An excerpt from Chapter 1, this document typifies America's view of itself at the end of the nineteenth century, and even today. Turner identified the frontier as the most important influence on American development, and it became another explanation for "American exceptionalism."

You can use the American characteristics that Turner identifies as developing on the frontier to help explain national values. Individualism, democracy, and ingenuity all point to positive aspects of the American character. However, Turner saw both sides of the coin. Negative aspects were lawlessness, waste, antisocial behavior, and materialism, but even some of these characteristics underlay the Republican distrust of concentrated power that American revolutionaries embraced. Turner's observations struck a respondent chord in the America of the 1890s and supported traditional values of the age.

CHAPTER 17
Industrial Supremacy

AP THEMES

- **Demographic Changes:** Immigration was an important source of labor during the late nineteenth century. However, the changing national origins of immigrants limited labor's ability to organize.
- **Economic Transformations:** As noted in Chapter 16, industrialization was a national and international phenomenon. The Industrial Revolution impacted both manufacturing and agriculture. Business consolidation changed the relationship between labor and capital.
- **Environment:** America's explosive industrial growth created enormous demand for natural resources, and spurred the development of the West. Industrialists looked to cut costs and boost production and profits, and a major result of that was pollution and waste.
- **Reform:** Labor issues are primary here. Business consolidation put the individual worker at a disadvantage, and although workers' absolute standard of living rose, their relative standard of living declined. Labor's search for power and position in industrial America is told through the history of the union movement.

CHAPTER SUMMARY

The development of the West was part of the remarkable economic transformation taking place in post–Civil War nineteenth-century America. However, technological advances that began before the war made the Industrial Revolution possible. The Bessemer furnace converted iron to steel, and later, the open-hearth process efficiently produced large quantities of steel. Pittsburgh, Pennsylvania, close to iron mines and already a center of iron production, became a center of steel production. Rapidly expanding railroads increased the demand for steel.

Increasingly mechanized factories needed lubricants, and Pennsylvanian **George Bissell** discovered that refined **petroleum** could be used for this, as well as for lamps and other purposes. In 1859 his well in Titusville, Pennsylvania, began pumping oil. By the 1870s oil was America's fourth largest export. The first **automobile** in the United States was made after the turn of the century, and **Henry Ford** followed with his soon after. The **Wright brothers** invented an **airplane** in 1903 but it was not a commercial proposition until the 1920s.

Rapid technological change inspired business leaders to stay ahead by sponsoring research. **General Electric, Bell Telephone, DuPont,** and **Eastman Kodak** were among the firms that supported research labs in the early twentieth century, and they also turned to universities to help make them more competitive. As production techniques evolved a new study following the principles of **Frederick Winslow Taylor,** called **"scientific management,"** arose. Taylor urged companies to specialize tasks in the production process to make workers more efficient and increase output. A consequence of Taylor's methods was to increase management's control over the workplace and reduce the need for highly skilled labor. Henry Ford's introduction of the **moving assembly line** in 1914 in his automobile plant exemplified scientific management; the production time for a **Model T** decreased from 12½ hours to 1½ hours; he reduced the hours and increased the wages of his workers. The price of the auto dropped from $950 in 1914 to $290 in 1929.

Railroads underlay the industrial growth of America in the late nineteenth century. They provided demand for many **heavy goods** and created a **national market** by connecting the country. **Chicago** became the railway hub of the central United States, and **time zones** were developed to make schedules easier to follow. In the last four decades of the nineteenth century miles of track increased more than six-fold, spurred in part by generous **government subsidies.**

New forms of business organizations worked to concentrate capital. The modern **corporation** could sell stock and offered **limited liability** to shareholders. It allowed businesses to raise the great sums of capital necessary to finance large business ventures. Also, these large corporations developed a class of managers who were often separate from ownership. This kind of business organization also allowed consolidation and concentration in many industries. **John D. Rockefeller** used a method called **horizontal integration** to expand in the oil industry. Using this method, Rockefeller initially acquired a substantial share of the nation's refineries and ultimately controlled the entire industry. He later expanded vertically, acquiring interests in all phases of the production of oil. By the 1880s he controlled access to 90 percent of the nation's refined oil. **Andrew Carnegie** used **vertical integration** to control all aspects of steel production from iron ore to sales of finished steel. In 1901 he sold his company to a group headed by **J. P. Morgan** to form the **United States Steel Corporation,** the first billion-dollar company in America.

Although these industrialists were firm believers in free enterprise, whenever possible they consolidated their interests to eliminate "cutthroat competition." **Pools** were informal agreements among companies to stabilize rates and divide markets, but they were not often successful. A more formal and more successful arrangement was the **trust,** an organization in which shareholders in individual corporations would exchange their shares of company stock for shares of a trust. The trustees could then exercise considerable control over an industry and distribute the profits to the trust's shareholders. The **holding company** was a variation of this business form. By 1900, 1 percent of America's corporations controlled over one-third of the nation's manufacturing output. However great this economic growth, the concentration of wealth and economic power in the hands of a few men was controversial.

American Industrialists	
Industrialist	**Industry**
Henry Ford	Automobiles
Cornelius Vanderbilt	Railroads
James J. Hill	Railroads
Collis P. Huntington	Railroads
Andrew Carnegie	Steel
J. Pierpont Morgan	Investment banking
Gustavus Swift	Meatpacking
Isaac Singer	Sewing machines
John D. Rockefeller	Oil

Capitalism and Its Critics

The rise of industrial capitalism and its effects spurred much debate about the role of the individual in a democracy. Supporters argued that the system provided expanded opportunity to gain wealth and become a **"self-made man." Herbert Spencer's** theory of **Social Darwinism** provided justification that the fittest survived and that great fortunes were a result of natural rules. Yale's **William Graham Sumner** supported this ideology by theorizing that individuals have the absolute freedom to compete and either succeed or fail. Although industrialists embraced this ideology, they did everything possible to eliminate competition and replace it with individual power in the marketplace. They also used bribery and corruption to gain the government's support for their industries. The idea of **laissez faire,** that government should not regulate or control business, was a prominent part of their philosophy.

Andrew Carnegie outlined the responsibility of the wealthy in his 1889 book *The Gospel of Wealth.* He argued that wealth should return to the society from which it came, and he, as well as others, devoted much of their fortunes to **philanthropy,** in his case to libraries and educational institutions, to provide a foundation for self-help. The popular promoter of this idea was **Horatio Alger,** whose **rags-to-riches** novels chronicled the rise from poverty to wealth.

Others criticized a system that simultaneously promoted vast wealth and poverty. The **Socialist Labor Party** led by **Daniel De Leon** attracted a modest following of intellectuals and an offshoot became the more enduring **American Socialist Party** in 1901. In 1879 **Henry George** published *Progress and Poverty,* which questioned the dilemma of the American economic system. For him the issue was the increasing value of land, and he proposed a **single tax** on land to destroy monopoly and redistribute wealth. Another popular author was **Edward Bellamy,** whose utopian novel, *Looking Backward,* explored what happened when a man fell asleep in 1887 only to awaken in 2000, finding a world where poverty and corruption were unknown. A single government-controlled trust distributed the nation's production equally among all the people. Few Americans questioned the basic capitalistic tenants, but many were concerned about the growing power of **monopoly** on which they blamed high prices and economic instability. Severe economic **panics** in 1873 and 1893, the threat of concentrated economic power on the individual's ability to advance, and the arrogance of the wealthy—which was publicly displayed in ostentatious consumption—bred growing resentment and criticism of both the wealthy and of the system responsible for its creation.

Industrial Workers in the New Economy

For workers, industrialism was a double-edged sword. They enjoyed a real rise in their standard of living but at the expense of long hours, low wages, and deteriorating conditions in the workplace. The workforce expanded dramatically as **rural workers** left the farm and migrated to the city, and **immigrants** came to America from Europe, Asia, Mexico, and Canada. After the end of the Civil War, immigration shifted from northern Europe to southern and eastern Europe by the end of the century. In the West, immigrants came from Mexico and Asia until the **Chinese Exclusion Act** of 1882 prohibited Chinese immigration. Immigrants were drawn to America by prospects of opportunity, much of it unrealized, and the desire to escape poverty and oppression in their homelands. Industry actively recruited foreign labor and was supported by the **Labor Contract Law,** legislation that allowed businesses to pay in advance for the passage of workers. These workers often worked for low wages, and ethnic tensions between foreign workers and American labor grew.

Although the absolute standard of living was rising, the average income of a worker was $400 to $500 a year, which put most workers very close to poverty. Industrial work imposed other hardships. Factory work was routine and impersonal during ten-hour days, six days a week. The principles of scientific management lowered the need for skills and transferred control from workers to managers. This led to the increased number of women and children working in factories. From 1870 to 1900 the number of women in the industrial labor force quadrupled to 17 percent, and 20 percent of all women were wage earners. The textile industry was the largest employer of women, and domestic work employed many others. More than 1.7 million children under the age of sixteen worked in factories or on farms in 1900. Many families could not survive without the additional income that women and children earned. The labor of these groups was particularly vulnerable to exploitation and injury and was increasingly seen as a social problem. Thirty-eight state legislatures passed **child-labor laws,** but most were ineffective, unenforceable, or both. For all workers, regardless of gender, conditions in the workplace were dangerous and exploitive, but few employers made efforts to improve the situation.

The workers, response to these problems mirrored their employers' tactics—they attempted to form combinations in a search for control. **Craft unions** had existed since the early republic, but they were local and could not hope to exert control in a national economy. The first attempt was the **National Labor Union** organized in 1866. Reform-oriented and with little direct connection to labor, it disintegrated after the Panic of 1873. A more radical and violent group was the **Molly Maguires** in the anthracite coal region of Pennsylvania. Their terror tactics were used by mine owners to turn public opinion against the union. However, that agitation was small compared to the **great railroad strike of 1877.** Started by the announcement of a 10 percent wage cut, strikers stopped rail service, destroyed equipment, and rioted in several cities. President Hayes ordered federal troops to restore order in West Virginia, and state militias were called out. The strike illustrated the widespread nature of labor issues, the deep resentment of labor toward employers, and the weakness of the labor movement, demonstrated by the strike's failure.

The first significant labor union was the **Knights of Labor** in 1869, a union open to all workers including women and African Americans. The loose organization and general reform platform—an eight-hour day, the abolition of child labor, reform of the capitalist system—was moderate. **Terrence V. Powderly** led the union in the 1870s and membership topped 700,000 in 1886. At that point, another rival and more successful union—the American Federation of Labor, or AFL—organized. Its structure differed from that of the Knights; it joined together autonomous craft unions of skilled labor. It did not allow women to join, but saw them as competitors to male workers. At the same time, it pushed for equal wages for men and women in order to make women less attractive workers and less able to compete with men for jobs. The AFL accepted capitalism but wanted a greater share of its rewards for workers. Its goals were better wages, shorter hours, and better working conditions. It preferred **collective bargaining** to achieve these goals, but was ready to strike when necessary. Its call for a **general strike** on May 1, 1886, if a national eight-hour day was not achieved, resulted in a protest in Chicago's **Haymarket Square,** where a strike against the McCormick Harvester Company was already underway. Someone threw a bomb at the policemen there, killing seven, and the police opened fire, killing four people. Most middle-class Americans were horrified; eight anarchists were convicted of murder on the basis that their statements had incited the bomb thrower. **Anarchism** became the new threat to social order and private property and was linked to the labor movement in the American mind. This spelled the demise of the Knights of Labor and provided a formidable obstacle to the acceptance of labor unions in America.

A series of violent strikes in the 1890s fueled anti-labor sentiment. In 1892, after wages were cut, the union at Andrew Carnegie's **Homestead Plant** struck. The plant's manager and Carnegie's chief aide, **Henry Clay Frick,** locked out the workers and hired **Pinkerton Agents** to protect the **strikebreakers** Frick planned to hire. After battling the workers, the agents surrendered and were ejected from the town. The company asked the National Guard to protect its property, and steel production at the plant resumed with strikebreakers. When an attempt to assassinate Frick failed, public opinion turned against the union, and the union was broken. An equally important strike occurred at the **Pullman Palace Car Company** near Chicago in 1894. **George Pullman,** the company owner, had built a "model" town that he rented to his workers. In the winter of 1893–1894, Pullman cut wages 25 percent but refused to lower rents in company housing. The workers struck and were supported by the **American Railway Union** headed by **Eugene V. Debs.** The union refused to run trains hauling Pullman Cars and equipment. Thousands of railway workers struck and rail transportation west of Chicago was paralyzed. The railroad owners appealed to the federal government that the strike was stopping the rails, and president Grover Cleveland sent 2,000 troops to Chicago. In addition a federal court issued an **injunction** against the union. Debs defied it and was arrested along with his associates. The strike dissolved.

The cards were stacked against the labor movement in post–Civil War America. Unions represented only a small proportion of the national labor force and often excluded unskilled workers, women, African Americans, and recent immigrants. Women attempted to form a union in 1903, the **Women's Trade Union League,** but it was unsuccessful. Also, ethnic tensions made it difficult to organize, and the workforce was mobile, with workers moving frequently. Gains for workers were few; real wages increased very little. Legislation, such as the establishment of an eight-hour day on government projects and for government employees, affected few workers. Ultimately the strength of labor's organization could not hope to match that of the corporations that enjoyed the support of government at all levels, as well as of public opinion. Even so, Americans were becoming more skeptical of free-enterprise capitalism and continued to question their individual place in its order.

Multiple-Choice Questions

1. The greatest significance for the worker of Frederick Taylor's scientific management was
   a. the need for fewer skilled workers, which led to greater employer control.
   b. increased wages for all workers from 1870 to 1900.
   c. forming workers into teams to make products.
   d. government support of unions to improve worker safety.
   e. longer hours but more fulfilling work in the factory.

2. All of the following contributed to the growth of industry in late nineteenth-century America *except*
   a. technological innovation such as the Bessemer furnace.
   b. a growing number of laborers fueled by immigration.
   c. the growth in canal mileage to transport raw materials and finished goods.
   d. government policies that supported commerce and industry.
   e. the discovery and exploitation of natural resources.

3. Andrew Carnegie became the major supplier of
   a. oil by using vertical integration to gain control of that industry.
   b. coal by using horizontal integration to monopolize coal mines.
   c. meatpacking by controlling railroads that serviced Chicago.
   d. sewing machines by holding the patent for a mechanical sewing machine.
   e. steel by using vertical integration to control all aspects of its manufacture.

4. The main reason business leaders looked to establish monopolies in their industries was to
   a. have sufficient wealth and power to bribe government officials.
   b. eliminate excessive competition, which made markets unstable.
   c. promote competition and free-enterprise capitalism.
   d. gain wealth that could later be used to help the poor.
   e. prove that the principles of Social Darwinism were true.

5. Henry George believed that the great inequality between rich and poor during the Industrial Revolution was a result of
   a. the survival of the fittest, which gave wealth to those who deserved it.
   b. the "Gospel of Wealth," where God determined who was rich and poor.
   c. the idea of the self-made man who had the opportunity to get ahead and become wealthy.
   d. rising land values that made owners wealthy at the expense of society.
   e. man's own plan for how society should be shaped.

6. Over the course of the late nineteenth century, immigration to the United States
   a. came mainly from Mexico, Canada, and Asia.
   b. shifted from southern and eastern Europe to northern Europe.
   c. included more Chinese as restrictions on immigration from that country ended.
   d. slowed as conditions for workers in American factories deteriorated.
   e. increasingly came from southern and eastern Europe.

7. Women became a greater part of the industrial labor force in post–Civil War America because
   a. opportunities opened up that were previously unavailable.
   b. working conditions in factories improved so owners believed it to be safe for females.
   c. many working-class families needed more than one income to survive.
   d. they could compete against low-paid immigrant labor better than men.
   e. the Victorian ideal of the "cult of domesticity" was declining.

8. The first major labor union that organized on a national scale was
   a. the Knights of Labor.
   b. the National Labor Union.
   c. the American Federation of Labor.
   d. the American Railway Union.
   e. the Congress of Industrial Organizations.

9. In late-nineteenth-century America, unions had difficulty prospering because
   a. workers saw no reason to organize because their wages were rising.
   b. middle-class values heralded individualism and private property, and unions were seen as a threat to these.
   c. immigrant laborers belonged to unions in their home countries, and would not join American unions.
   d. Union tactics and strikes were too radical for most workers.
   e. the federal government established an eight-hour day for public projects and employees.

10. The Pullman strike of 1894 broke new ground in labor-management relations because
    a. workers used violence and destroyed company property.
    b. armed Pinkerton detectives were used to keep strikers from entering the factory.
    c. the Illinois governor authorized the use of National Guard troops to stop the strike.
    d. the federal government became involved by sending troops, and issuing an injunction.
    e. police were killed in a riot in Haymarket Square.

11. The lesson from the novels of Horatio Alger is best summarized by the statement
    a. "Little women are little no longer."
    b. "The wealthy are trustees for their poorer brethren."
    c. "The public be damned."
    d. "Woman was created to be a man's companion."
    e. "Rags to riches."

12. Which of the following is an example of the influence of corporate power on politics in the decades following the Civil War?
    a. the use of state and federal troops to protect company property during strikes
    b. the repeal of the Contract Labor Law to promote immigrant workers
    c. establishing an eight-hour day for government employees
    d. low tariffs to protect American jobs
    e. passage of stringent child-labor laws to keep children out of factories

Free-Response Questions—Exam Tips

- Free-response questions often address the Industrial Revolution, and especially its effects on workers and the working class. Also familiarize yourself with both the ideological support for and criticism of free-enterprise capitalism.
- Learn about several specific industries and their representative tycoons such as Carnegie, Rockefeller, and Morgan. That will provide you with specific evidence about business practices to use in an essay.
- The birth of the labor movement is important also. Be able to compare and contrast the different unions, and the strengths and weaknesses of unions.

Free-Response Questions

1. Evaluate the successes and failures of the organized labor movement from 1866 to 1894.

2. Compare and contrast the development of the West with the industrial development of the East after the Civil War.

Document-Based Question

In what ways and to what extent were business leaders in the late nineteenth century industrial statesmen or robber barons?

Use the documents and your knowledge of the period 1870–1895 to construct your essay.

Document A

Source: From Baptist Minister Russell H. Crowell's lecture "Acres of Diamonds," 1880.

You have no right to be poor. It is your duty to be rich . . . It is cruel to slander the rich because they have been successful. It is a shame to 'look down' upon the rich the way we do. They are not scoundrels because they have gotten money. They have blessed the world. They have gone into great enterprises that have enriched the nation and the nation has enriched them. It is all wrong for us to accuse a rich man of dishonesty simply because he has secured money.

Document B

Source: "Eight Hour Day," a song to support labor's demand for a shorter working day, 1886. [*Annals* 11: 122].

We mean to make things over, we are tired of toil for naught,
With but bare enough to live upon, and ne'er an hour for thought;
We want to feel the sunshine, and we want to smell the flowers,
We are sure that God has willed it, and we mean to have eight hours.
We're summoning our forces from the shipyard, shop and mill.

Chorus: Eight hours for work, eight hours for rest, eight hours for what we will.
Eight hours for work, eight hours for rest, eight hours for what we will.

Document C

Source: President Grover Cleveland's 4th Annual Address to Congress, 1888. [Richardson, *Messages* VII: 5359–60.]

As we view the achievements of aggregated capital, we discover the existence of trusts, combinations, and monopolies, while the citizen is struggling far in the rear or is trampled to death beneath an iron heel. Corporations, which should be carefully restrained creatures of the law and servants of the people, are fast becoming the people's masters. . . . [the arrogance of government sponsored privilege] appears in the sordid disregard of all but personal interests, in the refusal to abate for the benefit of others one iota of selfish advantage, and in combinations to perpetuate such advantages through efforts to control legislation and improperly influence the suffrages of the people.

Document D

Source: Industrialist Andrew Carnegie in *The Gospel of Wealth*, 1889.

This, then, is held to be the duty of the man of wealth; . . . To set an example of modest . . . living, . . . to consider all surplus revenues which come to him simply as trust funds, which he is called upon to administer . . . in the manner which, in his judgment, is best calculated to produce the most beneficial results for the community – the man of wealth thus becoming the mere trustee and agent for his poorer brethren, bringing to their service his superior wisdom, experience, and the ability to administer, doing for them better than they would or could do for themselves.

Document E

Source: Oil refiner George Rice's testimony before the U.S. Industrial Trade Commission, 1899.

. . . my refinery has been shut down during the past three years, owing to the powerful and all-prevailing machinations of the Standard Oil Trust, in criminal collusion and conspiracy with the railroads to destroy my business . . . wholly by and through unlawful freight discriminations. I have been driven . . . from one railway line to another, . . . in the absolutely vain endeavor to get equal and just freight rates with the Standard Oil Trust, so as to be able to run my refinery at anything approaching a profit . . . because of their unlawfully acquired monopoly, by which they could temporarily cut only my customers' prices, and below cost, leaving the balance of the town, nine-tenths, uncut . . .

Document F

Source: Head of Standard Oil Company John D. Rockefeller's testimony before the U.S. Industrial Commission, 1899. [*Annals* 12: 314–15.]

It is too late to argue about advantages of industrial combinations. They are a necessity . . . Their chief advantages are:
(1) Command of necessary capital;
(2) Extension of limits of business;
(3) Increase of number of persons interested in the business;
(4) Economy in the business;
(5) Improvements and economies which are derived from knowledge of many interested persons of wide experience;
(6) Power to give the public improved products at less prices and still make profit for stockholders;
(7) Permanent work and good wages for laborers.

Multiple-Choice Answers

1. a. Taylor's principles of "scientific management" called for specialized tasks requiring few skills, thereby transferring power from the craftsman to the manager.

2. c. The canal boom was short-lived and ended well before the Civil War. Railroads provided both transportation and demand for the Industrial Revolution.

3. e. Andrew Carnegie gained control over all processes in the steel industry, or vertical integration, to gain a significant share of the domestic steel market.

4. b. The instability of the economy after the Civil War led entrepreneurs to combine to eliminate "cutthroat" competition, and ensure profits.

5. d. Henry George believed the rich gained undeserved wealth not through their toil, but because they owned land, which appreciated in value. He proposed a single tax on land.

6. e. The flow of immigration shifted from northern Europe to southern and eastern Europe by the end of the nineteenth century. This became known as the "new immigration."

7. c. Real wages fell so that working-class families could not survive on one income. Women and children entered the workforce to raise family income.

8. a. Knights of Labor was the first national organization of labor; it had few successes and disappeared after the Haymarket Square riot in 1886.

9. b. Labor unions found little public support for their cause because their basic premises and tactics appeared to violate traditional values of individual opportunity and private property.

10. d. The Pullman strike inaugurated a new phase in labor-management conflict. The company bypassed the state and asked the federal government to provide troops to protect company property; a federal court also issued an injunction against the strikers.

11. e. Horatio Alger's novels all revolved around one theme—that talent, tenacity, and luck gave any individual the opportunity to get ahead—thus the "rage to riches" formula.

12. a. Corporate influence was strong in government, and perhaps most evident in local, state, and the federal government's protection of corporate property from striking labor.

Free-Response Questions Commentary

1. Unions emerged from the nineteenth century with a mixed record. The broad-based unions with more general goals such as the National Labor Union and the Knights of Labor did not fare well. More focused unions with specific goals, like the AFL and ARU, did better but had little success in effecting significant change in the workplace for their members. Make a matrix with failures and successes, and try to categorize them according to general ideas to form a thesis. Successes might fall into more general areas such as the grudging public acceptance of labor unions, while failures might relate to specific working conditions such as wages, hours, and conditions. Create a strong thesis statement, take a clear position, and carefully analyze the successes and failures.

2. Although the overwhelmingly rural West and urban East might seem to have dramatically different development patterns, industrialism and its core values were national in scope. Although the West provided raw materials and food for the East, industrial values appear to have been significant. Mines, ranches, and farms all ended up as commercial rather than family enterprises. Also, railroads played a similar role in both the East and the West and had significant power. At face value there are many differences, but dig below the surface to look for the underlying nature of industrial development that was national in scope.

Document-Based Question Commentary

This question is one of the classic interpretive issues of late-nineteenth-century industrialization in the United States. Many middle-class Americans saw entrepreneurs as heroes who made possible a growing economy and rising standard of living after the Civil War. Factory workers and the poor viewed the great wealth denied them with anger and envy, recognizing that it was built upon their toil. This question asks you to determine in what ways and to what extent the businessmen of the late-nineteenth-century industrialists were "captains of industry" and in what ways they could be seen as "robber barons."

The documents fall into two neat categories. Documents A, D, and F support the industrial statesmen interpretation and provide the ideological basis for combination, monopoly, and great wealth as an asset to society as a whole. The remaining documents are critical of the capitalistic system as it developed in the United States, and look at it from three different perspectives: labor, government, and competing businessmen. Be sure to identify the point of view of the speaker as you address the issues.

Stronger answers will show that both interpretations have some validity but will take a clear position and analyze rather than describe the factual information. The hard part of the task is to identify in what specific ways the leaders were statesmen or barons. Thus, you can applaud Rockefeller's leadership in supplying low-cost petroleum products to America—the price of oil dropped dramatically—but also point out the illegal means he employed to supply the American market.

CHAPTER 18
The Age of the City

AP THEMES

- **Demographic Changes:** The late nineteenth century witnessed incredible growth in urban areas, fueled primarily by waves of immigrants from Europe and other parts of the world. Many of these so-called "new" immigrants came from southern and eastern Europe, gradually replacing the earlier patterns of immigration from northern Europe, known as the "old" immigration. In addition, a significant internal migration occurred following the Civil War, driven largely by men and women from rural areas and African Americans from the South who moved to cities in search of new economic opportunities.

- **Economic Transformations:** The development of railroads and other forms of transportation and communication helped to facilitate the growth of a national market in the post1865 period. As more and more Americans came to reside in urban areas, the growing prosperity produced by the Second Industrial Revolution, particularly among the middle class, helped to create a mass consumer society. Large retail chains and mail order houses took advantage of economies of scale to drive out smaller competitors, making their goods available to people in all parts of the country.

- **Culture:** Mechanization and greater efficiency of production changed how Americans used their time. The development of new American conceptions of leisure helped to produce greater emphasis on recreation and entertainment, especially in the areas of spectator sports, music and theater, and later, the movies. These new forms of recreation tended to have an intensely public character, although they often remained divided along racial, ethnic, class, and gender lines. In the intellectual realm, the growing popularity of Charles Darwin's theory of evolution produced an intellectual revolution in the United States, fueling the growth of the social sciences, but also creating a long-running split between its followers and its opponents, a split that continues today.

- **Politics and Citizenship:** Municipal governments, reflecting the period's individualist ethos, were unable to meet the growing needs of their largely immigrant populations. Urban political machines, which were frequently corrupt and dishonest but nonetheless provided needed services to their constituents, filled the vacuum. Middle-class Americans became concerned about this system, which they dubbed "boss rule," and gradually sought to replace these machines with more honest, efficient government, leading to the eventual emergence of the Progressive movement at the end of the nineteenth century.

- **American Identity:** The growth of the city in many ways transformed Americans' conception of their nation's character. Urbanization challenged the longstanding Jeffersonian ideal of a nation of small, independent farmers. The Hamiltonian vision of an industrial republic triumphed in the Civil War and continued into the postwar period. While the growth of cities brought numerous benefits, it also forced the United States to come to terms with many of the social problems that had plagued Europe and other parts of the world, undermining the long-running belief in American exceptionalism.

CHAPTER SUMMARY
The Urbanization of America

A wide variety of factors facilitated the growth of cities in the late nineteenth century, including the arrival of large numbers of new immigrants, the availability of factory and other jobs in urban areas, and the increasing ease of both domestic and international transportation. By 1920, a majority of Americans lived in what the census defined as "urban" areas, those with more than 2,500 people. Immigrants from southern and eastern Europe, as well as smaller numbers from Asia and Latin America (so called **"new immigrants"**), gradually replaced the more traditional patterns of immigration from northern European countries such as England, Ireland, and Germany **("old immigrants")**. These immigrants were driven by a combination of "push" factors, such as a desire to escape poverty, lack of opportunity, and persecution, and "pull" factors, such as the chance for land, economic opportunity, and political and social freedom in the United States.

Many of these new immigrants tended to form their own communities in a quest for mutual support and assistance. Tensions emerged as many old-stock Americans, as well as large numbers of second-generation Americans, pushed for the assimilation of these groups into American society and culture. By the late 1880s and early 1890s, partly in response to the economic downturn beginning in 1893, groups such as the **American Protective Association** (1887) and the **Immigration Restriction League** (1894) emerged to push for limiting the entry of immigrant groups.

The Urban Landscape

Urban growth produced great paradoxes, for it created unparalleled conveniences and opportunities as well as immense political and social dislocation that were beyond the scope of established institutions to solve. New public spaces such as parks and museums reflected the emergence of an "ordered vision" of urban growth, led by the efforts of men like landscape designer **Frederick Law Olmsted** and **Calvert Vaux,** who designed New York's **Central Park** in the 1850s. The 1893 **Columbian Exposition** in Chicago demonstrated the appeal of the urban ideal through its "Great White City" exhibit, which inspired the **"city beautiful"** movement, an effort to impose order and symmetry on urban development.

Despite these visions, the organization of city governments initially proved too limited to meet many of the challenges of rapid population increases. Housing proved one of the biggest challenges of urbanization. Well-to-do Americans lived in exclusive neighborhoods within the heart of their cities or in **"streetcar suburbs"** that allowed them to commute to their workplaces in the city. At the same time, however, many new immigrants lived in squalid **tenements.** In his 1890 book *How the Other Half Lives*, the reporter Jacob Riis exposed the squalid condition of the tenements.

In addition to housing, transportation proved to be another urban challenge. New York and other cities developed **elevated railways** starting in 1870. Electric trolley lines (1888) and subways (1897) soon followed. The development of the suspension bridge by John A. Roebling further facilitated ease of transportation and development. At the same time, advances in steel production and design led to the creation of the first skyscrapers, based largely on the pioneering work of the architect **Louis Sullivan** and his students, such as **Frank Lloyd Wright.** Wright went on to become one of America's preeminent and celebrated architects

Strains of Urban Life

Not surprisingly, growing cities faced hazards such as fires (most prominently in **Chicago** in 1871 and **San Francisco** in 1906), disease, environmental degradation, and poverty and crime. By about 1910, most cities had created sewage disposal systems (removing a major source of disease) and reformers such as **Alice Hamilton** pushed for reforms in public health. Groups such as the **Salvation Army,** founded in the United States in 1879, sought to address poverty by focusing on the moral state of those who lacked resources. Late-nineteenth-century Americans made a distinction between the "deserving poor" (those who genuinely could not help themselves) and the "undeserving poor." The deep commitment of most Americans to the ideals of self-help prevented more widespread efforts to help the poor for fear of creating a sense of dependence on charity.

Most urban problems proved well beyond the scope of existing city governments, leaving a power vacuum that was filled by urban political machines. These machines were political organizations led by so-called **"bosses,"** whose goal was to win votes for their parties. In exchange, they provided jobs, occasional relief, and government jobs to their supporters. The most famous of these machines was New York's **Tammany Hall,** led by Boss **William Marcy Tweed** (who was arrested in 1872 for fraud and fled the country for Spain after escaping from prison). Political machines eventually became the target of middle-class reformers who saw them as corrupt institutions serving to profit their leaders and exploit new immigrants. Reformers had mixed success— while they were able to drive machines from power in various cities, their emphasis on "clean" and "honest" government often had little appeal for members of the electorate who looked to political leaders for more tangible help.

The Rise of Mass Consumption

The Second Industrial Revolution led to greater income for almost all sectors of society, although growth was much slower for some groups, particularly women and minorities, than for others. New merchandising techniques and innovations in areas such food preparation and storage created new patterns of mass consumption in the late nineteenth century. The creation of national markets through improved transportation and communication fueled the rise of national grocery store chains, while mail order catalogs such as **Montgomery Ward** and **Sears** helped rural citizens gain access to goods that they had earlier lacked. Department stores like **Marshall Fields** in Chicago transformed the shopping experience for consumers and took advantage of **economies of scale** to sell goods at lower prices than their smaller competitors. Women in particular played a central role in the growth of mass consumption, and their influence as consumers gave them a growing social and economic role, as demonstrated through the growth of organizations like the **National Consumers League,** founded in 1894 by **Florence Kelley.**

Leisure in a Consumer Society

While most Americans had once considered leisure to be a sign of sloth or laziness, growing prosperity caused many to come to see it as a necessary and beneficial part of life. Many leisure activities, such as spending time in amusement parks or attending movies, had a mass, public character, but they nonetheless remained largely segregated along racial, class, and gender lines. Spectator sports such as baseball, football, and basketball, for example, drew largely male audiences, while women tended to watch sports such as golf and tennis. Some performance mediums did overcome ethnic and other barriers, as songwriters such as **George M. Cohan** and **Irving Berlin,** who had their origins in ethnic theater performances, eventually emerged on the national stage. **Thomas Edison** developed the technology used for motion pictures in the 1880s, leading to the beginning of a long-running American love affair with movies. Urban growth, higher literacy rates, and the increase in leisure time also fueled the growth of popular culture magazines and newspapers, leading to a circulation battle between publishers **William Randolph Hearst** and **Joseph Pulitzer,** apostles of so-called **"yellow journalism."**

High Culture in the Age of the City

Most foreign observers looked with disdain upon American culture, believing that it had produced little of originality or distinction. The urban explosion of the late nineteenth and early twentieth centuries did produce a number of writers who sought to chronicle the social realities of the city. These writers were collectively known as "realists." **Stephen Crane's** *Maggie: A Girl of the Streets* (1893) and Theodore Dreiser's *Sister Carrie* (1900) portrayed the plight of the urban poor, while writers like **Frank Norris, Kate Chopin,** and **William Dean Howells** dealt with other social issues that arose during the period.

Around the same time, American artists began to move away from classical styles and produce "modernist" works that portrayed many of the stark elements of American society. **Winslow Homer** reproduced maritime themes, while **James McNeil Whistler** introduced themes and conventions influenced by Japanese art. The so-called **"Ashcan School,"** influenced by modernism and French postimpressionism, produced a controversial exhibition known as the **Armory Show** in 1913.

The most influential intellectual trend of the time period was the theory of evolution, based on the work of the English naturalist **Charles Darwin.** Evolution gradually gained widespread acceptance in both the scientific and educational community. Darwin had argued in the 1850s that the human species had developed and evolved over time according to the process of natural selection, challenging the biblical account of creation and other central elements of American religious faith. Darwin's work and influence resulted in a split between his supporters and opponents that would have far-reaching consequences throughout the nineteenth and twentieth centuries. Some social scientists such as **William Graham Sumner** used these ideas to promote **Social Darwinism,** which justified the position of the elite in society, while others such as **William James** developed the idea of **pragmatism,** which held that ideas and institutions should be evaluated on the basis of scientific inquiry.

Toward Universal Schooling

As American society became increasingly based upon specialized skills and knowledge, education at all levels grew significantly. This growth was much more limited in rural areas and certain parts of the country, such as the South. Some educational reformers sought to provide practical education to African and Native Americans in hopes that they would absorb the values of white America and thus assimilate into the larger society. Women's colleges, such as Smith, Vassar, and Bryn Mawr, promoted the development of a distinctive women's community and helped to prepare women for a larger role in society (which they would undertake during the progressive era).

$\frac{8}{12} = \frac{3}{4} = 75\%$

Multiple-Choice Questions

1. Which of the following was the biggest contributor to urban population growth in the late nineteenth century?
   a. African Americans moving from the South in search of factory jobs
   b. young women from rural areas seeking new economic and social opportunities
   c. new immigrants, especially from southern and eastern Europe
   d. high birth rates among urban families
   e. farmers moving in response to declining agricultural opportunities

2. Congress in 1882 passed legislation restricting the entry of immigrants from which of the following countries?
   a. Japan
   b. Mexico
   c. Russia
   d. China
   e. Italy

3. All of the following characteristics are true of late-nineteenth-century political machines *except*
   a. they often provided constituents with needed jobs and resources.
   b. they were the target of many middle-class reformers.
   c. they gained widespread support from both immigrants and native-born Americans.
   d. they often served as money-making vehicles for political bosses and their associates.
   e. they helped to modernize city infrastructures and increase the role of city government.

4. Which of the following best characterizes American literature in the late nineteenth and early twentieth centuries?
   a. Most American writers sought to avoid controversial themes.
   b. Most American writers wrote about life abroad.
   c. The effort to capture social realities played a prominent role in many works.
   d. Literature played little role in American life during this period.
   e. Many works of fiction celebrated industrialization and urbanization.

5. All of the following writers played a role in chronicling negative American social conditions in the late nineteenth and early twentieth centuries *except*
   a. Stephen Crane.
   b. Theodore Dreiser.
   c. William Dean Howells.
   d. Upton Sinclair.
   e. Horatio Alger.

6. Which of the following was a major social repercussion of the widespread popularity of Charles Darwin's theory of evolution?
   a. a growing schism between the more cosmopolitan urban population and the more traditional rural population
   b. a tendency among scientists and intellectuals to look for absolute truths
   c. the development of more rigid, formalized educational practices
   d. the decline of organized Protestant fundamentalism
   e. greater scientific emphasis on abstract, as opposed to practical, ideas

7. Which of the following best characterizes American popular entertainment in the late nineteenth century?
   a. its ability to bridge differences of race, class, and gender in producing a mass culture
   b. its tendency to be confined to the home
   c. its intensely public character
   d. the fact that it was largely confined to the upper classes
   e. its reliance on European models and inability to develop distinctively American forms

8. Which of the following emerged as the most popular spectator sport in the post–Civil War United States?
   a. basketball
   b. football
   c. baseball
   d. boxing
   e. horse racing

9. Which of the following trends in income distribution had the most impact on the development of the late-nineteenth-century and early-twentieth-century consumer economy?
   a. the ability of a small elite to amass vast fortunes
   b. the growth and increasing prosperity of the middle class
   c. the emergence of a permanent working class
   d. the gradual loss of income among farmers
   e. the federal government's progressive income tax policies

10. Which of the following best characterizes late-nineteenth-century antipoverty efforts?
    a. an effort by reformers to address the role of one's environment in determining poverty levels
    b. a tendency to avoid making moral judgments in seeking to help those in need
    c. an effort to involve the federal government in eradicating poverty
    d. a tendency to differentiate between the "deserving" and "undeserving" poor
    e. a willingness to provide direct financial aid to the poor

11. The majority of women who received higher education in the post–Civil War period did so in
    a. coeducational institutions where they fought for equality with their male counterparts.
    b. foreign institutions that had longer traditions of allowing women access to colleges and universities.
    c. institutions that sought to prepare women for a marriage and motherhood.
    d. single-sex colleges that encouraged the development of a distinctive women's community.
    e. institutions that emphasized the development of practical skills for the workplace and encouraged women to adopt traditionally male values.

12. A major factor that promoted the growth of mass consumption in the late nineteenth century was
    a. the availability of inexpensive goods from abroad due to low American tariffs.
    b. inflation caused by government efforts to expand the currency.
    c. rising incomes among almost all segments of society.
    d. competition resulting from the decentralization of major industries.
    e. efforts by the federal government to promote consumer demand through fiscal and monetary policy.

Free-Response Questions—Exam Tips

Questions from this period often deal with the impact of immigration and urbanization on American society. Themes to consider could include how these immigrants fit into American society—were they able to assimilate or did they remain confined to their own communities? Be prepared to think about immigration in a comparative context, noting differences between pre– and post–Civil War trends, as well as how late-nineteenth-century immigration compares with that of the twentieth century.

Free-Response Questions

1. Evaluate the impact of urbanization between 1865 and 1920 in two of the following areas:
    Politics and government
    Popular culture and entertainment
    Economics

2. To what degree did immigration transform American society between 1865 and 1900?

Document-Based Question—Exam Tips

- Questions from the Civil War on will frequently use photographs and other visual sources (political cartoons, advertisements, and so on) as documents. Use the same criteria for assessing them that you would use for written sources: Who is the author? What prior knowledge can you bring that will help you analyze the document? What is the main idea of the document? What is the significance of the document considering both time and place? What symbols or images does the author use to convey the message? Why was the document produced when it was produced?
- Late-nineteenth-century questions will often include documents that deal with the growing gap between rich and poor. Keep in mind, though, that the growth of the middle class was extremely significant during this period.
- The growth of organized labor, intellectual trends such evolution and Social Darwinism, and changing ideas about time and place (the increasing separation between work and leisure time and home and workplace) are all things that had special significance during this time period.

Document-Based Question

Answer the following question using information from the accompanying documents, as well your knowledge of the time period.

To what degree did industrialization lead to an improved standard of living for Americans between 1865 and 1900?

Document A

Source: Andrew Carnegie, *The Gospel of Wealth* (1889).

The price which society pays for the law of competition, like the price it pays for cheap comforts and luxuries, is also great; but the advantages of this law are also greater still, for it is to this law that we owe our wonderful material development, which brings improved conditions in its train. . . .

This, then, is held to be the duty of the man of Wealth: First, to set an example of modest, unostentatious living, shunning display or extravagance; to provide moderately for the legitimate wants of those dependent upon him; and after doing so to consider all surplus revenues which come to him simply as trust funds, which he is called upon to administer, and strictly bound as a matter of duty to administer in the manner which, in his judgment, is best calculated to produce the most beneficial results for the community. . . .

Document B

Source: Henry George, *Progress and Poverty* (1879).

The association of poverty with progress is the great enigma of our times. . . . So long as all the increased wealth which modern progress brings goes but to build up great fortunes, to increase luxury and to make sharper the contrast between the House of Have and the House of Want, progress is not real and cannot be permanent.

Document C

Source: The Preamble and Declaration of Principles of the Knights of Labor, published in *Journal of United Labor* [Philadelphia, c. 1885).

TO THE PUBLIC:

The alarming development and aggressiveness of great capitalists and corporations, unless checked, will inevitably lead to the pauperization and hopeless degradation of the toiling masses.

It is imperative, if we desire to enjoy the full blessings of life, that a check be placed upon unjust accumulation, and the power for evil of aggregated wealth.

This much-desired object can be accomplished only by the united efforts of those who obey the divine injunction, "In the sweat of they face shalt thou eat bread."

Document D

Source: Testimony of Piano Manufacturer William Steinway before Senate Committee on the Relations between Labor and Capital (1883).

Question: The skilled laborers are paid less [in Europe]—how about labor that is not so much skilled?

Steinway: Unskilled labor is also paid less. In other words, it is very rare to see a workingman in Europe whose family can lay by anything, whereas here thrifty, skilled mechanics, blessed with health, and not meeting with sickness or other misfortune, have a chance to save money and do save money.

Question: Then you say that in this country the labor is much better off in his social and pecuniary conditions, and in the means of enjoying the comforts of life?

Steinway: Undoubtedly.

Document E

Source: Testimony by bronze worker Joseph Finnerty, before Senate Committee on the Relations between Labor and Capital (1883).

Question: Let me see if I understand you fully. You get less wages than you did fifteen years ago?

Answer: Yes.

Question: Now do you mean to say that the wages which you receive at present will buy as much as the comforts of life as the wages which you received then would?

Answer: By no means. I say that the rents are the same as they were fourteen years ago, but the man who had apartments of four or five rooms at that time is confining himself to perhaps three rooms now.

Question: How are the social surroundings of the workingmen now, as to the character of the neighborhoods in which they live; for I have noticed that there are some very fine neighborhoods in this city and some others that are very poor.

Answer: The bronze workers live in tenement houses. They are surrounded by the poorest class, the cheapest class; the cheapest element of the laboring people, and they are no better than anybody else.

Document F

Source: [http://xroads.virginia.edu/~MA01/Davis/photography/images/riisphotos/slideshow1.html].

Photograph captioned "Pedlar Who Slept in the Cellar of 11 Ludlow Street Rear" by Jacob Riis.

Document G

Source: Frederick Law Olmsted, "The Unplanned Growth of Cities."

The lives of women and children too poor to be sent to the country can now be saved in thousands of instances by making them go to the park. . . . The much greater rapidity with which patients convalesce and may be returned with safety to their ordinary occupations after severe illness, when they can be sent to the park for a few hours a day, is beginning to be understood. The addition thus made to the productive labor of the city is not unimportant.

Document H

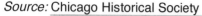
Source: Chicago Historical Society

Image of the Montgomery Ward Department Store

Document I

Source: S. Merlino, "Italian Immigrants and Their Enslavement," The Forum (April 1893).

"The Italian laborer does more than his share of work and receives less than his share of earnings; for as a matter of fact, the laws enacted with regard to this matter oppress the laborer and assist rather than hamper the contractor. Even supposing that the contractor does not succeed in importing contract labor, he finds in the market a large number of men entirely at his mercy, with not even the weak support of a promise to defend themselves against his greed."

Document J

Source: Bureau of the Census, *Historical Statistics of the United States: Colonial Times to 1970* (Washington, D.C., 1975).

Gross National Product, Total and Per Capita, 1869–1900

Year	Current prices		1958 prices	
	Total	Per Capita	Total	Per Capita
1900	18.7	246	76.9	1,011
1899	17.4	233	74.8	1.000
1898	15.4	210	68.6	933
1897	14.6	202	67.1	930
1896	13.3	188	61.3	865
1895	13.9	200	62.6	900
1894	12.6	185	55.9	819
1893	13.8	206	57.5	859
1892	14.3	218	60.4	920
1891	13.5	210	55.1	856
1890	13.1	208	52.7	836
1889	12.5	202	49.1	795
1879–1888	11.2	205	42.4	774
1869–1878	7.4	179	23.1	531

Document K

Source: Carroll D. Wright (future U.S. Labor Commissioner), "The Factory System as an Element in Civilization," *Journal of Science*, 16, (December 1882).

I am constantly obliged, in my everyday labors, to refute the assertion that wages under the factory system are growing lower and lower. The reverse is the truth, which is easily demonstrated; the progress of improvement in machinery may have reduced the price paid for a single article, yard, or pound of product, or for the services of a skilled and intelligent operative, but the same improvement has enabled the workman to produce in a greater proportion and always with a less expenditure of muscular labor and in less time, and it has enabled a low grade of labor to increase its earnings. At the same time, a greater number have been benefited, either in consumption or production, by the improvement.

Multiple-Choice Answers

1. c. While African Americans, women, and farmers did move to urban areas, they did so in numbers far smaller than new immigrants. Death rates were high among most urban families.

2. d. Congress would restrict Japanese immigration in the early twentieth century and the immigration of other groups during the 1920s.

3. c. The primary constituency for urban political machines was new immigrants who often lacked the knowledge and connections needed to succeed in American society and gravitated to those who could offer them immediate services.

4. c. The "realist" school of literature sought to portray the social realities of the period.

5. e. Horatio Alger wrote a large number of books celebrating the opportunity and upward mobility that he believed was available to those with ambition and drive.

6. a. As a result of the growing popularity of Darwin's theory of evolution, a split emerged between those who accepted his ideas (especially in urban areas) and those who opposed them (often in rural, heavily Protestant areas). This split became particularly acute in the 1920s.

7. c. While American popular entertainment was frequently divided by racial, class, and gender lines, most groups of Americans found some activities in which to take part, many of which were distinctively American (particularly in sports and musical theater).

8. c. While all of these sports attracted audiences in the late nineteenth century, baseball earned its place as "America's pastime" through its great popularity, and the first professional leagues were formed in the late 1860s.

9. b. Although the late nineteenth century was remarkable for the growth of large fortunes, the emergence of a professional middle class played a major role in the emergence of a consumer economy. The government did not levy an income tax until after the ratification of the Sixteenth Amendment in 1913.

10. d. Groups like the Salvation Army tended to focus more on moral uplift than upon addressing the structural causes of poverty. The American emphasis on a self-help ideology and fear of creating dependence on the poor helped to keep assistance limited.

11. d. One of the most significant developments in this period for women was the growth of women's colleges and universities, many of which helped prepare women for involvement in reform causes.

12. c. Most Americans saw increases in their incomes during this period, although these increases occurred much faster for some groups than for others.

Free-Response Questions Commentary

1. Urban growth led to major transformations in all three areas. In politics and government, urban political machines arose to fill the vacuum caused by the inabilities of existing city governments to provide jobs, sanitation, welfare, and other services to their residents. Middle-class reformers sought to replace the "boss" system with more efficient and honest government, finally succeeding in enacting a variety of municipal reforms beginning in the 1890s.

   In the realm of popular culture, urban population growth and the emergence of leisure time helped to spur a great American interest in new forms of recreation and entertainment. Spectator sports like baseball, basketball, football, boxing, and horse racing all drew large audiences, while music and theater proved popular as well. While a great deal of late-nineteenth-century recreation and culture was public in nature, private pursuits such as the reading of "dime" novels also increased.

Urban growth resulted in the emergence of a new middle class with the resources to purchase consumer goods on a large scale. New forms of transportation helped to promote the development of national markets. Department stores and retail chains helped to transform the experience of shopping, particularly for women. The idea of women as consumers gave them a new and distinctive public role that they had lacked previously.

2. Immigrants changed the face of American society significantly between 1865 and 1900. Whereas earlier immigrant groups had often moved west to buy land and or establish business, late-nineteenth-century immigrants tended to be poorer and took jobs in factories. Many of them formed ethnic communities to provide mutual assistance and to help to ease the painful adjustment to a new nation. In some cases, these communities made it more difficult for immigrants to assimilate into American society. Popular prejudice against immigrants caused Congress to pass the Chinese Exclusion Act in 1882 and led to the emergence of groups like the American Protective Association and the Immigration Restriction League in the 1890s. Overall, while immigrants adjusted to the new society with varying degrees of success, their arrival clearly transformed the face of the American city, making it far more diverse in 1900 than it had been in 1865.

Document-Based Question Commentary

Outside Knowledge—The issue of American economic development and its impact on the nation's class system and standard of living was the central topic of late-nineteenth-century America. The wealthy used the ideas of Social Darwinism to justify their position in society, although many argued that the wealthy had a responsibility to help the poor. While government remained slow to meet the needs of the poor, many workers looked to organized labor to help them improve their position in society, although unionization remained largely confined to skilled workers and overall improvement in wages and working conditions was minimal during this time period.

The Documents—There is evidence to point to both advances and declines in living standards. Carefully construct your thesis statement and then support it with the ample evidence provided in the documents. Avoid trying to straddle both sides. Overall, the American economy grew significantly in both total and per capita terms between 1869 and 1900 (as shown in Document I). A small minority made large fortunes, while the emergence of new professional opportunities fueled the growth of the middle class. Many groups, especially new immigrants and those living in areas like the South, did not share in the nation's prosperity.

Documents A, D, G, H, and K all point to positive trends. Andrew Carnegie argues that philanthropic efforts by the wealthy improve the lot of the poor; Steinway notes that even unskilled workers in America have much greater opportunities than those in Europe; the Montgomery Ward advertisement shows the wide availability of goods; Olmsted notes that urban development and planning can produce beneficial results for members of the lower classes; and Wright points to the fact that mechanization has in fact helped less-skilled workers produce more and thus have access to greater prosperity than they would have had in the pre-industrial period.

Documents B, C, E, F, and I all paint a different picture. Henry George demonstrates the concern that many intellectuals felt over the existence of poverty even during periods of apparent prosperity; the Knights of Labor remonstrate against the growing gap between rich and poor and show the efforts of organized labor to improve conditions for labor; Finnerty shows that skilled workers are experiencing a decline in their standard of living; Riis portrays the plight of the urban poor; and Merlino shows the desperate plight of immigrants and how they are often exploited in their new nation.

The best answers to this question will note that the standard of living improved for many, but that it was by no means a universal trend. Industrialization and urbanization provided new opportunities for work and made new goods and services available to many, yet a significant underclass emerged during the period. The documents should indicate that those who benefited from the new system were quick to sing its praises, while those who were left out had a different view (although intellectuals like George and journalists like Riis clearly saw reasons for great concern).

CHAPTER 19
From Crisis to Empire

AP THEMES

- **Economic Transformation:** Industrialization and modernization irrevocably altered the life of the American farmer. New technologies such as the mechanical reaper and the iron plow allowed farmers to cultivate more land than ever before but also imposed high costs, as farmers had to borrow to pay for the new machinery. Urban growth and railroads provided access to new markets but also forced farmers to confront high costs for shipping and storage. Many farmers advocated currency inflation to help them to reduce their debts, while the federal government remained committed to maintaining the gold standard.

- **Politics and Citizenship:** In the immediate post-Civil War period, few Americans believed in the need for an active federal government. Although the government provided aid to businesses through land subsidies, high tariffs, and pro-business intervention in labor disputes, the government had few other roles in American life. Throughout the late nineteenth century, Congress, heavily influenced by big business, dominated a series of weak presidents (in part a result of the pendulum swing against the power that the office had accumulated during the Civil War. American expansion played a role in the growth of the modern state and helped to change the American politicization experience). As the United States undertook new international responsibilities, the role of the government naturally began to expand. Although this was a slow and halting process, significant elements of a larger national government existed in the 1890s. President William McKinley, once seen as a relatively weak leader, helped to set in motion the creation of the modern presidency. The media played an important role in shaping public opinion on foreign and domestic policy, as more and more Americans had access to newspapers and magazines.

- **Reform:** In response to the challenges posed by industrialization, many farmers sought to organize to defend their interests, (going against the notion that farmers were by nature individualists). This movement ultimately took the form of the Populist, or People's Party, the largest third-party movement in American history. The Populists proposed a wide-ranging expansion of the power of the federal government in the public interest, laying the groundwork for the later Progressive movement. Although the Populists accomplished little in the form of specific pieces of legislation, their advocacy of a graduated income tax, measures such as the initiative, referendum, and recall, and the direct election of senators, all came to fruition within a few decades after the decline of the movement.

- **Globalization:** During the 1890s, the United States became much more directly involved in world politics than it had been prior to that point. While the United States was never in a strict sense isolationist, seeking commercial and other opportunities abroad since the end of the American Revolution, the nation's leaders sought to remain aloof from political commitments abroad throughout the nineteenth century (preferring to focus on expansion across the North American continent). Washington's farewell address had urged Americans to avoid permanent political connections with Europe but was less concerned with the dangers of commercial expansion. American foreign policy during the 1890s, influenced by a series of strategic, economic, and ideological motives, brought the country much more actively into the realm of international affairs.

- **War and Diplomacy:** American expansion during the 1890s brought the United States into a war with Spain, one that was successful militarily, largely as a result of Spain's military weakness, but that also exposed many of the underlying weaknesses of the American military, later spurring a series of reforms in an effort to modernize the nation's military establishment.
- **American Identity:** The agrarian challenge exposed the degree to which the country was divided across regional, class, and racial lines. The Populists represented in many ways a movement of the economically marginalized in the West and South against the forces of the more prosperous East. At the same time, racial differences between black and white farmers in the South ultimately prevented the development of a far-reaching challenge to the power of the economic elite in that region. The 1896 election represented a major realignment, whereby the Republican Party came to be the majority party for the next three decades, while the Democrats gradually began to be identified with the interests of the less fortunate elements of American society. The 1890s helped to significantly change both domestic and foreign views of the American national character. The United States had long prided itself on its ability to remain aloof from world affairs and from the selfish imperialism of the European powers. Territorial acquisitions in Puerto Rico, the Philippines, and Hawaii and indirect control over Cuba transformed the United States into an imperial republic. This would have far-reaching implications for America's role in the world throughout the rest of the twentieth century. A wide-ranging debate over the implications of empire divided the nation and foreshadowed the debates over World War I, World War II, and the Cold War. McKinley's reelection in 1900 was considered by many to be a mandate from the American people in support of United States imperialism.

CHAPTER SUMMARY
The Politics of Equilibrium

National politics in the late nineteenth century were marked by extraordinary voter participation. Despite the relative weakness of the federal government, voter turnout was high (almost 80 percent of eligible voters participated in presidential elections between 1860 and 1900). Regional differences, religion, and ethnicity shaped party loyalty more significantly than economic issues. Democrats tended to attract recent immigrants in northern cities and maintained a strong base in the South, while Republicans tended to favor measures limiting immigration and enjoyed popularity among "old-stock" Americans.

The federal government did relatively little during this period, with the significant exceptions including subsidies to railroads, primarily in the form of federal land grants, as well as intervention in labor-management disputes such as the **Pullman strike** in 1894. In addition, the federal government administered a massive system of **pensions** to Civil War veterans (some hoped to expand this into a permanent system of old-age pensions, but this died out, partly because the system was riddled with corruption and party patronage).

The role of the presidency during this period tended to be custodial—that is, the president "took care of" rather than took charge of the government and distributed government patronage in the form of jobs for party supporters. The Republican Party during this period split into two factions, the **Stalwarts** (supporters of traditional machine politics and patronage) and the **Half-Breeds,** reformers (although in reality both just wanted a larger piece of the patronage pie). **Rutherford B. Hayes** (1877–1881) sought to create an effective and honest civil service, an effort that dominated his presidency. Hayes' successor, Half-Breed **James A. Garfield,** was assassinated by a frustrated office-seeker in July 1881. Garfield's successor, **Chester A. Arthur** (1881–1884), had been a Stalwart throughout his career but sought to pursue an independent course upon taking office. In 1883, at Arthur's urging, Congress passed the **Pendleton Act,** which required a competitive written examination system for some federal jobs.

In the 1884 election, respectable New York reform Governor **Grover Cleveland** defeated **James G. Blaine** of Maine in an invective-filled campaign; the election was likely decided when Blaine failed to quickly repudiate the words of a Protestant minister who referred to the Democrats as the party of "rum, Romanism, and rebellion." Cleveland reflected the popular view that the federal government should play a limited role in American life. Cleveland particularly opposed protective tariffs, which he believed encouraged Congress to pass unnecessary legislation that would increase the federal government's size and scope. His efforts to reduce tariffs met significant Republican opposition, making the tariff a central issue in the 1888 presidential election. Cleveland was defeated by **Benjamin Harrison** (1889–1893) of Indiana in one of the closest elections in American history. It was the first election since the Civil War in which the Republicans and Democrats differed significantly on economic issues. This debate foreshadowed a series of spirited debates on such topics in the 1890s and the first several decades of the twentieth century.

Although Harrison was a passive president, his administration had to face some of the new issues arising in the public arena. In July 1890, Congress passed the **Sherman Antitrust Act,** a largely symbolic measure forbidding "combinations in restraint of trade." The measure was only haphazardly enforced, until more enforcement mechanisms were added after 1900. The Republicans also sought high protective tariffs to benefit American businesses embodied by the McKinley Tariff, passed by Congress in October 1890. This issue, however, contributed to heavy Republican losses in the midyear elections.

In 1892, Harrison and Cleveland undertook a rematch of the 1888 campaign, joined this time with third-party candidate **James B. Weaver** of the **People's Party.** Cleveland won a substantial victory, and the Democrats obtained a majority in both houses of Congress for the first time since 1878. Cleveland took few major initiatives, focusing primarily on tariff reform. The Senate weakened his original proposal, resulting in the compromise **Wilson-Gorman** tariff of 1894.

Despite the limited nature of the federal government, public support was increasing for more substantial reforms. In 1886, the Supreme Court in the so-called **Wabash Case** had overruled a series of state laws regulating railroads, arguing that these new state laws were an unconstitutional effort to control interstate commerce. In 1887, Congress responded with the **Interstate Commerce Act,** which prohibited rate discrimination in short and long hauls, required railroads to publish rate schedules, and declared that rail rates must be **"reasonable and just."** This, however, was loosely enforced for the next twenty years, until President Theodore Roosevelt urged Congress to pass legislation extending the federal government's power to regulate railroad rates.

The Agrarian Revolt

Although farmers were traditionally considered the most individualistic of Americans, they in fact exhibited a frequent tendency to organize to support their interests. The first major effort in this vein was the organization by Olliver H. Kelley in 1867 of the **National Grange of the Patrons of Husbandry,** popularly known as **"the Grange."** Although in its early years the organization was primarily a vehicle for social gatherings and education, the **depression of 1873** caused many of its members to form marketing cooperatives to allow farmers to bypass middlemen and hopefully raise their profits. In the 1870s the Grangers succeeded in controlling the state legislatures of many of the midwestern states. However, the temporary return of agricultural prosperity in the late 1870s and the overturning of the Granger laws by the Supreme Court caused the organization to decline rapidly by the end of the decade.

By the mid-1870s, farmers in both the South and the Midwest were forming so-called **Farmers' Alliances.** By 1880, the Southern Alliance had 4 million members. While the alliances were concerned primarily with local problems, some members sought larger reforms that would replace the competitive economy with a more cooperative system. The alliances were notable for the significant role played by women, epitomized by **Mary Ellen Lease,** best known for her admonition to farmers to "raise less corn and more hell!" By 1889, the alliances created a loose merger, and they met in Ocala, Florida, the following year, issuing the so-called **Ocala demands,** a preview of the more developed demands that the movement would articulate in the 1890s. Alliance members competed successfully in the off-year elections. By 1892, the movement was coherent enough to meet in Omaha, Nebraska, to nominate James B. Weaver as the candidate of the newly formed **People's Party** for president of the United States. Weaver gained 8.5 percent of the popular vote, while nearly 1,500 Populist candidates won seats in state legislatures.

While Populists sought to create a broad-based political coalition, their appeal was mainly limited to farmers, especially those farmers who worked in the areas that were threatened by the growth of mechanization and agricultural consolidation. Evidence indicates that many Populists were also "culturally marginal," feeling left out of the mainstream of American life. Populists generally failed in their efforts to attract organized labor, although this was less true in the Rocky Mountain states. One of the main tenets of populism was the demand for **"free silver."** Urban workers in eastern cities disliked the Populist idea of an expanded currency, fearing inflation and rising costs of living, and were also put off by the Populists' anti-immigrant stance. In the South, controversy existed over whether to allow blacks into the movement—once southern conservatives attacked the movement for undermining white supremacy, the interracial character of the movement quickly faded and the possibility of a widespread movement of the economically dispossessed against the region's economic elites ended.

The Populist program was best expressed in the **Omaha Platform** of 1892. Most notably, this called for the creation of **"subtreasuries,"** or warehouses, where farmers could store crops and use the crops as collateral until prices rose. The Populists also wanted the direct election of United States senators and regulation, and later, ownership, of railroads, telephones, and telegraphs. The Populist platform also demanded government-owned postal savings banks, a graduated income tax, and currency inflation.

Although some Populists were openly anti-Semitic and others expressed ideas that were based on mysticism and other dubious sources, the movement should be best remembered not as a challenge to capitalism and industrialization but as a challenge to the laissez-faire orthodoxy of the time.

The Crisis of the 1890s

The worst depression in American history to that point resulted from the collapse of the Philadelphia and Reading railroad, which triggered a stock market collapse, leading to the failure of banks that had invested heavily in the market. Overall, the **Panic of 1893** showed how interdependent the American economy had become, with failure in one area triggering failures in other areas. Prosperity did not truly return until 1901.

The depression naturally gave rise to some protest movements, most notably the march from Ohio to Washington led by **Jacob Coxey,** who advocated currency inflation and public works to stimulate the economy. **"Coxey's Army,"** as his group came to be known, only numbered about 500 upon reaching Washington and had little concrete impact on changing public policy. It did, however, indicate the sense of desperation that many Americans felt at the time.

The Panic of 1893 precipitated a deep debate over the basis of the currency of the United States. The government had traditionally recognized both gold and silver as circulating mediums, a system known as "bimetallism." In 1873, however, the government stopped coining silver because the market value of silver was much higher than the government-mandated 16:1 ratio (16 oz. of silver equaled 1 oz. of gold). In the 1870s, however, new discoveries of silver meant that the market value fell below 16:1, meaning that holders of silver would benefit from coinage at this ratio. Silver-mine owners and farmers seeking currency inflation sought to overturn the so-called **"Crime of '73."**

Cleveland believed that the nation's declining gold reserves were the result of the **Sherman Silver Purchase Act of 1890,** which required the government to purchase silver and pay for it in gold. In 1893, Congress repealed the act, although this split the Democratic Party. The currency issue came to be invested with great symbolic significance, as seen by the popularity of such books as William H. Harvey's *Coin's Financial School*, published in 1894.

"A Cross of Gold"

The Populists initially paid little attention to the silver issue, only embracing it as the party become more powerful on the national stage. In 1896, the Republicans nominated **William McKinley** of Ohio as their presidential candidate and adopted a conservative platform that opposed free coinage of silver except by agreement with the leading commercial nations of the world. The Democrats appeared ready to adopt the gold standard until Bryan's famous "Cross of Gold" speech at the end of their convention. Bryan was nominated as the youngest candidate ever by a major party, representing the interests and desires of rural, Protestant, middle-class Americans. The Democrats' adoption of the free-silver platform created a dilemma for the Populists, who feared (justifiably) losing their identity as a party if they undertook "fusion" with the major party. Nonetheless, the Populists nominated Bryan and Georgian **Tom Watson** as their candidates for president and vice president.

In 1896, the business and financial communities rallied behind McKinley, fearing the consequences of a Democratic victory. McKinley conducted a **"front porch"** campaign from his home in Canton, Ohio, while Bryan undertook the country's first truly national campaign, traveling systematically to visit all sections of the country. While this helped to form the modern system of presidential politics, it also antagonized many voters, especially urban immigrants who feared Bryan's emphasis on Protestant morality.

McKinley received 271 electoral votes to Bryan's 176. Bryan only won in those areas of the South and West where miners or economically struggling farmers predominated. The Democratic program was not sufficiently broad-based to win a national campaign. One of the major results of the election was the collapse of the Populist Party. The movement represented the most widespread protest against the excesses of industrialism—its failure meant that most Americans accepted industrial consolidation as a reality and sought to accommodate themselves with how best to use the power of the federal government to counterbalance, rather than to eliminate, the forces of big business. Farmers largely abandoned their efforts at reform and instead became part of the interest-group system that arose in the early decades of the twentieth century.

The McKinley administration presided over a period of relative domestic calm and stability, marked by the gradual return of economic prosperity. McKinley focused on raising tariffs, as shown by the **Dingley Tariff** of 1897, which raised duties to the highest point in American history. While the administration was more cautious in dealing with the silver issue, the Republicans enacted the **Currency** or **Gold Standard Act** of 1900, which confirmed the nation's commitment to the gold standard. New debates over America's role in the world dominated most of the administration's attention.

Although the free-silver movement failed, it raised important questions about the nature of the American economy. The growth of the money supply had not kept pace with the economic progress, and only through the dramatic growth of the gold available (due to new extraction techniques and discoveries in Alaska, South Africa, and Australia) were the Populist warnings of financial disaster avoided. The nation's commitment to the gold standard remained until the challenges of the Great Depression in the 1930s forced its abandonment.

Stirrings of Imperialism

While the United States undertook little in the way of expansion beyond its borders in the twenty years after the Civil War, focusing instead on consolidating its continental expansion, by the 1890s the nation began to look abroad for a variety of reasons, including the need for new markets and sources of raw materials; historian **Frederick Jackson Turner's** influential discussions of the influence of the closing of the frontier; reaction to the social unrest of the 1890s, the influence of European imperialism; and the continuation of the concept of Manifest Destiny, which had led to the destruction of the Native American tribes.

Many American leaders found a justification for imperialism in the doctrine of **Social Darwinism,** which contended that since nations underwent a constant struggle for existence, the domination of weak nations by strong ones was a fixed law of nature. Leading advocates of imperialism included **Josiah Strong,** a Protestant minister whose 1885 book, *Our Country,* argued that the Anglo-Saxon Christian race was divinely ordained to spread its institutions and values throughout the world. Captain **Alfred Thayer Mahan,** a naval officer, argued in his book, *The Influence of Sea Power upon History* (1890) that the countries that had built strong navies and were able to obtain control of the oceans were the most successful in world history. He thus urged that American leaders undertake the construction of a canal in Panama, acquisition of defensive bases, possession of overseas bases, and a program to expand the United States Navy.

The United States had played a leading role in the affairs of the Western Hemisphere. This region served as an area for the United States to undertake new ventures and initiatives as it sought a greater world role. Republican Secretary of State **James G. Blaine** sought to promote hemispheric cooperation through the 1889 PanAmerican Congress, which created the weak **Pan-American Union.** However, delegates failed to adopt Blaine's proposal for an inter-American customs union and arbitration for international disputes. In 1895, the United States supported Venezuela in a boundary dispute against Great Britain. England initially ignored American demands that the issue be subject to arbitration, and **Secretary of State Richard Olne** claimed that Britain was violating the Monroe Doctrine. President Grover Cleveland finally established an international commission to examine the issue, threatening war if Britain ignored the commission's finding and leading Britain to agree to arbitration.

Americans were also interested in pursuing economic gains in the Pacific. Beginning in the early nineteenth century, American missionaries and sugar planters had gradually built up strong influence in Hawaii. By 1887, the United States had negotiated a treaty to open a naval base at Pearl Harbor. The Hawaiian economy had become dependent on the export of sugar to the United States and was dealt a shock when the 1890 **McKinley Tariff** no longer allowed Hawaiian sugar to enter the country duty-free. Hawaii's **Queen Liliuokalani,** a nationalist who had been elevated to the throne in 1891, was deposed in 1893 by sugar planters who wanted annexation to the United States. The Democratic-controlled Senate refused to support the annexation agreement that had been negotiated between the United States and Hawaii, and a treaty was not passed until the Republicans returned to power in 1898.

The United States, Great Britain, and Germany all shared interest in the Pacific island of Samoa. In 1878, the United States was able to negotiate a treaty from Samoan leaders for a naval station at **Pago Pago.** In 1899, the United States and Germany finally agreed to divide the island between them and to compensate Great Britain with other Pacific territories.

War with Spain

The Spanish–American conflict of the 1890s was a direct result of Spanish tensions with Cuba, which had existed openly since 1868, when the Cubans undertook a ten-year revolt seeking independence from Spain. Rebellion broke out again in 1895, exacerbated by the loss of American markets for Cuban sugar due to the **Wilson–Gorman** tariff of 1894. The American press, led by "yellow journalists" **Joseph Pulitzer** and **William Randolph Hearst,** reported on Spanish atrocities in Cuba, ignoring the fact that atrocities existed on both sides. Such reports, along with lobbying efforts by Cuban refugees in the United States, caused many Americans to support U.S. intervention in Cuba. President Cleveland, however, resisted such calls.

After taking office in 1897,, McKinley took a stronger position and called for Spain to make extensive reforms in its Cuban policy. American demand for war was fueled by the **De Lome** letter, which was written by the Spanish Minister in Washington and was highly critical of President McKinley, and the explosion of the U.S.S. *Maine,* which occurred in Havana Harbor in February 1898. It was widely reported that the explosion was caused by a submarine mine; later evidence suggested that the *Maine* was destroyed by an internal explosion in one of the engine rooms.

Americans quickly adopted the slogan "Remember the *Maine,*" and Congress appropriated $50 million for military preparations. Last-minute negotiations failed, and Congress voted to declare war at the end of April, leading to the beginning of the Spanish–American War. Although the fighting itself was relatively short (Secretary of State John Hay dubbed the conflict **"A Splendid Little War"**), ending by August, the American war effort was not without problems. While 460 Americans were killed as a direct result of battle, there were approximately 5,200 others who died of disease. In addition, the American war effort was plagued by inefficiency and inadequate preparation. Racial conflict between black and white troops further hampered the American cause. Despite incredible incompetence, American troops succeeded in moving from Florida to Cuba in order to confront Cuban troops bottled up in Santiago Harbor. In a series of battles, most notably **San Juan Hill** (which made the reputation of Theodore Roosevelt), American troops made their way to Santiago. The Spanish government, meanwhile, decided to abandon the strategic port city of Santiago, and the Spanish fleet was destroyed by United States ships as it sought to leave the harbor.

Although the war had started over events close to the United States, the conflict quickly took on global dimensions. On the orders of Assistant Secretary of the Navy **Theodore Roosevelt,** Admiral George Dewey seized the Philippines, a longtime Spanish possession. This helped to shift the war from a conflict meant to free Cuba to a war to strip Spain of its colonies, but no immediate thought was given to what the United States would do with the territories it was suddenly acquiring. On August 12, Spain agreed to an armistice. Under its terms, Spain agreed to recognize Cuban independence, ceded Puerto Rico and Guam to the United States, and accepted continued American occupation of Manila pending the outcome of the fighting in the Philippines.

Ironically, the American occupation of Puerto Rico caused the least controversy in the United States. American troops had occupied the island during the Spanish–American War and remained there until 1900, when the **Foraker Act** ended military rule and established a formal colonial government. An American governor presided over a two-house legislature, with an upper house appointed by the United States and a lower house elected by the Puerto Rican people. In 1917, under pressure to clarify the American–Puerto Rican relationship, Congress passed the **Jones Act,** which declared Puerto Rico to be a United States territory and made all Puerto Ricans American citizens.

Overall, the addition of Puerto Rico to the United States was a boon to the island's sugar industry, as Puerto Rican sugar could enter the United States duty-free. The Puerto Rican economy came to be based on large sugar plantations owned by Americans and operated with native labor, which led to both a decline in Puerto Rican food preparation and greater dependence on international sugar prices.

The issues arising from the American occupation of the Philippines led to much greater debate than did the occupation of Puerto Rico. The **Treaty of Paris**, signed in December 1898, confirmed the original armistice terms but added the demand for annexation of the Philippines, bolstered by an American offer of $20 million for the islands, which the Spanish government accepted. Opponents of annexation, most notably members of the largely upper-class **Anti-Imperialist League,** made a variety of moral, racial, economic, and political arguments against acquisition of the Philippines. Supporters of annexation came out with an equal variety of arguments, with many noting that the American policy toward Native Americans had created a precedent for acquiring territory without absorbing the population. The treaty was ratified in February 1899. **William Jennings Bryan,** a noted anti-imperialist, surprisingly helped to gain passage of the treaty in the hope of making imperialism the central issue of the 1900 presidential campaign. Bryan's strategy backfired, as McKinley defeated him even more decisively than he had in 1896.

The Republic as Empire

While Hawaii, Alaska, and Puerto Rico offered relatively few problems for American governing officials, Cuba proved more difficult. United States troops occupied Cuba until 1902, helping to build the Cuban infrastructure, while also paving the way for American domination of the Cuban economy. In April 1898, Congress passed the **Teller Amendment,** stating that the United States would not attempt to annex Cuba. In 1901, Congress passed the **Platt Amendment,** which forbade Cuba from making treaties with other nations, allowed the United States to intervene to protect Cuban independence, and allowed the United States to maintain naval bases in Cuban territories. The United States also pressured Cuba into incorporating these terms into its constitution. Like Puerto Rico and Hawaii, the Cuban economy became heavily dependent on the export of sugar for the international market, making it subject to boom-and-bust cycles.

In the Philippines, American occupiers faced great opposition. A full scale rebellion was led by Filipino nationalist **Emilio Aguinaldo**. More than 4,300 American troops and likely at least 50,000 Filipinos were killed between 1898 and 1902. Aguinaldo was captured in 1901, and in the same year, the United States transferred control of the Philippines to **William Howard Taft,** who became the first American civilian governor. As had been the case in Cuba, American occupation officials introduced major reforms on the island, but also produced almost exclusive Filipino economic dependence on the United States. The Philippines finally received their independence from the United States in July 1946.

The American acquisition of the Philippines, which extended the nation's Pacific interests, increased American interest in China. In September 1898, responding to the growing encroachment of European and other powers in the face of Chinese weakness, McKinley enunciated the principle that the United States wanted an "open door" in China, meaning equal access for all nations but special privileges for none. Secretary of state **John Hay** further developed these principles the following year in a series of so-called **"Open Door Notes"** to Japan and other European powers. Although it was not really possible for the United States to force other nations to adhere to these policies, they did provide greater American access to the China trade.

The Spanish–American War had revealed serious problems with the organization of the American military, leading President McKinley to appoint influential lawyer Elihu Root to undertake a series of reforms of the American military following the conclusion of the Spanish–American War. These included enlarging the regular Army, establishing standards for the National Guard, creating a series of officer training schools, and establishing a body of military advisors to the secretary of war, which became known as the **Joint Chiefs of Staff.**

7/a

Multiple-Choice Questions

X 1. The Pendleton Act of 1883 dealt with which of the following issues?
   a. the free coinage of silver
   b. the government's ability to control trusts
   c. the reform of the nation's civil service
   d. he protective tariff
   e. the government's ability to control railroad rates

X 2. The "Granger laws" of the 1870s sought to do which of the following?
   a. control railroad rates and practices to prevent discrimination against small farmers
   b. establish the free coinage of silver to inflate the currency
   c. establish a system of warehousing cooperatives to raise farm prices
   d. lower tariffs to allow farmers access to foreign markets
   e. limit the power of trusts to allow farmers cheaper farm machinery prices

3. The Supreme Court's decision in the case of *Wabash* v. *Illinois* did which of the following?
   a. upheld states' abilities to regulate railroad rates in the public interest
   b. held that unions could be prosecuted for violations in restraint of trade
   c. limited states' abilities to pass legislation regulating railroads
   d. increased the federal government's power in antitrust cases
   e. limited the federal government's power to issue injunctions against unions

4. The election of 1896
   a. demonstrated Americans' deep frustration with conservative government policies.
   b. resulted in significant gains for the Populists.
   c. was a resounding victory for the forces of conservatism and stability.
   d. demonstrated few economic differences between the major parties.
   e. showed the unity of the Democratic Party.

X 5. The Populist Party
   a. sought to replace capitalism with a system of agrarian socialism.
   b. succeeded in gaining immediate passage of its demands.
   c. had little long-term influence on public policy.
   d. sought to curb the worst excesses of industrial capitalism.
   e. successfully reached beyond its agrarian base.

X 6. The "Crime of '73" refers to
   a. the government's intervention in labor disputes.
   b. the government's discontinuing the coinage of silver.
   c. the government's unwillingness to pursue antitrust actions.
   d. the Supreme Court's overturning of the Granger laws.
   e. the government's policy of purchasing silver.

X 7. The Panic of 1893
   a. caused the federal government to become more involved in American life.
   b. was a temporary downturn.
   c. exposed how failure in one economic sector could trigger a major depression.
   d. showed the growing power of the labor movement.
   e. awakened little popular protest.

8. Which of the following best characterizes the role of the popular American press in the period leading up to the Spanish–American War?
   a. It promoted balanced and informed debate over events in Cuba.
   b. It opposed potential American involvement in the conflict between Spain and Cuba
   c. It emphasized Spanish atrocities in Cuba to help inflame American public opinion.
   d. It took little interest in events in Cuba.
   e. It emphasized the atrocities committed by Cuban rebels.

9. What was the purpose of the Open Door Notes?
   a. They sought to promote American economic interests in Latin America.
   b. They served as a warning to Great Britain against interference in the Western Hemisphere.
   c. They sought to divide Samoa among Germany, Great Britain, and the United States.
   d. They sought to allow the United States equal access to trade with China.
   e. They sought to provide the United States with territorial control of the Philippines.

10. What was the impact of the Platt Amendment?
   a. It incorporated Puerto Rico into the United States.
   b. It gave the United States virtual control over Cuba
   c. It provided for the independence of the Philippines.
   d. It declared that the United States would not annex Cuba.
   e. It led to the annexation of Hawaii.

11. The results of the 1900 presidential election support the conclusion that
   a. imperialism played a role of little significance, as Americans seemed more interested in other issues.
   b. Bryan's efforts to spark debate on imperialism backfired, as Americans demonstrated clear support for McKinley's policies.
   c. the American people were evenly divided on the question of imperialism.
   d. voters offered a sharp protest against American imperialism.
   e. both major parties were united behind support for American imperialism.

12. The purpose of the Foraker Act of 1900 was to
   a. end American military rule in Puerto Rico and establish a formal colonial government.
   b. create provisions for the governing of American Samoa.
   c. provide guidelines for American government in the Philippines.
   d. grant American citizenship to all Puerto Ricans.
   e. establish guidelines for the eventual independence of the Philippines.

13. Which of the following best characterizes the American economic impact on Cuba, the Philippines, Puerto Rico, and Hawaii?
   a. American occupation produced a balanced economy.
   b. American occupation created a rising standard of living in each area.
   c. American occupation led to almost exclusive dependence on the United States.
   d. American influence led to industrialization and modernization in each area.
   e. American occupation had little significant economic impact.

Free-Response Questions—Exam Tips

- Questions covering this period often look at the role of the federal government and the growing challenges to the belief that the government should not play an active role in American society. The issue of whether the government in fact pursued a laissez-faire approach is a significant theme—while the self-help, individualistic American ideology meant that the government provided no direct assistance to the poor and dispossessed, American business could not have succeeded to the degree that it did without significant help from the federal government.
- The degree to which economic issues motivate political participation is another theme to consider. Despite the relatively weak federal government and uninspiring presidential candidates in the late nineteenth century, Americans divided over what historians call "ethnocultural" issues (Sabbath observance, temperance, English-only education) actively participated in elections at both the local and national level.

Free-Response Questions

1. How did farmers respond to social and economic change between 1865 and 1900? How successful was their response?

2. 2. Analyze national politics between 1865 and 1900. What major issues emerged between the Democratic and Republican parties?

Document-Based Question—Exam Tip

The Debate over Imperialism and American Identity: Debates over American foreign policy at key junctures have brought about significant questions about America's fundamental national mission and goals. Important questions include variations on the following themes: To what degree should the United States seek to spread its institutions and influence abroad? Should the United States concentrate its resources at home or abroad? In what ways and to what extent did the United States try to extend its hegemony beyond the Western Hemisphere? Many of the questions that emerge during the debate over imperialism in the 1890s reemerge during and after World War I and World War II and during and after the Cold War.

Document-Based Question

How did both supporters and opponents of the Spanish–American War and ensuing United States imperialism use their conception of American identity to support their positions between 1898 and 1900?

Use the documents that follow and your knowledge of the period to answer the question.

Document A

Source: Senator George Hoar, Speech, January 1899.

I deny the right to hold land or acquire any property for any purpose not contemplated by the Constitution. The government of foreign people against their will is not a constitutional purpose but a purpose expressly forbidden by the Constitution. Therefore I deny the right to acquire this territory and to hold it by the government for that purpose. . . .

Now, I claim that under the Declaration of Independence you cannot govern a foreign territory, a foreign people, another people than your own; that you cannot subjugate them and govern them against their will, because you think it is for their own good, when they do not; because you think you are going to give them the blessings of liberty. You have no right at the cannon's mouth to impose on an unwilling people your Declaration of Independence and your Constitution and your notions of freedom and notions of what is good.

Document B

Source: Charles Eliot Norton, Letter, November 1899.

We believe that America had something better to offer to mankind than those aims she is now pursuing, and we mourn her desertion of ideals which were not selfish nor limited in their application, but which are of universal worth and validity. She has lost her unique position as a potential leader in the progress of civilization and has taken up her place simply as one of the grasping and selfish nations of the present day. We all know how far she has fallen short in the past of exhibiting in her conduct a fidelity to those ideals which she professed, but some of us, at least, had not lost the hope that she would ultimately succeed in becoming more faithful to them.

Document C

Source: William Jennings Bryan, Speech, August 1900.

If we have an imperial policy we must have a great standing army as its natural and necessary complement. The spirit which will justify the forcible annexation of the Philippine Islands will justify the seizure of other islands and the domination of other people, and with wars of conquest we can expect a certain, if not rapid, growth of our military establishment. . . .

A large standing army is not only a pecuniary burden to the people and, if accompanied by compulsory service, a constant source of irritation but it is even a menace to a republican form of government. The army is the personification of force, and militarism will inevitably change the ideals of the people and turn the thoughts of our young men from the arts of peace to the science of war.

Document D

Source: Senator Albert Beveridge, Speech, September 1898.

Ah! As our commerce spreads, the flag of liberty will circle the globe and the highways of the ocean – carrying trade to all mankind – be guarded by the guns of the republic. And as their thunders salute the flag, benighted peoples will know that the voice of liberty is speaking, at last, for them; that civilization is dawning, at last, for them – liberty and civilization, those children of Christ's gospel, who follow and never precede the preparing march of commerce. . . .

Fellow Americans, we are God's chosen people. Yonder at Bunker Hill and Yorktown his providence was above us. At New Orleans and on ensanguined seas His hand sustained us. Abraham Lincoln was His Minister, and His was the Alter of Freedom the boys in blue set on a hundred battlefields.

Document E

Source: Charles Denby, "Shall We Keep the Philippines," *Forum* (November 1898).

The Philippines are a foothold for us in the Far East. Their possession gives us standing and influence. It gives us also valuable trade in both exports and imports. Should we surrender the Philippines, what will become of them? Will Spain ever conquer the insurgents, and, should she do so, will she retain the islands? To her they will be valueless; and if she sells them to any continental power she will, by that act, light the torches of war. . .

Dewey's victory is an epoch in the affairs of the Far East. We hold our heads higher. We are coming to our own. We are stretching out our hands for what nature meant should be ours. We are taking our proper rank among the nations of the world.

Document F

Source: Henry Watterson, Editorial, *Louisville Courier Journal* (April 1898)

There are those who diet on rice and peer through blue goggles, who whine that on legal grounds we have no right to interfere with Spain's belaboring her own ass, to dispute her sovereignty over Cuba her own territory. If they had prevailed, America today would be a slaveholding nation. They are deserving of no more serious consideration than the feather-headed maniacs who are bellowing for war only for war's sake. We are not going to the musty records of title archives to find our warrant for this war.

We find it in the law supreme—the law high above the law of titles in lands in chattels, in human bodies and human souls—the law of man, the law of god. We find it in our own inspiration, our own destiny. We find it in the peals of the bell that rang out our sovereignty from Philadelphia; we find it in the blood of the patriots who won our independence at the cannon's mouth. . . .

Multiple-Choice Answers

1. c. All of the choices were major issues in the late nineteenth century, but Congress was motivated by the assassination of President Garfield and public disillusionment with government corruption to make at least modest reforms to the federal civil service.

2. a. Farmers were concerned about all of the issues listed in the question, but discriminatory railroad rates that benefited large shippers formed the basis of the Granger movement's concerns.

3. c. The Supreme Court issued a series of conservative decisions in the 1870s and 1880s, tending to limit the power of federal and state governments. The *Wabash* case ruled that the so-called Granger laws of the 1870s infringed on Congress's exclusive power to regulate interstate commerce.

4. c. Republican William McKinley won a significant electoral and popular majority in the 1896 election, based largely on his support for the gold standard and business prosperity. Bryan failed to unite small farmers and urban immigrants despite his energetic campaign (in contrast to McKinley's "front-porch" campaign).

5. d. The Populists did not want to overturn the capitalist system but rather sought to make it more humane and cooperative. Although Populists saw few of their proposals enacted before 1900, many of their ideas formed the basis for later progressive era legislation.

6. b. While the federal government did relatively little to help farmers and workers during the late nineteenth century, farmers (and silver mine owners) became upset by the government's decision to discontinue the coinage of silver, as this foreclosed a potential avenue for inflating the currency and thus helping farmers to pay off debts.

7. c. The panic began with a downturn in the railroad sector, and quickly spread to banking and other areas. Widespread prosperity was not restored until 1901.

8. c. The "yellow press," especially the newspapers of William Randolph Hearst and Joseph Pulitzer, are often portrayed as key elements in creating a public outcry over Spanish policy toward Cuba and thus pressuring the McKinley administration to take stronger actions that resulted in war with Spain.

9. d. The Open Door Notes represented an effort by the United States to gain access to China's trade and economic opportunities there, with relatively little risk of a confrontation with other European powers there. Hay couched his notes in terms of a desire to protect China's territorial integrity, giving the United States a degree of moral authority, at least in rhetorical terms.

10. b. Although the Teller Amendment of 1898 had declared that the United States would not seek the annexation of Cuba, American officials were concerned when the postwar Cuban constitution made little reference to the United States. The Platt Amendment thus gave the United States virtual control over Cuban foreign policy and gave the United States the right to intervene in Cuba when American leaders deemed it necessary.

11. b. William Jennings Bryan supported the Treaty of Paris in an effort to make the 1900 election focus on imperialism in his rematch with McKinley. Although there were strong anti-imperialist voices, particularly among upper-class easterners, voters returned McKinley to office with an even greater margin than he had enjoyed in 1900.

12. a. Compared with Cuba and the Philippines, the American occupation of Puerto Rico created relatively little controversy. The Foraker Act withdrew American troops and created a governmental structure for the island. The Jones Act of 1917 gave Puerto Ricans American citizenship.

13. c. American occupation of the four areas addressed in the question produced a situation in which each became dependent on selling agricultural products for the American market, with little in the way of a balanced economy.

Free-Response Questions Commentary

1. Farmers faced significant challenges as a result of the nation's post-Civil War expansion. New farming technologies helped them to cultivate more land, but they were forced to pay high prices for farm machinery and faced high railroad charges to ship their goods to market. They also faced a fundamental dilemma: The more they produced in order to increase their income, the more that farm prices fell due to overproduction.

   In response, farmers (against their individual stereotype) organized to advance their interests, first on the local and then on the national level. The Granger movement of the 1870s, which began as a social movement but later took on political coloration, focused on the passage of state laws to regulate railroad rates. The Farmers' Alliances of the 1880s formed the basis of the Populist Party in the 1890s. The Populists introduced a wide-ranging series of demands, including a national income tax, federal regulation (and later ownership) of railroads, telegraphs, and telephones, and a federally supported program of warehouses to allow farmers to store goods until farm prices rose. However, the Populist agenda came to focus on free silver as the party entered the national arena. Following the 1896 election, the Populists declined as a party and movement.

   While the agrarian protest movement of the late nineteenth century had little direct effect in terms of legislative accomplishments on the national level, many of the Populist proposals, including the income tax, direct election of senators, and stricter government regulation of railroads, all became central parts of the Progressive reform agenda and were enacted by the federal government. The agrarian movement, as Brinkley notes, was one of the largest and best-organized protests against the excesses of industrial capitalism. Finally, although the Populist Party died out after 1896, it created a heritage of organization that helped farmers to belie their individualistic reputation and organize effectively in the twentieth century to represent their needs.

2. National politics in the late nineteenth century represented a paradox. On the one hand, both parties put forth a series of uninspiring candidates, while the federal government's role in American life was extremely limited. On the other hand, voter turnout was extremely high during the late nineteenth century. This was the result of several factors, including the fierce loyalty that the parties attracted in different regions of the country, as well as their emphasis on social and cultural (as opposed to economic) issues.

   On the presidential level, the Republican Party dominated, as only one Democratic president (Grover Cleveland) was elected between 1860 and 1912. Congress was much more evenly divided. The central issue in the 1870s and early 1880s was civil service reform, as the parties divided over the issue of federal patronage. Public disgust over this issue, fueled by President Garfield's assassination in 1881, spurred passage of the Pendleton Act in 1883. Economic issues, particularly the tariff and the currency issue, played a greater role starting at the end of the 1880s and became even more central following the Panic of 1893 (which lasted more or less for the next eight years). McKinley's decisive victory in 1896 demonstrated the country's general contentment with the politics of stability and showed the strength of the business community in terms of influencing politics (although this strength would be challenged with Theodore Roosevelt's ascension to the presidency in 1901).

Document-Based Question Commentary

Both supporters and opponents of the Spanish–American War and American imperialism use America's past to support their positions, albeit in very different ways. George Hoar hearkens back to the spirit of the Declaration of Independence and what he believes to be the original intent of the writers of the Constitution. By contrast, Henry Watterson argues that there is a "higher law" that gave the United States a duty to intervene in Cuba, making indirect reference to abolitionists who used the same argument in the 1850s to justify opposition to slavery.

Similarly, both Charles Eliot Norton and Charles Denby note that the United States has traditionally pursued a foreign policy different from the nations of Europe. Norton argues that taking control of distant territories will take away America's unique position as a nation that has resisted the desire for territorial gain beyond its borders, while Denby sees the potential American control of the Philippines as allowing the United States to properly accept a position among the leading nations of the world.

William Jennings Bryan argues that a large standing army will move the United States away from its republican roots and toward a more militaristic, bureaucratic society. Beveridge argues that expansion abroad is simply a continuation of America's march along God's chosen path and part of a pattern of divine providence.

Overall, such debates will always present a variety of different viewpoints about the fundamental nature of the American republic and imperialism. These arguments question the ideology of American expansion especially in the acquisition and control of territory and the spread of American democracy.

CHAPTER 20
The Progressives

AP THEMES

- **Reform:** The rise of industrial capitalism and the corresponding growth of urban centers in the late nineteenth century forced Americans to come to terms with a host of new social, political, and economic issues. The existing structure of government was unsuited to deal with the challenges posed by modernization, leading to new efforts to impose a sense of order on the chaos of American society. These efforts came to be grouped under the banner of "progressivism," a wide-ranging term that can be used to characterize those who shared a number of central assumptions, most notably the idea that the power of government could be used to transform society and that unregulated economic development produced harmful social, political, and economic results. Although progressive reformers experienced some successes on the state and local levels, many of their efforts foundered in the face of the size and scope of industrial combinations. Turning their efforts to the national level, it soon became clear that only a strong presidency could exercise the power necessary to create meaningful reforms. Progressives looked to the presidency to find ways to curb the power of big business, protect consumers, safeguard the natural environment, and promote an agenda of social justice.
- **Politics and Citizenship:** Progressive reformers first targeted the existing party system on the local and state level, which they saw as corrupt and unable to meet the challenges of the new industrial order. Many Progressives felt that the complex issues of the late nineteenth and early twentieth centuries should be in the hands of nonpartisan experts and managers, who could avoid the problems faced by members of the traditional political parties. They particularly sought to reduce the power of urban political machines, which they saw as mechanisms for taking advantage of new immigrants and enriching a small handful of professional politicians. National politics during the first two decades of the twentieth century witnessed a fundamental debate over the proper role of the federal government in an industrial republic. The central question was how the government could best use its power to protect the general welfare. Some argued that the government should seek to break up large business and other combinations to restore competition and allow individuals greater scope for their activity, while others argued that the federal government should act as a mediator between big business and other groups, helping to elevate them to a level that could counterbalance the power of industry. By the end of the period, it was increasingly clear that large-scale consolidation was to become a permanent feature of American life and that the United States was becoming increasingly dominated by large interest groups.
- **Environment:** For the first time during the presidency of Theodore Roosevelt, the federal government began to address the impact of industrial growth on the natural environment. The period witnessed the emergence of a debate between those who sought to preserve the natural environment for aesthetic reasons and those who sought to promote the rational development of the wilderness under the supervision of government experts. Federal actions during this period would have a deep influence on the nation's environmental policies throughout the twentieth century and beyond.
- **Economic Transformations:** One of the central hallmarks of the Second Industrial Revolution was corporate consolidation. The emergence of trusts forced a response

from both workers and reformers who sought ways to balance the power of business. Although mainstream unions such as the American Federation of Labor sought to avoid involvement in reform causes, the Industrial Workers of the World (IWW) and other unions sought to challenge the capitalist system and its perceived injustices more directly. A number of progressives produced works on the problem of monopoly that had profound influence on public policy in the first decades of the twentieth century.

- **Demographic Changes:** Economic changes in the late nineteenth century profoundly affected the structure of the American family, particularly the role of women. The increasingly sharp distinction between home and workplace, earlier schooling for children, and increasing levels of female education all helped to contribute to the emergence of the "new woman." Many of these women sought a greater social and political role outside the home and became active in a variety of causes, including the women's suffrage movement, consumer protection, and protective legislation for women and children in the workplace.

CHAPTER SUMMARY
The Progressive Impulse

While the reform wave known as progressivism appeared to be a diverse and even disparate movement that shared several assumptions. These included a belief in progress—but direct, ordered progress as opposed to the laissez-faire assumptions of the late nineteenth century. Three specific impulses helped to drive the reform crusades of the early twentieth century. One powerful trend was the spirit of "antimonopoly," motivated by a fear of concentrated power and the desire to limit and disperse wealth. A second strand of progressivism was based on a desire for social cohesion, which rested on a belief in social interdependence rather than the dominant individualism of the nineteenth century as the key to improving society. Other reformers found their motivation in a deep faith in knowledge—a belief that the principles of the natural and social sciences could be used to better society. Another hallmark of the progressive movement was the determination to impose efficiency on the structures of the society.

The growing availability of magazines and newspapers throughout the late nineteenth and early twentieth centuries fueled public consciousness of the social problems of the time. Crusading journalists known as **"muckrakers"** used their writings to expose economic, social, and political corruption. The most notable of these included **Ida Tarbell**'s study of Standard Oil and **Lincoln Steffens**'s study of political machines.

The muckrakers' sense of moral outrage at urban corruption and inequality found reflection in American religion. The Salvation Army offered both material and spiritual assistance to the urban poor, while both Protestant and Catholic theologians such as **Walter Rauschenbusch** and **Father John A. Ryan** sought to improve society through social reform. Rauschenbusch argued that Darwinism did not mean a struggle for survival among the fittest but rather offered the possibility for individuals to work together toward the evolution of a more just society.

Progressive reformers based much of their thinking on the influence of the environment as a cause of social problems such as poverty and crime, noting that the poor conditions in which most immigrants lived explained social problems. Unlike many earlier reformers, Progressives were less likely to make moral judgments about the poor or to differentiate between the "deserving" and "undeserving" poor. Many of the reformers, primarily young, college-educated women, seized on the **settlement house** model, which they adopted from England. **Hull House,** founded by **Jane Addams** in 1889, was at the forefront of the movement that resulted in the creation of more than 400 such institutions founded throughout the United States. Settlement houses sought to help new immigrants adjust to their new surroundings and helped to provide an impetus for the growing profession of social work, which became an outlet for young, educated women.

Many Progressives came to believe that scientific principles could be used to solve even nonscientific problems. Intellectuals moved from justifying the existing industrial system to working to create a new civilization. Social scientist **Thorstein Veblen,** in his book *A Theory of the Leisure Class* (1899), wrote of replacing the leadership of the current American system with a new class of highly trained engineers, while **Frederick Winslow Taylor** and his ideal of **scientific management,** which sought to use time and motion studies to make factory production more efficient, helped to produce a new generation of officials who worked to study and understand the structure of organizations.

The late nineteenth century witnessed the rapid growth of professional occupations, leading to the creation of the **"new middle class."** As fields such as law and medicine became increasingly complex, members of these professions sought to create clear standards that would distinguish skilled practitioners from amateurs and charlatans. Examples included the **American Medical Association** (1901), the **National Association of Manufacturers** (1895), and the **United States Chamber of Commerce** (1912). Even farmers, long considered the most individualistic of Americans, created the **National Farm Bureau Federation.**

Despite obstacles and opposition, a substantial number of middle-class women began to enter professional fields. While professions such as nursing, teaching, and library science shared an emphasis on training, expertise, and the creation of a professional identity, they tended also to be "helping professions" that involved working primarily with other women and children.

Women and Reform

The prominent role that women played in progressive reform served both to expand and confirm the idea of a separate **"women's sphere"** in society, as much of the reform work by women occurred in areas that were traditionally seen as female preserves. In addition, women often pushed for reform measures on the basis of a need to protect women, rather than on the basis of female equality with men. A series of changes in society, including the need to spend time with children, decreasing rates of childbirth, fewer hours devoted to housework, and increasing divorce rates, allowed women to define their identity outside of the home and play a greater role in society.

The rapid proliferation of **women's clubs** in the 1880s and 1890s provided a vehicle for women's involvement in reform causes. These clubs, consisting primarily of upper- and middle-class women, began mainly as social and cultural organizations but gradually shifted to political causes. While initially largely uncontroversial, these women's clubs gradually shifted toward issues such as gaining passage of state laws that regulated conditions for women and child workers, government inspection of working conditions, regulation of food and drug industries, and outlawing the manufacture and sale of alcohol. In 1912, female reformers succeeded in convincing Congress to create the **Children's Bureau** in the Department of Labor. Overall, these clubs gave women an outlet for public activity without challenging the male-dominated character of society. They tended to reinforce the dominant perspective of the "maternal" and "nurturing" character of women.

The movement for women's suffrage, initially presented on the basis of women's natural rights, did to some degree challenge the dominant ideas of **"separate spheres"** of society, where women's roles had been based on their roles as wives and mothers. By the early twentieth century, however, suffrage groups such as the **National American Woman Suffrage Association** became better organized than its opponents. Suffragists made a variety of arguments to support their cause, some maintaining that women would bring a special sensibility to social and political problems. Some argued that women's commitment to peace would make war obsolete, while others argued that giving middle-class women the right to vote would offset the votes of the poor and immigrants.

Starting in 1910, women won the vote in a series of states, and by 1919, thirty-nine states had given women the right to vote in at least some elections. By 1920, ratification of the Nineteenth Amendment allowed women to vote throughout the nation. Some feminists, most notably **Alice Paul** and the **National Woman's Party**, sought a constitutional amendment that would prohibit all forms of discrimination on the basis of gender. Many women, however, opposed this on the basis that it would put an end to the women's protective legislation that had been based on women's differences from men.

The Assault on the Parties

Almost all reformers agreed that increasing the power of government was necessary to ameliorate social problems. This would involve changing the corrupt, undemocratic nature of the nation's political institutions. Late-nineteenth-century attacks on party rule had succeeded in gaining adoption of the **secret ballot**. Reformers in the 1890s argued that party rule could be further broken either by giving more power to the people or by placing greater power in the hands of nonpartisan, unelected officials. Urban reformers gradually succeeded in lessening the power of political machines, although in the face of opposition from saloon owners, brothel keepers, business owners, and immigrants who received jobs and services from the machines. **Galveston,** Texas, was one of the first places in the nation to adopt a new form of government based on progressive reforms. This came as a result of the city government's failure to deal with the effects of a devastating tidal wave in 1900. Reformers gained approval of a new system that replaced the mayor and city council with an elected, nonpartisan commission. Other cities opted for the **city manager** plan, where elected officials would hire an outside expert to help them to govern the city. Almost 400 cities adopted the commission system and another 45 had city managers by the early twentieth century. Other cities had to settle for more conventional means such as making mayoral elections nonpartisan or holding them in years without presidential or congressional races. Cleveland Mayor **Tom Johnson** succeeded in battling the powerful streetcar interests in the city, while other reform mayors such as **Hazen Pingree** of Detroit and **Samuel "Golden Rule" Jones** of Toledo promoted reform causes.

On the state level, reformers gained passage of a number of measures that helped to place more power in the hands of the electorate and lessened the power of major economic interests. These included the **initiative**, which allowed reformers to submit new legislation directly to the voters; the **referendum,** which allowed actions of the legislature to be returned to the electorate; the **direct primary,** which took the nomination of candidates out of the hands of party bosses; and the **recall,** allowed voters the right to remove an official after a sufficient number of citizens had signed a petition. Other states passed limitations on lobbying efforts by businesses to lessen the power of trusts. Governor **Robert M. La Follette** of Wisconsin, first elected in 1900, helped to turn his state into a "laboratory of progressivism," through the implementation of direct democracy measures, regulation of railroads and utilities, workplace reforms, and state taxes on inheritances and corporate interests.

Overall, declining voter turnout in presidential elections after 1900 attests to the reformers' lessening the influence of political parties. New "interest groups" such as professional organizations, trade associations, and labor organizations, as well as social workers and women's clubs, all learned to work to advance their demands outside of the electoral process.

Sources of Progressive Reform

Labor unions and urban political machines had traditionally been two vehicles that represented the interests of the working classes. While the influential American Federation of Labor remained aloof from reform efforts, the **Union Labor Party** in San Francisco helped to promote reforms such as a child labor law, a workman's compensation law, and limitation for working hours for women. In many cases, political machines and their bosses, such as New York's Tammany Hall, realized that they needed to support reform causes in order to ensure their survival. Following the devastating **Triangle Shirtwaist Fire** in 1911, two Tammany Democrats, **Senator Robert E. Wagner** and **Assemblyman Alfred E. Smith,** proved to be two of the biggest supporters of new labor laws that placed stringent regulations on factory owners.

Western Progressives such as Senators **Hiram Johnson, George Norris,** and **William Borah** represented a tendency among westerners to focus their energies on the federal, rather than state, government. This was due to the fact that western states often faced issues such as water and land rights that demanded action at the federal level.

Although white Progressives placed relatively little emphasis on race, African Americans fought for a variety of different reforms. While many African Americans adopted **Booker T. Washington**'s advice that blacks should focus on education and self-help, others began to follow a new, more radical approach epitomized by **W. E. B. Du Bois,** who argued that political equality and civil rights were an inherent part of American citizenship. Du Bois challenged Washington's views. In works such as *The Souls of Black Folk* (1903), Du Bois argued that blacks should fight for immediate restoration of full civil rights. In 1905, Du Bois and a number of black and white civil rights activists launched the **Niagara Movement,** which formed the genesis of the **National Association for the Advancement of Colored People,** which was officially founded in 1909. The NAACP believed that civil rights could be secured by legislation and in the courts. It launched a series of lawsuits in federal courts, which resulted in such victories as the overturning of Oklahoma's grandfather clause (*Guinn v. United States*, **1915**) and striking down a Louisville, Kentucky, law requiring residential segregation (*Buchanan* v. *Worley*, **1917**).

Crusade for Social Order and Reform

Progressive reformers targeted alcohol as a key source of social problems: Urban workers squandered scarce wages in bars; drunkenness spawned domestic violence; workers were less efficient under the influence of alcohol; and saloons played a major role in upholding the power of urban bosses. In 1873, temperance advocates formed the **Women's Christian Temperance Union (WCTU),** which publicized the evils of alcohol, while the **Anti-Saloon League** (1893) sought the legal abolition of saloons, which eventually grew in scope to include calls for the complete prohibition of the sale and manufacture of alcoholic beverages. The "moral fervor" unleashed as a result of American entry into World War I helped to spur passage in January 1920 of the **Eighteenth Amendment,** which prohibited the manufacture, sale, or consumption of alcohol in the United States.

Reformers were varied in their responses to the problems caused by immigration. Some advocated the use of the emerging science of eugenics in order segregate and discriminate against races and ethnic groups according to rather loosely defined genetic qualities. **Madison Grant** in his book *The Passing of the Great Race* (1916) argued that the Anglo–Saxon race had to be protected from "pollution" by lesser races. The so-called **Dillingham Report,** composed by a federal panel of experts, argued that newer immigrant groups were less able to assimilate than earlier groups. These concerns gradually won support among Progressives, gaining further support as a result of World War I.

Challenging the Capitalist Order

Despite the wide variety of progressive causes and goals, all reformers were to some degree concerned about the character of the modern industrial economy. Support for radical critiques of the capitalist system reached their highest level between 1900 and 1914. Socialist **Eugene Debs** received nearly 1 million votes in the 1900 election, while a variety of reformers and intellectuals supported varieties of socialism. The most prominent among the radical groups was the **Industrial Workers of the World (IWW),** which advocated the general strike as a way toward abolishing "wage slavery" and sought to organize the most exploited workers in areas such as mining and timber.

While most progressive reformers agreed that excessive corporate consolidation was a threat to the nation's prosperity, they disagreed with how to combat this. Prominent lawyer **Louis Brandeis,** later appointed to the Supreme Court by Woodrow Wilson, argued on both moral and efficiency-based grounds that business must be regulated to ensure that large combinations did not emerge. Others argued that government should not necessarily fight "bigness" but should guard against abuses by large institutions, distinguishing between "good" and "bad" trusts. The most prominent spokesperson for this position was **Herbert Croly,** whose *The Promise of American Life* (1909) came to influence Theodore Roosevelt and others, who believed that government must find ways to coordinate the industrial economy.

Theodore Roosevelt and the Modern Presidency

While efforts to reform the industrial economy had some successes at the state and local levels, it soon became clear to many Progressives that the federal government must act to promote far-reaching changes in American society. More specifically, a strong presidency was needed to promote social change. **Theodore Roosevelt,** who ascended to the presidency following the assassination of **William McKinley** in 1901, proved to be the appropriate man for the times.

Although Roosevelt had obtained a reputation as somewhat of a wild man, it was more as a result of his personal style than as a result of any substantive challenges he posed to the Republican Party. Roosevelt promoted a vision of moderate change, believing that responsible reform efforts could serve to protect America from more radical challenges.

Roosevelt believed that the government should not serve as the champion of any particular interest but rather that it should serve as a mediator between various powerful groups in order to protect the public good. He believed that the power of educated public opinion could wipe out the worst corporate abuses, using government investigations through bodies such as the **Bureau of Corporations** to expose corporate malfeasance.

Roosevelt demonstrated his vision when he ordered the Justice Department to proceed with a case against the **Northern Securities Company,** a new railroad monopoly created by financiers J. P. Morgan, E. H. Harriman, and James J. Hill. Roosevelt also intervened in the 1902 **anthracite coal strike,** threatening to send federal troops to seize the mines if the mine owners failed to agree to arbitration. Workers ultimately won a 10 percent wage increase and a nine-hour day but failed to gain recognition of their union. This was more than they likely would have won without Roosevelt's intervention. It also represented the first time that the government did not openly side with business interests during a major industrial dispute.

Following his reelection campaign in 1904, in which he easily defeated Democrat **Alton B. Parker,** Roosevelt embarked on a number of new reform measures. He pushed Congress to pass the **Hepburn Act** (1906), which strengthened the government's right to regulate the railroad industry. He also urged passage of the **Pure Food and Drug Act,** which restricted the sale of dangerous medicines, and the **Meat Inspection Act,** which was sparked by the appalling descriptions of the meatpacking industry that were described in **Upton Sinclair's** *The Jungle.* After 1907, he began advocating even stronger measures, such as an eight-hour day for industrial workers, workmen's compensation, and progressive taxation, among others. Roosevelt's shift created a wide gulf between the president and congressional conservatives.

Due largely to his background as a sportsman and naturalist, Roosevelt believed in restricting private development on undeveloped government land. By modern standards, Roosevelt would be considered a **"conservationist,"** in that he sought to promote policies that would protect land for carefully managed economic development, rather than a **preservationist,** who sought to preserve the natural environment intact. Roosevelt and his chief forester, **Gifford Pinchot,** believed that government should act as a manager of the continuing development of the wilderness. The other significant element of Roosevelt's environmental efforts was support for public reclamation and irrigation projects. The **Newlands Act** (1902) provided federal funding for construction of dams, reservoirs, and canals in the West. This act set the precedent for massive federal aid for irrigation and, later, power development in the West that began in the 1930s and continued after World War II.

Although Roosevelt supported the conservationist vision of rational management of natural resources, he also shared some of the concerns of naturalists who wanted to preserve the natural shape of the land. Roosevelt supported the addition of federal land to several national parks and the creation of several new ones. Yellowstone was first, created in 1872.

The tension between conservationists and preservationists drew national attention as a result of the **Hetch Hetchy** controversy. This controversy began in 1906 with a dispute over whether to construct a dam in the **Hetch Hetchy** Valley. Following the devastating 1906 earthquake, San Francisco residents expressed increased support for creating a dam in the valley, which would have created a significant reservoir for the city. Preservationists such as **John Muir,** founder of the **Sierra Club,** argued that this would destroy the area's natural beauty. While construction of the dam finally began after World War I, the controversy served to mobilize a coalition opposed to the rational use of natural resources for economic development.

Economic issues never moved far from the center of national attention during this time. A serious financial panic and recession broke out in 1907 as a result of overproduction, weaknesses in the banking sector and the stock market, and irresponsible speculation. Financier **J. P. Morgan** helped to prop up a number of shaky financial institutions through stock purchases and other maneuvers, which helped to stem the recession. Roosevelt at least tacitly agreed not to pursue antitrust action against any purchases resulting from Morgan's actions. In a decision that he would later regret, Roosevelt decided to honor his promise not to run again in 1908.

The Troubled Succession

While **William Howard Taft,** who had served as Roosevelt's vice president, entered the presidency after having easily defeated **William Jennings Bryan** in the 1908 election (Taft had been Roosevelt's hand-picked successor.), Taft's term in office proved disastrous. Early in his term, Taft infuriated Progressives through his passivity in the debate over the **Payne–Aldrich Tariff,** which failed to lower duties, and even raised them in some cases. Taft further angered Progressives with his actions during the **Ballinger–Pinchot Affair (1909),** in which he fired Pinchot for urging congressional investigation of Taft's secretary of the interior, Richard Ballinger, for allegedly having turned over valuable coal lands in Alaska to a private syndicate for personal gain.

Although Roosevelt insisted that he had no plans to reenter politics during much of this controversial period, in September 1910, he delivered a significant speech to a group of Republican reformers in which he outlined the principles of the **"New Nationalism,"** which moved significantly beyond the "cautious conservatism" of his early presidency. Roosevelt argued that the federal government had a responsibility to promote and protect the social welfare of its citizens through measures such as graduated income and inheritance taxes, workers' compensation, regulation of female and child labor, and stronger corporate regulation. The 1910 congressional election, in which many conservative Republicans were defeated, demonstrated the growth of reform sentiment. The October 1911 announcement of an antitrust suit against **U.S. Steel** for actions that Roosevelt had approved during the 1907 panic pushed him toward seeking the presidential nomination. In February 1912, he announced his candidacy, challenging the incumbent Taft for the Republican nomination.

Although Roosevelt won all thirteen Republican presidential primaries, party leaders awarded almost all contested delegates to Taft. Roosevelt led his supporters out of the Republican Convention, leading to the creation of the **Progressive,** or **"Bull Moose,"** Party, based on his statement that he was as "fit as a bull mouse" following his return from an African safari.

Woodrow Wilson and the New Freedom

Meanwhile, Woodrow Wilson, former Princeton University president and reform governor of New Jersey since 1910, gained the Democratic nomination after forty-six ballots. While Wilson won only 42 percent of the popular vote, he benefited from the split in the Republican Party and captured 435 of 531 electoral votes. Wilson's program was known as the **"New Freedom,"** which differed from Roosevelt's New Nationalism most clearly in the apparent belief that monopoly should be destroyed, not regulated, as Roosevelt believed. Although the 1912 election was in some ways anticlimactic, it did offer voters several alternative visions of the proper role of the federal government in the modern era.

Wilson proved to be a "bold and forceful president" who concentrated power in the hands of the executive branch much more than Taft or even Roosevelt. He quickly pushed Congress to pass several major initiatives soon after taking office. First, the **Underwood–Simmons Tariff** significantly lowered tariff rates, with a graduated income tax to offset lost income. In the summer of 1913, Congress passed the **Federal Reserve Act,** which created a system of regional banks supervised by a presidentially appointed board to regulate the currency supply. Finally, to deal with the issue of monopoly, Congress created the **Federal Trade Commission,** which sought to work with businesses to determine whether their practices met government regulations. In addition, Congress passed the **Clayton Antitrust Act,** meant to help the government break up trusts. The Clayton Act was greatly weakened by conservative assaults with little objection from Wilson. This was an indication that he was moving closer to Roosevelt's position on antitrust issues.

In late 1915, responding to Republican gains in the 1914 elections, Wilson undertook a second wave of reform efforts, supporting bills for easier farm credit and extending workers' compensation to federal employees.. He also supported the 1916 **Keating–Owing Bill,** the first measure to regulate child labor on the national scale, although this was invalidated by the Supreme Court in 1918. He also supported the 1914 **Smith–Lever Act,** which gave federal matching grants to states that supported agricultural extension education programs. Wilson appointed antimonopolist **Louis Brandeis** to the United States Supreme Court. Brandeis became the first Jewish American to serve on the court.

Multiple-Choice Questions

1. Which of the following best characterizes the NAACP's strategy for combating racial oppression in the first two decades of its existence?
   a. Working patiently to achieve economic gains and prove its indispensability to the white population before seeking social equality
   b. Filing lawsuits in the federal courts as its principal weapon
   c. Violently challenging the existing social and political order in order to achieve its goals
   d. Advocating black separatism and even leaving the United States as a means to achieve equality with whites
   e. Using nonviolent resistance to create public awareness of inequality and discrimination

2. Most Progressives were united under which of the following sets of beliefs?
   a. That while human progress was possible, the growth of the power of government threatened human liberty and freedom
   b. That human progress was possible and that purposeful human intervention in the life of society was necessary
   c. That human characteristics were fixed and that only a select few individuals were capable of betterment
   d. That human progress was possible but that social change and reform could not occur under capitalism

e. That human progress could best be achieved through changing individuals rather through reforming institutions

3. Progressive reform efforts on the state and local level consistently focused on
   a. strengthening the role of established parties to increase public participation in politics.
   b. giving groups such as immigrants and the poor a direct voice in determining the policies that would best benefit them.
   c. replacing the existing party system with nonpartisan experts who could promote effective, efficient government.
   d. using the federal government to intervene directly to help promote municipal change.
   e. lessening the power of mayors and governors in order to disperse power to bodies such as city councils and state legislatures.

4. Advocates of women's suffrage used all of the following arguments to support their cause in the late nineteenth and early twentieth centuries *except*
   a. women's maternal influence could be used to curb men's belligerence and thus make war obsolete.
   b. women's natural rights made them deserving of equal treatment with men.
   c. women would be more sensitive than men to the need for equal treatment of immigrants and other minorities.
   d. women's moral sensibilities would help them to support legislation against alcohol and prostitution.
   e. giving women the right to vote would not challenge women's traditional roles in society.

5. The main goal of the settlement house movement was
   a. to help those from rural areas to adjust to urban life.
   b. to help new immigrants to preserve the customs and traditions they brought from their native lands.
   c. to prepare poor and working-class women with opportunities for leadership positions in American society.
   d. to help new immigrants to adapt to the United States by learning its language and customs.
   e. to help African Americans who migrated to urban areas in search of factory jobs.

6. All of the following contributed to the growing role that women played in reform activities in the late nineteenth and early twentieth centuries *except*
   a. a rejection of the notion of a separate women's sphere.
   b. new household technologies that allowed women more free time.
   c. declining rates of childbirth.
   d. higher levels of education for women.
   e. growing numbers of women who lived outside of traditional families.

7. Which of the following was the significance of the Hetch Hetchy controversy?
   a. It resulted in the firing of Gifford Pinchot.
   b. It led to a vast expansion of the federal domain dedicated to national parks.
   c. It helped to create a new coalition of activists committed to preservation of the natural environment.
   d. It demonstrated that there was little popular support for preservationist measures.
   e. It caused the federal government to become less involved in environmental issues.

8. What was the biggest difference between Roosevelt's New Nationalism and Wilson's New Freedom?
   a. Roosevelt believed in the regulation of business combinations, while Wilson believed in using the power of the government to break up monopolies.
   b. Roosevelt believed in committing the federal government to promoting social reform much more strongly than did Wilson.
   c. Roosevelt believed more strongly in breaking up all trusts, while Wilson sought to differentiate between "good" and "bad" trusts.
   d. Wilson believed more strongly in government cooperation with business leaders than did Roosevelt.
   e. Wilson believed in creating a stronger, more powerful government bureaucracy to regulate trusts than did Roosevelt.

9. As president, William Howard Taft
   a. alienated conservatives by supporting reform measures.
   b. sought to use the federal government to promote social reform.
   c. alienated Progressives through his conservative positions.
   d. showed little interest in pursuing antitrust measures.
   e. sided with conservationists over business interests.

10. Within two years after taking office, Wilson convinced Congress to pass legislation dealing with which of the following issues?
    a. child labor, workmen's compensation, and farm loans
    b. tariff reduction, banking regulation, and antitrust measures
    c. neutrality, relations with Mexico, and the Panama Canal
    d. government control of the railroad, banking, and fuel sectors
    e. women's suffrage, prohibition, and civil rights for African Americans

11. The biggest foreign policy threat in the first years of the Wilson administration came from events in which of the following countries?
    a. Germany
    b. Russia
    c. Mexico
    d. Panama
    e. Nicaragua

12. The biggest legacy of Roosevelt's environmental policies was
    a. a commitment to preserving the natural beauty of the land.
    b. his consistent opposition to greater governmental initiatives.
    c. his efforts to improve life for farmers on the Great Plains.
    d. his establishing the federal government's role in overseeing rational development.
    e. his commitment to preserving nature for ecological reasons.

Free-Response Questions—Exam Tips

Questions from this period can often deal with the impulses behind progressive reform. One key idea to consider is whether progressive reform was a grassroots movement with wide popular support, especially among the lower classes, or whether it was a movement by middle- and upper-class Americans to impose a degree of control on an increasingly chaotic industrial economy.

Free-Response Questions

1. Compare and contrast the populist and progressive movements in terms of sources of support and goals and objectives.

2. Assess United States policy toward Latin America between 1900 and 1917. What were the primary motivating factors of American policy in the regions?

Document-Based Question—Exam Tip

Questions from this period could deal with the changing role of government, the degree of change caused by progressive reform, or the factors behind specific reforms such as prohibition, antitrust legislation, or conservation.

Document-Based Question

Evaluate the ways in which progressive reformers challenged American traditional notions about the proper role of government between 1880 and 1910.

Use the documents that follow and your knowledge of the period to answer the question.

Document A

Source: Excerpt from Colorado Child Labor Law of 1887.

Be it enacted by the General Assembly of the State of Colorado:
123.28 Section 1. That any person who shall take, receive, hire, or employ any children under fourteen years of age in any underground works, or mine, or in any smelter, mill, or factory shall be guilty of a misdemeanor; and upon conviction thereof before any justice of the peace or court of record shall be fined not less than $10 nor than $50 for each offense.

Document B

Source: Robert M. La Follette, *La Follette's Autobiography: A Personal Narrative of Political Experience,* 1913 (quoted in Kevin Fernlund, *Documents to Accompany America's History,* p. 138).

No sooner had the taxation and direct primary bills been introduced than the lobby gathered in Madison in full force. . . . The railroads, threatened with the taxation bills, and the bosses, threatened by the direct primary, evidently regarded it as a death struggle. . . . The whole fight was centered on me personally. They thought that if they could crush me, that would stop the movement. How little they understood! Even if they had succeeded in eliminating me, the movement, which is fundamental, would still have swept on!

Document C

Source: George Nye Boardman, "Political Economy and the Christian Ministry," 1866 [in Edwards A. Park and Samuel H. Taylor, eds., Vol. XXIII, (Boston, 1866), in *Annals of America*, Vol. 10, p. 77.]

He who preaches the gospel to the poor will have no doubt . . . that governments and all social institutions are to be based on positive virtue, on morality, not on selfishness, not on each man's ability to take care of himself. He will have no hesitation in deciding that legislation in favor of the poor, in the form of poor laws, or as the compulsory support of free schools, is only the legitimate increase of the wages paid by the employer; it is the wages due to the family over and above that due to the individual.

Document D

Source: Lester F. Ward, "Plutocracy and Paternalism," Forum (November 1895), in *Annals of America*, 10, p. 32.

The degree to which the citizen is protected in the secure enjoyment of his possessions is a fair measure of the state of civilization, but this protection must apply as rigidly to the poor man's possessions as to those of the rich man. In the present system, the latter is not only encouraged but actually tempted to exploit the former. Every trust, every monopoly, every carelessly granted franchise has or may have this effect; and the time has arrived when a part at least of this paternal solicitude on the part of government should be diverted from the monopolistic element and bestowed upon the general public.

Document E

Source: Excerpt from Rutherford B. Hayes Diary, from *Diary and Letters of Rutherford Birchard Hayes*, Charles R. Williams, ed., Vol. IV (Columbus, 1924), pp. 277–78.

March 18. Thursday [1886]. At Toledo yesterday and until 1 p.m. today. At Father Hannan's St. Patrick's Institute last evening. I spoke of the dangers from riches *in* a few hands, and the poverty of the masses. General Comly regards the speech as important. My point is that free government cannot long endure if property is largely in a few hands and large masses of the people are unable to earn homes, education, and a support in old age. . .

Document F

Source: Cartoon from the Prohibition Party (http://prohibition.osu.edu/ProhParty/cartoon13.htm)

PERFECTLY NEUTRAL

The Saloon Wolf: "No matter which wins, my dinner is safe."

Document G

Source: Excerpt from Samuel Gompers, "The Laborer's Right to Life," *American Federationist,* (September 1894), in *Annals of America,* Vol. 11, p. 531.

What shall the workers do? Sit idly by and see the vast resources of nature and the human mind be utilized and monopolized for the benefit of the comparative few? No. The laborers must learn to think and act, and soon, too, that only by the power of organization and common concert of action can either their manhood be maintained, their rights to life (work to sustain it) be recognized, and liberty and rights secured.

Document H

Source: Excerpt from Jane Addams, "The Subjective Necessity for Social Settlements," in Johnson, *Reading the American Past,* Vol. II, p. 104.

The Settlement, then, is an experimental effort to aid in the solution of the social and industrial problems which are engendered by the modern conditions of life in a great city. It insists that these problems are not confined to any on portion of a city. It is an attempt to relieve, at the same time, the overaccumulation at one end of society and the destitution at the other. . .

Document I

Source: Excerpt from W. E. B. Du Bois, *The Souls of Black Folk, 1903* [quoted in Johnson, *Reading the American Past*, p. 118].

The question then comes: Is it possible, and probable, that nine millions of men can make effective progress in economic lines if they are deprived of political rights, made a servile caste, and allowed only the most meager chance for developing their exceptional men? If history and reason give any distinct answer to these questions, it is an, emphatic *No.*

Multiple-Choice Answers

1. b. Although all of the other choices were strategies that various civil rights advocates used to promote the fight for African American equality, filing lawsuits was the strategy most often used by the NAACP throughout its history.

2. b. The majority of progressive reformers believed that the power of the local and state, and later, federal governments should be used to help reform social institutions. Most Progressives did not seek to radically alter the fundamental nature of American society but rather to make changes within the existing framework.

3. c. Urban reformers found the existing city political system, particularly the urban machines, to be a significant obstacle to social reform. Through mechanisms like the city commission, the city manager, and in some cases through traditionally elected mayors, reformers in many cities were able to break the hold of the machines by the early twentieth century.

4. c. Many women's suffrage advocates based their arguments for women's suffrage on the idea that women had distinctive characteristics from men, in addition to earlier arguments based on women's "natural rights." A number of people began to argue that middle-class women would add to the constituency that supported limiting immigration.

5. d. The settlement house movement, which started in the United States with Chicago's Hull House and later saw the creation of 400 more such institutions under the leadership primarily of middle-class women, sought to help immigrants to assimilate into American society.

6. a. The increasing influence of the "new woman" emerged as a result of a variety of demographic and other factors but was in many ways based on the idea that women possessed different characteristics from men that helped to explain their involvement in reform activities.

7. c. The controversy over whether to erect a dam at the Hetch Hetchy Valley to create a reservoir for the city of San Francisco pitted preservationists, such as Sierra Club founder John Muir, who sought to retain the area's natural beauty, against conservationists, such as Gifford Pinchot, who believed that the needs of the region's residents were more important. Although a city referendum to create a dam passed by a wide margin, the fight against it helped to unite different groups committed to preservation of the natural environment. Pinchot was fired several years later following a dispute with Interior Secretary Richard Ballinger over the use of the nation's forest reserves.

8. a. The central issue between Roosevelt and Wilson in the 1912 presidential campaign was each candidate's conception of the role of the federal government in relation to trusts and economic consolidation. Roosevelt's "New Nationalism," a set of principles he first introduced in 1910, held that the federal government should regulate trusts. Roosevelt differentiated between "good" and "bad" trusts, with the later being those that abused their power and acted in a manner harmful to the public interest. Wilson's "New Freedom" platform argued that the federal government should seek to break up, rather than control, monopolies. Upon taking office, Wilson adopted a position closer to Roosevelt's, as he supported the creation of the Federal Trade Commission, a government regulatory agency, and did little to promote the Clayton Antitrust Act and offered little resistance to conservative efforts to weaken it.

9. c. Although Taft had strong progressive credentials upon taking office and was in fact much more vigorous than Roosevelt in pursuing antitrust measures, he took a number of steps that discredited him in the eyes of reformers. In particular, Taft took a relatively strict constructionist view of the Constitution and a more limited view of the role of the presidency than did either Roosevelt or Wilson. Among the results of his inaction was the Payne–Aldrich Tariff, which angered Progressives by maintaining high rates on a number of goods. He also sided with Interior Secretary Richard Ballinger over a decision to make significant amounts of federal forest reserves available for private development, a controversy that resulted in the firing of Forest Service chief Gifford Pinchot.

10. b. Upon taking office, Wilson was able to gain congressional passage of the Federal Reserve Act and the Underwood–Simmons Tariff and creation of the Federal Trade Commission and the Clayton Antitrust Act. In 1916, Wilson sought to address child labor and farm loans. Greater government control over the rail and fuel sectors occurred as a result of American involvement in World War I, while women's suffrage and Prohibition resulted from constitutional amendments following World War I. Foreign policy issues, except for relations with Mexico, played a relatively small role in Wilson's first years in office until the outbreak of World War I in the summer of 1914.

11. c. As Wilson took office in March 1913, Mexico was involved in a governmental crisis, and Wilson refused to recognize the new government of Victoriano Huerta, which was responsible for the murder of the deposed Fransisco Madero (who had been seen as hostile to American business interests by the outgoing Taft administration). In April 1914, Wilson sent American troops to seize the port of Veracruz after Huerta had formed a military dictatorship. Relations between the two countries continued to suffer well into Wilson's second term in office

12. d. Roosevelt was a committed outdoorsman who had spent a great deal of time in the West as a young man. As president, however, he was a firm believer in the ideas of conservation and in the use of experts to oversee the rational development of the nation's natural resources. His environmental policies, carried out by Gifford Pinchot, in some cases alienated him from preservationists who sought to keep the environment completely untouched. The ecological argument for environmental protection did not emerge until later in the twentieth century.

Free-Response Questions Commentary

1. Although they were concerned with many of the same issues, the populist and progressive movements differed widely in constituency, outlook, and effectiveness. First, despite their efforts to ally with industrial workers, the Populists remained by and large limited to rural or isolated areas of the country. Progressives tended to be much more heavily concentrated in urban areas and to be middle-class. Although

historians have disagreed widely about the outlook and ideology of the populist movement, many Populist leaders tended to glorify the nation's agrarian past and advocated a return to previous conditions even if they were in fact proposing a fairly revolutionary expansion of the government's role. Progressives, on the other hand, tended to be much more forward-looking, relying on knowledge, expertise, and efficiency to help them to formulate their vision of society. Ironically, despite their rapid decline following the election of 1896 and their decision to fuse with the Democratic Party, the Populists in fact proposed many of the key elements of the progressive agenda, including ideas of direct democracy, government regulation of business, and the income tax. Populists, however, were never able to break out completely of their isolation, while Progressives ended up having a great deal of influence on national politics during the administrations of Roosevelt, Taft, and Wilson.

2. United States policy toward Latin America between 1900 and 1917 represented an expansion of America's conception of its national interests and of the role of the presidency, both of which are congruent with domestic affairs during this period. Overall, American policy reflected a combination of strategic, economic, and ideological factors, with each president emphasizing one more than then other. Theodore Roosevelt's primary focus was strategic, Taft's economic, and Wilson's moral and ideological.

Roosevelt's approach to foreign policy was largely driven by his belief in the importance of the balance of power and of safeguarding the nation's national security through careful attention to strategic concerns (although more recent historians have also pointed out his emphasis on "civilization," as measured both by a nation's race and its level of economic development, as a key ideological motivation in his foreign policy). Influenced by the writings of strategic thinkers such as Alfred Thayer Mahan and Republican expansionists such as Henry Cabot Lodge, Roosevelt made the creation of a isthmusian canal a central part of his presidency (famously intervening in Panama during its revolution against Colombia to help Panama gain its independence and create favorable conditions for negotiation of a treaty that would allow the United States to complete the canal). In addition, he issued the "Roosevelt Corollary" to the Monroe Doctrine in 1904, which claimed the right of intervention for the United States in Western Hemisphere nations to maintain order and prevent European interference.

Taft's foreign policy is summed up by the phrase "dollar diplomacy." His administration had a heavy concentration of corporate lawyers, and his secretary of state, Philander Knox, was no exception. The goals of this approach were twofold: first, to promote American investment abroad and second, to use American banks to loan money to foreign governments. Taft several times sent American troops into Nicaragua to protect American business interests there. More complicated was his policy toward Mexico, where he resisted pressure from American businesses to intervene following the overthrow of dictator Porfirio Diaz in 1911, although he also prepared to recognize the reactionary Victoriano Huerta following the overthrow of Francisco Madero, who was seen as hostile to American business interests.

Wilson sought to use morality as a guide to American foreign policy toward Latin America, although the results of his policy were to increase American intervention in the region. Wilson sent United States troops to establish protectorates in Haiti and the Dominican Republic. Once again, the most complicated issues involved Mexico, where Wilson again intervened after his efforts to help bring about the overthrow of Huerta through nonrecognition of his government. American intervention at Veracruz, however, proved much bloodier than Wilson had expected and increased anti-American sentiment in Mexico. The new government of Venustiano Carranza proved hostile to the United States, while the bandit Pancho Villa conducted a series of raids on the American Southwest that brought the two nations near war. Concerned about events in Europe, however, Wilson withdrew American troops in March 1917 and recognized the Carranza government.

Overall, regardless of each president's motivations, American foreign policy became increasingly interventionist in the Western Hemisphere between 1900 and 1917. Reflecting a combination of strategic, economic, and ideological goals, Roosevelt, Taft, and Wilson created a strong precedent for American intervention and created a strong sense of anti-American sentiment in the region. It would be left to Herbert Hoover and Franklin Roosevelt to attempt to improve the American image in the region, more than a decade later.

Document-Based Question Commentary

Outside Information: One of the key social questions of the late nineteenth century was what role the individual would play in a society increasingly dominated by large organizations. In the words of historian Samuel Hays, the watchword of the period was "organize or perish." While government, labor, farmers, and other groups were slower to organize and consolidate than was big business, reformers gradually realized that they would need to form organizations that could challenge the power of big business. While their concerns gradually found their way into national politics during the administrations of Theodore Roosevelt, William Howard Taft, and Woodrow Wilson, this question is concerned with the development of reform ideas, especially regarding the role of the individual in a rapidly changing society.

Documents: The documents ask you to account for a variety of different sources of reform thought. Document A, an excerpt from Colorado's proposed child labor law, demonstrates the support for protective legislation on the local and state levels. Document B reflects the work of Governor Robert LaFollette in Wisconsin, one of the first governors to enact wide-ranging reforms as part of the so-called "Wisconsin Idea." Document C, from George Boardman's article, is an early example of the ideas that later took the form of the Social Gospel, noting the responsibility of both church and government to play a more active role in protecting the rights of the individual in modern society.

Document D, from the writings of sociologist Lester Frank Ward, shows the growing influence of the social sciences during this period, as many intellectuals sought to come to terms with the challenges of industrializing America. Although reform sentiment did not take root at the presidential level until Theodore Roosevelt's administration, the excerpt from Rutherford B. Hayes's postpresidential years (Document E) demonstrates that concern about the nation's growing inequality of wealth was becoming widespread and that government would have to play a more active role in stemming this tide.

Document F, a cartoon from the Prohibitionist Party, demonstrates the growing sentiment among many reformers that the two major political parties were under the control of various business interests. As a result, third-party movements of varying sizes and strength emerged in the late nineteenth century. In Document G, Samuel Gompers, the longtime head of the American Federation of Labor (AFL), notes the need for labor organization as a means of counterbalancing the power of business. In Document H, Jane Addams, the founder of

Chicago's Hull House, explains the role of the settlement house in helping to ameliorate urban problems. Finally, although the plight of African Americans drew relatively little support among even white reformers, W. E. B. Du Bois, one of the founders of the NAACP, here notes that African Americans can never succeed in American society without political rights and social equality.

Summation: One of the challenges of understanding reform movements such as progressivism is trying to make sense of all of the different groups advocating change. To avoid the tendency to simply make a "laundry list" of documents, one way to approach this question would be to note the different ways that the role of the individual was changing in the late nineteenth century and use the documents to fit into these categories. For example, one could discuss the changing role of the individual in the economic, political, and social realms. Several of the documents note the growing gap between rich and poor and advocate more active government (Documents D and E), as well as stronger labor organization (Document G). Politically, reformers sought to put more hands in the power of the people through measures to promote direct democracy such as the initiative, referendum, and recall (Document B), while minorities such as African Americans (Document I) sought greater political rights. Finally, in the social realm, religious reformers (Document C) sought to change the role of the church, while other groups sought to promote measures such as Prohibition in the political arena (Document F). Women played a central role in many aspects of the period, especially the settlement house movement (Document H).

CHAPTER 21
America and the Great War

AP THEMES

- **War and Diplomacy:** World War I transformed America's relationship with the world. The outbreak of war in Europe in the summer of 1914 initially seemed to have little to do with the United States. However, economic ties to Great Britain and France, the sympathies of various ethnic groups, and President Wilson's desire to protect American neutral rights all made it difficult for the United States to remain truly neutral. By early 1917, Wilson sought to use the influence of the United States to fashion a new world order based on the principles of free trade, self-determination, and collective security. His efforts to fashion a just and lasting peace met opposition from America's allies and from congressional leaders who feared the potential for the United States to be dragged into foreign conflicts.

- **Globalization:** The United States had been gradually moving away from its policy of political isolation from world affairs since the 1890s (and arguably before). American economic interests abroad grew significantly during the war through sales of munitions and other goods to the Allies. By the end of the war, the United States was the world's leading creditor nation. At the conclusion of World War I, the United States debated greater political involvement through the League of Nations, but this course was rejected. American commercial interests continued to grow during the postwar period, leading to a growing imbalance between the nation's significant economic influence abroad and its limited political role in international affairs.

- **Economic Transformation:** Wartime mobilization facilitated significant economic growth for the United States and also transformed the relationship between business and government, cementing a close alliance between the two that continued into the postwar period. While workers, farmers, and minority groups—particularly African Americans— benefited from the wartime boom, significant inflation and a deep postwar economic downturn erased the gains that they had made and left many worse off than they had been before the war. By and large, minority groups continued to struggle throughout the largely prosperous 1920s and into the Great Depression of the 1930s.

- **Politics and Citizenship:** The search for social unity following American entry into the war had important and far-reaching consequences for American society. The Wilson administration's propaganda efforts expanded beyond their original intent and in many cases became a mechanism for suppressing dissent and persecuting suspected radicals, members of minority groups, and others who did not fit the ideal of "100 percent Americanism." This ugly atmosphere continued into the postwar period and to some extent throughout the 1920s, as civil liberties frequently came under attack. Those who questioned American institutions and ideals were labeled as unpatriotic and un-American.

CHAPTER SUMMARY

The "Big Stick": America and the World, 1901–1917

Roosevelt's foreign policy (characterized by his citation of the adage "Speak softly and carry a big stick") was based on a distinction between "civilized" and "uncivilized" nations. While the distinction was often based on racial differences, Roosevelt also believed that modern, industrialized nations were civilized, while suppliers of markets and raw materials were uncivilized. Civilized nations had the right to intervene in uncivilized nations to ensure order and stability.

Seeking to prevent any power from dominating East Asia, Roosevelt agreed in 1905 to mediate an end to the **Russo–Japanese War,** winning the 1906 Nobel Peace Prize for his efforts. However, United States–Japanese relations declined as the Japan excluded American trade from many areas under its control, leading Roosevelt to send the **"Great White Fleet"** of sixteen American battleships around the world in 1907 in a show of American power.

Following a 1902 crisis in which British, Italian, and German ships blockaded the Venezuelan coast in response to that nation's inability to pay its foreign debts, Roosevelt realized that Latin American inability to fulfill financial and other commitments could lead to European intervention in the Western Hemisphere. In 1904, he enunciated the **"Roosevelt Corollary"** to the Monroe Doctrine, which stated that the United States not only opposed European intervention but also had the right to intervene in Western Hemisphere countries to preserve order and stability.

One of Roosevelt's most significant foreign policy accomplishments was the construction of the **Panama Canal** through Central America. Roosevelt's secretary of state, **John Hay,** had originally negotiated a treaty allowing the United States to construct a canal with Colombian officials, but Colombia changed its demands due to popular outrage at the terms. In November 1903, a revolution broke out in Panama and Roosevelt sent forces to "maintain order" and quickly recognized Panama as an independent nation, leading to a favorable treaty for the United States.

Taft continued to extend American investment in lesser developed nations, a policy critics termed **"dollar diplomacy."** This was most notable in **Nicaragua,** where Taft landed U.S. troops on several occasions to help increase American financial leverage.

Early in his administration, Wilson supported a series of interventions in Latin America that seemed to indicate that his policy in Latin America differed little from that of Taft and Roosevelt. However, Wilson's policy toward unrest in Mexico signaled a new approach, as he refused to recognize the reactionary government of **Victoriano Huerta,** who had opposed a popular predecessor who seemed to threaten American business interests there. Wilson sent U.S. troops to intervene in an effort to help topple the conservative government, although further troubles followed when the new government failed to accept American guidelines. Wilson finally with drew U.S. troops in early 1917 as the crisis in Europe drew greater American attention.

The Road to War

President Wilson's reaction to the outbreak of World War I in the summer of 1914 was to call upon Americans to be "impartial in thought as well as deed." This proved to be difficult for a number of reasons. Many Americans were bound by ethnic ties to the various belligerents, while others felt a cultural tie to England that caused them to sympathize with the Allied cause. Economic ties played a significant role in determining American sympathies as well, because of the high level of trade with Great Britain. This caused Americans to ignore the blockade against Germany and to continue to trade with Great Britain.

The emergence of **submarine warfare** in 1915 further pushed the United States closer to the Allied cause. In May 1915, Germany sank the British luxury *Lusitania*, killing 128 Americans. Wilson responded by asking Germany to affirm a commitment to neutral rights, including the right of American citizens to travel on the nonmilitary ships of belligerent nations. Germany announced in early 1916 that it would fire on unarmed Allied ships without warning, and several Americans were injured in an attack on the French steamer *Sussex*. Wilson responded by again calling upon Germany to abandon such actions, and the German government relented temporarily.

Americans remained widely divided over whether the United States should prepare to go to war. **Theodore Roosevelt** led calls for greater preparedness, while **William Jennings Bryan**, who had resigned as secretary of state over Wilson's refusal to warn Americans against traveling on belligerent ships, presented strong arguments for remaining neutral. The 1916 Democratic National Convention demonstrated the strength of the antiwar faction within the Democratic Party, producing the slogan "He kept us out of war" as part of Wilson's reelection campaign.

Following Wilson's narrow victory over **Charles Evans Hughes** in the 1916 presidential election, the president sought to find a way to address the continuing conflict between the United States and Germany. In early 1918, Wilson proposed his famous **Fourteen Points**, stating that the United States should fight to create a just world order on the basis of national self-determination, with a permanent organization to help maintain peace. Events in early 1917 played into Wilson's hands: Germany declared a resumption of unrestricted submarine warfare in January, while in late February the British intercepted the **Zimmerman Telegram**, which called upon Mexico to join Germany in the event of U.S.–German hostilities. The fall of the Tsarist regime in Russia in March of 1917 made it easier for Wilson to justify entry into the war on the basis of seeking to create a more just world order. Finally, in April 1917, Congress voted to declare war although six senators and more than fifty representatives voted against taking such a course.

"War Without Stint"

The immediate impact of American entry into the war occurred at sea. American destroyers assisted Britain in attacks on U-Boats, while U.S. warships escorted merchants across the Atlantic. As a result, Allied shipping losses fell precipitously in the months following American entry into the conflict. Despite this help, however, it was soon clear that given the massive losses suffered by France and Britain and Russia's withdrawal from the conflict, American ground troops would be needed to help defeat Germany.

Wilson and his advisors quickly realized that a draft would be needed to allow the United States to provide the necessary troops to assist in the European conflict. The **Selective Service Act,** passed in May 1917, drafted almost 3 million men into the armed services, and another 2 million Americans volunteered for service. The **American Expeditionary Force (AEF)** that went to Europe represented the largest and most sustained military effort outside of the nation's borders to that point in United States History. For the first time, women served in the military, although they were barred from combat. Four hundred thousand African Americans also served, although in segregated units, most of which were relegated to noncombat roles. Racial violence broke out in Houston in 1917, as black soldiers killed seventeen whites in response to continued provocations from the white community. This resulted in the hanging of thirteen black soldiers and life-in-prison terms for another forty soldiers.

American forces were involved in direct combat for a relatively short period of time, from the spring through the fall of 1918. American forces were able to help the French and the British to break the stalemate of trench warfare and advance against German positions. In June 1918, American troops helped the French to repel a German attack at **Chateau-Thierry**, while a month later they played a similar role at Rheims. In September, U.S. troops took part in the **Meuse–Argonne** offensive, which succeeded in pushing the Germans out of France and back toward their own border. By early November, Germany sought an armistice, and Allied leaders agreed, resulting in an end to fighting on November 11, 1918.

The United States lost approximately 112,000 men during World War I, half from influenza. France, Britain, Germany, Russia, and Austria-Hungary all suffered casualties in the millions. Overall, American casualty rates, while low in comparison to those of other combatants, were high in relation to other wars in American history. The high casualty rates in World War I were largely a result of new technologies, most notably mobile weapons such as tanks and flamethrowers, as well as chemical weapons, which made it possible to attack entrenched positions without direct engagement of soldiers.

War and American Society

The $32 billion that the United States spent as a result of its involvement in World War I dwarfed American expenses in all other wars to that point in the nation's history. Approximately two thirds of this money was raised through **"Liberty Bonds,"** while the other third was raised through new forms of taxation, most notably "excess profits" taxes on corporations and steeply graduated income and inheritance taxes.

In addition to raising needed funds, the United States also faced the challenge of mobilizing the nation's economy for war. After a process of trial and error, the Wilson administration settled upon the idea of a series of "war boards" to oversee various key areas of the economy such as food, fuel, and transportation. The center of domestic mobilization efforts was the **War Indus tries Board (WIB),** which Wilson put under the control of Wall Street financier **Bernard Baruch** in the early spring of 1918. Although Baruch was able to provide seeming order and efficiency to the process of allocating war materials, it was in fact the vast resources and productive capacity of the American economy that fueled the war effort. Although many progressives hoped that the WIB and other wartime agencies could serve to create a model for stronger government regulation of the economy, it was in fact business leaders who took the lead in mobilizing the economy. Many so-called **"dollar-a-year"** men, corporate executives who took paid leave from their positions, helped to bring business and government closer together during the war.

Organized labor was also heavily affected by the growing link between the public and private sectors. **The National War Labor Board**, which was formed to mediate labor disputes, helped workers to gain a number of concessions from industry leaders, including an eight-hour workday and the right of unions to organize and bargain collectively. At the same time, however, workers in various sectors of the economy continued to fight vigorously for greater rights and clashed with the forces of business. The bloodiest example of this occurred in Ludlow, Colorado, where striking workers at a coal mine owned by John D. Rockefeller were attacked by members of the state militia and strikebreakers. Thirty-nine people were killed in the so-called **Ludlow Massacre**.

The war created a period of significant economic growth for the United States, lasting from 1914 to 1919. Almost all sectors of the American economy benefited from the growth of wartime demand, and minority groups gained access to new work opportunities that had not been available to them in peacetime. Hundreds of thousands of African Americans moved from the rural south to northern industrial cities as part of the **"Great Migration,"** leading to tensions both with older, more established African American communities as well as resentful whites. In the years 1917 to 1919, racial violence broke out in **East St. Louis** and other metropolitan areas. Women also entered industrial jobs that had previously been considered men's work, although few women remained in the workforce after the war.

The Search for Social Unity

Although many progressives hoped that the war could be used to promote a sense of national unity and cohesion, the nation was in fact deeply divided over the war. Efforts, both public and private, to promote unity resulted in a series of episodes of repression. A wide variety of Americans supported the peace movement because of ethnic ties to various belligerents, religious principles, or ideological beliefs. The most sustained support for peace came from the women's movement. The **National American Woman Suffrage Association** threw its support behind the American war effort, but many other prominent feminists including **Jane Addams** opposed the war. Many women claimed that their status as wives and mothers gave them a moral obligation to oppose the war.

Once the United States entered the conflict, a majority of Americans supported the war effort, but many government leaders remained concerned about the influence of those groups that did oppose the war. The government agency responsible for "selling" the war effort was the **Committee on Public Information (CPI),** headed by journalist **George Creel**. The agency disseminated more than 75 million pieces of pro-war literature and sent thousands of "four minute men" around the country to deliver speeches in an effort to build support for the American cause. As the war progressed, the CPI's propaganda became more and more lurid in its portrayal of the Germans.

In addition to the efforts of the CPI, the government also passed several pieces of legislation meant to curb dissent. The **Espionage Act of 1917** allowed the government to ban "seditious" materials from the mail and established harsh punishments for spying, sabotage, or obstruction of the war effort. The **Sabotage Act and Sedition Act** of 1918 effectively made it crime to criticize the president or the government. Government efforts were primarily targeted at left-wing groups such as the IWW and socialist leaders such as **Eugene Debs**, who was sentenced to ten years in prison in 1918. Debs was subsequently pardoned in 1921. A series of private groups, most prominent among them the American Protective League, served to suppress dissent and target immigrant groups under the banner of promoting **"100 percent Americanism."** German Americans were the most heavily repressed groups, with large-scale efforts being made to root out virtually any form of German influence on American culture and society to the point of re naming sauerkraut "liberty cabbage" and hamburger "liberty sausage."

The Search for a New World Order

Wilson sought to use the American role in the war to provide him with the influence to help create a just and lasting postwar settlement. His major principles, which came to influence a foreign policy style known as **Wilsonianism,** are contained in his January 1918 message to Congress, in which he laid out a series of war aims that came to be known as the **Fourteen**

Points. The major tenets of this document included a series of proposals meant to lead to the creation of postwar territorial boundaries based on the principle of **self-determination**. Included are a series of principles for promoting international peace including free trade and freedom of the seas, open diplomacy, arms reductions, and impartial settlement of colonial claims, and a proposal for a League of Nations to resolve international disputes. Wilson's goals, while containing a number of serious flaws, reflected his optimistic worldview and belief that international relations could be conducted on the basis of rules and guidelines that would promote harmony between nations.

Almost from the beginning, Wilson's ambitious postwar plans encountered serious obstacles. British Prime Minister **David Lloyd George** and his French counterpart **Georges Clemenceau**, their nations exhausted and bloodied from the fighting, were in no mood to show generosity toward a defeated Germany. At the same time, Republican leaders bristled at Wilson's failure to include any of their party's leaders in the American delegation to the Paris Peace Conference. The president also miscalculated in calling upon the American voters shortly before the 1918 congressional elections to return Democratic majorities to Congress. Wilson believed that failure to elect a democratic Congress would be interpreted abroad as a sign of his political weakness in America and harm his negotiating position in Paris.

Despite these early obstacles, Wilson arrived to a grand welcome in Paris, although idealistic vision was quickly challenged. In addition to the war-weariness of the British and French, the continuing civil war in Russia unsettled many of the representatives at the peace talks. Wilson had ordered American troops to land in the Soviet Union, ostensibly to help to rescue 60,000 Czech troops trapped there, although the U.S. forces began to aid the white, or counterrevolutionary, forces in the U.S.S.R. As a result of these factors, Wilson was quickly forced to retreat on many of his proposals. The British found freedom of the seas and free trade an unacceptable challenge to their imperial position. In addition, the British had promised to transfer German colonies in the Pacific to Japan. The most damaging retreat for Wilson came in the area of reparations, as he was forced in the face of insistent Allied demands to accept the principle of German payments, which were eventually set in 1921 at $56 billion.

Given the difficult challenges that he faced, Wilson did manage to win some important victories at Paris, including the creation of a **mandate system**, in which many former imperial possessions were placed under League of Nations trusteeship. His most notable success was the creation of a permanent international organization to preserve peace and oversee international affairs. The Allies voted in January 1919 to accept the "covenant" for the League of Nations, with provisions for regular meetings of member nations to deal with international disputes. Although questions of enforcement and other issues were left unanswered, Wilson left Paris believing that his vision of a new world order would be fulfilled.

Wilson faced significant domestic opposition upon returning to the United States. A small group of primarily western isolationists in the Senate, known as **"irreconcilables,"** opposed the League covenant on the grounds of principles, while a larger group of so-called **"reservationists"** opposed the treaty for partisan and other reasons, although they would most likely have supported the treaty if Wilson had been willing to accept modifications. The leader of the reservationists was a bitter rival of Wilson—the Republican chairman of the

Senate Foreign Relations committee, Massachusetts Senator **Henry Cabot Lodge**. Suffering from poor health and convinced of the righteousness of his cause, Wilson refused to consider even the smallest changes to the Versailles Treaty and the League covenant. Realizing that he would most likely be unable to overcome his opposition in the Senate, Wilson took his case to the American people.

After an exhausting three-week tour across the country to win public support for American membership in the League of Nations, Wilson collapsed in **Pueblo,** Colorado, near the end of September 1919. He suffered a major stroke upon returning to Washington. A virtual invalid for the rest of his presidency, Wilson became even more stubborn, demanding that Senate Democrats vote down any version of the Versailles Treaty that deviated in the smallest detail from his version. In November 1919, Senate Democrats and Republican irreconcilables voted down an amended version of the treaty. An unamended version failed by a 38–55 Senate vote later that month. Although Wilson claimed that the 1920 election would be a **"solemn referendum"** on the League, the issue of American membership was essentially dead following the Senate votes.

A Society in Turmoil

The immediate postwar period demonstrated that few Americans wanted to continue the progressive reforms of the prewar and wartime periods, viewing new calls for reform with intense hostility. The decline in wartime demand, coupled with inflation resulting from the lifting of wartime wage and price controls, led to a major postwar recession. Organized labor, which sought to consolidate and build upon gains made during the war, responded with an unprecedented wave of strikes, a total of 3,600 in 1919 alone. The most notable of these were the **Seattle General Strike**, where a walkout by shipyard workers triggered a work stoppage that crippled the entire city; the **Boston Police Strike**, in which the strike by police officers in protest of wage cuts and layoffs led to rioting and looting resulting in the firing of the entire force and the hiring of a new one, and a September 1919 **steel strike**, in which 350,000 workers in a variety of different cities walked off the job. The latter strike collapsed in the face of determined opposition from steel company leaders, who employed force and nonunion labor to keep the mills running.

The wartime experience profoundly affected African Americans. Those who fought in the war, numbering nearly 400,000, sought greater rights and expanded economic opportunities in recognition for their sacrifices. Those who had obtained new economic opportunities during the war through factory work and other jobs also expected continued advancement and gains in the postwar period. In both of these demands they were sorely disappointed. Instead, there was a combination of overt discrimination and racial hatred, evidenced by a sharp increase in lynchings in the South, and economic discrimination, resulting in widespread layoffs in northern industrial areas. African Americans faced a series of difficult challenges. The charged racial atmosphere resulted in violent riots in Chicago and a number of other urban areas. The summer of 1919 was dubbed the **"Red Summer."** Some African American leaders urged retaliation while **Marcus Garvey,** a Jamaican immigrant, found wide support in the black communities with his calls for **black nationalism,** which urged African Americans to take pride in their heritage and develop their own institutions in an effort to reject assimilation. Garvey's movement suffered after he was charged with business fraud in 1923 and later deported to Jamaica.

The tense domestic and international environment triggered a sense of unease among many middle-class Americans and produced a determination to preserve order and stability, with violence if necessary. A series of bombings carried out by radical groups throughout 1919 and 1920 created a further sense of crisis. Nearly thirty states passed peacetime sedition laws, while acts of popular violence against suspected radicals contributed to the turmoil gripping the nation. On the federal level, in an effort to capture suspected radicals and communists, Attorney General **A. Mitchell Palmer** ordered a series of crusades known as the "Palmer Raids." These achieved little in terms of uncovering weapons or plots to overthrow the government although they did lead to the deportation of nearly five hundred alien radicals.

Although the Red Scare subsided following the failure of the Palmer Raids, its legacy continued to affect the nation throughout the rest of the 1920s. The case of two Italian immigrants, **Nicola Sacco** and **Bartolomeo Vanzetti**, who were tried and found guilty of murdering a paymaster in Braintree, Massachusetts, despite questionable evidence and clearly unfair trials, demonstrated how poisoned the national atmosphere had become. While public demonstrations calling for a pardon of the two men grew throughout the decade, the government refused to yield, and they were executed in August 1927.

The passage of the Nineteenth Amendment in August of 1920 granting women the right to vote signaled for many the culmination of many years of progressive struggle. Disillusioned with the results of the war effort and Wilson's idealistic crusade to create a new structure for international relations, the economic downturn after the war, racial strife, and the radical challenge, most Americans wanted stability and a retreat from governmental and social activism. In the 1920 presidential election, undistinguished Ohio Senator **Warren G. Harding** received more than 60 percent of the popular vote, based largely upon his promise of a return to "normalcy," signaling the end of the progressive fervent that had marked the first two decades of the twentieth century.

Multiple-Choice Questions

1. The "Roosevelt Corollary" to the Monroe Doctrine
   a. pledged the United States not to intervene in the Western Hemisphere.
   b. offered economic aid to Latin American nations.
   c. claimed the American right to intervene in Western Hemisphere nations.
   d. sought greater American cooperation with European nations in the Western Hemisphere.
   e. had little direct effect on U.S. relations with Latin America..

2. "America's greatest need is not heroics, but healing; not nostrums, but normalcy; not revolution, but restoration; . . . not surgery; but serenity." The speaker of this quotation is
   a. Woodrow Wilson.
   b. Henry Cabot Lodge.
   c. Warren G. Harding.
   d. Calvin Coolidge.
   e. Herbert Hoover.

3. Which of the following principles are associated with the foreign policy of Wilsonianism?
   I. Diplomatic negotiations between nations should be subject to public scrutiny.

II. The balance of power helped to preserve international peace and stability.

III. Trade barriers between nations should be removed.

IV. Peace could best be preserved through international institutions.

V. Defeated nations should be forced to pay reparations.

a. I, II, and III

b. I, II, and IV

c. I, III, and IV

d. I, II, III, and IV

e. All of the above

4. President Wilson is often criticized for which of the following in his handling of the Versailles Treaty and the League of Nations?

a. He remained aloof from many of the day-to-day details of the negotiations.

b. He was too willing to compromise with Republicans and thus retreated from his original vision.

c. He was unwilling to make a strong case for the League to the American people

d. He did not involve prominent Republicans in the negotiations at Versailles.

e. He was too willing to accommodate Russian postwar demands.

5. All of the following were significant sources of tension in the postwar period between 1919 and 1921 *except*

a. labor strikes.

b. demonstrations by disgruntled veterans.

c. antiradical sentiment.

d. race riots.

e. economic depression.

6. President Wilson responded to the sinking of the *Lusitania* by

a. warning Americans not to travel on the nonmilitary ships of belligerents.

b. asking Congress for a declaration of war against Germany.

c. creating a convoy system to help escort Allied ships across the Atlantic.

d. demanding that Germany commit to respecting neutral rights.

e. placing an embargo on American foreign trade.

7. The majority of the funds used to support the American war effort in World War I were raised through which of the following means?

a. The sale of war bonds

b. Loans from foreign nations

c. Taxes on corporate profits

d. Withholding taxes from wages and salaries

e. Currency inflation

8. Which of the following best characterizes the effect of World War I on the relationship between government and business?

a. The war effort increased government regulation of business as progressives had hoped.

b. The government allowed business a free hand to mobilize war production.

c. Business and government worked closely together in a mutually beneficial way.

d. The war effort alienated business and government from one another.

e. The war effort inspired government leaders to reduce the power of big business following the war.

9. The Zimmerman Telegram was designed to
    a. resume Germany's policy of unrestricted submarine warfare.
    b. convince Russia to sign a separate peace agreement with Germany.
    c. entice Mexico to ally with Germany against the United States.
    d. influence American public opinion against entering the war.
    e. convince Wilson that Germany would respect neutral rights.

10. Which of the following is not correctly matched with the wartime agency listed below?
    a. Food Administration—Herbert Hoover
    b. Committee on Public Information—George Creel
    c. War Industries Board—Bernard Baruch
    d. Railroad Administration—William Gibbs McAdoo
    e. National War Labor Board—A. Mitchell Palmer

11. During the 1916 presidential campaign, Wilson benefited heavily from
    a. his advocacy of military preparedness.
    b. the popular belief that he would keep the nation out of war.
    c. the pacifism of his Republican opponent, Charles Evans Hughes.
    d. popular support for his vision for the postwar world.
    e. bipartisan support for his policies toward the European conflict.

12. The most active element of the peace movement during World War I was
    a. German Americans and Irish Americans.
    b. socialists and intellectuals.
    c. women's groups.
    d. religious pacifists.
    e. midwestern isolationists.

Free-Response Questions—Exam Tips

Questions from this period can often deal with American reasons for entering World War I or questions focusing on why the United States did not join the League of Nations. Consider economic, strategic, and ideological factors in determining your answer. Keep in mind that the best answers will usually ascribe American entry into the war to multiple factors. In the case of World War I, for example, trade with Great Britain and France clearly tilted the United States in favor of the Allies. At the same time, however, evidence indicates that Wilson genuinely sought to create a more peaceful world order at the war's conclusion.

In responding to questions about the United States' failure to join the League, keep in mind the changing political climate in the United States during and after the war and that World War I was not a particularly popular war in the United States. Some historians argue that Wilson's stubbornness as well as a number of tactical blunders on his part destroyed any possibility of a bipartisan agreement. In addition, by the end of World War I, Americans had experienced a series of reform movements dating back to the Populists. Americans, weary of reform and moralism, were not ready to accept a leadership role in international affairs.

Free-Response Questions

1. The United States' failure to join the League of Nations resulted from the unwillingness of the American people to abandon the country's traditional policy of isolationism Evaluate this statement.

2. Analyze the impact of American involvement in World War I in three of the following areas:

Women's rights *women had jobs, went out of home*

The role of African Americans *formed unions*

Civil liberties

Labor rights *many were given*

Prohibition *alc. law was repealed*

Document-Based Question—Exam Tips

Questions from this period have dealt with whether Wilson or Congress was more responsible for American failure to join the League of Nations.

Document-Based Question

Following the outbreak of World War I in 1914, President Wilson called upon Americans to be neutral "in thought as well as deed." To what degree was the United States neutral in "thought as well as deed" between 1914 and 1917?

Document A

Source: Theodore Roosevelt, Letter to Sir Edward Grey, January 1915.

President Wilson is certainly not desirous of war with anybody. But he is very obstinate, and he takes the professorial view of international matters. I need not point out to you that it is often pacificists who halting and stumbling and not knowing whither they are going finally drift helplessly into a war, which they have rendered inevitable, without the slightest idea that they were doing so. A century ago this was what happened to the United States under Presidents Jefferson and Madison—although at that time the attitude of both England and France rendered war with one of them, and ought to have rendered war with both of them, inevitable on our part. . . .

Document B

Source: Secretary of State William Jennings Bryan. Letter to President Wilson, August 1914.

I beg to communicate to you an important matter which has come before the Department. Morgan Company of New York have asked whether there would be any objection to their making a loan to the French Government and also the Rothschilds—I suppose that is intended for the French Government. I have conferred with Mr. Lansing and he knows of no legal objection to financing this loan, but I have suggested to him the advisability of presenting to you an aspect of the case which is not legal but I believe to be consistent with our attitude in international matters. It is whether it would be advisable for this Government to take the position that it will not approve of any loan to a belligerent nation. . . .

The powerful financial interests which would be connected with these loans would be tempted to use their influence through the newspapers to support the interests of the Government to which they had loaned because the value of the security would be directly affected by the result of the war. We would thus find our newspapers violently arrayed on one side or the other, each paper supporting a financial group and pecuniary interest. All of this influence would make it all the more difficult for us to maintain neutrality, as our action on various questions that would arise would affect one side or the other and powerful financial interests would be thrown into the balance. . . .

Document C

Source: Henry Stimson, National Security League Bulletin, 1915 [*Annals of America*, 13, 572].

Taken as a whole, we find that the conditions of military unpreparedness of the United States is most serious and lamentable. We believe it is the duty of our citizens, without respect to party, to take the present occasion, when the interest of the country has been aroused by the European war, for insisting that Congress give to the subject its most earnest attention to the end that the forgoing deficiencies may be speedily remedied.

Document D

Source: Secretary of State William Jennings Bryan, Letter to U.S. Ambassador to Great Britain Walter Hines Page, December 1914.

The Government of the United States has viewed with growing concern the large numbers of vessels laden with American goods destined to neutral ports in Europe, which have been seized on the high seas, taken into British ports and detained sometimes for weeks by the British authorities. During the early days of the war this Government assumed that the policy adopted by the British Government was due to the unexpected outbreak of hostilities and the necessity of immediate action to prevent contraband from reaching the enemy. For this reason it was not disposed to judge this policy harshly or protest it vigorously, although it was manifestly very injurious to American trade with the neutral countries of Europe. This Government, relying confidently upon the high regard which Great Britain has so often exhibited in the past for the rights of other nations, confidently awaited amendment of a course of action which denied to neutral commerce the freedom to which it was entitled by the law of nations.

Document E

Source: The Bryce Report: Report of the Committee on Alleged German Outrages Appointed by His Britannic Majesty's Government and Presided Over by the Right Hon. Viscount Bryce, O.M., 1915.

The burning of the villages in this neighbourhood and the wholesale slaughter of civilians, such as occurred at Herve, Micheroux, and Soumagne, appear to be connected with the exasperation caused by the resistance of Fort Fleron, whose guns barred the main road from Aix la Chapelle to Liege. Enraged by the losses which they had sustained, suspicious of the temper of the civilian population, and probably thinking that by exceptional severities at the outset they could cow the spirit of the Belgian nation, the German officers and men speedily accustomed themselves to the slaughter of civilians.

Document F

Source: Woodrow Wilson, Speech to Congress, January 1917.

In every discussion of peace that must end this war, it is taken for granted that the peace must be followed by some definite concert of power which will make it virtually impossible that any such catastrophe should ever overwhelm us again. Every love of mankind, every sane and thoughtful man must take that for granted.

I have sought this opportunity to address you because I thought that I owed it to you, as the counsel associated with me in the final determination of our international obligations, to disclose to you without reserve the thought and purpose that have been taking form in my mind in regard to the duty of our Government in the days to come when it will be necessary to lay afresh and upon a new plan the foundations of peace among the nations.

It is inconceivable that the people of the United States should play no part in that great enterprise. To take part in such a service will be the opportunity for which they have sought to prepare themselves by the very principles and purposes of their polity and the approved practices of their government ever since the days when they set up a new nation in the high and honourable hope that it might, in all that it was and did, show mankind the way to liberty.

Multiple-Choice Answers

1. c. The Roosevelt Corollary to the Monroe Doctrine, issued in 1904 primarily in response to a crisis in the Dominican Republic, was an effort to forestall European intervention in the Western Hemisphere by claiming the United States' right to intervene in the domestic affairs of Latin American nations if they were unable to maintain order and stability. The corollary was used in support of numerous American interventions in the first three decades of the twentieth century, until it was repudiated by President Hoover following the onset of the Great Depression and subsequent defaults by Latin American nations on loans to the United States.

2. c. Harding first used the term "normalcy" during the 1920 presidential campaign and returned to it a number of times during his presidency. The term connoted a return to America's policy of remaining aloof from political commitments abroad and a retreat from progressive reforms, a marked difference from Harding's predecessor, Woodrow Wilson.

3. c. Open diplomacy, free trade, and a League of Nations were all part of Wilson's Fourteen Points, his program for maintaining permanent peace following World War I. Wilson believed that the European reliance on the balance of power had been largely responsible for the complex alliance system that ultimately helped lead to the outbreak of World War I. He opposed the Allied demand for German reparations at Versailles, although he was forced to accept this.

4. d. Wilson did not appoint any prominent Republicans to the American delegation at Versailles (Henry White, a Republican and career diplomat, played a minor role in the negotiations). Wilson became heavily involved in the details of the negotiations at Versailles. When he returned to the United States, he was unwilling to accept any reservations to his plan and took his case to the American people in an arduous cross-country tour. Wilson was hostile to Russia, which was not represented at Versailles

(Franklin Roosevelt would later be criticized by some for being too lenient in his negotiations with the Soviet Union during World War II).

5. b. World War I veterans marched on Washington in 1932 to seek early payment of their war bonuses to help them to cope with the Depression. The year 1919 witnessed the largest wave of strikes in American history, while a series of radical-inspired bombings led to the Red Scare of 1919–1920. Race riots brooks out in Chicago and other cities during the summer of 1919, while the economy underwent a serious downturn in 1920 and 1921.

6. Wilson demanded that Germany respect neutral rights, which the Germans agreed to (although tension between the two nations continued to grow). William Jennings Bryan resigned as secretary of state over Wilson's refusal to demand that Americans not travel on belligerent ships. Wilson asked Congress for a declaration of war in April 1917 following Germany's resumption of unrestricted submarine warfare, and implemented the convoy system soon after entering the war. Jefferson imposed an embargo in 1807 in response to British and French attacks on American shipping.

7. a. Approximately $23 million of the $32 million that the United States directly spent on the conflict came from the sale of Liberty Bonds. The United States became a net creditor by lending to other nations to finance their war efforts. "Excess profit" taxes were levied on some corporations. The system of payroll deductions began in 1943 during World War II. Although rapid inflation occurred during the war, the federal government did not seek to inflate the currency in order to finance the war effort.

8. c. Many corporate executives, known as "dollar-a-year" men (many received that amount from the government while still maintaining their corporate salaries), came to Washington to help with the war effort. While many progressives had hoped that the war would increase government oversight and regulation of business, the demands of mobilizing production meant that business and government were forced to work closely together (a trend that continued to some degree into the postwar period).

9. c. Germany sought to capitalize on tensions between the United States and Mexico by proposing in early 1917 that Mexico could regain territory that it had lost to the United States by allying with Germany. Germany did resume unrestricted submarine warfare in early 1917, while Russia signed a separate peace with Germany in early 1918. The telegram, once made public after having been intercepted by British intelligence, obviously turned American public opinion against Germany. The Sussex and Arabic pledges were earlier statements by Germany that it would respect neutral shipping.

10. e. Palmer served as an attorney general following the war and was best known for the "Palmer Raids" against suspected radicals. Hoover, Baruch, and McAdoo all played key role in heading war boards that helped to mobilize production and organize the war effort, while Creel played a significant role in "selling" the war effort (and helping to create a repressive climate that was hostile to any perceived dissent against the war effort).

11. b. Although Wilson never used the popular Democratic slogan "He kept us out of war," he did nothing to discourage Democrats who used the phrase. He also encouraged the idea that Hughes would lead the nation into war if elected. Although Wilson had supported a military preparedness program in 1915 and 1916, he did not emphasize this theme in the campaign. The electorate was sharply divided on both domestic and foreign issues, and Wilson received little support from Republicans.

12. c. Although all of these groups opposed the war to some extent, the women's peace movement formed the largest element of the antiwar movement. Among the women who played a large role in the antiwar movement were Jane Addams, Charlotte Perkins Gilman, and Carrie Chapman Catt (although Catt came to support the war following American entry). As in other segments of society, the impact of American involvement was divisive, as the National American Woman Suffrage Association supported the war and used this as a means to help gain support for women's suffrage, while other smaller women's groups continued their opposition even following American entry.

Free-Response Questions Commentary

1. Historians have disagreed widely over the reasons behind American failure to join the League of Nations following World War I. The classic debate was long between those who blamed Wilson for stubbornness and for a series of tactical errors and those who pointed to the intransigence of Senate Republicans, led by Henry Cabot Lodge, who failed to support the League due to a combination of personal hatred toward Wilson and a desire to take advantage of a partisan issue to discredit the president. Others, including William Leuchtenberg, have pointed to the fact that the American people were simply unwilling to take on a more significant role in world affairs following World War I and that neither a more flexible Wilson nor more cooperative Republican leadership in the Senate could have made American involvement in the League possible.

   Wilson's leading biographer, Arthur Link, has pointed out that the emphasis on the personal drama between Lodge and the president has obscured the fact that this was a debate over differing visions of America's role in the world. The American people, Link further observes, were less divided along purely partisan lines than according to what they believed the nation should do following the war. Wilson's emphasis on working through international institutions as the best means to safeguard American society and Lodge's emphasis on maintaining American freedom of action have echoed throughout the rest of American history, most recently in the debates over the proper United States response to the September 11, 2001, terrorist attacks and their aftermath.

   There is significant evidence to indicate that the American people were not strongly committed to isolationism after World War I and that they would have been willing to support American involvement in the League of Nations, with certain modifications. Wilson received a wildly enthusiastic hearing during his September 1919 cross-country trip to gain support for the League. Only a small handful of Senate "irreconcilables" unalterably opposed any American involvement in the League, and a two-thirds majority could almost certainly have been found for a compromise version of American League membership.

   Overall, it was less American isolationism that led to the League's defeat than a difference of opinion over the degree of American involvement in world affairs. A full commitment to the League, many feared, would surrender American sovereignty on a variety of issues, bring the nation into conflicts that did not affect the nation's vital interests, and potentially erode Congress's constitutional right to declare war. Public support for Republican diplomacy during the 1920s, which some historians have dubbed "independent internationalism," suggests that the public was not so much isolationist as desirous of protecting American freedom of action in world affairs.

2. The prominent impact that World War I had on American society brings up important questions about the role of war in promoting social change. As in other wars in American society, the results were mixed. New economic and social opportunities arose

for previously underrepresented groups although these opportunities, as is often the case, rapidly disappeared following the war's conclusion. The role of the federal government expanded, and the war created greater support for reforms that had been advocated prior to the war. On the other hand, wartime nationalism often crossed the line into intolerance and the postwar mood was one of disillusionment that eroded support for some of the war's more progressive results.

Women's roles had changed throughout earlier wars in American history, and World War I was no exception. The million or so women who entered industrial jobs during the war quickly lost those jobs upon the war's end. Much more important was the war's role in building support for women's suffrage, as many prominent activists emphasized their support for the war effort and tied America's struggle for democracy abroad to extending democracy at home by allowing women the right to vote. Wilson, who had originally opposed women's suffrage, became a supporter during the war although his support came after suffrage advocates had already made extensive headway in gaining popular support for their cause.

As they would do again during World War II, many African Americans moved north to take relatively well-paying factory jobs as part of the "Great Migration." While these jobs allowed African Americans greater economic opportunity than had been available to them in the South, they also caused social tension, as whites fearful of economic competition in northern cities were less than welcoming to the new arrivals. Wartime military service raised the expectations of many African Americans, who felt that they deserved a greater role in society as a result of their efforts during the war. The immediate postwar period, however, was marked by race riots and a sharp upsurge in lynchings, demonstrating that African American gains were only temporary.

A democracy also faces a precarious balance between maintaining liberty and security, and the American experience during World War I was no exception. More than one historian has noted that the Wilson administration's record on civil liberties represented "the ugliest blot" on his presidency. The Wilson administration passed a number of measures meant to limit criticism of the war effort and state and local governments largely followed the federal government's lead. More than 1,500 people were arrested during 1918 and this distrust of dissent continued into the postwar period. With the notable exception of Japanese Americans, the federal government's record in protecting civil liberties was much stronger during World War II.

Wartime demand led, at least temporarily, to improved conditions for workers. The National War Labor Board, a body set up to mediate industrial disputes, pushed industry leaders to grant concessions that included an eight-hour day, equal pay for women doing the same work as men, and the right to organize and bargain collectively. Union membership rose significantly between 1917 and 1919. At the same time, however, there existed strong public and government hostility toward radical labor groups. Members of the IWW became especially strong targets of persecution, as many of its leaders were arrested or subject to popular acts of vigilantism (1,200 striking workers were rounded up by sheriffs' deputies in Bisbee, Arizona, and transported to the desert and left there without food and water for two days before being rescued).

The temperance movement also used the war as a way to increase popular support for its program. Prohibition gained support as a war measure, both due to the need to conserve grain for the war effort and also because many popular beers bore German names. This helped to speed the movement toward ratification of the Eighteenth Amendment, in 1919, although local and state efforts had already put Prohibition into effect throughout much of the country. The Commission on Training Camp Activities also sought to prohibit alcohol use in the areas around military bases in an effort to improve conditions for American soldiers.

Document-Based Question Commentary

Background: While the United States apparently had little direct interest in the European conflict that broke out in the summer of 1914, it quickly became apparent that it would be difficult for the United States to remain completely neutral for a variety of reasons. American economic interests, the ethnic ties that many Americans had to belligerent nations, and President Wilson's commitment to protecting American neutral rights in the face of German submarine warfare all contributed to the American entry into the war. Ultimately, however, most historians agree that it was Wilson's conviction that the rules of international relations must be modified completely that was the decisive factor in his calling upon Congress for a declaration of war.

The Documents: The documents offer insight into some of the different factors that made true American neutrality difficult during World War I. In Document A, Theodore Roosevelt criticizes Wilson's "professorial" view of international affairs and suggests that Wilson's strong commitment to abstract principles may lead to a repeat of the events that led the United States into the War of 1812—that is, the efforts by Jefferson and Madison to protect American rights though a policy of commercial diplomacy without adequately preparing the nation for the possibility of war.

Document B, a letter from Secretary of State Bryan to Wilson shortly after the outbreak of the war, foreshadows the significant emphasis put on American economic ties with the Great Britain and France as a factor that made American neutrality impossible. This became especially prominent in the 1930s, as disillusionment with the outcome of World War I and renewed militarism in Europe caused many Americans to fear United States entry into another needless conflict.

As Document C demonstrates, a number of prominent Americans advocated a position of greater military preparedness as the war in Europe dragged on and as U.S.-German tensions over the German sinking of American ships increased. Wilson himself supported a program of military expansion in 1915 and early 1916 (although he backed away from this during the 1916 presidential campaign).

Document D demonstrates that the United States government was concerned with British as well as German actions toward American shipping. The fact that the United States was more willing to overlook British violations of American neutral rights than it was concerning German violations has led in some quarters to the conclusion that the United States always leaned to ward Great Britain. However, the qualitative difference between British seizure of American ships and the German threat to American lives through submarine warfare offers a clear reason why the United States was more concerned about German actions.

Document E, the Bryce Report on German atrocities in Belgium, helped to shift American public opinion against Germany and the Central Powers. Subsequent evidence that many of the al legations against the Germans were either false or exaggerated was later used to support the idea that a naïve United States was dragged into war by the duplicitous British.

By early 1917, it was clear that the United States would have great difficulty remaining out of the war. Wilson's "Peace Without Victory" speech (Document F) before Congress indicates his desire for the United States to play a leading role in the peace settlement and to help to reform international relations. Soon thereafter, the German government resumed unrestricted submarine warfare and offered an alliance with Mexico if it would fight alongside Germany against the United States.

Summation: Few Americans, including Wilson, wanted war in 1914. At the same time, it was very difficult for the United States to remain neutral in the conflict without accepting the emergence of a world very different than that which Wilson and many other Americans wanted to see. While ethnic ties, economic interests, British propaganda, and German U-Boat policies all worked against true American neutrality, most historians would agree that Wilson finally reached the conclusion that only through military involvement in the war could he reform international relations and create a lasting peace.

CHAPTER 22
The "New Era"

AP THEMES

- **Economic Transformation:** The period from 1921 to 1929 was a period of significant economic growth for the United States, fueled by new technologies, new forms of production, and new techniques in marketing and production. Business leaders sought to consolidate their operations and reduce harmful competition through industrywide agreements, often with government cooperation. At the same time, however, this prosperity was far from widespread. Union membership declined in the face of business, governmental, and popular hostility, while farmers continued to face serious problems of overproduction and an inability to organize to effectively communicate their demands.

- **Culture:** Economic prosperity had a significant influence, both positive and negative, on American culture. The availability of consumer goods, the growth of radio and movies, and the increasing use of the automobile helped to create a more national culture than had existed previously, as people across the country had access to shared experiences. Many intellectuals, disillusioned by the failure of World War I to reform the world order and by what they saw as the crass materialism of American society, responded either by producing works that critiqued life in the United States or by withdrawing from American society altogether.

- **American Diversity:** Following World War I, there existed a great deal of tension over who should be considered "American." The experience of fighting a wrenching foreign conflict, wartime patriotism, and fears of domestic subversion all contributed to hostility toward immigrants, minorities, and those who challenged the status quo. Congress responded during the 1920s by severely restricting immigration, while popular attitudes and actions resulted in a hostile climate for those perceived as "outsiders," as seen through the rebirth and rapid growth of the Ku Klux Klan and other groups. While the decade witnessed a flourishing of African American culture through the Harlem Renaissance, it was often a difficult decade for the nonwhite and non-Protestant.

- **American Identity:** The profound social, economic, and political changes facing the nation raised fundamental questions about the nation's identity. Many Americans, particularly those living in rural areas, sought to maintain what they saw as the nation's traditional ideals in the face of trends such as urbanization, secularization, and modernization. The result was a series of disputes over immigration, Prohibition, religion, and other cultural issues. These disputes between supporters of tradition and modernity have continued to exist in varying forms throughout the remainder of the twentieth century and into the twenty-first—indeed, the conflicts of the 1920s represent in some forms a forerunner to the "culture wars" of the 1990s.

CHAPTER SUMMARY
The New Economy

The United States underwent a period of sustained economic expansion following the postwar recession of 1921–1922, although this prosperity was by no means uniform throughout all sectors of the economy or the American population. The surge in American economic growth was the result of a variety of factors, the most important of which was a series of developments in technology that helped to transform patterns of both production and consumption. The automobile was the catalyst for the decade's prosperity, fueling the growth of other industries such as steel, glass, and rubber, as well as oil and, more indirectly, construction and housing. In addition, radio, aviation, and telephones further spurred the nation's economic growth.

As the American economy expanded, business leaders sought to create new forms of economic organization in order to limit competition and control production in an effort to avoid a repeat of the conditions that had led to frequent recessions in the late nineteenth and early twentieth centuries. Among the most prominent of these was the **trade association**, a national organization of manufacturers in various sectors that sought cooperation in both production and marketing. Industrial workers had a decidedly mixed experience in the 1920s. While some saw their standards of living rise, some—due to the so-called "**welfare capitalism**" of corporate employers—worked in situations in which employers sought to limit labor costs and keep profit levels high. As a result, wage increases generally lagged far behind increases in production. Organized labor made few gains during this period, as mainstream unions such as the **AFL** were unable to change the policies of corporate leaders.

Growing numbers of women and minorities in the workforce also faced difficulties in organizing effectively to improve their economic status. Many women entered low-paying service industries known as "**pink collar**" occupations, while African Americans, Mexicans , and Asian workers all faced varying degrees of hostility and discrimination from employers and received little or no assistance from labor unions.

Determined efforts by corporate and government leaders further hampered the efforts of organized labor to build upon the gains that had been made during World War I. Business leaders advocated the so-called "**American Plan,**" a campaign for the **open shop,** meaning that it was illegal for a worker to be required to join a union.. At the same time, a conservative Supreme Court declared picketing illegal and upheld the rights of courts to issue antistrike injunctions. Union membership fell from more than 5 million in 1920 to fewer than 3 million in 1929.

A variety of technological innovations helped farmers to bring millions of acres of new land under cultivation. The increasing use of tractors and other changes led to far greater productivity, but also caused agricultural production to outpace demand. Farmers responded with calls for "**parity,**" a formula in which the government would set prices for farm goods and guarantee that farmers would earn at least enough to cover their production costs. Congress twice passed the **McNary–Haugen Bill,** legislation requiring parity for certain products, but President **Calvin Coolidge** twice vetoed the proposals.

A New Culture

One of the biggest changes resulting from American industrialization was the emergence in the 1920s of a mass consumer culture, made possible by the fact that many Americans had significant amounts of discretionary income during this period. Goods such as home appliances and personal items helped to promote the consumer culture, but the automobile was the most significant factor in helping to create a mass culture. The car allowed Americans a geographic mobility that they had never known, made the vacation a central feature of American life, and led to the emergence of a distinctive youth culture as young people were able to move away from their parents.

Advertising helped to facilitate the growth of modern consumer culture, convincing Americans that buying certain products would help to transform their lives and lead them to new experiences. New forms of communication such as wire service news stories and mass-circulation of magazines such as *The Reader's Digest* (founded in 1921) and *Time* magazine (founded in 1923) made possible the enormous growth and success of advertising.

Both motion pictures and the radio further contributed to the growing sense of homogeneity in American culture. The emergence of sound in motion pictures beginning with Al Jolson's *The Jazz Singer* in 1927 helped to increase the already avid American interest in cinema. Radio, beginning with the first commercial broadcasting station in 1920, underwent a massive growth reaching 500 commercial stations by 1923.

The new consumer culture and its emphasis on personal fulfillment reached into organized religion, as many church leaders abandoned the more traditional elements of fundamentalist Christianity for a greater focus on living a fulfilling life in the present. At the same time, increasing numbers of middle-class Americans paid less and less attention to religion.

Middle-class women had access to relatively few opportunities outside the home although changing attitudes about motherhood and marriage helped to transform their experiences. **"Behaviorist"** psychologists argued that women did not necessarily possess innate maternal capabilities and that they should rely on outside experts to help them with child rearing. As a result of this changing perception of the maternal role, many middle-class women began to devote greater attention to their relationships with their husbands. The growing awareness and use of birth control, a result largely of the efforts of **Margaret Sanger** and others, allowed women to increase their sexual activity without concern about childbirth.

Many women embraced the ideal of the **"flapper,"** referring to a modern, liberated woman who was not bound by traditional moral standards and could smoke, drink, and pursue relationships with men as she pleased. While this image dominated popular perceptions of women during the 1920s, most women remained in traditional roles and were heavily dependent on men in both the workplace and the home. Some women's groups pressed for reforms to improve their position in society during the 1920s, including an unsuccessful push for an Equal Rights Amendment to the federal Constitution. The **Sheppard–Towner Maternity Act,** passed by Congress in 1921, provided federal funds to states to fund prenatal and child health-care programs, although it received opposition from some women's groups and the powerful American Medical Association. Congress finally terminated the program in 1929.

Another area of American culture that underwent a dramatic transformation was education. High school attendance more than doubled and enrollment in institutions of higher education more than tripled during the 1920s. Both the curriculum and the social functions of education expanded significantly, as many young people came to see high schools and colleges as an area for them to become involved in a wide variety of activities outside of the classroom. This helped fuel the development of a distinctive youth culture, as adolescence came to be seen as a period that allows young people to prepare for the challenges of adulthood.

The increasing consolidation and homogenization of American society contributed to the decline of both the reality and the ideal of the **"self-made man,"** one of the most cherished

American ideals. As a result of economic and social changes during the decade, men turned to a variety of different outlets, including fraternal societies and athletic events. Many turned to admiration of figures such as **Thomas Edison, Henry Ford,** and **Charles Lindbergh,** all of whom had managed to succeed in modern society without the benefit of formal education and embodied traditional American values of hard work and upward mobility.

Many artists and intellectuals experienced a deep sense of personal alienation from American society, resulting from their disillusionment with the results of World War I and their disgust with much of what they saw in contemporary culture during the 1920s. **Ernest Hemingway,** for example, portrayed the uselessness of war in works such as *A Farewell to Arms;* journalist **H. L. Mencken** relentlessly lampooned the "booboisie"—his name for middle-class Americans; and **Sinclair Lewis** criticized numerous aspects of American culture. **F. Scott Fitzgerald's** *The Great Gatsby* criticized Americans' obsession with money and success. Many members of what Gertrude Stein called **"The Lost Generation"** moved to France or took refuge in isolated parts of the United States where they could avoid contact with mainstream American society.

Other groups of intellectuals turned to an examination of their culture or regional heritages as a way to deal with the ills of modern society. Many black artists and intellectuals took part in the **"Harlem Renaissance,"** a movement that explored the richness of the African American heritage. Among the most notable contributors to this movement were writers **Langston Hughes, Zora Neale Hurston,** and **Claude McKay.** The work of artists, writers, dancers, and musicians began to attract the attention of white audiences, helping to expose segments of the wider public to the richness of the black experience.

A Conflict of Cultures

The self-indulgent culture that arose in the 1920s competed with traditional values resulting in social tension and conflict throughout the course of the decade. Prohibition, which had gone into effect in January 1920, was initially supported by a majority of middle-class progressives who considered it a **"noble experiment."** The measure reduced alcohol consumption, but it also led to significant increases in organized crime, especially in Chicago, where **Al Capone** built a huge illegal operation based largely on alcohol. By the latter part of the decade, most of Prohibition's remaining supporters were largely Protestant Americans from rural areas, who saw the crusade against alcohol as symbolic of their larger effort to maintain a hold over a society in which they were increasingly losing influence.

Growing support for immigration restriction represented another avenue through which old-stock Americans sought to influence the direction of American society. Congress passed an emergency immigration act in 1921 establishing a **quota system** limiting the numbers of immigrants from each country to 3 percent of the number of persons of that nationality who were in the United States in 1910, while the **National Origins Act** of 1924 reduced the numbers to 2 percent of the 1890 population and barred immigration from East Asia altogether. The final piece of immigration legislation was a 1929 act that limited the total number of immigrants to the United States to 150,000 per year.

Perhaps no trend demonstrated the prevalence of nativist sentiment and intolerance during the 1920s more than the growth of the **Ku Klux Klan.** While the organization had its roots in post-Civil War efforts to restrict the rights of blacks in the South, the newer incarnation of the Klan—started by a group of whites who met at **Stone Mountain** in Georgia in 1915—

widened its scope to anyone who challenged the traditional ideals of white, Protestant America, including recent immigrants, Jews and Catholics, political radicals, and women who defied traditional roles. It also expanded its geographical scope beyond the South, reaching into the West and into many northern industrial cities. The Klan reached a membership of 4 million by 1924.

American Protestantism was also split by cultural clashes. **Modernists** sought to adapt the teachings of Protestantism to modern culture, while **fundamentalists** sought to defend the traditional tenets of their faith, most notably by literal interpretation of the Bible. **Billy Sunday** and other evangelists traveled the country and found wide audiences for the fundamentalist message. The teaching of evolution became a focal point for the conflict between fundamentalism and modernism, as Tennessee and other states passed legislation outlawing the teachings of Darwin's theories in public schools. A young biology teacher named **John Scopes** took up an offer by the American Civil Liberties Union to defend any teacher who violated the Tennessee law. The resulting **"Scopes Monkey Trial"** featured celebrated defense attorney **Clarence Darrow** as a defender of Scopes and **William Jennings Bryan** as a defender of traditional values. While Scopes was convicted (although the sentence was later overturned on a technicality), the case discredited fundamentalists in the eyes of many Americans (even though it did little to dampen the fundamentalist zeal in promoting their values).

The Democratic Party was a victim of the cultural clashes of the decade, as it was unable to bridge the gap between its rural and urban wings. The party's 1924 convention, for example, split over resolutions calling for the repeal of Prohibition and a denunciation of the Ku Klux Klan (both narrowly failed). It took 103 ballots before settling upon bland compromise candidate **John W. Davis** for president. Four years later, the Democrats nominated New York Governor **Al Smith,** a Catholic and outspoken opponent of Prohibition. Smith ran well in urban areas but was also the first Democrat since the Civil War not to carry the South. Smith was soundly defeated by **Herbert Hoover.**

Republican Government

Between 1921 and 1933, both the presidency and Congress were under the control of the Republican Party. While the Republicans strongly supported corporate interests and enjoyed a warm relationship with the business community, the New Era governments by no means pursued a laissez-faire approach to economic issues. **Warren G. Harding** was an undistinguished Ohio politician who had been elected in 1920 on the basis of his pledge to restore "normalcy." Although he appointed a number of able cabinet members—**Charles Evans Hughes** as secretary of state; **Herbert Hoover** as secretary of commerce; and **Andrew Mellon** as secretary of the treasury—Harding also surrounded himself with a wide variety of party hacks and other unscrupulous figures who looked to government for personal gain. Harding's secretary of the interior, **Albert Fall,** was involved in the most notable scandal of the period, the **Teapot Dome** affair, in which Fall received loans from wealthy businessmen in exchange for allowing them to lease government-owned reserves in Teapot Dome, Wyoming, and Elk Hills, California. Harding died of a heart attack in the summer of 1923, before many of the scandals of his administration came to light.

Harding's successor, **Calvin Coolidge**, was in personal style Harding's opposite but very similar in his views about the role of government. Both believed that the federal government should intervene in national life as little as possible. Coolidge was easily elected in his own right in 1924 and would likely have won again in 1928 but chose not to run. Despite the passivity of Harding and Coolidge, the federal government worked closely with business to assure that the country's private economy achieved its full productive potential. Treasury Secretary Mellon promoted a program of tax cuts and stringent budgetary practices to reduce federal spending as well as the nation's World War I debt. Hoover worked with business leaders to promote his vision of **"associationalism,"** in which business leaders would work together to limit overproduction.

Hoover's election to the presidency in 1928 gave many progressives hope for the future, as they saw Hoover as a figure who could promote continued prosperity and help to ameliorate the nation's remaining economic problems. Less than a year after Hoover took office, the nation was plunged into the worst depression in its history. The depression revealed the weaknesses and limitations of the "New Era" economy.

Multiple-Choice Questions

1. Which of the following best characterizes the experiences of the majority of industrial workers in the United States between 1921 and 1929?
   a. They experienced wage increases commensurate with the levels of growth in their industries.
   b. They prospered due to the efforts of union leaders to ensure that workers received a significant share of increasing corporate profits.
   c. They took part in a series of violent sit-down strikes to gain union recognition in previously nonunionized industries.
   d. They experienced increases in their standards of living far below increases in corporate production and profits.
   e. They benefited from federal labor legislation guaranteeing the rights of collective bargaining.

2. Which of the following was the most significant factor in promoting American economic growth during the 1920s?
   a. government policies that emphasized national planning and centralized control of the economy
   b. a wide variety of technological innovations that spurred growth in both production and consumption
   c. the increasing globalization of the American economy, encouraged by the government's free-trade policies
   d. the increasingly even distribution of wealth, which led to balanced consumption by all groups in American society
   e. the success of business and agricultural leaders in controlling production and thus avoiding the conditions that had led to previous recessions

3. During the 1920s, farm groups advocated which of the following proposals to help them to deal with overproduction?
   a. government inflation of the currency to raise their prices and make it easier for them to pay creditors
   b. government subsidies to support their taking land out of production as a way to raise prices
   c. government price supports based on the principle of parity, which would have guaranteed farm profits at least equal to costs of production

d. government-owned warehouses to provide for crop storage until domestic and world prices rose

e. government education programs to promote more scientific and rational use of farmland

4. Which of the following best characterizes the experiences of the majority of both middle-class and working-class women during the 1920s?

a. Despite popular perceptions, most women remained heavily dependent upon men in both the public and private realms.

b. Women made widespread gains in employment opportunities and political rights throughout the decade.

c. Due to sustained governmental reform efforts, women's status in society improved significantly.

d. Most women shared the decade's conservative ethos and had little interest in promoting social or political changes.

e. Many women pressed for radical changes in a revolt against what they perceived as the patriarchal structure of American society.

5. The influence of nativist sentiment during the 1920s can be seen through all of the following *except*

a. the popularity of the Ku Klux Klan.

b. the passage of immigration restrictions.

c. the Harlem Renaissance.

d. the widespread provincial support for Prohibition.

e. the decision to execute Sacco and Vanzetti.

6. Which of the following best characterizes the differences between the post-Civil War and the post-1915 versions of the Ku Klux Klan?

a. The more modern version had less appeal among Americans due to a greater sense of tolerance among the population as a whole.

b. The more modern version widened its focus to include virtually all groups that it perceived as violating "traditional" ideals and social norms.

c. The more modern version had little appeal to women.

d. The more modern version made little effort to venture beyond the Deep South.

e. The more modern version sought to operate in secret to as great a degree as possible.

7. Which of the following best describes the role of the federal government between 1921 and 1929 under the administrations of Warren Harding and Calvin Coolidge?

a. The federal government pursued a policy of almost complete laissez-faire.

b. The federal government sought to restrict the power and influence of business.

c. The federal government took active steps to help business to operate with maximum efficiency but intervened in few other areas of American life.

d. The federal government pursued a vigorous program of social and economic reforms.

e. The federal government sought to serve as an impartial mediator between large interest groups.

8. All of the following writers produced important critiques of American society during the 1920s *except*
   a. Ernest Hemingway.
   b. F. Scott Fitzgerald.
   c. Sinclair Lewis.
   d. Bruce Barton.
   e. H. L. Mencken.

9. "I believe everything in the Bible should be accepted as it is given there; some of the Bible is given illustratively. For instance: 'Ye are the salt of the earth.' I would not insist that man was actually salt, or that he had flesh of salt, but it is used in the sense of salt as saving God's people. . ."
   The quotation above corresponds to which of the following?
   a. modernism
   b. fundamentalism
   c. agnosticism
   d. skepticism
   e. atheism

10. The "American Plan" received the majority of its support from
    a. members of the Ku Klux Klan.
    b. organized labor.
    c. business leaders.
    d. progressive reformers.
    e. recent immigrants.

11. The 1924 Democratic National Convention demonstrated which of the following?
    a. the predominance of the party's urban wing
    b. the continuing influence of Wilsonian ideals
    c. the party's united commitment to opposing Republican policies
    d. the party's sharp division between its rural and urban wings
    e. the predominance of the party's rural wing

12. The presidential administration of Warren G. Harding is best known for
    a. bold domestic initiatives.
    b. support for the League of Nations.
    c. a series of scandals implicating administration officials.
    d. a commitment to honesty and integrity.
    e. increasing presidential power and executive authority.

Free-Response Questions—Exam Tips

Themes in this period include the reasons behind economic and business expansion as well as causes of American prosperity and its decline. You should be able to discuss prosperity and its social implications, in terms of factors such as consumer culture, entertainment, and values, and be prepared to make comparisons with other periods. The late nineteenth century and the 1950s are particularly good areas of comparison.

Free-Response Questions

1. Analyze the impact of two of the following developments on American culture and society during the 1920s:

   The automobile *created Tech innovations, transport easier, news spread faster*

   Radio *passed news along, created entertainment*

   Motion pictures *entertainment*

2. In what ways and to what extent can the 1920s be called a decade of prosperity? Analyze with regard to two of the following:

   Women *created a name for memselves*

   Industrial workers *inflation, better living/working conditions*

   Farmers

   African Americans *created/shared the jazzy vibe, treated better could establish memselves as an individual more*

Document-Based Question—Exam Tips

Key themes in this period include the social and cultural tensions of the 1920s, as seen through disputes over religion, alcohol, race, and evolution, among others. Past questions have focused on the tension between tradition and modernity during the decade. You should note that while popular perceptions stress the prosperity and the growing urban culture of the decade, this was far from widespread. Large numbers of Americans, especially those in rural areas, clung to tradition in an effort to maintain their position in society and also to preserve their vision for the nation.

Document-Based Question

In what ways and to what extent did the 1920s represent a continuation of progressivism?

Use the documents and your knowledge of the period to answer the question.

Document A

Source: Calvin Coolidge, Address before the New York Chamber of Commerce (reprinted in Johnson, *Reading the American Past*, pp. 141–144).

I should put an even stronger emphasis on the desirability of the largest possible independence between government and business. . . . When government enters the field of business with its great resources, it has a tendency to extravagance and inefficiency, but, having the power to crush all competitors, likewise closes the door of opportunity and results in monopoly.

Document B

Source: Herbert Hoover, American Individualism (original publication?), in Fernlund, Documents to Accompany America's History.

Individualism cannot be maintained as the foundation of a society if it looks to only legalistic justice based upon contracts, property, and political equality. Such legalistic safeguards are themselves not enough. In our individualism we have long since abandoned the laissez faire of the 18th Century. . . . We have confirmed its abandonment in terms of legislation, of social and economic justice,—in part because we have learned that the foremost are not always the best nor the hindmost the worst—and in part because we have learned that social injustice is the destruction of justice itself.

Document C

Source: Manufacturer Record, September 1924 [Annals of America, 14, 422].

Because the Child Labor Amendment in reality is not legislation in the interest of children but legislation which would mean the destruction of manhood and womanhood through the destruction of the boys and girls of this country, the *Manufacturers Record* has been giving much attention to the discussion of the subject, and will continue to do so. . . .

This proposed amendment is father by Socialists, Communists and Bolshevists. They are the active workers in its favor. They look forward to its adoption as giving them the power to nationalize the children of the land and bring about in this country the exact conditions which prevail in Russia. These people are the active workers back of this undertaking, but many patriotic men and women, without at all realizing the seriousness of this proposition, thinking only of it as an effort to lessen child labor in factories, are giving countenance to it.

Document D

Source: Federal Prohibition Commissioner Roy Haynes, Speech, January 1927 [Annals, 14, p. 524].

We must remember that prohibition is the greatest effort for human advancement and betterment ever attempted in history, and that while the nearest approach, perhaps, was the destruction of human slavery, let us not forget that the revolutionary policy affected only one section of the nation—whereas the national prohibition policy called for changing the habits and customs of the people in all sections of the nation. Therefore, the most gratifying and enheartening feature of the situation is that so large a majority of our people respect the Constitution and observe this law, and this in spit of the fact there is a very considerable number of citizens of influence and position who, by nonobservance, are embarrassing the government in the promotion of its great task.

Document E

Source: Library of Congress.

Photograph of Passaic, New Jersey, textile workers picketing outside the White House, April 1926

Document F

Source: Justice G. Sutherland, *Adkins* v. *Children's Hospital*, April 1923 [*Annals*, 14, 392–393].

The authority to fix hours of labor cannot be exercised except in respect of those occupations where work of long-continued duration is detrimental to health. This Court has been very careful in every case where the question has been raised to place its decision upon the limited authority of the legislature to regulate hours of labor and to disclaim any purpose to uphold the legislation as fixing wages, thus recognizing an essential difference between the two. It seems plain that these decisions afford no real support for any form of law establishing minimum wages.

Document G

Source: Eleanor Roosevelt, "Women Must Learn to Play the Game as Men Do" *The Red Book Magazine* 50, no. 6 (April 1928): 78–79, 141–142 [available at http://newdeal.feri.org/er/er10.htm].

Remember, women have voted just ten years. They have held responsible positions in big business enterprises only since the war, to any great extent. The men at the head of big business or controlling politics are for the most part middle-aged men. Their wives grew up in an era when no public question was discussed in a popular manner, when men talked politics over their wine or cigars, and pulled their waistcoats down, on joining the ladies, to talk music, or the play or the latest scandal. Can you blame them if the adjustment to modern conditions is somewhat difficult?

Document H

Behind the Scenes
in
Candy Factories

❦

Investigation Conducted by
THE CONSUMERS' LEAGUE OF NEW YORK
1928

Frontpiece, "Behind the Scenes in Candy Factories," Consumers' League of New York, 1928

Source: Robert S. Lynd, "The People as Consumers," from *Recent Social Trends in the United States*, Vol. 2, Chapter 17 (1933).

Among the federal agencies operating in part to further consumer literacy is the Federal Trade Commission, set up in 1915 with the aim, among others, of helping to referee competitive commerce. . . . Originally intended only to prevent unfair competition between corporations, and functioning usually only where a competitor complains, its cases often have direct bearing on consumer deception. It has had before it, for instance, a number of cases involving the improper use of labeling based on federal specifications. In 1929 a special board was set up to deal with misleading advertising by competing manufacturers and dealers, and over five hundred proceedings were begun in the first year. Certain limitations on the capacity of the Trade Commission appeared in the reversal of its stand by the Supreme Court in the Marmola case in 1931 . . . The Court, while stating that "Findings, supported by evidence, warrant the conclusion that the preparation is one which cannot be used generally with safety to physical health except under medical direction and advice," held that the Commission had no power to ban these anti-fat pills on the ground of their harmfulness to the health of consumers, inasmuch as the Commission's duties do not concern unfair competition against the health of citizen's but rather unfair competition among business competitors.

Multiple-Choice Answers

1. d. While wages rose in most industries, they increased at a level far below increases in corporate profits. Organized labor was weak, as union membership fell during the 1920s and mainstream union leaders often cooperated with business in order to maintain industrial stability. The 1930s brought about sit-down strikes in the automobile industry and saw the passage of legislation guaranteeing labor's right to collective bargaining.

2. b. Technological innovations in the automobile industry, radio, and electronics, to name just three areas, all produced major growth that in turn helped to spur growth in ancillary areas. The federal government cooperated with business leaders to promote growth and efficiency but by and large left business a free hand. While American foreign investment increased during the 1920s, the country pursued a high tariff policy. The onset of the Depression was at least partly a result of overproduction, demonstrating that business leaders had not learned ways to curb production to prevent economic downturns.

3. c. The McNary–Haugen Bill, which twice passed Congress only to be vetoed by Coolidge, was based on the principle of parity. Inflation and warehousing had been proposed by the Populists in the late nineteenth century, while the idea of paying farmers to take land out of production and more scientific education for farmers came about in the 1930s as part of the New Deal.

4. a. While the idea of the "flapper" dominated popular perceptions of the decade, this reflected the experience of a relatively small number of women. Work opportunities remained scarce for women, as did opportunities in the political arena. Despite some reforms such as the Sheppard–Towner Maternity Act, the decade failed to live up to the expectations that many women had following their gains during the progressive era.

5. c. The Harlem Renaissance represented a growing awareness both among African Americans and among the population as a whole of the nation's rich black cultural heritage. The Ku Klux Klan's targeting of any groups not considered fully "American,"

the passage of three major pieces of immigration restriction legislation, the support for Prohibition on the basis that immigrant groups were more likely to consume alcohol than others, and the execution of Sacco and Vanzetti despite wide protests and the dubious evidence against them all demonstrate the decade's high degree of nativist sentiment.

6. b. The Ku Klux Klan during the 1920s had a much wider scope than the post-Civil War Klan and targeted Jews, Catholics, immigrants, and virtually anyone else that it believed violated traditional American morality. The 1920s Klan was popular in the South but also in parts of the Midwest and in some northern industrial areas, and it operated much more openly than the nineteenth-century Klan, even staging a march in Washington in 1926.

7. c. Although the federal government during the 1920s took a less active role than had previous administrations between 1901 and 1921, Harding and Coolidge by no means pursued a laissez-faire policy. The main goal of the federal government in their minds was to work with business to promote conditions that would facilitate prosperity and efficiency, while avoiding harmful competition. Treasury Secretary Andrew Mellon's program of tax cuts and commerce secretary Herbert Hoover's promotion of voluntary business–government cooperation were two central elements of the Republican vision.

8. d. Bruce Barton's *The Man Nobody Knows* was a celebration of advertising and consumer culture, which argued that Jesus Christ had been "a super salesman." Hemingway, Fitzgerald, Lewis, and Mencken all criticized various aspects of American culture and society during the decade through their works, the first three as part of the "Lost Generation" of writers and intellectuals, and Mencken as a master satirist in the journalistic realm.

9. b. The belief in the literal interpretation of Scripture and its divine inspiration represents the ideals of fundamentalism. This statement was made by William Jennings Bryan during his testimony in the Scopes trial. He had been called to testify as an expert on the Bible, and defense attorney Clarence Darrow sought to use Bryan's statements to expose his belief in Scriptural truth.

10. c. The "American Plan" was a campaign by business leaders to gain popular support for the "open shop" (one in which workers did not have to belong to a union to be hired). It was an effort to paint unions as "un-American" and may thus have gained some, but not its primary, support from members of the Ku Klux Klan. Organized labor and progressive reformers opposed the plan as harmful to the rights of workers. Recent immigrants may have benefited from the open hiring practices, as their willingness to work for low wages may have given them more opportunities, but immigration restrictions during the decade gave them little opportunity to express support for such measures.

11. d. The Democratic Party divided sharply over a number of issues during the 1920s, including support for Prohibition and the question of whether to denounce the Ku Klux Klan. In 1924, the party finally chose John W. Davis as a compromise presidential candidate palatable to both the rural and urban wings of the party. While Wilson had sought to make the 1920 election a "solemn referendum" on the League of Nations, the influence of his domestic and foreign policy program had declined significantly by 1924.

12. c. Harding died in 1923, just before public awareness of several major scandals, the largest implicating Interior Secretary Albert Fall in illegal transactions to turn leases of government-owned oil reserves in Teapot Dome, Wyoming, and Elk Hills, California, over to businessmen in exchange for his own financial enrichment. Harding's commitment to "normalcy" meant a retreat from domestic reform and international activism, as well as a belief in limited presidential authority.

Free-Response Questions Commentary

1. Developments in both transportation and communications touched almost all elements of American society. The automobile had extremely significant economic and social effects on American life, while the radio and motion picture industries helped to shape American culture during the 1920s. All three had both unifying and dividing effects on American life.

   Economically, the automobile industry stimulated the growth of the fuel, steel, glass, and rubber industries, among others. The automobile helped to fuel the growth of suburbs by making it possible for people to travel more easily to urban workplaces. By allowing Americans greater access to travel, it helped to broaden people's horizons and create a more national culture by allowing people to see different parts of the country. At the same time, however, it contributed to trends such as the separation of families, as young people were able to move further away from their parents. Traditional activities such as Sunday church attendance declined as people became more interested in leisure activities.

   Following the first commercial radio broadcast by Pittsburgh station KDKA in 1920, the nation witnessed an explosion in radio ownership, to the point where Americans had more than 2 million radios by mid-decade. Unlike motion pictures, radio was more decentralized and less subject to government control. As a result, local radio stations had the ability to air more controversial content than other media, a trend that can be seen even today. Socially, radio had both unifying and dividing effects on American culture. On one hand, the growth of radio and the popularity of radio programs caused Americans to spend more time in their own homes and involve themselves less in public life. At the same time, radio served both to unite families by providing common experiences for both parents and children and to allow community groups to congregate to listen to relevant programming.

   While the motion picture had existed several decades longer than the radio, the 1920s witnessed the addition of sound (with 1927's *The Jazz Singer*) and experienced an exponential growth in movie attendance. Much more than radio, films tended to be a nationwide experience that helped to create a common cultural reference point for Americans from a variety of different backgrounds. Culturally, movies tended to explore "safe" themes and avoid controversial topics.

   Overall, the 1920s was a decade that witnessed both the emergence of a growing national culture as well as a great deal of division, due largely to the tension between those who favored tradition and those who embraced modernity. The automobile, radio, and the motion picture helped to contribute to both unity and diversity in the modernizing America.

2. Early popular perception of the 1920s, shaped by journalists and other commentaries, created the image of the decade as one of widespread prosperity and carefree gaiety. Historians have long disputed this image of the 1920s, noting the presence of widespread dissent against the emerging decade's consumer culture and both the limited and uneven nature of the decade's prosperity—indeed, historian William Leuchtenberg's aptly titled *The Perils of Prosperity* chronicles much of this. Women, industrial workers, farmers, and African Americans all by and large failed to share in the decade's prosperity.

The popular image of the "flapper,"—that is, the carefree, independent young woman who often worked to support her enjoyable lifestyle—represented only a small minority of women. Similarly, the "new woman" who had emerged during the progressive era was again a small minority—most college-educated and middle-class women had to choose between marriage and a career. Overall, women in the workplace were poorly paid, especially in comparison with men. In the home, most women likewise maintained their earlier dependence on their husbands.

After World War I, workers sought to build upon their wartime gains, but popular revulsion over the 1919 labor strikes and the federal government's pro-business proclivities in the 1920s severely limited workers' progress. Employers did institute some benefits in the form of "welfare capitalism," such as paid vacations, pensions, shorter hours, and better workplace safety practices. At the same time, however, business leaders expected cooperation from pliable "company unions" and refused to tolerate organized labor efforts that sought greater worker control over the workplace. In short, industrial workers may have made small gains in wages and working conditions but at the price of surrendering control over their fates and at a rate much slower than overall growth in corporate profits.

Farmers had struggled economically since the late nineteenth century with the notable exception of World War I, and the 1920s saw a continuation of this problem. New technologies were at the root of the farmers' dilemma—they allowed the farmer to cultivate more land, but often forced the farmers to go into debt to purchase the new equipment. In turn, farmers sought to grow more, which drove prices down even further as supply outpaced demand. The four-fold increase in tractors during the 1920s resulted in more than 30 million new acres under cultivation, but the recovery of European agriculture after the war and other factors lowered demand. As a result, farmers looked in vain to the federal government for price supports such as the complicated McNary–Haugen program, which President Coolidge twice vetoed.

Similarly, African Americans sought to continue to improve their positions in society, as many had taken on better-paying industrial jobs or served in the armed forces during World War I. A group of African American writers, artists, and intellectuals flourished during the Harlem Renaissance. Overall, however, African Americans faced workplace discrimination and exclusion from the AFL and other unions, forcing them to take low-paying service jobs that whites did not want. The Brotherhood of Sleeping Car Porters, led by A. Philip Randolph, was an important exception in winning gains for black workers. The union would later play a significant in role in combating workplace discrimination during World War II.

Overall, the experience of women, industrial workers, farmers, and African Americans demonstrates that prosperity during the 1920s did not come close to reaching all groups. While each of these groups made some limited gains during the decade, these were mitigated both by accompanying losses as well as a sense of disappointment, as each had entered the post-World War I period with high hopes for a continuation of economic, social, and political gains made during the war.

Document-Based Question Commentary

Background: The degree to which the spirit of progressivism continued into the 1920s is one that has divided historians. Traditional views of the decade emphasize the pro-business elements of the Harding and Coolidge administrations, pointing to the era's waning reform spirit as seen though the anti-labor policies of the decade and the generally conservative decisions rendered by the Supreme Court, among other things. At the same time, measures such as the Sheppard–Towner Maternity Leave Act of 1921, support for a National Child Labor Amendment, and the role of prominent progressives such as Herbert Hoover as commerce secretary during most of the decade, are evidence of the degree to which the progressive spirit continued.

The Documents: Document A offers a classic statement of Coolidge's belief that the government should play as limited a role as possible in business affairs. Government, he suggests, has a tendency to inefficiency and monopoly, as its resources allow it to drive out competitors.

Document B provides a more tempered view of American individualism than Coolidge's on the part of Herbert Hoover, a central figure in the Republican administrations of the 1920s. Hoover believed that at least some degree of government intervention in society, economics, and politics was necessary to redress the balance between the haves and have-nots of society.

Document C demonstrates the strong opposition from the business community to the proposed Child Labor Amendment. The Supreme Court had twice declared federal efforts to outlaw child labor unconstitutional, and a national effort got underway for a constitutional amendment outlawing child labor in 1924 (The amendment failed to gain ratification.). Here, the *Manufacturer's Record* makes use of popular fears of domestic and foreign radicalism in an effort to discredit supporters of this reform.

In Document D, federal Prohibition Commissioner Roy Haynes provides an optimistic view of the progress of federal efforts under the Volstead Act, arguing that despite the fact that many Americans violated Prohibition, efforts to rid the nation of alcohol were making progress. Prohibition is widely seen as representing the failure of a progressive program due to widespread flouting of the law and the rise of organized crime, but declining alcohol consumption during the decade can be used to support the idea that progressive reforms had some effect during the decade.

Documents E and F can be used together to discuss the government's limited response to workers' demands during the 1920s. In Document E, a group of textile workers from Passaic, New Jersey, pickets the White House in response to President Coolidge's failure to listen to their complaints about a wage cut at their factory. Document F reflects the generally conservative tenor of the Supreme Court during the 1920s, as Justice Sutherland provides the majority opinion in *Adkins* v. *Children's Hospital,* a decision that struck down a Washington, D.C., minimum wage law.

Document G, an excerpt from an article in *The Red Book Magazine* by Eleanor Roosevelt, discusses the adjustments that women have had to make in their efforts to become more involved in the political arena. While the 1920s represented a disappointment to many women who had viewed the ratification of the Nineteenth Amendment as representing the dawn of a new era, Roosevelt points out that the newfound ability of women to exercise a political voice will take time.

Documents H and I represent two sides of consumer activism in the 1920s. The exposé of the candy industry in New York demonstrates the continued efforts of the National Consumer's League, founded in 1899 and an example of the progressive focus on investigation and publicity as keys to promoting reform. Document I, a chapter by the sociologist Robert Lynd in the publication *Recent Social Trends*, represents a continuing emphasis on the use of social science research to inform public policy. Lynd points to the continuing activity of the Federal Trade Commission (FTC), founded in 1914 at the height of the progressive era, in providing information to consumers. At the same time, the Supreme Court limited the FTC's power to protect consumers, noting that its mandate was limited to regulating unfair competition between businesses.

Summation: The documents indicate that the 1920s can by no means be viewed as a decade in which laissez-faire ideas dominated American thinking. While the Harding and Coolidge administrations clearly sought to retreat from the governmental activism of the Roosevelt and Wilson administrations, the prominent role of progressives such as Hoover indicate that a complete return to the limited vision of the nineteenth century was impossible. While few substantive reforms occurred during the 1920s, efforts by consumer activists, advocates of protective legislation, and workers themselves indicate that voices for reform still existed. In many ways, the debate over the reforms reflects the dominant theme of the decade: a period of conflict with no clear winner emerging.

CHAPTER 23
The Great Depression

AP THEMES

- **Economic Transformation:** Following the prosperity of the period from 1922–1929, the economic downturn that ensued from the stock market crash of 1929 shocked many Americans. The prolonged depression that followed exposed a series of structural weaknesses in the American economy, including the precarious banking structure, the unequal distribution of wealth, the weakness of the farm sector, and declining industries. The depth of the Great Depression would eventually force the federal government to take on new regulatory functions and greater responsibility for maintaining the economy.

- **Politics and Citizenship:** While President Hoover is often criticized for his response to the Depression, his efforts to combat the deep economic downturn represented the most ambitious peacetime expansion of the powers of the federal government. Hoover created a program of public works—federal aid and loans to states, localities, and businesses—and other efforts to stimulate the economy. Hoover, however, refused to extend federal power and influence beyond certain strictly defined limits, fearing that too great an extension of federal power would destroy individual initiative and lead to the regimentation and bureaucratization of American life as well as the creation of a welfare state. He ended his term in office largely discredited by the American people, although later historians would come to admire his restraint and moderation.

- **Culture:** The Great Depression had a profound effect on many aspects of American culture. Surprisingly, it initially did relatively little to erode the "success ethic" of the 1920s, which held that Americans could prosper on the basis of their own efforts provided they simply worked hard enough. The deep-rooted American belief in individual responsibility made many Americans ashamed to accept relief. Artists and intellectuals responded to the Depression by offering critiques of American society that found a more willing audience than they likely would have during times of greater prosperity. Critics of American capitalism enjoyed unprecedented popularity, although never enough to seriously challenge the nation's fundamental commitment to capitalism and democracy.

- **Globalization:** The Great Depression also had an important impact on America's relationship with the rest of the world. Hoover believed that the Depression was less the result of structural weaknesses in the American economy than the result of international factors. By protecting American markets through high tariffs and restoring public confidence in the economy, Hoover believed that he could best promote economic recovery. By cutting America off from global trade, however, Hoover's policies contributed to the growth of tariff barriers and economic nationalism that would have powerful political ramifications during the 1930s.

CHAPTER SUMMARY
The Coming of the Great Depression

The economic decline that started in 1929 came as a shock to most Americans, following as it did on the heels of a sustained period of economic growth and deep confidence in the strength of the American economy. Stock prices began a steady climb in February of 1928, which continued until the fall of 1929. Despite efforts by Wall Street bankers to prop up the stock market through stock purchases, the market crashed on October 29, known as **"Black Tuesday,"** and remained low for the next four years, not fully recovering for more than ten years.

Although historians and economists disagree about the causes of Great Depression, they do agree that several different factors, both domestic and foreign, contributed to the depth of the downturn. The lack of diversification in the American economy, with much of the decade's prosperity based on the automobile and construction industries, meant that any slackening of demand in these sectors could lead to a much deeper decline in the overall American economy. Maldistribution of purchasing power further contributed to the weakness of the American economy, as there was insufficient consumer demand to sustain economic growth indefinitely, especially once industrywide layoffs began. A third major factor was the credit structure of the economy, as the farm sector in particular was burdened by heavy debts. Furthermore, many bank failures deepened the worsening economic crises.

In addition to the underlying weaknesses of the domestic economy, several international factors further contributed to the depth of the Depression. A fourth overall factor was that the American international trade position weakened as European demands for American goods declined, because of both the recovery of the European economy and financial problems in Weimar Germany and elsewhere. The international debt structure following World War I was a fifth contributing factor, as many European nations were unable to pay their war debts and were also unable to sell their goods in the United States due to high American tariffs.

Following the stock market crash, a series of events exposed the deeper underlying weaknesses of the American economy. First, the banking system collapsed, as more than 9,000 banks ceased operation between 1930 and 1933 and depositors lost more than $2 billion. The resulting decline in the money supply led to severe deflation and caused many employers to cut production and lay off workers. The nation's gross national product (GNP) declined by one-third between 1929 and 1932, and unemployment reached as high as 25 percent by 1932.Many other workers were subject to reduced hours and wages.

The American People in Hard Times

The Depression caused a great human toll, which was particularly acute given the deep sense of individual responsibility that most Americans felt for their own fate and the shame that the unemployed often experienced as a result of their joblessness. Even as many Americans reluctantly turned to state and local public relief systems, they found that these were not able to handle increased demand for relief. Declining tax revenues and public officials fearful of creating dependence on the government limited the funds available for relief efforts. Both city and countryside experienced great deprivation. In urban areas, Americans lined up at Salvation Army and Red Cross soup kitchens. In the countryside, farmers were forced to confront one of the nation's worst droughts, which began in 1930 and turned much of the Great Plains into a **"Dust Bowl."** Amazingly, despite these conditions, American farmers still produced far more than the American people could consume, driving agricultural prices even lower.

African Americans were especially hard hit by the Depression. In the South, blacks hurt by the collapse of the farm sector went to urban areas in search of work, only to find resentment and discrimination from whites who believed that they should be given work before African Americans. Many responded by moving to the North, where there was less outright hostility but not necessarily more economic opportunity. The most publicized example of racial discrimination was the **Scottsboro case**, in which nine young black men were accused of raping two white women on an Alabama train and were convicted by a local jury despite extensive evidence that indicated that the women were not raped. The Supreme Court overturned the conviction, and the retrials gained national attention as the NAACP and other organizations sought to aid the young men—all of whom eventually regained their freedom.

Other minority groups also struggled mightily during the Depression. There were approximately 2 million Mexicans and Mexican Americans living in the United States during the 1930s, both in agricultural regions of the Southwest and in larger urban areas where they worked in low-skill positions at the bottom of the industrial ladder. Unlike African Americans, Mexican immigrants had not had the opportunity to develop their own educational, religious, and other institutions as a way to help them to deal with either discrimination or the economic depression. Asian Americans also struggled as they sought to balance both work and life within their own communities while seeking to enter into mainstream society, where they faced hostility and discrimination.

For women, the Depression served to reinforce the traditional ideal that women should not work outside the home. Despite this sentiment, many married women did enter the workplace out of economic necessity, many in service-sector jobs that men would not seek but were less subject to economic fluctuations than industrial jobs. African American women in the South were hard-hit by the decline of domestic service jobs, although a much larger percentage of black women worked than did white women. The Depression had a significant impact on the American family. While many households expanded as more distant relatives came to live under one roof, others broke up, either through divorce or—more commonly—informal breakups in which unemployed men would simply abandon their families.

The Depression and American Culture

Although the Depression seemed to pose serious challenges to the materialism and consumerism of the 1920s, many Americans redoubled their commitment to the traditions of individual initiative and responsibility. Many of the unemployed refused to leave their homes out of a sense of shame at what they perceived as their own failures, while books such as Dale Carnegie's *How to Win Friends and Influence People* (1936) found a wide audience for their message of how to "get ahead" in American society.

At the same time, many artists and intellectuals sought to produce works meant to arouse the American social conscience. Photographers employed by the Farm Security Administration helped to expose widespread rural poverty in the South, while writers such as Erskine Caldwell, Richard Wright, John Dos Passos, and John Steinbeck all portrayed various elements of the downside of American life and culture. The two most popular cultural mediums of the 1930s, however, were radio and motion pictures, both of which served to distract Americans from the Depression. The vast majority of American families owned radios during the 1930s, and they listened primarily to comedies, adventure stories, and other entertainment programs that helped them to escape the problems of their day-to-day lives. Although movie attendance fell in the early years of the Depression, by the mid-1930s Americans flocked to the theaters. Some movies, such as the comedies of Frank Capra, and a series of popular gangster films, all held some either implicit or explicit social and political messages. The majority of Hollywood films, however, provided for increasingly lavish forms of escape for an American people struggling with great difficulties and did little to challenge conventional patterns in matters such as race, class, and gender.

Print media did more to challenge conventional patterns of American existence than did radio or movies. Many Americans read *Life* magazine (founded in 1936), which focused on lavish photographic spreads (many of which detailed social events), as well as novels such as Margaret Mitchell's *Gone with the Wind* (1936). **Dos Passos** in his *U.S.A. Trilogy* and **James T. Farrell** in *Studs Lonigan* (1932), among others, presented stories and ideas that challenged the conventional belief in the essential soundness of American values and institutions.

As the 1930s progressed, political writing on the left tended to take on a more positive, although still decidedly radical, approach to social problems. The development of the **Popular Front,** a coalition of left-wing groups, the most prominent of which was the American Communist Party, promoted a strong critique of American capitalism and economic inequality. During the Depression, the Communist Party had its largest membership in American history. The party took a strong stand against racial injustice and sought to represent the economically marginalized. Despite its efforts to put forth a less hostile image of American capitalism and democracy, the party nonetheless still remained subservient to Moscow and followed the Soviet Union's order to abandon the Popular Front after the Soviet Union signed the Nazi–Soviet Pact in August 1939. The **Socialist Party** also sought to organize the poor, but did not achieve success during the Depression.

Overall, the economic crisis of the 1930s fostered more criticism of American capitalism. Works by filmmakers and artists were deeply critical of the excesses of the capitalist system. Less radical, but nonetheless effective, was the book *Let Us Now Praise Famous Men* (1941) by novelist James Agee and photographer Walker Evans, which chronicled the lives of three southern sharecropper families and exposed Americans to the difficult challenges many Americans experienced.

The Unhappy Presidency of Herbert Hoover

Herbert Hoover became president in 1929 before the Depression began. The high hopes that he and other Americans had were quickly dashed by the onset of the Depression. Hoover took strong action in an effort to curb the Depression and used the power of the federal government more strongly than any other peacetime president. Hoover's refusal to abandon many of his deepest convictions about the government's role in society hampered his efforts to solve the economic challenges facing the nation. Hoover's initial response to the crisis was to seek voluntary cooperation between business and labor in an effort to restore public confidence in the economy. Although he believed strongly in the need for a balanced budget, Hoover promoted increased government spending to speed the process of economic recovery through federal public works programs. In 1929, Congress passed the **Agricultural Marketing Act**, which provided federal loans to marketing cooperatives and farm corporations. At the same time, Hoover sought higher tariffs to protect American farmers, most notably the **Hawley–Smoot Tariff** of 1930.

The continuing Depression eroded Hoover's popularity and led to Democratic successes in the 1930 election. The collapse of the Austrian central bank and other European financial institutions in 1931 made it clear that the Depression would not end quickly or easily. In early 1932, at Hoover's urging, Congress created the **Reconstruction Finance Corporation (RFC),** which gave loans to businesses and to state and local governments to fund public works programs. While the program received more than $1.5 billion for public works, it limited its lending primarily to large institutions and failed to pump enough money into the economy to promote large-scale stimulus.

Although most Americans were initially too shocked to undertake large-scale protests at the outset of the Depression, by mid-1932 a different mood emerged. In Iowa, a group of farmers formed the **Farmers' Holiday Association**, which proposed withholding agricultural goods from the market in an effort to raise prices. More significant nationally was a protest movement by veterans of World War I, who wanted Congress to move payment of their war bonuses forward from 1945 to 1932. More than 20,000 veterans formed the **Bonus Expeditionary Force**, or "**Bonus Army**," and set up camps around Washington, D.C., while waiting for Congress to approve their bonus. Hoover became increasingly upset by the presence of the marchers, and after the local police were unable to clear them out, he ordered the U.S. Army under the command of Army Chief of Staff General **Doulgas MacArthur** to complete the process. The military dispersed the veterans by force, in a manner that did extensive damage to Hoover's already-tarnished reputation.

As the 1932 election approached, most observers agreed that Hoover, who was unenthusiastically renominated by the Republican Party, had little chance against popular New York Governor **Franklin Roosevelt**. Pledging a "new deal" for the American people, Roosevelt won more than 57 percent of the popular vote and a wide majority in the Electoral College. In the four-month period between the election and the inauguration, Hoover sought to gain assurances from Roosevelt that he would not make drastic economic changes, requests that Roosevelt rebuffed on several occasions. Roosevelt remained deliberately vague in his public statements before taking office, leaving the American people hopeful about what would await them once he assumed power.

Multiple-Choice Questions

1. Which of the following best characterizes America's position in the international economy on the eve of the Great Depression?
   a. American leaders sought to forgive European war debts as a way to help promote European economic recovery.
   b. The United States provided economic aid to help rebuild the European economies following the war.
   c. The United States refused to forgive European war debts while also maintaining high tariff levels that restricted the entry of European goods into American markets.
   d. The United States pursued a free-trade policy in order to allow European nations access to American markets as a means of promoting European economic recovery.
   e. The United States worked through international organizations to promote agreements that would help to stabilize the European economic situation.

2. President Hoover promoted all of the following to help alleviate the Great Depression *except*
   a. voluntary cooperation by business and labor leaders to restore public confidence in the economy.
   b. a program of public works programs in an effort to stimulate the economy.

c. a large-scale program of federal deficit spending in an effort at "pump-priming."

d. a program of loans to farm cooperatives in an effort to raise agricultural prices.

e. a program of economic recovery loans to businesses and local governments.

3. President Hoover responded to the Bonus Army's encampment in Washington, D.C., by
   a. agreeing to meet privately with its leaders to address the concerns.
   b. ordering the police to clear the veterans from their camps.
   c. urging Congress to pass legislation providing immediate payment to the veterans.
   d. publicly praising the veterans for their contributions during World War I.
   e. initially denouncing the men as communist sympathizers.

4. Which of the following best characterizes the efforts of the American Communist Party between 1935 and 1939?
   a. It openly stressed patriotism and cooperation with other groups on the left, while remaining closely tied to the Soviet Union.
   b. It disavowed its connection with the Soviet Union both publicly and privately.
   c. It denounced Socialists and other left-wing groups as "social fascists" and worked toward the overthrow of the United States government.
   d. It avoided involvement in pressing social issues in the United States, focusing instead on the growing crisis in Europe.
   e. It denounced Franklin Roosevelt's New Deal measures as efforts to prop up a declining capitalist system.

5. A key to Franklin Roosevelt's success in his 1932 bid for the presidency was his
   a. emphasis on Prohibition and other cultural issues.
   b. well-defined program for combating the Depression.
   c. promise, if elected, to cooperate with Hoover in the period between the general election and the inauguration.
   d. ability to unite Democrats on the basis of their economic grievances.
   e. commitment to respond actively to the declining world political situation.

6. During the Great Depression, the films of Frank Capra
   a. emphasized the glamour of urban life.
   b. provided a harsh critique of American society and culture.
   c. offered a form of escape with little social message.
   d. contained implicit or explicit social and political messages.
   e. awakened Americans to events abroad.

7. The Scottsboro case brought attention to
   a. the continued presence of nativist sentiment in the United States.
   b. the high degree of racial tensions in the South.
   c. the federal government's intolerance of dissent.
   d. the anti-union tenor of the Supreme Court.
   e. the Supreme Court's willingness to support growing federal power.

8. Which of the following factors contributed to the onset of the Great Depression in the United States?

    I. heavy competition from European goods
    II. lack of diversification in the American economy
    III. large federal budget deficits
    IV. weakness of the American banking sector
    V. maldistribution of purchasing power

    a. I, II, and II
    b. I, II, and IV
    c. II, III, and IV
    d. d. II, IV, and V
    e. I, II, III, IV, and V

9. Which of the following is not correctly matched with the literary work?
    a. John Steinbeck—*The Grapes of Wrath*
    b. Richard Wright—*Native Son*
    c. Erskine Caldwell—*Tobacco Road*
    d. Dale Carnegie—*Studs Lonigan*
    e. John Dos Passos—*U.S.A.*

10. Which of the following is true of American families during the Depression?
    a. Divorce rates increased, but overall family size decreased.
    b. Both marriage and birth rates fell.
    c. Marriage rates increased, but birth rates fell.
    d. Marriage rates fell, but birth rates increased.
    e. Both marriage and birth rates increased.

11. The stock market crash of October 1929 was immediately followed by
    a. the collapse of several European central banks, leading to a deepening of the global depression.
    b. the collapse of the American farm sector, causing a mass exodus of farmers from the Great Plains to the West Coast and urban areas.
    c. the collapse of the American banking system, which triggered a significant contraction of the money supply.
    d. the collapse of international trade, creating a series of global tariff increases.
    e. the collapse of American industry, leading to a drastic decline in the nation's gross national product.

12. The Federal Reserve Board's response to the Depression was to
    a. lower interest rates in an effort to increase the nation's money supply.
    b. urge the Hoover administration to take the nation off the gold standard.
    c. urge the Hoover administration to undertake a program of large-scale deficit spending to stimulate economic growth.
    d. raise interest rates in an effort to protect its own solvency.
    e. urge member banks to make low-interest loans to stimulate recovery.

Free-Response Questions—Exam Tips

The causes of the Great Depression and the federal government's response to the Depression are central themes for free-response questions. You should be able to account for the relationship between the stock market crash and the ensuing Depression and be able to discuss why the Depression lasted as long as it did. Consider the Hoover administration's response to the Depression, both in terms of how it represented an expansion of the federal government's role in American life as well as the factors that limited further action.

Free-Response Questions

1. The Great Depression was the direct result of World War I and would not have occurred without the conflict.
   Assess the validity of this statement.

2. Compare the federal government's response to the Great Depression with one of the following:
   Panic of 1837
   Panic of 1893
   Panic of 1907

Document-Based Question—Exam Tip

The comparison between Herbert Hoover and Franklin Roosevelt in their responses to the Depression is a natural one. Past questions have asked students to assess whether the labels "conservative" and "liberal" apply to the two men. Bases for comparison could include their attitudes on government spending, relief for the unemployment, and whether each viewed the Depression as primarily international or domestic in its causes.

Document-Based Question

Hoover versus Roosevelt: In what ways and to what extent did Herbert Hoover and Franklin D. Roosevelt differ in their characterization of the Depression and proposed responses?

Use the documents that follow and your knowledge of the period to answer the question.

Document A

Source: Herbert Hoover, Speech, June 1931.

For the first time in history the Federal government has taken an extensive and positive part in mitigating the effects of depression and expediting recovery. I have conceived that if we would preserve our democracy this leadership must take the part not of attempted dictatorship but of organizing cooperation in the constructive forces of the community and of stimulating every element of initiative and self-reliance in the economy. . . .

We have reversed the traditional policy in depression of reducing expenditures upon construction work. We are maintaining a steady expansion of ultimately need construction work in cooperation with the states, municipalities, and industries. Over two billions of dollars are being expended, and today a million men are being given direct and indirect employment through these enlarged activities. We have sustained the people in twenty-one states who faced dire disaster from the drought. We are giving aid and support to the farmers in marketing their crops, by which they have realized hundreds of millions more in prices than the farmers of any other country. Through the tariff we are saving our farmers and workmen from being overwhelmed with goods from foreign countries where, even since our tariff was revised, wages and prices have been reduced to much lower levels than before.

Document B

Source: Franklin D. Roosevelt, Commonwealth Club Address, September 1932 [*Annals of America*, 15, p. 163].

A glance at the situation today only too clearly indicates that equality of opportunity as we have known it no longer exists. Our industrial plant is built; the problem just now is whether under existing conditions it is not overbuilt. . . . Our system of constantly rising tariffs has at last reacted against us to the point of closing our Canadian frontier on the North, our European markets on the East, many of our Latin American markets to the South, and a goodly proportion of our Pacific markets on the West, through the retaliatory tariffs of those countries. It has forced many of our great industrial institutions which exported their surplus production to such countries, to establish plants in such countries, within the tariff walls. This has resulted in the reduction of the operation of their American plants and opportunity for employment.

Document C

Source: Franklin D. Roosevelt, Speech, October 1932 [*Annals of America*, 15, p. 185].

The first principle I would lay down is that the primary duty rests on the community, through local government and private agencies, to take care of the relief of unemployment. But we then come to a situation where there are so many people out of work that local funds are insufficient.

It seems clear to me that the organized society known as the state comes into the picture at this point. In other words, the obligation of government is extended to the next higher unit. . .

I am very certain that the obligation extends beyond the states and to the federal government itself, if and when it becomes apparent that states and communities are unable to take care of the necessary relief work.

Document D

Source: Herbert Hoover, Speech, October 1932.

Our economic system has received abnormal shocks during the past three years, which temporarily dislocated its normal functioning. These shocks have in a large sense come from without our borders, but I say to you that our system of government has enabled us to take such strong action as to prevent the disaster which would otherwise have come to our nation. It has enabled us further to develop measures and programs which are now demonstrating their ability to bring about restoration and progress. . . .

It is by the maintenance of equality of opportunity and therefore of a society absolutely fluid in freedom of movement of its human particles that our individualism departs from the individualism of Europe. We resent class distinction because there can be no rise for the individual through the frozen strata of classes, and no stratification of classes can take place in a mass livened by the free rise of its particles. Thus in our ideals the able and ambitious are able to rise constantly from the bottom to leadership in the community.

Multiple-Choice Answers

1. c. The Harding and Coolidge administrations refused to forgive European war debts, while the 1924 Fordney–McCumber Tariff maintained high levels. The Smoot–Hawley Tariff of 1931 later raised rates to even higher levels. Hoover later declared a one-year moratorium on war debts as the Depression became increasingly severe. Following World War II, the United States would provide large-scale aid and open its markets in an effort to promote European economic recovery and avoid a repeat of the Great Depression.

2. c. While Hoover took an increasingly active series of steps in an effort to stem the Depression, he was unwilling to run large budget deficits to stimulate the economy, even proposing a tax increase in the middle of his administration in an effort to increase government revenues. The concept of large-scale deficit spending as a "pump-priming" measure was introduced to Americans by British economist John Maynard Keynes during the 1930s.

3. b. Hoover badly damaged his already declining public image by ordering the police to clear the veterans from their camp on the outskirts of Washington, D.C. When marchers threw rocks at the police, Hoover ordered the United States Army to clear the protesters from their camps. More than 100 of the marchers were injured as military forces under General MacArthur forcibly removed the men from camps and burned their tent city.

4. a. Between 1935 and 1939, the American Communist Party cooperated with other groups on the left and praised Franklin Roosevelt as part of Soviet leader Joseph Stalin's Popular Front strategy, an effort to gain allies in the likely event of conflict between the Soviet Union and Germany. Following the Nazi–Soviet Pact in August 1939, party leaders followed Stalin's order to denounce other groups on the left. The Communist Party did take a strong stand for racial justice and helped to organize the unemployed.

5. d. The Democrats had been extremely divided between the party's urban and rural wings throughout the 1920s, but Roosevelt was able to unite the party by his focus on economic issues. Roosevelt offered few specifics beyond promising a "new deal" in his speech accepting the Democratic nomination and later refused Hoover's request that he commit to a continuation of current policy during the transition period. Roosevelt did not focus primarily on international events until his second term.

6. d. Capra's films, especially *It's a Wonderful Life* and *Mr. Smith Goes to Washington*, emphasized the essential goodness of ordinary Americans in contrast to the greed and materialism of the wealthy. While Capra was critical of some elements of American society, he also believed that there was much good in the ordinary American. During World War II, he worked with the government to produce a series of films helping to mobilize support for the American war effort.

7. b. The convictions of nine young black men by Alabama courts on highly dubious rape charges, later overturned by the Supreme Court, became a highly publicized issue involving the NAACP, the American Communist Party, and other groups, while drawing attention to the continued racial tensions in the United States. The Sacco–Vanzetti execution in 1927 dealt with nativism, and several Supreme Court cases during and after World War I highlighted the federal government's intolerance of dissent. Cases restricting the rights of organized labor had emerged in the 1920s, while the proper role of the federal government became a central issue during the New Deal.

8. d. An unbalanced economy especially weak in the farm sectors and in "sick" industries such as mining and textiles, an uneven distribution of wealth, and the presence of many potentially failing banks were all serious weaknesses that were exposed following the stock market crash in October 1929. American protectionism and the relative weakness of Europe's postwar economies meant that the United States faced little foreign

competition, while the stringent budgetary policies of the Republican administrations of the 1920s meant that budget deficits were not a significant issue facing the country.

9. d. Dale Carnegie's *How to Win Friends and Influence People* was a popular self-help manual that gained a popular audience from Americans looking to find a way out of their economic plight James T. Farrell had written *Studs Lonigan,* which portrayed the difficult life of a youth during the Depression. The remaining authors and works all represent critiques of various elements of American culture and society during the Great Depression.

10. b. For the first time since the early nineteenth century, both marriage and birth rates decreased, as couples deferred marriage and having children in the face of economic uncertainty. Divorce rates actually fell, although likely due to the fact that many people could not afford a legal separation (many men simply drifted away from their families due to their inability to provide support).

11. c. The stock market crash almost immediately exposed the underlying weakness of the American banking system, as many struggling banks (many had already seen a large number of defaults even before the crash) were forced to declare bankruptcy. This in turn caused a significant deflation, which caused businesses to cut back on production and lay off workers. The decline in international trade and the collapse of several European central banks, particularly those of Austria and Germany, followed between 1930 and 1932.

12. d. The Federal Reserve, in a decision that later economists and historians blame for contributing to the depth of the Depression, decided to raise interest rates in 1931 in an effort to protect its solvency. The Roosevelt administration later took the nation off the gold standard and used deficit spending as efforts to promote economic recovery during the New Deal.

Free-Response Questions Commentary

1. This question can be used as the basis for a discussion over the degree to which the Depression was ultimately caused more by foreign or domestic factors and whether it resulted from structural weaknesses in the American economy or from disruptions caused by World War I. Both contemporary political leaders and later historians have differed on this issue and the only real consensus is that a variety of factors led to the Depression and account for its severity.

   Factors that would support the argument that the Depression resulted from World War I could include the issues of war debts, German reparations, and slow European economic recovery following the war. Germany, hampered by the demands of paying reparations to France and Britain, could not afford to buy foreign goods, helping to depress demand for American products. European nations relied on loans from American banks to help them to pay off their war debts, a precarious system that destabilized once American banks reduced their lending following the downturn that started in 1929. Another factor related to World War I was the ability of leaders such as Adolf Hitler and Japanese militarists to gain power in their countries by exploiting nationalist resentments and tying economic problems to the policies of England, France, and the United States.

   Structural problems in the American economy and questionable federal government policies suggest that the Depression may have occurred even without World War I. The stock market speculation and irresponsible lending policies of many American banks that emerged in the mid- to late-1920s and led to the great crash of 1929 suggest domestic responsibility for the Great Depression. The Harding and Coolidge administrations' tax-cut policies during the 1920s reduced government revenues, while federal policy did little to aid the ailing farm sector or other ailing sectors of the American economy. During the Depression, the Federal Reserve raised interest rates and the Hoover administration raised taxes, both of which arguably made the downturn last longer than it would have had different policies been pursued.

Historians note a combination of domestic and international factors behind the Great Depression and can ultimately only agree that it was caused by a number of different issues. World War I clearly disrupted the international economy and left lingering resentments that had both economic and political results. On the other hand, American exuberance and questionable federal government policies in the 1920s and 1930s most likely prolonged the Depression and helped to account for its severity and length.

2. Comparison with earlier downturns demonstrates the degree to which the Hoover administration sought to marshal the power of the federal government to restore prosperity. In both 1837 and 1893, the Van Buren and Cleveland administrations pursued conservative, orthodox economic policies based on contracting the currency, similar to those pursued by the Federal Reserve System in 1931. In 1907, Roosevelt sought to work with business leaders to restore confidence. Hoover pursued elements of both approaches but also worked to stimulate the economy through increased public works spending and work relief, laying the groundwork for Franklin Roosevelt and the New Deal.

The Panic of 1837 offers an instructive parallel, as similar factors helped to cause the downturn. Following an economic boom in the mid-1830s, the federal government sought to return its surplus to the states. This was the first and only time in United States history that the government was out of debt to the states. This placed pressure on the state banks in which the government had deposited funds following the end of the Second Bank of the United States in 1836. Jackson sought to curb the speculative boom the nation faced by accepting only gold and silver for purchase of public lands. Rather than simply ending speculation, however, the result of the circular was to trigger a heavy string of bank and business failures that lasted for the next five years. The Van Buren administration generally sought to avoid federal intervention in the economy. Its policies of borrowing to pay government debts and accepting only specie for tax payments actually exacerbated the Depression. Van Buren sought to replace the Bank of the United States with an "independent treasury" plan that placed federal funds in an independent treasury in Washington and other cities in order to separate the federal government from the banking system. This finally passed in 1840.

The Panic of 1893 was the worst depression in American history prior to the Great Depression. Triggered by a combination of railroad bankruptcies and bank failures, falling agricultural prices, and European depression, the downturn lasted for eight years. President Cleveland opposed federal intervention in the economy and believed that currency stabilization was the best method for restoring prosperity. Cleveland called a special session of Congress to repeal the Sherman Silver Purchase Act, leading to a sharp split within the Democratic Party. Cleveland ignored calls for increased spending on public works and other forms of relief for the American people.

In 1907, President Roosevelt worked with business leaders to curb a serious financial panic resulting from stock market speculation, industrial overproduction, and bank failures. Roosevelt, despite his reputation as an enemy of big business, worked with business leaders to restore economic confidence. J. P Morgan marshaled the resources of several New York banks to prop up the nation's financial system, with Roosevelt's assurances that the acquisition of several failing businesses would not be subject to antitrust actions. President Taft would later order prosecution of several of these actions.

The Hoover administration went further than previous administrations in its response to the Great Depression, although its emphasis on economic orthodoxy and on voluntary cooperation with business leaders was reminiscent of earlier administrations. Hoover was clearly a transitional figure, caught between commitment to the policies of the past and his philosophical convictions and new circumstances that ultimately required a more fundamental rethinking of the federal government's proper role.

Document-Based Question Commentary

Background: Hoover and Roosevelt disagreed on a number of points. Most notable in these documents are their characterizations of the structural soundness of the economy, the international elements of the Depression and the appropriate American policy toward foreign trade, and the proper role of the federal government in relief efforts.

The Documents: In Document A, Hoover succinctly lays out his program for combating the Depression. Increased federal public works spending, aid to farmers and business, and protective tariffs are the centerpieces of Hoover's program. The president emphasizes the degree to which voluntary cooperation between business and government is ultimately the key to restoring prosperity. In Document D, three years after the stock market crash, Hoover reiterates his commitment to the fundamental soundness of the American economy and his belief that reliance on traditional American values such as equality of opportunity is the best path to recovery.

Roosevelt's Commonwealth Club speech, his most significant and detailed programmatic speech during the 1932 campaign expresses his belief that American industry had saturated the domestic market. The Hoover administration's high tariff policy forced businesses that had previously relied on the export of their surpluses to move their operations abroad, reducing employment opportunities for Americans.

Summation: While Hoover and Roosevelt were not nearly as far apart on many issues as traditional historical accounts would suggest, there were nonetheless important philosophical differences between them. Hoover saw little reason to question the fundamental soundness of the American economy, while Roosevelt believed that modern economic conditions necessitated a questioning of whether the ideals of equal opportunity and self-help stilled applied.

CHAPTER 24
The New Deal

AP THEMES

- **Reform:** The Great Depression created new opportunities for reform and allowed Franklin Roosevelt more flexibility for changing the role of the federal government than any president before him. Among other things, the New Deal created the basis for a federal welfare system, especially through the creation of a federal program of Social Security, which would help to provide for the elderly, the sick, the disabled, and those with dependent children. While limited by the standards of many other industrial countries, New Deal programs nonetheless acknowledged a new level of government responsibility for the nation's citizens. The New Deal also put into place the idea of the "broker state," in which the federal government would act as a mediator between large interest groups. New Deal policies helped to elevate labor and farm groups to the level at which they could, at least in some cases, balance the power of corporate interests.

- **Economic Transformations**: Although the New Deal failed to restore prosperity and end the Great Depression, it did create a number of important regulatory mechanisms that allowed the federal government to prevent the conditions that had led to the economic disaster of the late 1920s through the regulation of the stock market and the banking sectors. The New Deal provided a basis for post-World War II experiments in federal fiscal policy, as Roosevelt began to experiment on a limited basis with macroeconomic tools such as deficit spending to stimulate economic growth. The New Deal also promoted economic growth in the South and West, helping to improve lives in those regions and bring them to a standard of living closer to that enjoyed by people living in other parts of the country.

- **Politics and Citizenship:** The New Deal helped create a Democratic coalition that would shape national politics until the late 1960s. While the party had been badly divided between its urban and rural wings during the 1920s, FDR was able to shift the Democrats from a focus on divisive cultural issues to an emphasis on economic issues and thus unite a number of different constituencies. By the end of his first term in 1936, Roosevelt had brought together African Americans, organized labor, women, urban residents, southerners, and traditional liberals and progressives, creating a powerful coalition that made the Democratic Party the nation's majority political party for several decades.

- **American Identity:** The New Deal fundamentally transformed how Americans thought about themselves and their relationship to the state. Traditional American ideology had stressed the nation's abundance and the equality of opportunity that was open to all who were willing to work hard in pursuit of prosperity. The Great Depression caused Americans to question their unbounded optimism and faith in individual initiative as the key to material progress and well-being. While the New Deal was criticized by conservatives for bringing the government into people's lives to too great a degree and by those on the left for not going far enough, the acceptance of FDR's programs by the vast majority of Americans represented their acceptance of a new belief in the possibilities of government and its ability to positively affect their lives.

CHAPTER SUMMARY
Launching the New Deal

Roosevelt's first task upon taking office was to stem public panic over the failure of the banking system. Much of FDR's early success in restoring confidence in the American economy came from his optimistic personality, his **"fireside chats,"** and frequent informal press conferences. Almost immediately after taking office, FDR declared a **"bank holiday"** that closed all American banks for four days until Congress could meet to consider banking legislation. Congress quickly passed the **Emergency Banking Act,** which allowed the Treasury Department to inspect all banks before they were allowed to reopen. The following day, Congress passed the **Economy Act,** which proposed measures to balance the federal budget through salary cuts to federal employees and reductions in veterans' benefits. Finally, FDR signed a bill legalizing the manufacture and sale of beer with a 3.2 percent alcohol content.

Once he had temporarily restored a semblance of calm to the nation, FDR turned to more long-range programs. The **Agricultural Adjustment Act (AAA),** passed by Congress in May 1933, was the first comprehensive New Deal measure. It sought to reduce crop production in an effort to raise prices, with the government providing subsidies to farmers for leaving some of their land idle. While this helped to raise farm incomes, it tended to favor larger farmers and did little to protect those who worked the land such as sharecroppers and tenant farmers. The Supreme Court in 1936 struck down the AAA, arguing that the government had no right to force farmers to limit production. Congress quickly passed legislation that paid farmers to reduce production on the grounds of soil conservation, with no objection from the Supreme Court. The administration also undertook efforts to help poorer farmers, mainly through the **Resettlement Administration** and the **Farm Security Administration.** The **Rural Electrification Administration** (1935) made electric power available to thousands of farmers for the first time.

To help stimulate industrial production, Congress passed the **National Industrial Recovery Act** in June 1933, under which the government would suspend some antitrust provisions in exchange for business recognition of the right of workers to collective bargaining through unions. While the **National Recovery Administration (NRA)** initially appeared to be a great success under the forceful leadership of **Hugh Johnson,** it was soon plagued by lack of enforcement mechanisms and domination by large-business owners. In 1935, the Supreme Court struck down the NRA, arguing that its regulation of a Brooklyn poultry business run by the **Schechter Brothers** overran Congress' constitutional authority to regulate only interstate commerce.

Many New Dealers favored some type of economic planning but disagreed about whether private interests or the government should be the chief agent in this process. The **Tennessee Valley Authority (TVA),** which authorized the federal completion of a major dam project at Muscle Shoals, Alabama, and other locations along the Tennessee River, reflected the latter approach and proved to be one of the New Deal's most notable successes. The program helped to eliminate flooding, provided electricity to thousands for the first time, and caused a decrease in private power rates throughout the nation.

To help restore prices, FDR removed the United States from the **gold standard,** a measure that would have far-reaching consequences on the relationship between the public and private sectors. The abandonment of the gold standard meant that the government could manipulate the value of the dollar through its policies. Roosevelt also urged Congress to pass the **Glass-Steagall Act** (1933), which established the **Federal Deposit Insurance Corporation (FDIC),** which guaranteed all bank deposits up to $2,500. In 1934, Congress created the **Securities and Exchange Commission** to regulate the stock market.

Although relief of the unemployed was not the New Deal's most important goal, as FDR and many of his advisors feared that it would create dependency on the federal government, several major New Deal measures dealt with this area. **The Federal Emergency Relief Act (FERA)** gave money to states to support failing relief efforts. The **Civil Works Administration (CWA),** passed in 1933, employed 4 million people to work on temporary projects, while the **Civilian Conservation Corps (CCC)** put millions of young men to work on environmentally beneficial projects. The administration also took steps to provide mortgage relief to farmers and homeowners.

The New Deal in Transition

Roosevelt enjoyed nearly unprecedented popularity during his first several years in office, but the continuing severity of the Depression caused him to come under increasing criticism in 1934 and 1935. Many of the early criticisms of the New Deal came from the right, as business leaders formed the **American Liberty League** in 1934, objecting to the New Deal's restrictions on individual enterprise. Most threatening to the administration, however, was criticism from three men who defied easy classification: **Dr. Francis E. Townsend, Father Charles E. Coughlin,** and **Huey Long.** Townsend proposed a system of government pensions for retirees over age sixty, which helped to build later support for Social Security. Popular radio priest Coughlin, later known for his support of fascism and anti-Semitism, proposed a series of monetary reforms including nationalization of banks. Former Louisiana Governor Long proposed using the tax system to take money from the wealthy and redistribute it to the poor, a program he dubbed **"Share Our Wealth."**

Long's challenge in particular helped to cause FDR and his advisors to realize the need to do something to counter the strength of these critics. They feared that Long's popularity among voters on the left could rob support from the Democrats and allow the Republicans to capture a close election. Responding to political pressures and the continuing economic crisis, FDR in 1935 shifted the emphasis in his **"Second New Deal,"** which represented a more open effort to attack corporate interests. The **Holding Company Act of 1935** sought to break the power of major utilities; several tax reform proposal sought to "soak the rich"; while the **National Labor Relations Act of 1935,** also known as the **Wagner Act,** allowed unions the right to organize and bargain collectively.

Organized labor had struggled during the 1920s and was relatively weak at the onset of the Depression. During the 1930s, more militant labor organizations responded to the challenge of the Depression in their efforts to increase the power of workers. While the American Federation of Labor (AFL) remained committed to the **craft unionism,** new constituencies emerged seeking to promote **industrial unions,** under which all workers in given industries would be organized in one large union. In 1936, the **Congress of Industrial Organizations** was formed as an offshoot of the AFL and sought to organize the automobile and steel industries. The two unions later merged in 1955 to form the AFL–CIO. Workers in the automobile industry were able to win recognition of their union from **General Motors** in February 1937 through the **sit-down strike**. In the steel industry, **U.S. Steel** recognized the efforts of steelworkers to organize, although its competitors, collectively known as **"Little**

Steel," held out, with the police opening fire on pro-union marchers on Memorial Day 1937. By 1941, Little Steel had given in and more than 10 million workers, as opposed to 3 million in 1932, belonged to unions.

In 1935, FDR provided public support to the **Social Security Act,** which would provide social insurance to the elderly and unemployed. The base of the system was a program of matching employee–employer payroll contributions, which would fund the retirement of workers. In addition, the program also provided a system of unemployment insurance as well as need-based assistance to the elderly, those with disabilities, and dependent children and their mothers. Although the program was based on the idea of "insurance" as opposed to "welfare," it soon took on proportions far greater than those envisioned by the Roosevelt administration.

Despite efforts such as Social Security, the administration still needed to meet the needs of the millions of unemployed, and in 1935 FDR created the **Works Progress Administration** (WPA), which under the creative direction of **Harry Hopkins** employed an average of 2.1 million workers and helped to stimulate the economy. As federal relief and welfare programs grew, New Deal programs tended to treat men and women differently. Men tended to benefit from work relief programs, while women in need tended to receive cash assistance, particularly through programs such as the Aid to Dependent Children section of Social Security.

Roosevelt won a resounding victory over Kansas Governor **Alf Landon** in 1936, winning almost 61 percent of the popular vote and capturing all but two states, demonstrating the new political realignment caused by the New Deal. FDR and the Democrats gained the support of farmers in the South and West, the urban working class and organized labor, African Americans in northern cities, the poor and unemployed, and traditional liberals and progressives. This coalition helped the Democrats to play a dominant role in national politics until the end of the 1960s.

The New Deal in Disarray

Although Roosevelt stood at the height of his popularity following the 1936 election, he soon faced a series of setbacks, some the result of his own mistakes and others the result of factors beyond his control. Following his victory in 1936, FDR sought to reform the Supreme Court, which had invalidated the NRA and the AAA. He proposed a plan to add six new justices to the court, ostensibly to aid the court in its work but mainly to add new liberal judges. Opponents dubbed this as **"court packing."** Soon after the proposal's introduction, however, the court assumed a more moderate position than it had in the past, upholding a number of New Deal measures. The court reform bill was defeated in Congress.

Economic recovery by the spring of 1937 convinced FDR to attempt to balance the budget by cutting appropriations for the WPA and other relief efforts, which contributed to an economic downturn dubbed **"the Roosevelt Recession."** FDR responded by asking Congress for an emergency relief appropriation of $5 billion and by coming before Congress in the spring of 1938 to denounce concentrations of economic power. That year, the administration gained passage of the **Fair Labor Standards Act,** which established a nationwide minimum wage and mandated a forty-hour workweek. The New Deal, however, faced increasing conservative opposition. Circumstances forced FDR to turn his attention to events abroad.

Limits and Legacies of the New Deal

While many New Dealers sought to reorder American capitalism to create a harmonious, ordered economic world, it was soon clear that this was impossible. Instead, the federal government became a mediator, or **broker,** between competing interest groups such as organized labor, farmers, and consumers, which had grown in power to the point where they could challenge the unlimited influence of the corporate world. One of the enduring legacies of the New Deal was to make the federal government a protector of interest groups that were in competition for government assistance.

Overall, the New Deal did relatively little to help African Americans, as FDR refused to challenge southern conservatives by supporting legislation to make lynching a federal crime or oppose the poll tax. New Deal relief programs were often segregated by race, discriminating against African Americans. However, by 1935 perhaps one quarter of all African Americans received some form of government aid. After African American opera singer Marian Anderson had been refused access to the Daughters of the American Revolution Hall, Eleanor Roosevelt facilitated an Easter Sunday concert for her on the steps of the Lincoln Memorial. Seventy-five thousand people attended the concert, which in effect became one of the first modern-day civil rights demonstrations. FDR appointed a number of African Americans to midlevel administration posts, forming the **"black cabinet."** By 1936, 90 percent of African Americans were voting Democratic, a historic shift away from the Republican Party.

Under the influence of **John Collier,** the commissioner for Indian Affairs, the New Deal undertook a shift away from the assimilation policy that had held sway since the 1887 Dawes Act. Influenced by the ideas of **cultural relativism,** which held that no culture was inherently superior to another, Collier sought to restore collective tribal land ownership and help promote traditional Native American culture, resulting in the **Indian Reorganization Act** of 1934. This fostered significant gains in tribal landholding and Native American income, although Indians remained the poorest segment of the American population.

The New Deal did not oppose feminist goals but did little to actively support them either, largely due to a lack of political support even among women. FDR appointed **Frances Perkins** as secretary of labor, the first female cabinet secretary, and appointed more than 100 other women to various federal government positions. Women continued to be divided, however, on the most appropriate goals of federal action: Perkins and other progressives tended to argue for the continuation of special protective legislation such as limits on women's work hours and the Aid to Dependent Children section of the Social Security Act. This went against the view of many feminists that women should seek gender equality with men in the form of an Equal Rights Amendment and other mechanisms. Perkins and others also tended to accept the traditional notion that women should leave the workplace in favor of men during difficult economic times.

The West and the South benefited disproportionately from New Deal programs. Western farmers tended to receive large amounts of New Deal aid. The need for new water and power sources led to massive public works projects such as the **Grand Coulee Dam** on the Columbia River. New Deal administrators came to recognize that the South did not have a sufficient economic infrastructure relative to the rest of the nation, and the region benefited greatly from programs such as rural electrification.

Many critics note that the New Deal failed to end the Depression, significantly alter the distribution of power within American capitalism, or alter the distribution of wealth. New Dealers never completely embraced the idea of using federal spending as an economic stimulus measure. On the other hand, the New Deal did help to elevate important groups such as farmers and labor to a position that could sometimes challenge corporate power, stabilized important sectors of the economy such as banking and the stock market, and developed tools of federal fiscal policy. It also created the outlines of a federal welfare state, abandoning to some degree, at least, the federal government's reluctance to offer aid to the needy.

The New Deal's greatest legacy was perhaps how it changed American government and politics. The power of the federal government was clearly supreme over state and local government. FDR placed the presidency at the center of the political process, and the Democratic Party formed a powerful majority coalition. The New Deal also created the expectation that it was the federal government's responsibility to regulate, maintain, and control the economy of the nation.

Multiple-Choice Questions

1. During the First New Deal, the Supreme Court
   a. upheld Roosevelt's programs expanding federal power.
   b. played little role in addressing controversial issues.
   c. struck down several key New Deal measures.
   d. sought to promote minority rights.
   e. issued decisions restricting civil liberties.

2. The biggest threat to Franklin Roosevelt and the New Deal during FDR's first administration came from
   a. conservative groups such as the Liberty League.
   b. left-wing groups such as the Communist and Socialist parties.
   c. groups on the far-right including the American Fascist Party.
   d. populist critics such as Charles Coughlin and Huey Long.
   e. protests by the poor and unemployed.

3. All of the following groups were part of the New Deal Coalition *except*
   a. urban workers.
   b. southern farmers.
   c. African Americans.
   d. business leaders.
   e. traditional progressives.

4. Which of the following characterizes the New Deal by 1938?
   a. Facing conservative opposition, Roosevelt halted further reform efforts.
   b. Concerned about criticism from the left, Roosevelt sought deeper changes in the American economy in order to bring about a redistribution of wealth.
   c. Having achieved some economic recovery and growing international tensions, Roosevelt's priorities shifted away from seeking to implement more New Deal measures.

d. Seeking to weaken his conservative opposition, Roosevelt urged Congress to enact a far-reaching program of business regulation.

e. Realizing that the New Deal had not given sufficient priority to helping minority groups, FDR sought to focus legislation on addressing their needs.

5. During the 1930s, the Congress of Industrial Organizations (CIO) sought to
   a. gain practical improvements such as shorter hours and better pay.
   b. organize workers along craft lines.
   c. work closely with corporate leaders to avoid labor strife.
   d. organize previously unprotected workers into industrial unions.
   e. overthrow the capitalist system through violent means if necessary.

6. Which of the following best characterizes New Deal policies toward women and African Americans?
   a. The New Deal was not actively hostile to their aspirations, and was in many ways supportive, but failed to challenge existing cultural norms.
   b. The New Deal paid little attention to their needs, focusing its energy on helping primarily white males to return to work.
   c. The New Deal vigorously promoted policies and programs that would help members of these groups to achieve greater equality.
   d. The New Deal actively opposed efforts for greater equality, fearing that these would lead to a loss of support for other New Deal programs.
   e. The New Deal leadership of Franklin Roosevelt and his advisors wanted greater equality but could not convince Congress to pass such legislation.

7. The largest and most effective New Deal relief program was
   a. the Civil Works Administration.
   b. the Public Works Administration.
   c. the Works Progress Administration.
   d. the Civilian Conservation Corps.
   e. the National Youth Administration.

8. Which of the following statements about the New Deal's impact on the American economy are accurate?

   I. It elevated union and farm groups to the point where they could to some degree balance the power of corporate America.
   II. It brought about economic recovery from the Great Depression.
   III. It promoted lasting economic development in the West and South.
   IV. It increased the federal government's regulatory function in the banking and stock market sectors.
   V. It promoted the widespread redistribution of wealth.

   a. I, II, and III
   b. I, II, and IV
   c. I, III, and IV
   d. II, III, and IV
   e. III, IV, and V

9. Which of the following legalized collective bargaining by unions and provided an enforcement mechanism through the National Labor Relations Board?
   a. Section 7A of the National Industrial Recovery Act
   b. the Works Progress Administration
   c. the Wagner Act
   d. the Social Security Act
   e. the Fair Labor Standards Act

10. Federal Native American policy during the New Deal sought to
    a. promote the assimilation of Native Americans into white culture.
    b. eliminate collective tribal land ownership.
    c. withdraw official recognition of tribes as legal entities.
    d. promote tribal autonomy by restoring collective land ownership rights.
    e. honor previous obligations by paying reparations to tribes that had lost land due to broken treaties.

11. A key difference between the labor strife of 1919 and 1937, each of which witnessed more than 4,000 strikes, was
    a. the conciliatory attitude of business leaders toward labor demands in 1937.
    b. the lack of violence in the 1937 strikes.
    c. the more favorable public attitude toward the 1919 strikes.
    d. the fact that a vast majority of the 1937 strikes were settled in workers' favor.
    e. the increase in union membership following the 1919 strikes.

Free-Response Questions—Exam Tips

You should be prepared to assess the New Deal's success in promoting economic recovery. Other important themes include Roosevelt's expansion of presidential power and how New Deal policies affected specific groups, particularly business, farmers, organized labor, and minorities.

Free-Response Questions

1. To what degree did the First New Deal accomplish the three goals of reform, relief, and recovery?

2. Compare New Deal policy toward organized labor with one of the following periods: 1877–1894 or 1900–1912.

Document-Based Question—Exam Tips

The New Deal was criticized from both sides of the political spectrum. Critics on the left argued that the New Deal did not go far enough in helping the poor, while those on the right argued that Roosevelt's programs did too much to restrict business and prevented recovery by stifling individual initiative.

Document-Based Question

Analyze the major criticisms leveled against Franklin D. Roosevelt and the New Deal.

Use the documents that follow and your knowledge of the period to answer the question.

Document A

Source: Huey Long, Radio Speech, January 1935.

Our plan would injure no one. It would not stop us from having millionares—it would increase them tenfold, because so many more people could make $1 million if they had the chance our plan gives them. Our plan would not break up big concerns. The only difference would be that maybe 10,000 people would own a concern instead of 10 people owning it.

But, my friends, unless we do share our wealth, unless we limit the size of the big man so as to give something to the little man, we can never have a happy or free people. God said so! He ordered it.

Document B

Source: Norman Thomas, "The Future: Socialism?" 1936.

To carry out a socialist program. It is necessary that at least the key industries be taken over under a concerted plan. For example, good as publicly owned electric plants may be, it will be found unsatisfactory to try to carry on a socialized or partially socialized power industry under the capitalist economy. TVA is now doing a remarkably good job. It success is an encouragement for the future. It is worth while as a yardstick. But the yardstick theory, or any other theory of piecemeal socialization within the confines of capitalism, has its disadvantages in waste and confusion.

Document C

Source: Herbert Hoover, Speech to the Republican National Convention, June 1936.

We have seen the most elemental violations of economic law and experience. The New Deal forgets it is solely by production of more goods and services that we advance the standard of living and security of men. If we constantly decrease costs and prices and keep up earnings, the production of plenty will be more and more widely distributed. These laws may be restitched in new phrases but they are the very shoes of human progress.

Document D

Source: Charles E. Coughlin, Speech, June 1936.

My friends, what have we witnessed as the finger of time turned the pages of the calendar? Nineteen hundred and thirty three and the National Recovery Act which multiplied profits for the monopolists; 1934 and the AAA which raised the price of foodstuffs, by throwing back God's best gifts in His face; 1935 and the Banking Act which rewarded the exploiters of the poor, the Federal Reserve bankers and their associates, by handing over to them the temple from which they were to have been cast!

Multiple-Choice Answers

1. c. The Supreme Court declared both the National Industrial Recovery Act and the Agricultural Adjustment Administration unconstitutional during Roosevelt's first term, asserting that both exceeded the powers granted to Congress and the president. Following his landslide reelection in 1936, FDR launched an unsuccessful effort to "pack" the Supreme Court by adding two additional justices for each justice over a certain age (although the court did take a more liberal stance in a number of subsequent cases despite Congress' defeat of FDR's court reform).

2. d. Although Roosevelt had been able to stem some of the worst crises of the Depression during his first two years in office, criticisms of the New Deal began to emerge when it was clear that full recovery was far away. The most potent threat came from Long, who criticized the New Deal for not going far in enough in redistributing wealth and caused FDR to fear that he would draw support from the president in the 1936 election. The far left did gain followers in the 1930s but never to the degree that would make it a serious force in electoral politics, while conservatives were largely in disrepute due to their being associated with the factors that helped to cause the Depression.

3. d. By 1936, FDR had managed through his New Deal programs to bring up a major realignment in American politics. The Democratic Party had been severely divided over cultural issues in the 1920s, and FDR managed to bring together a coalition of African Americans, the urban poor, the South, women, and traditional progressives and intellectuals that would be a major force in American politics for more than thirty years. Business leaders generally opposed what they saw as the excessive regulation of the New Deal.

4. c. By 1938, FDR had achieved an impressive series of reforms, although the American economy had not yet fully recovered. Conservatives, both Republican and Democratic, made further reforms difficult, while fascist aggression in Europe drew greater attention from Roosevelt. FDR had shifted to the left late in his first term, partly in order to disarm opposition on the left. Many historians criticize the New Deal for never fully addressing the needs of racial minority groups.

5. d. The CIO differed from other major unions such as the AFL in its emphasis on industrial unionism and its desire to organize all, not just skilled, workers. More militant than the AFL, the CIO used the sit-down strike to organize the automobile industry, although it also suffered a temporary defeat in its efforts to organize the steel industry (which finally recognized unions in 1941).

6. .a. New Deal policies achieved ambivalent results in their efforts to help African Americans, women, and other minorities. While the New Deal was in many ways more sympathetic to minority aspirations than any other administration in the twentieth century, the results of its relief programs did not challenge wage differentials based on race or gender. Roosevelt frustrated African American leaders by refusing to press for a

legislation making lynching a federal crime or opposing the poll tax for fear of alienating southern Democrats whose support he needed for New Deal measures.

7. c. Established in 1935, the Works Progress Administration was led effectively and creatively by Harry Hopkins and given a much larger budget than earlier relief efforts. The other agencies were effective to certain degrees but were either more specialized in focus or more limited in funding than the WPA.

8. c. The New Deal was able to help unions and farmers balance the power of corporate interests; benefit less-developed areas of the country through electrification, public works, and other programs; and provide greater regulation of the stock market and banking industries. Not until after the outbreak of World War II, and especially following American entry into the war in 1941, did the country's economy fully recover from the Depression. A frequent criticism of the New Deal is that it benefited those groups that were already powerful enough to advocate their interests and never really sought to address the needs of the poor by redistributing wealth.

9. c. The National Labor Relations Act of 1935, or the Wagner Act, recognized labor's right to collective bargaining and provided an enforcement mechanism through the creation of the National Labor Relations Board. Section 7A of the NIRA had recognized the rights of unions to organize and bargain collectively but contained no enforcement mechanisms and was invalidated when the NIRA was declared unconstitutional by the Supreme Court in 1935.

10. d. Under the commissioner of Indian affairs, John Collier, New Deal policy used measures such as the Indian Reorganization Act of 1934 to allow Native American tribes to resume collective land ownership in an effort to restore tribal autonomy. This reversed the policy of assimilation instituted under Dawes Act of 1887. The federal government undertook the policy of withdrawing legal recognition of tribes in 1953 (known as "termination"). It sought to provide reparations in the face of Native American protests in the late 1960s and the early 1970s.

11. d. More than 80 percent of the 1937 strikes were settled in favor of workers, due largely to government policies recognizing the rights of labor to organize, despite the fact that there was extensive violence in many of the year's labor disputes. In 1919, government, business, and public hostility led to the defeat of many of that year's strikes. Union membership declined significantly during the 1920s.

Free-Response Questions Commentary

1. A key element in answering this question is the ability to show that the New Deal emphasized different goals at different points. Roosevelt initially focused on economic recovery. Although the New Deal was never particularly successful in restoring prosperity, it did manage to stabilize the economy. A discussion of economic recovery should discuss the NRA, the AAA, and banking reform measures.

   New Deal relief programs focused on work relief and sought to avoid anything that resembled "the dole." The centerpiece of New Deal work relief was the WPA, which dwarfed all other relief programs. While millions received jobs from New Deal programs, the programs tended to reinforce traditional employment patterns, overwhelmingly assisting men and not challenging wage disparities on the basis of race and gender.

   FDR's focus shifted toward reform in the so-called Second New Deal of 1935. An answer dealing with this section should focus on labor relations, business regulation and taxation, and Social Security.

2. New Deal labor policies, which extended federal protection to unions to an unprecedented degree, can be evaluated in comparison with two other key periods in the development of organized labor. The Gilded Age of the late nineteenth century witnessed great labor strife (the Rail Strike of 1877; the Homestead Strike of 1892; the Pullman Strike of 1894), with the federal government usually intervening on the side of business owners.

Progressive-era policies were more supportive of the aspirations of organized labor (Theodore Roosevelt's mediation of the anthracite coal strike; the eight-hour day in the railroad industry), although labor militancy was much less than during the New Deal. The Great Depression served to both make labor more militant and increase the scope for federal action, helping to account for the greater success of New Deal policies.

Document-Based Question Commentary

By 1934, groups on both the right and left began to grow impatient with the New Deal's inability to restore the nation to full prosperity and to effect a major redistribution of wealth and power in the United States. Louisiana Senator Huey Long advocated an ambitious "Share Our Wealth" plan that threatened to steal support from Roosevelt. Socialist Norman Thomas argued that the New Deal policies, as long as the United States remained under a capitalist system, would never succeed in bringing economic and social justice to the United States. Hoover, who had competed against Roosevelt in the 1932 election, continued his critique of the New Deal throughout the 1930s, arguing that New Deal policies were leading the nation toward European collectivism. Coughlin, a former New Deal supporter, later turned violently against FDR, criticizing him especially for his failure to reform the nation's financial institutions. An answer to this question should note that FDR shifted to the left in 1935 as part of the Second New Deal, helping him to neutralize his opposition on the left and further isolate his conservative opponents.

CHAPTER 25

The Global Crisis, 1921–1941

AP THEMES

- **War and Diplomacy:** During this period, the United States was faced with the dual challenge of dealing with the issues remaining from World War I as well as the emerging challenges as the world prepared for a second global conflict throughout the 1930s. American leaders rejected Wilson's plan for the United States to play a leading role in the League of Nations as a part of the former president's plan to create a world order based on international cooperation. At the same time, Republican presidents during the 1920s wanted to safeguard American security and ensure the success of American business interests abroad. As another major war became more and more likely, President Hoover and his successor, Franklin Roosevelt, faced growing isolationist sentiment. Many Americans keenly remembered the nation's experiences during World War I and felt that the nation had made significant sacrifices with little to show for them.

- **Globalization:** Wilson had sought to promote American involvement throughout the globe as a way to ensure the nation's security and economic prosperity. His Republican successors, however, responded to the period's challenges by seeking to limit American involvement abroad. Following the onset of the Great Depression in 1929 and viewing its growing severity, American leaders chose to put into place extremely high tariffs to protect American markets. They chose to believe that the Depression was caused by the weakness of European economies and that the United States could restore itself to prosperity by cutting itself off from Europe. Although Franklin Roosevelt would emerge as a dedicated internationalist by the late 1930s, he also chose to focus on solving the nation's economic problems and refused cooperation with European nations in seeking a program of global recovery.

CHAPTER SUMMARY

The Diplomacy of the New Era

Critics characterized American foreign policy during the 1920s as isolationist, but the United States in fact played a more active role than at almost any other time in its history. The goal of American foreign policymakers between 1921 and 1929 was to expand the nation's influence abroad while preserving the widest possible scope for American freedom of action. Republican leaders believed that the Wilsonian emphasis on the League of Nations would have forced the nation into unwanted international commitments.

After having secured legislation declaring an end to the conflict with Germany in 1921, Secretary of State **Charles Evans Hughes** hoped to find ways to prevent future wars without committing the United States to burdensome international responsibilities. One of his most important contributions was the **Washington Conference** of 1921, which led to agreements between the United States, Great Britain, and Japan on naval armaments, with separate agreements to maintain the Open Door policy in China, and mutual respect for each country's Pacific possessions.

The **Kellogg–Briand Pact** of 1928, eventually signed by more than sixty nations, was the culmination of New Era diplomacy, with all signatories pledging to outlaw war as an instrument of national policy.

One of the most significant foreign policy challenges of the 1920s was the European debt crisis, as England and France struggled to find ways to repay the $11 billion in loans they had acquired from the United States. In 1924, American banker **Charles Dawes** proposed a plan by which Germany would take on loans from American banks and use these to make reparations payments to Britain and France, which would then repay their war debts. This was an unstable system that relied on an increasing cycle of debt to American banks. High American tariffs based on the 1922 **Fordney–McCumber Act** made it difficult for European nations to recover, as it deprived them of an important market to sell their goods abroad. Overall, the 1920s saw the growing influence of American banks and corporations throughout Europe and Latin America, bolstered in the latter region by the frequent presence of American troops.

By the end of the 1920s, President Hoover faced an array of international problems that he was ill-equipped to handle. The Great Depression had both economic and political consequences that eroded the decade's earlier optimism and spirit of international cooperation. In Latin America, Hoover made an effort to ease the resentment caused by American economic domination of the region by repudiating the Roosevelt Corollary to the Monroe Doctrine and undertaking a ten-week goodwill tour prior to his inauguration. Hoover refused to cancel European war debt although he did propose a one-year moratorium, which contributed to even greater economic instability in the region. In Asia, Hoover and Secretary of State Henry Stimson issued the **Stimson Doctrine,** which withheld diplomatic recognition for the Japanese takeover of Manchuria but did nothing to stop Japanese expansion in the region.

Isolationism and Internationalism

Upon taking office in 1933, Franklin Roosevelt recognized that the United States could not remain isolated from world affairs. Although Roosevelt's actions at times seemed contradictory, his background and beliefs made him a decided internationalist. In 1920 he had had run as a vice-presidential candidate on the Democratic ticket in strong support of the League of Nations. FDR repudiated Hoover's efforts to resolve the war debt issue and maintain the gold standard, while seeking to improve the U.S. position in world trade through the **Reciprocal Trade Agreement Act of 1934,** which sought mutual tariff reductions between the United States and other nations.

In 1933, the United States put ideology aside and extended diplomatic recognition to the Soviet Union in the hopes of finding new markets, and Stalin sought a possible ally against Japanese expansion. This agreement, however, failed to live up to the expectations of either side, as American businesses failed to capitalize on the new Soviet market and the United States showed little inclination to work with the Soviet Union in containing Japanese expansion. In Latin America, Roosevelt and Secretary of State **Cordell Hull's** policy of trade reciprocity increased American trade with Western Hemisphere nations more than 100 percent during the 1930s. While the Roosevelt administration formally renounced the right of intervention in Latin American affairs, easing tensions with nations to the south, its **Good Neighbor** policy extended American economic dominance throughout the region.

Most Americans responded to the growing international instability of the 1930s by seeking to isolate the United States from conflict. The **Nye Committee** argued that American bankers and business leaders had pressured the Wilson administration to intervene during World War I, and many Americans accepted this argument. The Senate defeated a bill for American entry into the **World Court** in 1935 and passed a series of **Neutrality Acts** in 1935, 1936, and 1937. The goal of these acts was to prevent a repeat of the events that led to World War I by establishing a mandatory arms embargo in military conflicts and empowering the president to warn Americans that they could travel on belligerent ships only at their own risk. The 1937 act established the principle of "cash and carry"—the United States would sell only nonmilitary goods, but they must be paid for in cash and carried by the buyers in their own ships. The power of isolationist opinion was clear following FDR's **Quarantine Speech** of October 1937, which he gave in response to Japan's renewed aggression in China. Even vague, modest proposals about the need to contain militaristic nations by FDR met significant isolationist opposition.

Beginning in 1936, Hitler sought to expand German power and territory with little opposition from the United States and Europe. After Hitler proclaimed an *Anschluss* (or union) between Germany and Austria in 1938, he sought to annex the western part of Czechoslovakia, where many ethnic Germans lived. He met with French and British leaders at **Munich,** where he assured them that the takeover of the Sudetenland would be his last territorial conquest. Eager to avoid a repeat of their costly World War I experience, Britain and France followed a policy of **"appeasement,"** believing that agreeing to Hitler's territorial demands would satisfy German ambitions and prevent conflict. British Prime Minister **Neville Chamberlain,** encouraged by FDR, declared that the Munich Conference had achieved a lasting European peace. In early 1939, Hitler quickly violated the Munich Conference and began to threaten Poland. Britain and France sought diplomatic measures to stem Hitler's advances, but these were too late. By September 1939, Hitler attacked Poland and Europe was at war.

From Neutrality to Intervention

While isolationist opinion was strong, the majority of Americans clearly supported the Allies in their efforts against Nazi Germany. In 1939, FDR gained congressional approval to extend the principle of cash and carry to military goods. Germany won an alarming series of victories in the spring of 1940. Americans found the fall of France in June of 1940 to be particularly distressing. FDR sought to aid the Allies by providing Britain with fifty American destroyers in exchange for the chance to build bases on Britain's Western Hemisphere possessions, and in September 1940, Congress enacted the first peacetime draft. Isolationist opinion continued to play a significant role, primarily through the **America First Committee.**

While FDR initially made it unclear whether he would break from tradition and run for a third term in 1940, his willingness to accept a "draft" made it impossible for any rival Democrat to seek the nomination. FDR also skillfully maintained a middle ground in the debate on intervention in Europe, leaving the Republicans with little room to attack him. Republican candidate **Wendell Willkie** mounted an impressive campaign, but FDR still won the election by a significant margin.

By the end of 1940, Britain's financial exhaustion forced FDR to take more drastic measures to aid the Allies. He proposed a program of **"lend–lease,"** which would allow him to provide arms to any nation deemed vital to American defense, which Congress approved by a wide margin.

FDR then faced the challenge of making sure that these arms reached Great Britain, which he did by committing the United States to protect Allied shipping in the western Atlantic as far as Iceland. Starting in September 1941, Germany began a campaign against American vessels, to which FDR responded by instituting a "shoot-on-sight" policy. Further, he met with Churchill in April 1941 and issued **the Atlantic Charter,** which committed the United States to work with Great Britain to assure the destruction of Nazi power. The United States was clearly committed to the conflict, but FDR realized that only a direct attack on the United States or its forces would gain sufficient support for a declaration of war.

Continuing Japanese expansion in East Asia after 1939 necessitated that the Roosevelt administration respond with greater urgency than it had earlier in the decade. Following the Japanese takeover of Indochina in July 1941, FDR froze all Japanese assets in the United States and imposed a complete trade embargo on Japan. Japan faced the choice of either pulling back to restore American trade or moving further toward taking over British and Dutch possessions in the East Indies. Although the Japanese government initially appeared open to negotiations, the United States demanded assurances that Japanese diplomats were not empowered to make. By late November 1941, the breakdown of negotiations and American intelligence made it clear to American leaders that a Japanese attack was virtually inevitable.

The Japanese attack on Pearl Harbor has been a subject of a long debate. Some historians have argued that Roosevelt knew about the planned Japanese attack and did little to prevent it in order to create conditions that would allow him to secure a declaration of war from Congress. Although United States officials had evidence that the Japanese were planning an attack on American possessions, they were unclear about where such an attack would take place. Few believed that a Japanese attack on the American naval base at **Pearl Harbor** was actually possible. Following the death of more than 2,000 American servicemen, FDR on December 8 sought a declaration of war against Japan, which succeeded unanimously in the Senate and by a vote of 388 to 1 in the House of Representatives. Representative Jeanette Rankin of Montana was the only person to vote against American entry into both World Wars I and II.

Multiple-Choice Questions

1. Which of the following best characterizes American foreign policy from 1921 until 1928?
   a. active international involvement through international bodies such as the League of Nations
   b. political and economic isolation from other nations
   c. efforts to maintain a world balance of power through alliances
   d. efforts to prevent future conflicts while maintaining American freedom of action
   e. active efforts to help Europe recover from the ravages of World War I.

2. President Hoover and Secretary of State Henry Stimson responded to Japanese aggression in Asia with
   a. a vigorous appeal to the League of Nations to punish Japan for its actions.
   b. a threat of using American troops to remove Japan from Manchuria.
   c. a refusal to grant diplomatic recognition to Japanese territories acquired by force.

     d. an economic blockade against Japan and freezing of Japanese assets in the United States.

     e. a proposed alliance with Great Britain against Japan and other aggressors.

3. The public response to Roosevelt's Quarantine Speech in 1937 indicated that
     a. the American people were growing increasingly concerned about the world crisis.
     b. there existed a very strong fear of any steps that might commit the United States to action abroad.
     c. many people felt that Roosevelt was not moving strongly enough to stop aggressor nations.
     d. the American people were willing to follow FDR's lead in foreign affairs, just as they had in domestic affairs during the First New Deal.
     e. traditional American concern for the fate of China manifested itself in a desire to help that nation against Japanese aggression.

4. A major conclusion of the Nye Committee was that
     a. the United States had entered World War I because of legitimate threats to American national security.
     b. pressure from American bankers and businessmen had been a primary factor pushing the United States to enter World War I.
     c. British propaganda had caused the United States to enter World War I.
     d. Wilson's insistence on protecting America's neutral rights was the major factor behind United States involvement in World War I.
     e. Germany could have been defeated without American military involvement in World War I.

5. In comparison to Wilson, FDR responded to the outbreak of hostilities in Europe in 1939
     a. by calling on Americans to take an even more truly neutral stance than they had in response to World War I.
     b. by urging Congress to put the nation on a full war footing in preparation for possible American involvement in the war.
     c. by declaring American neutrality but also noting that not all Americans would be neutral in their thoughts.
     d. by following his predecessor's lead and calling on Americans to be neutral in both thought and deed.
     e. by articulating a clear vision of his goals for American involvement in the war and in the postwar world.

6. The impact of the Dawes Plan was to
     a. use American aid to promote European economic recovery following World War I.
     b. provide European nations with assurances of American assistance in cases of fascist aggression.
     c. create a precarious trans-Atlantic economic balance based on the accumulation of enormous German and European debts to United States banks.
     d. open American markets to European goods to promote their economic recovery.
     e. decrease the United States economic presence in Germany and other European nations.

7. Which of the following are true of the United States between 1939 and 1941?
      I.   The United States instituted the first peacetime draft in its history.
      II. President Roosevelt successfully defied the nation's two-term precedent.
      III. Isolationist sentiment fell into disrepute.
      IV. The United States became involved in an undeclared naval war against Germany.
      V.   Congress insisted on enforcement of the Neutrality Acts.
   a. I, II, and III
   b. I, II, IV
   c. I, II, V
   d. I, III, IV
   e. I, III, V

8. All of the following are evidence of American isolationism prior to December 1941 *except*
   a. the results of the Senate vote on World Court membership.
   b. the findings of the Nye Committee.
   c. the popularity of the America First Committee.
   d. the response to the *Panay* incident.
   e. the policy of lend–lease.

9. What was the impact of FDR's Good Neighbor policy?
   a. It reduced political tensions between the United States and Latin America, while increasing American economic dominance over the region.
   b. It continued the American commitment to upholding the Roosevelt Corollary to the Monroe Doctrine.
   c. It expanded trade and political relations with the Soviet Union in effort to help the U.S.S.R. lessen its self-imposed isolation.
   d. It committed the United States to work with other nations in a program of international currency stabilization.
   e. It permanently forgave European war debts in an effort to help promote economic recovery in those nations.

10. The agreements reached at the Washington Naval Conference represented
   a. a lasting effort to maintain international peace and stability.
   b. the culmination of Woodrow Wilson's international vision.
   c. a well-intentioned effort to maintain peace that lasted less than a decade.
   d. the assumption of a global leadership position by the United States.
   e. a continuation of traditional, pre–World War I diplomatic practices.

11. The official American policy of neutrality during the Spanish Civil War served to
   a. provide a major advantage to the fascists, who received aid from Germany and Italy.
   b. assist the sitting Republican government in its struggle against the fascists.
   c. give the United States a strong moral position in the face of growing European conflict.
   d. position the United States to help to serve as the mediator in the conflict.
   e. convince Roosevelt that further efforts to influence the European conflict were fruitless.

12. "Revisionist" accounts of the Japanese attack on Pearl Harbor argue that
   a. the Roosevelt administration failed to correctly interpret intelligence indicating a Japanese attack on Hawaii.

b. the Roosevelt administration deliberately withheld information about the planned Japanese attack in order to maneuver the United States into war against Japan.

c. the Roosevelt administration underestimated Japanese skill and daring in undertaking the attack on Hawaii.

d. the Roosevelt administration expected a Japanese attack on British or Dutch possessions in East Asia and thus failed to predict the attack on Hawaii.

e. the Roosevelt administration's weakness in its negotiations with Japan emboldened the Japanese to attack Hawaii.

Free-Response Questions—Exam Tips

The experience of World War I had a significant influence on both the American public and American policymakers during the pre-1941 period. Congress passed neutrality legislation during the 1930s in an explicit attempt to prevent a repeat of the experiences that led to involvement of the United States in World War I. This is a good place to consider the use of historical analogies to guide decision making, and students should be able to consider key similarities and differences between the conditions that led to American involvement in each war.

Free-Response Questions

1. How successful was the United States in upholding the Open Door policy in East Asia between 1900 and 1940?

2. Compare America's response to the outbreak and course of European war between 1914 and 1917 and between 1939 and 1941.

Document-Based Question—Exam Tips

A major theme from the interwar period is the issue of isolationism. Historians once used the term to describe American foreign policy from the end of World War I until the outbreak of World War II. Many historians prefer terms such as "independent internationalism" to describe American policy during the 1920s, noting the degree to which American foreign investment involved the United States with other nations.

Document-Based Question

To what degree can the term "isolationist" be used to characterize American foreign policy between 1919 and 1941?

Use the documents that follow and your knowledge of the period to answer the question.

Document A

Source: Calvin Coolidge, Speech, May 1923.

Our country is at peace, not only legal but actual, with all other peoples. We cherish peace and goodwill toward all the earth, with a sentiment of friendship and a desire for universal well-being. If we want peace it is our business to cultivate goodwill. It was for the promotion of peace that the Washington Conference on the Limitation of Armaments and Pacific Questions was called. For the first time in history the great powers of the earth have agreed to a limitation of naval armaments. This was brought about by American initiative in accordance with an American plan, and executed by American statesmanship. . . .

Document B

Source: James Randolph, "Can We Go to Mars?" *Scientific America,* August 1928.

Rockets are possible that could shoot halfway around the earth, carrying loads of hundreds of tons—and this offers interesting possibilities for the next war. They could be steered to a limited extent, the pilot staying in the rocket until the last possible moment, and then going off in a landing plane.

Decided changes in world politics would follow the introduction of such a weapon. The armored horseman brought in the feudal system. The gun restored democracy. The modern battleship suppressed piracy and abolished the rights of small nations. The airplane made the League of Nations a necessity by bringing possible enemies entirely too close for comfort. The rocket would bring America and Russia as close together, in a military sense, as France and Germany now are.

Document C

Source: Edwin L. James, "Our World Power and Moral Influence," *International Digest,* October 1930.

The Material situation of the United States of America is such that the resulting political influence is enormous, so enormous that a failure to place its true value on it may be explained by the circumstance that it has not yet made its real force felt to a degree that will surely materialize.

There is not country where the power of the dollar has not reached. There is no capital which does not take the United States into consideration at almost every turn. Conversely, there is no zone where our interests are not involved. Isolation is a myth. We are not isolated and cannot be isolated. The United States is ever present.

Document D

Source: Franklin D. Roosevelt, Letter to Maxim Litvinov, November 1933.

I am very happy to inform you that as a result of our conversations the government of the United States has decided to establish normal diplomatic relations with the government of the Union of Soviet Socialist Republics and to exchange ambassadors.

I trust that the relations now established between our peoples may forever remain normal and friendly, and that our nations henceforth may cooperate for their mutual benefit and for the preservation of the peace of the world.

Document E

No Foreign Entanglements

Document F

Source: Bennett Champ Clark, Article, *Harper's Monthly*, December 1935.

We know that however strong is the will of the American people to refrain from mixing in other people's quarrels, that will can be made effective only if we have a sound, definitive policy from the beginning.

Such a policy must be built upon a program to safeguard our neutrality. No lesson of the World War cannot be improvised after war breaks out. It must be determined in advance, before it is too late to apply reason. I contend with all possible earnestness that if we want to avoid being drawn into this war now forming, or any other future war, we must formulate a definite, workable policy of neutral relations with belligerent nations.

Document G

These grand and fatal movements toward death: the grandeur of the mass
Makes pity a fool, the tearing pity For the atoms of the mass, the persons, the victims, makes it seem monstrous To admire the tragic beauty they build. . . .

To change the future. . . I should do foolishly. The beauty of modern
Man is not in the persons but in the Disastrous rhythm, the heavy and mobile masses, the dance of the Dream-led masses down the dark mountain.

Document H

Source: Franklin D. Roosevelt, Speech, October 1937.

It seems to be unfortunately true that the epidemic of world lawlessness is spreading. When an epidemic of physical disease starts to spread, the community approves and joins in a quarantine of the patients in order to protect the health of the community against the spread of the disease. . . .

We are determined to keep out of war, yet we cannot insure ourselves against the disastrous effects of war and the dangers of involvement. We are adopting such measures as will minimize our risk of involvement, but we cannot have complete protection in a world of disorder in which confidence and security have broken down.

Document I

Source: Committee to Defend America by Aiding the Allies, Advertisement, *New York Times*, June 1940 [*Annals*, 16, p. 6].

If Hitler wins in Europe—if the strength of the British and French armies and navies is forever broken—the United States will find itself alone in a barbaric world—a world ruled by Nazis, with 'spheres of influence' assigned to their totalitarian allies. However different the dictatorships may be, racially, they all agree on one primary objective: *'Democracy must be wiped from the face of the earth.'*

Document J

Source: Charles Lindbergh, Speech, April 1941.

In time of war, truth is always replaced by propaganda. I do not believe we should be too quick to criticize the actions of a belligerent nation. There is always the question we, ourselves, would do better under similar circumstances. But we in this country have a right to think of the welfare of America first of their own country when they encouraged the smaller nations of Europe to fight against hopeless odds. When England asks for us to enter the war, she is considering her own future and that of her Empire. In making our reply, I believe we should consider the future of the United States and that of the Western Hemisphere.

Multiple-Choice Answers

1. d. American foreign policy during the 1920s consisted of a type of "limited internationalism" that sought to protect American interests, especially economic, while also preserving American freedom of action. The United States rejected League of Nations membership but did try to promote international stability through efforts such as the Washington Naval Conference and the Kellogg–Briand Pact.

2. c. The policy of refusing to recognize territorial acquisitions undertaken by force came to be known as the Stimson Doctrine. Japan later withdrew from the League of Nations after a League-appointed commission condemned Japanese actions in Manchuria. The

United States would pursue a policy of economic pressure against Japan in 1940 in the face of Japanese expansion in Southeast Asia.

3. b. The hostile public response to Roosevelt's speech, which had not proposed any specific steps by the United States, indicated the growth of isolationist opinion and the limited room that FDR faced in foreign policy, a marked contrast to his early experience in domestic affairs. While Americans traditionally felt sympathy for China, they were also hesitant to support any measure that would commit the United States to military action there.

4. b. The Nye Committee hearings, chaired by North Dakota Senator Gerald Nye, reached the conclusion that American banking interests had pressured President Wilson to enter World War I to protect their loans. The impact of the Nye Committee report was to strengthen isolationist opinion in the United States and limit Roosevelt's ability to respond to events abroad.

5. c. Roosevelt declared shortly after the outbreak of war in 1939 that the United States would remain neutral, "but I cannot ask that every American remain neutral in thought as well." Roosevelt would articulate his vision for the postwar world with the Atlantic Charter in the summer of 1941 and sought to find ways to increase aid to the Allies short of war until the Japanese attack on Pearl Harbor in December 1941.

6. c. The Dawes Plan provided loans to Germany, which the Weimar Republic used to make reparations payments to France and England but at the cost of massive German debts to American banks. The result was to significantly increase the American economic presence in Germany and Europe. The United States would not provide direct government aid to Europe until after World War II with the Marshall Plan and other measures.

7. b. The United States instituted its first peacetime draft in the spring of 1940; FDR was able to defy Washington's time-honored precedent of two terms given the growing international crisis; and beginning in the summer of 1941, American ships began escorting British merchant ships and informing the British of Nazi ship movement (FDR followed soon after by ordering American ships to "shoot on sight" at German submarines). Despite the growing American involvement, the strength and influence of the America First Committee and other groups indicated the persistence of strong isolationist opinion. Congress voted to overturn the "cash and carry" provision of the 1937 Neutrality Act in allowing the United States to provide "lend–lease" aid to the Allies beginning in 1939.

8. e. Roosevelt convinced Congress to pass a "lend–lease" bill in 1941 that allowed the United States to "eliminate the dollar sign" by lending or leasing armaments to any nation that President Roosevelt deemed "vital to the defense of the United States." The Senate had voted to reject American membership in the World Court in 1935; the Nye Committee strengthened isolationist sentiment by ascribing U.S. entry into World War I to put pressure on the Wilson administration from American bankers; the America First Committee advocated American noninvolvement in the growing European conflict; and the United States responded meekly to the Japanese sinking of the *Panay* in 1937.

9. a. FDR continued the policy started by Hoover of seeking to improve United States relations with Latin America by increasing trade (which further increased American economic dominance in the region), while also refraining from intervention (a repudiation of the Roosevelt Corollary to the Monroe Doctrine). FDR had refused to cooperate with other nations on currency stabilization at the World Economic Conference and signed a congressional bill forbidding American banks to make loans to nations in default on their debts.

10. c. The agreements reached at the Washington Naval Conference began to break down soon after the start of the Great Depression in 1929, as the London Naval Conference of 1930 showed that England and France were unwilling to accept meaningful limits on naval armaments. In rejecting the League, the United States had rejected Wilson's vision of international relations. Although the agreements represented a shift away from traditional European balance-of-power diplomacy, the lack of any meaningful enforcement mechanism or willingness by the United States to use force meant that it was unwilling to take a position of global political leadership.

11. a. The Spanish Falangists, a fascist group under General Francisco Franco, received extensive aid from Germany and Italy, while the Republican government received no assistance from France, Britain, or the United States (Soviet aid to the Republicans was provided more in a manner to benefit Stalin's interests than those of the Spanish). The United States policy of neutrality limited its influence over affairs in Europe. Roosevelt, concerned about American isolationist sentiment in the face of growing fascist expansion, gradually began to seek ways to circumvent the neutrality laws and find ways to oppose German, Italian, and Japanese aggression.

12. b. Beginning with Charles Beard in 1948 and continuing to the present day, a school of "revisionist" historians has argued that the Roosevelt administration knew that the Japanese were going to attack Pearl Harbor and withheld this information in order to provoke a Japanese attack that would allow the United States to enter the war through a "back door." Other historians have emphasized the failure to interpret intelligence (Roberta Wohlstetter), the daring and skill of the Japanese (Gordon Prange), and the American anticipation of an attack elsewhere (Richard Current). Revisionists argue that the United States took an extremely hard, rather than weak, diplomatic stance to encourage the Japanese attack.

Free-Response Questions Commentary

1. Discussion of the Open Door policy provides students with the opportunity to discuss two key themes of American foreign policy. First, the policy, articulated by Secretary of State John Hay at the turn of the twentieth century and a central theme of American policy in Asia for the next several decades, was driven by a combination of self-interest and idealism. American leaders sought to protect Chinese territorial integrity and felt a sense of paternalistic concern for the Chinese people, while they also sought access to Chinese markets as an outlet for American surplus production and capital. The Open Door policy also demonstrates the tension between rhetoric and reality, as American pronouncements about East Asia carried little weight in the face of the power of Japan and other European nations; it was not until the United States entered World War II that it could meaningfully influence events in the region.

2. Presidents Woodrow Wilson and Franklin Roosevelt faced a series of challenges in response to European conflict and responded in differing manners. Wilson, initially concerned with the rights of American neutral shipping and American national honor, called on Americans to be neutral in both thought and deed at the outset of the war. Roosevelt, much more concerned with the direct threat that fascism posed to American national security, made no such effort at true neutrality. Wilson gradually came to see the war as a way to promote a new world order on the basis of the League of Nations; Roosevelt, once able to overcome American isolationist sentiment, was able to more firmly commit the United States to a position of global leadership. Wilson was arguably more defensive in his response to German aggression, as events such as the German decision to undertake unrestricted submarine warfare and the Zimmerman telegram gradually increased American sentiment for involvement in the war. Roosevelt, facing greater opposition, took a series of steps—including involving the United States in an

undeclared naval war with Germany and placing severe economic pressure on Japan—
that sought to support the Allied cause without directly involving the United States in
the war. The Japanese attack on Pearl Harbor and Hitler's subsequent declaration of
war on the United States finally brought the nation into the war.

Document-Based Question Commentary

Background: The United States, despite the rejection of the League of Nations, was not
particularly isolationist during the 1920s. Efforts such as the Washington Naval Conference
and the Kellogg–Briand Pact demonstrate a belief in the need for mechanisms to preserve
peace— American leaders were concerned about doing so while also preserving American
freedom of action. As the global crisis became more likely during the 1930s, Congress and
other groups responded with neutrality legislation and other efforts meant to prevent a
repeat of World War I.

Document A, a speech by Vice President Coolidge, attests to the attempts by the United
States to remain involved in international peacekeeping efforts through efforts such as the
Washington Naval Conference.

Documents B and C could be further grouped together to demonstrate that isolationism
was not a viable policy given conditions in the world. Document B presciently notes that
technological developments such as the rocket could present major threats to American
security in the future, while Document C, by foreign correspondent Edwin James, notes that
the extent of American economic power means that the United States can no longer isolate
itself from the rest of the world.

Document D deals with Roosevelt's decision to recognize the Soviet Union in 1934, an effort
to end American economic isolation and Soviet political isolation (although the results were
not what either side had hoped for).

Document E, a cartoon by Herblock, demonstrates the tension between efforts by American
leaders, especially in the Senate, to remain aloof from European political affairs, while at the
same time seeking to promote American economic interests abroad.

Documents F and G can easily be paired together. In Document F, Senator Clark of Missouri
advocates for a policy of neutrality—this is a good opportunity for students to bring in their
knowledge of the Neutrality Acts of 1935, 1936, and 1937. Poet Robertson Jeffers notes the
dangers of war in his poem, "Rearmament," in Document G.

Document H, Roosevelt's "Quarantine Speech," offered vague proposals to contain fascist
aggression. Students should note here that the negative public reaction to the speech
demonstrated the strength of isolationist opinion.

Documents I and J demonstrate the diverging American responses to the war in Europe.
Document I, from a New York Times advertisement bought by advocates of American
support for England and France, notes the dangers for the United States if Hitler conquered
Europe. In Document J, by contrast, the influential Charles Lindbergh notes that the United
States should maintain a focus on its own interests in the Western Hemisphere.

Summation: The documents show a strong divergence of American opinions on foreign policy during the 1920s and 1930s. The documents from the 1920s demonstrate relatively little in terms of complete isolation; American leaders sought to preserve the nation's freedom of action and avoid being dragged into conflicts not related to American interests. The debate over American foreign policy grew much sharper in the 1930s, as the global crisis called for both greater support for isolationism and a stronger American response. Only the Japanese attack on Pearl Harbor, however, brought the United States into the war and to some degree silenced the advocates of isolationism.

CHAPTER 26
America in a World at War

AP THEMES

- **War and Diplomacy:** World War II transformed the United States more fundamentally than any conflict since the Civil War. It revolutionized American foreign policy by causing the nation's leaders to realize that the United States must commit itself to playing a leading role in postwar collective security efforts to avoid a repeat of the events that led up to the war; it expanded the role of the federal government in myriad ways; it ended the Great Depression; and it changed the role of women and minority groups, fueling postwar demands for greater rights among groups that helped to maintain the nation's freedom during wartime.

- **Economic Transformations:** World War II succeeded where the New Deal failed—in ending the Great Depression. Federal spending increased more than tenfold between 1939 and 1945; at the same time, Americans saved money due to the shortage of consumer goods, helping to spark a massive postwar economic boom. The war also spurred economic growth in the West, where federal military and infrastructure spending helped to transform the region's economy. The war led to unprecedented government spending on research and development, which produced a host of new innovations, with both military and civilian applications. Increased taxation, including the first federal withholding taxes, helped to finance the costly war effort.

- **American Diversity:** The struggle against Nazi ideas of racial superiority forced the United States to grapple with the issue of racial and ethnic diversity in the United States. The United States placed more than 100,000 Japanese Americans in internment camps in the name of protecting national security, a controversial decision that evoked little popular opposition at the time. Despite this action, the federal government and the American people largely came to see the nation's ethnic diversity as a source of its strength, a major difference from World War I, when government efforts to promote national unity helped spark anti-foreign hysteria. African Americans demanded a greater role in the war effort and an end to discrimination in defense industries. Their military efforts led to the desegregation of the armed forces soon after the war's end.

- **Culture:** Despite the natural anxiety caused by the war, the conflict also demonstrated the resilience of American culture and society. Americans came to believe that they were fighting to uphold the ideals of democracy and material prosperity. They looked forward to a postwar age in which peace and economic stability would be the order of the day. Families were strained as a result of the demands of military services, women joining the workforce and the uncertainty of the outcome of the war. Marriage and birth rates increased significantly during the war, and Americans became even more mobile to meet the demands of the military and the expansion of the industrial workforce.

CHAPTER SUMMARY
War on Two Fronts

Following the attack on Pearl Harbor in December 1941, the Japanese achieved a series of victories against U.S. forces, culminating with the surrender of the Philippines in early May of 1942. The United States planned to defeat the Japanese through a two-pronged approach, with forces under General **Douglas MacArthur** moving north from Australia and an

American fleet under Admiral **Chester Nimitz** moving west from Hawaii to ultimately reach the Japanese mainland. American forces won decisive victories at the battles of **Coral Sea** and **Midway** in the spring of 1942 before undertaking a six-month campaign to take **Guadalcanal** from the late summer of 1942 to the spring of 1943.

On the western front, Roosevelt was torn with regard to American strategy in Europe. Army Chief of Staff **George Marshall** favored a large-scale Allied invasion of France in May 1943, while Winston Churchill and British leaders sought to weaken Germany with attacks in North Africa and Italy. Soviet leader Joseph Stalin hoped for an Allied invasion of France as early as possible to take pressure off the Soviet Union, which had been involved in bitter fighting with Germany since Hitler had invaded in June 1941. Roosevelt agreed to support the British proposal and in the late fall of 1942, American troops landed in North Africa. Despite early difficulties, they were able to help British forces clear North Africa of German troops by May 1943.

Roosevelt agreed at **Casablanca** in January 1943 to help the British in a campaign against Italy, which would help drive Italy out of the war and tie up German divisions in France. The campaign was costly and time-consuming. The Allies captured Rome only in June 1944. The Allied effort in Italy delayed the invasion of France for close to a year, further embittering Stalin but allowing Soviet troops to move further east, which would have important effects on the postwar world.

By early 1942, American leaders had clear evidence of a concerted German effort to exterminate European Jews and other minority groups. Despite public pressure, FDR and his administration refused to order the bombing of the rail lines to the death camp at **Auschwitz,** Poland. The United States also refused to admit large numbers of Jewish refugees into the United States largely because of anti-Semitism among State Department officials. The administration argued that winning the war as quickly as possible was the best way to help end the Holocaust.

The American People in Wartime

The American war effort succeeded in ending the Depression, as federal spending put more money into the economy than all New Deal agencies combined. The gross national product nearly doubled between 1939 and 1945, because many Americans were putting their earnings into savings due to a shortage of consumer goods. The West Coast, particularly California, benefited more than any other part of the nation from federal spending, as its location made it a staging ground for much of the naval war against Japan. The Pacific coast became a center for the American aircraft and shipbuilding industry and was transformed into one of the most vital manufacturing centers in the nation.

The economic boom during the war caused a 20 percent increase in the size of the civilian labor force and led to an increase of 2.5 million union members. Labor leaders, however, agreed to several measures that limited workers' wartime gains, including a 15 percent limit on wartime wage increases and a "no-strike pledge." Congress passed the **Smith–Connally Act,** following a strike by the United Mine Workers in May 1943. The act required a thirty-day waiting period before strikes and empowered the president to seize plants where strikes were occurring.

In late 1942, the **Office of Price Administration** was forced to take measures to stem wartime inflation, freezing farm prices, wages, rents, and salaries. To finance the war, which necessitated twice as much federal spending as had occurred in the previous 150 years of America's existence, the government passed the **Revenue Act of 1942,** which raised income taxes on the highest tax brackets and imposed income taxes on lower-income families as well. The bill also imposed a payroll withholding tax for the first time.

The government experienced difficulty in economic mobilization efforts. In early 1942, FDR created the **War Production Board (WPB),** which was unable to overcome conflicts with the military and between large and small business. FDR transferred much of the agency's power to the **Office of War Mobilization,** which had little more success. Overall, despite inefficiencies, the American economy did manage to meet the needs of the war effort.

The United States government was willing to pour massive resources into scientific research and development to help overcome the lags that had occurred in the 1920s and 1930s. World War II proved to be an unprecedented period in the development of scientific and technological innovations. In 1940, the government established the **National Defense Research Committee,** which spent more than $100 million on military technology. The conversion of American mass-production mechanisms into military purposes helped the Allies to overcome early German advantages. Particularly important were advances in radar and sonar technology; the development and production of four-engine bombers; new navigation systems; and intelligence, achieved through systematic decoding operations (the British **Enigma** machine and the American **Magic** operation), which allowed the Allies to anticipate German and Japanese military movements.

African Americans sought to use World War II as a means to advance their struggle for equality. They were much more forceful in their demands than they had been during World War I. **A. Philip Randolph** of the Brotherhood of Sleeping Car Porters threatened a massive march on Washington, D.C., to protest discrimination in defense plants in 1941. In response, Roosevelt created the **Fair Employment Practices Commission (FEPC),** which was charged with investigating discrimination against blacks in war industries. Although the FEPC's enforcement powers were weak, its establishment was an important symbolic victory for African Americans. The war produced a second **Great Migration** of African Americans from the South to northern cities, in even greater numbers than during World War I. Racial tensions once again emerged, as was the case in Detroit in June 1943, where rioting led to the death of thirty-four people, the majority of them African Americans. The **Congress on Racial Equality (CORE),** which was formed in 1942, protested discrimination and laid the groundwork for the later civil rights movement. The military gradually began to shift from its traditional belief in having segregated units and using blacks only in combat support roles, due largely to the realization that such practices were militarily inefficient and deprived the United States of an important manpower source.

Other minority groups also played significant roles in the American war effort. Twenty-five thousand Native Americans served directly in the war, while others worked as **"code talkers,"** who helped facilitate Allied military communications. Many Native Americans left reservations for work in war industries. This undermined support for tribal autonomy, leading to the resignation of the commissioner of Indian Affairs, John Collier, in 1945.

Due to the wartime labor shortage, the American and Mexican governments agreed to the *bracero* **(contract labor)** system, under which Mexicans were allowed to enter the United States for certain jobs. Farm workers were allowed access to jobs they had lost during the Depression, and many Mexicans migrated to cities in search of work. In Los Angeles, the site of large concentrations of Mexican Americans, tensions emerged as a result of white concerns over the actions of street gangs (*pachucos*). The **Zoot Suit Riots**—named for a distinctive clothing style worn by Mexican teenagers—erupted in June 1943 when white sailors with the tacit support of local police attacked Mexican American teenagers.

The war opened new opportunities to women. The percentage of women in the paid workforce rose from one-quarter in 1940 to one-third by 1945. The symbol of **"Rosie the Riveter"** demonstrated the power of women in the industrial workforce. Many other women became **"government girls,"** working long hours in wartime agencies as clerks and typists. Many of the female workers were older and more likely to have children than their World War I counterparts. (Because of a lack of child-care facilities, some children were left temporarily unattended and were known as **"latchkey children"** or **"eight-hour orphans."**)

While the war led to the development of high levels of anxiety over the fates of those at war, it also demonstrated the resilient strain in American life and culture. Americans believed they were fighting to preserve a democratic society based on freedom, economic security, and liberty. This was a recurring theme among those on the home front and those on the battle front. To compensate for the rigors of wartime, soldiers romanticized their thoughts of home. The **USO** sponsored dances, while government-supported **"dance brigades"** helped to give servicemen healthy social outlets.

World War II produced much less wartime hysteria and fewer violations of civil liberties than did World War I—one exception being. Japanese Americans, who faced deep discrimination from both the government and private citizens. Among the 127,000 Americans of Japanese descent, about one-third were unnaturalized immigrations (*Issei*) and two-thirds were naturalized or native citizens (*Nisei*). In February 1942, the government created the **War Relocation Authority** to supervise the movement of Japanese Americans from the West Coast to relocation camps in the interior, in one of the most serious violations of citizens' civil rights in American history.

The Supreme Court ruled in the 1944 case *Korematsu v. U.S.* that internment was allowed under the Constitution and later that year barred the internment of loyal citizens—with the government given the latitude to determine the criteria for loyalty. By the end of 1944, most internees had been released but not compensated for loss of income or property. In 1988, Congress voted to provide reparations to survivors and their descendants.

To help improve relations with China, in 1943 the United States government repealed the Chinese Exclusion Act, which had been in effect since 1882, and allowed small numbers of Chinese immigrants to enter the United States (with larger allotments for war brides and fiancées of American servicemen. Overall, Chinese Americans strongly supported the war effort, with many serving in the armed forces or working in war-related industries.

In 1943, FDR publicly stated that **"Dr. New Deal"** should become **"Dr. Win-the-War,"** reflecting both his own concerns and political realities brought about by the growing strength of conservatives in Congress. In 1944, FDR ran for a fourth term as president against popular New York Governor **Thomas Dewey,** having agreed to replace his liberal vice president, **Henry Wallace,** with the more moderate **Harry Truman** of Missouri. Despite concerns over his health and the nation's economic state, and the war, FDR won reelection by a healthy margin and the Democrats retained control of Congress.

The Defeat of the Axis

To ease the Allied invasion of France, American and British planes began a massive bombing campaign against German factories and other significant targets, including a highly controversial firebombing raid on the city of Dresden that killed 135,000 people. On June 6, 1944, vast Allied forces landed on the coast of Normandy, providing a foothold from which German forces were gradually pushed back through France and Belgium. A massive German counteroffensive in late 1944, the **Battle of the Bulge,** was finally halted and paved the way for the Allied entry into Germany. While American forces fought a frustrating campaign on the Asian mainland, by the late spring of 1944, American naval forces had reached within 1,500 miles of Tokyo. In a series of battles beginning with the **Battle of Leyte Gulf,** the largest naval battle in history, American forces moved toward the Japanese mainland. Fearing a continuation of battles as that which occurred at **Iwo Jima** in February 1945, the bloodiest battle in Marine Corps history, American forces firebombed Tokyo, killing 80,000, to weaken Japanese resistance.

Efforts by German scientists to create an atomic bomb spurred a massive effort beginning in 1939 by the United States to be the first to create such a weapon. During the course of the war, the American government dedicated nearly $2 billion to the **Manhattan Project,** the top-secret program dedicated to creating an atomic weapon. The first test occurred in mid-July 1945 near Alamogordo, New Mexico, after the end of the war in Europe but in time for possible use against Japan.

President Truman first learned about the explosion while at a conference of Allied leaders in **Potsdam,** Germany. He quickly issued an ultimatum to the Japanese, demanding that they surrender by August 3, 1945, or face ultimate destruction. Japan failed to accept these terms, insisting on the retention of their emperor, leading to the dropping of bombs on **Hiroshima** on **August 6** and **Nagasaki** on August 9, which resulted in the immediate deaths of nearly 200,000 civilians and the injuries and illnesses of countless others. While Truman's decision has been the subject of intense controversy among historians, he believed that he was making a clear military decision that would help facilitate a quick end to the war. Later historians argued that Truman sought to intimidate the Soviet Union in order to forestall communist expansion and pave the way for American economic domination of the postwar world. In early September, the Japanese government formally surrendered, paving the way for an uneasy transition to the postwar world.

$$\frac{6}{12}$$

Multiple-Choice Questions

1. What was the goal of A. Philip Randolph's proposed March on Washington in 1941?
   a. to gain an end to segregation of public facilities
   b. to gain protection for African American voting rights
   c. to end discrimination in the defense industry
   d. to gain FDR's support for federal anti-lynching legislation
   e. to end segregation in the armed forces

2. Working women in World War II differed from their World War I counterparts in that
   a. they were more likely to challenge traditional social mores.
   b. they were more likely to be older and have children.
   c. they were more likely to use war work to promote postwar feminist goals.
   d. they received genuine equality with men in the workplace.
   e. they worked more in factories than in service-sector jobs.

3. The Supreme Court during World War II ruled that Japanese internment
   a. was an unconstitutional violation of the Fourteenth Amendment.
   b. was allowed in wartime for those the government considered disloyal.
   c. was allowed only for those who were not American citizens.
   d. unfairly singled out members of one ethnic group.
   e. violated the Fifth Amendment rights of those whose property was taken.

4. The biggest diplomatic obstacle to concluding the war between the United States and Japan in 1945 was
   a. the fate of American prisoners of war.
   b. the issue of postwar reparations.
   c. the question of retaining the emperor.
   d. the issue of assigning war guilt.
   e. the question of how to deal with Japanese territorial acquisitions.

5. During the course of the war, President Roosevelt sought to
   a. use wartime mobilization as a way to increase government regulation of business.
   b. increase his commitment to social reforms for minority groups.
   c. signal his commitment to liberals in the Democratic Party by choosing Harry S. Truman as his running mate.
   d. place less emphasis on reform and more on the issues of military strategy and postwar planning.
   e. purge conservatives from wartime government agencies and replace them with New Deal supporters.

6. The United States and Great Britain made major technological innovations in all of the following areas during World War II *except*
   a. synthetic rubber.
   b. intelligence gathering and decoding.
   c. radar and sonar development.
   d. the development of the hydrogen bomb.
   e. the production of bomber planes.

7. Which of the following are true about American strategy during World War II?
   I. The United States had less freedom of action in the European theater than it did in the Pacific.
   II. The first significant European fighting by American troops occurred in France.
   III. American troops made significant progress in reducing Japanese control over mainland Chinese territory during the war.
   IV. Truman and other American leaders had few doubts about whether to use atomic weapons to conclude the war against Japan.
   V. The Allies were unwilling to negotiate surrender terms with the Axis powers.

a. I, II, III
b. I, II, IV
c. I, IV, V
d. II, IV, V
e. III, IV, V

8. Which of the following is true of Mexican Americans during World War II?
   a. They assimilated easily into American society.
   b. They had little record of service in the United States military.
   c. They were deported from the United States in large numbers.
   d. They found few opportunities for agricultural labor.
   e. They migrated to urban areas and found factory jobs for the first time.

9. Wartime production increases most benefited which of the following regions?
   a. the West Coast
   b. the Midwest
   c. the South
   d. the Northeast
   e. the Southwest

10. All of the following are true of organized labor during World War II *except*
    a. union membership increased significantly during the course of the war.
    b. union leaders agreed to limits on wartime wage increases.
    c. union leaders signed a "no-strike" pledge.
    d. new workers in defense plants were automatically enrolled in unions.
    e. few work stoppages occurred during the war.

11. American leaders responded to the Holocaust by
    a. increasing quotas of Jewish refugees allowed into the United States.
    b. bombing the rail lines leading to Auschwitz and other death camps.
    c. focusing on defeating Hitler as quickly as possible as the best way to help his victims.
    d. working closely with Great Britain to save as many Jewish lives as possible.
    e. urging third-party countries to accept more refugees and providing them with financial incentives for doing so.

12. In comparison to World War I, the federal government during World War II
    a. made a more concerted effort to censor dissident publications
    b. portrayed ethnic differences as harmful to the American war effort
    c. made little effort to differentiate between the peoples from enemy nations and their governments
    d. committed relatively few civil liberties violations, with the exception of the internment of Japanese Americans
    e. used wartime patriotism as an opportunity to weaken left-wing groups.

Free-Response Questions—Exam Tips

A central theme from this period is the connection between World War II and the Cold War between the United States and the Soviet Union. As you read this chapter and the next, keep in mind the degree to which the wartime actions of Roosevelt and Stalin influenced the postwar relationship between the two nations.

Free-Response Questions

1. Assess Franklin D. Roosevelt's diplomacy in the period between 1941 and 1945.

2. Analyze the impact of World War II on the American home front in two of the following areas:
    Economic development
    The role of the federal government
    The treatment of minorities

Document-Based Question—Exam Tips

Most document-based questions contain at least one visual source, if not more. During wartime, political cartoons and propaganda posters often play a role in shaping public opinion. Remember to use captions and titles, along with symbols contained within the visual sources, to help you to determine the author's point of view and motivation. Once you have done that, you can use the source more easily and effectively to support your argument.

Document-Based Question

Propaganda Posters: Wartime propaganda posters can offer significant insights about popular attitudes in a given period. World War II recruiting posters reveal a great deal about the role of women in the United States during World War II. Analyze the three posters that follow, considering what they reveal about women's role in the war effort and about gender roles in the 1940s.

Document A

Keep These Hands Off!

Document B

Victory Waits on Your Fingers

Document C

Attention Women!

Multiple-Choice Answers

1. c. Randolph, the leader of the Brotherhood of Sleeping Car Porters, threatened to march on Washington with 100,000 demonstrators to protest the lack of opportunities for African Americans in the defense industry. Roosevelt responded by issuing Executive Order 8801, which established a Fair Employment Practices Commission (FEPC) to investigate claims of discrimination against blacks in the defense industry.

2. b. The number of women in the workforce rose by 60 percent during the war, and these women were more likely to be older and married than were their earlier counterparts in the workforce. The majority of World War II women worked in service-sector, not factory, jobs. Most of these women returned to their prewar roles after the war, and a new wave of feminism did not emerge until the 1960s.

3. b. In the 1944 case *Korematsu v. U.S.,* the Supreme Court upheld the constitutionality of internment and held in another case that year that the government could not imprison "loyal" citizens but allowed the government the discretion to define who was considered loyal. By the end of 1944, in any event, most internees had been released and were allowed to return to the West Coast in 1945

4. c. Following the successful tests of American atomic weapons, President Truman demanded that the Japanese surrender or face complete destruction. While there was some evidence that the Japanese might be willing to surrender in exchange for an agreement that they be allowed to retain the emperor, the United States rejected this and insisted on "unconditional surrender." Following the experience of World War I, the United States did not want to insist on reparations; the issue of war guilt would be dealt with in the Nuremberg War Crimes Trials through the trials of high-ranking German and Japanese officials.

5. d. In 1943, Roosevelt famously declared that "Dr. New Deal" had become "Dr. Win the War." Roosevelt had to accept greater influence from business leaders and conservatives in the wartime mobilization effort and accept the diminishing of New Deal programs in order to focus on military strategy. His decision to drop Henry Wallace and make Missouri Senator Harry Truman vice president was an effort to put a more moderate figure on the Democratic ticket.

6. d. The hydrogen bomb, which relied on the fusion of atoms (rather than the fission that powered the World War II atomic weapons), was not developed until the early 1950s. Innovations in the other four areas all played key roles in the Allied defeat of the Axis powers.

7. c. Because of the need to coordinate with the British and Soviets, American leaders had relatively little flexibility in Europe. Truman and most of his closest advisors had little doubt that they would use the atomic bomb once it was developed. At the Casablanca Conference, Roosevelt, Churchill, and Stalin agreed that they would fight until receiving the unconditional surrender of the Axis powers.

8. e. The wartime labor shortage, in both rural and urban areas, caused the federal government to reverse the policy of deporting Mexican Americans that it had undertaken during the 1930s. However, while Mexican Americans had worked on farms in the Southwest for some time, they found factory jobs in significant numbers for the first time during World War II.

9. a. Wartime shipbuilding and aircraft production needs led to a major economic boom in the West, particularly in the Pacific Northwest. The federal government made more than $40 billion in capital investment in the West during the war, and 10 percent of federal government spending between 1940 and 1945 went solely to California.

10. e. Despite the fact that union leaders agreed to a "no-strike" pledge, there were nonetheless nearly 15,000 work stoppages during the course of the war, most of which were "wildcat" strikes (meaning that they were not authorized by union leadership).

11 c. Roosevelt and other administration leaders argued that the best way to save the lives of potential Holocaust victims was to focus on defeating Hitler as quickly as possible, arguing that bombing death camps themselves or the rail lines leading them to would be militarily unfeasible and refusing to raise refugee quotas.

12 d. With the exception of the internment of Japanese Americans, the federal government actually committed relatively few civil liberties violations during World War II. One of the biggest differences between World War I and World War II was that whereas ethnic diversity was seen as dangerous in the former case, it came to be seen as a source of America's strength in the latter case.

Free-Response Questions Commentary

1. As a wartime leader, Franklin Roosevelt sought to emphasize the broad principles for which the United States was fighting, while at the same time focusing on defeating Germany and Japan as quickly as possible. An answer to this question could begin with discussion of the Atlantic Charter and also note Roosevelt's efforts to ensure that the United States played a major role in a postwar collective security organization. Some historians have criticized Roosevelt for failing to foresee the long-term diplomatic implications of American strategy, for example, in his failure to push for an earlier cross channel invasion of France, which helped to alienate the Soviet Union in the postwar period; others have criticized him for failing to take a stronger line against the Soviet Union at Yalta and failing to realize the impact of allowing Soviet troops to move deep into Germany. While some of Roosevelt's decisions can be questioned, he led the United States through a harrowing war and left it, at the time of his death, ready to assume a position of world leadership.

2. An answer to this question should stress the far-reaching impact of the war in terms of economic development and the role of the federal government. While some minority groups made gains during the war, many of these were halted or reversed in the aftermath of the war. The key themes in economic development are the restoration of prosperity, the development of the West, and the nation's impressive wartime production War invariably expands the role of the federal government, and World War II was no exception. Federal spending and taxation policies, wage and price controls, and support for science and technology were three significant areas of government wartime activity, many of which set the tone for the more activist government of the post-World War II era. Minorities frequently had difficult experiences during the war, particularly Japanese Americans. The war did galvanize African Americans and generated the seeds of the civil rights movement. The war also saw the movement of African Americans from the rural South to the industrialized northern cities. Mexican Americans moved into urban areas and gained factory jobs on a widespread basis for the first time during the war. Wartime developments in all of these areas had a significant influence on the shape of the postwar United States.

Document-Based Question Commentary

As is frequently the case with propaganda, the themes presented here are not subtle. In Document A, an innocent-looking woman and her child, dressed in white, are about to fall into the grasp of two demonic sets of hands representing Germany and Japan. There is a clear connection drawn between a certain action, in this case buying war bonds, and the prevention of harm to women and children.

Document B presents a different theme, in this case calling upon a patriotic woman to work as a typist or clerk. These types of jobs were actually much more prevalent for women during this period than the highly publicized factory jobs of "Rosie the Riveter." Finally, Document C, calling upon women to serve in the Women's Auxiliary Corps, presents a much more masculine-looking woman—notice her leather gloves, upright posture, and the whistle that she is holding. These posters demonstrate that traditional views of femininity coexisted with less traditional images. Women contributed to the massive effort to win the war. The roles of women in American society were significantly changed as a result of World War II.

CHAPTER 27
The Cold War

AP THEMES
- **War and Diplomacy:** Although the United States experienced relatively little in the way of armed conflict in the immediate post-World War II period, the nation faced a series of tense crises with the Soviet Union between 1945 and 1950. The two wartime allies had vastly different conceptions of the shape of the postwar world, and each perceived the other's actions through a lens of distrust and suspicion. The United States gradually developed a policy of containment in an effort to prevent the expansion of Soviet power. By the end of the 1940s, communism had spread to China and other parts of Asia. Between 1950 and 1953, the United States fought a costly and inconclusive war in Korea, the first armed conflict of the Cold War.
- **Globalization:** The expansion of the containment policy, as well as the process of helping to rebuild war-torn Western Europe and Japan, transformed America's relationship with the rest of the world. The United States developed a substantial aid program to Western Europe in the form of the Marshall Plan and occupied Japan from 1945 until the 1950s. American foreign policy became heavily focused on preserving democracies throughout Europe and Asia and later to other parts of the world in an effort to develop reliable allies in the anticommunist struggle. At the same time, the United States sought to promote a liberal world economic order based on free trade in an effort both to maintain foreign markets and prevent the spread of economic autarchy, which American policymakers saw as having been central to the eventual outbreak of World War II.
- **Politics and Citizenship:** America's activist foreign policy required extensive domestic mobilization and significantly increased the power of the national state. Although President Truman had sought to keep defense spending limited in the early years of the Cold War, by 1950 American leaders believed it was necessary to undertake a major increase in defense spending to combat the Soviet threat. The nation's intelligence, military, and diplomatic institutions were all reorganized to give the president greater power and authority to conduct foreign policy.
- **Culture:** The Cold War had profound effects on virtually all aspects of American culture. Most apparent was the pervasive fear of communism that gripped much of the American public and eventually found form in the anticommunist crusade known as McCarthyism although the phenomenon went much deeper than the Wisconsin senator and his followers. Long accustomed to living relatively isolated from any direct threats to the nation's security, Americans had to become accustomed to a series of threats ranging from internal subversion and espionage to the potential threat of nuclear war.

CHAPTER SUMMARY
Origins of the Cold War

While historians disagree about whose actions were more responsible for the emergence of Cold War tensions, most agree that both the United States and the Soviet Union contributed to the post-World War II atmosphere of distrust and confrontation. At the heart of the Soviet-American rivalry were two fundamentally different conceptions of international relations. Roosevelt and many Americans accepted the ideals of the **Atlantic Charter,** announced by FDR and Churchill in 1941, in which an international organization would help to protect each nation's right of self-determination. Churchill and Stalin envisioned something much closer to the traditional European balance of power, in which great powers would control areas of strategic interest.

At **Casablanca** in January 1943, FDR and Churchill agreed that they would only accept **unconditional surrender** on the part of the Axis powers to help assure Stalin that the U.S.S.R. would not be forced to fight Germany alone. In November 1943, the three powers met at Teheran, with Stalin agreeing to enter the war in the Pacific soon after the end of European hostilities. The United States and Britain pledged to open a Second Front within six months. The seeds for future discord were apparent, however, as there was disagreement over the composition of the postwar Polish government.

At **Yalta** in February 1945, FDR, Churchill, and Stalin met to address a number of issues. Stalin renewed his pledge to enter the war against Japan, and FDR agreed to the restoration of Russian territory lost during the Russo–Japanese War. The sides also agreed to the creation of a postwar international organization with a General Assembly and a Security Council with each of the five major powers having veto power. However, Poland once again arose as a source of disagreement. Stalin made a vague promise to include some pro-western Poles in the postwar government and to hold "free and unfettered" elections in the future. Each side left the conference believing it had accomplished its goals, although FDR was soon dismayed by Soviet efforts to set up procommunist governments throughout Eastern Europe.

The Collapse of the Peace

Almost immediately after taking office following FDR's death in April 1945, President Truman decided to pursue a "get tough" policy toward the Soviet Union, although his leverage was limited by the military realities in Eastern Europe and elsewhere. Truman agreed to recognize the pro-Soviet government in Poland, hoping for greater noncommunist participation in the future. At the Potsdam conference in July 1945, the two sides disagreed over German reparations, and it soon became clear that Germany would remain divided into pro-western and pro-Soviet zones.

In Asia, a central part of the Allied hopes for a stable postwar world rested on a strong China. However, the nationalist government of **Chiang Kai-shek** was corrupt and unrepresentative, leading many Chinese to support the communists under **Mao Zedong.** The United States was left with few options other than to continue to support Chiang, although he clearly had little chance of winning the civil war against the communists. Realizing China's weakness, United States policy soon shifted to include support for a revived Japan to promote Asian stability.

Responding to European events in 1946, the United States abandoned its efforts to create an open world order and instead sought to find ways to contain the expansion of Soviet power and influence. The doctrine of **containment** based largely upon the ideas of diplomat **George Kennan,** became the centerpiece of American foreign policy for the next four decades. On March 12, 1947, Truman went before Congress and asked for $400 million to support Greece, which was involved in a civil war between communist and noncommunist forces, and Turkey, where Stalin was applying pressure to try to control sea lanes to the Mediterranean. Congress easily approved the measure.

American policymakers soon realized that they would need to facilitate the economic recovery of Western Europe in order to implement containment. In June 1947, Secretary of State **George Marshall** announced a plan, which became known as the **Marshall Plan,** under which the United States would provide aid to all European nations that would help to draft a recovery program. The U.S.S.R. and its satellites refused to participate, so the United States provided more than $12 billion in aid to Western Europe.

In 1947 and 1948, the United States undertook a number of efforts to maintain a high state of military readiness, including reinstitution of the **Selective Service System** and a **draft** in 1948. The **National Security Act** of 1947 established a National Security Council and a Department of Defense, as well as the **Central Intelligence Agency (CIA),** all of which provided the president with greater power to pursue American goals abroad.

In an effort to bolster Western Europe's military capacity, France, Great Britain, and the United States agreed to merge their three zones of occupation in Germany into one including Berlin, which was well within the Soviet occupation zone. In June 1948, Stalin imposed a tight blockade around the city, and for more than a year, the United States undertook a major airlift that brought several million tons of materials to the citizens of Berlin. Stalin abandoned the airlift, and by the spring of 1949, Germany was officially divided into two separate nations. In April 1949, twelve nations signed a treaty forming the **North Atlantic Treaty Organization (NATO),** providing for collective self-defense. The U.S.S.R. responded with the **Warsaw Pact,** formed in 1955.

The Soviet explosion of an atomic bomb and the collapse of the Chinese nationalist government in 1949 convinced Truman that stronger measures were needed to protect American society. A review of American policy issued in 1950, commonly known as **NSC-68,** shifted U.S. policy toward seeking to stop communist expansion in all parts of the world instead of differentiating between areas of vital and lesser interest to American security. NSC-68 also called for a drastically expanded American defense budget.

American Society and Politics After the War

The end of the war in the Pacific created serious economic problems, as consumers were impatient for a return to a peacetime economy. Although government spending decreased rapidly in 1946, increased consumer demand prevented an economic recession. The **Servicemen's Readjustment Act,** better known as the **GI Bill of Rights,** helped to provide economic assistance to veterans and supported the economy. A bigger problem was inflation, as Truman eliminated wage and price controls in the spring of 1946.

Labor unrest further contributed to the nation's economic problems. **John L. Lewis** and the **United Mine Workers** went on strike in April 1946, while at the same time the railroads shut down as two major unions went on strike. Truman threatened to seize the railroads and use the army to run trains, ending the dispute. Many women and minorities struggled with reconversion, as they were forced out of well-paying jobs that they had come to depend upon. Truman quickly issued a major set of domestic proposals that became known as the **Fair Deal,** in which he called for extension of Social Security, a rise in the federal minimum wage, a permanent **Fair Employment Practices Commission,** and, weeks later, national health insurance. These goals, however, were met with conservative opposition. Republicans won control of both houses of Congress in the 1946 elections. Conservatives wanted to lessen the power of organized labor, passing the controversial **Taft–Hartley Bill** of 1947 over

Truman's veto. The bill outlawed the **closed shop,** in which workers would have to be union members in order to be hired, and allowed states to pass **right-to-work laws,** which prohibited **union shops,** in which workers had to join a union after being hired. It also allowed the president to call for a **"cooling off period"** in the case of work stoppages that endangered national health or security.

Truman's personal unpopularity and commitment to reform helped to splinter the Democratic Party before the 1948 elections. Southern conservatives walked out of the Democratic convention and formed the **States Rights** or **"Dixiecrat," Party** in response to the creation of a civil rights plank in the Democrat platform. The left wing of the Democratic Party formed the **Progressive Party** and nominated **Henry Wallace** as its candidate. Truman faced popular New York Governor **Thomas Dewey** as the Republican nominee. Despite Dewey's apparently insurmountable lead, Truman continued to campaign hard, criticizing the "do-nothing" Republican Congress. To the surprise of many, he was reelected, capturing 303 electoral votes to Dewey's 189.

Following his reelection, Truman sought to promote his reform agenda, gaining an expansion of Social Security, an increase in the minimum wage, and the creation of a public housing program. However, he was unable to get Congress to pass legislation on education, health care, or civil rights. Truman moved to desegregate the armed forces and ordered an end to discrimination in the hiring of federal employees.

The advent of nuclear weapons understandably caused great anxiety among the American people. Air raid drills, fallout shelters, and frequent tests of the emergency broadcast system all reminded Americans of the imminent danger of nuclear war. At the same time, however, Americans learned that nuclear technology could be harnessed as a source of cheap electric power and as a means to greater prosperity for the nation.

The Korean War

Korea was divided along the 38th parallel at the end of World War II, with the United States occupying the south and a procommunist government in the north. The south was relatively weak, tempting the communists to seek unification by armed force. The United States inadvertently made this desire stronger by indicating that South Korea was not part of the American **"defense perimeter."** In late June, North Korean forces attacked South Korea. Truman sought and received a United Nations resolution pledging the UN to assist South Korea. UN forces, primarily consisting of American troops under **Douglas MacArthur,** succeeded in pushing North Korean troops back across the 38th parallel. MacArthur received permission from Truman to pursue North Korean troops in an effort to **"liberate"** Korea.

While the American-led offensive was initially successful, in early November, Chinese forces intervened in response to fears over the approach of western forces to the Chinese borders. American troops were pushed back, although by the spring of 1951, the situation stabilized, as the communists once again retreated past the 38th parallel. Truman sought a negotiated settlement, a position that was heavily and publicly criticized by MacArthur, forcing Truman to remove him from command in April 1951. Truman faced heavy criticism for this decision, although this criticism abated in the face of military leaders testifying to the soundness of Truman's decision.

The American domestic commitment to the war remained relatively limited, although Truman did establish an **Office of Defense Mobilization** to combat inflation and seized the railroads in response to a 1951 strike. The Supreme Court invalidated Truman's seizure of the steel mills in 1952. Despite the economic boom caused by the war, Americans quickly became frustrated by the nation's inability to prevail in a seemingly limited conflict, coming to believe that there must be great incompetence, or even deliberate sabotage, behind these failures.

The Crusade Against Subversion

In the face of failures in Korea, the Republicans capitalized on the issue of communist subversion in government to discredit the Democrats. Starting in 1947, the **House Un-American Activities Committee (HUAC)** investigated the film industry most famously in the case of the **"Hollywood Ten,"** and later turned its attention to subversive activity in the government. Most alarming to the American public was the case of **Alger Hiss,** a former State Department official who had passed classified documents on to the Soviet Union in the late 1930s. Hiss was convicted of perjury and spent several years in jail in a case that helped to raise widespread public fears of large-scale communist infiltration of the federal government.

In response to popular anticommunist sentiment and to gain support for its foreign policy initiatives, the Truman administration in 1947 created a loyalty program in which the government investigated the "loyalty" of federal employees. More than 2,000 employees resigned and another 200 were dismissed as a result of the loyalty program. In 1950, Congress passed the **McCarran Internal Security Act** over Truman's veto, requiring all communist organizations to register with the federal government.

The Soviet explosion of an atomic bomb in September 1949 further intensified American fears about the nation's security, and widespread suspicions of espionage emerged. **Julius and Ethel Rosenberg,** a couple who were Communist Party members, were accused of masterminding a scheme to pass atomic secrets to the Soviet Union and were executed in June 1953 after a series of unsuccessful appeals. The overall coincidence of a variety of factors paved the way for the rise of Wisconsin Senator **Joseph McCarthy.** McCarthy made a bold speech in February 1950 claiming that he had a list of more than 200 communists in the State Department. Beginning in 1952, McCarthy conducted a series of investigations of federal agencies, badgering and intimidating witnesses, without uncovering evidence of communist influence. McCarthy's popularity resulted from his attacks on the eastern "Establishment" and as an outlet for frustrated Republican ambitions.

Truman, facing widespread criticism for his handling of the economy and the war in Korea, and for allowing corruption within his administration, withdrew from the 1952 presidential race in favor of Illinois Governor **Adlai Stevenson.** Despite Stevenson's personal appeal, particularly among liberal Democrats, he stood little chance before the Republican nominee, **Dwight D. Eisenhower,** the hero of World War II. Anticommunist Congressman **Richard Nixon** was nominated as Eisenhower's vice president. Eisenhower swept to victory on the basis of his personal popularity and his promises to end corruption in Washington and bring a halt to the Korean conflict.

Multiple-Choice Questions

1. All of the following issues were resolved among the Grand Alliance at Yalta *except*
   a. plans for the creation of a postwar international organization.
   b. the decision to allow the Soviet Union to recover territory lost in the Russo–Japanese War.
   c. the shape of the postwar Polish government.
   d. the division of Germany into "zones of occupation."
   e. the issue of Soviet entry into the war against Japan.

2. "I believe that it must be the policy of the United States to support free peoples who are resisting attempted subjugation by armed minorities or by outside pressures." This quotation represents which of the following?
   a. the Marshall Plan
   b. the North Atlantic Treaty Organization
   c. the Truman Doctrine
   d. the Long telegram
   e. the Iron Curtain speech

3. NSC-68 reflected which of the following assumptions about American foreign policy?
   a. that the United States must differentiate between areas of vital and peripheral interest to American security
   b. that there are differences among communist nations and that the United States could exploit these
   c. that the United States must act to protect all areas that were under threat from communist attack or subversion
   d. that American resources were limited and that the United States must rely heavily upon its allies for the defense of those resources
   e. that the advent of Soviet nuclear capabilities meant that the United States must pursue a less confrontational approach toward the Soviet Union

4. All of the following were proposed elements of Truman's Fair Deal *except*
   a. right-to-work laws.
   b. civil rights legislation.
   c. national health insurance.
   d. federal aid to education.
   e. extension of Social Security benefits.

5. The main source of disagreement between Truman and General MacArthur during the Korean War arose over which of the following issues?
   a. Truman's desire to give other nations a stronger role in the UN military effort
   b. Truman's desire to avoid provoking China and widening the war
   c. Truman's desire to make the South Korean regime more democratic
   d. MacArthur's desire to limit the use of American ground troops
   e. MacArthur's plan to land UN troops at Inchon

6. The election of the 80th Congress in 1946 reflected which of the following trends among the American electorate?
   a. the desire for a vigorous anti-Soviet foreign policy
   b. the desire for a continuation of New Deal-style domestic reforms
   c. the desire to reduce government involvement in the economy and a return to peacetime conditions
   d. a strong mandate for Truman's handling of the domestic economy
   e. the desire for bipartisan cooperation between Democrats and Republicans

7. All of the following factors contributed to American domestic anticommunism *except*
   a. frustration with American lack of progress in the Cold War.
   b. clear proof of large-scale communist infiltration of the federal government.
   c. a desire by Republicans to find an issue with which to discredit Democrats.
   d. President Truman's federal loyalty program.
   e. the persuasive tactics of Senator McCarthy.

8. The decision to create the North Atlantic Treaty Organization (NATO) occurred largely in response to which of the following?
   a. the Greek Civil War
   b. the Korean War
   c. the Berlin Blockade
   d. the Soviet atomic bomb explosion
   e. the formation of the Warsaw Pact

9. Soon after taking office following the death of Franklin Roosevelt, President Truman
   a. sought to continue FDR's policy of accommodation with the Soviet Union.
   b. sought to work through the United Nations to accomplish American foreign policy goals.
   c. sought to retreat to an isolationist policy.
   d. sought to pursue a tougher policy toward Soviet influence in Eastern Europe.
   e. sought to reach an agreement with the Soviet Union based on respect for each nation's sphere of influence.

10. In response to nationalist weakness and communist success during the Chinese Civil War, American policy in Asia gradually shifted toward
    a. putting pressure on Chiang Kai-shek to make reforms to increase his popularity among the Chinese peasantry.
    b. considering options for U.S. military intervention in the conflict.
    c. looking toward Japan as an anticommunist bulwark in Asia and promoting rapid recovery instead of reform as an occupation goal there.
    d. seeking an accommodation with Chinese communist leaders in order to prevent them from forming a close connection with the Soviet Union.
    e. seeking a "Third Force" as an alternative to both the nationalists and the communists.

11. A key factor in Truman's surprise victory in the 1948 election was
    a. his ability to unify the Democratic Party on civil rights.
    b. his strong support from Democratic liberals and intellectuals who saw him as the heir to FDR.
    c. his ability to relate to ordinary voters during his "whistle-stop" campaign.
    d. his decision to downplay his commitment to the Fair Deal.
    e. his success in handling the conversion to a peacetime economy.

12. A key difference between the immediate post-World War I and World War II periods was
    a. the difficulties in converting from a wartime to a peacetime economy.
    b. the spirit of domestic conservatism among much of the American public.
    c. the desire of Congress to assert itself against the president once the war ended.
    d. the attitude of the American people toward membership in an international peacekeeping organization.
    e. the widespread desire to end wartime regulations as quickly as possible.

Free-Response Questions—Exam Tips

In the years following World War II, historians studying the Cold War tended to blame the aggressiveness of the Soviet Union and Stalin's appetite for more territory for the breakdown of the wartime Grand Alliance. Starting in the early 1960s, many "new left" historians looked to American economic expansionism, especially a desire to maintain free trade and open markets, as the major contributor to Cold War tensions. In the 1970s and beyond, "post-revisionist" historians noted that the Cold War was largely the result of misunderstanding between the two nations and that it was impossible to single out one for blame. This cycle of "orthodoxy," "revisionism," and "postrevisionism" can often be applied to historiographical trends with other periods as well.

Free-Response Questions

1. Account for the rise of American anticommunism between 1945 and 1955.

2. Analyze the impact of two of the following on U.S.–Soviet relations between 1941 and 1947:
    Wartime military issues
    Eastern Europe
    Atomic weapons

Document-Based Question—Exam Tips

Scholars have often divided America's leaders into two camps with regard to foreign policy: "realists" (those who believe that foreign policy should be based purely on considerations of national power and promotion of the national interest) and "idealists" (those who argue that American foreign policy should be based on the promotion of larger principles such as democracy and self-determination). Theodore Roosevelt and Woodrow Wilson are often cited as the classic examples of realism and idealism, respectively. Some historians—George Kennan was among the most notable—have argued that American foreign policy during the early Cold War was based too heavily on the idealistic promotion of abstract principles and not enough on rational calculations of the national interests, leading the United States to undertake heavy commitments that unnecessarily drained the nation's resources.

Three essential documents for studying the Cold War are President Truman's speech of March 1947, known as the "Truman Doctrine" speech; the article "Sources of Soviet Conduct," published in the journal Foreign Affairs in July 1947 under the pseudonym "X" who was later revealed to be State Department official George Kennan, and the 1950 document NSC-68, which brought about a major shift in American Cold War strategy.

Document-Based Question

In what ways and to what extent was the American response to Soviet actions during the Cold War justified?

Use the documents and your knowledge of the time period to support your answer.

Document A

Source: Harry S. Truman, Speech, March 12, 1947.

At the present moment in world history nearly every nation must choose between alternative ways of life. The choice is too often not a free one.

One way of life is based upon the will of the majority, and is distinguished by free institutions, representative government, free elections, guarantees of individual liberty, freedom of speech and religion, and freedom from political oppression. The second way of life is based upon the will of a minority forcibly imposed upon the majority. It relies upon terror and oppression, a controlled press and radio, fixed elections, and the suppression of personal freedoms.

I believe that it must be the policy of the United States to support free peoples who are resisted subjugation by armed or outside pressures.

Document B

Source: George Kennan, "The Sources of Soviet Conduct," *Foreign Affairs*, July 1947.

In these circumstances it is clear that the main element of any United States policy toward the Soviet Union must be that of a long-term, patient but firm and vigilant containment of Russian expansive tendencies. It is important to note, however, that such a policy has nothing to do with outward histrionics—with threats or blustering or superfluous gestures of outward "toughness." . . . Like almost any other government, it can be placed by tactless and threatening gestures in a position where it cannot afford to yield even though this might be dictated by its sense of realism . . . .

In the light of the above, it will be clearly seen that the Soviet pressure against the free institutions of the Western world is something that can be contained by the adroit and vigilant application of counterforce at a series of constantly shifting geographical and political points, corresponding to the shifts and maneuvers of Soviet policy, but which cannot be charmed or talked out of existence.

Document C

> *Source:* National Security Council, NSC 68 (1950).
>
> Our position as the center of power in the free world places a heavy responsibility upon the United States for leadership. We must organize and enlist the energies and resources of the free world in a positive program for peace which will frustrate the Kremlin design for world domination by creating a situation in the free world to which the Kremlin will be compelled to adjust. Without such a cooperative effort, led by the United States, we will have to make gradual withdrawals under pressure until we discover one day that we have sacrificed positions of vital interest.
>
> It is imperative that this trend be reversed by a much more rapid and concerted build-up of the actual strength of both the United States and the other nations of the free world. The analysis shows that this will be costly and will involve significant domestic financial and economic adjustments.

Multiple-Choice Answers

1. c. The issue of Poland proved to be a central issue in the emerging Cold War between the United States and the Soviet Union, as Stalin sought a communist-dominated government there, while Churchill and Roosevelt wanted a democratically elected government.

2. c. President Truman made this statement in appealing to Congress for $400 million in aid for Greece and Turkey in March 1947.

3. c. NSC-68, formulated in early 1950, was based on the premise that the United States was locked in a global struggle with the Soviet Union and that it must combat communist expansion wherever it might occur.

4. a. Right-to-work laws, which allowed states to ban union shops in which workers were required to join a union as a condition of being hired, were part of the Taft–Hartley Act, which was passed by the Republican Congress over President Truman's veto in 1947.

5. b. Following Chinese military intervention in November 1950, Truman feared provoking China into a wider war and began to seek a negotiated settlement to the conflict. MacArthur argued that the United States should take stronger military measures against China, even advocating bombing Chinese forces massing near the Korean border.

6. c. The 1946 congressional elections returned significant Republican majorities in both the House and the Senate, as the Republicans relied on the slogan "Had Enough?" This demonstrated a desire among the American public to return to peacetime conditions and not focus on domestic reforms.

7. b. Despite their efforts, groups such as the House Un-American Activities Committee (HUAC) and Senator Joseph McCarthy's later Senate subcommittee never produced evidence of widespread communist infiltration of the federal government.

8. c. The Berlin Blockade of 1948 and 1949 was the most significant Cold War crisis to that point. It confirmed the division of Europe and convinced the United States and its Western European allies of the necessity of creating a military alliance to halt further Soviet advances.

9. d. Although it was unclear what Roosevelt might have done if he had not died in April 1945, Truman sought to pursue a "get tough" policy toward the Soviet Union, in an effort to get Stalin to honor the agreements that had been made at Yalta.

10. c. While American leaders did hope that they could convince Chiang Kai-shek to make necessary reforms, they gradually came to the conclusion that his cause was lost and that a better option for American foreign policy in Asia would be to support Japan as its major anticommunist ally in Asia.

11. c. Truman conducted a vigorous campaign with speaking engagements across the country, in which he blasted the "do-nothing" 80th Congress, a factor that helped him to overcome disunity among the Democratic Party and his earlier unpopularity among voters.

12. d. Although the United States made a smoother domestic transition after World War I than after World War II, many of the same challenges presented themselves. The biggest difference between the two eras was the willingness of both Congress and the American public to support the nation's membership in the United Nations at the end of World War II.

Free-Response Questions Commentary

1. This question provides an opportunity to discuss both discrete events as well as the historiography of the time period. The breakdown of U.S.-Soviet relations in the immediate aftermath of World War II clearly led to a strong distrust of communism and a fear of its influence in the United States, fears that were exacerbated by later events such as the loss of the American atomic monopoly fueling suspicions of espionage, the Chinese communist victory leading to distrust of State Department officials who had offered a realistic appraisal of the post-World War II situation in China, and the Korean War in which the military stalemate convinced some Americans that sabotage must have played a role in the war's course. Historians have offered widely varying explanations for the depth of anticommunist sentiment and the emergence of a second "Red Scare." Some see it as a legitimate movement against a real threat; others see support for Joseph McCarthy as stemming from antipathy toward the eastern elite that was running the country; a third explanation argues that the Republican Party was simply looking for an issue with which to discredit the Democrats following Truman's upset victory in the 1948 election.

2. This question deals with the origins of the Cold War. As mentioned in Chapter 26, it is impossible to understand the origins of the Cold War without reference to World War II. Soviet distrust of the West as a result of the Anglo–American failure to open a second front until 1944 and controversy over Soviet entry into the war against Japan were two of the key issues that arose in the military realm. Eastern Europe demonstrated the clash of Soviet and American views of the postwar world—Roosevelt sought an open world based on the ideals of the Atlantic Charter, while Stalin sought a sphere of influence in the region as a way to protect Soviet security. The American decision to drop atomic bombs on Hiroshima and Nagasaki has been portrayed by some as a measure to intimidate the Soviet Union; whatever Truman's intentions were in 1945, the issue of atomic weapons came to dominate the postwar world. The Soviet Union undertook a crash atomic weapon program that succeeded in ending the American nuclear monopoly by 1949.

Document-Based Question Commentary

Three key issues in understanding American foreign policy in the early Cold War period are the U.S. perception of the motivations behind Soviet foreign policy, the relationship between Soviet intentions and capabilities, and the appropriate American response. Truman and the authors of NSC-68 portray the struggle in ideological terms and view the Soviet Union as seeking world domination. The result is that both advocate responses that call upon the United States to commit resources to many different parts of the world. Truman, in asking for aid to Greece and Turkey, asserts that it is American policy to aid "free peoples" resisting outside domination. The authors of NSC-68 go much further, advocating a massive increase in military spending, as the world context had significantly changed since 1947, notably that the world was much more dangerous to the United States in 1950 than it had been in 1947. Kennan, although known as the architect of containment, placed less emphasis on Soviet ideology and urged American leaders to distinguish between vital and peripheral interests as they sought to stop Soviet expansion.

CHAPTER 28
The Affluent Society

AP THEMES

- **Economic Transformation:** The most notable characteristic of the 1950s was the economic boom fueled by the growing availability of consumer goods. Despite the sometimes conservative rhetoric of the Eisenhower administration, most governmental leaders came to accept the principle that the federal government had a responsibility to promote economic prosperity through its spending and taxation policies. The Cold War helped to fuel federal spending on science, technology, and transportation, all of which had a significant impact on the American economy and society.

- **Culture:** The postwar period witnessed important changes in American culture, especially the growth of the middle class. The wide availability of consumer goods and new media such as television helped to create a society that valued economic prosperity and mass consumption. Popular images of the decade emphasize a widespread sense of conformity. As the decade progressed, however, many intellectuals came to see the society as sterile and unimaginative. Furthermore, a new youth culture emerged, demonstrating an increasing sense of alienation with America's middle-class culture and helping to lay the groundwork for the more widespread protests of the 1960s.

- **Demographic Change:** Postwar prosperity helped to create a new generation of baby boomers, as the end of the Great Depression and World War II made Americans more willing to start families. Inexpensive housing and dissatisfaction with urban life led to the proliferation of suburbs, while the American West grew significantly as a result of government spending and internal migrations. Cities became increasingly populated by African Americans, Latinos, and other minority groups, who faced significant poverty even as the country as a whole prospered.

- **American Diversity:** While middle-class white Americans seemed to dominate the American landscape, African Americans and other groups began a struggle to achieve an equal role in American society. The Supreme Court's 1954 decision to end segregation in America's public schools brought civil rights into the forefront of the national consciousness. African American activists began a long battle against segregation with protests in Montgomery, Alabama, and elsewhere. Civil rights became an issue that Americans found impossible to ignore by the end of the decade.

- **War and Diplomacy:** The Eisenhower administration faced growing challenges outside of Europe, particularly in the Middle East and Southeast Asia. Although Eisenhower sought to limit American defense spending and its foreign commitments, the Cold War had spread to most corners of the globe by the time Eisenhower left office in 1960. The Cold War had unfortunate domestic ramifications, as Senator Joseph McCarthy capitalized on popular fears in an effort to uncover communist influence in the government and other arenas of American life.

CHAPTER SUMMARY
The "Economic Miracle"

Overall, the nation underwent a period of spectacular economic growth between 1945 and 1960. Government spending on schools, the interstate highway system, public welfare, and especially military spending all contributed to the nation's rapid growth. The **baby boom** led to a 20 percent increase in the population during the decade. This enormous population growth in turn increased consumer demand, the growth of **suburbs**, and the housing and automobile industries.

Due largely to government spending, investment in infrastructural projects, and military contracts, the West more than any other region underwent a period of dramatic growth in the postwar period. Increased automobile use and the development of the federal highway system during the 1950s stimulated the oil industry in places such as Texas and Colorado. The creation of irrigation projects that provided adequate water supplies to the area led to a significant migration to the Southwest, as many Americans sought the warm, dry climates there.

Two major ideas dominated the economic thinking of the 1950s and beyond. The first was the belief in **Keynesian economics,** named for the British economist John Maynard Keynes, which argued that the government could use both **fiscal policy** (controlling spending and taxation) and **monetary policy** (controlling the currency supply) to stimulate economic growth without direct intervention in the American economy. The second key idea was a belief that the American economy was capable of producing permanent economic growth. This caused a shift among reformers, who now argued that increased production, rather than redistribution of wealth, could be used to eliminate poverty.

Consolidation marked the development of both the corporate and agricultural sectors in the postwar period. Business leaders made a number of concessions to the now-powerful unions in the automobile, steel, and other large industries, known as the **"postwar contract,"** under which unions accepted significant increases in salary and benefits in exchange for not raising issues such as workplace control and planning of production. A significant turning point for organized labor was the merger of the **AFL and CIO** in 1955, which led to the gradual lessening of tensions between the two organizations. Despite a number of successes, organized labor became stagnant and corrupt in some cases. Unorganized workers in the South and other areas made few gains.

The Explosion of Science and Technology

The postwar period saw a series of major changes in medical science, particularly through the development of antibacterial drugs capable of fighting infection. While researchers made progress in developing vaccines against both bacterial and viral infections in the pre-World War II period, many of these were not widely used until after World War II. In 1954, American scientist **Jonas Salk** produced a vaccine against polio, which was distributed free to the public beginning in 1955, while **Albert Sabin** developed an oral vaccine after 1960. These and other advances led to declines in the infant mortality rates and an increase in average life expectancy. During World War II, scientists discovered the compound known as **DDT,** which was extremely toxic to insects and used to combat insect-borne tropical disease such as malaria and typhus. It only later became clear that it had harmful effects on humans and animals.

Among the advances in the postwar period were the development of commercially viable televisions, transistors capable of amplifying electrical signals much more efficiently than were vacuum tubes, and integrated circuits, which helped to make possible the development of the computer. During the 1950s, computers began to be used in commercial tasks for the first time. CBS News used computers to help predict the results of the 1952 election and raise public consciousness of their utility. By the mid-1950s, **International Business Machines (IBM)** had introduced data processing computers for business purposes.

While many of the period's technological developments were used for civilian purposes, the ongoing Cold War meant a continued emphasis on developing new military technologies. The United States exploded the first **hydrogen bomb** in 1952 and was followed by the Soviet Union a year later. By relying on the power of atomic **fusion** rather than **fission,** as early atomic weapons had, the hydrogen bomb possessed vastly greater destructive power. This sped up efforts by both the Soviets and the United States to develop unmanned missiles and rockets to deliver these weapons. Both the United States and the Soviet Union sought to develop **Intercontinental Ballistic Missiles (ICBMs)** that could reach the other's soil. By the early 1960s, each nation had developed land- and sea-based missiles capable of reaching distant targets.

The Soviet launch of the satellite *Sputnik,* which orbited the earth in October 1957, convinced the American government of the necessity of devoting far greater resources to scientific education and research than it had done previously. The United States launched its own satellite, *Explorer I,* in January 1958. The **National Aeronautics and Space Administration (NASA),** founded the same year, focused on developing a manned space program. The Soviet Union was the first to launch a man into space, although the United States **Apollo Program** succeeded in landing men on the moon by 1969. Later efforts focused on a **"space shuttle,"** which was capable of navigating in space and landing on earth in the manner of a conventional aircraft.

People of Plenty

The growing middle class of the 1950s became obsessed with obtaining new consumer goods, fueled by the growth of advertising and the ease of obtaining consumer credit. National consumer crazes such as the **hula hoop** and the popularity of **Walt Disney-**related products demonstrated the powerful effects of marketing and new patterns of consumption. Another cultural change that resulted from the expansion of the middle class during the 1950s was the virtually unprecedented growth of the suburbs. Americans left cities for a variety of reasons, including a desire for greater privacy and safety, better schools, greater contact with nature, and, in some cases, to escape the impacts of racial and ethnic diversity.

Innovations in homebuilding by developers such as William Levitt, whose developments in Long Island and other places became known as **"Levittowns,"** led to the creation of communities of modestly priced, nearly identical homes affordable to the middle class. While there was a significant degree of diversity among suburban communities, the majority of them consisted of middle- and lower-middle-class white families one step removed from urban living. While popular expectations about child rearing and the role of men in providing for their families created pressure for women to remain at home during the 1950s, economic realities in fact led to an increase in the number of married working women. Feminism ebbed during the early 1950s, but the frustration of increasing work demands, and economic necessity, helped to lay the groundwork for the feminist movement of the 1960s.

A revolution in communications occurred as a result of the expansion of commercial television during the 1950s. This new industry emerged directly from the radio industry, as the three major networks had all started as radio companies. The new medium, like radio, was driven by advertising. While television tended to reinforce traditional gender and racial roles, either by its portrayal of the two-parent nuclear family or by portraying minorities in ways that were not threatening to whites, it also inadvertently helped to increase the potential for social discord by making Americans more aware of the conditions in which they lived and showing vivid images of social upheavals such as the early civil rights movement.

The growth of travel and consumer recreation, fueled by the increasingly common practice of the paid vacation, increased Americans' interest in having access to the wilderness and preserved natural areas. Particularly significant was the fight over **Echo Park** located near the borders of Utah, Colorado, and Wyoming, where the government sought to build a dam to create a source of hydroelectric power. A number of prominent American intellectuals, writers, and environmental activists led a successful fight to maintain Echo Park in its natural state. This in turn helped to create more widespread environmental consciousness.

Middle-class culture was not without its critics. As white-collar workers increased and corporate, labor, and other bureaucracies grew significantly during the 1950s, large numbers of Americans began to grow concerned about the impact of these developments on the nation's culture and society. Education became increasingly focused on preparing individuals for successful careers. Writers such as **William Whyte** in *The Organization Man* and **David Reisman** in *The Lonely Crowd* focused on the decline of individualism and the growing conformity within American society. Among the most vocal critics of American middle-class conformity were a group of young writers and artists known as **"beats"** or **"beatniks."** In works such as **Allen Ginsberg's "Howl"** and **Jack Kerouac's *On the Road* (1957),** they signaled a widespread alienation and restlessness among American youth, much of which resulted from that nation's prosperity. Societal expectations stressed unlimited possibilities, yet placed great restrictions on what young people could in fact do. Greater attention was paid to "juvenile delinquency" in films such as *The Blackboard Jungle*, while the popularity of icons such as the rebellious **James Dean** caused fear and concern among older Americans.

[handwritten margin note: elvis played music in this]

A new style of popular music known as **rock 'n' roll** helped to give voice to the growing needs and aspirations of American youth. Musicians such as **Elvis Presley,** drawing from an eclectic set of influences—especially the African American genres of rhythm and blues and gospel music—greatly appealed to the young during the decade and helped to define the generation. Popular television programs such as *American Bandstand* and radio **disc jockeys** further fueled this phenomenon.

The "Other America"

As in other prosperous periods in American history, there were significant numbers of people who did not share in the nation's overall prosperity. In 1962, socialist **Michael Harrington** published a book entitled *The Other America,* in which he chronicled the existence of a significant group of Americans who lived in a condition of permanent poverty. Harrington's book led to a questioning of the assumption that economic growth could be used as a tool to put an end to poverty in the United States. One group that had suffered significantly since the late nineteenth century, with the exception of a few periods of prosperity, was farmers. Due largely to agricultural surpluses creating falling farm prices, those involved in agriculture suffered significant declines in their percentage of the national income in the late 1940s and 1950s. Sharecroppers and tenant farmers in the South and coal-mining population of the Appalachians were particularly affected by structural changes in the economy.

Cities also experienced growing poverty. Between 1940 and 1960, large numbers of African Americans and Latinos moved into urban areas. These urban minorities faced great poverty, for a variety of reasons. Some have argued that these new migrants suffered as a result of their own work habits and values, while others have argued that the existence of a "culture of poverty" in the inner cities—a result of crime, poor schools, and institutionalized racism—relegated these groups to this condition. The major public policy response to decaying urban conditions was the policy of **"urban renewal,"** which generally meant destroying buildings in the poorest areas and replacing them, in some cases, with public housing projects, and in others, office buildings, stadiums, or middle-class high-rise housing.

The Rise of the Civil Rights Movement

World War II and its aftermath moved the issue of segregation closer to the forefront of the national consciousness. Professional baseball was desegregated in 1947 when **Jackie Robinson** began to play for the Brooklyn Dodgers. President Truman had desegregated the armed forces by executive order in the 1950s. Racial issues became a central struggle of the 1950s. In May 1954, the Supreme Court issued the landmark ruling in *Brown v. Board of Education of Topeka,* which declared that segregated schools were "inherently unequal." The following year, the court's **"Brown II"** decision ordered that desegregation occur with "all deliberate speed." While some areas desegregated quickly, many southerners reacted with the doctrine of **"massive resistance,"** working through their local governments and organizations such as the **White Citizens' Councils** to obstruct desegregation. In October 1957, Eisenhower, who had been unenthusiastic about the *Brown* decision, sent federal troops to **Little Rock,** Arkansas, to protect black students and enforce the Supreme Court order, in the face of opposition from **Governor Orville Faubus** and segments of the Arkansas public.

Following the *Brown* decision, a series of greater challenges to discrimination emerged in the South, most notably in **Montgomery,** Alabama. A black seamstress named **Rosa Parks** refused to give up her seat to a white passenger as required by local law. Her arrest sparked a yearlong boycott, which caused bus companies to end their discriminatory seating policies. In 1956 the Supreme Court outlawed segregation in public transportation. The larger significance of the Montgomery boycott was the fact that it exposed **Martin Luther King Jr.** to the national spotlight and that it raised awareness of King's nonviolent approach to oppression, based on the teachings of Mahatma Gandhi and Henry David Thoreau. Congress passed a weak **Civil Rights Bill** in 1957, the first since Reconstruction, which gave federal protection to African Americans seeking to register to vote.

A number of different factors contributed to the rise of the civil rights movement. These included the experience of World War II, which gave both war veterans and factory workers a broader view of the world and higher expectations. The rise of an urban black middle class, along with the greater visibility of racial injustice that was revealed to many unsuspecting Americans by television, further contributed to the growing civil rights movement. In addition, white Americans became more sensitive to black aspirations, partly due to the pressures of the Cold War, in which racial discrimination damaged America's image abroad, as well as the growing influence of blacks within the Democratic Party.

Eisenhower Republicanism

In domestic affairs, Eisenhower was a moderate who favored a relatively limited role for the federal government, although he made no attempts to roll back the welfare state gains of the New Deal. He appointed wealthy corporate executives to his cabinet, although most of these supported the major ideas of the Keynesian state, which they believed could help to promote prosperity and social order. Eisenhower, rather than dismantling the New Deal, in fact extended the Social Security system to an additional 10 million people and increased the federal minimum wage. His administration's most far-reaching domestic accomplishment was the **Federal Highway Act** of 1956, the largest public works program in American history. Eisenhower easily defeated Stevenson again in 1956, although the Democrats retained control of both houses of Congress and extended these margins in the elections of 1958.

Although the Eisenhower administration initially did little to discourage anticommunist sentiment in the United States, by 1954 popular support for Senator McCarthy and his tactics had begun to decline. McCarthy's downfall came when he began to investigate the armed services, at which point Congress created a special committee to investigate the charges. The televised investigation became known as the **Army–McCarthy hearings.** McCarthy was exposed as a bully and a thug, and the Senate voted in December 1954 to censure him for inappropriate behavior.

Eisenhower, Dulles, and the Cold War

Eisenhower and his secretary of state, **John Foster Dulles,** came into office denouncing what they perceived as the passivity of the Truman administration's foreign policy and instituting the policy of **"rollback"** against communist expansion, although Dulles was forced to moderate his policies considerably upon taking office. Dulles's most significant innovation was his policy of **"massive retaliation,"** which held that the United States would use its nuclear deterrent ability, rather than conventional forces, to stop communist expansion. Such a policy would help the budget-conscious Republican administration to achieve "more bang for the buck" in its foreign and defense policies.

The Eisenhower administration had been able to achieve a quick settlement of the crisis in Korea, but events in Southeast Asia began to lay the groundwork for a long, bitter struggle in Vietnam. Following the final defeat of French forces at **Dienbienphu** in May 1954, Vietnam was temporarily divided at the 17th parallel in anticipation of national elections in 1956. The Eisenhower administration strongly supported the noncommunist government of **Ngo Dinh Diem** in the south against the procommunist northern government under **Ho Chi Minh** and accepted Diem's decision not to participate in the 1956 elections once it was clear that Ho would easily prevail in a nationwide vote.

While the Eisenhower administration largely followed the containment doctrine as it had inherited it in its broad outlines, much of the decade's focus came to rest in the nonwestern world. In the Middle East, the Eisenhower administration used the CIA to help support the overthrow of a left-wing prime minister in Iran who had threatened the position of American corporations. In Egypt, the United States sought to punish **Gamal Abdel Nasser** for his leanings toward the Soviet Union by withdrawing funds for a massive dam project, although it opposed an effort by Israel, Britain, and France to retain western control of the **Suez Canal** in 1956. In Latin America, the administration supported the overthrow of a left-wing government in **Guatemala** at the urging of American business interests. In Cuba, the pro-American dictator **Fulgencio Batista** was overthrown by **Fidel Castro** in 1959. The United States cut diplomatic ties with Castro once he began to expropriate foreign businesses. Castro responded to his isolation by drawing closer to the Soviet Union.

Although direct confrontations between the United States and Soviet Union seemed to have lessened by the mid-1950s, the Soviet crushing of an uprising in **Hungary** in 1956 convinced many Americans that there was little change in Soviet policy. New Soviet premier **Nikita Khrushchev** demanded in 1958 that the NATO powers give up their position in Berlin, which they refused. Khrushchev and Eisenhower made plans for a summit in Paris in 1960, although this failed when an American **U-2 spy plane** was shot down over the Soviet Union and its pilot was captured shortly before the summit was scheduled to begin.

As Eisenhower left office, Cold War tensions were perhaps greater than they had been when he took office. However, he had managed to stem calls for greater foreign activism and a buildup of the military establishment. In his farewell address, Eisenhower warned of the dangers of the so-called **"military–industrial complex,"** which he believed had obtained too great an influence over American government and politics.

Multiple-Choice Questions

1. Which of the following is a central principle of Keynesian economics?
   a. The government should intervene in the economy as little as possible.
   b. The government should heavily regulate businesses to help ensure a more equal distribution of wealth.
   c. The government should use fiscal and monetary policy to stimulate the economy without intervening directly in the private sector.
   d. Government should cooperate closely with business leaders in developing plans to promote economic prosperity.
   e. The government should rely on balancing the budget to promote economic prosperity.

2. The publication of Michael Harrington's *The Other America* raised public awareness of
   a. the continuing discrimination against African Americans.
   b. the plight of Native Americans.
   c. the widespread dissatisfaction among American women.
   d. the disillusionment and alienation of many American youth.
   e. the existence of significant levels of poverty in the United States.

3. The biggest difference between the economic prosperity of the 1920s and 1950s was
   a. the significant role of automobile and transportation developments in each decade.
   b. the degree of government spending in each decade.
   c. the equality of distribution of wealth in each decade.
   d. the degree of corporate consolidation in each decade.
   e. the role of new communication technologies.

4. The Eisenhower administration faced Cold War crises in all of the following areas *except*
   a. Cuba.
   b. Egypt.
   c. the Dominican Republic.
   d. Guatemala.
   e. Iran.

5. The Eisenhower administration responded to French calls for aid during the siege of Dien Bien Phu in the spring of 1954 by
   a. bombing Vietminh positions in an effort to relieve the French garrison.
   b. calling on Congress to pass a resolution giving the president authority to introduce ground troops to assist the French.
   c. refusing to intervene on the basis of the inability to reach an agreement with Great Britain on the terms of Anglo–American involvement.
   d. threatening to use nuclear weapons in an effort to utilize the policy of brinkmanship.
   e. calling upon the United Nations to send a "police force" into the area in an effort to prevent further communist aggression.

6. President Eisenhower's main reason for sending federal troops to Little Rock, Arkansas, to enforce a federal court school desegregation order was
   a. his belief that federal power should be used to promote black equality.
   b. his personal sympathy for the African American cause.
   c. his desire to support Earl Warren, whom he had appointed chief justice of the Supreme Court.
   d. his belief that he had a constitutional duty to uphold federal authority in the face of state resistance.
   e. his desire to improve America's image abroad during the Cold War.

7. The Hetch Hetchy and Echo Park controversies were similar in that both
   a. had outcomes favorable to environmentalists.
   b. helped to galvanize groups committed to preserving the environment.
   c. showed that most Americans cared little about environmental preservation.
   d. demonstrated the unwillingness of Congress to address the concerns of environmentalists.
   e. represented victories for those who believed that development of the nation's resources was more important than preservation.

8. Senator Joseph McCarthy declined in popularity after 1954 due primarily to
   a. the vigorous public effort by President Eisenhower to discredit him.
   b. public disclosure of the fact that he had done little to expose actual communist infiltration of the United States government.
   c. the public perception that the Cold War threat was waning.
   d. public disgust at his tactics during televised Army–McCarthy hearings.
   e. public sympathy for the groups and individuals who had been targeted during the anticommunist efforts since the late 1940s.

9. All of the following works offered critiques of 1950s conformity *except*
   a. William H. Whyte—*The Organization Man.*
   b. David Reisman—*The Lonely Crowd.*
   c. Gunnar Myrdal—*An American Dilemma.*
   d. Saul Bellow—*Herzog*
   e. J. D. Salinger—*The Catcher in the Rye.*

10. "We conclude that in the field of public education the doctrine of 'separate but equal' has no place. Separate educational facilities are inherently unequal."
Which of the following are true regarding this quotation?
  I. It overturned the Supreme Court's 1896 ruling in *Plessy* v. *Ferguson*.
  II. It aroused little popular opposition.
  III. It required a separate court ruling to provide rules for its implementation.
  IV. It was enthusiastically supported by President Eisenhower.
  V. It reflected the unanimous decision of the Supreme Court.
  a. I, II, III
  b. I, II, IV
  c. I, III, IV
  d. I, III, V
  e. I, IV, V

11. An immediate impact of the Montgomery bus boycotts was to
  a. raise Martin Luther King Jr. to national prominence and make nonviolent protest a central part of the new stage of the civil rights movement.
  b. force the nation's leaders to consider legislation ending segregation in public facilities.
  c. bring about a heated debate between advocates of nonviolence and those who promoted using violence to achieve equality.
  d. spark a series of violent racial confrontations in other cities throughout the country.
  e. motivate civil rights activists to begin a campaign to register African Americans to vote throughout the South.

12. In domestic affairs, President Eisenhower is best characterized as
  a. a conservative who sought to roll back many of the gains of the New Deal period and severely limit the federal government's role in American life.
  b. a moderate who introduced few new initiatives and preferred private enterprise to extensive federal activities.
  c. a liberal who supported the extensive use of Keynesian measures to promote economic development.
  d. a reformer who sought to use the power of the federal government to promote equality.
  e. a radical who proposed to revolutionize the relationship between the federal government and the American people.

Free-Response Questions—Exam Tip

The ability to analyze presidential leadership is crucial to understanding many different periods in American history, and the 1950s are no exception. President Eisenhower, like the decade during which he served as president, was long considered a passive president who was more interested in playing golf than in running the country. More recent historians, however, have emphasized his behind-the-scenes leadership and argue that his apparent lack of activity reflected more of a philosophical belief that the nation needed stable, calm leadership—especially during a time of global crisis—and a restrained use of federal power after two decades of Democratic activism, rather than laziness.

Free-Response Questions

1. Analyze the growth of the African American civil rights movement between 1945 and 1961.

2. To what degree did the Cold War policies of Dwight D. Eisenhower and John Foster Dulles represent a departure from those of the Truman administration?

Document-Based Question—Exam Tip

An important skill for the AP Exam is to be able to differentiate between popular perceptions of a particular period and the more nuanced view that frequently emerges as scholarship develops. Both the 1920s and the 1950s, for example, are often considered decades of prosperity, cultural conformity, and conservatism in the popular imagination. Below the surface, however, significant sources of protest existed in each decade. Many of the protest movements that emerged full-blown during the 1960s had significant roots during the 1950s

Document-Based Question

To what degree do the terms "consensus" and "conformity" characterize the period from 1945 to 1961?

Use the documents that follow and your knowledge of the period to construct your essay.

Document A

Source: Brigadier General Frank T. Hines, Speech, November 1944.

One of the finest and most unselfish things which the Legion has ever done, in my judgment, was to conceive, formulate, and take a leading part in the enactment of the GI Bill of Rights. . . .

Because of the great interest the Legion has taken in community affairs and the work you have already done in mapping future benefits for veterans of World War II, your members will be in a position to take a leading part in bringing to the United States a stronger and better disciplined citizenship. In other words, Legionnaires will be in a position to influence for good the construction of strong communities, truly American homes, and to fight for the ideals which your forefathers intended should be the basis of our government and of the welfare of our country.

Document B

Source: J. Edgar Hoover, Speech, March 1947.

I feel that once public opinion is thoroughly aroused as it is today, the fight against communism is well on its way. Victory will be assured once Communists are identified and exposed, because the public will take the first step of quarantining them so they can do no harm. Communism, in reality, is not a political party. It is a way of life—an evil and malignant way of life. It reveals a condition akin to disease that spreads like an epidemic, and, like an epidemic, a quarantine is necessary to keep it from infecting the nation.

Document C

TV happiness shared by all the family!

The Fifties Family

Document D

Source: Russell Davenport, et al, *U.S.A.: The Permanent Revolution*, 1951.

What counts is that the concept that the owner has a right to use his property just the way he pleases has evolved into the belief that ownership carries social obligations, and that a manager is a trustee not only for the owner but for society as a whole. Such is the Transformation of American Capitalism. In all the world there is no more hopeful economic phenomenon.

Document E

Source: *Fortune*, "The Changing American Market," 1955.

The middle-class Suburbia, rapidly growing larger and more affluent, is developing a way of life that seems eventually bound to become dominant in America. It has been a major force in the phenomenal rise in the nation's birth rate. . . . It has centered its customs and conventions on the needs of children and geared its buying habits to them. It has made the 'ranch house' nationally popular.

Document F

Source: Resolution of the State of South Carolina, Feb. 14, 1956.

. . . The right of each of the States to maintain at its own expense racially separate public schools for the children of its citizens and other racially separate public facilities is not forbidden or limited by the language or the intent of the Fourteenth Amendment. . . . Be it enacted by the General Assembly of the State of South Carolina. . . . That the States have never delegated to the central government the power to change the Constitution nor have they surrendered to the central government the power to prohibit to the States the right to maintain racially separate but equal public facilities.

Document G

Source: Levittown Public Library / Associated Press.

Levittown

Document H

Source: Allen Ginsberg, "Howl," 1956.

I saw the best minds of my generation destroyed by madness, starving hysterical naked, dragging themselves through the negro streets at dawn looking for an angry fix, angelheaded hipsters burning for the ancient heavenly connection to the starry dynamo in the machinery of night, who poverty and tatters and hollow-eyed and high sat up smoking in the supernatural darkness of cold-water flats floating across the tops of cities contemplating jazz. . . .

Document I

Source: Harvey Swados, "The Myth of the Happy Worker," *Nation*, August 17, 1957.

The working-class family today is not typically held together by the male wage earner, but by multiple wage earners, often of several generations, who club together to get the things they want and need—or are pressured into believing they must have. It is at best a precarious arrangement; as for its toll on the physical organism and the psyche, that is question perhaps worthy of further investigation by those who currently pronounce themselves bored with Utopia Unlimited in the Fat Fifties.

Document J

Source: Newton Minnow, Speech, 1961.

I invite you to sit down in front of your television set when your station goes on the air and stay there without a book, magazine, newspaper, profit and loss sheet or rating book to distract you— and keep your eyes glued to that set until the station signs off. I can assure you that you will observe a vast wasteland.

You will see a procession of game shows, violence, audience participation shows, formula comedies about totally unbelievable families, blood and thunder, mayhem, violence, sadism, murder, western badmen, western good men, private eyes, gangsters, more violence, and cartoons. And, endlessly, commercials—many screaming, cajoling, and offending. And most of all, boredom.

Multiple-Choice Answers

1. c. Keynesian economics, named for the British economist John Maynard Keynes and first used in the United States during the New Deal, argued that macroeconomic tools such as federal spending could be used to stimulate economic growth. During the 1930s his biggest contribution was the argument that federal deficit spending was sometimes necessary to restore prosperity in times of economic downturn.

2. e. Harrington, a socialist, published *The Other America* in 1962. The book brought home to many Americans the existence of large pockets of poverty, in both rural and urban areas, which continued to exist even during times of overall prosperity.

3. b. A number of similarities emerge when one examines the economic prosperity of the 1920s and the 1950s. A key difference, however, was that the federal government maintained higher levels of spending in the 1950s, based largely on greater outlays for defense and programs such as Social Security, which had not existed in the 1920s.

4. c. The Eisenhower administration faced significant crises in each of the areas listed except for the Dominican Republic. President Lyndon Johnson sent American troops there in 1965 after the election of a left-wing government that was seen as a threat to stability in the region.

5. c. The Eisenhower administration did not want to become directly involved in helping the French war effort, which was clearly doomed to fail. Eisenhower proposed a program of "United Action" with Great Britain, a proposal that many historians suspect was meant to fail and thus provide the United States with a rationale for nonintervention.

6. d. Eisenhower had little personal sympathy for the African American civil rights cause and had a relatively limited conception of the role of the federal government; his main reason for ordering troops to Little Rock was his belief that the states did not have the right to defy federal authority and that he had a duty to uphold the Constitution.

7. b. Although the outcomes were different (those who sought to stop the building of a dam in the Hetch Hetchy Valley were defeated, while those who sought to stop the development of Echo Park were successful), both helped to bring together various groups committed to environmental preservation.

8. d. The Army–McCarthy hearings proved to be McCarthy's undoing. While a group of senators began to prepare for censure proceedings against him, the effort to stem his power was facilitated by growing public concern about his tactics as the American public had more opportunity to see him on television. Broadcaster Edward R. Murrow further criticized McCarthy on the program "See It Now," something other journalists had hesitated to do previously.

9. c. Gunnar Myrdal, a Swedish sociologist, had published *An American Dilemma* in 1944, noting the deep-rooted nature of American racial problems. All of the other works dealt with the difficulty of the individual in finding a role in an increasingly conformist society.

10. d. The court's decision received widespread opposition most immediately in the South, although it was also very difficult to enforce in northern cities and provoked significant opposition there when the Supreme Court resorted to busing students from different districts to achieve racial balance. Eisenhower believed that the court's decision had a very negative effect on race relations.

11. a. Although all of the other choices eventually occurred, they were more prominent in the following decade. The success of the Montgomery boycott made King a household name throughout the country.

12. b. Eisenhower's "Modern Republicanism" accepted many of the basic principles of the New Deal, at least tacitly, although Eisenhower took few major domestic initiatives during his two terms in office (with the exception of the Federal Highway Act of 1956).

Free-Response Questions Commentary

1. The civil rights movement was an issue that was in the forefront of the national consciousness by the end of the Eisenhower administration, setting the stage for the momentous struggles and accomplishment of the 1960s. Various factors account for the movement's growth in the decade and a half after 1945. Key factors include the impact of World War II and President Truman's leadership. The president ordered the desegregation of the armed forces in 1948. There was also fragmentation within the Democratic Party that forced white liberals to take sides (note the formation of the Dixiecrat Party as a result of the effort to include a civil rights plank in the 1948 Democratic platform). The role of the Supreme Court in promoting school desegregation polarized white opposition in the South where the doctrine of "massive resistance" and groups such as the White Citizens' Councils emerged following Brown. There was also the desire by American leaders to improve America's image as a result of the Cold War. Most important, however, were the growing efforts of African Americans themselves, beginning with the Montgomery bus boycott and growing with the sit-in movement, the "freedom rides," the emergence of organizations such as the SCLC and the SNCC, and the growth of older organizations such as CORE.

2. The Eisenhower administration, despite Republican rhetoric during the 1952 presidential campaign, found that it had to adhere to many of the policies adopted by the Truman administration. The threat of nuclear weapons, meant to be a less costly deterrent to Soviet actions than conventional forces, proved to be increasingly difficult to use as the Soviet Union approached nuclear parity; at the same time, the Republican calls for the "liberation" of Eastern Europe were equally unworkable in light of the overwhelming Soviet preponderance of power in the region as seen by the meek American response to the Soviet invasion of Hungary in 1956. Eisenhower, responding to changing conditions in the 1950s (especially the increasingly global scope of the Cold War as the Third World gained greater importance), relied more upon covert operations (Iran and Guatemala, for example) and building alliances (SEATO, CENTO), than had his predecessor. Overall, despite that fact that Republican policies never lived up to their early rhetoric, Eisenhower arguably succeeded in leading the United States through a dangerous period without unduly inflaming the fears of the American people although his paltry efforts to put an end to the excesses of McCarthyism and control defense spending are disappointing aspects of his record. He managed to avoid the types of open-ended commitments that his Democratic successors made in Vietnam during the following decade.

Document-Based Question Commentary

Background: While the idea of cultural conformity is well-known with regard to the 1950s, the term "consensus" is an important concept as well. The decade's economic prosperity, growth of middle-class culture, and apparently widespread acceptance of a set of fundamental principles—including government responsibility for economic prosperity; the belief that government, business, and organized labor could work together to promote economic growth that would benefit the nation as a whole; and the belief that communism and other ideological systems that questioned the fundamental premises of American society had no place in the national debate—caused many to believe that the nation's experience was marked much more by agreement and harmony than by conflict. David Potter and Richard

Hofstadter were two prominent historians who produced interpretations of American history based on the "consensus" idea during the 1950s.

The documents can be divided fairly easily into two groups: those that promote and support the consensus and conformity interpretation and those that question it. Documents A through E, as well as G, represent themes that would support the idea that conformity marked the period.

The Documents: In Document A, an American military official notes that the returning veterans from World War II can play an important role in promoting traditional American values, especially as they are able to enter colleges and universities as a result of the GI Bill. In Document B, FBI Director J. Edgar Hoover calls upon the American public to root out communist sympathizers who threaten the nation's values and institutions, helping to signal the beginning of a period of strong anticommunist sentiment among much of the American public.

Documents C, D, E, and G deal with the relationships among economic prosperity, consumer culture, and social harmony. Document C shows the nuclear family sitting in front of the television and sharing enjoyment of this new medium. Document G shows a typical "Levittown," an example of how the availability of affordable housing made the development of suburbs a key pattern of American development in the postwar period. Documents D and E note how a "revolution" in American business has made a future of abundance possible for a wide variety of Americans. In Document D, Russell Davenport notes the emergence of a new ethic of social responsibility among American business leaders, while the editors of *Fortune* celebrate the growth of middle-class suburban culture, which they see as being made possible by the ever-growing American productive capacity.

The later documents show, however, that this idyllic view of the 1950s covered over many fissures in American society. In Document F, the South Carolina legislature pledges "massive resistance" to the Supreme Court's *Brown* decision, an example of the surfacing racial tensions that marked the late 1950s and especially the 1960s. Allen Ginsberg's "Howl," published in 1956 and excerpted in Document H, became an anthem of the "beat generation," which questioned many of the dominant cultural values of the 1950s. In Document I, Harvey Swados questions the belief in the "happy worker," arguing that pursuit of the middle-class dream causes more harm than good, forcing families to go into debt to acquire consumer goods in order to keep up with their neighbors. Finally, in Document J, FCC Chairman Newton Minnow notes the negative influence of television on American culture, as the medium represents a "vast wasteland" that leads to a deep sense of boredom and emptiness.

Summation: Most periods in American history defy easy categorization, and the period after World War II is no exception. Economic prosperity and a belief in the values of consumerism, abundance, and loyalty to the "American way of life" clearly represented the experience of a substantial number of people, (mainly those who were white and had the economic resources to take part in that period's version of the "American Dream"). Minorities had little access to middle-class prosperity or culture, and many who did take part in middle-class life struggled mightily to meet the demands of maintaining such an existence. Many of the fissures that lay just below the surface of American life during the 1950s emerged full-blown during the following decade.

CHAPTER 29
Civil Rights, Vietnam, and the Ordeal of Liberalism

AP THEMES

- **Politics and Citizenship:** Following the 1950s, Presidents John F. Kennedy and Lyndon Johnson committed themselves to a strong, active presidency in both foreign and domestic policy. African Americans took unprecedented steps to combat racial discrimination, resulting in federal legislation to eliminate segregation and preserve voting rights. Despite these victories, however, many civil rights advocates remained disillusioned with the slow pace of change, as economic discrimination, urban poverty, and a host of other social problems led to significant outbreaks of violence in many urban centers throughout the country.

- **Reform:** Lyndon Johnson undertook the most ambitious reform program since the New Deal, as his Great Society program sought to increase medical coverage for the poor and elderly, eradicate poverty, and improve housing and other social services in urban areas. While these efforts created a host of new entitlement programs and expanded the federal welfare state in a way that benefited many of the nation's poorest citizens, many of these programs also drew criticism from conservatives who objected to the expanded role of the federal government and the costs involved. Johnson was ultimately unable to balance his high domestic hopes with the need to maintain the American commitment to South Vietnam.

- **War and Diplomacy:** The Cold War remained dangerous throughout much of the 1960s. John F. Kennedy, perceived by Soviet leaders as young and untested, faced a number of confrontations in his early years in office, the most serious of which was a showdown over the Soviet decision to place missiles in Cuba. Kennedy, reflecting the era's liberal activism and belief in the limitlessness of American resources, also vastly increased the commitment of American advisors to the defense of South Vietnam. Lyndon Johnson inherited and expanded this commitment further, leading to a disastrous war that ultimately caused many to question the fundamental premises of the containment policy that had caused the United States to enter the conflict.

CHAPTER SUMMARY
Expanding the Liberal State

Both presidential candidates in 1960, Democrat **John F. Kennedy** and Republican **Richard Nixon,** promised to offer the nation bold, active leadership as an antidote to the perceived passivity of the Eisenhower administration. Despite his youth and concerns about his Catholicism, Kennedy was able to win a narrow victory. Kennedy's ambitious domestic program was dubbed the **New Frontier,** although a combination of conservative Democrats and Republicans frustrated many of his efforts. Kennedy's charm and charisma helped him to maintain popular support, and the nation grieved when he was assassinated on November 22, 1963, by **Lee Harvey Oswald.** Although a federal commission found that Oswald had acted alone, many believe that the action was part of a larger conspiracy.

Lyndon B. Johnson could not have been more unlike Kennedy. Johnson came from a background of rural poverty in Texas but rose to become Senate majority leader during the 1950s, largely as a result of his mastery of the legislative process. Despite his rough personality, he shared Kennedy's commitment to activist government, creating a wide-ranging reform program known as the **Great Society.** In the 1964 presidential election, Johnson won the largest popular majority in American history against Republican **Barry Goldwater,** a conservative Arizona senator.

For the first time since the New Deal, the federal government under Johnson took significant steps to extend the welfare state. Central to this effort was **Medicare,** which provided federal funds to the elderly for health care, and **Medicaid,** which did the same for the poor. Johnson also launched a **"war on poverty,"** under the **Office of Economic Opportunity (OEO).** The "war on poverty" was a large-scale but controversial program that sought to involve members of the poor communities in planning programs under the banner of **community action.** The antipoverty program fell short due to lack of funding and increasing American involvement in the Vietnam War.

The federal government also sought to address the critical conditions of cities and especially urban schools with a series of aid programs. Johnson created the **Department of Housing and Urban Development (HUD)** in 1966, along with the **Model Cities Program,** which gave federal funds for urban redevelopment pilot programs. Johnson also overcame traditional fears from both Catholic and non-Catholic groups about federal aid to education, gaining passage of the **Elementary and Secondary Education Act of 1965,** which provided aid to schools on the basis of students' economic needs, not the schools themselves. Another significant piece of legislation was the **Immigration Act of 1965,** which eliminated the "national origin" system that had existed since the 1920s and allowed immigration from all parts of Europe, Africa, and Asia, helping to greatly increase the diversity of the American population.

Growing budget deficits caused by increased federal spending on social programs as well as the war in Vietnam, coupled with the failure of certain programs, caused many Americans to become disillusioned with the Great Society's efforts to use federal power to alleviate social problems. At the same time, however, the Great Society succeeded in reducing hunger and bringing about the greatest decline in poverty in American history.

The Battle for Racial Equality

Kennedy had been very much a moderate on civil rights issues, seeking to build on existing laws and using the courts to overturn segregation, without alienating large segments of the public and influential southern Democrats in Congress. However, as African Americans undertook greater and more direct efforts to combat segregation, the federal government had little choice but to act more vigorously.

Starting in 1960 with efforts by African American college students in Greensboro, North Carolina, to desegregate a lunch counter at a Woolworth's, a rapid series of events led to a much greater need for federal action. Some of the student sit-in veterans and others formed the **Student Nonviolent Coordination Committee (SNCC)** to further the battle against segregation. The **Congress of Racial Equality (CORE),** which had formed during World War II, started a series of so-called **"freedom rides"** in an effort to force desegregation of bus stations, while the **Southern Christian Leadership Conference (SCLC)** undertook grass-roots efforts to mobilize black workers, housewives, farmers, and other groups to combat discrimination.

At the same time, the federal courts continued their efforts to enforce the desegregation of public education, with **James Meredith** enrolling in the University of Mississippi in October 1962. In 1963, Martin Luther King Jr. helped lead a series of demonstrations to desegregate Birmingham, Alabama, in the face of massive and violent opposition from police Commissioner **Eugene "Bull" Connor** and Governor **George Wallace.**

The growing confrontations in Alabama and Mississippi convinced Kennedy that greater presidential action was necessary, and he responded in the summer of 1963 with a speech that called civil rights a "moral issue" and soon after proposed a bill outlawing segregation in public accommodations. In August, approximately 200,000 demonstrators took part in a march on Washington, where King delivered his revered **"I have a dream"** speech in support of Kennedy's bill. The president's assassination in November 1963, along with strong pressure from Johnson after taking office, allowed for passage of the milestone **Civil Rights Act of 1964.**

The civil rights movement then shifted its focus from desegregation to voting rights, with thousands of black and white activists taking part in the **"freedom summer,"** seeking to register black voters in Mississippi and other parts of the South. Three of the early workers, two black and one white, were murdered by Ku Klux Klan members in Mississippi. The freedom summer led to the creation of the **Mississippi Freedom Democratic Party (MFDP),** an integrated challenger to the regular state Democratic Party. The MFDP won the right to sit as observers at the 1964 Democratic National Convention. In March 1965, Martin Luther King Jr. led a large voting rights demonstration at **Selma, Alabama,** with harsh and violent opposition from Sheriff **Jim Clark** and local authorities. Television cameras captured the violence and helped to spur popular support for the **Voting Rights Act** of 1965, which offered federal protection to blacks seeking to register to vote.

By the mid-1960s, the focus of the struggle against discrimination began to shift from the South to northern cities, where blacks faced discrimination in jobs and housing. In many cases, the battles moved from combating de jure segregation (the result of laws) to de facto segregation (the result of popular practices) in northern industrial cities. Many activists began to argue that not only should employers abandon discriminatory practices but they should also adopt measures to right past injustices (Johnson tentatively supported the idea of **"affirmative action"** in the fall of 1965). King led a campaign against housing and job discrimination in Chicago in 1966 that received a lukewarm public response.

Starting in the summer of 1964 but escalating rapidly with a race riot in the **Watts** section of Los Angeles in the summer of 1965, a series of major racial disturbances occurred throughout many of America's major cities—there were more than fifty race riots in the summers of 1966 and 1967. Johnson appointed a special **Commission on Civil Disorders** (known as the **Kerner Commission**), which called for national action to combat discrimination and address black poverty and other social problems (although much of the American public believed that urban disorder called for stronger action against lawbreaking).

Disillusionment with the idea of peaceful progress in cooperation with whites caused growing numbers of blacks to embrace the philosophy of **"black power,"** in which African Americans found ways to emphasize their own cultural traditions and instill a sense of pride in themselves. Politically, black power meant eschewing cooperation with organizations such as the NAACP and the SCLC that worked in tandem with sympathetic whites. In

Oakland, California, the **Black Panther Party** threatened to use violence if necessary to achieve its goals, although party members were more frequently victims of police violence, rather than its perpetrators.

As the black power movement grew, a nationalist group known as the **Nation of Islam,** which called on its members to live by strict codes of conduct and discipline and reject dependence on whites, gained greater prominence. The most famous member, **Malcolm X,** who had changed his name from Malcolm Little, using the X to symbolize his lost African surname, advocated black self-defense, violent if necessary, against all forms of oppression and discrimination. Even after his murder in 1965, Malcolm X remained one of the most influential symbols of the civil rights struggle.

"Flexible Response" and the Cold War

Kennedy came into office critical of the Eisenhower administration's emphasis on nuclear weapons and sought in particular to increase America's ability to compete with the Soviet Union in the "emerging areas" of the so-called Third World. Kennedy supported the creation of special forces, popularly known as **"Green Berets,"** who were trained for guerrilla warfare. He also sought to improve relations with Latin America through an aid program known as the **Alliance for Progress** and helped to create the **Agency for International Development (AID),** which coordinated U.S. assistance programs to other countries. He also created the **Peace Corps,** which helped harness the idealism of many young Americans by sending them abroad to work in developing nations.

Soon after taking office, the Kennedy administration supported a disastrous effort by a group of Cuban exiles to overthrow the Castro regime. The project's planning had started under the Eisenhower administration. The **Bay of Pigs** invasion was easily crushed by Castro's forces. Following the Bay of Pigs crisis, Kennedy and Soviet leader **Nikita Khrushchev** met in Vienna in June of 1961. Khrushchev, believing he could intimidate Kennedy, called on the United States to abandon its commitment to West Berlin. In the summer of 1961, Khrushchev responded to the exodus of East Germans to the western part of the city by constructing a wall between East and West Berlin.

In the summer and fall of 1962, the United States and the U.S.S.R. faced their most dangerous confrontation over the Soviet Union's decision to place missiles in Cuba. After Kennedy declared a naval and air blockade around Cuba to prevent weapons from arriving, Khrushchev agreed to remove the missile bases in exchange for a U.S. pledge not to invade Cuba. Events in the Western Hemisphere continued to play a large role in American foreign policy after Kennedy's assassination. Johnson, who had virtually no experience in foreign affairs upon assuming the presidency, seized on disorder in the **Dominican Republic** in 1965 to dispatch 30,000 American troops to prevent the rise of a pro-Castro government in that country.

The Agony of Vietnam

Following the end of World War II in 1945, the United States was faced with appeals for support in Vietnam from the French, who sought to reassert the colonial control that they held from the late nineteenth century until the early part of World War II, and Vietnamese nationalists under the banner of the **Vietminh,** who sought freedom from French control. Vietminh leader **Ho Chi Minh** unsuccessfully sought U.S. support in his independence efforts, as Cold War pressures caused the United States to increase its commitment to supporting France. Eisenhower rebuffed calls for U.S. military intervention to relieve French forces besieged at **Dien Bien Phu**.

The French defeat at Dien Bien Phu occurred against the backdrop of negotiations over the future of Vietnam taking place at Geneva. The United States took little direct role in the negotiations, although it played a role in subsequent events. The conference agreed to divide Vietnam along the 17th parallel, with a procommunist government in the North and a pro-western regime in power in the South, with national elections to be held in 1956.

As the French withdrew from Vietnam following the Geneva Conference, the United States stepped in to provide large amounts of aid to South Vietnamese leader **Ngo Dinh Diem,** a nationalist who sought to consolidate his control over a fragmented South Vietnamese society. The United States supported Diem's decision not to participate in the 1956 elections, correctly reasoning that Ho Chi Minh would be elected easily.

In 1959, the Vietminh formed the **National Liberation Front (NLF)** to combat Diem's largely successful efforts to root out communist influence in the South and began assassinating South Vietnam officials. Diem responded with increasingly authoritarian efforts to control his society and precipitated a major crisis by limiting the rights of Buddhists, who responded with a series of public self-immolations that led to increasing disenchantment with Diem's leader ship. The United Sates supported Diem's overthrow in 1963, although not the assassination of him and his brother shortly before Kennedy's own assassination.

When Johnson took office, he faced widespread pressures to expand the American commitment to South Vietnam, which was consistent with the past twenty years of American Cold War policy. While Johnson initially did little to expand Kennedy's commitment of advisors, he used an attack on American destroyers in the **Gulf of Tonkin** to ask Congress for a resolution giving him broad authority to defend South Vietnam with American armed forces if necessary. Subsequent evidence casts serious doubts on the administration's version of the alleged attack. Congress nonetheless easily passed the Gulf of Tonkin Resolution, paving the way for the Johnson administration to introduce significant numbers of American ground troops into Vietnam in the spring of 1965. Although a fairly stable South Vietnamese government was in place by the end of 1965, procommunist forces still controlled much of the Vietnamese countryside.

The United States soon became heavily involved in a frustrating military effort. American strategy sought to use conventional forces and weapons to win a conflict against an enemy that used unconventional guerrilla forces and tactics. Most significantly, the communists were able to establish a rapport with the population that the United States and many of the South Vietnamese forces were unable to emulate, a concept known as winning the **"hearts and minds"** of the Vietnamese population. In addition, the United Sates relied heavily on bombing, which failed to disrupt the flow of supplies, weapons, and men from the North to the South along the **Ho Chi Minh Trail.**

Beginning with a series of **"teach-ins"** at the University of Michigan in 1965, growing numbers of Americans had begun to question the U.S. military effort in Vietnam. By 1967, large numbers of American students were protesting the war, while journalists who frankly conveyed the difficulties faced by U.S. forces in Vietnam and some members of Congress began to join the growing number of voices questioning the war effort. Johnson also faced growing economic challenges as the American military commitment grew, as he was unable to fund both the war and his domestic programs. He had promised both **"guns and butter"** to the American people.

The Traumas of 1968

A massive offensive by communist forces against a series of American bases throughout South Vietnam in January 1968 created widespread public disillusionment with the war effort. Although American forces inflicted crushing casualties on the communists, images of communist infiltration of the American embassy in Saigon and isolated acts of apparent brutality by South Vietnamese military officials created a sense of anger among the American people and led to a sharp drop in support for both the war and for Johnson.

With support from Democratic activists, Minnesota Senator **Eugene McCarthy** emerged to challenge President Johnson in the New Hampshire primary. After McCarthy's strong showing, New York Senator **Robert Kennedy** entered the race, bringing strong supporters from racial and economic minorities to the anti-Johnson effort. Despite Kennedy's strong showing in many primaries, Vice President **Hubert Humphrey** retained strong support from the party establishment and became the party's front-runner.

In early April 1968, Martin Luther King Jr. was assassinated in Memphis. He was there to help organize a strike by sanitation workers. His assassination caused widespread grief and anger throughout the nation, particularly among African Americans. Riots broke out in more than sixty American cities. Two months later, Robert Kennedy was killed by a young Palestinian on the evening of his momentous victory in the California presidential primary. Vice President Humphrey then faced little opposition in his efforts to gain the Democratic nomination. Clashes between the police and rioters outside the convention in **Chicago** caused widespread public dismay and increased support for stronger measures to preserve public order and stability.

During the 1968 campaign, growing public concern over the nation's disorder manifested itself in support for conservative candidates. Alabama Governor **George Wallace** gained the most popular support of any third-party candidate in more than sixty years by criticizing busing to promote school integration, the proliferation of federal social programs, and governmental laxness against race riots and antiwar demonstrations. Republican nominee **Richard Nixon** more successfully captured the concerns of the so-called **"silent majority,"** offering to provide law and order, less federal intervention in American life, and **"peace with honor"** in Vietnam. Despite a late charge from Humphrey, Nixon carried the 1968 race with a slim popular margin.

Multiple-Choice Questions
1. A major conclusion of the Kerner Commission report was that
   a. a stronger commitment to law and order was needed to prevent racial violence.
   b. government actions could do little to change deep-seated racial attitudes
   c. emphasis on desegregation and voting rights was the best means to end racial strife in the United States.
   d. massive government spending to improve urban conditions and reduce black poverty was necessary to eliminate racial problems.
   e. racial problems were limited to the parts of the country that had been heavily involved in slavery.

2. President Johnson announced that he would not run for reelection following
   a. the Tet Offensive.
   b. the violent Chicago Democratic National Convention.
   c. the 1968 New Hampshire primary.
   d. the assassination of Martin Luther King Jr.
   e. the public outcry over the My Lai Massacre.

3. Upon assuming office, President Kennedy believed that the biggest Cold War challenge that the United States faced was
   a. matching the Soviet Union in nuclear capabilities.
   b. maintaining a balance between the Soviet Union and China.
   c. continuing to bear the financial costs of containment while maintaining a high standard of living.
   d. finding ways to contain the spread of communism in the Third World.
   e. maintaining the support of European allies.

4. The accompanying map reflects which of the following about the election of 1968?

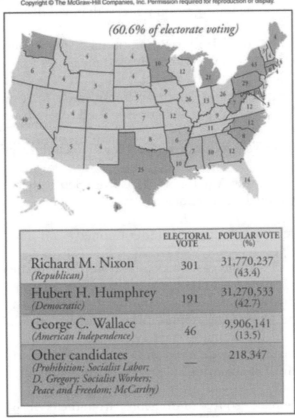

Copyright © The McGraw-Hill Companies, Inc. Permission required for reproduction or display.

(60.6% of electorate voting)

	ELECTORAL VOTE	POPULAR VOTE (%)
Richard M. Nixon *(Republican)*	301	31,770,237 (43.4)
Hubert H. Humphrey *(Democratic)*	191	31,270,533 (42.7)
George C. Wallace *(American Independence)*	46	9,906,141 (13.5)
Other candidates *(Prohibition; Socialist Labor; D. Gregory; Socialist Workers; Peace and Freedom; McCarthy)*	—	218,347

   a. The majority of the American electorate supported the Great Society.
   b. The Democratic Party maintained support from traditionally loyal regions.
   c. The majority of American voters supported candidates who opposed the direction they believed the nation had taken during the 1960s.
   d. The majority of American voters perceived little need for governmental change.
   e. The civil rights legislation passed earlier in the decade had little effect on changing voting patterns.

5. President Kennedy responded to the Soviet decision to place missiles in Cuba by
   a. ordering a series of air strikes against the missile sites.
   b. emphasizing diplomacy and negotiations to avoid provoking a Soviet attack on the United States.
   c. offering Soviet leaders a public exchange whereby the United States would remove its missiles in Turkey for a Soviet missile removal from Cuba.
   d. ordering a naval and air blockade around Cuba to prevent the missiles from arriving in Cuba.
   e. threatening a full-scale invasion of Cuba with American ground troops.

6. Which of the following statements about the Immigration Act of 1965 is accurate?
   a. It did away with the system of limiting the total number of immigrants allowed into the United States to 170,000.
   b. It gave preference to immigrants of European birth.
   c. It did away with restrictions on Latin American immigration.
   d. It allowed immigrants from Africa and Asia to enter the country on an equal basis with Europeans
   e. It continued many of the immigration policies that had been in place since the 1920s.

7. Under the terms of the Gulf of Tonkin Resolution, President Johnson
   a. was given the authority to take strictly limited measures to preserve the independence of South Vietnam.
   b. was forced to reduce the American troop commitment to South Vietnam
   c. was given the authority to provide an open-ended commitment to the preservation of South Vietnamese independence.
   d. was allowed to increase American support for Ngo Dinh Diem and his circle of advisors.
   e. was required to withdraw American troops from South Vietnam after sixty days without a congressional declaration of war.

8. American military strategy in Vietnam under Kennedy and Johnson consisted of all of the following *except*
   a. attempting to inflict enough casualties on the North Vietnamese to eliminate their will to continue fighting.
   b. relying on bombing to eliminate the communists' war-making capacity.
   c. seeking to win the "hearts and minds" of the southern population in an effort to reduce communist support in the countryside.
   d. relocating villagers to refugee camps and cities in an effort to control the countryside.
   e. attacking communist sanctuaries in Laos and Cambodia.

9. By the late 1960s, the major source of division within the civil rights movement was
   a. whether African Americans should concentrate on economic advancement or on achieving social equality with whites.
   b. whether African Americans should work with moderate white groups or use more radical approaches to achieve their goals.
   c. whether African Americans should oppose or support the Vietnam War.
   d. whether African Americans should continue to work for reforms in the South or spread their efforts to northern cities.
   e. whether African Americans should work through the federal courts or advocate legislation to advance their goals.

10. In pursuing his New Frontier domestic policy, President Kennedy experienced
    a. great success on the basis of his skill and experience in dealing with Congress.
    b. great success due to large Democratic majorities in both houses of Congress.
    c. great success due to his ability to use his personal charisma to appeal directly to the American people in support of his legislative program.
    d. frustration due to the coalition of conservative Democrats and Republicans who blocked many of his programs.
    e. frustration due to his inability to convert his large electoral mandate into legislative success.

11. Advocates of "community action" during the 1960s believed that
    a. the poor should be given a role in planning and administering government programs designed to help them.
    b. Vietnamese peasants should be trained to police their villages to prevent communist infiltration.
    c. African Americans in the South should organize to combat segregation at the local level.
    d. citizens in urban areas should band together to preserve order and stability in the face of crime and other disturbances.
    e. antiwar opponents should take direct measures against the draft.

12. All of the following were Great Society proposals or programs *except*
    a. civil rights for African Americans.
    b. immigration reform.
    c. federal aid to education.
    d. universal national health care.
    e. federal aid to urban areas.

Free-Response Questions—Exam Tip

The key to writing a successful free response essay on the AP United States History exam is to create a clear, precise thesis statement that fully addresses every aspect of the question, takes a position with regard to the question, and provides categories for analysis. Do not assume that the only acceptable form of organization for the "bullet" essays that follow are to use the topics outlined in the prompt as your categories. Within each topic listed, try to create clear categories that demonstrate that you have analyzed every aspect of the question very carefully. Support your thesis with accurate factual information. Do not assume that the facts will "speak for themselves." Strong analysis is the key to a high score on essay questions. Carefully examine both the New Deal and the Great Society. Recognize that the question contains an inherent comparison between the two.

Free-Response Questions

1. To what degree did the Great Society represent a continuation of New Deal policies? Discuss with regard to two of the following three areas:
    Race relations
    Poverty
    Fiscal policy

2. To what degree did American foreign policy toward the Third World between 1950 and 1965 support nationalist aspirations? Discuss with regard to two of the following three areas:

Asia
Latin America
The Middle East

Document-Based Question—Exam Tip

When writing a document-based essay question, be careful not to quote too much material directly from the documents. The question asks you to analyze the assumptions and beliefs of Kennedy, King, and Johnson, and then to synthesize those assumptions in an essay that reflects on the future of the United States. Rather than direct quotations, you should paraphrase key concepts from the documents. Avoid long quotations of material from the documents. Again, analysis is the key. Give reasons for the beliefs of each speaker. Evaluate the assumptions and beliefs. Avoid mere description of the documents and the time period. Be sure to read the question for what the question is asking and for what the question is asking you to do.

Document-Based Question

What assumptions and beliefs do the speeches by Kennedy, King, and Johnson reflect about the United States and its future possibilities?

Use the documents that follow and your knowledge of the period to develop a short essay in response to this question.

Document A

Source: John F. Kennedy, Inaugural Address, January 20, 1961.

Let the word go forth from this time and place, to friend and foe alike, that the torch has been passed to a new generation of Americans—born in this century, tempered by war, disciplined by a hard and bitter peace, proud of our ancient heritage—and unwilling to witness or permit the slow undoing of those human rights to which this nation has always been committed, and to which we are committed at home and around the globe.

Let every nation know, whether it wishes us well or ill, that we shall pay any price, bear any burden, meet any hardship, support any friend, oppose any foe to assure the survival and success of liberty. . . .

To those new states whom we welcome to the ranks of the free, we pledge our word that one form of colonial control shall not have passed away merely to be replaced by a far more iron tyranny. We shall not always expect to find them supporting our view. Be we shall always hope to find them strongly supporting their own freedom—and to remember that, in the past, those who foolishly sought power by riding the back of the tiger ended up inside.

Document B

Source: Martin Luther King Jr., Speech, August 28, 1963.

Read the speech in its entirety.

http://www.americanrhetoric.com/speeches/mlkihaveadream.htm

Document C

Source: Lyndon B. Johnson, Speech, May 22, 1964.

The Great Society rests on abundance and liberty for all. It demands an end to poverty and racial injustice, to which we are totally committed in our time. But that is just the beginning. The Great Society is a place where every child can find knowledge to enrich his mind and to enlarge his talents. It is a place where leisure is a welcome chance to build and reflect, not a feared cause of boredom and restlessness. It is a place where the city of man serves not only the needs of the body and the demands of commerce but the desire for beauty and the hunger for community.

It is a place where man can renew contact with nature. It is a place which honors creation for its own sake and for what it adds to the understanding of the race. It is a place where men are more concerned with the quality of their goals than the quantity of their goods. But most of all, the Great Society is not a safe harbor, a resting place, a final objective, a finished work; it is a challenge constantly renewed, beckoning us toward a destiny where the meaning of our lives matches the marvelous products of our labor.

Multiple-Choice Answers

1. d. The President's Commission on Civil Disorders, or the Kerner Commission, concluded in 1968 that the violence that had engulfed many of the nation's major cities for several years was a result of the desperate poverty that African Americans faced and that government spending to eliminate these problems was necessary to alleviate racial tensions.

2. c. Johnson, weakened by the Tet Offensive and disillusionment with his Vietnam policies, announced his withdrawal from the presidential campaign on March 31, 1968, several days after the New Hampshire primary (antiwar candidate Eugene McCarthy had captured 42 percent of the vote to Johnson's 49 percent).

3. d. Kennedy believed that Latin America, Africa, and Asia were crucial to the Cold War. He responded to Khrushchev's 1959 statement that the Soviet Union would support "wars of national liberation" in the developing world by increasing American foreign aid, developing the U.S. counterinsurgency capability, and developing programs such as the Peace Corps.

4. c. The fact that Republican Richard Nixon and Independent George Wallace carried almost 57 percent of the popular vote demonstrated public concern over the course of the war in Vietnam, racial and other tensions unleashed by the civil rights movement, and a perceived breakdown of order and stability in American life.

5. d. Kennedy, in a series of tense meetings with his closest advisors, rejected the counsel of those who advocated air strikes against the missile sites and chose instead an air and naval blockade, or "quarantine," of Cuba to prevent the missiles from arriving.

6. d. The Immigration Act of 1965 continued to limit the total number of immigrants into the United States to 170,000 but allowed Africans and Asians to enter on an equal basis with Europeans, thus setting the stage for a dramatic increase in the nation's Asian population.

7. c. The Gulf of Tonkin Resolution, passed unanimously by the House of Representatives and with two dissenting votes in the Senate in August 1964, gave President Johnson the authority to take "all necessary measures" to preserve South Vietnam's independence.

8. e. The United States attacked communist sanctuaries in Cambodia and Laos under President Nixon, Johnson's successor. All of the other choices were attempted at various points between 1961 and 1969.

9. b. By the late 1960s, particularly following the assassination of Martin Luther King Jr., many African Americans were impatient with the results that had been achieved following the passage of the path-breaking civil rights legislation of 1964 and 1965. As a result, many "black power" advocates argued that African Americans should reject moderation and instead use all necessary means, including violence, to achieve full equality with whites.

10. d. Kennedy, elected president by a slim margin in 1960, faced a Congress with small Democratic majorities. Many Democrats, especially those from the South, were more conservative than Kennedy and unwilling to support the ambitious New Frontier.

11. a. "Community action" was one of the more controversial Great Society programs, allowing the poor to play a role in implementing federal programs on the local level. While the program had some successes, it suffered as a result of the general disillusionment with the war on poverty that emerged by the late 1960s.

12. d. Although many critics argued that congressional passage of Medicare and Medicaid would lead to "socialized medicine," the programs nonetheless maintained many elements of the nation's largely private health-care system and came nowhere close to providing universal health care, limiting federal assistance to the elderly and indigent.

Free-Response Questions Commentary

1. The New Deal and the Great Society represent the two most significant domestic reform movements in American history. Both expanded the role of the federal government, particularly in the realm of social welfare policy, to greater levels than it had ever been before. The Great Society differed from the New Deal in that it emerged during a period of overall prosperity, whereas the New Deal had represented a response to the worst economic downturn in the nation's history. Also, while the New Deal placed little emphasis on civil rights and relied on more traditional American ideals such as work relief, the Great Society placed racial justice at the center of efforts and began to provide welfare money directly to poor Americans. In terms of fiscal policy, the New Deal had represented a revolution in terms of the use of Keynesian deficit spending to stimulate the economy; these efforts helped to stem the worst of the depression, although they did not succeed in returning the nation to prosperity. Johnson's Great Society, coupled with the expenses of the Vietnam War and the president's desire to avoid raising taxes, resulted in the emergence of significant deficits and helped to set the stage for the nation's economic troubles in the 1970s.

2. As the Cold War spread from Europe to the underdeveloped world during the 1950s, the United States and the Soviet Union faced the challenge of attempting to win allies among the so-called Third World. The United States struggled to find leaders in these nations who shared its commitment to democracy and capitalism, particularly since many of the nationalist leaders who had the greatest legitimacy were communists or socialists. As a result, the United States was in a number of cases forced to support conservative, authoritarian leaders who they believed would support order and stability to a greater degree than left-wing leaders.

In Asia, the two greatest nationalist challenges were in China and Vietnam. The emergence of Mao Zedong and the Chinese communists after 1949 forced the United States to rely on Chiang Kai-shek as a major ally. In Vietnam, the United States after 1954 supported Ngo Dinh Diem, a nationalist with impeccable anti-French and Japanese credentials, but with much less support than the communist Ho Chi Minh. Latin America posed a similar challenge. Fidel Castro overthrew the autocratic Batista regime in 1959, but faced hostility from the United States upon taking power (the degree to which this drove him closer to the Soviet Union is a debated question). In Guatemala in 1954 and the Dominican Republic in 1965, the United States supported the overthrow of democratically elected left-wing leaders who were seen as threats to hemispheric stability. In the Middle East, the United States supported the overthrow of the leftist Mossadegh regime in Iran. In the Suez Crisis of 1956, however, the United States did oppose British, French, and Israeli attempts to intervene against Gamel Abdul Nasser's efforts to nationalize the Suez Canal.

Document-Based Question Commentary

Few periods in American history can match the optimism of the early 1960s. Following the perceived passivity of the Eisenhower administration in the 1950s, John F. Kennedy came into office believing that he could reinvigorate the nation's idealism, especially in helping to combat communism across the globe. Martin Luther King Jr.'s speech, one of the most famous pieces of oratory in American history, represents an important watershed in the period leading up to the passage of the Civil Rights Act of 1964 and the Voting Rights Act of 1965. Johnson, attempting to take up the Kennedy mantle, lays out perhaps the most ambitious agenda of all, pledging the United States to end poverty and racial injustice, but also to improve the quality of life for all Americans in myriad ways.

Kennedy and King were both assassinated, while Johnson left office in disgrace due to his inability to balance the demands of an ambitious domestic agenda and an unwinnable war. While the efforts of these three men in the early 1960s represented inspirational leadership that produced important accomplishments, by the end of the decade, Americans were coming to terms with the fact that the nation was entering an age of limits.

CHAPTER 30
The Crisis of Authority

AP THEMES

- **Culture:** The United States underwent a significant cultural shift in the late 1960s, in which American youth challenged many of the accepted cultural norms and values of previous decades. Many young people challenged traditional conventions in areas such as dress, personal behavior, and morality, while also offering a deeper critique of the values of consumerism, conformity, and militarism that they believed dominated American society. This emergence of youth culture proved deeply polarizing, as many older Americans and young ones as well reacted negatively to the changes that they saw happening in the society around them.

- **American Diversity:** The mobilization of minorities proved to be one of the most far-reaching movements of the 1960s and 1970s. Building on the example of the African American civil rights movement, women, Latinos, Native Americans, and gays and lesbians all sought greater rights and recognition in American society. The efforts by these groups resulted in a number of gains, although some observers have argued that the new identity politics of the 1960s resulted in the emergence of a fragmented society in which the search for common values is subordinated to the desire of various groups to advocate their own goals and interests.

- **War and Diplomacy:** Richard Nixon and his closest foreign policy advisor, Henry Kissinger, came into office looking for a way to extricate the United States from Vietnam while also maintaining American credibility before both our allies and enemies. They sought to turn the war effort over to the South Vietnamese, while at the same time continuing a policy of heavy bombing of North Vietnam and neighboring areas. Nixon's "Vietnamization" policy was part of a larger "Grand Design" in foreign policy, in which he and Kissinger hoped to improve relations with the Soviet Union and China and gradually allow the United States to expend fewer resources in costly interventions throughout the globe.

- **Politics and Citizenship:** Richard Nixon's administration ended with his resignation after Watergate, one of the biggest political scandals in the nation's history. While evidence showed that Nixon and members of his administration had been engaged in a series of unsavory activities meant to discredit opponents and undermine the democratic process, a number of historians and commentators have placed his actions in the context of the trend toward an "imperial presidency," beginning with FDR in the 1930s. Nixon's resignation and the events around it bred or confirmed the mistrust many Americans felt and still feel toward politics and government.

- **The Environment:** While Americans' consciousness of the need to protect the world's natural environment had developed in fits and starts throughout the twentieth century, the 1960s and 1970s witnessed a growing awareness of the dangers posed by unchecked economic development and consumption of natural resources. Spurred by the new science of ecology, environmental groups promoted the need for both legislative measures and private efforts to preserve the nation's natural heritage.

CHAPTER SUMMARY
The Youth Culture

Members of the postwar baby boom generation became increasingly assertive in the 1960s for a variety of reasons, with the initial impetus for their activism coming primarily from the civil rights movement. As many university students, large numbers of whom had grown up in comfortable surroundings, became exposed to racial prejudice, they began to question many of the values of the society around them. In 1962, a group of students met in Michigan and formed the **Students for a Democratic Society (SDS),** which issued a manifesto known as the **Port Huron Statement** that expressed their disillusionment with and alienation from contemporary America. Two years later, students at the University of California at Berkeley became involved in a **free speech movement,** which began as a dispute with university administrators over the right to disseminate political literature on campus but soon developed into a larger debate about the fundamental nature of the university.

Antiwar sentiment t and opposition to the draft further fueled the youth movement, as students seized buildings and administration offices at colleges and universities throughout the nation. One of the most prolonged crises of the 1960s was the 1969 battle over **"People's Park"** in Berkeley, California. Students seized a vacant lot that the university sought to convert into a parking garage and gained support from the vast majority of the student body. While relatively few student activists embraced violence, there were radical groups such as the **"Weathermen,"** a revolutionary offshoot of the SDS, that became more prevalent in the later 1960s. Many Americans came to see the student movement as chaotic and disruptive. Large antiwar protests such as the **"spring mobilization"** of April 1968 and the Vietnam **"moratorium"** in 1969 helped to make the direction of the war a central issue in American politics.

Related to the New Left was an emerging youth culture that openly rejected the values of middle-class America and expressed this rejection in their styles of clothing, speech, and tastes, as well as other elements of their lifestyle. The most notable members of the counterculture were so-called **hippies** and other groups who sought to drop out of society and create rural communes. The central message of the counterculture was that the individual's first responsibility was to find ways to achieve personal fulfillment. One of the most potent symbols of the counterculture was rock music. Groups such as the Beatles changed from expressing innocent, nonthreatening themes in the early 1960s to much more radical, experimental, even mystical, ideologies by the end of the decade. Others used music to express social and political protest themes. The rock festival at **Woodstock, New York,** in the summer of 1969 was in many ways the most visible manifestation of the counterculture's growing influence.

The Mobilization of Minorities

Native Americans in many ways had the worst grievances of any group in American society. For most of the postwar period, federal policy toward Native Americans was aimed toward the goal of assimilating them into mainstream American society. The **"termination policy,"** based on legislation passed by Congress in 1953, withdrew official legal recognition of tribes as part of a larger effort to encourage Native Americans to become part of the larger society. These policies were largely unsuccessful, due to corruption and abuse by white officials and the efforts of Native Americans themselves for greater tribal self-determination.

Beginning with a meeting of members of more than sixty tribes in Chicago in 1961, Native Americans expressed a growing sense of self-consciousness and sought a redress of grievances from the federal government. Among the most notable Native American organizations was the **American Indian Movement (AIM),** which drew support from both urban and reservation dwellers. In response to a 1968 struggle over fishing rights in Washington State, a group of Indian activists seized **Alcatraz Island** in San Francisco Bay, leading the Nixon administration to make a number of reforms that did little to stem protest. The best-known of the protests occurred at **Wounded Knee,** site of the 1890 massacre of Sioux by federal troops, where Indian activists seized the reservation and demanded reforms in its administration and government adherence to treaty obligations.

Federal court decisions in many ways did more than violent protests to advance Native American goals. Like other civil rights movements, the Native American movement struggled to achieve a coherent identity and reconcile the conflicting goals of tribal autonomy and equality for their group as a whole. Overall, however, the movement helped Native Americans to confront the discrimination they faced and raise the consciousness and commitment of the government and American people of their grievances and means to address them.

Latinos, or Hispanic Americans, were the fastest-growing minority group in the United States. Like Native Americans, Latinos had no single, coherent identity, as their community ranged from groups with deep roots in the United States to new immigrants, with vast differences in socioeconomic status. Although in the early 1950s, the government had started to attempt to deport illegal immigrants, Mexican and other Hispanic immigrants continued to enter the country in large numbers. Despite many struggles and setbacks, Mexican Americans achieved some modest degree of influence in the late 1960s. Activists embraced the term **"Chicano,"** and groups such as **La Raza Unida** in the Southwest helped to raise public awareness of the concerns of Mexican Americans. Perhaps the best-known representative of Chicano issues was union activist **Cesar Chavez,** who formed the **United Farm Workers** and promoted organizing efforts that caused grape farmers and others in the Southwest to make important concessions to migrant farm workers.

The efforts of African Americans, Indians, Latinos, and Asians challenged the traditional American belief in assimilation, popularly known as the **"melting pot"** ideal. Instead, activists promoted a vision of **cultural pluralism,** in which ethnic and racial groups could take pride in their own heritage and live by their own cultural norms. These efforts helped to promote ethnic studies departments in colleges and universities and became reflected in law through a series of **affirmative action programs.**

Despite long-standing public unwillingness to discuss and acknowledge homosexuality, the movement for greater recognition and rights inspired the gay community as well. One of the precipitating events, the "**Stonewall Riots**" of 1969, resulted from gays fighting back against a police raid and series of arrests of patrons at New York's Stonewall Inn simply for frequenting the nightclub. This event and subsequent growing awareness and recognition of the issues around homosexuality caused many gay men and women to become more open and assertive about their sexual orientation, although tangible progress in the area of public policy has remained slow and controversial as seen in President Clinton's unsuccessful efforts to end the military's ban on openly gay and lesbian men and women serving in the armed forces in the early 1990s.

The New Feminism

Although women form a numerical majority of the nation's population, they began in the 1960s to identify with the minority groups seeking a greater voice in American society. While the publication of **Betty Friedan's** *The Feminine Mystique* in 1963 is often seen as the catalyst for the "new feminism" of the 1960s and 1970s, it in fact simply gave voice to a movement that was already taking shape. Kennedy had established the **President's Commission on the Status of Women,** while his administration had sought to prevent the practice of paying women less than men for equal work and extended women the same protection as African Americans under Title VII of the Civil Rights Act of 1964.

The new women's movement was in many ways driven by the conflict between the popular image of women living in happy, fulfilling domestic roles and the larger reality of their increasing role in the workplace. In 1966, Friedan and other activists formed the **National Organization for Women (NOW)** to demand greater opportunities for women in education and the workplace. By the late 1960s, influenced by the civil rights and antiwar movements, many feminists replaced the earlier emphasis on personal fulfillment with a larger critique of the overall male-dominated American power structure. This led to the founding of a wide variety of institutions, ranging from coffee shops and bookstores to rape crisis centers and abortion clinics, that sought to create a separate sense of community for women.

By the early 1970s, women began making a series of gains in their status and in gaining public recognition of their needs. The government in 1971 extended affirmative action guidelines to include women, while women gained growing acceptance in the professions, academia, and professional sports. Congress passed an **Equal Rights Amendment** to the Constitution in 1972, although this failed to gain ratification from the states by 1982 due to rising objections from men, conservative religious groups, and a growing number of women, many of whom feared the social impacts of such a change.

While abortions had once been performed in much of the country, states passed laws restricting the practice in the early twentieth century. Growing emphasis on the **"right to privacy"** first recognized in the 1965 case *Griswold* **v.** *Connecticut* formed the basis of the Supreme Court's decision in *Roe* **v.** *Wade* (1973) to overturn laws prohibiting abortion in the first three months of pregnancy.

Environmentalism in a Turbulent Society

While environmentalists (or conservationists) had longed based their commitment to preserving the natural habitat on moral or aesthetic grounds, scientists in the postwar period began to focus on the ideas of **ecology,** which stressed the interrelatedness of the natural world. Influenced heavily by the work of naturalist **Aldo Leopold** and later **Rachel Carson** (whose 1962 book *Silent Spring* publicized the dangers of pesticides), ecologists developed a scientific rationale for preserving the environment and gained strong influence among the public. The rise of academic ecology was helped by the growing strength of nonprofit environmental advocacy organizations dedicated to lobbying and influencing public policy. Among these were the **Sierra Club,** the **National Audubon Society,** and the **National Wildlife Federation,** which had existed well before the rise of the modern environmental movement, but gained new levels of strength and influence.

John Muir

In addition to the work of ecologists, other forces drove Americans to take more of an active interest in preserving the environment. While public figures such as President Johnson's wife, **Lady Bird Johnson,** promoted popular programs of "beautification," growing issues such as water and pollution, which were driven in many ways by the rapid levels of postwar economic growth, caused Americans to take steps to halt the destruction of the natural environment.

Beginning on April 22, 1970, millions of Americans annually observed **Earth Day,** an opportunity for people across the political spectrum to celebrate the environment and its preservation. In addition, Congress passed legislation in 1970 to create the **Environmental Protection Agency,** a government body to enforce antipollution standards. The **Clean Air Act** and the **Clean Water Act,** both passed in the early 1970s, further helped the government to fight environmental damage. Overall, environmentalism served several functions, both as a movement that influenced public policy and as a larger national goal, all of which contributed to its success and influence.

Nixon, Kissinger, and the War

Richard Nixon had come into office pledging to achieve **"peace with honor"** in Vietnam, although he did little to clarify how he would achieve that objective. **Henry Kissinger,** Nixon's national security advisor, proved to be the most influential figure in helping him to shape foreign policy. Nixon and Kissinger sought to limit dissent against the Vietnam War by gradually doing away with the draft and through a policy of **Vietnamization,** which involved the training and equipping of South Vietnamese forces to replace American troops.

Nixon and Kissinger soon came to believe that the best way to promote the success of the war effort was to destroy communist bases in Cambodia, first with air strikes and then, in the spring of 1970, with ground troops. This new military escalation stirred the antiwar movement to unprecedented levels. On May 4, four college students were killed by National Guardsmen at **Kent State** University in Ohio, while two black students were killed at **Jackson State** soon after.

Congress soon began to limit the president's war-making powers, while public opinion was further inflamed by the publication of the **Pentagon Papers,** a secret government study of the war's origins that was leaked to *The New York Times* and published in 1971. The same year, Lieutenant **William Calley** was tried for his role in the 1968 massacre of more than 300 South Vietnamese civilians at **My Lai.** The Nixon administration responded to the growing public outcries by stepping up efforts to discredit domestic opponents, supporting a South Vietnamese invasion of neighboring Laos, and bombing targets near Hanoi and Haipong, a major port, in North Vietnam.

The administration sought a breakthrough in negotiations with the North Vietnamese prior to the 1972 election, and Kissinger announced that "peace is at hand" several weeks before the election. Following the so-called **"Christmas bombing,"** in which the administration ordered heavy air raids on North Vietnamese targets and suffered the loss of significant numbers of American planes, the United States and North Vietnam finally signed a peace agreement in January 1973. The agreement allowed the South Vietnamese government to remain in power but also allowed North Vietnamese troops in the South to remain. The North Vietnamese agreed to return several hundred American prisoners of war.

The Paris agreements quickly broke down, with bitter fighting among the Vietnamese factions. In the spring of 1975, the North Vietnamese launched a successful offensive that led to the surrender of the South and the reunification of Vietnam under communist rule. Soon after, a genocidal communist group known as the **Khmer Rouge** came to power in Cambodia, with their policies resulting in the deaths of more than one-third of the country's population. The American war effort, at the cost of more than $150 billion and more than 55,000 American lives and countless more Vietnamese, was now ended, but with serious implications for America's role abroad.

Nixon, Kissinger, and the World

Nixon and Kissinger sought to create a new international order based on the ideal of **"multipolarity,"** in which China, Japan, and Western Europe would play an increasing role, replacing the **"bipolar"** U.S.–Soviet system that had existed since the end of World War II. They also pursued a policy of **détente** (meaning "lessening of tensions") with the Soviet Union and China, believing that rigid adherence to the containment doctrine was draining American resources. In February 1972, following months of secret negotiations, Nixon shocked many by visiting communist China, laying the groundwork for the opening of formal diplomatic relations between the two nations. Later in 1972, Nixon helped to take further steps toward greater international stability by signing the first **Strategic Arms Limitation Treaty (SALT I)** with the Soviet Union, which kept both nations' nuclear missiles at current levels.

Despite Nixon and Kissinger's emphasis on great power relationships, events in the so-called "Third World" proved to be volatile. The United States sought to keep its involvement in such conflicts limited, using as a guide the **Nixon Doctrine,** which held that America would provide aid and support to allies but that the major responsibility for defense stood with these nations themselves. The United States did support the overthrow of Marxist **Salvador Allende** in Chile in the early 1970s. Allende was subsequently murdered and replaced by a repressive military regime. In the Middle East, growing American dependence on Arab nations for oil forced the United States to press Israel to limit potential gains in the **Yom Kippur War** of 1973.

Politics and Economics Under Nixon

A central goal of Nixon's domestic agenda was to return some degree of power from the federal government to the states, under the umbrella of the so-called **"New Federalism."** Although Nixon sought to dismantle many of the social programs of the Great Society, he did undertake an effort to revise the nation's welfare system. His **Family Assistance Plan** proposed a guaranteed annual income for all Americans; although the program passed the House in 1970, opposition from a variety of different groups led to its failure in the Senate.

Members of the so-called "silent majority" reacted negatively to many of the decisions rendered by the Supreme Court under the leadership of **Chief Justice Warren.** These cases had, among other things, expanded the rights of criminal defendants, declared school prayer unconstitutional, and limited the federal government's power to curb pornography, as well as requiring reapportionment of state legislative districts to ensure equal representation to all citizens. Reapportionment increased the influence of African Americans, Hispanics, and other minorities living in urban areas.

Nixon sought to create a more conservative court, replacing Earl Warren with **Warren Burger** and nominating justices with a known conservative record. Despite Nixon's efforts, the Supreme Court in the early 1970s actually moved further in the direction of social reform in the areas of school integration, affirming the use of busing to achieve racial balance, capital punishment, and reproductive rights, striking down state laws forbidding abortion.

Despite Nixon's inability to enact all of his programs, the president was in a strong position for the 1972 campaign. An assassination attempt that resulted in the paralysis of **George Wallace** removed an important threat to Nixon's support among disgruntled middle- and working-class voters, while the Democrats' nomination of liberal **George McGovern** played into Nixon's hands. Nixon won more than 60 percent of the popular vote and failed to carry only Massachusetts and the District of Columbia.

The transformation of the American economy in the early 1970s represented perhaps the greatest long-term challenge to the Nixon administration. Rising energy costs, driven by the growing bargaining power of the **Organization of Petroleum Exporting Countries (OPEC),** helped to fuel massive levels of inflation in the United States. A deeper underlying cause of the nation's economic troubles was the gradual decline of the American industrial sector, driven by growing international competition. Nixon sought to respond to the nation's economic troubles by seeking to curb inflation with higher interest rates and tight control of the nation's money supply. Despite these efforts, inflation did not subside, while economic growth remained slow. This combination of factors known as **"stagflation,"** continued through much of the 1970s. Overall, despite going so far as to impose a system of mandatory wage and price controls, the Nixon administration was able to do little to provide a coherent solution for the nation's economic problems.

The Watergate Crisis

In addition to the economic problems that the nation faced during the early 1970s, a series of scandals involving Nixon and his administration further occupied public attention. Nixon, while himself secretive and defensive, came into office in an atmosphere of foreign and domestic crisis that caused him and his advisors to believe that they could justify virtually any effort to stifle dissent against their policies. The most damaging event was the break-in at the Democratic National Committee offices located in the Watergate office building in Washington—hence the popular identification of the Nixon scandals with the name **Watergate**. Although Nixon apparently did not order or have prior knowledge of the break-in, the revelations of a secret taping system in the Oval Office led to a heated battle between Nixon and Congress over release of tapes that would prove whether Nixon participated in the administration's efforts to cover up the affair by interfering in a federal investigation. Although Nixon claimed **"executive privilege,"** he was finally forced to give up the tapes.

Nixon's presidency was further damaged by the resignation of **Vice President Spiro Agnew** in late 1973 on charges of income tax evasion, precipitated by revelations that he had accepted bribes while serving as governor of Maryland and as vice president. This laid the groundwork for popular House Minority Leader **Gerald Ford** to become vice president. In April 1974, the House Judiciary Committee recommended three articles of impeachment against Nixon, which would likely have passed the House and led to his conviction in the Senate. In August, Nixon's release of tapes, under unanimous order of the Supreme Court, indicated that he had ordered the FBI to halt the investigation of the Watergate affair. This forced his resignation in the face of almost inevitable impeachment and conviction. Nixon's resignation revealed and illustrated the deep sense of disillusionment many Americans felt about the presidency and the nation's direction in the mid 1970s.

Multiple-Choice Questions

1. All of the following played a role in the initial formation of the New Left *except*
   a. the generational influence of parents of college students.
   b. the experience of working in the civil rights movement.
   c. the writings of 1950s social critics such as C. Wright Mills.
   d. the antiwar movement.
   e. the example of Third World revolutionaries such as Che Guevara.

2. President Nixon's "Vietnamization" strategy reflected his belief that
   a. the United States should make the Third World the central battleground of the Cold War.
   b. the United States must continue to use American combat troops as long as necessary to maintain an independent South Vietnam.
   c. the United States should rely on its allies to take a greater share of responsibility for their own defense.
   d. the United States should abandon the bankrupt containment policy.
   e. United States should use its vast economic resources to replace military force as the key component of American Cold War policy.

3. Many environmental advocates in the 1960s and 1970s based their arguments on
   a. the belief that the earth's natural beauty should be preserved for aesthetic reasons.
   b. the belief that government should work with business leaders to promote the rational development of the nation's national resources.
   c. the belief that the United States should become more self-sufficient for national security reasons.
   d. the ecological idea that damaging one aspect of the environment risked harming all others.
   e. the belief that programs supporting the environment would have economic benefits.

4. Betty Friedan's *The Feminine Mystique* argued that
   a. women had certain inherent qualities that made them well-suited to be wives and mothers.
   b. women should unite to confront and overthrow the patriarchal structure of the society around them.
   c. women should overcome their unhappiness by seeking personal fulfillment.
   d. women should take the lead in reform movements in the United States due to their unique moral sensibilities.
   e. women should withdraw from the society around them and establish their own communities and institutions

5. All of the following were significant decisions rendered by the Warren Court *except*
   a. *Gideon* v. *Wainwright.*
   b. *Escobedo* v. *Illinois.*
   c. *Bakke* v. *Board of Regents of California.*
   d. *Miranda* v. *Arizona.*
   e. *Baker* v. *Carr.*

6. President Nixon responded to the nation's economic difficulties in the early 1970s by
   a. urging Americans to sacrifice and accept potentially lower standards of living to preserve the nation's resources.
   b. shifting unsuccessfully between anti-inflation and anti-recession efforts.
   c. undertaking a consistent policy of Keynesian deficit spending to stimulate the economy.
   d. adhering to a policy of strictly controlling government spending in an effort to curb inflation.
   e. maintaining a limited government role in the economy in an effort to allow market forces to restore prosperity.

7. "Our long national nightmare is over." This quotation was spoken by
   a. Gerald Ford, referring to Watergate.
   b. Richard Nixon, referring to Vietnam.
   c. Lyndon Johnson, referring to segregation.
   d. Richard Nixon, referring to the OPEC crisis.
   e. John F. Kennedy, referring to the Cuban missile crisis.

8. In foreign affairs, Nixon and Kissinger sought to promote
   a. a multipolar world in which power was balanced between the United States, the Soviet Union, China, Japan, and Western Europe.
   b. a bipolar world in which the U.S.-Soviet relationship dominated world politics.
   c. a unipolar world in which the United States stood unchallenged as the dominant power.
   d. a world order based on Wilsonian principles of collective security, free trade, and disarmament.
   e. a world order in which national self-determination would allow underdeveloped nations to choose the social, political, and economic system that best suited them.

9. All of the following contributed to the growing pressure on Richard Nixon in 1973 and 1974 to resign his office *except*
   a. the resignation of Vice President Agnew and his replacement by Gerald Ford, which made Nixon's opponents less fearful of his replacement.
   b. the president's refusal to turn over tapes from White House conversations to the special prosecutors appointed to investigate the Watergate scandal.
   c. the emergence of evidence that proved the president's role in planning and approving the Watergate break-in.
   d. the discovery that the president had ordered the FBI to stop investigating the Watergate break-in.
   e. the implication of many of Nixon's closest aides in the effort to cover up evidence about the break-in, which led to questions about the extent of the president's involvement.

10. The protests at Kent State and Jackson State Universities occurred in response to
    a. public disclosure of details about the My Lai massacre.
    b. President Nixon's decision to order an invasion of Cambodia without congressional approval.
    c. President Nixon's decision to expand the draft.
    d. the assassination of Martin Luther King Jr.
    e. the decisions by university officials to accept government contracts for military-related research.

11. The Port Huron Statement was a document that reflected
    a. the frustration of African Americans with the slow progress of civil rights.
    b. the grievance of women who sought equal treatment with men.
    c. the disillusionment of college students with contemporary American society.
    d. the desire of Native Americans for government reparations as compensation for broken treaties.
    e. the desire of Latinos for an end to economic and social discrimination.

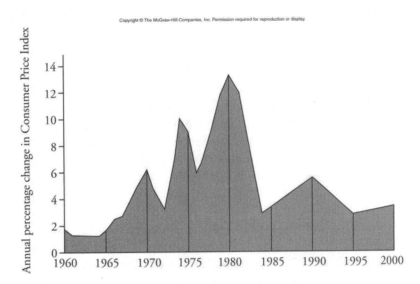

Copyright © The McGraw-Hill Companies, Inc. Permission required for reproduction or display.

12. The accompanying chart reflects all of the following *except*
    a. the impact of growing budget deficits as a result of the combination of federal spending on both military and social programs during the 1960s
    b. increased competition for raw materials from Third World countries and a resulting increase in prices.
    c. the difficulty that Presidents Nixon, Ford, and later Carter faced in developing effective policies to curb inflation.
    d. the dependence of the United States on foreign oil.
    e. the fact that the nation's economy was operating at nearly full employment.

Free-Response Questions—Exam Tip

President Nixon, like Herbert Hoover earlier, has undergone a transformation in how historians have perceived him. Nixon's legacy will always be tainted by his being forced to resign from office as a result of his involvement in covering up the Watergate break-in, part of a larger pattern of corruption and "dirty tricks" in his administration. However, historians have pointed to the influence of his policy of détente toward the Soviet Union and China as paving the way for the end of the Cold War. In domestic policy, he was surprisingly moderate, as advances were made in areas such as environmental protection, worker safety, and civil rights during his administration. Overall, Nixon was effective in many areas of public policy, making his egregious errors in judgment with regard to dealing with opponents and dissent all the more unfortunate.

Free-Response Questions

1. What factors account for the growing movement for minority rights in the period between 1960 and 1975? Discuss with regard to two of the following three groups:
   Women
   Latinos
   Native Americans

2. Trace the emergence and growth of concern for the environment in the period from 1901 to 1975.

Document-Based Question—Exam Tip

It is easy to use many of the terms from the turbulent period of the 1960s and early 1970s interchangeably. However, there were differences between two of the most significant protest movements of the period. Members of the New Left focused on combating the nation's social and political problems, especially racism, poverty, and war. Members of the counterculture, while critical of the dominant values of the society, tended much more to withdraw from society and seek individual fulfillment in response to the society around them.

An easy tendency in dealing with questions from periods such as the 1960s and early 1970s is to be overly simplistic in analyzing them—for example, the jazz age of the 1920s; the conservative 1950s, the turbulent 1960s, and so forth. Popular images of the 1960s involve young people dressed in outlandish fashions, listening to rock 'n' roll, and engaging in drug use. While this clearly took place, the 1960s were a more complicated time in which many young people offered a serious critique of the society around them. When dealing with a period like this, it is important to be able to point to specific ideas, trends, groups, and individuals in answering free-response or document-based questions. Think about the following as you read the documents below:

Document-Based Question

Analyze the immediate and long-term problems that student protestors sought to combat in the 1960s and early 1970s? What tactics did they employ in an effort to get authority figures to remedy the problems they identified? How successful were their efforts?

Use the documents that follow and your knowledge of the period to answer the question.

Document A

> *Source:* Student Nonviolent Coordinating Committee, Statement of Purpose (1960).
>
> We affirm the philosophical and religious ideal of nonviolence as the foundation of our purpose, the presupposition of our faith, and the manner of our action. Nonviolence as it grows from JudaicChristian tradition seeks a social order of justice permeated by love. Integration of human endeavor represents the crucial first step toward such a society.
>
> Through nonviolence, courage displaces fear; love transforms hate. Acceptance dissipates prejudice; hope ends despair. Peace dominates war; faith reconciles doubt. Mutual regard cancels enmity. Justice for all overthrows injustice. The redemptive community supersedes systems of gross social immorality.

Document B

Source: Students for a Democratic Society, Port Huron Statement, June 1962.

We are people of this generation, bred in at least modest comfort, housed now in universities, looking uncomfortably to the world we inherit.

When we were kids the United States was the wealthiest and strongest country in the world; the only one with the atom bomb, the least scarred by modern war, an initiator of the United Nations that we thought would distribute western influence throughout the world. Freedom and equality for each individual, government of, by, and for the people—these American values we found good, principles by which we could live as men. Many of us began maturing in complacency.

As we grew, however, our comfort was penetrated by events too troubling to dismiss. First, the permeating and victimizing fact of human degradation, symbolized by the Southern struggle against racial bigotry, compelled most of us from silence to activism. Second, the enclosing fact of the Cold War, symbolized by the presence of the Bomb, brought awareness that we ourselves, and our friends, and millions of abstract "others" we knew more directly because of our common peril, might die at any time. We might deliberately ignore, or avoid, or fail to feel all other human problems, but not these two, for these were too immediate and crushing in their impact, too challenging in the demand that we as individuals take the responsibility for encounter and resolution.

Document C

Source: Free Speech Movement Newsletter, "Do Not Fold, Bend, Mutilate, or Spindle," 1964.

The source of their power is clear enough: the guns and the clubs of the Highway Patrol, the banks and corporations of the Regents. But what is the source of our power?

It is something we see everywhere on campus but find hard to define. Perhaps it was best expressed by the sign one boy pinned to his chest: "I am a UC student. Please don't bend, fold, spindle or mutilate me." The source of our strength is, very simply, the fact that we are human beings and so cannot forever be treated as raw materials—to be processed. Clark Kerr has declared, in his writings and by his conduct, that a university must be like any other factory—a place where workers who handle raw material are themselves handled like raw material by the administrators above them. Kerr is confident that in his utopia "there will not be any revolt, anyway, except little bureaucratic revolts that can be handled piecemeal."

Document D

Source: Herbert A. Deane, Article, *Graduate Faculties Newsletter* (Columbia University), June 1967.

The new student attitude—and for want of a better term let me call it the 'anarchistic' or 'nihilistic' attitude—seems to reject all existing institutions and patterns of behavior. It seems to reject the state, the legal system, political parties, churches, colleges, and universities, and seems to deny objective standards of excellence in literature, the arts, and morals. I want, however, to distinguish between the attitude and the students. Although I cautiously use the term 'nihilism,' I do not wish to describe any of the students as outright nihilists. A few of them seem to speak and behave as if they thought destruction were the only suitable solution for existing ill; but other are less dogmatic, and still other have more limited targets for their hostility.

Document E

We . . . believe in the right of all people to participate in the decisions that affect their lives. An institution is legitimate only if it is a structure for the exercise of this collective right. The people who are affected by an illegitimate institution have the right to change it.

Columbia University has been governed undemocratically. An administration responsible only to the Trustees has made decisions that deeply affect students, faculty, and the community. It has expropriated a neighborhood park to build a gym. It has participated, through IDA, in the suppression of self-determination throughout the world. It has formulated rules and disciplined students arbitrarily and for the purpose of suppressing justified protest. The actions of the administration in the present crisis have exposed it to students and faculty as the antidemocratic and irresponsible body it has always been.

Multiple-Choice Answers

1. d. The New Left emerged in the public consciousness largely as a result of the 1962 formation of the Students for a Democratic Society (SDS), before the antiwar movement emerged. Antiwar efforts began in earnest with the "teach ins" that started in 1965 and fueled more significant efforts as the American troops commitment in Vietnam increased.

2. c. Vietnamization was part of the larger "Nixon Doctrine," in which the president called upon American allies to play a greater role in their own defense. Vietnamization involved gradually withdrawing American troops as South Vietnamese forces assumed a greater share of the war effort against North Vietnam.

3. d. While earlier environmental debates had often pitted so-called preservationists (those who believed in maintaining the natural environment in its pristine state) against conservationists (those who believed in the rational use of the nation's resources), many environmentalists in the 1960s and 1970s based their argument on the developing field of ecology, which emphasized the close relationship of many elements of the natural world.

4. c. Friedan's book, both a catalyst for the renewal of the feminist movement and a reflection of many larger changes that were already taking place, argued that women must escape the "comfortable concentration camp" of suburbia and middle-class life by seeking to fulfill their own potential.

5. c. The Warren Court, among the most influential in American history, issued a number of decisions on race relations, free speech, and the rights of accused criminals, among other areas. The *Bakke* case, decided in 1978 under the court headed by Chief Justice Burger, upheld the principle of affirmative action, while also putting restrictions on its use and application.

6. b. The Nixon administration was never able to establish a consistent policy for dealing with the nation's economic problems, some of which resulted from government overspending and some of which reflected larger systemic factors in the global economy. Nixon initially relied upon politically unpopular efforts to reduce inflation, and then shifted to a program of greater federal spending to restore prosperity (neither worked particularly well).

7. a. Gerald Ford, chosen as Nixon's vice president and succeeding to the presidency upon Nixon's resignation in August 1974, made this statement in reference to the end of the Watergate scandal in an effort to help the nation move forward as quickly as possible.

8. a. Nixon and Kissinger promoted a "realist" vision in foreign affairs, one that relied on the balance of power to maintain order and stability in world politics (most previous American leaders had distrusted the balance of power as a manifestation of corrupt Old World practices, one which had produced World War I, among other conflicts).

9. c. No evidence ever emerged to prove that Nixon approved or even knew about the Watergate break-in before it occurred. The central issues in the chain of events leading to his resignation involved the extent to which he conspired with aides to cover up the Watergate affair.

10. b. President Nixon's decision to order an invasion of Cambodia in the spring of 1970 led to a resurgence in antiwar activity. The protests at both Kent State in Ohio and Jackson State in Mississippi turned deadly when National Guardsmen fired on student protesters.

11. c. The Port Huron Statement, issued by the Students for a Democratic Society (SDS) at the University of Michigan in 1962, provided a wide-ranging critique of many of the ills of modern American society, including racism, poverty, and militarism. It is in many ways the founding document of the New Left.

12. e. While inflation often results from high levels of employment and economic activity, the 1970s introduced the term "stagflation," which refers to a period of both high inflation and slow economic activity. The nation experienced these conditions throughout most of the 1970s, with inflation only falling significantly several years into Ronald Reagan's term of office.

Free-Response Questions Commentary

1. One of the most notable features of the 1960s and 1970s is the growth of minority-group consciousness. Women, Native Americans, and Latinos all drew from the experience of the African American civil rights movement in their demands for improved conditions, but also had unique factors rooted in their collective experiences that helped to account for their growing protests. Overall, the movement for minority rights represented part of a "rights revolution" that has had a lasting impact on American society since the 1960s, both positive and negative.

Following African Americans, women were the first group to undertake a large-scale movement for civil rights; indeed, a number of women became members of the feminist movement as a result of their experiences in the civil rights movement. A general dissatisfaction with their traditional roles as wives and mothers, as well as the persistence of economic discrimination for working women, helped to fuel the growing demands for greater rights. Key events in the formation of the "new feminism" include the publication of Betty Friedan's *The Feminine Mystique* (1963), the formation of the National Organization of Women (NOW) in 1966, and the fight for the Equal Rights Amendments which stalled by the early 1980s. While the efforts of women themselves were central to the gains of the feminist movement, factors such as the Supreme Court's willingness to expand its definition of rights, most notably the right to privacy in *Griswold* v. *Connecticut* (1962), formed the basis for the 1973 *Roe* v. *Wade* decision that legalized abortion, further helped women to achieve more independence and control over their lives.

Native Americans also sought redress for many of their grievances, which were among the most serious of any group in American society. Federal policy since World War II had sought to assimilate Native Americans into white society and weaken tribal identities, a policy that many Indians opposed. As other minority groups were doing, Native Americans became more organized and assertive beginning in the 1960s, reflecting a new sense of cultural consciousness and protesting unjust government policies. A series of occupations and sit-ins, most notably the protest at Wounded Knee in 1973 by members of the military American Indian Movement, raised national awareness of Native American issues. The government responded with measures guaranteeing Indians more rights, while the Supreme Court ended the "termination" policy and allowed tribes more authority over businesses within reservation boundaries.

Although often less homogenous and less organized than other minority groups, Latinos fought against long-standing patterns of discrimination on two fronts. First, Cesar Chavez organized migrant farm workers in the Southwest and won significant concessions for workers in grape fields and other areas. More middle-class in nature was La Raza Unida, a political party in the Southwest that sought to separate from the white society in Texas and create an autonomous state for Mexican Americans. The Supreme Court supported the aspirations of Chicano activists by ruling in 1974 that non-English-speaking students had the right to education in their native language.

Overall, the movements for minority rights occurred as a result of efforts to combat long-standing patterns of discrimination. These movements were facilitated by a larger tendency to question many of the dominant values of traditional America as a result of the African American civil rights movement and the growth of student protest and later the antiwar movement. The relatively liberal Kennedy and Johnson administrations and even to some degree the Nixon administration,, as well as the Warren and Burger Courts, helped to some degree to legitimize these demands through legislation and court decisions. While no group achieved all that it hoped for, these efforts helped to create a more culturally pluralistic society that has been both more tolerant and more fractured.

2. Concern over the natural environment and its conservation has developed at different rates over the course of the twentieth century. While it has become a fundamental part of the national consciousness today, the process by which this occurred has been relatively long and slow. Two periods, the progressive era and the 1960s and 1970s, saw perhaps the largest growth in environmental concern, although for different reasons. In the progressive era, Theodore Roosevelt and other progressives became concerned about the potential damage caused by unchecked industrial growth. Roosevelt and Gifford Pinchot, head of the Forest Service, sought to promote the rational use of natural resources. At the same time, preservationists also grew in power and influence, galvanized by the fight over the Hetch Hetchy Dam, a losing battle that nonetheless raised popular awareness of environmental issues.

The battle over the preservation of Echo Park in the mid-1950s demonstrated that even in supposedly conservative periods, Americans still had a desire to practice good stewardship of the natural environment. The 1960s, however, represented a watershed in the growth of environmental consciousness, especially due to the influence of the growth of the science of ecology. Works such as Rachel Carson's *Silent Spring* (1962), as well as a series of highly publicized examples of the harm caused by pollution and degradation of the natural environment, caused a growth in environmental activism. The federal government responded with measures such as the creation of the Environmental Protection Agency and the Clean Air and Clean Water Acts.

Debates over the environment reflect larger debates over the proper role of government in regulating business and, more broadly, protecting the general welfare. As the scope of the federal government grew throughout the twentieth century, so did its role in protecting the environment. While debates over the proper use of natural resources continue today, the growth in environmental consciousness over the course of the twentieth century changed many of the terms of the debate, as few would argue that completely unregulated development is a viable and sustainable path.

Document-Based Question Commentary

Student protests both drove and reflected the larger pattern of the 1960s: a decade that started with great hope and optimism and ended with a great deal of disillusionment and bitterness. The optimistic tone of the decade is reflected by the Student Non-Violent Coordinating Committee (SNCC) in its 1960 statement of purpose. This statement notes a commitment to nonviolent protest. By the mid-1960s, SNCC was divided over issues such as whether to continue to work with sympathetic whites or to take more radical measures.

Perhaps the most famous student protest document is the Port Huron Statement, issued by the Students for a Democratic Society (SDS) in 1962. The group's "Agenda for a Generation" notes the discomfort that these middle-class students feel about the society around them. Early photos of the SDS reveal their relatively conservative and clean-cut appearance, a marked contrast with the popular image of the student protester. SDS members were particularly concerned about the militarism of American foreign policy and the nuclear threat. You should note the emergence of this critique prior to large-scale United States involvement in Vietnam.

Many student protesters first became active in the civil rights movement and the free speech movement, which began at Berkeley in 1964. This protest was led by students who had taken part in civil rights work during the previous summer. Though the immediate issue at Berkeley was whether students should be allowed to distribute political literature on campus, the movement soon moved on to provide a larger critique of the university itself. Many students became upset with the fact that their university leaders saw their mission as merely providing training to allow people to enter mainstream careers in corporate America and other similar venues.

Another issue that student protesters focused on was the larger issue of the university's social responsibility. The Columbia University protests of 1968, which are dealt with in Document E, occurred primarily as a result of the university administration's decision to buy property in a largely black Harlem neighborhood to build a gymnasium, as well as the university's accepting money from the federal government for defense-related research.

Herbert A. Deane, an administrator at Columbia, summed up his view of the student protest movement in a 1967 article based on a speech he had given that year. He noted the rejection of established institutions and values that was at the center of the student movement. He accurately notes that violence was a relatively small part of the student movement espoused only by the Weather Underground and a few other fringe groups but that many students shared the rejection of the nation's previously dominant social and cultural values.

CHAPTER 31
From the "Age of Limits" to the Age of Reagan

AP THEMES

- **Demographic Changes:** One of the most significant developments of the late 1970s and beyond was a shift of population, along with political power and influence, to the "Sunbelt." This reflected a number of different trends, including the growth of a largely conservative population of older Americans, along with a relative decline in power and influence of the nation's former industrial heartland in the upper Midwest. Many businesses were attracted to the South and Southwest for lower labor costs and the lesser degree of taxation, regulation, and pro-union sentiment that existed in these regions.

- **Religion:** As the nation's power center shifted away from the East Coast, another development that helped to move the United States in a more conservative direction emerged as well: the growing number and increasing political involvement of evangelical Christians. While many conservative Christians had previously avoided political involvement, growing numbers were attracted to the Republican Party for a variety of reasons, some of which included the growing debate over cultural issues such as abortion and rights and the debate over the teaching of evolution in schools.

- **War and Diplomacy:** Following the end of the Vietnam War in 1975, Jimmy Carter had come into office pledging the United States to a greater commitment to upholding human rights and placing less emphasis on rigid adherence to an anticommunist foreign policy, particularly when it meant opposing nationalist sentiments in other nations. By the end of his term in office, however, Carter faced major crises in Afghanistan and Iran, which led to a major defense buildup in his last days in office and setting the stage for the more aggressive policies of Ronald Reagan. Reagan and his successor, George Bush, presided over a period in which the Soviet Union gradually withdrew from the Cold War. Whether this was due to American policy or internal problems within the Soviet Union is still subject to debate.

CHAPTER SUMMARY
Politics and Diplomacy After Watergate

President Gerald Ford faced the challenge of attempting to restore public confidence in the presidency and to restore prosperity following Nixon's resignation and the nation's poor economic performance in the early 1970s. Although most Americans saw Ford as a man of integrity, his popularity suffered because of his immediate pardon of Nixon. Many suspected a deal between the two men. Continuing inflation plagued the administration, despite Ford's efforts to impose voluntary wage and price controls.

In foreign policy, Ford and his secretary of state, Henry Kissinger, laid the groundwork for another arms control agreement, known as SALT II, through negotiations with the Soviet Union. They also made an agreement recognizing the postwar European borders, which many conservatives saw as legitimizing Soviet control over Eastern Europe. The Soviets agreed to increase respect for human rights as part of the **Helsinki Accords**. Ford's policies came under criticism from both left and right. In the 1976 election, despite a strong final push, the president suffered a narrow defeat at the hands of former Georgia Governor **Jimmy Carter.**

Carter inherited many of the problems that Ford had faced and experienced little success in his efforts to solve them. Continuing hikes in oil prices kept inflation at high levels, while Carter's policy efforts were hurt by his alienation of experienced Washington political figures. He delivered a noted televised address in the summer of 1979 in which he spoke of the "crisis of confidence" among the American people. This became popularly known as the "malaise" speech, despite the fact that Carter never actually used that term.

Carter spoke frequently about committing American foreign policy to the defense of "human rights," although he offered relatively few specific proposals for accomplishing this. His administration negotiated a treaty to turn control of the Panama Canal over to Panama. This was a highly controversial measure that barely passed the Senate. His biggest success was mediating a peace agreement between Egypt and Israel, known as the Camp David Accords. His administration completed negotiation of the SALT II agreement with the Soviet Union, although this fell victim to conservative opposition. Carter eventually withdrew the treaty from Senate consideration following the Soviet invasion of Afghanistan in late 1979.

The Middle East proved to be a significant challenge to Carter, particularly Iran. The United States had supported the Shah of Iran since his ascent to power in the early 1950s. In 1979, the Shah fled Iran due to a popular revolution against his repressive policies, leaving the door open for the rise to power of an Islamic fundamentalist government under Ayatollah Ruhollah Khomeini. The new government seized the American embassy and held fifty-three American hostages for more than a year. The United States experienced another crisis when, in December 1979, the Soviet Union invaded Afghanistan, which Carter and many Americans saw as a threatening expansionist move. Carter responded by imposing a series of economic sanctions on the Soviet Union and boycotting the 1980 Summer Olympics in Moscow.

The Rise of the New American Right

Perhaps the most significant demographic phenomenon of the 1970s was the rise of the "Sunbelt," consisting of parts of the Southeast, Southwest, and California, which grew in population to surpass the older, industrial regions of the Northeast. This population shift tended to produce hostility to federal regulations and social programs, creating more support for conservative political candidates. The Sagebrush Rebellion in the late 1970s, for example, arose in opposition to federal environmental regulations. This trend was further helped by the growth of suburbanization, as areas such as Orange County, California, became centers of right-wing politics.

The conservatism that flourished in the Sunbelt was reinforced by the fact that beginning in the 1970s, the United States underwent perhaps its largest religious revival since the Second Great Awakening of the early nineteenth century. Evangelical Christians who believed in being "born again" and having a direct personal relationship with Jesus Christ became an increasingly powerful voice in American society and politics through organizations such as the Moral Majority and the Christian Coalition.

The evangelical movement helped to fuel the rise of the New Right, a coalition of conservative groups that grew rapidly in the 1970s and 1980s. With great success in fundraising and the rise of new leaders, such as former California Governor Ronald Reagan who replaced Barry Goldwater as the movement's informal leader after the 1964 campaign, the New Right became a growing force in the late 1970s. The movement's success was fueled by public dissatisfaction with Ford's domestic and foreign policy, which many saw as contributing to a decline in American power and influence.

Beginning with Proposition 13, a popular movement against property tax rates in California in 1978, conservatives seized on the issue of opposition to taxes to propel them into a position of even greater political power and influence. Rather than attacking federal social programs such as Social Security and Medicare directly, and thus alienating the groups that benefited from these programs, conservatives instead sought to capitalize on popular dissatisfaction with high taxes.

Carter attracted little popular support in his reelection efforts, despite holding off a Democratic primary challenge from liberal Massachusetts Senator **Edward Kennedy.** Reagan, emphasizing opposition to federal taxes and a desire to regain American strength and prestige abroad, easily defeated Carter in the general election. The Republicans also captured control of the Senate for the first time since 1952. The Iranian government released the American hostages on the day of Reagan's inauguration.

The "Reagan Revolution"

While Reagan had benefited from popular disillusionment with Carter and his policies, he also benefited from the rise of a new coalition of conservative groups. One element of this coalition consisted of traditional, "free market" conservatives, primarily made up of corporate leaders who opposed both federal interference with business and costly social programs as being hurtful to economic growth. A second element consisted of so-called "neo-conservatives," many of whom were former radicals disillusioned by what they believed to be excesses of the 1960s and who thus sought to regain control of American culture from the influence of the left.

Despite being the oldest man ever to serve as president, Reagan was able to project an image of energy and vigor. While he was not heavily involved in the day-to-day running of government, he surrounded himself with effective advisers who carried out policies based on the president's larger principles. Reagan was also able to defend his policies through effective rhetoric during his television appearances.

Reagan sought to restore economic growth through a program known as **"supply side economics,"** or **"Reaganomics,"** which was based on the assumption that tax cuts (particularly for large businesses and wealthy individuals) would free up funds for new investments. In 1981, Congress passed significant tax cuts, which became the centerpiece of Reagan's overall effort to reduce the role of the federal government in American life. Despite a serious recession in 1982, the country began to return to prosperity in 1983, partly as a result of Reagan's policies and partly as a result of other factors such as falling energy prices and staggering budget deficits.

Despite Reagan's promise to balance the federal budget within four years of taking office, his administration in fact presided over an unprecedented growth in the national debt, resulting from the 1981 tax cuts, large increases in military spending, and increasing costs for federal "entitlement" programs such as Social Security and Medicare. The administration sought to cut "discretionary" programs such as food stamps, federal subsidies for low-income housing, educational programs such as school lunches and student loans, and federal aid to cities and states, but these cuts could not compensate for the growth in other areas.

Reagan came into office arguing that the United States should offer vigorous support to those opposing the spread of communism throughout the world. In a famous 1983 speech, he referred to the Soviet Union as the **"evil empire."** Reagan proposed an ambitious program called the **Strategic Defense Initiative (SDI),** popularly known as "Star Wars," which sought to make nuclear weapons obsolete by providing a shield to block incoming missiles. Foreign and domestic opponents of the program argued that it would in fact elevate the arms race to new levels.

In the Third World, Reagan pledged support to opponents of communism everywhere, a policy known as the **Reagan Doctrine.** This was particularly relevant to Latin America, where the administration supported anticommunist efforts in El Salvador, Nicaragua, and Grenada. In the Middle East, American peacekeepers sought to help provide stability in Lebanon following a 1982 Israeli invasion of that country. Reagan withdrew U.S. troops following a 1983 terrorist bombing that killed 241 Americans. Reagan easily won reelection in 1984 against former Vice President **Walter Mondale** and New York Representative **Geraldine Ferraro,** the first woman to appear on a national ticket. Democrats, however, gained a seat in the Senate and maintained control of the House of Representatives.

America and the Waning of the Cold War

Reagan's two terms in office came at a time when deep changes were occurring in the communist world. In the face of a costly war in Afghanistan and long-term economic problems, new Soviet leader **Mikhail Gorbachev,** who came to power in 1985, pledged new policies of openness (*glasnost*) and reform and rebuilding (*perestroika*). As a result of these policies, the communist states of Eastern Europe transformed from Soviet satellites into conventional, left-wing democracies in a short span of time. In 1991, communism fell in the Soviet Union, as Gorbachev resigned in the face of growing fragmentation and declining legitimacy. In China, pro-democracy movements were less successful, as the Chinese government brutally put down a demonstration in **Tiananmen Square** in June 1989. The Chinese government continued to modernize its economy using western, capitalist methods. Despite Regan's initial skepticism of Gorbachev's sincerity, the United States and the Soviet Union signed an important agreement in 1988 to eliminate Soviet and American intermediate-range nuclear forces (INF) in Europe.

Although Reagan drew popular support through identification with the changes occurring in the world, a series of scandals throughout his second term eroded the president's credibility. In the domestic realm, the government was forced to bail out large numbers of savings banks, many of which had rapidly, and sometimes corruptly, expanded as a result of government deregulation of the industry. The most damaging scandal for the administration, however, was the Iran–Contra Affair, in which it was revealed that the administration had sold weapons to the Iranian government in an effort to gain the release of American hostages in the Middle East, despite the president's pledge that his administration would not negotiate with terrorists. Furthermore, despite congressional bans the administration had funneled some of the money from the sale of these weapons to support the anticommunist opposition, known as contras, in Nicaragua.

Democrats were hopeful that the declining support for Reagan would translate into a victory for their party in the 1988 election, relying on former Massachusetts Governor **Michael Dukakis** as their presidential candidate. Dukakis was an uninspiring campaigner and offered little response to the negative and highly partisan campaign of **Vice President George Bush,** who won a relatively easy victory despite trailing early in the campaign.

The Bush administration achieved a number of successes in international affairs, although these were in many ways more a result of cooperation with Gorbachev and his successors than of any bold vision on Bush's part. Domestically, Bush had less success. Despite pledging **"no new taxes"** in 1988, he agreed to support a tax increase in 1990 to help balance the federal budget. He also alienated Democrats and Republican moderates by taking conservative positions on issues such as abortion and affirmative action to firm up his support among the Republican right wing. The biggest challenge that his administration faced was a recession that gripped the country starting in 1990 and continuing into 1992.

The fall of the Soviet Union left the United States with a choice of lessening its military commitments and concentrating on domestic issues or continuing to use its power to defend its interests abroad. The Bush administration chose the latter. In 1989, an American invasion of Panama led to the overthrow of military dictator **Manuel Noriega** and his replacement by an elected, pro-American government. In 1990 and 1991, the United States became involved in an effort to oust Iraqi leader **Saddam Hussein** and his military forces from the neighboring nation of Kuwait, an oil-rich entity. The United States and its allies, following an intense bombing campaign, were able to defeat Iraqi forces in a major ground offensive that lasted less than a week. While the war was popular in the United States, Hussein remained in power for more than a decade after the first Persian Gulf War.

Despite broad popularity following the Gulf War, Bush's inability to deal with the nation's recession left him vulnerable to challenges in his reelection campaign. Arkansas Governor **Bill Clinton** emerged as the Democratic candidate and skillfully exploited concern over the nation's economy, while Texas billionaire **Ross Perot** tapped into continuing American dislike of federal bureaucracy. Clinton was elected with 43 percent of the popular vote to 38 percent for Bush and 19 percent for Perot, with the Democrats retaining control of both houses of Congress.

Multiple-Choice Questions

1. In his policy toward the Third World, President Reagan believed that
   a. the United States should make the promotion of economic development and social progress the key theme of American relations with underdeveloped nations.
   b. the United States should be wary of supporting undemocratic leaders, even if they appeared to align themselves with American foreign policy goals.
   c. the United States should vigorously support anticommunist efforts throughout the underdeveloped world.
   d. the United States could work closely with left-wing nationalist groups, as long as they were not closely aligned with the Soviet Union or China.
   e. the United States should concentrate its resources on the Cold War in Europe, which was more central to American interests than other regions.

2. President Carter's efforts to maintain his "outsider" status during the 1976 presidential campaign resulted in
   a. his ability to undertake sweeping reforms upon assuming office.
   b. opposition from veteran congressional leaders that made it difficult for Carter to accomplish many of his programs.
   c. his ability to maintain high levels of popularity with the American people throughout his term in office.

d. a desire by the American people to make great sacrifices in order to preserve the nation's foreign policy.

e. the implementation of a series of dramatic initiatives that significantly shifted American foreign policy toward the Soviet Union.

3. President Carter's most successful foreign policy accomplishment was his
   a. negotiation of the Panama Canal Treaty.
   b. handling of the SALT II negotiations.
   c. effort to negotiate a treaty between Israel and Egypt.
   d. response to the Iranian hostage crisis.
   e. Resumption of formal diplomatic relations with China.

4. A major result of President Reagan's economic policies was
   a. a significant increase in federal spending for new social programs.
   b. an increase in inflation levels over those of the previous decade.
   c. an increase in federal assistance to state and city governments.
   d. a decrease in federal spending for national defense.
   e. an increase in both federal budget deficits and the national debt.

5. An analysis of presidential elections between 1968 and 1988 would reveal evidence of all of the following *except*
   a. the continuing dominance of the New Deal coalition at the national level.
   b. the growing influence of the "Christian right" on American politics.
   c. the Democratic loss of control over the "Solid South."
   d. the growing electoral influence of the Southwest.
   e. the ability of the Republican Party to form successful electoral coalitions.

6. George Bush was elected president in 1988 as a result of all of the following *except*
   a. the uninspired campaigning of Democratic nominee Michael Dukakis. ✓
   b. his rhetorical skills and inspirational campaigning style.
   c. his being identified with the policies that were leading to the end of the Cold War.
   d. his pledge of "no new taxes" if he was elected. ✓
   e. his relentless attacks on Dukakis and liberalism in general. ✓

7. The slogans "It's Morning in America" and "America Is Back" represent the themes emphasized by
   a. Gerald Ford.
   b. Jimmy Carter.
   c. Ronald Reagan.
   d. George Bush.
   e. Bill Clinton.

8. President Carter responded to the Soviet invasion of Afghanistan by
   a. pursuing a policy of negotiation with Soviet leaders.
   b. calling for economic sanctions and boycotting the 1980 Moscow Olympics.
   c. attempting to assure the American people that the Soviet move was largely defensive in nature.
   d. threatening nuclear retaliation as a possible American option.
   e. calling upon the United Nations to assemble an international military coalition to remove Soviet troops

9. United States involvement in the first Persian Gulf War resulted from
    a. concern over the spread of communism in the region.
    b. efforts to stem the increase of Islamic radicalism.
    c. a desire to reverse Iraq's invasion of Kuwait.
    d. a desire to punish Iraq for its actions during the Iran–Iraq war.
    e. a desire to support Israel against Arab territorial claims.

10. During his presidency, Gerald Ford pursued policies that
    a. represented a retreat from Nixon's policy of détente.
    b. frequently angered conservative members of his party.
    c. successfully resolved the nation's economic problems.
    d. included bold new domestic initiatives.
    e. sought to punish Nixon and others who had been involved in Watergate.

11. Evangelical Christians in the 1970s and 1980s differed from their early twentieth-century counterparts in that
    a. they were much more likely to live in rural areas.
    b. they tended to avoid involvement in politics.
    c. they were more likely to belong to the middle class and to be more assertive.
    d. they were largely dismissed by secular political and social leaders.
    e. they were poorly organized and had little way to spread their message.

12. The most significant demographic trend of the 1970s and 1980s was
    a. the movement of African Americans from the South to northern cities.
    b. the influx of immigrants seeking jobs in heavy industry.
    c. the rapid population growth in the Northeast and Midwest.
    d. the continuation of high birth rates that had started in the immediate postwar period.
    e. the internal migration of Americans to the South and Southwest.

Free-Response Questions—Exam Tip

One good way of organizing your understanding of American history is to understand the nature of party competition in each major era, particularly at the presidential level. In the early republic, Hamiltonian Federalists and Jeffersonian Republicans were the two dominant parties. From the 1830s to the early 1850s, the Jacksonian Democrats competed against the Whigs. The period from the beginning of the Civil War until the election of 1932 was one of Republican dominance on the presidential level (only two Democrats, Grover Cleveland and Woodrow Wilson, were elected). From 1933 until 1969, the Democratic Party held the presidency for all but eight years, during the Eisenhower presidency, largely on the strength of the New Deal coalition that Roosevelt assembled. The Republican Party dominated presidential politics between 1968 and 1992, winning all but one election, beginning with Nixon's ability to tap dissatisfaction among former Democrats and continuing with the rise of the neoconservatives.

Free-Response Questions

1. Account for the rise and growth of the "New Right" between 1968 and 1988.

2. To what extent did American foreign policy efforts between 1968 and 1989 contribute to the eventual fall of the Soviet Union and the end of the Cold War?

Document-Based Question—Exam Tip

Political leaders are often influenced by past events as they formulate public policy. In the case of American Cold War policy, for example, many of the assumptions that the United States made about Soviet behavior came from the experience of the 1930s and the rise of Hitler (leading American policymakers to assume that the Soviet Union was bent on world domination and sought to subordinate all communist movements under its control). Following the end of the Vietnam War in 1975, American policymakers assessed most of our foreign policy endeavors through the lens of our experience in Vietnam. Questions that ask you to interpret foreign policy decisions will often involve thinking about how policymakers used historical assumptions and past experiences to arrive at their understanding of the world around them.

Document-Based Question

To what extent did American involvement in Vietnam cause American leaders to reassess the fundamental assumptions behind the policy of containment?

Use the documents that follow as well as your knowledge of the period from 1954 to 1980 to construct your answer.

Document A

Source: Dwight D. Eisenhower, Press Conference, April 1954.

Q. Robert Richards, Copley Press:

Mr. President, would you mind commenting on the strategic importance of Indochina to the free world? I think there has been, across the country, some lack of understanding on just what it means to us.

A. The President.:

You have a row of dominoes set up, you knock over the first one, and what will happen to the last one is the certainty that it will go over very quickly. So you could have a beginning of a disintegration that would have the most profound influences.

[handwritten margin note: one goes, they can go]

Document B

Source: Lyndon Johnson, Speech, April 1965.

Over this war and all Asia is another reality: the deepening shadow of communist China. The rulers in Hanoi are urged on by Peking. This is a regime which has destroyed freedom in Tibet, which has attacked India and has been condemned by the United Nations for aggression in Korea. It is a nation which is helping the forces of violence in almost every continent. The contest in Vietnam is part of a wider pattern of aggressive purposes.

[handwritten note: It must be stopped because its extremely aggressive and violent.]

Document C

Source: Senator J. William Fulbright, Speech, April 1966.

There is a kind of voodoo about American foreign policy. Certain drums have to be beaten regularly to ward off evil spirits; for example, the maledictions which are regularly uttered against North Vietnamese aggression. . . . Certain pledges must be repeated every day lest the whole free world go to rack and ruin—for example, we will never go back on a commitment no matter how unwise; we regard this alliance or that as absolutely 'vital' to the free world; and, of course, we will stand stalwart in Berlin from now until Judgment Day.

Document D

Source: Robert F. Kennedy, Speech, February 1968.

The fourth illusion is that the American national interest is identical with—or should be subordinated to—the selfish interest of an incompetent military regime.

We are told, of course, that the battle for South Vietnam is in reality a struggle for 250 million Asians—the beginning of a Great Society for all of Asia. But this is a pretension. We can and should offer reasonable assistance to Asia; but we cannot build a Great Society there if we cannot build one in our own country. We cannot speak extravagantly of a struggle for 250 million Asians, when a struggle for 15 million in one Asian country so strains our forces, that another Asian country, a fourth-rate power which we have already once defeated in battle, dares to seize an American ship and hold and humiliate her crew.

Document E

Source: Richard Nixon, Speech, November 1969.

The defense of freedom is everybody's business—not just America's business. And it is particularly the responsibility of the people whose freedom is threatened. In the previous administration we Americanized the war in Vietnam. In this administration we are Vietnamizing the search for peace.

Document F

Source: John F. Kerry, Testimony before the Senate Foreign Relations Committee, April 1971.

We found that not only was it a civil war, an effort by a people who had for years been seeking their liberation from any colonial influence whatsoever, but also we found that the Vietnamese whom we had enthusiastically molded after our own image were hard put to take up the fight against the threat we were supposedly saving them from.

Document G

Source: Henry Kissinger, Press Conference, April 1975.

Question: Mr. Secretary, looking toward the future, has America been so stunned by the experience of Vietnam that it will never again come to the military or economic aid of an ally? . . .

Secretary Kissinger: As I pointed out in a speech a few weeks ago, one lesson we must learn from this experience is that we must be very careful in the commitments we make, but that we should scrupulously honor those commitments we do make.

Document H

Source: Jimmy Carter, Inaugural Address, January 1977.

Our nation can be strong abroad only if it is strong at home, and we know that the best way to enhance freedom in other lands is to demonstrate here that our democratic system is worthy of emulation.

To be true to ourselves, we must be true to others. We will not behave in foreign places so as to violate our rules and standards here at home, for we know that the trust which our nation earns is essential to our strength.

Document I

Source: Ronald Reagan, Speech, August 1980.

Can we doubt that only a Divine Providence placed this land, this island of freedom, here as a refuge for all those people in the world who yearn to breathe free? Jews and Christians enduring persecution behind the Iron Curtain; the boat people of Southeast Asia, Cuba and of Haiti; the victims of drought and famine in Africa; the freedom fighters in Afghanistan; and our countrymen held in savage captivity.

Multiple-Choice Answers

1. c. The Reagan Doctrine pledged the United States to work closely with anticommunist groups in the Third World, particularly in Latin America, which Reagan saw as central to American foreign policy interests.

2. b. Carter's efforts to distance himself from the so-called Washington Establishment helped him to defeat Gerald Ford in the 1976 election. Once he took office, however, Carter's decision to rely on many of his Georgia advisors and ignore the advice of more established Washington insiders cost him support and stymied many of his initiatives.

3. c. Carter was able to mediate between Israel and Egypt and convince the leaders of the two nations, Menachem Begin and Anwar Sadat, to sign the Camp David Accords in March 1979 after nearly two years of negotiations.

4. While Reagan's policies played a role in helping the United States recover from the "stagflation" that had plagued it for much of the 1970s, the president's combination of deep tax cuts and increased defense spending—along with spending on federal entitlement programs such as Social Security—led to high annual budget deficits and corresponding increases in the overall national debt.

5. a. While Democratic candidates often continued to be successful in state and local elections, Republicans dominated the presidency during these twenty years—winning five of six presidential elections—leading some commentators to argue that Republicans could be the nation's natural majority party.

6. b. Bush, Reagan's vice president from 1980 to 1988, was not an inspiring campaigner or public speaker. He benefited from identification with the administration's policy toward the Soviet Union and his national security experience. The most important factor in the Republican victory, however, was the combination of Dukakis's weakness as a candidate and Bush's relentless attacks upon him.

7. c. Reagan emphasized the economic recovery that the United States had undergone during his first term, as well as the return to a more activist foreign policy, in his 1984 reelection campaign. Partly as a result of this optimism, Reagan won landslide reelection over Democratic nominee Walter Mondale.

8. b. Carter responded strongly to the Soviet Union's invasion of Afghanistan in December 1979 and called for economic sanctions and boycotted the 1980 Moscow Olympics.

9. c. When Saddam Hussein invaded Kuwait and announced that he intended to annex the region in the summer of 1990, the United States responded by leading a multinational effort to force Iraq to reverse its actions and retreat from Kuwait. The U.S.-led force quickly succeeded in its immediate military objective, although Hussein remained in power.

10. b. Ford, a moderate, alienated conservatives and others by pardoning Nixon, continuing the policy of détente which made the United States seem weak, and seeking to heal the wounds of Vietnam by proposing amnesty for draft resisters. Ford faced a spirited challenge from Ronald Reagan at the 1976 Republican convention and was renominated only narrowly.

11. c. Evangelical Christians, many of whom prospered and joined the middle class in the post-1945 period, became increasingly active in the 1970s and 1980s, taking up a number of different social and political causes. They represented a well-organized force that tended to support the Republican Party and had significant political influence.

12. e. The growth of the "Sunbelt"—including Florida, Texas, Arizona, and California—occurred as Americans moved away from the Northeast and industrial Midwest. This trend had important implications for American politics and society, helping to account for the nation's conservative shift during this period.

Free-Response Questions Commentary

1. The biggest political shift since the emergence of the New Deal coalition in the 1930s occurred with the growth of the rise of neoconservatism in the 1970s and 1980s. This process occurred for a variety of social, political, and economic reasons. A major factor behind the surge in conservative sentiment was a deep sense of dissatisfaction with the direction that the United States was taking, particularly as a result of the social programs of the Great Society. Many lower-class whites who had earlier embraced the Democratic Party's focus on economic issues became disillusioned with the party's increasing liberalism on civil rights and social issues. Demographic changes, particularly the aging population and the increasing population shift away from the industrial Northeast and Midwest, tended to create a larger grouping of people who were in favor of less government involvement in American life. California, for example, experienced a "tax revolt" in the late 1970s as many of its citizens sought to roll back property taxes. Religious conservatives, who had earlier remained largely uninvolved in politics, became an increasingly important constituency that supported the Republican Party for its stance on issues such as civil rights, abortion, gay rights, and school prayer. Finally, many conservative politicians, such as Ronald Reagan, found a willing audience for

their attacks on the Nixon–Kissinger policy of détente, as well as the seeming weakness of the United States in the post-Vietnam era, as seen in events such as the Iranian hostage crisis.

2. The degree to which the end of the Cold War resulted from the efforts of American policymakers, as opposed to internal problems within the Soviet Union, is a question that awaits fuller resolution until more Soviet documents are made available. Those who argue that American policy played a key role in the Soviet Union's decline point primarily to three factors: the détente policy pursued by Nixon and Kissinger, the American emphasis on human rights under Ford and Carter, and President Reagan's policy of increased defense spending and efforts to roll back communism in the Third World.

    Détente allowed the United States to play the Soviet Union and China off against one another. Also, by pursuing a policy of "linkage" through offering food sales and other forms of economic assistance, Nixon and Kissinger hoped to gain some degree of influence over Soviet behavior and restrain Soviet leaders from making aggressive moves. The Ford administration angered conservatives by signing the Helsinki Accords. While these did recognize the postwar European borders, they also allowed the United States to insist on greater adherence to human rights by the Soviet Union. Carter and, to a lesser degree, Reagan also frequently pointed to the treatment of Soviet dissidents as a way to emphasize the differences between the United States and the Soviet Union. Finally, some commentators argue that the massive defense spending increase under Reagan, as well as American support for anticommunist groups in areas such as Latin America and the Middle East, helped to contribute to the downfall of the Soviet Union by forcing it into bankruptcy in an effort to keep up with the United States.

Document-Based Question Commentary

Background: American involvement in the Vietnam War emerged as a logical outgrowth of the policy of containment and also caused American policymakers to reassess many of the fundamental premises of the containment policy. Several assumptions about the nature of Soviet, and more generally, communist, behavior emerged in the first decade or so of the Cold War. These included the ideas of monolithic communism, the fact that the United States had the resources to both maintain a vibrant democratic society and aid other nations in creating their own democratic societies, and that the United States had a duty to both intervene abroad and support anticommunist allies, even if our allies were less than ideal in their records in areas such as human rights. The Vietnam War caused American policymakers to question many of these assumptions in the latter stages of the conflict and in the immediate postwar period. Still, many influential figures began to reassert the earlier premises of American Cold War policy in the late 1970s and beyond.

The Documents: Documents A and B, President Eisenhower's famous espousal of the "domino theory" and President Johnson's April 1965 speech outlining the link between events in Vietnam and Chinese expansionism in Asia, put forth several key premises of Cold War policy. These include the interest of the United States in stopping communism throughout the world and the connection between Soviet and Chinese expansion and other communist movements in the Third World.

Documents C, D, E, and F demonstrate the breakdown of the Cold War consensus that occurred as a result of both the growing American military commitment in Vietnam and the lack of American success in achieving the major goals behind intervention. In Document C,

Senator J. William Fulbright, the chair of the Senate Foreign Relations Committee who had been instrumental in steering the Gulf of Tonkin Resolution through the Senate, begins to question the assumption that all areas of the globe are equally vital to American security, an assumption that was contained in NSC-68. Robert Kennedy, on the verge of challenging Johnson for the Democratic nomination, questions the American support for the military regime in Saigon, as well as the idea that the United States can promote meaningful social reform in Asia when it cannot do so at home. He also makes reference to the seizure of the U.S.S. *Pueblo* by North Korean forces as a symbol of America's loss of international prestige. In Document E, President Nixon, elected at least to some degree on the basis of his pledge to end the war, outlines his "Vietnamization" strategy, one that involves removing American troops and replacing them with South Vietnamese forces. John Kerry, a leading member of the Vietnam Veterans Against the War, testifies to Congress about the atrocities of American soldiers and the fact that the conflict in Vietnam is a civil conflict with little or no impact on American security, and no ideological meaning for the South Vietnamese in the Winter Soldier Investigations of 1971 (Document F).

Documents G through I deal with the aftermath of the war and the "lessons" of Vietnam. In Document G, Secretary of State Kissinger acknowledges that while the United States will continue to honor its commitments abroad, it must be careful in making future commitments. A major factor behind the Nixon–Kissinger détente policy was the belief that a more stable international system would lessen the need for the United States to intervene across the globe. Document H, an excerpt from President Carter's inaugural address, reflects the new president's belief that the United States should focus on improving American society before seeking to promote democracy abroad. Carter sought to bring a greater emphasis on human rights into American foreign policy, although events toward the end of his term forced him to return to a more traditional, security-minded foreign policy. Ronald Reagan, who believed that the United States should break out of its post-Vietnam hesitancy to use force, uses rhetoric more reminiscent of the early Cold War period in his pledge that the United States should support freedom everywhere. Reagan's support for anticommunist regimes throughout the Third World and his emphasis on heavy defense spending attest to the fact that the challenge to the containment policy resulting from the Vietnam War was by no means complete and permanent.

Summation: Most commentators argue that Vietnam represented a misapplication of the containment policy and that the United States went into the war without clearly understanding the nature of the conflict there, the relationship between events in Vietnam and the larger Cold War context, and the ability of the United States to influence events in Third World countries. Much of the debate in the middle to later stages of American involvement and in the immediate aftermath of the war reflects an acceptance of the limits of American power. By the late 1970s and early 1980s, however, many American policymakers and segments of the American public were willing to retest some of the original assumptions behind containment and escape from the "lessons" of Vietnam.

CHAPTER 32
The Age of Globalization

AP THEMES

- **Economic Transformations:** The last two decades of the twentieth century were marked by an impressive economic recovery from the stagflation of the 1970s. This surge of economic growth was driven primarily by investments in new technology in areas such as finance and information; the downside was that it often occurred as companies sought to reduce their labor costs through mergers and employee downsizing. The result was a steadily increasing gap between rich and poor in the United States.

- **Globalization:** The United States experienced a dramatic change in both its political and economic relationship with the rest of the world during this period, as trade barriers between nations decreased and a wider variety of goods entered the United States, while American products flooded the rest of the world. While many around the world welcomed the influx of American products and culture, others—especially in the Muslim world—opposed what they saw as American cultural hegemony.

- **War and Diplomacy:** Presidents George Bush and Bill Clinton struggled to define America's role in the immediate post-Cold War period, although by the late 1990s American foreign policy increasingly focused on intervening to promote humanitarian goals. Following the September 11, 2001, terrorist attack on the United States, President George W. Bush undertook military operations against Afghanistan and Iraq as part of a bold American initiative to promote democracy abroad, even when it meant overthrowing undemocratic regimes abroad.

- **Culture:** The nation faced another significant challenge during this period in the polarizing debates over a series of contentious cultural issues, including abortion and gay rights. At the same time, while mass media, retail chains, and popular culture continued to attract large audiences, an increasing tendency toward specialized marketing in a large variety of different areas signaled the continued fragmentation of American culture.

- **Politics and Citizenship:** American politics demonstrated significant polarization at century's end. Nowhere was this more apparent than in the largely partisan effort to remove Bill Clinton from office in 1998 and the tightly contested 2000 election between George W. Bush and Al Gore. Increasing partisanship and the seeming disappearance of the moderate center helped to create a political climate in which governing the nation became an increasingly difficult task.

CHAPTER SUMMARY
A Resurgence of Partisanship

Upon entering office, Bill Clinton faced a series of political challenges, including a slim Democratic majority in Congress and an adversarial Republican leadership, as well as personal challenges brought about by his reckless personal behavior. Clinton brought an ambitious agenda to the office and experienced a mix of successes and failures during his first years in the White House. He failed to overturn the ban on openly gay men and women in the military, settling for the "don't ask, don't tell" policy. He won passage of a budget that raised taxes on the wealthiest Americans and offered tax credits to low-income men and women while cutting spending. The result was a balanced federal budget after several decades of growing deficits. His commitment to free trade was reflected in the creation of the **North American Free Trade Agreement (NAFTA)** and the **General Agreement on Tariffs and Trade (GATT).** His most ambitious proposal, reform of the nation's health-care system, fell victim to conservative attacks and was never enacted. In foreign policy, the Clinton administration helped to broker an agreement for the partition of **Bosnia** in the former Yugoslavia to help end the brutal civil war between Christians and Muslims there.

The failure of health-care reform, among other things, paved the way for the Republicans to regain control of the House and Senate for the first time in forty years in the 1994 congressional elections. The new speaker of the House, **Newt Gingrich,** had gotten many Republican congressional candidates to agree to the so-called **"Contract with America,"** a set of conservative principles that included drastically reducing taxes and federal spending. Clinton moved his policies to the center in response to the Republican successes, but the two sides could not create a workable budget, leading to the shutdown of the federal government for several days in 1995 and 1996. Public opinion turned heavily against Gingrich and the Republicans for their failure to compromise on a way to allow the government to continue its operations during the budget negotiations.

Clinton's recovery following the 1994 elections put him in a strong position for his 1996 campaign against Republican Senator **Robert Dole** of Kansas. In the period leading up to the election, Congress passed bills raising the minimum wage and extending health coverage to Americans who had left jobs and who were ill when applying for coverage. Most important, Congress passed a **welfare reform bill** that reduced benefits for those without jobs and shifted them to low-income workers. Clinton won a relatively easy victory over Dole and Ross Perot.

Clinton's popularity grew after the 1996 election, as a soaring economy and the first federal budget surpluses in nearly thirty years helped him in public opinion polls. In 1998, however, the president's popularity was tested by a major scandal over his relationship with a young intern named **Monica Lewinsky.** Clinton's presidency had already weathered questions about his personal financial dealings, Democratic fundraising in the 1996 elections, and allegations of sexual harassment while he had been governor of Arkansas. Independent counsel **Kenneth Starr,** who had been investigating Clinton's financial dealings for several years, subpoenaed Clinton to appear before a grand jury, forcing him to admit to an "improper relationship" with Lewinsky. Despite this, Clinton remained popular in the polls and the Democrats actually gained ten House seats in the 1998 elections.

Despite Clinton's popularity, congressional Republicans pursued impeachment charges against him for lying under oath and obstruction of justice. In early 1999, after the charges passed the House, the Senate acquitted Clinton easily (neither of the charges received even a majority vote). Following his acquittal, Clinton focused primarily on foreign affairs for the remainder of his presidency, ordering bombing strikes against Iraq as a result of Saddam Hussein's failure to honor agreements he had made at the end of the first Gulf War. The most serious crisis the administration faced was in **Kosovo,** part of the former Yugoslavia, where the Kosovan minority faced large-scale atrocities from the majority Serbian population. Under United States and NATO pressure, exerted through bombing strikes and other means, Serbian troops withdrew from Kosovo in May 1999.

The 2000 election between Democratic Vice President **Al Gore** and Republican **George W. Bush,** the governor of Texas, proved uninspiring to many Americans, as the two men argued primarily over how they would use projected budget surpluses. The election, however, proved to be agonizingly close, with the final results dependent on the outcome of voting in Florida. Initial reports appeared to indicate that Gore had won Florida, but then Bush was declared the winner, a result contested by the Democrats. After a mandatory recount, state officials declared Bush the winner, which the Democrats again challenged. The issue was finally resolved in early December, when the U.S. Supreme Court by a 5–4 vote overruled the Florida Supreme Court's recount order, allowing Bush to assume the presidency.

Bush entered office pledging to reduce taxes, and Congress cooperated by passing the largest tax cut in American history. Republican efforts to move further with their agenda suffered when Republican Senator **James Jeffords** of Vermont declared that he would vote with Democrats in protest against the Bush administration's conservative direction. This broke the 50–50 deadlock in the Senate and made it difficult for Bush to carry out his agenda.

The Economic Boom

The slow growth and stagnation of the 1970s forced American businesses to change their practices by reducing labor costs, investing in new technologies, and seeking mergers to increase efficiency. In addition, new technology-based industries emerged in the 1990s particularly, helping to fuel a new period of economic growth. The result was nearly twenty years of almost unprecedented economic growth and productivity between 1983 and 2000, interrupted only by a brief recession in 1992–1993.

Much of the prosperity of the 1990s was driven by investment in Internet-based companies, causing some government officials to warn of the dangers of overinvestment in this area. Beginning in 2001, the technology sector of the economy fell dramatically as many investors sought to sell off their stocks, leading to a recession beginning in the fall of 2001. The end of the so-called Internet "bubble" coincided with revelations of improper accounting practices and other scandals as a result of the collapse and subsequent congressional investigation of Enron, a giant Houston-based energy firm. This was the first in a series of corporate scandals that would occur over the next several years.

Despite the remarkable growth of the American economy, the prosperity was less widely shared than in the earlier times. The gap between wages and salaries for workers with higher education and those without access to such education was particularly acute. The decline of American heavy industry and greater emphasis on knowledge-based industries helped to increase this gap. Perhaps the most significant change in the American economy was the degree to which it was increasingly tied to the international economy, a process known as "globalization." This process led to the availability of a wider variety of products, often at lower prices, for the American consumer. At the same time, it led to the loss of many manufacturing jobs, as American companies moved their operations overseas or collapsed in response to foreign competition.

Science and Technology in the New Economy

The proliferation of new technologies was nowhere more apparent than in the massive increase in computer usage in virtually all areas of American life. This was due to advances in the use of the **microprocessor**, which allowed smaller computers to carry out functions previously possible only with much larger machines. Beginning in the late 1970s and increasing exponentially in the 1980s, computer companies **Apple** and **IBM** began a battle to control the burgeoning market for personal computers. The new computer revolution spawned new enterprises such as computer manufacturing and software producers. The best-known software company, Microsoft, managed to achieve a virtual monopoly on operating systems, leading to a series of antitrust suits launched by the United States Justice Department (the case was initially decided against the company, although much of its impact was reduced through appeals).

Alongside the computer revolution emerged a new source of information and communication, the Internet, which allowed people from all parts of the world to communicate with one another. Growing out of government-funded research in cooperation with the Department of Defense and other agencies, the Internet was allowed to develop independently when the Defense Department pulled out of the project for security reasons. In 1989, a laboratory in Geneva developed the **World Wide Web,** which allowed individual users to publish information for the Internet.

The area of genetics underwent massive growth in the second half of the twentieth century and beyond. The discovery of DNA in 1944 and the later discovery in 1953 of its structure by scientists Francis Crick and James Watson allowed for the identification of genetic codes. In 1989, the federal government began funding the **Human Genome Project** in an effort to identify all human genes. In 1997, Scottish scientists cloned a sheep, known as **Dolly,** while DNA testing came to play a significant role in criminal trials. The relatively new science of genetic engineering has proven controversial, especially in the area of stem cell research, which uses genetic material obtained from undeveloped fetuses. While this offers the promise of helping to cure many diseases, many believe that it endangers the lives of unborn children. In 2001, President Bush issued an order banning the use of federal funds to support new stem cell research.

A Changing Society

American society faced several important demographic changes at the end of the twentieth century. Birth rates began to decline in the 1970s and remained low in the 1980s and 1990s, leading to an increase in the proportion of elderly citizens. This has put greater pressure on government programs such as Social Security pensions and has increased health-care costs significantly. In addition, it has led to changes in the workforce and a potential labor shortage during the next several decades.

Following the Immigration Reform Act of 1965, which eliminated quotas on the basis of national origin and allowed immigrants to enter on a first-come, first-served basis, the percentage of non-European immigrants in the United States increased dramatically. The growth of Latino and Asian immigration has been particularly significant. The civil rights movement helped to support the dramatic growth of an African American middle class, which made up more than half of the African American population by the end of the twentieth century. African American education levels rose exponentially following the civil rights legislation of the mid-1960s, while black participation in major professions grew apace.

Along with the growth of the black middle class occurred the growth of an African American "underclass," which lived primarily in poor urban areas. African Americans suffered from growing public impatience with affirmative action and other social programs, as well as lack of access to educational and economic opportunities. Racial tensions became apparent in rioting in Los Angeles following the acquittal of four white police officers charged with beating motorist **Rodney King,** while several years later racial differences over the guilt or innocence of former football star **O. J. Simpson,** a black man accused of killing his former wife and another young white man, further illustrated the gap between the races.

Growing drug use, based especially on the spread of "crack" cocaine, increased significantly among the poor and spawned crushing social problems in many areas, disproportionately affecting poor urban neighborhoods. Even more damaging was the growth of AIDS (acquired immune deficiency syndrome), first documented in 1981. Although this disease initially appeared among male homosexuals, by the late 1990s the most rapid increases began occurring among heterosexuals. Although scientists began developing effective treatments for the disease, the drugs needed for such treatments remained prohibitively expensive for many Americans.

The late 1990s witnessed an unexpected drop in crime, due to factors such as economic prosperity and tougher sentencing policies that took many criminals off the streets for long periods of time. This decline in crime helped to produce a high degree of social contentment among Americans.

A Contested Culture

The 1980s and 1990s witnessed heated battles over the character of American culture, nowhere more than in the area of feminism, particularly abortion rights. Many conservatives opposed abortion on a variety of religious and other grounds and sought to overturn the 1973 Supreme Court decision of *Roe* v. *Wade.* Although the Supreme Court appeared to be moving in that direction in the late 1980s, the election of Bill Clinton in 1992 paved the way for the appointing of several justices who supported abortion rights.

In addition to the struggle over reproductive rights, growing public awareness of issues such as the need for child care and the prevalence of sexual harassment fueled debate over public policy (the latter issue was particularly keen in the debate over the nomination of Supreme Court Justice **Clarence Thomas,** accused of sexual harassment by a former employee, although the appointment was eventually confirmed by a narrow margin).

Following the end of the Vietnam War, the New Left faded rapidly as many former activists retreated to enter more conventional careers or sought to work through traditional channels or on the local level to produce reform movements. The environmental movement, driven by a number of major catastrophes in the 1970s and 1980s and by warnings over the effects of pollution on the atmosphere and **global warming,** sought to influence the government to take greater measures to safeguard the world's natural environment. However, both Bush administrations rejected international agreements imposing stricter environmental standards. Overall, the post-Vietnam period demonstrated a major trend in American culture, which was the movement away from protests based on issues of economic class and toward issues that dealt with individual and community life.

Despite the emergence of a standardized mass culture, based on the growth of massive retail chains and the ability of media such as radio and film to create entertainment appealing to people across the country, the period from the late 1970s on has witnessed a growing fragmentation in American culture. This has resulted from, among other things, the practice of marketers targeting certain segments of society with their products, as well as the massive proliferation of television stations and the rise of the Internet, which allows virtually anyone to publish and disseminate their views.

The class-based controversies that had dominated public debate for much of the twentieth century gave way in the 1980s and 1990s to increasing debate over the nature of American culture. Particularly acute was the argument over issues such as how or whether to commemorate the 500th anniversary of Columbus's first voyage to the Western Hemisphere, which many argued represented the racist, imperialistic nature of western culture. This and other issues became part of a schism in which the left complained of the conservative ascendancy that limited freedom of expression, while those on the right decried the tyranny of **"political correctness,"** in which cultural radicals displayed intolerance in their efforts to defend the rights of women and other minorities.

The Perils of Globalization

The increasing globalization of the world, while greeted with enthusiasm by many, raised opposition on both ends of the political spectrum. Many opposed the increasingly interventionist United States foreign policy, as seen in Somalia and the Balkans, while others focused on the economic basis of the emerging international order. Those on the left argued that the growth of free trade hurt American workers and led to exploitative working conditions in less developed countries. The result was large-scale protest against multinational organizations such as the **World Trade Organization (WTO)** and the **International Monetary Fund (IMF)** that worked to promote a new global economy.

Among many parts of the world, globalization produced large-scale protests based more on culture and religion than on economic grounds. This was particularly true in areas such as Iran where an Islamic revolution gained power in 1979 and other parts of the Middle East, where Islamic fundamentalists sought to defend traditional culture against the inroads of the West. One result of this effort was the growing commitment of some groups and individuals to use violence to halt the western encroachment on their societies.

While acts of terrorism had occurred throughout the world in the twentieth century, Americans generally thought of terrorism as a force affecting other parts of the world until the events of September 11, 2001, which had far-reaching effects on American society, as well as U.S. foreign policy. President Bush declared a "war against terrorism," which quickly resulted in the removal of the radical Taliban government in Afghanistan and spread to Iraq and other parts of the world as well. In January 2002, President Bush spoke of an **"axis of evil"** consisting of Iran, Iraq, and North Korea. While September 11 and its aftermath caused many Americans to question their long-held assumptions about the nation's safety and security—reflected in the emergence of a host of new government regulations in areas such as travel, immigration, and banking—it also created unprecedented displays of heroism and patriotism.

The "war on terror" resulted in the fall of the Taliban regime in Afghanistan and the capture of a number of leaders of Al Qaeda, the terrorist network that planned and carried out the September 11 attacks. The United States also invaded Iraq in March 2003, based on claims that Iraq was supporting terrorist efforts throughout the world and that the Iraqi leader possessed or was close to possessing "weapons of mass destruction." While the primarily American and British military force succeeded in capturing Baghdad and overthrowing Saddam Hussein, the country entered a period of strife and instability that continues today.

The invasion of Iraq proved to be the most visible example of President Bush's bold effort to overthrow regimes that opposed freedom, despite the risks that such a course posed.

Multiple-Choice Questions

1. Bill Clinton and John F. Kennedy were similar in all of the following areas *except*
   a. they both had slim Democratic majorities in Congress that made it difficult for them to implement their domestic agendas.
   b. they were both elected by extremely thin electoral margins.
   c. they were both young, charismatic candidates who relied on their personal charm to help them to get elected.
   d. they were both relatively unknown on the national stage before their first presidential runs.
   e. they were both among the youngest presidents ever elected to office.

2. Which of the following best characterizes the American economy for the majority of the 1980s and 1990s?
   a. a combination of high inflation and slow economic growth
   b. an emphasis on maintaining heavy industry as the basis of the national economy
   c. an increased emphasis on the high-technology and knowledge-based enterprises
   d. a policy of high tariffs to protect domestic markets
   e. a decreasing gap between rich and poor as new economic opportunities became available to wider groups of people

3. President Clinton responded to the Republican successes in the 1994 midterm elections by
   a. aggressively promoting liberal causes such as universal national health care.
   b. attacking the Republicans for polarizing the nation's political debate.
   c. focusing primarily on foreign policy for his final six years in office.
   d. moving closer to the center of the political spectrum and thus limiting Republican gains.
   e. forging cooperative relationships with Republican leaders in a bipartisan effort to govern the country.

4. The elections of 1876 and 2000 were similar in that
   a. their final results were largely dependent on disputed electoral vote returns from Florida.
   b. they both attracted widespread popular interest and voter participation.
   c. they were both decided on the basis of political compromises between the major parties.
   d. they were both decided in a manner that involved little controversy.
   e. they both resulted in Democratic presidential administrations taking power.

5. All of the following were major demographic trends of the last two decades of the twentieth century *except*
   a. declining birth rates.
   b. increases in life expectancy.
   c. increasing ethnic diversity.
   d. significant growth of the African American middle class.
   e. increases in native-born workers between ages twenty-five and fifty-four.

6. Both the Rodney King and O. J. Simpson cases served as examples of
   a. the decline in racial tensions since the civil rights movement of the 1960s.
   b. the continued divide between whites and African Americans, especially regarding their perceptions of the justice system.
   c. the degree to which the media shied away from covering controversial legal cases.
   d. African American defendants being found guilty of crimes even with questionable evidence against them.
   e. largely white juries acquitting black defendants.

7. All of the following were major arguments against economic globalization *except*
   a. that the process moved jobs from advanced to less developed nations.
   b. that the process led to the creation of virtual slave labor systems in modernizing nations.
   c. that the process hurt the global environment by shifting production to nations without sufficient regulatory mechanisms.
   d. that the process enriched a small number of multinational corporations.
   e. that it kept the United States reliant on its aging industrial infrastructure.

8. The American military campaigns in Iraq and Afghanistan succeeded in
   a. capturing the leaders who planned the September 11 attack on the United States.
   b. finding evidence that each possessed "weapons of mass destruction."
   c. overthrowing undemocratic leaders who were hostile to American interests.
   d. bringing immediate order and stability to these nations.
   e. helping to improve the image of the United States abroad.

Free-Response Questions—Exam Tips

There will be very few questions directly from this period on the AP United States History Exam. A few multiple-choice questions may be drawn from the period since 1980, but no free-response questions will come exclusively from this period. Do not spend a great deal of time studying material from this chapter. You may want to consider asking your parents or an adult who lived through the 1980s and 1990s for their memories of the period; even if they are not experts in United States history, their insights might help you to be more familiar with some of the material used on the multiple-choice questions.

Free-Response Questions

1. Analyze the differences and similarities in American society and culture in the 1920s and the 1990s.

2. President Nixon and President Clinton both deserved to be removed from office. Assess the validity of this statement.

Multiple-Choice Answers

1. b. While Kennedy was elected by less than 1 percent over Richard Nixon in 1960, Clinton won a relatively comfortable victory over incumbent George Bush and third-party candidate Ross Perot in 1992 (he had only 43 percent of the popular vote but more than twice as many electoral votes as Bush).

2. c. The relatively rapid economic growth of the last two decades of the twentieth century was driven primarily by new knowledge-based industries, especially in areas such as finance and information technology; opportunities in these areas tended to be limited to those with strong educational backgrounds.

3. d. Following the success of the Republican "Contract for America," President Clinton emphasized traditionally Republican ideas such as welfare reform, tax cuts, and balancing the federal budget.

4. a. Both elections were decided only after weeks of dispute; in both cases, the electoral votes from the state of Florida played a key role in determining the outcome.

5. e. Due to declining birth rates and the aging of the American population, the number of native-born Americans between ages twenty-five and fifty-four will not increase in the first decade of the twenty-first century, forcing employers to rely on older or immigrant workers.

6. b. Both the Rodney King and O. J. Simpson cases broke down along racial lines; African Americans, and many whites were upset by the acquittal of the four white police officers accused of beating King, while in the Simpson trial large numbers of whites believed he was guilty of murder and many African Americans believed he was innocent.

7. e. While many different groups criticized globalization, it did force many American companies to become more efficient by opening United States companies to greater competition from abroad although often at the cost of jobs.

8. c. The military campaign in Afghanistan succeeded in bringing down the Taliban regime, while that in Iraq brought down Saddam Hussein; some of the longer-term goals of each capturing (Osama bin Laden; bringing order and stability to the Middle East) have yet to be accomplished.

Free-Response Questions Commentary

1. This free-response prompt gives you a wide variety of possible directions to take. A strong essay will most likely find ways to discuss major similarities and differences, while being able to qualify each; an essay that makes blanket parallels without qualifications and analysis will likely be less successful. Possible themes to explore include the role of economic prosperity in each decade, the new technologies, and the high degree of social and cultural conflict in each period. Obvious differences might include the differences between the Republican administr ations of the 1920s and the Democratic leadership of Bill Clinton throughout most of the 1990s; the much wider scope of federal activity in the 1990s; the emergence of relatively new cultural issues such as privacy and gay rights; and the generally more tolerant culture of the 1990s.

2. This is a question that has the potential to arouse strong opinions; the key is to be able to craft an objective answer that avoids partisan coloration. A strong answer will obviously need to identify the major cases against each president and then be able to evaluate the arguments for and against each president's removal. One tendency is to evaluate Nixon and Clinton in terms of public versus private behavior; some have argued that Nixon sought to undermine the two-party political system, while Clinton was simply guilty of poor personal judgment. Others have argued that presidents such as John F. Kennedy and Clinton showed patterns of dangerous recklessness in their personal behavior, patterns that could easily have influenced how they conducted public policy. Another way to assess the issue would be to examine the degree of support for their removal in the House and Senate and whether these efforts could be seen as largely partisan or as reflecting a widespread popular sentiment for removal.

PRACTICE EXAM I
AP United States History Examination

SECTION I

Multiple-Choice Section

Time—55 Minutes

80 Questions

Directions: Each question that follows has five answer choices. Choose the letter that correctly answers the question and write that letter in your exam booklet.

1. The economic salvation of the Virginia colony in its first century was
   a. the cultivation of cotton.
   b. the manufacture of silk.
   c. production of rice
   d. the growing of tobacco.
   e. production of sugarcane.

2. The main reason British imperial policy with respect to North America changed at the end of the French and Indian War in 1763 was due to
   a. the enormous national debt England incurred as a result of the war.
   b. no longer feeling the need to station any more regular troops there.
   c. the fact that England had not enjoyed peace before in the eighteenth century.
   d. Britain's need to concentrate its forces in India after defeating the French.
   e. Britain's acquisition of many French Caribbean islands in the peace treaty.

3. Alexander Hamilton supported ratification of the federal Constitution because
   a. it contained sufficient authority to provide the order and stability liberty required.
   b. it gave unchecked power to large states such as New York, where he lived.
   c. Washington and Jefferson both actively supported the new Constitution.
   d. he supported the idea of the new capital city located on the Potomac River.
   e. it contained provisions to support small farmers and agriculture.

4. Between 1840 and 1860, most Americans moved west
   a. by sailing around Cape Horn to the West Coast.
   b. by railroad, across the plains.
   c. by barge along rivers and canals to California.
   d. through the Panama Canal.
   e. along the overland trails.

5. Fort Sumter became an issue in the secession crisis because
   a. Union forces attacked it to regain claim to federal property.
   b. allowing the Union to supply the fort would make the Confederacy look weak.
   c. South Carolina seized it after seceding from the Union despite federal protests.
   d. it contained specie that the new Confederacy desperately wanted.
   e. a major Union force would be lost if the fort surrendered.

6. Populist and progressive reformers shared a belief that
    a. inflating the currency would be beneficial for the nation as a whole.
    b. cultural, racial, and ethnic diversity was a major source of strength for the United States.
    c. the power of the federal government should be used to limit the power of large corporations.
    d. the nation should return to its agrarian roots.
    e. the common people could not be trusted to make decisions about the nation's future.

7. The Scopes trial involved a dispute over
    a. an alleged murder committed by two anarchists.
    b. the rights of a group of African Americans accused of rape.
    c. the right to teach evolution in public schools.
    d. the rights of two young men accused of a gruesome murder in Chicago.
    e. the limits on the federal government's right to limit interstate commerce.

8. Franklin Roosevelt faced the most significant opposition from Congress in his
    a. efforts to pass legislation protecting labor's right to collective bargaining.
    b. efforts to expand the nation's welfare system through the creation of Social Security.
    c. efforts to raise farm prices by giving farmers subsidies to stop growing on parts of their land.
    d. efforts to change the size and composition of the Supreme Court.
    e. efforts to stop depositors from removing their funds from the nation's banks.

9. President Eisenhower's biggest domestic initiative occurred in the area of
    a. race relations.
    b. social welfare policy.
    c. labor relations.
    d. transportation.
    e. immigration policy.

10. Which of the following is true about the results of the Korean War?
    a. They increased President Truman's popularity significantly.
    b. They demonstrated the failure of the principle of collective security.
    c. They showed the limits of American power in attempting to combat communism abroad.
    d. They were an overwhelming victory for the United States.
    e. They demonstrated China's lack of influence as a military and diplomatic power.

11. Before European contact, early American Indian cultures
    a. were very diverse with some civilizations rivaling those of Europe.
    b. subsisted mainly on hunting and gathering with simple social structures.
    c. were more elaborate and wealthy in northern climates because of abundant resources.
    d. relied mainly on home manufactures for subsistence.
    e. used technologies that were on a par with those of Europe and Asia.

12. The eighteenth-century Great Awakening arose in response to all of the following *except*
    a. the movement toward secularism and away from piety in society.
    b. influential English evangelists preaching throughout the American colonies.
    c. colonial instability such as epidemics moving people to seek solace in God.
    d. churchgoers becoming dissatisfied with traditional Puritan church services.
    e. people turning to God for help during the French and Indian War.

13. The main reason for the establishment of the Democratic–Republican Party in the 1790s was
    a. fear that the strong government the Federalists were creating would lead to tyranny.
    b. to create a party that supported federal power and business interests.
    c. to oppose the radical ideas of Thomas Jefferson.
    d. the threat posed by states' rights and the nullification theory.
    e. support for internal improvements to build a national economy.

14. All of the following were considered justifications for America's Manifest Destiny in the 1830s and 1840s *except*
    a. the idea that the United States needed to acquire foreign bases to supply its navy.
    b. that both America's history and God sanctioned America's expansion over North America.
    c. that it was America's duty to civilize the savage peoples in the Americas.
    d. that it was necessary to acquire new territory to preserve economic opportunity.
    e. that our mission was to expand our institutions to new areas.

15. An ambitious goal of Reconstruction, but a goal that was not successfully attained, was
    a. improvements in education for both black and white Southerners.
    b. raising the income of former slaves.
    c. establishing free black churches.
    d. redistributing land to freedmen.
    e. the beginning of the physical rebuilding of the South.

16. The main idea of the "Gospel of Wealth" was
    a. to accumulate vast fortunes by any means.
    b. the fittest survive by gaining wealth through legal means.
    c. "greed is good" if it leads to wealth.
    d. human spirit and wealth are what is important.
    e. fortunes should be returned to the society.

17. "Is it possible and probable that nine million men can make effective progress in economic lines if they are deprived of political rights, made a servile caste, and allowed only the most meager chance for developing their successful men?"
    This quotation most closely reflects the philosophy of
    a. Booker T. Washington.
    b. W. E. B. Du Bois.
    c. Marcus Garvey.
    d. Eugene Debs.
    e. Malcolm X.

18. The most significant economic impact of World War II was
    a. the government's increased power to regulate business.
    b. the extension of new rights to organized labor.
    c. the availability of new goods and services to the American people.
    d. the restoration of prosperity due to increased federal spending.
    e. the continued dominance of the East Coast and Midwest as the
       nation's manufacturing centers.

19. The most significant demographic trend during the 1950s was
    a. increased immigration from non-European areas.
    b. the continued increase in birth rates following World War II.
    c. the decrease in birth rates following World War II.
    d. the movement of African Americans from the South to rural areas in the North.
    e. the movement of population from the Northeast and Midwest to the South and
       Southwest.

20. Lyndon Johnson faced a major dilemma over Vietnam policy as president because
    a. he was willing to consider using nuclear weapons against North Vietnam
       but feared alienating the more liberal members of the Democratic Party.
    b. he wanted to increase the numbers of ground troops there but deferred
       to American military leaders who wanted to rely on South Vietnamese troops.
    c. he wanted to focus on domestic affairs but feared attacks from conservatives
       if the United States withdrew from Vietnam.
    d. he did not believe that the United States should devote its resources to defending
       South Vietnam but felt he had to due to pressure from European allies.
    e. he did not accept the major premises of the containment policy but felt he could
       not abandon South Vietnam without losing both domestic and foreign support.

21. The United States economy faced all of the following challenges during the 1970s *except*
    a. rising prices of oil and other raw materials.
    b. increased competition from other industrialized nations such as Germany and Japan.
    c. inflation resulting from federal spending during the 1960s.
    d. deflation due to the nation's reliance on a shrinking supply of gold reserves.
    e. slow economic growth and high unemployment.

22. John Winthrop proclaimed Massachusetts Bay a "city upon a hill" to
    a. celebrate the Puritan settlement on the hills of Boston.
    b. claim that after a long search his congregation had found heaven.
    c. silence opposition to his choice of settling in Massachusetts.
    d. serve as a righteous and civil model for the world, and particularly England.
    e. deter local Indians from attacking their highly defensible settlement.

23. Both the Articles of Confederation and state constitutions drafted during the same
    period were Republican in nature due to
    a. the role of a strong executive to maintain order during wartime.
    b. the significant role played by officials appointed for life by the legislature.
    c. a weak executive with sovereign authority resting in the people.
    d. the prohibition of slavery.
    e. granting women the right to vote in states that approved.

24. In the 1830s Thomas Dew and John C. Calhoun defended slavery by arguing that
    a. slavery was more harmful to whites than to blacks.
    b. slavery was a positive good for all in Southern society.
    c. Southern aristocracy provided opportunity for all to improve their position.
    d. free blacks in Northern states were in a poorer position than slaves.
    e. slaves were spared the worst jobs, which were done by European immigrants.

25. The effect of the Emancipation Proclamation was to
    a. free no slaves immediately because the Union had no control over areas
       to which it applied.
    b. free slaves in the border states of Kentucky, Missouri, Maryland, and Delaware.
    c. end slavery immediately throughout the United States and the Confederacy.
    d. free slaves in the Union but not the Confederacy.
    e. offer compensation to slaveholders who agreed to free their slaves.

26. Urban political machines grew and thrived in the late nineteenth century due to
    a. their support from middle-class reformers.
    b. their reputation for honesty and efficiency.
    c. the failure of existing city government to provide necessary services.
    d. the favorable attention that they received in newspapers and popular
       journals of the day.
    e. the lack of voting power among immigrant groups.

27. All of the following were significant factors contributing to the onset
    of the Great Depression *except*
    a. the lack of diversification in the American economy.
    b. the excessive spending of the federal government.
    c. the weakness of the nation's farm sector.
    d. the high level of European war debt.
    e. the unequal distribution of purchasing power.

28. The major impetus for the internment of Japanese Americans was
    a. the discovery of information indicating sabotage at Pearl Harbor
       in an effort to assist the Japanese military's attack there.
    b. the breaking of the Japanese military code and consequent discovery
       of communications between military officials and Japanese Americans.
    c. the deliberate efforts of the United States government to stir up anti-Japanese
       sentiment through propaganda.
    d. the long-standing American suspicion of the Japanese, coupled with anger
       over the attack on Pearl Harbor.
    e. the belief that this action would hasten the surrender of Japan by lessening its morale.

29. The Alger Hiss trial was significant in that it
    a. catapulted Joseph McCarthy onto to the national stage.
    b. increased the suspicions of many Americans about the communist infiltration
       of the federal government.
    c. demonstrated that the Soviet Union had access to American atomic secrets.
    d. discredited the efforts of those who sought to investigate communist influence
       in the federal government.
    e. allowed the Truman administration to focus on containing communism abroad
       without worrying about domestic anticommunism.

30. Most American leaders between 1945 and 1960 believed that the best way to end poverty was to
    a. raise taxes on the wealthy and redistribute the money to the poor directly.
    b. provide job training to the poor and involve them directly in programs that were meant to assist them.
    c. create a system of universal military service that would help American national defense and provide job training for members of the lower classes.
    d. promote continued economic growth through government support for private industry and thus allow the poor greater access to the benefits of this growth.
    e. develop large-scale public works programs that would employ people regardless of the level of private-sector economic activity.

31. Unlike Dwight Eisenhower, John F. Kennedy's initial Cold War strategy sought to
    a. rely primarily on American nuclear strength to deter Soviet expansion.
    b. win the support of newly independent Third World nations through United States economic aid and other related measures.
    c. use covert operations to overthrow leaders who opposed American interests.
    d. pursue negotiations with the Soviet Union and China.
    e. build a system of mutual defense pacts to help protect American security.

32. King Philip's War and Bacon's Rebellion were both caused by
    a. royal efforts to consolidate control over the English colonies.
    b. expansion by neighboring colonies into Virginia and Massachusetts.
    c. religious tensions between Protestants and Catholics in Maryland.
    d. Dutch and German settlers trying to regain lands taken by the English.
    e. issues concerning European expansion onto Indian lands.

33. Many anti-federalists came to support ratification of the new Constitution when
    a. Shays' Rebellion showed the instability of the Confederation government.
    b. agreement was reached that a Bill of Rights would be added later.
    c. Indians threatened attack in the Northwest Territory.
    d. states were given the authority to veto federal legislation.
    e. they read the series of essays by Alexander Hamilton, James Madison, and John Jay.

34. At the close of the War of 1812, the Hartford Convention
    a. settled all outstanding claims between England and the United States.
    b. offered President Madison advice on what war strategy to pursue.
    c. expressed outrage over the British attack on Washington, D.C.
    d. proposed constitutional amendments to protect New England's political influence.
    e. ended with Republican delegates upset about the unresolved issues.

35. Life on the overland trail for women was
    a. dangerous and deadly because of the threat of Indian attack.
    b. not very different from their lives at home on the frontier.
    c. less onerous than that of men because women rode on wagons most of the way.
    d. harder than a man's work because women had to continue work when the wagon stopped.
    e. the same as that for men, as women gained full equality on the journey.

36. Enthusiasts for the "New South" included all of the following *except*
    a. Southerners who sought industrial expansion for their region after the Civil War.
    b. Confederates who fought for an independent Southern nation during the Civil War.
    c. Northern carpetbaggers who gained fortunes in the South after the Civil War.
    d. former plantation owners who wished to reestablish their former labor system.
    e. former Southern Democrats who wanted to start a Southern Republican Party.

37. The so-called "Granger laws" of the 1870s sought to
    a. control railroad rates and practices to prevent discrimination against small farmers.
    b. establish the free coinage of silver to inflate the currency.
    c. establish a system of warehousing cooperatives to raise farm prices.
    d. lower tariffs to allow farmers access to foreign markets.
    e. limit the power of trusts to allow farmers cheaper farm machinery prices.

38. The census of 1920 was significant in first revealing
    a. the closing of the frontier.
    b. the emergence of a majority urban population.
    c. that immigrants outnumbered native-born Americans.
    d. that the country's rural population was growing faster than its urban counterpart.
    e. the enormous population shift away from the Northeast to the South and Southwest.

39. The majority of ordinary Americans responded to the Great Depression by
    a. questioning and ultimately rejecting many of the traditionally dominant values of American society.
    b. joining political organizations in order to protest what they saw as the government's inadequate response to the crisis.
    c. maintaining and even increasing their commitment to the values of hard work and individual responsibility.
    d. looking abroad to other countries for answers as to how the United States should respond to the Depression.
    e. supporting third-party political candidates who offered more radical solutions than those offered by the Democratic and Republican Parties.

40. Following the passage of the 1964 Civil Rights Act, Martin Luther King Jr. and other civil rights leaders organized protests in Selma, Alabama, in an effort to
    a. promote desegregation of the city's restaurants.
    b. push for greater access to jobs and economic opportunities in the city.
    c. demand desegregation of the city's transportation facilities.
    d. demand the right for African American voter registration.
    e. allow African American students to attend a university there.

41. One of the most significant medical developments of the 1940s and 1950s was the development of
    a. antibiotic drugs to prevent infections during surgery.
    b. advances in heart and other organ transplants.
    c. a series of vaccines against viruses such as polio, influenza, and tuberculosis.
    d. radiation treatments for cancer.
    e. an understanding of the causes of HIV-AIDS.

42. One of the most effective tactics colonists used to protest the Stamp Act, Townshend Duties, and other British actions before the Revolutionary War was
    a. the economic pressure put on British merchants by the boycott.
    b. the colonial refusal to quarter and provision British troops stationed in America.
    c. increased trade with the Spanish and French islands instead of with England.
    d. appeals to the British public that their rights too were threatened by unchecked government power.
    e. not to use the official stamped paper if it was not necessary.

43. The most dangerous and direct challenge to George Washington and the national government came from
    a. rebelling slaves led by Nat Turner in Virginia.
    b. dissatisfied Indians when they found they were awarded no rights in the Constitution.
    c. western farmers who refused to pay the excise tax on whiskey.
    d. New England merchants who opposed the tariffs limiting trade.
    e. political opposition to his retirement after two terms.

44. Which of the following did not contribute to the industrial revolution after the War of 1812?
    a. President Madison's support of internal improvements, especially roads and canals
    b. merchant capital amassed during the war
    c. domestic demand for goods created by wartime conditions
    d. technological innovation in the textile industry
    e. a higher tariff that protected domestic industry

45. The Marshall Court is best known for its decisions regarding
    a. the right of slavery to exist and to expand.
    b. strong federal authority and private property.
    c. the supremacy of the state authority within its borders.
    d. the political rights of African Americans.
    e. federal authority over all Indian lands.

46. The most important new role for women during the Civil War was
    a. teaching Union veterans after they came home from the war.
    b. entering the field of nursing even though there was some resistance.
    c. working in factories to replace men who went off to battle.
    d. becoming military doctors even though men claimed they were too weak.
    e. teaching former slave women to do domestic work in their free households.

47. All of the following were major political issues at the national level during the Gilded Age *except*
    a. the protective tariff.
    b. child and female labor.
    c. railroad regulation.
    d. civil service reform.
    e. the federal currency.

48. Which of the following is true of the movement for women's suffrage in the early twentieth century?
    a. Women were more likely to receive the vote in eastern states than in the West.
    b. Women first received the right to vote in western states.
    c. Feminists were united in seeing the vote as a key to doing away with the notion of "separate spheres."
    d. The conservative mood that swept the country during World War I proved to be a hindrance to women's efforts to achieve the vote.
    e. Women campaigned for the right to vote because they believed it would allow them to do more to help immigrants, the poor, and other minority groups.

49. Which of the following events is not matched with the correct American response?
    a. Italian invasion of Ethiopia—First Neutrality Act
    b. Japanese aggression in China—FDR's Quarantine Speech
    c. German invasion of Poland—Revision of Neutrality Acts
    d. Japanese invasion of Indochina—U.S. trade embargo
    e. Spanish Civil War—cash-and-carry extended to military goods

50. Which of the following statements accurately characterizes the New Left and other student protest movements of the 1960s and early 1970s?
    a. They were able to successfully mobilize minorities and the poor in an effort to reform American society.
    b. They were generally restricted to a small but vocal and articulate minority of students at the nation's elite colleges and universities.
    c. They represented the views and outlook of a majority of the nation's college students during the period.
    d. They drew little response or attention from the media and the American general public.
    e. They had relatively little influence upon the nation's politics and society during this period.

51. Bill Clinton's biggest success during his two terms in office was his
    a. reform of the nation's health-care system.
    b. ability to convince military leaders to allow openly gay men and women to serve in the armed forces.
    c. ability to help the Democrats maintain control of the House and Senate between 1993 and 2001.
    d. ability to balance the federal budget after years of growing deficits.
    e. ability to overcome the partisan divisions between Democrats and Republicans.

52. The first written document establishing a civil government on American soil was
    a. the Mayflower Compact.
    b. the Fundamental Orders of Connecticut.
    c. the Halfway Covenant.
    d. the Maryland Act of Toleration.
    e. the Fundamental Constitution for Carolina.

53. Historians have labeled the period of colonial history before 1763 as a time of "Salutary Neglect" because
   a. colonists ignored Indian needs during this time and the response was continual warfare.
   b. neglect of religious concerns in the early eighteenth century led to witchcraft outbreaks.
   c. individual colonies focused on their own concerns, and not those of other colonies, promoting economic prosperity.
   d. British inattention to enforcing colonial policy led to growth and prosperity.
   e. royal governors were more interested in seeking fortunes and thus neglected colonial politics.

54. Territory gained as a result of the Mexican War included which of the following? Use the accompanying map to answer the question.

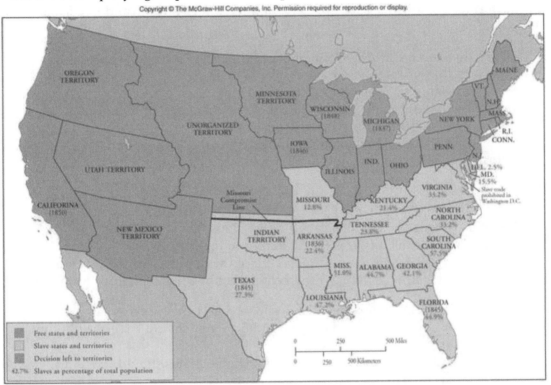

   I. California
   II. Utah Territory
   III. New Mexico Territory
   IV. Texas

   a. I
   b. I and II
   c. I, II, and III
   d. I, II, III, and IV
   e. I and III

55. Brothers Tecumseh and the Prophet responded to white efforts to move westward
    a. by successfully defending their tribal lands in defeating William Henry Harrison's forces at the Battle of Tippecanoe.
    b. ruthlessly raiding white settlements in Georgia and South Carolina.
    c. succumbing to divisions among their Indian tribes caused by Caucasian intervention.
    d. believing that negotiation backed by force would protect their tribal lands.
    e. using both religion and politics to unite Mississippi River Valley tribes against whites settling on their lands.

56. Radical Reconstruction ended in the South after
    a. Andrew Johnson was impeached by the House.
    b. Rutherford B. Hayes was elected president in 1877.
    c. the Reconstruction Act of 1867 was passed by Congress.
    d. Grant opposed Radical Republicans in the House of Representatives.
    e. the former Confederate states were readmitted under Lincoln and Johnson's programs.

57. The rise of modernism in American art and during the first several decades of the twentieth century resulted in
    a. a greater reliance on European conventions.
    b. a greater emphasis on the portrayal of themes that appealed to the elite.
    c. a greater emphasis on formal styles and standards.
    d. a greater emphasis on portraying social realities and day-to-day themes.
    e. a greater appreciation for traditional themes from the nation's past.

58. The results of the 1912 election suggest
    a. an overwhelming popular support for Woodrow Wilson.
    b. that most Americans did not support reform causes.
    c. that the Republican Party was the nation's minority party.
    d. that the split between Roosevelt and Taft cost the Republicans the election.
    e. that there were no substantive disagreements among the American electorate.

59. Henry Cabot Lodge's foreign policy philosophy is best characterized as
    a. an isolationist one that argued that the United States should have as little contact with the outside world as possible.
    b. an internationalist one that argued that the United States should cooperate with other nations in an effort to preserve international peace.
    c. a realist one that argued that the United States should act unilaterally to protect its own national interests when threatened.
    d. a universalist one that argued that the United States should seek to become the world's most powerful nation by spreading its institutions across the globe.
    e. a pragmatic one that argued that the United States should rely on more powerful European nations such as England to safeguard American security.

60. African Americans made gains in all of the following areas as a result of World War II *except*
    a. an executive order ending discrimination in the defense industry.
    b. increased sentiment for desegregation of the armed forces.
    c. challenges to segregation through the formation of civil rights organizations.
    d. a federal law desegregating all public facilities in Washington, D.C.
    e. the opportunity to move from the South to northern cities for factory jobs.

61. Central to Puritan religion and settlement was
    a. the idea of covenant with its emphasis on mutual ties and responsibilities.
    b. the separation of church and state as established by Anne Hutchinson.
    c. a commitment to toleration and the equal treatment of all people, even Indians.
    d. the county seat as the center of the community for all matters.
    e. the participation of all in both church and town affairs.

62. British advantages in the War for Independence included all of the following *except*
    a. the most powerful navy in the world.
    b. an established government with a command structure.
    c. a strong manufacturing sector.
    d. a military alliance with France.
    e. a system in place to finance the war.

63. A major reason for the declaration of war in 1812 was
    a. the French sale of Louisiana to the United States included significant territory Britain claimed.
    b. three British officials named X, Y, and Z demanded bribes from American diplomats.
    c. the British attack and burning of public buildings in Washington.
    d. British attempts at stopping American vessels from impressing English seamen.
    e. the election to Congress of nationalist War Hawks in 1810.

64. The Wilmot Proviso was continually defeated because
    a. Southern senators opposed its slavery prohibition as against their section's interests.
    b. many opposed its provision to extend the Missouri Compromise line to the West Coast.
    c. its provision for popular sovereignty in new territories angered northerners.
    d. it did not deal with the issue of slavery in the territories.
    e. Northerners objected to its provisions for lower tariff rates.

65. The largest source of financing for the Union's expenses incurred during the Civil War came from
    a. confiscating Confederate property and then selling it.
    b. printing greenbacks that were not backed by specie.
    c. loans from both American citizens and businesses.
    d. levying an income tax with rates as high as 10 percent.
    e. loans from foreign nations.

66. Theodore Roosevelt's "New Nationalism" and Woodrow Wilson's "New Freedom" were primarily focused on their approaches toward
    a. the proper course that the United States should take in its approach to the rest of the world.
    b. the proper approach to business consolidation.
    c. the best way to ensure protection of the civil rights of minority groups.
    d. the issue of how best to conserve the nation's environmental resources.
    e. the issue of women's suffrage.

67. Both Warren Harding and Calvin Coolidge were successful in
    (a.) surrounding themselves with able, energetic cabinet members who made
        up for many of their personal shortcomings.
    b. presenting Congress with ambitious legislative agendas and following
        through on gaining passage of key measures.
    c. using their personal charisma and rhetorical abilities to gain widespread
        popular support for their programs.
    d. promoting honesty and integrity in the federal government.
    e. implementing reforms to expand federal protections for the less fortunate
        in American society.

68. The Berlin Crisis of 1948 and 1949 was a major turning point in the early
    Cold War because
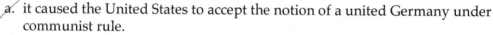
    a. it caused the United States to accept the notion of a united Germany under
        communist rule.
    b. it led to widespread questioning of the wisdom of the containment doctrine
        among the American people.
    c. it convinced American leaders that while they could not stop communist
        expansion in Europe, they should focus their efforts on non-western areas.
    (d.) it hastened the formation of a divided Europe through rival alliance systems.
    e. it convinced American leaders that Soviet leaders were open to the possibility
        of negotiations.

69. Which of the following is true of the movement for an Equal Rights Amendment
    in the twentieth century?
    a. It was first introduced as part of the renewed feminism movement of the 1960s
        and 1970s.
    b. It was first raised during the 1920s and once again during the 1960s, although
        it was never presented to the states for ratification.
    c. It found little or no popular support in either the 1960s or 1970s.
    (d.) It initially found significant support in the 1960s and 1970s, although
        it was never ratified due to rising conservative opposition.
    e. It was passed by Congress and finally ratified by the states in 1982.

70. A major trend in American immigration since the 1960s has been
    a. a decrease in the number of illegal immigrants.
    (b.) a significant increase in Asian immigrants.
    c. the continued preponderance of those of European descent.
    d. unlimited immigration from Latin America.
    e. a decrease in overall numbers of immigrants by the end of the twentieth century.

71. The central idea of Whig ideology was that
    a. peaceful obedience to government policy gained groups a voice in government.
    b. a strong central government would provide order and security.
    (c.) concentrated power invariably led to corruption and tyranny.
    d. opposition to the king was disrespectful and promoted tyranny.
    e. an enlightened aristocracy was the group most able to rule a country wisely.

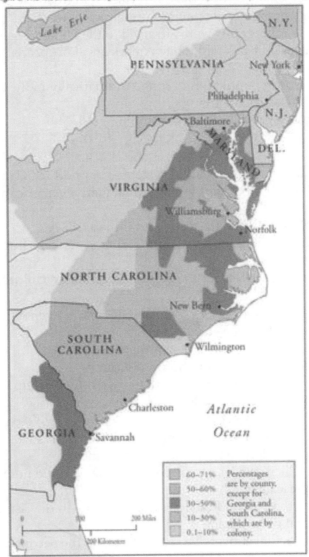

72. The accompanying map indicates that
    a. black majorities existed throughout the southern colonies.
    b. despite its Quaker foundations, there was a substantial slave population in Pennsylvania.
    c. only South Carolina had a slave majority.
    d. Maryland had more slaves than Virginia.
    e. black slaves were not a significant proportion of any colony.

73. Following the example set during the American Revolution, Jefferson
    a. wanted to resolve the crisis with Britain in 1806–1807 by military warfare.
    b. tried to ally with France to oppose English transgressions.
    c. believed continued negotiation would lead to a successful result.
    d. attempted to use economic warfare by proposing an embargo.
    e. refused to pay tribute to England to stop the impressments of American seamen.

74. All of the following characterized the California Gold Rush *except*
   a. that California's population expanded dramatically from 1848 to 1852.
   b. the first Chinese immigrants were attracted to the United States.
   c. immigrants included black and white Americans, Europeans, South Americans, and Mexicans.
   d. the Native American population declined dramatically in the two decades following the discovery of gold.
   e. most immigrants gained wealth from finding gold.

75. One of the major effects of the Dawes Act was
   a. the strengthening of the reservation system to support tribal culture.
   b. the transfer of much tribal land to individual Native Americans or white owners.
   c. continued warfare between the army and Indian tribes.
   d. successful assimilation of most western Native Americans into mainstream American society.
   e. the end of boarding schools for the education of Indian children.

76. Which of the following is true of vaudeville in the early twentieth century?
   a. It was only accessible to the elite.
   b. It was open to African American performers.
   c. It excluded members of recent immigrant groups.
   d. Its performers rarely reached beyond their own ethnic group.
   e. It remained limited to small-scale, inexpensive venues.

77. A major difference between the First and Second Red Scares was the
   a. sense of postwar anxiety that fueled each movement.
   b. use of antiradicalism as a way to persecute those who did not fit popular notions of "Americanism."
   c. degree to which the Second Red Scare was focused on the issue of subversion within the federal government.
   d. large number of actual subversives caught during the Second Red Scare.
   e. fear of international communist expansion.

78. The event that had the most negative impact on American public opinion during the Vietnam War was
   a. congressional passage of the Gulf of Tonkin resolution.
   b. Senator J. William Fulbright's hearings on the war.
   c. the Tet Offensive.
   d. the release of the Pentagon Papers.
   e. President Nixon's Christmas bombing.

79. Rachel Carson's *Silent Spring* was significant in that
   a. it highlighted the problems faced by women who could not find a voice in American society.
   b. it promoted the growth of ecology by warning of the dangers caused by the pesticide DDT.
   c. it warned of the harmful effects of Agent Orange on the environment in Vietnam.
   d. it caused chemical company executives to voluntarily change harmful environmental practices.
   e. its reception demonstrated the widespread popular indifference to environmental issues.

80. The impeachment efforts against Richard Nixon and Bill Clinton differed in that
   a. Nixon resigned before a full House vote on impeachment, while Clinton was acquitted by the Senate of all charges.
   b. Nixon was acquitted by the full Senate, while Clinton resigned before he could be convicted.
   c. the House of Representatives voted overwhelmingly to impeach Nixon but failed to attract enough votes to impeach Clinton.
   d. the charges against Nixon were conducted entirely along partisan lines, while those against Clinton attracted widespread support from both parties.
   e. Republicans feared the ascension of Gerald Ford to the presidency, while Clinton's threat to resign caused Republican senators to vote against conviction.

United States History

SECTION II
Part A
(Suggested writing time—45 minutes)
Percent of Section II score—45

Directions: The following question requires you to construct a coherent essay that integrates your interpretation of Documents A through I and your knowledge of the period referred to in the question. High scores will be earned only by those essays that both cite key pieces of evidence from the documents and draw on outside knowledge of the period.

To what degree did the African American civil rights movement achieve its goals of full social, political, and economic equality in the period between 1945 and 1975?

Document A

Source: Harry Truman, Speech before Congress, February 1948.

The protection of civil rights is the duty of every government which derives its powers from the consent of the people. This is equally true of local, state, and national governments. . . .

The federal government has a clear duty to see that constitutional guarantees of individual liberties and of equal protection under the laws are not denied or abridge anywhere in our Union. That duty is shared by all three branches of the government, but it can be fulfilled only if the Congress enacts modern, comprehensive civil rights laws, adequate to the needs of the day, and demonstrating our continuing faith in the free way of life.

Document B

Source: Bettman/Corbis.

Little Rock An African American student passes by jeering whites in Arkansas on her way to Little Rock High School newly integrated by federal court order.

Document C

Source: United States Constitution, Amendment XXIV

Passed by Congress August 27, 1962. Ratified January 23, 1964.

Section 1.
The right of citizens of the United States to vote in any primary or other election for President or Vice President, for electors for President or Vice President, or for Senator or Representative in Congress, shall not be denied or abridged by the United States or any State by reason of failure to pay poll tax or other tax.

Document D

Source: Stokely Carmichael, "What We Want," *New York Review of Books*, September 1966.

Ultimately, the economic foundations of this country must be shaken if black people are to control their lives. The colonies of the United States—and this includes the black ghettoes within its borders, North and South—must be liberated. For a century, this nation has been like an octopus if exploitation, its tentacles stretching from Mississippi and Harlem to South America, the Middle East, southern Africa, and Vietnam; the form of exploitation varies from area to area but the essential result has been the same—a powerful few have been maintained and enriched at the expense of the poor and voiceless colored masses. This pattern must be broken. As its grip loosens here and there around the world, the hopes of black Americans become more realistic. For racism to die, a totally different America must be born.

Document E

African American
Migration, 1950–1980

Document F

Source: National Commission on Civil Disorders Report, 1968.

This is our basic conclusion: Our nation is moving toward two societies, one black, one white— separate and unequal.

Reaction to last summer's disorders has quickened the movement and deepened the division. Discrimination and segregation have long permeated much of American life; they now threaten the future of every American.

This deepening racial division is not inevitable. The movement apart can be reversed. Choice is still possible. Our principal task is to define that choice and to press for a national resolution.

To pursue our present course will involve the continuing polarization of the American community and, ultimately, the destruction of basic democratic values.

The alternative is not blind repression or capitulation to lawlessness. It is the realization of common opportunities for all within a single society.

This alternative will require a commitment to national action—compassionate, massive and sustained, backed by the resources of the most powerful and the richest nation on this earth. From every American it will require new attitudes, new understanding, and, above all, new will.

The vital needs of the nation must be met; hard choices must be made, and, if necessary, new taxes enacted.

Document G

Source: Historical Statistics of the United States.

Median Wage or Salary Income, 1955–1970		
Year	White	Black and other races
1970	$5,490	$4,674
1969	5,168	4,231
1968	4,700	3,677
1967	4,394	3,363
1966	4,152	2,949
1965	3,960	2,713
1964	3,859	2,674
1963	3,723	2,368
1962	3,601	2,278
1961	3,480	2,325
1960	3,410	2,372
1959	3,306	2,196
1958	3,225	1,988
1957	3,107	1,866
1956	2,958	1,637
1955	2,870	1,637

Document H

Source: United States Supreme Court, *Swann* v. *Charlotte Mecklenburg Board of Education*, April 1971.

Absent a constitutional violation there would be no basis for judicially ordering assignment of students on a racial basis. All things being equal, with no history of discrimination, it might well be desirable to assign pupils to schools nearest their homes. But all things are not equal in a system that has been deliberately constructed and maintained to enforce racial segregation. The remedy for such segregation may be administratively awkward, inconvenient, and even bizarre in some situations and may impose burdens on some; but all awkwardness and inconvenience cannot be avoided in the interim period when remedial adjustments are being made to eliminate the dual school systems.

Document I

Source: Third National Institute for Black Elected Public Officials, Statement of Principles, December 1975.

The needs of black Americans today are not too different than they have been for the last decade and, therefore, the specific concerns and demands of this document are not new. They are a reaffirmation of what the country has been told over the years. . . .
In an era of declining economy and a clear withdrawal by the country from its constitutional commitment for justice, it is essential for black elected officials to become more vigilant and forceful in meeting the needs of their constituents. The general moral decline shall not deter us from the drive for economic justice for all Americans.

United States History

SECTION II
Part B and Part C
(Suggested total planning and writing time—70 minutes)
Percent of Section II score—55

Part B
Directions: Choose ONE question from this part. You are advised to spend 5 minutes planning and 30 minutes writing your answer. Cite relevant historical evidence in support of your generalizations and present your arguments clearly and logically.

1. "The Industrial Revolution increased individual opportunity."
   Evaluate the validity of this statement in the period from 1800 to 1840.

2. Analyze the impact of slavery on the development of American political parties between 1840 and 1860.

Part C
Directions: Choose ONE question from this part. You are advised to spend 5 minutes planning and 30 minutes writing your answer. Cite relevant historical evidence in support of your generalizations and present your arguments clearly and logically.

1. Analyze the emergence of the "new woman" between 1900 and 1930 and evaluate whether this phenomenon was more myth or reality.

2. To what degree did Wilsonian principles influence the foreign policy of Franklin Roosevelt between 1933 and 1945?

PRACTICE EXAM ANSWERS
Multiple-Choice Answers

1. d. Virginia struggled mightily with disease and death in its early years; the discovery of new tobacco cultivation techniques by John Rolfe helped to salvage the colony and its settlers.

2. a. Great Britain's debt more than doubled as a result of the French and Indian War, leading Chancellor of the Exchequer Grenville to seek to make the colonies bear a greater share of the cost of their defense.

3. a. Hamilton strongly believed that liberty could only exist under a strong central government that could provide order and believed that the Articles of Confederation had failed in not placing enough power in Congress, resulting in anarchy.

4. e. The internal migrations of this period occurred primarily along the Oregon Trail and to a lesser degree, the Santa Fe Trail, as this was the most feasible mode of travel.

5. b. President Lincoln was determined to resupply Fort Sumter, while Confederate leaders were determined to resist these efforts, reasoning that it was worse to appear to be weak before federal efforts than to be the aggressor in attacking Sumter.

6. c. While the populists and progressives differed in their constituency and outlook, as well as in a number of aspects of their program, both groups believed that increased federal power was necessary to combat the power of big business.

7. c. This 1925 trial, brought on by a challenge to Tennessee's antievolution law, became a flashpoint for the cultural conflict between the urban and rural parts of the country.

8. d. FDR's so-called "court-packing" plan, a reaction to the Supreme Court's overturning of several key New Deal measures, aroused such significant opposition from members of Congress who saw it as a threat to the system of checks and balances that the president was forced to abandon it.

9. d. Eisenhower believed in a relatively limited role for the federal government, but the Federal Highway Act of 1956 appropriated $25 billion for highway construction and had a major impact on the nation's travel and residential patterns.

10. c. Much of the frustration that the American public had over the Korean conflict resulted from the fact that it was a limited war that the United States was unable to win, having to settle for a stalemate after having repelled North Korea's initial incursion into the South.

11. a. While many of the early tribes lived in nomadic bands that relied on hunting and gathering, over time the Aztecs, Inca, and Maya at various points all achieved levels rivaling those of many European civilizations before the Spanish arrival in the Western Hemisphere.

12. e. The French and Indian War occurred after the Great Awakening, which moved through the colonies in the 1730s and 1740s.

13. a. The Democratic–Republican Party formed in opposition to the Federalist program, especially the creation of the Bank of the United States, which its members saw as an unconstitutional measure that put too much power in the hands of that nation's elite.

14. a. Alfred Thayer Mahan and other proponents of expansion argued for the acquisition of foreign bases in the 1890s, much later than the other rationales for Manifest Destiny.

15. d. While some freedmen believed that they would be given "forty acres and a mule" during Reconstruction, land redistribution in the South never occurred.

16. e. Andrew Carnegie, John D. Rockefeller, and other industrialists believed that they had a responsibility to use large portions for their wealth to support philanthropic causes.

17. b. Du Bois believed strongly in educating what he referred to as the "talented tenth," African Americans who could enter leadership positions in society and hope to lift the black race overall.

18. b. While unemployment remained high (above 15 percent) until the outbreak of World War II in 1939, the war's massive federal spending resulted in a return to full employment and prosperity much more effectively than the New Deal had been able to do.

19. b. The so-called "baby boom" following World War II helped to facilitate other important demographic trends of this period, such as suburbanization, as young couples with children moved to the suburbs in search of what they believed to be safer conditions and better schools.

20. c. Johnson's main focus was his Great Society program, but he feared a repeat of the anticommunist backlash against Truman and his advisors, who were accused of "losing" China in 1949, if he withdrew from Vietnam.

21. d. The United States had gone off of the gold standard during the 1930s; among the decade's most significant problems was not deflation but rather inflation due to rising oil prices and other related factors.

22. d. Winthrop's famous sermon, delivered upon the arrival of the Puritans at Massachusetts Bay, called upon the colony's settlers to serve as an example to a corrupt England, as he and his followers hoped eventually to reform the corrupt Anglican Church.

23. c. Both the national and state governments formed during the Revolution reflected the fear of centralized executive power that the newly independent former colonies held due to their experience under British rule and widespread belief in the tenets of Whig ideology.

24. b. Thomas Jefferson and other Southerners had argued that slavery was a "necessary evil" through the 1820s; the growth of the abolitionist movement and slave resistance changed the terms of the arguments as Southerners began to argue that slavery was in fact a "positive good."

25. a. The Emancipation Proclamation freed slaves in areas that were in rebellion against the Union; Lincoln wanted to use the proclamation as a war measure, reasoning that freeing slaves in Confederate areas that came under Union occupation would hurt the South's military effort.

26. c. Urban political machines such as New York's Tammany Hall, while enriching their leaders, also filled a necessary vacuum left by the inadequacy of existing political structures through providing jobs, limited welfare, and other services for new immigrants.

27. b. The Republican administrations of the 1920s sought to cut federal spending and balance the federal budget; federal spending thus had little impact on the emergence of the Depression.

28. d. No direct evidence was ever found linking Japanese Americans to the attack on Pearl Harbor or to the Japanese war effort; the policy of internment was largely the result of long-standing hostility toward the Japanese, especially on the West Coast, as well as American anger over the Japanese attack on Pearl Harbor.

29. b. The Hiss trial of 1948, in which Hiss was found guilty of perjury (the statute of limitations on espionage had run out), helped to increase the fear of the American people about communist involvement in government; it also helped to increase the status of Richard Nixon as an anticommunist and helped to lay the groundwork for the later popularity of Joseph McCarthy.

30. d. The seemingly limitless economic growth of the 1950s convinced American leaders that increased production, rather than efforts to limit what the wealthy could acquire and redistribute wealth, was the best way to eliminate poverty.

31. b. Kennedy, responding to Soviet leader Nikita Khrushchev's pledge to support "wars of national liberation" in the newly independent nations, sought to use programs such as the Peace Corps and the Alliance for Progress to win support in the so-called Third World; he believed that the Eisenhower administration had relied too heavily upon nuclear weapons and failed to cultivate the forces of nationalism abroad.

32. e. These two conflicts, both occurring in the mid-1670s, highlighted the conflicts between the white expansionist desires and Native American efforts to defend their land in Massachusetts Bay and Virginia, respectively.

33. b. Anti-federalists opposed the Constitution largely due to the increased centralized power envisioned in the document; they felt that a Bill of Rights would protect their liberties and prevent a repeat of the colonial experience under Great Britain.

34. d. New England Federalists, concerned about what they believed was the excessive influence of the "Virginia Dynasty" or Democratic–Republican presidents, sought to make it more difficult for the United States to acquire new territory, make trade embargos, and declare war.

35. d. Women on the overland trail struggled as they had to take on additional tasks due to the new circumstances of their journey, while continuing the "domestic" tasks that continued when the wagon train stopped.

36. b. Many who fought to establish a separate Confederate nation based on slavery, agrarianism, and limited government opposed the efforts of both northerners and southerners to create an industrialized "New South."

37. a. Farmers were upset by the fact that they frequently had to pay higher rates to ship their goods than those who were able to ship larger amounts of goods over longer distances; elimination of the "short haul/long haul" distinction was a major goal of the Granger laws passed on the state level.

38. b. The urban–rural division was a key theme of the 1920s; the 1920 census showed that a majority of Americans lived in urban areas for the first time in the nation's history.

39. c. Despite the depth and severity of the Depression, the majority of Americans avoided looking for radical solutions to the crisis and instead simply sought to work harder and assume a greater sense of personal responsibility for their plight.

40. d. Once the Civil Rights Act of 1964 forbade segregation in public places, civil rights leaders turned their attention to voting rights, making Selma a major target and thus influencing passage of the 1965 Voting Rights Act.

41. c. Following the end of World War II, scientists were able to build upon earlier advances in the understanding of viruses to develop vaccines against several of the most devastating diseases of the early twentieth century; these advances led to declines in infant mortality rates and increases in life expectancy.

42. a. Colonial resistance to British taxation measures centered on boycotting British goods, an effort to appeal to the economic self-interest of English merchants

43. c. Farmers in western Pennsylvania rebelled against the excise tax on whiskey in 1794; Washington responded by personally leading a large military force against the rebellion in a strong assertion of federal power.

44. a. Although Madison adopted a number of federalist-style programs after the War of 1812, he believed that a constitutional amendment was necessary to allow the federal government to fund internal improvements.

45. b. John Marshall, chief justice from 1801 to 1835, issued a series of decisions asserting the power of the federal government over the states (most notably *McCullough* v. *Maryland*) and the rights of private property (*Dartmouth College* v. *Woodward*).

46. b. Nursing had been dominated by men prior to the Civil War; the conflict caused a shift whereby nursing became an almost entirely female-dominated profession by the late nineteenth century.

47. b. Gilded Age issues included political corruption and reform, early efforts at business regulation, and the gold standard and tariffs; not until the progressive era did protection for workers become a national issue.

48. b. The western states gave women the right to vote earlier than states on the East Coast; traditional historians note the influence of frontier egalitarianism as the major factor, while more recent interpretations stress the fact that women's suffrage in western states was less tied with controversial social issues such as temperance and prohibition.

49. e. During the Spanish Civil War, the United States Congress passed the Neutrality Act of 1937, which forbade the sale of arms to either side in a civil war; this clearly helped the Spanish fascists under Francisco Franco, who received substantial military aid, while France, England, and the United States agreed not to help arm the Republicans.

50. b. Despite popular stereotypes of the 1960s (helped by the media's focus on student protests), most college students remained fairly conventional in their attitudes and actions; highly visible protests at the University of California at Berkeley and Columbia University, among others, account for the prominent image of the student protester.

51. d. Clinton went against the stereotype of the Democrats as the party of federal spending; through cuts in defense spending and fiscal disciplines in domestic programs, he was able to balance the federal budget.

52. a. A group of forty-one Pilgrims, or Separatists, agreed to form a "Civil Body Politik" through the Mayflower Compact upon their arrival at Plymouth Rock in 1620, a document that began the tradition of written governmental charters in the English colonies.

53. d. Before 1763, British officials loosely enforced colonial trade regulations to the mutual benefit of both England and the colonies; increased British debt as a result of the French and Indian War led to a shift toward tighter regulations.

54. c. Texas had joined the Union by a joint resolution of Congress in early 1845; one of the precipitating issues in the Mexican War was the dispute between the United States and Mexico over the Texas boundary.

55. e. Tecumseh and the Prophet sought to create a pan-Indian movement to oppose the movement of white settlers into Indian lands; Tecumseh sought cooperation with the British and tribal alliances, while the Prophet emphasized messianic prophecies and Indian religious revival until their forces were defeated at the Battle of Tippecanoe in 1811.

56. b. Hayes was elected as a result of the disputed election of 1876, receiving disputed electoral votes from three southern states in exchange for a pledge to end the federal occupation of the South as part of the Compromise of 1877.

57. d. Movements such as the Ashcan School reflected an emphasis on portraying urban life and other themes associated with everyday life; this was a movement away from the earlier reliance on classicism and formalism.

58. d. Wilson won less than 50 percent of the popular vote; the split between Roosevelt and the progressive wing of the Republican Party and Taft and the more conservative wing most likely cost the Republican Party the election.

59. c. Lodge, the influential chairman of the Senate Foreign Relations Committee during World War I, opposed U.S. entry into the League of Nations because he wanted to safeguard the United States' ability to preserve its freedom of action and not get dragged into conflicts that were not direct threats to American security or interests.

60. d. Although some D.C. restaurants were desegregated during the war, complete desegregation awaited the later civil rights movement and the 1964 Civil Rights Act.

61. a. The Puritan community relied on the covenant ideal as a way to bind its members together as they sought to create their ideal settlement in Massachusetts Bay.

62. d. France sought revenge against Great Britain following the end of the Seven Years' War in 1763; the American Revolution provided a perfect opportunity for France to exact this.

63. e. Westerners, known as War Hawks, desired territorial expansion and wanted to stop Britain's violation of America's rights as a neutral nation.

64. a. The Wilmot Proviso twice passed the House of Representatives; equal representation in the Senate allowed the South to kill the measure, which would have banned slavery in the areas acquired as a result of the Mexican War.

65. c. For the first time, the federal government undertook a program to sell bonds to ordinary citizens rather than just the wealthy, resulting in a program of mass financing of a war that helped to create a model for the two world wars.

66. b. Roosevelt and Wilson differed, at least rhetorically, on their approaches toward big business; Roosevelt leaned toward regulation of business, Wilson toward breaking up large combinations to ensure greater competition.

67. a. While both Harding and Coolidge believed in a limited presidential role, they relied heavily on able advisors such as Secretary of State Charles Evans Hughes, Commerce Secretary Herbert Hoover, and U.S. Treasury Secretary Andrew Mellon.

68. d. The Berlin Crisis hastened the formation of NATO by making European and American leaders fear the Soviet military threat to Western Europe; the Soviet Union responded by creating the Warsaw Pact in 1955.

69. d. The ERA passed both houses of Congress and received support in many states throughout the 1970s; rising conservative opposition in the late 1970s, however, stalled it short of the necessary three-fourths majority in 1982.

70. b. The Immigration Act of 1965 led to a significant increase in non-western immigration, especially Asian immigrants who had been limited by earlier acts.

71. c. Colonial resistance to Great Britain was heavily based on Whig ideology, drawn from English opposition thinkers who feared the growth of central power in England.

72. c. South Carolina proved the exception among England's American colonies in that it was the only one with a black majority.

73. d. Jefferson feared the harmful domestic effects of large military establishments; he believed instead that commercial warfare could achieve American goals short of armed conflict.

74. e. While diverse groups of people flooded into California in search of riches, few actually found them; the gold rush was more important in creating a heterogeneous, unstable population than in producing widespread wealth for new immigrants to the region.

75. b. The Dawes Act encouraged Indian ownership of private property and hastened the end of communal tribal ownership of land by Indians.

76. b. Vaudeville was the most popular urban entertainment form in the early twentieth century; aspects of it built upon the earlier minstrel performances of African Americans, making it one of the few areas open to black performers.

77. c. The First Red Scare focused primarily on anarchist, communist, and other radical groups operating in American society; the Second Red Scare shared many of these concerns but focused much more heavily on the role of alleged communist subversion in the federal government.

78. c. A majority of Americans supported the United States military effort in Vietnam prior to the Tet Offensive of January 1968; after that, while other events caused further erosions in public support, the major damage had already been done.

79. b. Carson's influential 1962 book warned of the harm caused by DDT; although it enraged chemical company executives, it helped to fuel popular concern over environmental issues and led the federal government to ban DDT in 1972.

80. a. Nixon resigned after it became clear following the release of the transcript of tapes showing his role in covering up the Watergate break meant that he would be impeached by the House and convicted by the Senate; although Clinton was impeached by the House, the Senate failed to attract even a simple majority for the two charges against Clinton.

SECTION II

Part A

The strongest essays will have a sophisticated thesis that addresses the progress of the civil rights movement in all three categories (political, social, and economic), with body paragraphs that treat all three areas relatively equally; that uses a substantial number of documents; and is well organized, without major errors. Most likely, you will find differences in the three areas; African Americans may have moved closer to equality in some areas than in others.

Among the documents, political equality is probably the most straightforward to address. President Truman calls for comprehensive civil rights legislation in Document A; possible background knowledge to bring in might be the split in the Democratic Party in 1948. The Twenty-Fourth Amendment, Document D, outlawed the poll tax; you will most likely want to refer as well to the Voting Rights Act of 1965, which gave federal protection to those attempting to register to vote.

Social equality is more difficult to measure. The most obvious place to begin is education. A strong essay should analyze *Brown* v. *Board of Education* and discuss its impact and implementation. The picture of the African American student entering Little Rock's Central High School surrounded by jeering whites provides an opportunity to discuss white resistance to school integration; Document H alludes to the continued *de facto* segregation through the Supreme Court's sanction for busing. You may want to discuss the reaction to busing in northern cities such as Boston to show that the difficulties of desegregation were not confined to the South.

Economic equality became an increasing focus of civil rights advocates following the passage of civil rights legislation in the mid-1960s. Stokely Carmichael, an advocate of "black power," the members of the President's Commission on Civil Disorders, and members of the Third National Institute for Black Public Officials all suggest that economic inequality remains the single biggest problem facing African Americans. Despite African American complaints about continuing economic inequality, the chart shows that median minority incomes increased at a faster rate than white incomes from 1955 to 1970.

You should offer a conclusion that once again addresses the progress that African Americans made in the political, social, and economic realms; you will probably be more successful if you qualify your analysis by noting that the civil rights movement was more successful in some areas than in others. You will also be more successful if you are able to offer a sense of why more progress was made in some areas than in others and what accounts for different results in the political versus the social and economic realms.

Part B

1. This is a broad question that invites a variety of different answers and should allow you to analyze a number of different types of information. The most important element of this essay is for you to define what types of opportunity existed; also, you should qualify your essay in terms of different groups for whom opportunity increased or decreased. An essay that makes a blanket statement for all groups in society will probably not be particularly successful. A strong essay will also address the impact of industrialization and economic opportunity in different regions of the country. Finally, you should try to show trends and changes during the forty years covered in the question.

An essay on this topic should discuss the process of industrialization and its social impacts; areas to include could be the role of the War of 1812 in spurring industrialization; the impact of technological innovations and the emergence of the factory system; the initial development of labor unions; and the growth of urban areas, especially in the Northeast. The main focus should be on how the process of industrialization affected different groups. Examples should include a discussion of the recruitment process for factory labor and the fact that over time factory owners found it increasingly difficult to maintain the relatively high wages and good working conditions that existed in places such as Lowell because large-scale immigration after 1840 brought in a new source of labor. Another theme to consider would be the decline of the independent artisan, which led to the emergence of workingmen's political parties and early labor unions. The issue of wealth distribution is also significant because many groups, slaves, Native Americans, poor farmers, and unskilled workers were almost always left out of the nation's prosperity. Evidence shows that even with more white male skilled workers, there was a growing gap between rich and poor during this period. As occurred in the Second Industrial Revolution, the middle class was the fastest growing group during this period.

A strong essay will conclude with a reiteration of your thesis. Be sure to be as specific as possible in noting who received increased opportunities and to what extent.

2. This essay requires you to develop a thesis and essay that demonstrates how and why slavery transformed American political parties between 1840 and 1860. Specifically, a strong essay needs to show that the existing political party system of Democrats and Whigs in the 1830s and 1840s could not deal effectively with the issue, leading to the emergence of a new party system in the 1850s. In addition, a strong essay should show factors that changed over the period between 1840 and 1860 that made compromise over slavery more difficult. These factors should include the growing popular mobilization, the increasing moral argument over slavery; and the loss of a generation of compromise-minded leaders such as Henry Clay and Daniel Webster in the early 1850s.

The body of your essay should include a discussion of the Mexican War and its aftermath; the Compromise of 1850; the publication of *Uncle Tom's Cabin* in 1852; the split of the Whig Party following the 1852 election; the Kansas–Nebraska Act and the emergence of the Republican Party; the Dred Scott decision and its impact on the Democratic Party; the Lincoln–Douglas debates of 1858 (especially Lincoln's "House Divided" speech); and the election of 1860, which made secession and war almost inevitable, as the South felt slavery and its interests could no longer be defended under the existing political system. Keep in mind that Lincoln's name did not even appear on the ballot in the South.

Your conclusion should again stress the transformative effect of slavery on the party system, noting that the existing political parties in 1840 could not effectively diffuse slavery as a volatile political issue. Over time, as slavery came to be increasingly cast in moral terms, compromise became less possible. The formation of the sectional-based Republican Party and the division of the Democrats created further conflict. Many historians argue that only the Civil War could finally resolve the slavery question.

Part C

1. This question will allow you to look at the extent to which the idea of the "new woman" was myth and reality. Essentially, the question is asking you to evaluate the extent of change that occurred in the roles of women during the first three decades of the

twentieth century. The most successful essays will likely be those that note that the period represented both gains and disappointments for women. A strong essay should also note who claimed the label of "new women" and how representative they were of the larger female community as this phenomenon was largely restricted to white urban middle-class women. Immigrants, African Americans, farm wives, and poor women in urban areas experienced few of these changes.

Your essay should discuss reasons for the emergence of new ideas about the role of women at the end of the nineteenth century. These can include changing ideas about the role of the family, as women were required to spend less time in child rearing and running the household; increased access to education; and limited professional growth. Manifestation of women's desire for a new role include the growth of women's clubs; the women's suffrage movement; and the widespread female involvement in movements such as temperance, consumer protection, and child labor restrictions. An essay on this topic should also examine the 1920s, when the high expectations following ratification of the Nineteenth Amendment were to some extent disappointed. You will want to note the factors that limited changes for women, especially if your essay emphasizes the lack of gains during the period.

Your essay should provide a strong conclusion that reiterates your argument about how widespread the phenomenon of the "new woman" was and accounts for why changes did or did not occur. The ability to show changes and important turning points during this period will strengthen your essay.

2. This essay question requires you to demonstrate your knowledge of Wilsonian foreign policy and its major principles, as well as the foreign policies beliefs and actions of Franklin Roosevelt. A successful essay will demonstrate that Roosevelt's policies were more Wilsonian at some points than at others, as FDR was willing to adapt to circumstances and adopt policies appropriate to changing conditions. You may also qualify your essay by noting that Roosevelt focused on certain aspects of Wilson's vision more than others.

Your essay should briefly summarize the major tenets of Wilson's foreign policy especially those that you relate to FDR's policies. You will probably want to address the foreign and domestic issues that FDR faced when he took office. Focus on the impact of the Depression and American public opinion on his policies. A substantial portion of your essay should analyze FDR's response to the world economic and diplomatic crises of the 1930s as well as World War II, and Roosevelt's vision for the postwar world. Specific examples that could be related to Wilson may include the Atlantic Charter, the concept of the "Four Freedoms," his goals for a postwar United Nations. and his views on European colonialism.

Your conclusion should emphasize the degree to which Roosevelt can be considered Wilsonian in his views, as well as provide a more specific discussion of the degree to which he developed his own foreign policy.

PRACTICE EXAM II
AP United States History Examination

SECTION I

Multiple-Choice Section

Time—55 Minutes

80 Questions

Directions: Each question that follows has five answer choices. Choose the letter that correctly answers the question and write that letter in your exam booklet.

1. Which of the following statements about early settlement in the Chesapeake and New England is *not accurate*?
   a. The Chesapeake environment proved less healthy than New England's.
   b. Supply ships bound for the Chesapeake hit rough weather, and some were lost.
   c. Generally, single men settled the Chesapeake and families settled New England.
   d. The Chesapeake colony had friendly relations with Native Americans while the Pilgrims were actively hostile.
   e. The goal of Chesapeake settlers was commercial profit, and the goal for New England settlers was to worship without interference.

2. One of the biggest reasons for the changing public opinion about independence was
   a. Thomas Paine's argument in *Common Sense* that America's ties with England were broken.
   b. Tory propaganda pushing for reconciliation.
   c. the British proclamation that colonists could not settle beyond the Appalachian Mountains.
   d. Mercy Otis Warren's satirical plays about oppressed women.
   e. the closing of the port of Boston to subdue the rebellion.

3. Despite Jefferson's rhetoric, his most significant accomplishment as president was
   a. reducing the national debt.
   b. limiting the size of the national government.
   c. refusing to pay tribute to and appeasing the Barbary States.
   d. doubling the size of the United States by purchasing Louisiana.
   e. reducing the influence of Federalists in the judiciary.

4. During the nullification crisis in 1833, President Jackson
   a. supported South Carolina in its policy with regard to the tariff.
   b. played a minor role and let the Supreme Court decide the issue
   c. sent troops to enforce the law when the state refused to do so.
   d. urged Congress to change the law because it was unfair to southern states.
   e. showed his willingness to use force to uphold federal law.

5. After the Civil War, black codes were enacted to
   a. give former slaves the right to move freely and work without restraint throughout the South.
   b. assert white control and supremacy over freed slaves in the former Confederacy.
   c. carry out the provisions of the Supreme Court's *Plessy* v. *Ferguson* ruling.
   d. ensure the civil rights of blacks through congressional legislation.
   e. stop freedmen from testifying in court against their former masters.

6. The photographs of Jacob Riis raised public awareness of
   a. the plight of southern sharecroppers and tenant farmers.
   b. the desperate conditions of the urban poor.
   c. the continuing discrimination against African Americans.
   d. the appalling conditions in the meatpacking industry.
   e. the corruption of big business.

7. A major domestic impact of World War I was
   a. the desegregation of the armed forces.
   b. increased support for women's suffrage at the national level.
   c. the widespread internment of German Americans.
   d. increased appreciation for America's ethnic diversity.
   e. permanent government control of the nation's railroads.

8. The event that had the most significant effect on American public opinion prior to the United States entry into World War II was
   a. the Japanese invasion of China.
   b. Mussolini's invasion of Ethiopia.
   c. the Nazi–Soviet Pact.
   d. Hitler's invasion of Poland.
   e. the fall of France.

9. Which of the following would support the idea that the 1950s was not a decade of conformity?
   a. the growth of the suburbs
   b. the importance of advertising
   c. the emergence of the beat movement
   d. television programming
   e. the growing influence of corporate America

10. The Environmental Protection Agency was established during the administration of
    a. Theodore Roosevelt.
    b. Franklin Roosevelt.
    c. Richard Nixon.
    d. Jimmy Carter.
    e. George H. W. Bush.

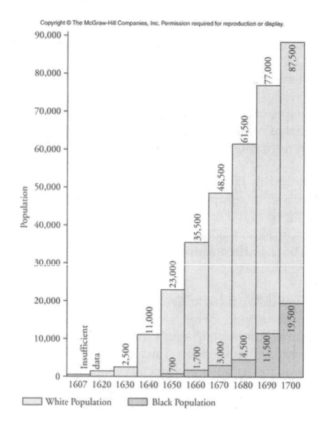

White Population   Black Population

11. The accompanying chart suggests that
    a. the white population of the Chesapeake grew much more rapidly
       after the first half of the seventeenth century.
    b. the black population grew more rapidly than the white population after 1640
    c. the white population grew more rapidly than the black population after 1640.
    d. the mortality rate for blacks was significantly higher than that for whites.
    e. the last two decades of the century were a period of extraordinary
       population growth.

12. The correct chronological order for the following events is
    a. Declaratory Act, Stamp Act, Tea Act, Coercive Acts, Boston Tea Party.
    b. Declaratory Act, Stamp Act, Tea Act, Boston Tea Party, Coercive Acts.
    c. Stamp Act, Declaratory Act, Tea Act, Boston Tea Party, Coercive Acts.
    d. Stamp Act, Declaratory Act, Tea Act, Coercive Acts, Boston Tea Party.
    e. Declaratory Act, Stamp Act, Coercive Acts, Tea Act, Boston Tea Party.

13. In the early years of the United States, women adopted the role of
    a. domestics and blurred the lines between home and the outside world.
    b. model citizens, and artists used women to model republican liberty.
    c. deputy wives who were on an equal basis with their husbands in
       running family businesses.
    d. housewives with no role to play in politics and business.
    e. Republican mothers who were to teach children virtue.

14. The significance of the Dred Scott case was
    a. the Missouri Compromise was constitutional and slavery could
       not be established in Northern territories.
    b. blacks were citizens and could sue for freedom in the courts as
       Dred Scott did.
    c. slave auctions were no longer legal in the District of Columbia.
    d. Congress had no right to prohibit slavery in the territories.
    e. citizens had an obligation to return fugitive slaves to their owners.

15. Union advantages at the start of the Civil War included all of the following *except*
    a. familiarity with Southern territory since it always was part of English America.
    b. a population twice as large as the Confederacy.
    c. an advanced industrial economy.
    d. better railroads and transportation.
    e. a naval fleet.

16. Unlike earlier immigrants, those who came to the United States in the late nineteenth
    century generally
    a. possessed enough capital and education to become prosperous and successful.
    b. sought to move west to set up their own businesses in urban areas or buy
       farmland in rural areas.
    c. were able to assimilate into American society quickly and easily.
    d. settled in cities on the East Coast and took unskilled jobs.
    e. faced little opposition from native-born Americans.

17. All of the following transformed American life and culture during the 1920s *except*
    a. the increasing popularity of the radio.
    b. the growth of television.
    c. the increasing availability and use of the automobile.
    d. the advent of the motion picture.
    e. the growth of advertising and consumer credit.

18. The biggest source of controversy between the Allies during World War II was
    a. the question of how best to defeat Japan.
    b. timing the opening of a Second Front in Europe.
    c. how Nazi war criminals should be treated after the war.
    d. how to respond to the Holocaust.
    e. the question of whether Germany and Japan should be forced to surrender
       unconditionally.

19. The dominant approach among civil rights activists in the 1950s and early 1960s was
    a. violent protest against racism and segregation.
    b. lobbying the nation's white leaders to pass civil rights legislation.
    c. nonviolent protest and direct action against segregation.
    d. promoting black nationalism and separatism.
    e. working with the Communist Party and other left-wing groups to promote
       desegregation.

20. The "spring mobilization" of April 1968 was held to protest
    a. the assassination of Martin Luther King Jr.
    b. the war in Vietnam.
    c. the mistreatment of Native Americans.
    d. the continued inequality of women.
    e. the lack of progress in the war on poverty.

21. The Spanish conquistadors' greatest advantage in their conflicts
    with native populations was
    a. the introduction of smallpox that killed many natives.
    b. the use of firearms to subdue the natives.
    c. their ability to negotiate and resolve disputes peacefully.
    d. their willingness to use Spanish wealth to compensate Indians for territory.
    e. a willingness to accept Indian culture and allow it to coexist with Spanish culture.

22. Both the Articles of Confederation and state constitutions drafted during the same
    period were republican in nature due to
    a. the strong executive to maintain order during wartime.
    b. the significant role played by officials appointed for life by the legislature.
    c. a weak executive with sovereign authority resting in the people.
    d. the prohibition of slavery.
    e. granting women the right to vote in states that approved.

23. In antebellum America, romanticism and nationalism were expressed in all of the
    following *except*
    a. paintings of the Hudson River School.
    b. Walt Whitman's *Leaves of Grass*.
    c. James Fenimore Cooper's "Leatherstocking Tales."
    d. Nathaniel Hawthorne's *Scarlet Letter*.
    e. Horatio Alger's *Bound to Rise*.

24. During his first inaugural address, Lincoln made it clear that his primary goal
    as president was to
    a. stop the expansion of slavery in United States territory.
    b. preserve the Union at any cost.
    c. abolish slavery throughout the United States.
    d. avoid war as long as neither side started a fight.
    e. compromise on slavery's expansion by extending the Missouri Compromise line
       west.

25. Which of the following became the nation's largest labor union between 1880 and 1920?
    a. the National Labor Union
    b. the Knights of Labor
    c. the Industrial Workers of the World
    d. the American Federation of Labor
    e. the Congress of Industrial Organizations

26. Members of the "Lost Generation" were artists and intellectuals
    a. who lamented the South's defeat in the Civil War.
    b. who criticized urban ills and corporate power at the turn of the twentieth century.

c. who felt alienated from American society following World War I.
d. who criticized the conformity and materialism of 1950s America.
e. who protested against the Vietnam War and American globalism.

27. Unlike Herbert Hoover, Franklin Roosevelt was able to
   a. articulate a consistent philosophy of government that guided his efforts in office.
   b. implement an effective economic recovery program that helped to restore the nation's prosperity.
   c. project a sense of confidence and optimism to the American people.
   d. work effectively with the leaders of the other nations to deal with the Depression as an international phenomenon.
   e. win the trust of the nation's business and financial community as part of his efforts to combat the Depression.

28. The power and scope of the federal government increased significantly during World War II in all of the following areas *except*
   a. the federal budget.
   b. support for science and technology.
   c. taxation.
   d. social welfare programs.
   e. economic mobilization.

29. Which of the following best characterizes George Kennan's Cold War policy?
   a. A policy of firmness by the United States would contain the expansion of the Soviet Union.
   b. Communism anywhere in the world was a direct threat to America's vital interests.
   c. Nationalism was a much less significant force than communism in world affairs.
   d. The Soviet Union was driven by communist ideology to expand to the point where it achieved world domination.
   e. The Third World was the most important battleground of the Cold War.

30. One advantage that Lyndon Johnson had over John F. Kennedy in pursuing his Great Society program was
   a. his relationship with liberal intellectuals, who loyally supported his domestic reform efforts.
   b. his ability to deal with Congress due to his experience in the House and Senate.
   c. his personal charisma and ability to capture the imagination of the American people.
   d. his ability to successfully balance the demands of domestic reform and fighting a war in Vietnam.
   e. the nation's desire for active presidential leadership following the perceived passivity of the Eisenhower administration in the 1950s.

31. Upon taking office, Ronald Reagan's biggest priority was
   a. negotiating the release of American hostages held by Iran.
   b. working with Soviet leaders to lessen the arms race.
   c. undertaking a program of Keynesian deficit spending on public works programs to stimulate the economy.
   d. implementing a conservative social agenda of outlawing abortion and resuming prayer in public schools.
   e. cutting taxes to stimulate economic growth, and limiting inflation.

32. A rigid system of slavery for life based on race became an American institution in part because
  a. slavery had been an English institution since the Middle Ages.
  b. whites assumed blacks were inferior and of a lower status.
  c. white indentured servants served only for a fixed time period.
  d. Africans practiced their own religion and would not accept Christianity.
  e. Africans were the last people to settle in America and were therefore left outside the established social hierarchy.

33. Hamilton's financial plan included all of the following provisions *except*
  a. funding the national debt at face value.
  b. the assumption of state debts by the national government.
  c. a high tariff to protect newly establish American industries.
  d. not repaying debt to countries that did not support America's Revolution.
  e. the creation of a national bank.

34. The emergence of the Whigs in the 1830s was mainly
  a. the response of those opposed to President Jackson's ideology and policies.
  b. a reaction to the power-hungry politics of President Adams.
  c. an attempt to return to an earlier period of dignified political debate.
  d. an action to halt the states' rights movement growing in the West.
  e. to stop the expansion of slavery in the territories.

35. The Lincoln–Douglas debates changed the political landscape by
  a. showing Douglas to be compassionate and worthy to be president.
  b. making Lincoln a prominent national political figure.
  c. having two important leaders agree on the issue of slavery.
  d. introducing the idea of a national debate during the presidential election.
  e. showing that an abolitionist could be the leader of a national party.

36. Impeachment charges against Andrew Johnson included
  a. excessive use of the veto against Democratic legislation.
  b. his opposition to Secretary of State Seward's purchase of Alaska.
  c. abuses of the presidential power of pardon.
  d. treason as governor of a state that seceded.
  e. failure to obey the Tenure of Office Act.

37. Mass production of goods by way of the moving assembly line was pioneered by
  a. Henry Ford's production of automobiles.
  b. Andrew Carnegie's production of steel.
  c. Isaac Singer's manufacture of sewing machines.
  d. Alexander Graham Bell's telephone.
  e. Gustavus Swift in meatpacking.

38. D. W. Griffith's pioneering film *The Birth of a Nation* played a significant role in
  a. helping Americans to celebrate and seek and a return to the spirit of equality contained in the Declaration of Independence.
  b. whipping up patriotic enthusiasm for American involvement in World War I.
  c. helping to stimulate a revival of racism and the rebirth of the Ku Klux Klan.
  d. helping to promote progressive social reforms.
  e. helping to gain support for American colonization efforts abroad.

39. The group that benefited most directly from New Deal legislation was
    a. women.
    b. tenant farmers and sharecroppers.
    c. industrial workers.
    d. African Americans.
    e. the urban poor.

40. Following the passage of the Voting Rights Act of 1965, civil rights leaders found
    a. widespread support from northern whites as they sought to fight discrimination in urban areas outside of the South.
    b. hostility and indifference to their efforts to combat issues such as poor housing, inferior schools, and economic discrimination.
    c. increasing unity within their movement as they shifted from issues of political to economic equality.
    d. renewed emphasis on nonviolence and interracial cooperation in an effort to spread the fight for equality beyond the South.
    e. widespread encouragement from President Johnson and his successors for further advances in civil rights such as "affirmative action."

41. All of the following are true of Richard Nixon's foreign policy *except* that he
    a. believed the United States should pursue a policy of negotiation with the Soviet Union and China.
    b. believed that the United States should combine increased bombing with greater reliance on South Vietnamese troops in the Vietnam conflict.
    c. supported increasing American troop levels in Vietnam if that was necessary to preserve South Vietnam's independence.
    d. was willing to use the CIA to assist in the overthrow of foreign leaders who opposed American interests abroad.
    e. believed that the United States should use its concrete interests, and not abstract moral principles, as a guide to American foreign policy.

42. The consequences of the Revolutionary War for the American economy included
    a. stronger economic ties with England once the peace treaty was signed.
    b. a dramatic growth in America's wartime manufacturing.
    c. expanded trade with Britain's Caribbean Islands.
    d. the opening up of new markets without the navigation system.
    e. destruction of the American merchant fleet by the British navy.

43. The Second Great Awakening clearly illustrates
    a. the strong evangelical strain in the American character.
    b. the tendency for Americans to support a limited number of religious denominations.
    c. passive piety and a willingness to leave individual affairs in God's hands.
    d. the continued and powerful influence of the Puritan Church in America.
    e. the importance of reason to gain access to salvation.

44. After the "Era of Good Feelings" ended,
    a. there was little party strife since nationalism was overwhelming.
    b. the Federalist Party was reinvigorated over the issue of the 2nd BUS.
    c. new parties arose over ideological differences between John Quincy Adams and Andrew Jackson.
    d. political parties divided over the issue of slavery after the Compromise of 1820.
    e. the political party system disintegrated into many insignificant factions.

45. The Compromise of 1850 included which of the following provisions?
    I. admission of Kansas as a slave state
    II. admission of California as a free state
    III. a strengthened fugitive slave law
    IV. no restrictions on the slave trade in Washington, D.C.
a. I
b. I and II
c. II and III
d. II, III, and IV
e. I, II, and IV

46. Northern views on the emancipation of slaves during the Civil War
    a. changed little until victory was assured.
    b. always favored immediate freedom for all citizens.
    c. overwhelmingly agreed that compensation should be paid to slave owners to end the fighting.
    d. accepted Lincoln's opinion that the nation could survive half slave and half free.
    e. accepted it as a war goal as the war progressed.

47. Which of the following statements about urbanization in the late nineteenth and early twentieth centuries is accurate?
    a. New immigrants settled in ethnic neighborhoods and resisted assimilation for several generations.
    b. The federal government provided extensive assistance to urban areas during this period.
    c. Cities remained a source of attraction for many different groups because of the opportunities they provided.
    d. City leaders devoted few resources to the creation of shared public space.
    e. Urban life broke down class distinctions by bringing people of different economic levels into contact with one another.

48. The emergence of the "new woman" of the 1920s was most facilitated by
    a. changing ideas about motherhood and birth control among middle-class women.
    b. the abandonment of traditional ideals of motherhood and the family in previously conservative regions such as the South and Midwest.
    c. the large growth of professional opportunities in previously male realms.
    d. the significant political influence that women wielded as a result of the ratification of the Nineteenth Amendment.
    e. the increasingly popular feminist belief that women should work to overthrow the patriarchal structure of the society around them.

49. The African American migration during and after World War II differed from that of World War I in that
    a. there existed little significant white opposition to the latter movement.
    b. the percentage of African Americans living in urban areas grew in both relative and absolute terms during the latter migration.
    c. those who migrated during the latter period usually benefited significantly from government urban renewal programs and were less likely to live in poverty.
    d. fewer African Americans moved north in the latter period.
    e. the earlier migration led to a mass exodus of whites from urban areas.

50. The assassination of Ngo Dinh Diem was an important turning point for American leaders because
    a. it caused them to question whether the United States should commit resources to supporting the independence of South Vietnam.
    b. it caused the American public to turn against the United States effort there.
    c. it convinced them not to participate in the nationwide elections that were called for by the Geneva Conventions.
    d. it created a power vacuum in South Vietnam that the United States felt a responsibility to fill.
    e. it led to the founding of the National Liberation Front and thus presented a major challenge to South Vietnam's independence.

51. A major source of Jimmy Carter's strength as a presidential candidate was
    a. his expertise in foreign policy.
    b. his long experience in national politics.
    c. his reputation for personal honesty and integrity.
    d. his personal wealth and colorful family history.
    e. his ties to traditional Democratic interest groups.

52. The principle of religious toleration in the American colonies was
    a. universally accepted in all the English colonies because of persecution in England.
    b. only accepted on an individual basis if a person could show signs of salvation.
    c. practiced in some colonies, but religious conformity was enforced in others.
    d. practiced by all with the exception of Catholics and Quakers.
    e. only agreed to by Maryland in its Act of Toleration.

53. The French and Indian War in America
    a. was part of the larger global conflict between England and France.
    b. concerned struggles between the French and the Indians over Canadian lands.
    c. was mostly an internal conflict between various Indian tribes rather than European interests.
    d. had very little effect on the coastal English colonies.
    e. had begun earlier in Europe and spread to the American colonies later.

54. Henry Clay opposed territorial expansion in the 1830s and 1840s for the reason that
    a. Texas was a province of Mexico and the United States had no reason to seek territory there.
    b. the United States had so much unsettled territory in Louisiana that there was no great desire for more.
    c. Indians were enough of a problem in existing United States territory without adding more to the problem.
    d. more territory would reopen the contentious issue of slavery.
    e. the Monroe Doctrine had settled the issue of colonization and expansion in the Western Hemisphere.

55. In *Uncle Tom's Cabin*, Harriet Beecher Stowe
    a. revealed her experiences as a slave woman and gave support to abolitionists.
    b. used true slave stories from her family's plantation to expose slavery's evils.
    c. used fiction to bring the antislavery message to new and wider audiences.
    d. along with her sister Sarah Grimke discussed slavery's "irresponsible power."
    e. linked the issues of women's political rights and slavery.

56. After the Civil War, the "Cattle Kingdom" depended upon
    a. fencing in the open lands to keep cattle from straying away from ranches.
    b. western farmers to grow grain to feed the large herds.
    c. new strains of cattle to withstand the harsh western climate.
    d. a large western population to consume beef supplied by ranchers.
    e. open range for free grazing of livestock without restriction.

57. In his 1895 speech to the Cotton States Exposition, Booker T. Washington
    urged African Americans to
    a. fight for access to higher education in order to train a core of African
       American leaders.
    b. move to the North in search of better economic opportunities and greater
       social equality.
    c. focus on immediate economic gains rather than long-term social change.
    d. form organizations to agitate for civil rights legislation.
    e. separate themselves from white society and create their own institutions.

58. As secretary of commerce during the 1920s, Herbert Hoover supported
    a. voluntary cooperation between business and government in an effort to stabilize
       economic conditions and promote efficiency and organization.
    b. increasing the federal government's role in regulating business.
    c. total rejection of progressive reforms and a return to the limited governmental
       role of the late nineteenth century.
    d. free-trade policies that would allow American businesses to capture overseas
       markets and thus avoid overproduction in the domestic market.
    e. efforts of organized labor to develop to the point where workers could balance
       the power of corporate leaders.

59. Throughout the 1930s, Franklin Roosevelt responded to events abroad by
    a. asserting a bold vision for American world leadership.
    b. moving cautiously toward bringing the United States into a more active world
       role without antagonizing isolationist leaders.
    c. assuming an isolationist stance until the United States was forced into action by
       the Japanese attack on Pearl Harbor.
    d. supporting the appeasement of fascist powers in an attempt to preserve peace at
       all costs.
    e. advocating a policy in which the world's most powerful nations maintained control
       over their spheres of influence.

60. In the 1952 presidential campaign, Dwight Eisenhower and Richard Nixon based their
    appeals to the American people on
    a. their desire to continue the Truman administration's containment policies.
    b. their efforts to downplay the issue of domestic anticommunism and separate
       themselves from the tactics of McCarthy.
    c. their ability to end the war in Korea and lessen communist influence in government.
    d. their desire to increase American conventional forces and intervene with ground
       troops wherever necessary to contain communism.
    e. the potential danger of nuclear war and the need for an acceptance of the limits
       of American power abroad.

61. The most significant political conflict between royal governors and colonial assemblies was over
    a. raising colonial militias to provide defense from Indian attacks.
    b. the power to tax and spend in the provinces.
    c. the changing status from charter to royal colonies.
    d. governors granting their friends exclusive trading rights.
    e. the use of British troops to preserve order in the colonies.

62. The American Revolution was part of a larger trend because
    a. other British colonies were fighting for their independence from British rule.
    b. French and Spanish colonial empires were revolting at the same time.
    c. it was the first of a series of revolutions based on Enlightenment political ideas.
    d. European empires could no longer afford to hold on to their colonies.
    e. Napoleon was fighting for the same principles in France.

63. William Lloyd Garrison was attacked and reviled by many northerners because his views
    a. demanded an immediate, uncompensated abolition of slavery and challenged the Constitution.
    b. supported the colonization of freed slaves in Africa.
    s. contradicted the ideas in slave narratives such as that of Frederick Douglass.
    d. on gradual emancipation were too mild and would take too long.
    e. supporting slave rebellions in the South terrified most citizens.

64. During the Civil War, the Republican Party's program of economic development included all of the following *except*
    a. the Homestead Act to promote free-soil ideology.
    b. a protective tariff to support domestic industry.
    c. the Morrill Land Grant Act to aid education.
    d. support for the Erie Canal to link the Great Lakes and East Coast.
    e. support for a transcontinental railroad.

65. A key similarity between the Jacksonian era and the Gilded Age was
    a. the identification of political parties with strong personalities.
    b. the high degree of political participation among the electorate.
    c. the expansion of voting rights that occurred in both periods.
    d. the lack of corruption and high standards for government appointments.
    e. the dominance of one party at both the presidential and congressional levels.

66. All of the following were direct results of American foreign policy in the 1890s *except*
    a. a significant increase in American trade and investment abroad.
    b. the abandonment of the traditional policy of avoiding permanent peacetime alliances.
    c. the acquisition of an overseas empire.
    d. the willingness to employ the ideas in the Monroe Doctrine.
    e. the recognition for the need of an isthmusian canal in Latin America.

67. During the Great Depression, commercial radio and movies generally
    a. provided a sharp critique of American society and its values.
    b. enthusiastically supported the New Deal and its programs.
    c. raised awareness of the Depression's efforts abroad.
    d. offered escapist programming that helped Americans forget their problems.
    e. called on Americans to persevere and sacrifice through hard times.

68. Which of the following is true of women during World War II?
    a. They were barred from union membership in factory jobs.
    b. They were more likely to work in factories than in service-sector jobs.
    c. They benefited heavily from government child-care programs.
    d. They were treated equally in factories where they worked.
    e. They made some limited progress by taking on jobs in heavy industry that had previously been reserved for men.

69. The Fair Deal represented a departure from the New Deal in
    a. the degree to which it made civil rights a part of its agenda.
    b. its belief that the government had a responsibility to promote economic conditions that would produce full employment.
    c. its efforts to protect the interests of organized labor.
    d. its belief that the federal government should provide for the welfare of those citizens least able to care for themselves.
    e. its efforts to reduce the role of the federal government in American life.

70. The efforts of Cesar Chavez focused on which of the following issues?
    a. creating a separate Mexican–American state in the Southwest
    b. gaining improved conditions for migrant farm workers
    c. mandating access to bilingual education
    d. reforming the nation's immigration system
    e. improving conditions in urban ghettos

71. Pennsylvania followed a policy like that of Rhode Island with respect to
    a. the separation of church and state.
    b. creating an aristocracy living on large landed estates.
    c. making the Puritan Church the established church.
    d. buying the land for white settlement from the Indians.
    e. establishing a center for the slave trade in the colony

72. Texas fought for its independence from Mexico after
    a. Mexico no longer supported a territory largely peopled by United States exiles.
    b. settlers there claimed Texas was part of the Louisiana Purchase.
    c. Mexico's government imposed stricter control over its provinces in the 1830s.
    d. civil war erupted between American settlers and native Mexicans in Texas.
    e. Mexico moved to legalize slavery in Texas.

73. A major transcendentalist effort at social reform occurred
    a. at Brook Farm, a community where work and leisure were shared equally by all.
    b. in the area of temperance, headed by Horace Mann.
    c. at Oneida, where traditional marriage and family were emphasized.
    d. during the camp meetings of the Second Great Awakening.
    e. with Dorothea Dix and the movement for improved education

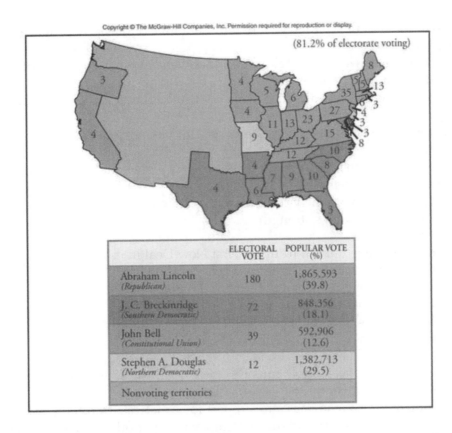

(81.2% of electorate voting)

	ELECTORAL VOTE	POPULAR VOTE (%)
Abraham Lincoln (Republican)	180	1,865,593 (39.8)
J. C. Breckinridge (Southern Democratic)	72	848,356 (18.1)
John Bell (Constitutional Union)	39	592,906 (12.6)
Stephen A. Douglas (Northern Democratic)	12	1,382,713 (29.5)
Nonvoting territories		

74. Using the information from the accompanying map, one could conclude which of the following about the election of 1860?
    a. Abraham Lincoln received a majority of both the popular and electoral vote.
    b. The four candidates split the vote so the election was decided in the House of Representatives.
    c. Abraham Lincoln received the greatest number of popular votes and thus won the election.
    d. The vote for president divided along clear sectional lines.
    e. Douglas carried Missouri because it was his home state.

75. "The existence of an area of free land, its continuous recession, and the advance of settlement westward, explain American development."
    This statement best typifies the ideas of
    a. Frederick Jackson Turner's Frontier Thesis.
    b. Helen Hunt Jackson's *A Century of Dishonor.*
    c. Mark Twain's *Roughing It.*
    d. Henry Nash Smith's *Virgin Land.*
    e. Frederick Remington's *The Winning of the West.*

76. As a presidential candidate in 1896, William Jennings Bryan
    a. made little effort to venture beyond his home area.
    b. forcefully represented the interests of rural, Protestant America.
    c. appealed successfully to urban, immigrant Democrats.
    d. gained the support of the nation's business leaders.
    e. paid little attention to the currency issue.

77. Jane Addams and Florence Kelley were representative of the early progressive movement in that
   a. they came from lower-class backgrounds and believed in mobilizing the poor to advocate on their own behalf.
   b. they were educated, middle-class women who sought meaningful outlets for their reform sentiments.
   c. they rejected the notion of a separate sphere for women and believed in full equality with men in all realms.
   d. they believed that the problems of rural America were equally important as those of urban America.
   e. they sought to promote the virtues of immigrant culture and diversity as a source of the nation's strength.

78. The Second New Deal differed from the First New Deal in its
   a. stronger focus on business–government cooperation.
   b. greater focus on helping promote the civil rights of minority groups.
   c. more open split with the philosophy of big business.
   d. more limited focus on foreign affairs.
   e. focus on economic recovery rather than on reform.

79. A key source of the appeal of folk music in the 1960s and 1970s was its
   a. emphasis on individual middle-class values.
   b. celebration of patriotic themes and support for America's traditional politics.
   c. rejection of musical styles and themes from earlier periods in American history.
   d. ability to provide a seemingly authentic alternative to American consumer culture.
   e. emphasis on high-quality production values and elaborate concerts by the genre's popular artists.

80. Which of the following is true of the Supreme Court under Chief Justice Earl Warren between 1954 and 1969?
   a. It came under attack from conservatives for a series of decisions that protected and extended the rights of the less powerful members of society.
   b. It did little to expand the court's role, relying on a strict interpretation of the Constitution and avoiding controversial rulings.
   c. It issued a series of conservative rulings that frustrated President Johnson's Great Society efforts.
   d. It did little to extend the protections offered under the Bill of Rights.
   e. Its major rulings dealt primarily with business regulation and economic issues, angering the business community with its perceived antibusiness bias.

United States History

SECTION II

Part A

(Suggested writing time—45 minutes)

Percent of Section II score—45

Directions: The following question requires you to construct a coherent essay that integrates your interpretation of Documents A through H and your knowledge of the period referred to in the question. High scores will be earned only by those essays that both cite key pieces of evidence from the documents and draw on outside knowledge of the period.

To what degree did the American political system and public opinion accept broad construction of the Constitution in antebellum America?

Document A

Source: McCullough v. Maryland, Supreme Court Decision, 1819.

The powers of the general government, it has been said, are delegated by the States, who alone are truly sovereign; and it must be exercised in subordination to the States, who alone possess supreme domination. It would be difficult to sustain this proposition. . . . The government of the United States, then, though limited in its powers, is supreme. . . . [Commanger, *Documents:* 213]

Document B

Source: The Missouri Compromise, 1820.

And be it further enacted, that in all that territory ceded by France to the United States, under the name of Louisiana, which lies north of 36°30′ N latitude, not included with the limits of the state [Missouri], slavery and involuntary servitude, otherwise than in the punishment of crimes . . . . shall be, and is hereby, forever prohibited. . . . [Annals IV: 592]

Document C

Source: Hugh S. Legaré, Review in the *Southern Review*, 1828.

". . . the government has been fundamentally altered by the progress of opinion; that instead of being any longer one of enumerated powers and a circumscribed sphere, as it was beyond all doubt intended to be, it knows absolutely no bounds but the majority of Congress; that instead of confining itself in time of peace to the diplomatic and commercial relations of the country, it is seeking out employment for itself by interfering in the domestic concerns of society, and threatens, in the course of a very few years, to control, in the most offensive and despotic manner, all the pursuits, the interests, the opinions, and the conduct of men. [Annals V: 276]

Document D

Source: James Madison, letter to Edward Everett, 1830.

This brings us to the expedient lately advanced, which claims for a single state a right to appeal against an exercise of power by the government of the United States decided by the state to be unconstitutional. . . . Can more be necessary to demonstrate the inadmissibility of such a doctrine than it puts in the power of the smallest fraction over one-fourth of the United States. . . . giving such a power to such a minority over such a majority would overturn the first principle of free government. . . . [Annals V: 402]

Document E

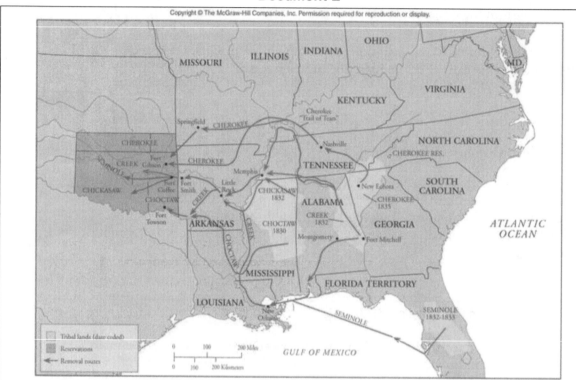

The Expulsion of the Tribes, 1830–1835

Document F

King Andrew the First political cartoon, 1832

Document G

Joseph Smith reviewing his troops

Document H

Whatever is good or evil in the local institutions of Texas will remain her own, whether annexed to the United States or not. None of the present states will be responsible for them any more than they are for the local institutions of each other. [Annals VII: 287]

United States History

SECTION II

Part B and Part C
(Suggested total planning and writing time—70 minutes)
Percent of Section II score—55

Part B

Directions: Choose ONE question from this part. You are advised to spend 5 minutes planning and 30 minutes writing your answer. Cite relevant historical evidence in support of your generalizations and present your arguments clearly and logically.

1. How closely did America adhere to George Washington's foreign policy principles in TWO of the periods listed below?
    1805 to 1825
    1844 to 1865
    1880 to 1900

2. Analyze the role of women and minorities in antebellum reform movements.

Part C

Directions: Choose ONE question from this part. You are advised to spend 5 minutes planning and 30 minutes writing your answer. Cite relevant historical evidence in support of your generalizations and present your arguments clearly and logically.

1. "World War I was the culmination of progressivism in America."
    Evaluate the validity of this statement during the period 1901–1921.

2. Compare and contrast the role of religion in society and politics in the 1920s and the 1950s.

PRACTICE EXAM ANSWERS
Multiple-Choice Answers

1. d. Relations between Pilgrims and local Indians were friendly compared with those between the Chesapeake settlers and the Powhatan tribe.

2. a. *Common Sense* was published in January 1776 and made a strong argument in straightforward prose for a break with England.

3. d. Jefferson's policy changes were not radical, but the Louisiana Purchase had a dramatic effect on the development of the United States.

4. e. With the passage of the Force Bill, Jackson was ready to send troops to South Carolina to collect the tariff. A compromise tariff defused the crisis.

5. b. Much like the slave codes, the black codes were designed to keep African Americans in a subservient position.

6. b. Riis took photographs of tenements, sweatshops, and poor neighborhoods in New York City to promote reforms.

7. b. Wilson had originally opposed women's suffrage, but the fact that war was being fought to "make the world safe for democracy" increased support for the suffrage movement.

8. e. With France no longer resisting Hitler, England alone remained the line of defense for American democracy in the Atlantic.

9. c. The beats were the opposite of conformity, constantly challenging convention.

10. c. Republican Richard Nixon organized the EPA after the environmental movement began, inspired by Rachel Carson's *The Silent Spring.*

11. b. In proportional, not absolute, terms, the black population grew more rapidly than the white population.

12. c. The Declaratory Act asserted Parliament's right to legislate for the colonies; the Tea Act set off the chain of events culminating in the passage of the Coercive Acts.

13. e. According to republican ideology, a republic depended on virtuous citizens, and it fell to mothers to teach children to grow up to be good citizens.

14. d. The Supreme Court decision in Dred Scott ruled that blacks could not sue in court, but a larger uproar came from its finding that the Missouri Compromise was unconstitutional.

15. a. Union forces did not have the intimate knowledge of the South that Confederates did.

16. d. The "new" immigrants settled in cities with their own countrymen, and, because they had few skills, they took whatever jobs were available.

17. b. Television was not invented until after World War II.

18. b. The Soviet Union pushed for an early attack on mainland Europe to relieve the pressure on its forces; England wanted to wait until preparations were complete.

19. c. All direct protest actions against segregation were planned to be nonviolent.

20. b. The planning was to protest the Vietnam War; later assassinations inspired race riots.

21. a. European disease was the biggest killer of Native Americans.

22. c. Government by consent of the governed was the main republican principle. A weak executive was a check on concentration of power.

23. e. Alger wrote about the national dream after the Civil War.

24. b. Lincoln followed the Republican platform and would not interfere with slavery where it existed.

25. d. The AFL, a craft union of skilled labor, had more members than any other union.

26. c. These people were intellectuals disillusioned by the direction in which America was going and by the unfulfilled promise of the Treaty of Versailles.

27. c. Hoover projected an air of pessimism with the depression's effects; FDR tried to lift the American spirit.

28. d. Victory held the highest priority; social welfare was low on the list of priorities.

29. a. Kennan wanted to stop the expansion of communism but in areas of vital interest to the United States, such as countries bordering the Soviet Union.

30. b. LBJ was one of the most effective Senate majority leaders before becoming vice president and later president.

31. e. Reagan took office during a period of stagflation; his first priority was the economy.

32. b. Prejudice and white bias assigned "blacks" an inferior status.

33. d. Hamilton's plan called for repaying all foreign debt.

34. a. The Whig Party borrowed its name from the party opposed to the English king. It compared Jackson's actions to those of a corrupt monarch.

35. b. Lincoln was known only within Illinois before this series of debates.

36. e. Johnson dismissed Secretary of War Stanton without Senate approval as specified by the act.

37. a. Ford's assembly line revolutionized manufacturing and increased productivity.

38. c. Griffith's 1916 film glorified the Klan's role during the Reconstruction and thus helped to spur its revival in the 1920s.

39. c. The New Deal focused on workers and the growth of businesses.

40. b. America appeared to be tiring of civil rights, especially when it began to affect all areas of the country.

41. c. Nixon campaigned on a platform of "Peace with Honor," promising the American withdrawal from Vietnam.

42. d. Without the restrictions of British policy, American merchants found new markets for trade.

43. a. Christian evangelism was unleashed during this series of revivals.

44. c. The end of the Federalist Party ushered in a period of political peace until the election of 1824 between Adams and Jackson.

45. c. This compromise ended the slave trade in Washington; Kansas became an issue four years later.

46. e. Northern public opinion accepted the Emancipation Proclamation by the end of 1862.

47. c. With established immigrant populations and the prospect of work, cities were the destination of most immigrants.

48. a. The changes concerning a woman's role came largely from middle-class urban women who embraced modernism.

49. b. The migration north to take advantage of urban manufacturing jobs significantly increased the African American northern population.

50. d. Diem's assassination in 1963 led to a series of unstable, short-lived governments in South Vietnam and increased American intervention.

51. c. Carter stressed that he would never lie to the American people, an asset in the period in which people distrusted government following Watergate.

52. c. Religious toleration was more the exception than the rule in early colonial America.

53. a. France and England were competing for Atlantic hegemony, and the colonial wars were a part of this.

54. d. Clay had brokered the Missouri Compromise and knew firsthand that the issue of slavery's expansion was very divisive and contentious.

55. c. *Uncle Tom's Cabin* emotionally combined romantic fiction with the antislavery political message in Stowe's best-selling novel.

46. e. The open range allowed cattle to feed at no cost to the rancher. The fencing of the plains spelled the end of this enterprise.

57. c. Washington believed that once blacks became indispensable to the economy, political and social rights would follow, unlike W. E. B. Du Bois.

58. a. Hoover accepted the Republican ideology of laissez-faire but also was progressive in his focus on scientific practices and efficiency.

59. b. FDR saw fascism as a growing threat to American democracy but was well ahead of American public opinion on this issue.

60. c. Eisenhower promised to seek an end to the fighting in Korea. He also promised to fight domestic communist influence but was not a supporter of McCarthy.

61. b. The rise of the assemblies as a political force was a result of gaining the "power of the purse."

62. c. The American Revolution was part of the "Age of Revolution" inspired by the ideas of Enlightenment political thinkers such as John Locke.

63. a. Garrison's ideas embraced the immediate end of property in slavery and labeled the Constitution as a "covenant with death."

64. d. The Erie Canal was completed in 1825 with support from New York state.

65. b. The expansion of democracy during the Age of Jackson mirrored the use of the vote by political bosses.

66. b. Despite its imperial ambitions, the United States continued to avoid foreign alliances in the 1890s.

67. d. Radio programs and films mostly provided entertainment for Americans.

68. e. Women such as "Rosie the Riveter" were the minority but did break employment barriers during World War II.

69. a. New Deal programs made little effort to address issues of African Americans.

70. b. Chavez's United Farm Workers focused on the poor conditions faced by migrant farm workers and helped win several major victories over California grape growers.

71. d. Both William Penn and Roger Williams purchased the right to settle lands from Native Americans.

72. c. Mexico's increasing restrictions on Americans in Texas inspired the revolt.

73. a. Transcendentalism was mainly an individual movement, but Brook Farm was an attempt to create a utopia where the individuals could realize their full potential.

74. d. The map's information points to the clear division between the South and North.

75. a. Turner saw the end of an era with the closing of the American frontier.

76. b. Bryan's strongest appeal was to populists and farmers.

77. b. Like many progressives, these well-to-do women wanted to reform urban America.

78. c. The New Deal's inability to end the depression led FDR to take a stronger antibusiness stance during the Second New Deal.

79. d. Folk music appealed most to primarily young Americans who rejected the consumerism and materialism of American culture.

80. a. Conservatives criticized the Warren Court for its rulings in race relations, criminal defendants' rights, and privacy issues, among other areas.

Free-Response Questions

Part A

1. This question looks at the question of the development of American national government during the antebellum period, specifically 1815–1845. You will want to keep your focus within that time period, but it may be appropriate to briefly mention the War of 1812 and the Hartford Convention, even though they are outside the period. Focus on what the question asks: To what degree did the American political system and public opinion accept broad construction of the Constitution in antebellum America? Explore the degree of acceptance of this ideology, not whether it was accepted. You also must take a balanced look at both public opinion and politics.

The documents themselves fall fairly neatly into the two opposing camps, although your background information might add to their obvious points. Stronger essays might look at the map of Indian removals as expressing federal authority but also as an expression of state will with Jackson's failure to enforce the court order in *Worcester* v. *Georgia*; the issue of the states being able to decide the issue of slavery south of the 36°30' line could weaken the idea of federal authority. One straightforward way to answer this question would be to look at it geographically; the South did not fully accept the concept of the Missouri Compromise, while the North embraced federal authority to limit the spread of slavery and regulate tariffs. Public opinion can be ascertained in Legaré's editorial, the political cartoon, and the Mormon exodus.

Arguments can be made for assertion of both strong state and strong federal power during this time period. It is a wide-open question just as it was during the time period, and the political system ultimately could not settle the question of ultimate sovereignty without war. Point out both sides of the issue in your essay and use the nullification crisis of 1832, decisions of the Marshall court, and the slavery question as prominent issues to support your arguments. You can also use a thesis that is based in economics to support the geographical divide—northern commerce as opposed to southern agriculture—and the reasons for supporting one interpretation or the other. Continually refer to the question, "to what extent," and analyze the degree to which broad construction of federal power was accepted in America.

Part B

1. This political and diplomatic question is typical of many that ask you to choose among time periods in which to frame your answer. In addition, it asks you to assess "how closely" Washington's foreign policy principles were followed; do not simply answer whether they were followed.

   To construct a complete answer, it is important to explain Washington's policies. Refer to the Neutrality Proclamation and his farewell address as examples. Then move on to look at two of the periods listed. The first includes American involvement in the War of 1812 and the Monroe Doctrine. You can interpret the impact of these policies on either side of the issue. Between 1844 and 1865 the United States annexed Texas and Oregon and fought the Mexican War and Civil War. Although American diplomacy inserted the nation more deeply into negotiations with Europe and Latin American nations, you might argue that the focus was on the North American continent, thus true to Washington. The last period, 1880–1900, encompasses American imperialism and the Spanish–American War. More than the other periods, this made the United States a player in the world and more involved in issues outside the United States borders.

   In terms of framing an argument, you might simply argue that in any of the three periods, the United States never formed permanent alliances and so was true to Washington. Be sure to explain why and how international involvement supports your position. Another way to proceed would be to point to a gradual movement away from isolation to the acquisition of a global empire by 1900, which resulted in the repudiation of Washington's principles.

2. This social history question is asking you to analyze the role of women and minorities in the antebellum reform movements. In order to receive a high score, you must deal with both groups in a balanced manner. Although reform movements were broad-based, only the abolition movement had a significant number of African Americans and women participating.

454 Practice Exam II

Part of your task is to show why the reform movements developed in this period. Using the Second Great Awakening, religion, and the influence of the Transcendentalists provides a way for you to include both women and African Americans as part of your discussion. Clear analysis of specific reform movements and their goals and accomplishments will help you answer this question. The antislavery movement used freed slaves such as Frederick Douglass and Sojourner Truth as speakers and authors. The restrictions on natural rights inherent in the women's suffrage movement with Lucretia Mott and Elizabeth Cady Stanton found sympathy with the abolition movement. Dorothea Dix, Harriet Beecher Stowe, the Grimke sisters, and Emma Willard all played major roles in their respective reform movements. As victims of drunkenness, women played a large role in the temperance movement.

One way to approach this question might be to explain how the role of reform usually fell outside the "mainstream," as it was in one sense attacking accepted norms. This then provides an opening to show how it was easier for women and minorities to find a larger role in these movements than in society as a whole.

Part C

1. Many historians have posited that the government's strong role in fighting the war abroad, and directing the economy to supply its own forces and its allies, was the high point of the progressive impulse in the twentieth century. First, define what aspects of progressivism you think are pertinent; you might look at morality, scientific efficiency and organization, and the role of government in achieving national goals to support the statement. On the other hand, the United States government inhibited democracy by limiting civil liberties and increasing its power. You must weigh both sides and decide which you can best argue.

   The time period specified invites you to look at the growth of progressivism before the war. Attempts to regulate the economy and break up trusts in the period before 1914, and discourage "immoral" behavior, especially in urban areas heavily populated by immigrants, can be shown to continue during the war with the centralization of economic functions under government control (for example: the War Industries Board, Food Administration, Fuel Administration, and Shipping Board). Attempts to control morality among soldiers can be illustrated by rules prohibiting bars and brothels near military camps. On the other side, government power grew stronger, taking initiative away from individuals and businesses. Civil liberties were restricted by the Espionage and Sedition Acts, and the Creel Committee presented one-sided and heavy-handed propaganda supporting the war. The opportunity exists to present a strong case, and the most sophisticated answers will be in the form of "In fighting World War I, the United States government exhibited many progressive actions and tendencies, but the pressures of war also moved the government away from progressive principles."

2. Like many other free-response questions, this one asks you to do several tasks, and you must demonstrate balance between the areas and time periods you are asked to analyze. You must evaluate the role of religion in both society and politics during two decades. In addition, you must also show the ways in which the two decades are similar and different. Be sure to address all these various aspects and to provide balance so that you do not neglect nor overemphasize one aspect.

In both these decades there was a conflict between secularism and traditional religious fundamentalism. You might establish the differences between the two to introduce your argument. The tension between the two has occurred throughout our history but was sharp during these decades. In terms of comparison you might mention that fundamentalism had strong appeal during both the 1920s and 1950s. In both decades religion was used as a defense against "radicalism" or modernism. Issues differed: evolution culminated in the Scopes trial, and religion was enlisted to fight communism during the Cold War.

Keep your focus on the central tension between secularism and Christian evangelism. In politics, secularism supported different types of candidates in the two decades, and in social terms it divided largely between urban and rural, and in the major issues of the decade.